SALO WITTMAYER BARON

JUBILEE VOLUME

SALO WITTMAYER BARON

JUBILEE VOLUME

ON THE OCCASION OF HIS EIGHTIETH BIRTHDAY

ENGLISH SECTION

VOLUME I

JERUSALEM 1974

AMERICAN ACADEMY FOR JEWISH RESEARCH

Distributed by

COLUMBIA UNIVERSITY PRESS

NEW YORK AND LONDON, 1974

© Copyright 1974 by

THE AMERICAN ACADEMY FOR JEWISH RESEARCH
Library of Congress Catalog Card Number: 74–82633
ISBN : 0-231-03911-5

Published with Subventions from the

LOUIS AND MINNA EPSTEIN FUND

ALEXANDER KOHUT MEMORIAL FOUNDATION

LUCIUS N. LITTAUER FOUNDATION

GUSTAV WURZWEILER FOUNDATION AND MR. IRWIN BRATER

PRINTED IN ISRAEL
AT CENTRAL PRESS, JERUSALEM

FOREWORD

At a meeting held in February 1968, the executive committee of the American Academy of Jewish Research voted to publish a Jubilee Volume on the occasion of the seventy-fifth birthday (May 1970) of Doctor Salo Wittmayer Baron as a token of its love and admiration for one of the foremost scholars of our generation, the historian par excellence of the Jewish people, the many-times president of the Academy.

The editor invited a number of outstanding scholars here and abroad, personal friends of Doctor Baron, to contribute to the Volume. The replies to the invitation are represented in these three volumes.

It goes without saying that the responsibility of the articles rests wholly with their authors.

The invitations were sent out in March 1969, and we regret very much that the appearance of these volumes has been delayed some six years. They are herewith tendered to Doctor Baron on his eightieth birthday, accompanied by the ardent prayer of his friends and admirers for good health, continuous creative scholarship, and fruitful activity in the many projects under his guidance.

It should be noted that the contents of this Volume reached the editor some four years ago, and their authors can hardly be held responsible for ignoring publications on their subjects which have appeared since then.

I am grateful to Professor Zalman Dimitrowsky and to Professor Leon Feldman for reading part of the Hebrew pageproofs. Our sincerest thanks are due te the Louis and Minna Epstein Fund, to the Alexander Kohut Memorial Foundation, to the Lucius N. Littauer Foundation, to the Gustav Wurzweiler Foundation and to Mr. Irwin Brater through the good offices of Mr. Russel S. Knapp which made it possible to publish these volumes in their present size.

Saul Lieberman, Editor

Arthur Hyman, Associate Editor

TABLE OF CONTENTS

TABLE OF CONTENTS OF THE HEBREW SECTION

A BIBLIOGRAPHY OF THE PRINTED WRITINGS OF SALO WITTMAYER BARON

JEANNETTE MEISEL BARON

PREFACE

THE RICH AND VARIED SCOPE of the bibliography of an individual scholar requires, I believe, an explanatory note. Professor Baron who decided to dedicate his life to Jewish history felt that he could accomplish this only by acquiring a very broad base from which to work. He, therefore, studied history, political science, economics, and jurisprudence as well as the more traditional Jewish and Semitic subject matter and received his doctorates from the University of Vienna in Philosophy (History as a major, Semitic Languages as a minor), 1917; Political Science, 1922; Jurisprudence, 1923; and his rabbinical degree from the Jewish Theological Seminary in Vienna in 1920. With this background he now felt that he was able to specialize primarily in the field of modern Jewish history. However, he was sidetracked by such general works as his *The Jewish Community* and *A Social and Religious History of the Jews*, particularly its second edition on which he has spent the past twenty-five years working in the ancient and medieval areas.

From many parts of the world including Europe, Israel, Latin America, and even Australia have come queries about the size and competence of his research staff. The answer to these queries is that he has NO outside assistants and for the last two decades has had none other than his wife who has been his principal research assistant throughout the years (from 1934 to date). Although trained as an economist, she had taken a minor in Jewish History for her degree at Columbia University. In addition he has had the services of a secretary, either full or part-time, who has done his manuscript typing. Therefore, it should be stressed that this is the output of one man who, despite his extreme dedication to his work, found time actively to engage in lecturing and in working on a multitude of communal projects; some, like the co-founding of the Conference on Jewish Social Studies and its quarterly, *Jewish Social Studies*, and the organization of Jewish Cultural Reconstruction, Inc. have left a lasting imprint on scholarship and Jewry at large. But this is neither the place nor the time to write a biographical sketch detailing Professor Baron's manifold activities.

Of necessity there will be many omissions in this bibliography. Interviews which have appeared in the press and in university publications are too numerous and scattered to make them easily available to the researcher or reader. They span more than four decades and five continents. For the same reason tape recordings of public addresses delivered during the last twenty years are not listed. Some are in Professor Baron's possession, others are in the libraries of the sponsoring institutions and organizations. The scope of their subject matter bears witness to his far-ranging and varied interest in the field of Jewish and general historical and sociological studies. Similarly unpublished manuscripts of books and articles, secretarial transcripts of several lecture courses at Columbia University, and the numerous memoranda and inter-office communications submitted by Professor Baron to governmental, communal, and scholarly agencies are not indicated. Nor are even important reviews of his books and biographical sketches which have appeared in the course of time in newspapers and in general and Jewish periodicals enumerated here.[1]

In addition to his own writings he has supervised some two-score Ph.D. dissertations at Columbia University's History Department

---

[1] This bibliography is in part based on that published in *Essays in Jewish Life and Thought Presented in Honor of Salo Wittmayer Baron*, ed. by J. L. Blau, P. Friedman, A. Hertzberg, and I. Mendelsohn (New York, 1959), pp. xv–xxx, which listed the publications through 1955. I am grateful to Columbia University Press for allowing me to use that material. I have made a considerable number of corrections and additions to it. I also have been able to use some titles which Professor Baron's secretaries had, through the years, filed in his office.

which range from the biblical to the contemporary periods. He has also been actively involved in many others, written under the auspices of the Departments of Religion, Public Law, Economics, and Sociology, Teachers College, and the Schools of Business and Law, as well as of the Jewish Theological Seminary of America. Many of these dissertations, which were acclaimed upon their publication, are now being used as standard reference works at universities both here and abroad. A number of Master's Essays written under his guidance have also appeared in print. Professor Arnold J. Band of UCLA in his survey of "Jewish Studies in American Liberal Arts Colleges and Universities," states that "Over 80 per cent of the professors listed have received their graduate training in the United States.... The men who are teaching in the better universities were also trained in fine graduate schools. The contribution of Columbia, often that of Salo W. Baron, is overwhelming."[2]

Professor Baron through his teaching and writings opened new horizons for the understanding of Jewish history. No longer is Jewish history a *Leidens- und Gelehrtengeschichte* taught only at theological seminaries or tucked away under the wing of a Semitics Department at the colleges and universities of the world. "By his teaching and his books he has made the study of Jewish history a recognized part of that comprehensive learning which is an essential goal of the University."[3] Jewish history has become a discipline *inter pares* with the other disciplines in the secular institutions of the United States and foreign countries.

His students are scattered throughout the world in professions as varied as meteorology (involved with moon exploration) and diplomatic service, administration, law, medicine, social work, library service, engineering and the pure sciences, the rabbinate and the Church. In the academic profession they range from a university president to deans, and up the ladder from lowly in-

---

[2] *American Jewish Year Book*, Vol. 67 (1966), p. 15.

[3] Meyer Schapiro, University Professor, Columbia University, *Letter*, May 8, 1965.

structor to named-chair professors, many teaching non-Jewish subjects. They also have been represented in the British Parliament, the Israeli government, and the various branches of the United States government, local, state, and federal. It is a great source of pride to hear the President of the State of Israel, Zalman Shazar (who attended Salo Baron's Columbia seminar for an academic year), publicly address him as "my teacher and my master, disciple of my teachers, the first in the historiography of Judaism of our day."[4]

ABBREVIATIONS

ADL   Anti-Defamation League
AHR   American Historical Review
AJHQ   American Jewish Historical Quarterly (continuation of *PAJHS*)
JBL   Journal of Biblical Literature
JQR   Jewish Quarterly Review
JSS   Jewish Social Studies
JSSQ   Jewish Social Service Quarterly
MGWJ   Monatsschrift für Geschichte und Wissenschaft des Judentums
MJ   Menorah Journal
PAAJR   Proceedings of the American Academy for Jewish Research
PAJHS   Publications of the American Jewish Historical Society (changed to *AJHQ*, 1963)
REJ   Revue des études juives
ZGJD   Zeitschrift für die Geschichte der Juden in Deutschland

---

[4] Zalman Shazar, President of the State of Israel, *Cablegram*, May 19, 1965.

1912

1 "חזיון מעציב" (A Sad Phenomenon), המצפה, IX, No. 43 (November 8), 3. Under the pseudonym שבא.

2 "משבר־הכסף" (Financial Crisis), *ibid.*, IX, No. 44 (November 15), 2–3. Under the pseudonym שבא.

3 "שאלת הצדקה ותקוניה" (The Problem of Social Welfare and Its Reforms), *ibid.*, IX, No. 46 (November 29), 1–2. Under the pseudonym שבא.

4 "תקון סדר הבחירה לסים הגליצאי" (Reform of the Electoral System for the Galician Diet), *ibid.*, IX, No. 49 (December 20), 1–2. Under the pseudonym שבא.

1913

5 "אותות הזמן" (Portents of the Day), המצפה, X, No. 27 (July 11), 2–3.

6 "הבויקוט הפולני" (The Polish Boycott), 5 parts, *ibid.*, X, No. 7 (February 14), 1–2; No. 8 (February 21), 1–2; No. 9 (February 28), 3–4; No. 10 (March 7), 2–3; No. 11 (March 14), 3–4. Under the pseudonym שבא.

7 "על מפתן התקופה" (On the Threshold of a New Period), *ibid.*, X, No. 36 (September 12), 4–5. Under the pseudonym שבא.

1914

8 "ליובלו של 'המצפה'" (On the Anniversary of the המצפה), 2 parts, המצפה, XI, No. 17 (April 24), 2–3; No. 18 (May 1), 3.

9 "מרדכי דוד ברנדשטטר (ליובל השבעים שלו)" (Mordecai David Brandstaetter), 3 parts, הצפירה, XL, No. 94 (May 7), 1; No. 95 (May 8), 4; No. 97 (May 11), 1–2.

10 "שאלת הזמן" (The Problem of the Day), 2 parts, המצפה, XI, No. 3 (January 16), 2–3; No. 4 (January 23), 2–3.

1918

11 "Graetzens Geschichtsschreibung," *MGWJ*, LXII, 5–15. See Nos. 381, 417.

12 "Nation oder Sprache?" *Die Wage*, XXI, No. 18 (May 4), 276–80.

1920

13 *Die Judenfrage auf dem Wiener Kongress. Auf Grund von zum Teil ungedruckten Quellen dargestellt.* Vienna and Berlin. 211 pp.

1923

14 *Die politische Theorie Ferdinand Lassalles.* Leipzig, 122 pp. Beihefte zum Archiv für die Geschichte des Sozialismus und der Arbeiterbewegung, hrsg. von Carl Grünberg, Heft 2.

1925

[15] "פרדיננד לסל היהודי" (Ferdinand Lassalle, the Jew), התקופה, XXIII, 347–62.

[16] "Yudayajin to Sekaiheiwa" (Jewish People and World Peace), *Revue Internationale* (Japanese), 1925–26, pp. 106–7.

[17] Review of Josef Klausner, היסטוריה ישראלית. שעורים בדברי־ימי־ישראל, Vols. II–IV (Berlin, 1924–25). In *Literarische Wochenschrift*, No. 27 (December 5), pp. 840–41.

1926

[18] "Jüdische und Palästina Fragen auf dem Zehnten Kongress der Internationalen Union der Völkerbundligen," *Zionistische Korrespondenz*, VI, No. 27 (July 9), 1–5.

[19] "Unveröffentlichte Aktenstücke zur Judenfrage auf dem Wiener Kongress (1814–1815)," *MGWJ*, LXX, 457–75.

[20] "אדמים, עזריה מן" (De' Rossi, Azariah), אשכול (Hebrew Encyclopedia), קונטרס לדוגמה, Berlin, pp. 28–29. See Nos. 41, 381.

[21] "Für den Schutz der Minderheiten. Der Kongress der Völkerbundligen," *Wiener Morgenzeitung*, VIII, No. 2644 (July 4), 2.

[22] "Eine Palästinadebatte auf dem Kongress der Völkerbundligen," *ibid.*, VIII, No. 2646 (July 6), 2.

[23] "Der zehnte Kongress der Internationalen Union der Völkerbundligen," *ibid.*, VIII, No. 2650 (July 10), 2.

[24] Review of Simon Dubnow, *Weltgeschichte des jüdischen Volkes*, Vol. I (Berlin, 1925). In *Literarische Wochenschrift*, Nos. 3–4 (January 20), pp. 72–73.

[25] Review of N. M. Gelber, *Aus zwei Jahrhunderten* (Vienna, 1924); and *Die Juden und der polnische Aufstand 1863* (Vienna, 1923). In *MGWJ*, LXX, 134–35.

[26] Review of Ferdinand Lassalle, *Nachgelassene Briefe und Schriften*, hrsg. v. Gustav Mayer, V. Bd. (Stuttgart, 1925). In *Archiv für Geschichte des Sozialismus*, XII, 449–50.

1927

[27] "Azariah de' Rossi's Attitude to Life," in *Jewish Studies in Memory of Israel Abrahams*, New York, pp. 12–52. See No. 381.

[28] "Artom, Isacco," *Jüdisches Lexikon*, Berlin, I, 486–87.

[29] Review of I[sidor] Kracauer, *Geschichte der Juden in Frankfurt a. M.* (*1150–1824*), Vol. I (Frankfurt, 1925). In *Literarische Wochenschrift*, No. 7 (February 13), pp. 166–67.

1928

[30] "Ghetto and Emancipation. Shall We Revise the Traditional View?" *MJ*, 515–26. Also reprint, New York, 12 pp. See No. 385.

31 "La Méthode Historique d'Azaria de' Rossi," *REJ*, LXXXVI, 151–75; LXXXVII, 43–78. Also as a pamphlet, Paris 1929, 62 pp. (Publications de la Société des études juives). See No. 381.

32 "האיש ,ז"ל דוד בראנדשטטר מרדכי קבר על" (Obituary of Mordecai David Brandstaetter), הדאר, VIII, No. 28 (June 3), 440–41.

33 "הרב צ.פ. חיות בתור חוקר ומורה" (Rabbi H. P. Chajes as Scholar and Teacher), שבילי החנוך. IV, No. 1, 37–45. Also reprint, New York, 8 pp.

34 "The Study of Jewish History," *Jewish Institute Quarterly*, IV, No. 2 (January), 7–14.

35 "Research in Jewish History," *ibid.*, IV, No. 4 (May), 1–8.

36 "Eskeles, Bernard, Freiherr von," *Jüdisches Lexikon*, II, 513.

37 "Fischhof, Adolf (Abraham)," *ibid.*, II, 673–74.

38 "Friedjung, Heinrich," *ibid.*, II, 822–23.

39 Review of *The Legacy of Israel*, ed. by Edwyn R. Bevan and Charles Singer (Oxford, 1927). In *Journal of Religion*, VIII, No. 3 (July), 477–79.

1929

40 "Nationalism and Intolerance," *MJ*, XVI (June), 405–15; XVII (November), 148–58. Also reprint, New York, 23 pp. See No. 437.

41 "אדמים, עזריה מן" (De' Rossi, Azariah), אשכול (Hebrew Encyclopaedia), I, 689–93. Revised from No. 20. See also No. 381.

42 "תשובה בשפה איטלקית מאת ר' אברהם גראציאנו" (An Italian Responsum of Abraham Graziano), in *Studies in Jewish Bibliography and Related Subjects in Memory of Abraham Solomon Freidus*. New York and Vienna, pp. 122–37.

43 Introduction to Filip Friedmann, *Die galizischen Juden im Kampfe um ihre Gleichberechtigung (1848–1868)*. Frankfurt a. M.

1930

44 *The Jews in Roumania. Report Submitted to the Eighth Session of the American Jewish Congress*. New York, 15 pp. An extract of this Report appeared under the title, "The Situation of the Jews in Roumania," in *Jewish Tribune*, XCVII, No. 17 (October 24), 4.

45 "The Authenticity of the Numbers in the Historical Books of O.T.," *JBL*, XLIX, Part 3, pp. 287–91.

46 "I. M. Jost, the Historian," *PAAJR*, I, 7–32. See No. 381.

47 "Teaching Jewish History." Interview by Dr. Dora Askowith. In *Jewish Tribune*, XCVI, No. 7 (February 14), 2, 7. Appeared also in Polish trans. in the literary supplement to *Chwila*, No. 3988 (Lwów, May 4, 1930), pp. 9–10.

48 "Berliner, Abraham (1833–1915)," *Encyclopaedia of Social Sciences*, II, 523–24.

1931

49 "Zur ostjüdischen Einwanderung in Preussen, Aktenstücke," *ZGJD*, N.S., III, 193–203.

50 "Żydzi w Rumunji," *Miesięcznik żydowski*, I, No. 4 (March), 322–35. Trans. of No. 44.

51 "Frankel, Zecharias (1801–75)," *Encyclopaedia of Social Sciences*, VI, 418–19.

52 "Graetz, Heinrich," *Encyclopaedia Judaica*, VII, 645–52. See No. 381.

53 Review of George A. Barton, *A History of the Hebrew People from the Earliest Times to the Year 70 A.D.* (New York, 1930). In *Historical Outlook*, October, p. 305.

1932

54 "Jewish Emancipation," *Encyclopaedia of Social Sciences*, VIII, 394–99.

55 "Karo, Joseph ben Ephraim (1488–1575)," *ibid.*, VIII, 547–48.

56 Interview in *Der Wiener Tag*, July 3.

1933

57 "אוכלוסי ישראל בימי המלכים" (The Israelitic Population under the Kings), in *Abhandlungen zur Erinnerung an Hirsch Perez Chajes*, Vienna, pp. 76–136. See No. 462.

58 "Jewish Influence on Christian Reform Movements," *JQR*, XXIII, 405–10. Review of L. I. Newman's work on this subject.

59 "Jews and the Syrian Massacres of 1860," *PAAJR*, IV, 3–31.

60 "Żydzi a żydowstwo" (Jews and Judaism: the Interrelation between Society and Religion in Jewish History), *Miesięcznik żydowski*, III, Part 2, Nos. 11–12 (November–December), 193–207. Essentially trans. from ms. of Chap. I in No. 75. Also reprint. Warsaw, 1933, 15 pp.

61 Resumé des communications présentées au VIIe Congrès internationale de sciences historiques, Warsaw. Vol. II, p. 455.

62 Review of Fannie A. Andrews, *The Holy Land under Mandate* (2 vols., Boston, 1931); and of Angelo S. Rappoport, *History of Palestine* (London, 1931). In *Historical Outlook*, XXIV (March), 160–161.

1935

63 *Jewish Studies in Memory of George A. Kohut.* Edited by Salo W. Baron and Alexander Marx. New York: Bloch Publishing Co. XCIII + 619 + 149 pp.

64 "Abraham Benisch's Project for Jewish Colonization in Palestine (1842)," *ibid.*, pp. 72–85.

65 "Germany's Ghetto, Past and Present. A Perspective on Nazi Laws against Jews," *Independent Journal of Columbia University*, III, No. 3 (November 15), 3–4.

66–67 "An Historical Critique of the Jewish Community," *JSSQ*, XI, 44–49. Also in *Jewish Education*, X, (1936), 2–8.

68 "The Historical Outlook of Maimonides," *PAAJR*, VI, 5–113. See No. 381.

69 "Maimonides, Guia y Legislador de su Pueblo," *Revista Hispanica Moderna*, I, No. 4 (July), 303–7. Trans. of Address at Maimonides Celebration. See No. 135.

70 "לתולדות יהודי גרמניה בא״י" (On the History of German Jews in Palestine), in מנחה לדוד: ספר היובל לר׳ דוד ילין (The David Yellin Jubilee Volume), Jerusalem, pp. 113–28.

71 Review of Jacob de Haas, *Palestine, the Last Two Thousand Years* (New York, 1934). In *Annals of the American Academy of Political and Social Science*, 178 (March), 235–36.

72 Another review of the same work. In *AHR*, XL, No. 3 (April), 545–46.

73 Review of M. I. Zwick, *Berthold Auerbachs sozialpolitischer und ethischer Liberalismus* (Stuttgart, 1933). In *Germanic Review*, No. 1 (January), 50–51.

1936

74 Review of Marcel Bulard, *Le Scorpion, symbole du peuple juif dans l'art religieux des XIVe, XVe, XVIe siècles* (Paris, 1935). In *AHR*, XLI, No. 2 (January), 412–13.

1937

75–77 *A Social and Religious History of the Jews*. 3 vols. New York: Columbia University Press. xii + 377; ix + 462; xi + 406 pp. 2d Impression, 1938–40.

78 "מתולדות הישוב היהודי בירושלים" (From the History of the Jewish Settlement in Jerusalem), in ספר קלוזנר ... מוגש לפרופסור יוסף קלוזנר (Josef Klausner Jubilee Volume), Jerusalem, pp. 302–12.

79 "סכסוך קהלות בוירונה עפ״י תשובת ר׳ מרדכי בשאן בסוף המאה השבע־עשרה" (A Communal Controversy in Verona), in ספר־היובל לפרופיסור שמואל קרויס (Professor Samuel Krauss Anniversary Volume), Jerusalem, pp. 217–54. Also reprint with 4 pages of Addenda and Corrigenda.

80 Review of Fritz Baer, *Die Juden im christlichen Spanien*. Erster Teil, Urkunden und Regesten. Zweiter Band, Kastilien, Inquisitionsakten (Berlin, 1936). In *AHR*, XLIII, No. 1 (October), 101–3.

81 Review of Albert Lewkowitz, *Das Judentum und die geistigen Strömungen des 19. Jahrhunderts* (Breslau, 1935). In *Review of Religion*, II, No. 1 (October), 80–83.

1938

82 "A propos de mon 'A Social and Religious History of the Jews'," *REJ*, N.S., IV (CIV), Nos. 1–2 (July–December), 139–46. Answer to Solomon Zeitlin's review, *ibid.*, N.S., II, 141–43.

83 "Democracy and Judaism," *Hadassah Newsletter*, January, pp. 66–67.

84 "Freedom and Constraint in the Jewish Community. A Historic Episode," in *Essays and Studies in Memory of Linda R. Miller*, New York, pp. 9–23.

85 "The Jewish Question in the Nineteenth Century," *Journal of Modern History*, X, No. 1 (March), 51–65.

86 "Palestine and the Refugee Problem," *Story Behind the Headlines*, December 6, 23 pp. [Collaborated with Caesar Searchinger's broadcast.]

87 "לתולדות ההשכלה והחינוך בווינה" (A Study in the History of Jewish Enlightenment and Education in Vienna), in ספר טורוב (Touroff Anniversary Volume), New York, pp. 167–83, 374–79.

88 "סאציאל־רעליגעזע פארשוגנען אין אידישער געשיכטע" (Socioreligious Research in Jewish History: A Lecture), די צוקונפט, XLIII, No. 5 (June), 341–47.

89 Review of Isaac Da Costa, *Noble Families among Sephardic Jews* (New York, 1936). In *AHR*, XLIII, No. 3 (April), 608–10.

90 Review of Franz Kobler, *Juden und Judentum in deutschen Briefen aus drei Jahrhunderten* (Vienna, 1935). In *Historia Judaica*, I, No. 1 (November), 74–75.

1939

91 Ed., *Jewish Social Studies* (*JSS*). A Quarterly Journal Devoted to Contemporary and Historical Aspects of Jewish Life. Published by the Conference on Jewish Relations, subsequently called the Conference on Jewish Social Studies. Vol. I. Also of all subsequent issues to date.

92–94 "Emphases in Jewish History," *JSS*, I, No. 1 (January), 15–38. Appeared also in *Jewish Education*, XI, No. 1 (April), 8–22; and, with some variations, in *JSSQ*, XV, No. 2 (December 1938), 219–35. See Nos. 381, 482.

95–96 "Cultural Problems of American Jewry," in *Harry L. Glucksman Annual Lectures*, No. 1, New York: Jewish Welfare Board, pp. 16–26. Also appeared in *Jewish Center*, XVII, No. 2 (June), 7–11. See No. 450.

97–98 "משה כהן בעלאינפאנטע א משכיל פון נאפאלעאנס צייטן" (Moses Cohen Belinfante, a Maskil of the Napoleonic Period), ייווא בלעטער, XIII, Nos. 5–6 [Wachstein Memorial Volume] (September–October), 429–59. See No. 169. An abridged trans. under the title of "Un iluminista sefardí de la época napoleónica" appeared in *Judaica*, VII, Nos. 73–75 (July–September), 68–77.

99–100 Review of Mortimer Cohen, *Jacob Emden: A Man of Controversy* (Philadelphia, 1937). In *JSS*, I, No. 4 (October), 483–87. Supplemented by comments of author and reviewer, *ibid.*, II, 1 (January 1940), 117–23.

101 Review of Sigmund Freud, *Moses and Monotheism* (New York, 1939). In *American Journal of Sociology*, XLV, No. 3 (November), 471–77. See Nos. 442, 460, 462.

102 Review of Jewish Historical Society of England, *Transactions, 1932–35*, Vol. XIII (London, 1936); and *Miscellanies*, Vol. III (London, 1937). In *JSS*, I, No. 4 (October), 467–69.

103 Review of Jacob R. Marcus, *The Jew in the Medieval World, a Source Book, 315–1791* (Cincinnati, 1938). In *AHR*, XLIV, No. 2 (January), 421–22.

104 Review of *Occident and Orient* (ed. by Bruno Schindler and A. Marmorstein). Studies in honor of Haham Dr. M. Gaster's 80th Birthday (London, 1936). In *JSS*, I, No. 3 (July), 370–73.

105 Review of James Parkes, *The Jew in the Medieval Community* (London, 1938). In *MJ*, XXVII, No. 1, 102–7.

106 Review of Hans Zucker, *Studien zur jüdischen Selbstverwaltung im Altertum* (Berlin, 1936). In *JSS*, I, No. 2 (April), 264–65.

107 Booknote on Joshua Bloch, *Early Hebrew Printing in Spain and Portugal* (New York, 1938). *Ibid.*, I, No. 3 (July), 391–92.

108 Booknote on Ernst Hoffman, *Die Liebe zu Gott bei Moses Ben Maimon* (Breslau, 1937). *Ibid.*, I, No. 3 (July), 391.

109 Booknote on W. O. E. Oesterley, *Sacrifices in Ancient Israel* (New York, 1938). *Ibid.*, I, No. 3 (July), 389–90.

110 Booknote on Michael Traub, *Die jüdische Auswanderung aus Deutschland*, etc. (Berlin, 1936). *Ibid.*, I, No. 3 (July), 392.

1940

111 "Jewish Social Studies, 1938–39: A Selected Bibliography," *JSS*, II, No. 3 (July), 305–88; No. 4 (October), 481–605. See No. 132.

112 "The Future of European Jewry," *Jewish Forum*, XXIII, No. 9 (October), 164–65, 171. A radio address.

113 "Great Britain and Damascus Jewry in 1860–61: an Archival Study," *JSS*, II, No. 2 (April), 179–208.

114 Necrology: "Zevi Diesendruck," *PAAJR*, X, 3–4 (signed by Salo W. Baron and Shalom Spiegel).

115 Necrology: "Zevi Diesendruck," *AHR*, XLVI, 255–56.

116–17 "Reflections on the Future of the Jews of Europe," *Contemporary Jewish Record*, III (July–August), 355–69. Reprint, 15 pp. Appeared also, with some variations, in *JSSQ*, XVII, No. 1, pp. 5–19.

118 "על שיטתו ההיסטורית של שמעון דובנוב" (Simon Dubnow's Historical Approach), בצרון, II, No. 3 (December), 212–15.

119 Review of Louis Finkelstein, *The Pharisees* (2 vols., Philadelphia, 1938). In *Review of Religion*, IV, No. 2 (January), 196–99.

120 Another review of the same work. In *JBL*, LIX, No. 1 (March), 60–67.

121 Review of *Judaism and Christianity*, 3 vols., ed. by W. O. E. Oesterley, H. Loewe, and Erwin I. J. Rosenthal (New York, 1937–38). In *AHR*, XLV, No. 2 (January), 358–61.

122 Review of *Letters to Emma Lazarus in the Columbia University Library*, ed. by Ralph L. Rusk (New York, 1939). In *JSS*, II, No. 1 (January), 108–9.

123 Review of מסעות חבשוש, trans. from Arabic into Hebrew with an Intro. and Notes by S. D. Goitein (Tel-Aviv, 1939). *Ibid.*, II, No. 2 (April), 226–27.

[124] Review of Manfred Reifer, *Ausgewählte historische Schriften* (Cernauti, 1938). *Ibid.*, II, No. 2 (April), 220.

[125] Review of Cecil Roth, *Magna Bibliotheca Anglo-Judaica*. New ed. revised and enlarged (London, 1937). *Ibid.*, II, No. 1 (January), 97–99.

[126] Review of *Scritti in Onore di Dante Lattes*, ed. by Guido Bedarida (Città di Castello, 1938). *Ibid.*, II, No. 2 (April), 223–26.

[127] Review of Oskar Wolfsberg, *Zur Zeit- und Geistesgeschichte des Judentums* (Zurich, 1938). In *Historia Judaica*, II, No. 2 (October), 119–20.

[128] Booknote on Saul Mézan, *De Gabirol à Abravanel* (Paris, 1936). In *JSS*, II, No. 1 (January), 113.

[129] Booknote on D. Sidersky, *Quelques portraits de nos maîtres des études sémitiques* (Paris, 1937). *Ibid.*, II, No. 1 (January), 112–13.

[130] Booknote on ספר־מסעות כתוב בידי עצמו הרפתקאותיו של אשר הלוי: (Asher ha-Levi's Book of Travels Written by Himself), ed. by Abraham Yaari (Jerusalem, 1938). *Ibid.*, II, No. 1 (January), 114.

[131] Introduction to Manoah L. Bialik, *The Cooperative Credit Movement in Palestine*, Ann Arbor, Michigan.

1941

[132] *Bibliography of Jewish Social Studies, 1938–39*. New York. iv + 291 pp. Jewish Social Studies, Publications, No. 1. Revised edition of no. 111 with Additions, Corrections, and Index, pp. 213–91.

[133] Ed., *Essays on Maimonides; an Octocentennial Volume*. New York: Columbia University Press. [VIII +] 316 pp. See No. 403.

[134] "The Economic Views of Maimonides," in *Essays on Maimonides*, pp. 127–264. See No. 462.

[135] "Maimonides, the Leader and Lawgiver," *ibid.*, pp. 12–18. See No. 69.

[136] "Rashi and the Community of Troyes," in *Rashi Anniversary Volume*. New York: American Academy for Jewish Research, pp. 47–71. Texts and Studies, I. See Nos. 446, 462.

[137] "Yehudah Halevi: An Answer to a Historic Challenge," *JSS*, III, No. 3 (July), 243–72. See Nos. 155, 462.

[138] Review of Albert M. Hyamson, *The British Consulate in Jerusalem in Relation to the Jews of Palestine, 1838–1914*. Part I: 1838–1861 (London, 1939). *Ibid.*, III, No. 3 (July), 343. See No. 162.

[139] Review of *The Jewish Theological Seminary*, ed. by Cyrus Adler (New York, 1939); and *The Hebrew University* (Jerusalem, 1939). *Ibid.*, III, No. 1 (January), 99–102.

[140] Review of Israel Klauzner, תולדות הקהילה העברית בוילנה (History of the Jewish Community in Wilno), Vol. I (Wilno, 1938). *Ibid.*, III, No. 4 (October), 419–20.

141 Review of Arthur Ruppin, *Jewish Fate and Future* (New York, 1940). In *Jewish Digest*, January, pp. 89–92.

142 Review of A. L. Sachar, *The Jew in the Contemporary World* (New York, 1939). In *AHR*, XLVI, 455–56.

143 Review of Joseph Vogt, *Kaiser Julian und das Judentum* (Leipzig, 1939). In *JSS*, III, No. 2 (April), 220.

144 Booknote on Solomon F. Bloom, *World of Nations: A Study of the National Implications in the Work of Karl Marx* (New York, 1941). *Ibid.*, III, No. 4 (October), 438–39.

145 Booknote on H. Wheeler Robinson, *The History of Israel* (New York, 1938). *Ibid.*, III, No. 1 (January), 118–19.

146 Booknote on Royal Institute of International Affairs, *Great Britain and Palestine, 1915–39* (London, 1939); and Ben M. Edidin, *Rebuilding Palestine* (New York, 1939). *Ibid.*, III, No. 1 (January), 121–22.

147 Booknote on *Cultural Approaches to History*, ed. by Caroline F. Ware (New York, 1940). *Ibid.*, III, No. 4 (October), 439–40.

1942

148–50 *The Jewish Community: Its History and Structure to the American Revolution.* 3 vols. Philadelphia: Jewish Publication Society of America. 1942–5702. xii+374; 366; 572 pp. 3d Impression, 1948. The Morris Loeb Series. See Nos. 466–68.

151 *American and Jewish Destiny: A Semimillennial Experience.* Address delivered under auspices of the Synagogue Council of America on Monday Evening, October 12, 1942, at Spanish and Portuguese Congregation Shearith Israel of New York. 12 pp. See No. 450.

152 *Effect of War on Jewish Community Life.* Harry L. Glucksman Memorial Lecture for 1942, New York. 15 pp. See No. 450.

153 ״לתולדות החלוקה ופדיון השבויים במאה הי״ז (מפנקסי קורפו)״ (A Contribution to the History of Palestine Relief and the Ransom of Captives), ספר השנה ליהודי אמריקה (American Hebrew Year Book), [VI], תש״ב, pp. 167–79. Also reprint, New York, 13 pp.

154 "Jewish Factor in Medieval Civilization," *PAAJR*, XII, 1–48. See Nos. 407, 462.

155 "Judá Leví: Respuesta a un desafío histórico," *Judaica*, X, Nos. 112–14 (October–December), 165–83. See Nos. 137, 462.

156 "Modern Capitalism and Jewish Fate," *MJ*, XXX, No. 2, 116–38. See Nos. 381, 482.

157 "Prospects for Peace in Palestine," in *The Near East; Problems and Prospects*, ed. by Philip W. Ireland, Chicago (Lectures on the Harris Foundation), pp. 103–40.

158 "David Yellin" (Obituary). In *JSS*, IV, No. 2 (April), 191.

[159] "What War Has Meant to Community Life," *Contemporary Jewish Record*, V, No. 5 (October), 493–507. See No. 450.

[160] Correspondence, *JQR*, XXXII, No. 3 (January), 321–25. Answer to S. Zeitlin's review of *Essays on Maimonides, ibid.*, No. 1, pp. 107–14.

[161] Review of Cecil Roth, *A History of the Jews in England* (Oxford, 1941). In *Journal of Modern History*, XIV, 522–23. See also No. 173.

[162] Review of *Transactions of the Jewish Historical Society of England, 1935–39*, Vol. XIV (London, 1940); and of Albert M. Hyamson, *The British Consulate in Jerusalem*, Part II, 1862–1914 (London, 1941). In *JSS*, IV, No. 4 (October), 403–7. See No. 138.

[163] Booknote on David Druck, *Yehuda Halevy* (New York, 1941). *Ibid.*, IV, No. 3 (July), 286.

[164] Booknote on George Vernadsky, *Bohdan, Hetman of Ukraine* (New Haven, 1941). *Ibid.*, IV, No. 3 (July), 286.

[165] Foreword to *Essays on Antisemitism*, ed. by Koppel S. Pinson. New York: Jewish Social Studies, Publications, No. 2. See No. 189.

1943

[166] *Palestinian Messengers in America, 1849–79... A Record of Four Journeys.* New York: Conference on Jewish Relations, 116 pp. Together with Jeannette M. Baron. Reprinted from *JSS*, Vol. V, Nos. 2–3. See No. 450.

[167] *President's Report 1940–1943.* Conference on Jewish Relations, New York.

[168] "Israel's Present" (Symposium on "Israel's Present and Future"), in *Man's Faith and This Crisis* (Addresses delivered at 38th Council of Union of American Hebrew Congregations, April 2–4, 1943). New York, pp. 78–82.

[169] "Moses Cohen Belinfante: A Leader of Dutch-Jewish Enlightenment," *Historia Judaica*, V, No. 1 (April), 1–26. Revised trans. of No. 97 with supplementary documents.

[170] "לתולדות הישוב היהודי בטבריה וישיבתה בשנות תק״ב–ד״י" (On the History of the Jewish Settlement in Tiberias in 1742–44), in ספר היובל לכבוד פרופיסור אלכסנדר מארכס (A Tribute to Professor Alexander Marx), ed. by David Fränkel. New York, pp. 79–88.

[171] "Saadia's Communal Activities," in *Saadia Anniversary Volume*. New York: American Academy for Jewish Research, pp. 9–74. Texts and Studies, II. See No. 462.

[172] "Vienna, Congress of (1814–1815)," *The Universal Jewish Encyclopedia*, X, [418]–[419].

[173] Review of Cecil Roth, *A History of the Jews in England* (Oxford, 1941). In *JSS*, V, No. 1 (January), 61–63. See No. 161.

[174] Review of יידן אין פראנקרייך (The Jews in France), 2 vols., ed. by E. Tcherikower (New York, 1942). *Ibid.*, V, No. 1 (January), 67–70.

175 Booknote on *The Jewish Quarterly Review*, N.S., XXXIII, Nos. 2–3 (Saadia Anniversary Issue) (Philadelphia, 1943). *Ibid.*, V, No. 4 (October), 408.

176 Booknote on F. A. Teilhaber, *The Graphic Historical Atlas of Palestine*, Vol. I (Tel-Aviv, 1941). *Ibid.*, V, No. 4 (October), 407–8.

1944

177 "Migration Speeds Progress," *Rescue: Information Bulletin of the HIAS*, I, Nos. 3–4 (March–April), 3, 15–16.

178 "לתולדות קהלות קורפו וארגונן" (On the History of the Corfu Communities and Their Organization), in קובץ מדעי (Studies in Memory of Moses Schorr). New York, pp. 25–41.

179 "Bernstein, Herman," *Dictionary of American Biography*, Vol. XXI, Supplement One, New York, pp. 77–79.

180 "Ismar Elbogen (1874–1943)" (Obituary), *JSS*, VI, No. 1 (January), 91–92.

181 Review of ספר זכרון לאשר גולאק ולשמואל קליין ז״ל (Studies in Memory of Asher Gulak and Samuel Klein) (Jerusalem, 1942). *Ibid.*, VI, No. 3 (July), 275–78.

182 Review of Hans Kohn, *The Idea of Nationalism. A Study in its Origins and Background* (New York, 1944). *Ibid.*, VI, No. 4 (October), 408–11.

1945

183 "At the Turning-Point," *MJ*, XXXIII, No. 1 (April–June), 1–10. Address delivered at the Thirtieth-Year Dinner of the *Menorah Journal* in New York City on November 29, 1944.

184 "The Jewish Community of Tomorrow," in *Moral and Spiritual Foundations for the World of Tomorrow*. The Centenary Series of Addresses and Other Papers Prepared for the Celebration of the Hundredth Anniversary of Congregation Emanu-El, 1845–1945. New York, pp. 75–83.

185 "Levi Herzfeld, the First Jewish Economic Historian," in *Louis Ginzberg Jubilee Volume*. On the Occasion of His Seventieth Birthday, English section. New York, pp. 75–104. See No. 381.

186–87 "The Spiritual Reconstruction of European Jewry," *Commentary*, I, No. 1 (November), 4–12. Also reprint 9 pp. Appeared also in a different form in the *Yearbook of the Central Conference of American Rabbis*, LV, 193–206. Also reprint 14 pp.

188 Booknote on Henry Charles Lea, *Minor Historical Writings and Other Essays*, ed. by Arthur C. Howland (Philadelphia, 1942). In *JSS*, VII, No. 1 (January), 94.

1946

189 Foreword to *Essays on Antisemitism*, ed. by Koppel S. Pinson. Second edition, revised and enlarged. New York: Jewish Social Studies, Publications, No. 2. See No. 165.

190 Foreword to *Tentative List of Jewish Educational Institutions in Axis-Occupied Countries.* Supplement to *JSS*, VIII, No. 3 (July), 5–8.

191 Introductory Statement to *Tentative List of Jewish Cultural Treasures in Axis-Occupied Countries.* Supplement to *ibid.*, VIII, No. 1 (January), 5–11. See No. 212.

1947

192 *Modern Nationalism and Religion.* The Rauschenbusch Lectures for 1944 (Colgate-Rochester Divinity School, Rochester, N.Y.). New York: Harper and Brothers. x + 363 pp. See Nos. 324, 449.

193 "Dr. Baron Calls on JWB to Change from Service Agency to Central Guiding Body," JWB *Circle*, II, No. 6, (June–July), 5, 14. Opening Address at JWB Annual Meeting in Pittsburgh, May 10, 1947 by Chairman of Survey Commission. See No. 213.

194 *President's Report 1943–1946.* Conference on Jewish Relations, New York.

195 "How S. A. [South African] Jewry Should Plan Its Future," *Jewish Affairs*, II, No. 4 (April), 4–9.

196 "Prospects for the Diaspora," *New Palestine*, XXXVII, No. 20 (June 20), 143–46.

197 *Religious Liberty: Area of Investigation.* Seminar on Religion and Democracy. Columbia University. 6 pp. mimeographed.

198 "Work Among Our Youth," *Proceedings of the Plenary Session, Canadian Jewish Congress, May 31–June 2, 1947*, Montreal, pp. 55, 61–64.

199 "The Year in Retrospect," *American Jewish Year Book*, XLIX (1947–48), 103–22.

201 Booknote on George Antonius, *The Arab Awakening: The Story of the Arab National Movement* (New York, 1946). In *JSS*, IX, No. 2 (April), 191–92.

202 Booknote on Corliss Lamont, *Peoples of the Soviet Union* (New York, 1946). *Ibid.*, IX, No. 2 (April), 190–91.

203 Booknote on C. J. Friedrich, *American Policy toward Palestine* (Washington, D.C., American Council on Public Affairs, 1944). In *Journal of Modern History*, XIX, 386.

204 Foreword to *Tentative List of Jewish Periodicals in Axis-Occupied Countries.* Supplement to *JSS*, IX, No. 3 (July), 7–9.

1948

205–206 *The Jewish Community and Jewish Education.* American Association for Jewish Education, New York, 17 pp. Also appeared in *Jewish Education*, XIX, No. 2 (March), 7–13, 42. (Paper read before a special session on "Communal Responsibility for Jewish Education" at a meeting of the Board of Governors of the American Association for Jewish Education in New York City, October 19, 1947.) See Nos. 408, 450.

207 Review of Mordecai M. Kaplan, *The Future of the American Jew* (New York, 1948). In *New York Times*, Book Review, May 2, p. 12.

208 Review of James Parkes, *The Emergence of the Jewish Problem 1878–1939* (London, 1946, under the auspices of the Royal Institute of International Affairs). In *Middle East Journal*, II (January), 96–97.

209 Booknote on Kuno Trau and Michael Karyan, אדם בעולם צבי פרץ חיות (Biographical Sketch of H. P. Chajes) (Tel-Aviv, 1947). In *JSS*, X, No. 1 (January), 97–98.

210 Foreword to "Papers given at the Seminar on Religion and Democracy of Columbia University," *Review of Religion*, XII, No. 2 (January), 116.

211 Introduction to *Tentative List of Jewish Publishers of Judaica and Hebraica in Axis Occupied Countries*. Supplement to *JSS*, X, No. 2 (April), 5–7.

212 Preface to *Addenda and Corrigenda to Tentative List of Jewish Cultural Treasures in Axis-Occupied Countries*. Supplement to *JSS*, X, No. 1 (January), 3–4. See No. 191.

213 Letter of Transmittal to Frank L. Weil, in *JWB Survey*, by O. I. Janowsky, New York: The Dial Press, pp. vii–ix. See No. 193.

1949

214 "A Diplomatic Episode in the Spanish-Portuguese Community of London (1841)," *Bulletin Congregation Habonim*, IX, No. 9 (September), 12–16. Issue dedicated to Dr. Adolf Kober on occasion of his 70th Birthday. Mimeographed.

215 "The Impact of the Revolution of 1848 on Jewish Emancipation," *JSS*, XI, No. 3 (July), 195–248. See No. 485.

216 "The Revolution of 1848 and Jewish Scholarship, Part I," *PAAJR*, XVIII, 1–66. See No. 224.

217 Review of Arnold J. Toynbee, *Civilization on Trial* (New York, 1948). In *Political Science Quarterly*, LXIV, No. 1 (March), 110–13.

218 Review of Chaim Weizmann, *Trial and Error* (2 vols., New York, 1949). In *New York Times*, Book Review, January 23, p. 1.

1950

219 "American Jewish History: Problems and Methods," *PAJHS*, XXXIX, No. 3 (March), 207–66. See No. 450.

220 "Moritz Steinschneider's Contribution to Jewish Historiography," in *Alexander Marx Jubilee Volume*, New York, pp. 83–148. See No. 381.

221 "Opening Remarks" to the Conference on "Problems of Research in the Study of the Jewish Catastrophe 1939–45" held at the New School for Social Research, New York City. In *JSS*, XII, No. 1 (January), 13–16.

1951

222 Ed. (with Ernest Nagel and Koppel S. Pinson), *Freedom and Reason: Studies in Philosophy and Jewish Culture in Memory of Morris Raphael Cohen.* Glencoe, Ill. Jewish Social Studies, Publications, No. 4, viii + 468 pp.

223 "New Horizons in Jewish History," *ibid.*, pp. 337–53.

224 "The Revolution of 1848 and Jewish Scholarship, Part II," *PAAJR*, XX, 1–100. See No. 216.

225 Review of Ben Zion Bokser, *The Legacy of Maimonides* (New York, Philosophical Library, 1950). In *New York Times*, Book Review, February 18, p. 25.

226 Review of Saul Lieberman, *Hellenism in Jewish Palestine: Studies in the Literary Transmission Beliefs and Manners of Palestine in the I Century B. C.E–IV Century C.E.* (New York, 1950: Texts and Studies of the Jewish Theological Seminary of America, Vol. XVIII). In *New York Times*, Book Review, July 29, p. 7.

227 Review of Cecil Roth, *The Great Synagogue, London, 1690–1940* (London, 1950). In *JSS*, XIII, No. 3 (July), 261–62.

228 Review of Jean Stengers, *Les Juifs dans les Pays-Bas au moyen-âge* (Académie Royale de Belgique, Classe des lettres, et des sciences morales et politiques, Mémoires, XLV, 2, Brussels, 1950). In *Speculum*, XXVI, No. 2 (April), 407–9.

229 Review of *A Documentary History of the Jews in the United States 1654–1875*, ed. by Morris U. Schappes (New York, 1950). In *JSS*, XIII, No. 1 (January), 77–80. See No. 450.

230 Review of R. Walzer, *Galen on Jews and Christians* (London, 1949: Oxford Classical and Philosophical Monographs). In *Journal of the History of Medicine and Allied Sciences*, VI, 428–29.

231 Booknote on Louis Gottschalk, *Understanding History; a Primer of Historical Method* (New York, 1950). In *JSS*, XIII, No. 3 (July), 280–81.

232 Booknote on *Hitler Directs His War; the Secret Records of His Daily Military Conferences, Selected and Annotated... from the Manuscript in the University of Pennsylvania Library*, ed. by Felix Gilbert (New York, 1950). *Ibid.*, XIII, No. 3 (July), 283.

233 Booknote on Jacques Petitpierre, *The Romance of the Mendelssohns* (New York, 1950). *Ibid.*, XIII, No. 3 (July), 282.

234 Booknote on Walter A. Kaufmann, *Nietzsche: Philosopher, Psychologist, Anti-Christ* (Princeton, 1950). *Ibid.*, XIII, No. 3 (July), 283–84.

235 Booknote on Manfred Reifer, *Dr. Mayer Ebner, ein juedisches Leben* (Tel-Aviv, 1949). *Ibid.*, XIII, No. 3 (July), 284–85.

236 Booknote on *South African Jews in World War II* (Published by the South African Jewish Board of Deputies, Johannesburg, 1950). *Ibid.*, XIII, No. 3 (July), 285–86.

1952

237-38 *A Social and Religious History of the Jews.* Second edition, revised and enlarged. Vols. I–II: Ancient Times. New York: Columbia University Press, and Philadelphia: The Jewish Publication Society of America. ix + 415; vi + 493 pp. The "Index" to both volumes (II, 439–93) was omitted from the 4th impression (1962) on because of the intervening publication of the more inclusive *Index*, No. 323. See Nos. 277, 285–86, 299–300, 421–22, 465.

239 "Aspects of the Jewish Communal Crisis in 1848," *JSS*, XIV, No. 2 (April), 99–144.

240-41 "Hebrew Civilization," *Encyclopedia Americana* (1952) under *Middle East*, Section No. 5, Vol. XIX, 38k–38n. Also in *Background of the Middle East*, Cornell University Press, Chap. V, pp. 33–42.

242 "Impact of Wars on Religion," *Political Science Quarterly*, LXVII, No. 4 (December), 534–72. See Nos. 450, 482.

243 "A Revolutionary Transformation of Jewish Community," *ADL Bulletin*, IX, No. 5 (May), 2. With comments thereon by Benjamin R. Epstein in "The Side of the Angels," *ibid.*, pp. 2, 8.

244 Review of Rufus Learsi, *Fulfillment: The Epic Story of Zionism* (Cleveland and New York, 1951). In *Saturday Review*, April 12, p. 37.

245 Review of Malcolm Hay, *The Foot of Pride* (Boston, 1950); and Ludwig Lewisohn, *The American Jew: Character and Destiny* (New York, 1950). In *New Republic*, January 21, pp. 19–20.

246 Booknote on Moses Hadas, *A History of Greek Literature* (New York, 1950); and *A History of Latin Literature* (New York, 1952). In *JSS*, XIV, No. 3 (July), 277–78.

1953

247 "Church and State Debates in the Jewish Community of 1848," in *Mordecai M. Kaplan Jubilee Volume.* New York: The Jewish Theological Seminary of America, pp. 49–72.

248 "The Cold War and Jewry," *American Zionist*, Abba Hillel Silver Anniversary Issue, XLIII, No. 7 (February 5), 21–24.

249 "Jewish Immigration and Communal Conflicts in Seventeenth-Century Corfù," in *The Joshua Starr Memorial Volume; Studies in History and Philology.* New York: Conference on Jewish Relations, pp. 169–82. Jewish Social Studies, Publications, No. 5.

250 "שד״ל והמהפכה בשנות התר״ח–ט" (Samuel David Luzzatto and the Revolution of 1848), ספר אסף (Simha Assaf Jub. Vol.), pp. 40–63.

251 "Eugen Täubler" (Obituary), *PAAJR.* XXII, pp. xxxi–xxxiv (cosigner, Ralph Marcus).

252 Review of Israel Cohen, *Contemporary Jewry, a Survey of Social, Cultural, Economic and Political Conditions* (London, 1950). In *JSS*, XV, No. 1 (January), 90–92.

253 Review of Gerald de Gaury, *The New State of Israel* (New York, 1952). In *Political Science Quarterly*, LXVIII, No. 2 (June), 287–88.

254 Review of David Hedegard, *Seder R. Amram Gaon*, Part I. Hebrew Text with Critical Apparatus Translation with Notes and Introduction (Motala, Sweden, 1951). In *JSS*, XV, No. 2 (April), 178–79.

255 Review of Simha (Simone) Luzatto, מאמר על יהודי ויניציה (Discourse on the Status of Jews in Venice), translated from the Italian by Dante Lattes, with introduction by Riccardo Benjamin Bachi and M. S. Shulvass, edited by the late A. Z. Aeshcoly (Jerusalem, ספריה היסטוריוגרפית [Historiographic Library], Mosad Bialik, 1951). *Ibid.*, XV, Nos. 3–4 (July–October), 313–14.

256 Review of Abraham A. Neuman, *Landmarks and Goals: Historical Studies and Addresses* (Philadelphia: Dropsie College Press, 1953). In *New York Times*, Book Review, October 25, p. 46.

257 Booknote on Ray Allen Billington, *The Protestant Crusade 1800–1860: The Growth of Bigotry and the Anti-Catholic Movement in America* (New York: 1938; second printing, 1952). In *JSS*, XV, Nos. 3–4 (July–October), 331–32.

258 Booknote on S. G. F. Brandon, *The Fall of Jerusalem and the Christian Church: A Study of the Effects of the Jewish Overthrow of A.D. 70 on Christianity* (London: Society for the Promotion of Christian Knowledge, 1951). *Ibid.*, XV, No. 1 (January), 93.

259 Booknote on Zevi (Hirsch) Perez Chayes, נאומים והרצאות (Addresses and Lectures). Hebrew trans. by Israel Lewin (Boston: Hebrew Teachers College, 1953). *Ibid.*, XV, Nos. 3–4 (July–October), 329.

260 Booknote on William Chomsky, *David Kimhi's Hebrew Grammar (Mikhlol): Systematically Presented and Critically Annotated* (New York, 1952). *Ibid.*, XV, Nos. 3–4 (July–October), 328.

261 Booknote on Frank S. Mead, *Handbook of Denominations in the United States* (New York and Nashville, 1951). *Ibid.*, XV, Nos. 3–4 (July-October), 332.

262 Booknote on Manfred Reifer, *Menschen und Ideen. Erinnerungen* (Tel-Aviv, n.d.). *Ibid.*, XV, Nos. 3–4 (July–October), 329.

263 Booknote on Priscilla Robertson, *Revolutions of 1848: A Social History* (Princeton, 1952). *Ibid.*, XV, Nos. 3–4 (July–October), 330.

1954

264 *Jerusalem: City Holy and Eternal.* New York: Hemisphere Publications, Inc. 32 pp. + 63 plates.

265 *Judaism: Postbiblical and Talmudic Period* (in collaboration with Joseph L. Blau). Ed. with an Introduction and Notes. New York: Liberal Arts Press. xxvi + 245 pp. Library of Religion, Series of Readings in Sacred Scriptures and Basic Writings of the World's Religions, Past and Present. See No. 347.

266–67 "American Jewish Communal Pioneering," Presidential Address, American Jewish Historical Society, February 20, 1954. *PAJHS*, XLIII, No. 3

(March), 133–50. Also appeared in Yiddish trans. in די צוקונפט, LIX, 251–59. See Nos. 361, 438, 450.

268 "עתידה של יהדות אמריקה" (The Future of American Jewry), גשר, Nos. 2–3, pp. 9–17.

269 "אמונה והיסטוריה בתולדות ישראל" (Faith and History in the Jewish Past), מגילות, March, pp. 5–14.

270 Address: "Report on Israel," delivered at Fourth Session, Part II, Saturday morning, March 7, 1953, Seventh Annual Conference on Middle East Affairs sponsored by the Middle East Institute. Published in *Evolution in the Middle East—Reform, Revolt and Change*, Washington, D.C., pp. 77–85.

271 "Three Hundred Years of American Jewry," "*300*" (September), 3, 5. See No. 272.

272 "Trescientos años de vida judía en los Estados Unitos," *Tribuna israelita*, 120 (November), 26–27. See No. 271.

273 Review of Oscar Handlin, *Adventure in Freedom*, and Rufus Learsi, *The Jews in America: A History*. In *New York Times*, Book Review, September 12, p. 6.

274 Foreword to Stuart Rosenberg, *The Jewish Community in Rochester, 1843–1925*. New York.

275 Foreword to Arnold Wiznitzer, *The Records of the Earliest Jewish Community in the New World*. New York.

1955

276 *Are the Jews Still the People of the Book*? Oscar Hillel Plotkin Lecture, 1955, Glencoe, Illinois. 20 pp. See No. 450.

277 היסטוריה חברותית ודתית של עם ישראל (Tel Aviv, Massada). Vol. I (Hebrew translation of No. 237, Chaps. I–VI by I. M. Grintz). 269 pp. + 21 illus.

278 "Opening Statement," and "Communal Responsibility for Jewish Social Research," in *Papers and Proceedings of the Tercentenary Conference on American Jewish Sociology*. Convened by the Conference on Jewish Relations, Commodore Hotel, New York, November 27–28, 1954. *JSS*, XVII, No. 3 (July), 175–76, 242–45.

279 "President's Report 1953–55," *PAJHS*, XLIV, No. 4 (June), 243–47.

280 "Some of the Tercentenary's Historic Lessons," *ibid.*, 199–209. See No. 450.

281 Review of Erwin R. Goodenough, *Jewish Symbols in the Greco-Roman Period* (New York, 1953, Bollingen Series XXXVII). Vol. I: The Archeological Evidence from Palestine; Vol. II: The Archeological Evidence from the Diaspora; Vol. III: Illustrations. In *JBL*, LXXIV, 196–99.

282 Review of Moses Hadas, *Third and Fourth Books of the Maccabees* (New York, 1953. Dropsie College Edition, Jewish Apocryphal Literature). *Ibid.*, 280–81.

283 Booknote on *The Age the Reformation* by E. Harris Harrison (Ithaca, New York: Cornell University Press, 1955). In *JSS*, XVII, No. 4 (October), 359.

1956

284 *Great Ages and Ideas of the Jewish People*, by Salo W. Baron [and others], ed. with an Introduction by Leo W. Schwarz. New York: Random House. xxvi + 515 pp. includes "The Modern Age," pp. 315–484, 494–98. See Nos. 394, 482.

285 *Histoire d'Israël vie sociale et religieuse* (Paris: Presses Universitaires de France). Vol. I (French translation of No. 237 by V. Nikiprowetzky). 589 pp. Sinaï Collection des sources d'Israël.

286 היסטוריה חברותית ודתית של עם ישראל (Tel Aviv: Massada). Vol. II (Hebrew translation of Nos. 237–38, Chaps. VII–XI by I. M. Grintz). 230 pp. + 10 illus.

287 יעקב שאצקי‎ (1956–1893)" (Jacob Shatzky: An Obituary), ייווא בלעטער, XL, 234–37.

288 "תנועת השחרור ויהודי אמריקה" (The Emancipation Movement and American Jewry), ארץ־ישראל, Vol. IV (Ben Zvi Jub. Vol.), Jerusalem: Israel Exploration Society, pp. 205–14. See No. 450.

289 "Maimonides' Significance to Our Generation," in *Maimonides; His Teachings and Personality*, ed. by Simon Federbusch. New York, pp. 7–16. See No. 303.

290 "Second and Third Commonwealth: Parallels and Differences," in *Israel: Its Role in Civilization*, ed. by Moshe Davis. New York, pp. 58–66.

291 "חרם וילנא והממשלות האדירות" (A Vilna Excommunication and the Great Powers), חורב, XII (September), 62–69.

292 Review of Izhak Ben-Zvi, ארץ־ישראל ויישובה בימי השלטון העותמאני (Eretz-Israel under Ottoman Rule: Four Centuries of History) (Jerusalem, 1955). In *Middle Eastern Affairs*, VII, Nos. 8–9 (August–September), 302.

293 Review of Justine Wise Polier and James Waterman Wise, eds., *The Personal Letters of Stephen Wise* (Boston, 1956). In *New York Times*, Book Review, July 8, p. 18.

294 Review of David and Tamar de Sola Pool, *An Old Faith in the New World: Portrait of Shearith Israel, 1654–1954* (New York: Columbia University Press, 1955). In *AHR*, LXII, No. 1 (October), 246–47.

295 Foreword to the American edition of *Monumental Inscriptions in the Burial Ground of the Jewish Synagogue at Bridgetown, Barbados*. Transcribed with an Introduction by E. M. Shilstone. New York, pp. i–ii. Copies of this edition were inscribed "in memory of… Elias and Minna Baron."

1957

296–98 *A Social and Religious History of the Jews*. Second edition, revised and enlarged. Vols. III–V: High Middle Ages, 500–1200. Vol. III: Heirs of

Rome and Persia. Vol. IV: Meeting of East and West. Vol. V: Religious Controls and Dissensions. New York: Columbia University Press, and Philadelphia: The Jewish Publication Society of America. xii + 340; vi + 352; vi + 416 pp. See Nos. 338–39, 380, 393, 423–25.

299 *Histoire d'Israël vie sociale et religieuse* (Paris: Presses Universitaires de France). Vol. II (French translation of No. 238 by V. Nikiprowetzky). 727 pp. Sinaï Collection des sources d'Israël.

300 היסטוריה חברותית ודתית של עם ישראל (Tel Aviv: Massada). Vol. III (Hebrew translation of No. 238, Chaps. XII–XV by I. M. Grintz). 254 pp. + 5 illus.

301 "בעיות היסוד של התפוצות החופשיות" (Basic Problems of the Dispersions in the Free World), Ideological Conference, Jerusalem, 1957, חזית, IV (1957–58), 230–36. See Nos. 310, 315–17, 367.

302 "Conference Theme," *The Writing of American Jewish History*, ed. by Moshe Davis and Isidore S. Meyer. New York, pp. 137–40. Reprint of *PAJHS*, XLVI, No. 3 (March).

303 "En lisant Maïmonide," *Dix ans après la chute de Hitler, 1945–1955*, ed. by Jonah M. Machover. Paris, pp. 67–76. French translation of No. 289.

304 ארץ־ישראל, ההתיישבות החדשה (1800–1882) ב. הישוב היהודי (Palestine, History, The New Settlement, 1800–1882, Part 2: The Jewish Settlement), האנציקלופדיה העברית (Encyclopedia Hebraica), VI, 504–508.

305 Foreword to Meir Ben-Horin, *Max Nordau, Philosopher of Human Solidarity*. New York. Jewish Social Studies, Publication No. 6.

1958

306–308 *A Social and Religious History of the Jews*. Second edition, revised and enlarged. Vols. VI–VIII: High Middle Ages, 500–1200. Vol. VI: Laws, Homilies, and the Bible. Vol. VII: Hebrew Language and Letters. Vol. VIII: Philosophy and Science. New York: Columbia University Press, and Philadelphia: The Jewish Publication Society of America. vi + 486; vi + 321; vi + 405 pp. See Nos. 404, 426–28.

309 "Can American Jewry be Culturally Creative?" *Jewish Heritage*, I, No. 2 (Spring), 11–14, 53. See Nos. 450, 478.

310 "Diaspora and Zion," *Jewish Frontier*, XXV (July), 7–12. Part of No. 308, an address delivered in Hebrew at the Ideological Conference, Jerusalem, 1957. See Nos. 301, 315–317, 367.

311 "A Historian Looks at South African Jewry," *Jewish Affairs*, 2 Parts, May, pp. 4–8; June, pp. 13–16.

312 "מקומה של יהדות אמריקה בתולדות ישראל" (The Role of American Jewry in Jewish History), הדאר, XXXVIII, No. 17 (February 21), 303–304; No. 18 (February 28), 323–24.

1959

313 "Community, Jewish." *Standard Jewish Encyclopedia*. Ed.-in-Chief, Cecil Roth. Garden City, New York, pp. 469–75. See Nos. 405, 415, 440, 444, 455.

314 "Concluding Remarks" to the Joint Conference on "The Impact of Israel on the American Jewish Community," *Papers and Proceedings of the Joint Conference on the Impact of Israel on the American Jewish Community*. Convened by the Conference on Jewish Social Studies and the Theodor Herzl Institute. New York, December 22–23, 1954. *JSS*, XXI, No. 1 (January), 87–88. Also reprint.

315 "The Dialogue Between Israel and the Diaspora," *Forum* for the Problems of Zionism, Jewry and the State of Israel, Vol. IV: Proceedings of the Ideological Conference held in Jerusalem, 1957, pp. 236–44. (English translation of No. 301). See Nos. 310, 316–17, 367.

316 "Le Dialogue entre Israël et la Diaspora," *L'Arche*, No. 36 (December), 26–30. See Nos. 301, 310, 315, 317, 367.

317 "Diaspora and Zion," *The Jewish Digest*, IV, No. 11 (August), 60–70. Condensed from No. 310. See Nos. 301, 315–16, 367.

318–19 "The Jewish State and the Jewish People from the Historic Perspective." Address delivered at the seventh session of the *Symposium on the Jewish State and the Jewish People*, Fourth Plenary Assembly of the World Jewish Congress, Stockholm, August 1959, Booklet No. 3, pp. 27–40. Also in *Proceedings of the Fourth Plenary Assembly of the World Jewish Congress, Stockholm, 1959* (Geneva), pp. 148–64.

320 "Moses Maimonides (1135–1204)." In *Great Jewish Personalities in Ancient and Medieval Times*, ed. by Simon Noveck. B'nai B'rith Great Books Series, Vol. 1 (New York), pp. 204–30. Also reprint. See No. 406.

321 Booknote on *Demographic Yearbook 1957*. Statistical Office of the United Nations (New York, 1957). In *JSS*, XXI, No. 3 (July), 214.

322 Foreword to Zvi Ankori, *Karaites in Byzantium*, New York.

1960

323 *A Social and Religious History of the Jews*. Second edition, revised and enlarged. Index to Vols. I–VIII. New York: Columbia University Press, and Philadelphia: The Jewish Publication Society of America. xi + 163 pp. See No. 238.

324 *Modern Nationalism and Religion*. Paperback. New York: Meridian Books, Inc., and Philadelphia: The Jewish Publication Society of America. xiv + 363. Reprint of No. 192. See No. 449.

325 ספר-יובל ליצחק בער: במלאת לו שבעים שנה (Yitzhak F. Baer Jubilee Volume: On the Occasion of his Seventieth Birthday). Edited by S. W. Baron, B. Dinur, S. Ettinger, I. Halpern. Jerusalem: The Historical Society of Israel. 484 + XXVII pp.

326 "Etapas de la emancipación judía," *Diógenes*, No. 29 (March), pp. 71–101 (Spanish translation of No. 331.) See No. 327.

327 "Étapes de l'Emancipation juive," *Diogène*, No. 29 (March), pp. 65–94. (French translation of No. 331). See No. 326.

328 "The Image of the Rabbi in Traditional Literature," *Proceedings* of the Rabbinical Assembly of America, XXIV, pp. 84–92. Address delivered at the Sixtieth Annual Convention of the Rabbinical Assembly of America, May 9, 1960. See Nos. 341, 450.

329 "Introductory Remarks" to Proceedings of the Herzl Centennial Celebration (April 28) under the auspices of Columbia University and the Herzl Institute. *Herzl Year Book*, III, 11–14, 26, 35, 48.

330 "בימי הביניים' 'מלוא הריבונות האפוסטולית' ו'שעבוד היהודים' ("'Plenitude of Apostolic Powers' and 'Medieval Jewish Serfdom'"), in ספר־יובל ליצחק בער (Y. F. Baer Jubilee Volume), Jerusalem, pp. 102–124. See No. 462.

331 "New Approaches to Jewish Emancipation," *Diogenes*, No. 29 (Spring), pp. 56–81. See Nos. 326–27.

332 "Philip Friedman" (Obituary), *PAAJR*, XXIX, 1–7. Also reprint.

333 "Qui est Juif? Quelques considérations historiques," *L'Arche*, No. 46 (November), pp. 48–51. The cover reads: "Qui est Juif? Le questionnaire de Ben Gurion. La réponse du Prof. Baron." The Table of Contents: "Qui est Juif? Le point de vue de l'historien." See Nos. 334–35, 359, 381.

334 "Who is a Jew?" *Midstream*, VI, No. 2 (Spring), 5–16. Based on addresses delivered at the Y.M.H.A., New York, and at the Washington Hebrew Congregation, Washington, D.C. See Nos. 333, 335, 359, 381, 440.

335 מיהו יהודי? קמץ הרהורים בהסטוריה (Who is a Jew? Some Historical Reflections). New York, 20 pp. Reprinted from הדאר, XL, Nos. 24–25. (Hebrew translation of No. 334.) See also Nos. 333, 359, 381, 440.

336 Review of Selma Stern, *Josel von Rosheim: Befehlshaber der Judenschaft im Heiligen Römischen Reich Deutscher Nation* (Stuttgart, c. 1959). In *AHR*, LXV, No. 3 (April), 670.

337 Foreword to *Guide to Jewish History under Nazi Impact*, ed. by Jacob Robinson and Philip Friedman. New York.

1961

338–39 *Histoire d'Israël vie sociale et religieuse* (Paris: Presses Universitaires de France). Vol. III (French translation of No. 296 by Léo Lacks), 420 pp.; Vol. IV (French translation of No. 297 by Andrée R. Picard), 426 pp. Sinaï Collection des sources d'Israël.

340 "Der Hass auf den Anderen. Aussagen im Eichmann-Prozess in Jerusalem," *Frankfurter Allgemeine Zeitung*, No. 113, May 17, p. 13.

341 הדאר, "הרב לפנים בישראל – ודמותו היום באמריקה", XLV, No. 27, pp. 476–78. (Hebrew translation of No. 328.) See also No. 450.

342 "Isaiah Sonne 1887–1960" (Obituary), *JSS*, XXIII, No. 2 (April), 130–32.

343 – 44 "Jewish Interdependence and the Alliance," *The Alliance Review*, XV, No. 35 (Winter), 23–29. Appeared in Spanish under the title: "Interdependencia judía y la Alianza," in *Revista de la Alliance*, No. 35 (October), 25–31. Both journals are published by the American Friends of the Alliance Israelite Universelle, New York.

345 "Koppel Shub Pinson" (Obituary), *JSS*, XXIII, No. 3 (July), 138–42.

346 "The Long Road That Led to Israel." Review of Ben Halpern, *The Idea of the Jewish State* (Cambridge, Mass., 1961). In the *New York Times*, Book Review, January 22, pp. 7, 35.

1962

347 *Judaism. Postbiblical and Talmudic Period* (in collaboration with Joseph L. Blau). Ed. with Introduction and Notes. New York: The Liberal Arts Press. Paperback. xxvi + 245 pp. The Library of Religion, Vol. III. See No. 265.

348 *Últimas chronicas do judaísmo europeu*. Rio de Janeiro: Instituto Brasileiro Judaico de Cultura. 40 pp. Ediçãos Comentário, IX (Portuguese trans. of No. 352.) See Nos. 368, 429, 482.

349 *World Dimensions of Jewish History*. New York: Leo Baeck Institute. 26 pp. Leo Baeck Memorial Lecture No. 5. See Nos. 357, 376, 482.

350 "Anti-Semitism," *Encyclopaedia Britannica*, II, 75–78F. See No. 414.

351 "Exilarch," *ibid.*, VIII, 967–68. See No. 416.

352 "From a Historian's Notebook. European Jewry Before and After Hitler," *American Jewish Year Book*, Vol. 63, pp. 3–51. With an extract from the official transcript of his testimony at the trial of Adolf Eichmann, Jerusalem, April 24, 1961. App. pp. 52–56. Also reprint, 56 pp. See Nos. 348, 368, 429, 482.

353 "The Future of Jewish Culture in the United States." Condensed from a Paper presented at the 74th Jewish Publication Society Annual Meeting held in Philadelphia, May 20, 1962. In *JPS Bookmark*, IX, No. 2, pp. 7–9.

354 "The Jewish Commonwealths and the Dispersions," in *The Ethic of Power: The Interplay of Religion, Philosophy, and Politics*, ed. by Harold D. Lasswell and Harlan Cleveland (New York), pp. 3–25. See No. 482.

355 "Josel of Rosheim," *Encyclopaedia Britannica*, XIII, 150. See No. 419.

356 "Medieval Nationalism and Jewish Serfdom," in *Studies and Essays in Honor of Abraham A. Neuman* (Philadelphia), pp. 17–48. See No. 462.

357 "היהודית" ממדיה העולמיים של ההיסטוריה" (World Dimensions of Jewish History), הדאר, XLII, Nos. 24 (April 13), 382–84; 25 (May 4), 416–18. (Hebrew translation of No. 349.) See Nos. 376, 482.

358 "Pharisees," *Encyclopaedia Britannica*, XVII, 689–90. See No. 420.

359 "Quién es Judío? Algunas reflexiones historicas," *Davar*, 92, pp. 64–82. (Spanish translation of No. 334.) See also Nos. 333, 335, 381.

360 "Some Recent Literature on the History of the Jews in the Pre-Emancipation Era (1300–1800)," *Journal of World History*, VII, No. 1, pp. 137–71.

361 "Trois siècles d'esprit pionnier dans les communautés juives," *L'Arche*, Nos. 67–68 (August–September), 58–62. See Nos. 266–67, 450.

362 "Introductory Remarks," in *Papers and Proceedings on the Emergence of New African States and World Jewry* of the Annual Meeting, Conference on Jewish Social Studies, New York, 1961. *JSS*, XXIV, No. 2 (April), 67–68.

363 "Berichtigung" (to Guido Kisch's 'Zur Frage der Aufhebung jüdisch-religiöser Jurisdiktion durch Justinian' [in *SZ*, LXXVII, 1960, pp. 395–401]). *Zeitschrift der Savigny-Stiftung für Rechtsgeschichte*, LXXIX, 547–48.

1963

364 *The Jews of the United States, 1790–1840. A Documentary History*, ed. in collaboration with Joseph L. Blau. 3 vols. New York: Columbia University Press, and Philadelphia: The Jewish Publication Society of America. xxxv + 1034 pp.

365 Co-editor with Moshe Davis and Allan Nevins, *The History of the Jews of Milwaukee* by Louis J. Swichkow and Lloyd P. Gartner. Philadelphia: The Jewish Publication Society of America, xix + 533 pp. Regional History Series of the American Jewish History Center of the Jewish Theological Seminary of America, I.

366 "American Jewish Scholarship and World Jewry," *AJHQ*, LII, No. 4 (June), 274–82. Address delivered at the Sixty-First Annual Meeting of the American Jewish Historical Society in New York, April 21. See No. 450.

367 "The Dialogue Between Israel and the Diaspora." Reprinted in *The Mission of Israel*, ed. by Jacob Baal-Teshuva. New York. Pp. 306–20. See Nos. 301, 310, 315–17.

368 עדויות (Testimonies at the Eichmann Trial). Published by the Legal Counsel for the State Against Adolf Eichmann. 2 vols. Jerusalem. Vol. I, pp. 5–41. See Nos. 348, 352, 429, 482.

369 "Israel Spanier Wechsler 1886–1962" (Obituary), *JSS*, XXV, No. 2 (April), 100–1.

370 "Jewish College Students Are More Religious." Interview with Gabriel M. Cohen in *The National Jewish Post and Opinion*, XVIII, No. 26 (March 1), 4–5.

371 "Newer Emphases in Jewish History." *JSS*, XXV, No. 4 (October), 235–48. See Nos. 381, 399, 482.

372–73 "The Problem of Teaching Religion." *Columbia College Today*, X, No. 3, pp. 25–27. Reproduced in the *Bulletin* of the National Foundation for Jewish Culture, Vol. III, No. 1.

374 "A Reply" at the conferral of the Lee M. Friedman Award by the American Jewish Historical Society on April 20. *AJHQ*, LII, No. 4 (June), 332–33.

375 "David Rosenstein 1895–1963" (Obituary), *JSS*, XXV, No. 3 (July), 172–73.

376 "World Dimensions of Jewish History," in *Simon Dubnov, l'homme et son oeuvre*. Publié à l'occasion du centenaire de sa naissance (1860–1960). Ed. by Aaron Steinberg (Paris: Section française du Congrès juif mondial); also with an English title page reading: *Simon Dubnow. The Man and His Work. A Memorial Volume on the Occasion of the Centenary of his Birth (1860–1960)*, pp. 26–40. Reproduced from No. 349 with additional annotations. See also Nos. 357, 482.

377 Booknote on Richard W. Diel, *Der Parlamentarier Eduard Lasker und die parlamentarische Stilentwicklung der Jahre 1867–1884* (Diss. Erlangen, Germany, 1956). In *JSS*, XXV, No. 1 (January), 93–94.

378 Booknote on Robert A. Kann, *A Study in Austrian Intellectual History. From Late Baroque to Romanticism* (New York, 1960). *Ibid.*, XXV, No. 1 (January), 93.

1964

379 *The Russian Jew under Tsars and Soviets*. New York: The Macmillan Company. xv + 427 pp. See No. 483.

380 *Histoire d'Israël vie sociale et religieuse* (Paris: Presses Universitaires de France). Vol. V (French translation of No. 298 by Andrée R. Picard), 374 pp.

381 *History and Jewish Historians: Essays and Addresses*. Compiled with a Foreword by Arthur Hertzberg and Leon A. Feldman. Philadelphia: The Jewish Publication Society of America, xviii + 504 pp.

Part 1: Essays in History

1) Who Is a Jew? pp. 5–22. See Nos. 333–35, 359; 2) World Dimensions of Jewish History, pp. 23–42, 345. See Nos. 349, 357, 376, 482; 3) Modern Capitalism and Jewish Fate, pp. 43–64. See Nos. 156, 482; 4) Emphases in Jewish History, pp. 65–89, 345–47. See Nos. 92–94, 482; 5) Newer Emphases in Jewish History, pp. 90–106, 347–48. See Nos. 371, 399, 482.

Part II: Maimonides

6) The Historical Outlook of Maimonides, pp. 109–163, 348–404. See No. 68.

Part III: Jewish Historians and their Viewpoints

7) Azariah de' Rossi: A Biographical Sketch, pp. 167–173, 405; revised translation from the Hebrew. See Nos. 20, 41; 8) Azariah de' Rossi's Attitude to Life, pp. 174–204, 406–422. See No. 27; 9) Azariah de' Rossi's Historical Method, pp. 205–239, 422–42, revised translation from the French. See No. 31; 10) I. M. Jost the Historian, pp. 240–62, 442–46. See No. 46; 11) Heinrich (Hirsch) Graetz, 1817–1891: A Biographical Sketch, pp. 263–69, 446–48, revised translation of No. 52; Graetz and Ranke: A Methodological Study, pp. 269–75, 448–49, revised translation from the German. See No. 11; 12) Moritz Steinschneider's Contributions to Jewish Historiography, pp. 276–321, 449–70.

See No. 220; 13) Levi Herzfeld: The First Jewish Economic Historian, pp. 322–43, 471–79. See No. 185.

382 "Action Through Knowledge," *The Torch*, XXIII, No. 3 (Summer), 5–7. A reply at the conferral of the Citation and Award for Distinguished Service to American Jewry presented by the National Federation of Jewish Men's Clubs on April 19.

383 "The Cultural Potential of American Jewry," *Hadassah*, 45, No. 6 (February), 6, 28.

384 "From Colonial Mansion to Skyscraper: An Emerging Pattern of Hebraic Studies," *Rutgers Hebraic Studies*, I, 3–24. Address at the Inaugural Convocation of the Department of Hebraic Studies, Rutgers — The State University, New Brunswick, N.J. Also reprint, 24 pp. See No. 450.

385 "Ghetto and Emancipation," in *The Menorah Treasury: Harvest of Half a Century*. Ed. by Leo W. Schwarz, Philadelphia, pp. 50–63. Reprint of No. 30.

386 "Medieval Folklore and Jewish Fate," *Jewish Heritage*, VI, No. 4 (Spring), 13–18. See Nos. 398, 445.

387 "The Nazi Impact on European Jewry" (Summary), in *Life, Struggle and Uprising in the Warsaw Ghetto*, Chicago, pp. 10–11. YIVO Exhibit, YIVO Institute for Jewish Research, Documentary Projects.

388 "Whither American Jews?" *Jewish Chronicle* (London), September 4, pp. 49–50.

389 Foreword to Jacob Agus, *The Meaning of Jewish History*, 2 vols., New York.

390 Foreword to Stuart E. Rosenberg, *America is Different. The Search for Jewish Identity*. New York. See No. 442 a.

1965

391–92 *A Social and Religious History of the Jews*. Second edition, revised and enlarged. Late Middle Ages and Era of European Expansion, 1200–1650. Vol. IX: Under Church and Empire. Vol. X: On the Empire's Periphery. New York: Columbia University Press, and Philadelphia: The Jewish Publication Society of America. x + 350; vi + 432 pp.

393 היסטוריה חברותית ודתית של עם ישראל (Tel Aviv: Massada). Vol. IV (Hebrew translation of No. 296 [Vol. III] by Zvi Ankori). 295 pp. + 6 illus.

394 *La Época moderna*. Vol. VI of *Grandes épocas e ideas del pueblo judío* (Buenos Aires, Argentina: Paidos). Paperback (Spanish translation of No. 284 by Matilde Horne). Biblioteca Ciencia e historia de las religiones, I. See No. 482.

395 "Some Historical Lessons for Jewish Philanthrophy," in *The Critical Challenges to Philanthropy*, pp. 2–9. Mimeographed. Address delivered at a Symposium under the sponsorship of the Federation of Jewish Philanthropies of New York, October 21. See No. 450.

396 "In Historic Perspective," *Our Age*, Vol. VII, No. 2 (October 31), 1–3. A Teen-Team Interview.

397 "John Calvin and the Jews," in *Harry Austryn Wolfson Jubilee Volume: On the Occasion of his Seventy-Fifth Birthday* (Jerusalem: American Academy for Jewish Research). English Section, Vol. I, pp. 141–63. See Nos. 462, 482.

398 "Medieval Folklore and Jewish Fate," in *Jewish Heritage Reader*, Selected, with Introduction by Morris Adler, ed. by Lily Edelman (New York: Taplinger Publishing Co. Inc.), pp. 13–18. Reprint of No. 386. See No. 445.

399 "הדגשים חדשים בהיסטוריה היהודית" (Newer Emphases in Jewish History), הדאר, XLV, No. 27 (May 28), 485–88. (Hebrew translation of No. 371.) See Nos. 381, 482.

400 "Interview with Professor Salo W. Baron," *Reconstructionist*, XXI, No. 9 (June 11), 12–21.

401 Foreword to Marnin Feinstein, *American Zionism 1884–1904*. New York.

402 Foreword to Mark Wischnitzer, *A History of Jewish Crafts and Guilds*. New York.

1966

403 Ed., *Essays on Maimonides. An Octocentennial Volume* (New York: AMS Press). Reprint. See No. 133.

404 היסטוריה חברותית ודתית של עם ישראל (Tel Aviv: Massada). Vol. VII (Hebrew translation of No. 306 [Vol. VI] by Yehoshua Amir). 367 pp. + 4 illus.

405 "Community, Jewish," *Standard Jewish Encyclopedia*, new ed., pp. 469–75. See Nos. 313, 415, 440, 444, 455.

406 "Moses Maimonides [1135–1204]," in *Molders of the Jewish Mind* (Washington, D.C.: B'nai B'rith Adult Jewish Education), pp. 75–101. Reprint of No. 320.

407 "An Incurable Disease," *The Alliance Review*, XX, No. 40 (Spring), 11–13. Excerpts from No. 154.

408 "The Jewish Community and Jewish Education," in *Judaism and the Jewish School*, ed. and intro. by Judah Pilch and Meir Ben-Horin. New York, pp. 2–14. See also Nos. 205–6, 450.

409 "[Jews and Germans: a] Millennial Heritage." *World Jewry*, IX, No. 5 (September/October), 19–20. Excerpts of Address delivered at the Fifth Plenary Assembly of the World Jewish Congress, Brussels, July 31– August 9. See Nos. 413, 418.

410 Introduction: "Georg Brandes and Lord Beaconsfield," to Georg Brandes, *Lord Beaconsfield: A Study of Benjamin Disraeli*. New York, pp. v–xiv.

1967

411–12 *A Social and Religious History of the Jews*. Second edition, revised and enlarged. Late Middle Ages and Era of Expansion, 1200–1650. Vol. XI:

Citizen or Alien Conjurer. Vol. XII: Economic Catalyst. New York: Columbia University Press, and Philadelphia: The Jewish Publication Society of America. x + 422; viii + 359 pp.

413 *Deutsche und Juden.* Beiträge von Nahum Goldman, Gershom Scholem, Golo Mann, Salo W. Baron, Eugen Gerstenmaier, Karl Jaspers. Frankfurt am Main: Suhrkamp Verlag. Includes ["Deutsche und Juden. Ein tausendjähriges Erbe"], pp. 70–95. Translated into German by Helmut Heck. See Nos. 409, 418.

414 "Anti-Semitism," *Encyclopaedia Britannica*, II, 81–90. Revised No. 350.

415 "Comunidade Judia," *Enciclopedia Judaica.* Rio de Janeiro: Editore tradição, pp. 343–50. See Nos. 313, 405, 440, 444, 455.

416 "Exilarch," *Encyclopaedia Britannica*, VIII, 963. Revised No. 351.

417 "Graetzens Geschichtsschreibung. Eine methodische Untersuchung," in *Wissenschaft des Judentums im deutschen Sprachbereich. Ein Querschnitt*, ed. by Kurt Wilhelm. Tübingen. Vol. I, pp. 353–60. Schriftenreihe Wissenschaftlicher Abhandlungen des Leo Baeck Institut, No. 16. See also No. 11; and in an abridged English translation, No. 381.

418 "Jews and Germans: A Millennial Heritage." *Midstream*, XIII, No. 1 (January), 3–13. Based on an address delivered at the Fifth Plenary Assembly of the World Jewish Congress, Brussels, Belgium, August, 1966. See Nos. 409, 413.

419 "Josel of Rosheim," *Encyclopaedia Britannica*, XIII, 86–87. Revised No. 355.

420 "Pharisees," *Ibid.*, XVII, 794. Revised No. 358.

1968

421–28 *Historia social y religiosa del pueblo judío*, Vols. I–VIII. Buenos Aires: Editorial Paidos. (Spanish translation of Nos. 237–38, 296–98, 306–8 by Eduardo Goligorsky under the supervision of Marshall T. Meyer.) Vol. I: Época Antigua, Parte 1; Vol. II: Época Antigua, Parte 2. Alta Edad Media, 500–1200: Volumenes III–VIII; Vol. III: Herederos de Roma y Persia; Vol. IV: El Encuentro de Oriente y Occidente; Vol. V: Controles y conflictos religiosos; Vol. VI: Las leyes, las homilías y la biblia; Vol. VII: El idioma y la literatura hebreas; Vol. VIII: Filosofía y ciencia. 434 pp., 33 illus. + 8 col. plates; 451 pp., 38 illus. + 9 col. plates; 330 pp., 24 illus. + 8 col. plates; 340 pp., 28 illus. + 5 col. plates; 393 pp., 31 illus. + 6 col. plates; 461 pp., 37 illus. + 5 col. plates; 304 pp., 26 illus. + 5 col. plates; 378 pp., 31 illus. + 8 col. plates.

429 "From a Historian's Notebook," in *Out of the Whirlwind: a Reader of Holocaust Literature*, ed. by Albert H. Friedlander. New York, pp. 133–54. See Nos. 348, 352, 368, 482.

430 "Herencia medieval y realidades modernas en las relaciones entre judíos y Protestantes," *Diógenes*, XVI, No. 61 (January–March), 31–48 (Spanish translation of No. 433). See No. 431.

431 "Héritage médiéval et réalités modernes dans les relations entre juifs et protestants," *Diogène*, No. 61 (January–March), 36–58 (French translation of No. 433 by Marguerite Derrida). See No. 430.

432 "פרץ צבי, חיות" (Hirsch Perez Chajes), האנציקלופדיה העברית (Encyclopaedia Hebraica), XVII, 351–53.

433 "Medieval Heritage and Modern Realities in Protestant-Jewish Relations," *Diogenes*, No. 61 (Spring), 32–51. Lecture delivered at the Harvard Divinity School, October 1966. Revised and annotated. See Nos. 430–31.

434 "Nationalism in the Middle East" [A Discussion], in *Proceedings* of the First Annual Conference of American Professors for Peace in the Middle East, pp. 35–37.

435 "נוסח בלתי-שכיח של חרם בפרנקפורט" (An Unusual Excommunication Formula from Frankfurt), in מחקרים בקבלה ובתולדות הדתות מוגשים לגרשם שלום (Studies in Mysticism and Religion Presented to Gershom G. Scholem), Jerusalem, pp. 29–34.

1969

436 *A Social and Religious History of the Jews.* Second edition, revised and enlarged. Late Middle Ages and Era of European Expansion, 1200–1650. Vol. XIII: Inquisition, Renaissance, and Reformation; Vol. XIV: Catholic Restoration and Wars of Religion. New York: Columbia University Press, and Philadelphia: The Jewish Publication Society of America. x + 463; viii + 412 pp.

437 "Impact of Nationalism," in *Readings in English for Students of the Social Sciences and Humanities.* Selected and edited by N. A. Berkoff, Batya Ariel, and Jane Falk. Jerusalem: Hebrew University, Department of English, pp. 50–51. See No. 40.

438 "Jewish Communal Pioneering." Reprinted in *The Jewish Experience in America: Selected Studies from the Publications of the American Jewish Historical Society.* Ed. with an Intro. by Abraham J. Karp. 5 vols. Waltham, Mass.: American Jewish Historical Society, New York: Ktav Publishing House. Vol. I, pp. 1–18. See Nos. 266, 361, 450.

439 "Jewish Pioneering. A Lesson of Jewish History," *Jewish Heritage*, II, No. 4 (Summer), 53–55. Response to Four Addresses when presented with the 1969 Jewish Heritage Award for Excellence in Literature on January 19th in New York.

440 "קהילה" (Community, Jewish), אנציקלופדיה של היהדות. Ramat Gan: Massada. Hebrew translation of No. 313 by Israel Eldad. See Nos. 405, 415, 444, 455.

441 "Who is a Jew? Some Historical Reflections," in *Readings in English for Students of the Social Sciences and Humanities.* Selected and edited by N. A. Berkoff, Batya Ariel and Jane Falk. Jerusalem: Hebrew University, Department of English, pp. 142–49. See Nos. 333–35, 359, 381.

442 "A Review of Freud," in *Monotheism and Moses: the Genesis of Judaism*. Ed. by Robert J. Christen and Harold E. Hazelton. Lexington, Mass., pp. 39–43. Problems in Europeans Civilization. See Nos. 101, 460, 462.

442a Foreword to Stuart E. Rosenberg, שונה היא אמריקה. Ramat Gan: Massada. Hebrew translation of No. 390.

1970

443 Co-editor with Moshe Davis and Allan Nevins, *History of the Jews of Los Angeles* by Max Vorspan and Lloyd P. Gartner. San Marino, California: The Huntington Library, and Philadelphia: The Jewish Publication Society of America. Regional History Series of the American Jewish History Center of The Jewish Theological Seminary of America [II]. xii + 362 + 22 pp. Constitution of The Hebrew Benevolent Society appearing only in JPS ed.

444 "Community," *Standard Jewish Encyclopedia*, New ed., pp. 469–75. See Nos. 313, 405, 415, 440, 455.

445 "Medieval Folklore and Jewish Fate," *Jewish Affairs*, XXV, No. 3 (March), 14–19. Reprinted from *Jewish Heritage*. See Nos. 386, 398.

446 "Rachi et la Communauté de Troyes," *L'Arche*, Nos. 162–63 (26 September to 25 October), pp. 61–68. French translation by Reine Silbert of text of No. 136, without notes. See No. 462.

447 "הרהורים על הדמוגרפיה ההיסטורית היהודית בימי קדם ובימי הבינים" (Reflections on Ancient and Medieval Jewish Historical Demography) in בנתיבי הגות ותרבות (Aryeh Tartakower Jubilee Volume). Ed. by Yosef Shapiro. Tel Aviv: Brit Ivrit Olamit, pp. 31–45. See No. 462.

448 Foreword to Yosef Yerushalmi, *From Spanish Court to Italian Ghetto: Isaac Cardoso, a Study in Seventeenth-Century Marranism and Jewish Apologetics*. New York: Columbia University Press. Publications of the Center of Israel and Jewish Studies, I.

1971

449 *Modern Nationalism and Religion*. Freeport, New York: Books for Library Press, x + 363 pp. Essay Index Reprint Series. See Nos. 192, 324.

450 *Steeled by Adversity: Essays and Addresses on American Jewish Life*. Edited by Jeannette Meisel Baron. Philadelphia: The Jewish Publication Society of America. xi + 729 pp.

Part I: Introduction
1) Ages of Anxiety, pp. 3–12.

Part II: Gradual Unfolding 1654–1879
2) American and Jewish Destiny: A Semimillennial Experience, pp. 15–25. See No. 151; 3) American Jewish History: Problems and Methods, pp. 26–73,

575–91. See No. 219; 4) A Documentary History of the Jews in the United States 1654–1875. Ed. by Morris U. Schappes. A Book Review, pp. 74–79. See No. 229; 5) The Emancipation Movement and American Jewry, pp. 80–105, 592–98. See No. 288; 6) From Colonial Mansion to Skycraper: An Emerging Pattern of Hebraic Studies, pp. 106–126, 598–602. See No. 384; 7) American Jewish Communal Pioneering, pp. 127–46, 603–4. See Nos. 266–67, 361; 8) The Image of the Rabbi, Formerly and Today, pp. 147–57, 604–5. See Nos. 328, 341; 9) Palestinian Messengers in America, 1849–79: A Record of Four Journeys, pp. 158–266, 605–25. See No. 166.

Part III: Climax of Immigration

10) United States 1880–1914, pp. 269–414, 625–79.

Part IV: Twentieth Century Problems

11) Impact of Wars on Religion, pp. 417–53, 679–85. See Nos. 242, 482; 12) The Second World War and Jewish Community Life, pp. 454–72, 686–87. See Nos. 152, 159; 13) Some of the Tercentenary's Historic Lessons, pp. 473–84, 687–89. See No. 280; 14) Some Historical Lessons for Jewish Philanthropy, pp. 485–94, 690. See No. 395; 15) Cultural Pluralism of American Jewry, pp. 495–505. See Nos. 95–96; 16) Are the Jews Still the People of the Book? pp. 506–17, 690. See No. 276; 17) The Jewish Community and Jewish Education, pp. 518–31, 690. See Nos. 205–6, 408; 18) American Jewish Scholarship and World Jewry, pp. 532–41. See No. 366; 19) Can American Jewry Be Culturally Creative? pp. 542–51, 691. See Nos. 309, 353, 478; 20) Reordering Communal Priorities, pp. 552–72, 691. See No. 459.

451 Co-editor with Moshe Davis and Allan Nevins, *Immigrants to Freedom: Jewish Communities in Rural New Jersey since 1882* by Joseph Brandes in association with Martin Douglas. Philadelphia: The University of Pennsylvania Press, and The Jewish Publication Society of America. Regional History Series of the American Jewish History Center of The Jewish Theological Seminary of America, III.

452 "Anti-Semitism," *Encyclopaedia Britannica*, II, 81–90. Updated No. 414.

453 "Cecil Roth" (Obituary), *AHR*, 76, No. 2 (April), 591–92.

454 "A Collection of Hebrew-Latin Aphorisms by a Christian Hebraist," in *Studies in Jewish Bibliography, History and Literature in Honor of I. Edward Kiev.* Ed. by Charles Berlin. New York: Ktav Publishing House, pp. 1–10.

455 "Community," *Standard Jewish Encyclopedia*, New ed., pp. 469–75. See Nos. 313, 405, 415, 440.

456 "Cultural Reconstruction of Russian Jewry." Condensed from a Paper delivered at the 83rd Annual Meeting of The Jewish Publication Society of America held in Philadelphia on May 15, 1971. In *JPS Bookmark*, XVIII, No. 2 (June), 4–5, 10.

457 חלום שנתגשם (A Dream Come True). Tel Aviv: University of Tel Aviv,

5732. Inaugural lecture at the Opening of the Chaim Rosenberg School of Jewish Studies at the University of Tel Aviv, October 19th. 47 pp.

458 "Nationalismus und Religion in der heutigen Welt," *Saeculum*, XXII, Heft 2–3, pp. 305–16. Revised and annotated version of an Address delivered at the Institut für Judaistik at the University of Vienna on June 16, 1969. See No. 488.

459 "Transmitting and Enriching the Heritage of Judaism," *Assembly Papers* of the 39th General Assembly of the Council of Jewish Federations and Welfare Funds held at Kansas City, Mo. November 11–15, pp. 1–15. Address delivered at General Assembly on November 14th. See No. 450.

460 "Book Review of Moses and Monotheism," in *Psychoanalysis and History*. Ed. with an Intro. by Bruce Mazlish. New York: Grosset and Dunlop, pp. 50–55. The Universal Library, Paperback. See Nos. 101, 442, 462.

461 Review of *The Letters and Papers of Chaim Weizmann*. Ed. by Leonard Stein in collaboration with Gedalia Yogev. Series A: Letters. Vol. I: Summer 1885–29 October 1902 (London: Oxford University Press, 1968), in *Political Science Quarterly*, LXXXVI, No. 2 (June), 359–62.

1972

462 *Ancient and Medieval Jewish History: Essays*. Edited with a Foreword by Leon A. Feldman. New Brunswick: Rutgers University Press. xxiv + 588 pp. Introduction: Analysis and Synthesis, pp. xv–xxiii.

Part I: Antiquity

1) Monotheism and Moses, pp. 3–9. See Nos. 101, 442, 460; 2) Reflections on Ancient and Medieval Jewish Historical Demography, pp. 10–22, 373–80. See No. 447; 3) The Israelitic Population under the Kings, pp. 23–73, 380–99. English translation of No. 57.

Part II: Medieval Islam

4) Some Medieval Jewish Attitudes to the Muslim State, pp. 77–94, 399–403; 5) Saadia's Communal Activities, pp. 95–127, 403–33. See No. 171; 6) Yehudah Halevi: An Answer to a Historic Challenge, pp. 128–48, 433–43. See Nos. 137, 155; 7) The Economic Views of Maimonides, pp. 149–235, 443–501. See No. 134.

Part III: Medieval Europe

8) The Jewish Factor in Medieval Civilization, pp. 239–67, 502–17. See Nos. 154, 407; 9) Rashi and the Community of Troyes, pp. 268–83, 518–25. See No. 136; 10) 'Plenitude of Apostolic Powers' and 'Medieval Jewish Serfdom,' pp. 284–307, 525–33. English translation of No. 330; 11) Medieval Jewish Nationalism and Jewish Serfdom, pp. 308–22, 533–44. See No. 356; 12) Medieval Heritage and Modern Realities in Protestant–Jewish Relations, pp.

323–37, 544–48. See No. 433; 13) John Calvin and the Jews, pp. 338–52, 548–54. See No. 397; 14) The Council of Trent and Rabbinic Literature, pp. 353–71, 555–64. See No. 484.

463–64 היסטוריה חברותית ודתית של עם ישראל. Tel Aviv: Massada. Vol. V (Hebrew translation of No. 297 [Vol. IV] by Zvi Baras); Vol. VI (Hebrew translation of No. 298 [Vol. V] by Joseph Nedava). 260; 336 pp.

465 *A Social and Religious History of the Jews.* Second edition, revised and enlarged. Vol. I: Ancient Times. 6th impression. New York: Columbia University Press, and Philadelphia: The Jewish Publication Society of America. See No. 237.

466–68 *The Jewish Community: Its History and Structure to the American Revolution.* 3 vols. Westport, Connecticut: Greenwood Press. Reprint of Nos. 148–50.

469–74 *Encyclopaedia Judaica.* 16 vols. Jerusalem: Keter Publishing Co.
Calvin, John, V, cols. 66–68;
Chajes, Hirsch (Zevi) Perez, *ibid.*, cols. 325–26;
Conference on Jewish Social Studies, *ibid.*, col. 874;
Economic History, XVI, cols. 1266–96;
Israelitisch-Theologische Lehranstalt, Vienna, Vol. IX, cols. 1067–68;
Population, XIII, cols. 866–903.

475 Foreword to Arthur J. Zuckerman, *A Jewish Princedom in Feudal France 768–900.* New York and London: Columbia University Press. Publications of the Center for Israel and Jewish Studies, II.

476 Introduction to Naomi W. Cohen, *Not Free to Desist: The American Jewish Committee.* Philadelphia: The Jewish Publication Society of America.

1973

477 *A Social and Religious History of the Jews.* Second edition, revised and enlarged. Late Middle Ages and Era of European Expansion, 1200–1650. Vol. XV: Resettlement and European Expansion. New York: Columbia University Press, and Philadelphia: The Jewish Publication Society of America, viii + 550 pp.

478 "היכולה יהדות אמריקה להיות מוקד יצירה מבחינה תרבותית?" ("Can American Jewry be Culturally Creative?"). In הגות עברית באמריקה (A Collection of Essays), ed. by Menahem Zahari. Jerusalem. (Hebrew trans. of No. 309). See No. 450.

479 Review of Alexander Altmann, *Moses Mendelssohn: a Biographical Study* (Tuscaloosa, Alabama, 1973). In *The Jerusalem Post*, Magazine, July 27, p. 18.

480 Introduction to Aron Freimann, *Union Catalogue of Hebrew Manuscripts.* Vol. I. New York: American Academy for Jewish Research.

In press

481 *Cultural Reconstruction of Russian Jewry*. Allan Bronfman Lectureship. Revised and enlarged address delivered in Montreal, November 18, 1971.

482 *História e Historiografia*. Collected Essays in Portuguese translation. São Paulo, Brazil: Editôra Perspectiva.

Section I:
1) World Dimensions of Jewish History. See Nos. 349, 357, 376, 381; 2) Emphases in Jewish History. See Nos. 92–94, 381; 3) Newer Emphases in Jewish History. See Nos. 371, 381, 399.

Section II:
1) John Calvin and the Jews. See Nos. 397, 462; 2) Modern Capitalism and the Jews. See Nos. 156, 381.

Section III:
1) The Jewish Commonwealths and the Dispersions. See No. 354; 2) The Impact of War on Religion. See Nos. 242, 450; 3) From a Historian's Notebook. See Nos. 348, 352, 368, 429.

Section IV:
1) The Dynamics of Emancipation. See Nos. 284, 394; 2) The Impact of Nationalism. See Nos. 284, 394; 3) The Enduring Heritage. See Nos. 284, 394; 4) The Challenge of Material Civilization. See Nos. 284, 394; 5) The Emergence of Israel. See Nos. 284, 394.

483 *The Russian Jew under Tsars and Soviets*. Second edition, revised and enlarged. New York: The Macmillan Company.

484 "The Council of Trent and Rabbinic Literature," in the *Isidore Epstein Memorial Volume*. See No. 462.

485 "The Impact of the Revolution of 1848 on Jewish Emancipation," in *The Jewish Social Studies Reader*, ed. by Abraham G. Duker *et al*. See No. 215.

486 "The Journal and the Conference on Jewish Social Studies," *ibid*.

487 "Judaism, a History of: General Observations," *Encyclopaedia Britannica*.

488 "Nationalism and Religion in the Contemporary World," *Greek Orthodox Theological Quarterly*. Translated into English and considerably enlarged from No. 458.

489 "A Noteworthy Letter of Heinrich Graetz," in the *Raphael Mahler Jubilee Volume*.

490 "Solomon ibn Ya'ish and Sultan Suleiman the Magnificent," in the *Joshua Finkel Jubilee Volume*.

491 Foreword to Tuvia Preschel, *The Alexander Kohut Memorial Foundation. A Review of Activities (1915–1972)*. New York: American Academy for Jewish Research.

492 Preface to *Die Hebräischen Handschriften in Osterreich*. Ed. by Arthur Zacharias Schwarz, D. S. Loewinger and E. Roth. American Academy for Jewish Research, Texts and Studies, Vol. IV.

LETTERS FROM DOHM
TO MENDELSSOHN

ALEXANDER ALTMANN

IN 1892 LUDWIG GEIGER published and analyzed excerpts from eleven letters written by Christian Wilhelm Dohm to Friedrich Nicolai, his intimate friend and publisher of his famous treatise *Ueber die bürgerliche Verbesserung der Juden* (1781; revised edition 1783; Second Part 1783).[1] The letters belong to the period from May, 1781 to November, 1783 and contain valuable information about the circumstances in which the treatise was edited, re-edited and expanded by a second part. They also offer striking evidence of Dohm's angry reaction to the critical review in the *Göttingische Anzeigen*. There is, however, an interval of eight months between letters 1 and 2, dated May 11, 1781 and January 9, 1782 respectively. Similar lacunae occur also at later stages in the correspondence. As a result, the sequence of events can be reconstructed only in patches. The paucity of the material is also responsible for some erroneous conclusions drawn by Geiger.

Fortunately, eight letters written by Dohm to Moses Mendelssohn during roughly the same period have been preserved in the family archive owned by Herr Robert von Mendelssohn and kindly put at my disposal.[2] In addition, one more letter has been discovered by me among the papers of Felix Mendelssohn Bartholdy

---

[1] Ludwig Geiger, "Aus Briefen Dohms an Nicolai," *Zeitschrift für die Geschichte der Juden in Deutschland* (*ZGJD*), V (1892), 75–91 (referred to hereafter as Geiger).

[2] "Depositum Robert von Mendelssohn" (DRvM), Staatsbibliothek der Stiftung Preussischer Kulturbesitz, Berlin, Serie C I, Nos. 6–13. I wish to express my thanks to Herr Robert von Mendelssohn for his kind permission to publish these letters.I also thank the Leo Baeck Institute, New York for allowing me the use of the xerox copies of these letters which are extant in the Moses Mendelssohn archive of the Institute.

filed in the so-called *Grüne Bücher* at the Bodleian Library, Oxford.[3] These nine letters enable us to fill in some of the blank pages in the story of Dohm's treatise and to elucidate more fully the degree of cooperation that obtained between Dohm and Mendelssohn. They are presented here in chronological order with a running commentary. I consider it a privilege to dedicate this incursion into history — a field not specifically my own — to our eminent historian, Professor Salo W. Baron.

Letter 1
(DRvM, C I, Nr. 6)

P. P.

Endlich habe ich das Vergnügen Ihnen hierbey den Schluss meiner Schrift zu schicken. Der Anhang u[nd] Vorwort werden nicht über 1½ Bogen mehr betragen. Wenn es H[err] Moses erlauben, werde ich Ihnen auch diese noch zuschicken, u[nd] Sie bitten sie durchzusehen, da ich bey dem französischen meinem Auge nicht genug traue. Wenn ich die K[orrektur] Bogen heute wieder erhalte, könnte das morgen abgedruckt werden.

Da eine Schrift doch immer mehr Eindruck macht, wenn sich jemand zu ihr nennt, da in der meinigen nichts enthalten ist, was ich abläugnen dürfte, auch die Censur sie durchaus approbirt hat; ohnedem der Verfasser doch immer bekannt wird; so habe ich beschlossen meinen Nahmen auf den Titel zu setzen, welches H[errn] Nicolai auch sehr lieb seyn wird. Haben Sie noch keine Briefe aus Strasburg? Wenn Sie dieselben erhalten, bitte ich um gefällige Mittheilung des mir so wichtigen Urtheils.

H[err] Wessely könnte seine Berichtigungen mir entweder als einen Anhang mittheilen, oder sie in einer besondren kleinen Schrift nachfolgen lassen, worin er füglich die Hauptsache bestä-

---

[3] The *Grüne Bücher* (GB) contain Felix Mendelssohn Bartholdy's correspondence and they are deposited at the Bodleian Library. The late Miss Margaret Deneke, Oxford, who owned them, gave me permission to edit letters selected by me (see my publication of letters by Joseph Mendelssohn to his nephew Felix in *Bulletin des Leo Baeck Instituts*, ed. Hans Tramer, Nr. 42, Vol. XI (1968), 73–88).

tigte. Letzteres halte ich selbst für besser, da ersteres auch noch aufhalten würde. Jedoch hängt es von Ihrer Verabredung mit H[errn] W[essely] ab. Ich wünsche sehr, dass er über diese Sache schreiben möge, u[nd] dies allein wird schon ein Vortheil meines Schreibens seyn.

Dohm

d[en] 24*ten* Aug. 81.

On May 11, 1781 Dohm had informed Nicolai of his expectation to finish the treatise at the beginning of July. It is clear from the above letter that the work was not completed until about the end of August. The appendix (*Anhang*) comprising the *Mémoire sur l'état des Juifs en Alsace* (pp. 155–200) and the preface do indeed amount to hardly more than the size (1½ *Bogen*) indicated in the letter. One gathers from the first sentence that Dohm had sent Mendelssohn proofs regularly as and when they came to hand. Naturally, the purpose of letting Mendelssohn read the proofs was above all to receive his critical observations and suggestions for changes. In the case of the *Mémoire*, which was a mere reprint, proof-reading by Mendelssohn was intended as an additional safeguard against printing errors since Dohm did not trust his eyes to spot all misprints in a French text.

The *Mémoire* had been dispatched to Herz Cerf Berr in Strassburg the year before. Dohm mentions in the treatise (p. 78 f.) that "ein *im vorigen Jahre* [the italics are mine] dem Königl. Staatsrath [viz. of France] von der elsassischen Judenschaft vorgelegtes *Mémoire*" had come to his notice. He adds that this document had seemed to him very important both on account of the interesting facts recorded therein and because of its noble, dignified diction. He, thus, adroitly conceals the fact of his consultative role in the final draft of this document. The praise he bestows on the style of the *Mémoire* does not belie the common assumption that he had a hand in its composition.[4] It indicates,

---

[4] See W. Gronau, *Christian Wilhelm von Dohm nach seinem Wollen und Handeln* (Lemgo, 1824), p. 84 f.; Geiger, p. 79.

however, that in his view the credit for its merits belonged to Mendelssohn.[5] The reference to the *Mémoire* in the treatise (pp. 78–82) and its reproduction as an appendix were obviously designed to keep the still unresolved issue of the Alsatian Jews before the public eye. Dohm's question in the letter, "Haben Sie noch keine Briefe aus Strasburg?" and his request to be informed about the *Urtheil* must be understood to refer to the Jewish situation in Alsace, the term *Urtheil* most probably being meant to denote a royal order or cabinet decision. The rather modest result of the *Mémoire* (and of the French edition of Dohm's treatise) was eventually the issuance, in July 1784, of Louis XVI's *Letters Patentes*.[6]

An interesting piece of information that emerges from the letter relates to the scruples and anxieties which Dohm felt about the book. From the announcement of his decision to put his name on the title page we learn that he had previously intended to publish the work either anonymously or under an assumed name. The reason that had motivated his earlier decision can easily be guessed. His official position as *Kriegsrath* Dohm was a dual one: he was Registrar of the Prussian State Archive (*Geheimes Archiv*) and Counsellor at the Ministry of Foreign Affairs under von Hertzberg, the Minister. Although he enjoyed the confidence of his superior, he had to cope with a great deal of envy and intrigue.[7] Having been called from Kassel to Berlin only in 1779, he was still somewhat of a novice who had to watch his steps. As his letter of May 11, 1781 to Nicolai shows, it had been his original idea to publish his treatise outside Prussia: "Ich habe Ihnen gesagt, dass ich die Schrift auswärts gedruckt zu haben wünschte,

---

[5] Geiger, ibid., mistakenly infers from Dohm's letter of November 15, 1782 to Nicolai that Dohm received an honorarium only for his work on the *Mémoire*. In contrasting *die bei dem ersten Theil eintretenden Umstände* with the circumstances obtaining in regard to the Second Part of the treatise, Dohm clearly speaks of the two parts of the treatise.

[6] See Gabriel Hemerdinger, "Le Dénombrement des Israélites d'Alsace," *Revue des Études Juives*, XLII (1901), pp. 254 ff.

[7] See Gronau, op. cit., pp. 44–84.

und Sie wissen die Gründe davon."[8] Now, however, he pointed out, that he was hesitant to carry out this intention since he was anxious to do the proof-reading himself and, secondly, was afraid of difficulties that might be raised by a foreign censor. He had, therefore, asked the Berlin theologian Teller whether he was prepared to act as censor and, having obtained his consent, he now suggested to Nicolai that he be the publisher.[9] As the letter to Mendelssohn reveals, his fears had not been entirely allayed. Although he was ready to publish the treatise in Berlin, he shrank from presenting himself publicly as its author. Not until the latter part of August, when the writing was completed, did he summon enough courage to drop the desire for anonymity. It seems that in the course of his work he had become so immersed in his ideas and convictions that he felt the urge to secure the maximum success of the book through the acknowledgement of his authorship: a piece of writing, he argues in the letter, makes, after all, more of an impression when it bears somebody's name. He gives three more reasons for his change of mind: the treatise contains nothing which he could not openly avow; it had been passed by the censor; and the secret of the author's identity is in any event bound to leak out.

The final paragraph of the letter refers to the critical observations on the treatise that were eventually published under the title *Anmerkungen zu der Schrift des Herrn Dohm, über die bürgerliche Verfassung der Juden* (Altona, 1782). The title page of this short tract (32 pp.) carries the initials J. C. U. [Johann Christoph Unzer], although Moses Wessely (1737–1792), Mendelssohn's friend, who lived as a merchant and writer in Hamburg, was the real author. Unzer was a noted physician and poet who held the post of professor of natural science at the Altona Gymnasium and was closely connected with Wessely. He had obviously no objection to the use of his initials on the title page of Wessely's pamphlet.

---

8 Geiger, p. 75.
9 Geiger, p. 75 f.

He realized, no doubt, that launching it under a Christian writer's flag would help the cause. As is apparent from our letter, it was Mendelssohn who steered the whole enterprise. The purpose of it was a twofold one. The pamphlet was to express, in the first place, full moral support for Dohm's treatise.[10] It was to "confirm the essential thing," as the letter puts it. It was, secondly, to offer "corrections" (*Berichtigungen*) with regard to Dohm's advocacy of Jewish "autonomy" as practiced until then. The burden of Wessely's plea was to be a vigorous rejection of the rabbis' right to excommunicate dissenters or otherwise unruly members. Dohm (p. 124) had seen no harm in granting the Jewish community the right of excommunication and, if necessary, its enforcement by the secular arm. Other denominations, he recalled, enjoyed the very same right. Nor was there any need for the state to feel concern about the exercise of this *Bannrecht* since it did not interfere with the civil and political status of the person thus penalized. Mendelssohn strongly objected to this way of thinking and he eventually expressed his disapproval in the clearest terms in his preface to Manasseh Ben Israel's *Rettung der Juden* (1782).[11] He did not attempt, however, to correct the passage in Dohm's work at the proof stage. All he did then was to inform Dohm of his objection and arrange, with Dohm's knowledge and consent, the procedure

[10] It should be noted that the pamphlet misquotes the title of Dohm's treatise on its title page by calling it *über die bürgerliche Verfassung* [instead of: *Verbesserung*] *der Juden*. This change of name may be due to negligence or, possibly, imply a critique of the ambiguity of the term *Verbesserung*. As Jacob Katz has pointed out, Mendelssohn, in discussing Dohm's proposals, "characteristically dropped the term *bürgerliche Verbesserung*, substituting in its stead *bürgerliche Aufnahme* (see Jacob Katz, "The Term 'Jewish Emancipation': Its Origin and Historical Impact," *Studies in Nineteenth Century Jewish Intellectual History*, ed. Alexander Altmann [Cambridge, Mass., 1964], p. 14 f.). The term *Aufnahme* occurs also in Michaelis' review (*Orientalische und Exegetische Bibliothek*, 19. Theil (1782), p. 2) and in the letter by v. W. reproduced by Dohm in the second part of his treatise, p. 118. This term is adopted from the legal literature on the *Judenrecht* and translates the term *ius recipiendi*.

[11] GS III, 193–206.

referred to in the letter. It seems that at the time he was averse to expressing himself publicly on the issue concerned. In Wessely he found a suitable mouthpiece of his ideas. As the letter shows, Dohm left it entirely to Mendelssohn and Wessely to determine whether the *Berichtigungen* should appear as an appendix to his book or as a separate pamphlet. His preference, however, was for the second alternative and his wishes were respected. The pamphlet seems to have appeared in February, 1782, for on February 15 Dohm sent Nicolai a copy (see the text of the letter as quoted by Geiger, p. 77). Geiger's assumption that the words "Hierbey die Schrift von Wessely" refer to Hartwig Wessely's *Dibrei Shalom we-Emmet* (1782) is untenable.

Letter 2
(DRvM, C I, Nr. 7)

P. P.

H[err] Basedow hat mir beykommende verschiedene Schriften, *Frieden zwischen Vernunft und Urchristenthum*, e[t] c[etera] über-schickt, um sie Ihnen, theuerster H[err] Moses zuzustellen. Von den lateinischen Colloquien sollen Sie eins für sich behalten, und die übrigen Ex[emplare] unter einige Judenfamilien, deren Kinder Latein lernen, auszutheilen.

Von unserer französischen Uebers[etzung] habe ich seit einiger Zeit nicht gehört, ich vermuthe H[err] Bernoulli ist desto fleissiger. Von Dessau habe ich die Nachricht, dass die Buchh[andlung] der Gelehrten die Sache gern übernehmen will und der Druck ist dort auch 25 rt. [Reichsthaler] wohlfeiler als hier.

Dohm
d[en] 2*ten* Oct. 81.

Johann Bernhard Basedow (1723–1790), the well-known liberal theologian and pioneer in pedagogy, was on friendly terms with Mendelssohn.[12] The exact title of the book mentioned in the letter is: *Vorschlag an die Selbstdenker des Jahrhunderts zum Frieden*

---

[12] See my *Moses Mendelssohn: A Biographical Study* (University, Alabama, 1973), pp. 323 f.

zwischen dem wohlverstandenen Urchristenthum und der wohlgesinnten Vernunft (1780). The Latin colloquia are Basedow's *Chrestomathie aus Corderii et Ludov. Vivis colloquiis scholasticis* (1781).[13] Johann Bernoulli, a member of the famous family of savants and a fellow of the Royal Academy of Sciences in Berlin, had undertaken a translation of Dohm's treatise into French. Judging from the letter, he had commenced work sometime during the summer of 1781. The "Buchhandlung der Gelehrten" in Dessau published the translation under the title *De la réforme politique des Juifs* (Dessau, 1782).

Letter 3
(DRvM, C I, Nr. 8)

P. P.

Ich weiss nicht, ob H[err] Moses die Büschingische Zeitung lesen, und überschicke also hierbey den Beschluss s[einer] Recens[ion] der so günstig ist, als wir ihn nur von ihm erwarten konnten. Ich lege zugleich einen Brief des Fürsten von Dessau bey, der Ihnen interessant seyn wird, da er sich so sehr in die Materie einlässt. Ich habe mit H[errn] Bernoulli schon über die Hälfte seiner Uebersetzung durchgelesen, und gefunden, dass unsre letzte Erinnerung sehr gut gewirkt habe. Er übersetzt itzt weit französischer, dünkt mich, und weniger sclavisch. Unsrem Wunsch, dass ein guter französischer Grammaticus noch die letzte Durchsicht übernehmen möchte, ist H[err] B[ernoulli] auch zuvor gekommen, indem er seine Arbeit schon einem solchen Mann (den Uebersetzer von *Erasmus Lob der Narrheit* und andrer Sachen) gegeben hat. Ich hoffe also in kurzem einen Anfang nach Dessau schicken zu können. Den Extract eines Briefes über die Seedienste der Juden in Holland bitte ich mir bald aus, damit er gehörigen Orts eingeschaltet werden könne. — Anliegendes Avertis[sement] über Lamberts Schriften bitte ich in H[errn] B[ernoullis] Nahmen doch gelegentlich bekannt zu machen.

Dohm
d[en] 23*ten* Oct. 81.

13 See *Allgemeine Deutsche Biographie*, II, 122.

Dohm's friend Anton Friedrich Büsching (1724–1793), theologian, geographer and director of the Gymnasium zum Grauen Kloster in Berlin,[14] reviewed the treatise favorably in his periodical *Wöchentliche Nachrichten von neuen Landcharten, geographischen... und historischen Büchern*, Vol. 9, 1781, pp. 299–302, 319–320, 331–335.[15] Dohm sent Mendelssohn the *Beschluss*, i.e. the last instalment of the review. This letter is clear evidence of the fact that Dohm's treatise was published not later than toward the end of September, 1781. For, assuming that the final of the three weekly instalments of Büsching's review appeared on October 23, the date of the above letter, the first must be dated October 9. Allowing a two weeks' interval between the date of publication and the commencement of the reviewing of it leads us to suppose that the treatise came out at about the time suggested. This disposes of Geiger's surmise that the printing took a long time and that the book saw the light of day only about or after January 9, 1782.[16] The "interesting" letter written to Dohm by the Prince of Dessau seems lost.

Mendelssohn took an active part in the supervision of the French translation of the treatise by Bernoulli. This is attested by Dohm's remark that Bernoulli had responded to "*our* last admonition" and to "*our* desire" to entrust the final revision to an expert in French grammar.

The extract from a letter concerning the maritime services of the Jews in Holland which Dohm requests for insertion in the appropriate place was received by him and used to good purpose. The French version of the treatise contains on p. 214 a passage introduced by the words, "On a lu dans les Gazettes" which reports the outstanding bravery shown by a Portuguese Jew in the battle between the English and the Dutch fleet on August 5, 1781. Conscious of the kindness of the Dutch Government toward the Jews, many members of the Dutch Jewish community, we are told,

14 On his friendship with Dohm, see Gronau, op. cit., pp. 30 f., 53.
15 See Volkmar Eichstädt, *Bibliographie zur Geschichte der Judenfrage*, I (Hamburg, 1938), p. 8, Nr. 90.
16 See Geiger, p. 76.

volunteered to serve in the Navy and did so with the consent and blessing of the Chief Rabbi of Amsterdam. Dohm incorporated this story also in Part Two of his treatise (p. 239 f.).

The *Avertissement* of Lambert's *Schriften* is the announcement of the edition by Johann Bernoulli of "Joh. Heinrich Lamberts logische und philosophische Abhandlungen," the first volume of which appeared in Berlin and Dessau, 1782. Volume 2 was published in Berlin and Leipzig, 1787. Bernoulli edited also Lambert's learned German correspondence (*Deutscher gelehrter Briefwechsel J. H. Lamberts*, Berlin, 1782-84). He knew of Mendelssohn's great admiration for Lambert[17] and, therefore, had no hesitation to enlist his help in propagating these writings.

Letter 4

(DRvM, C I, Nr. 9)

P. P.

Ich überschicke hierbey die Uebersetzung, soweit sie fertig und schon nach der Durchsicht eines Franzosen, ausgebessert ist. Es würde mir lieb seyn, wenn sie H[err] Moses noch einmal durchlaufen und mir Ihre Meynung davon sagen wollten; wenn ich sie auf übermorgen wieder bekomme, werde ich sie alsdann noch nach Dessau schicken. Hierbey noch einige Avert[issements] von Lamberts [...]

Dohm

d[en] 1*sten* Nov. 81

The letter offers additional evidence of the active part Mendelssohn took in the preparation of the French version for the press.

---

[17] See my *Moses Mendelssohns Frühschriften zur Metaphysik* (Tübingen, 1969), p. 263. On the affinities between Lambert's and Mendelssohn's thought see the page references in the index, p. 394, s.v. Lambert.

Letter 5
(DRvM, C I, Nr. 10)

P. P.

Ich will H[errn] Cerf Beer [sic] noch nicht wieder mit einem Schreiben beschwerlich werden. Aber ich bitte ihn zu ersuchen mir doch baldigst gefällig zu melden:

1. Ob er alle Exempl[are] die in meinem Briefe angegeben, richtig erhalten habe?
2. Ob der Verkauf verstattet und welche Maasregeln er mit Buchhändlern deshalb getroffen?
3. Wie es sonst mit der Sache der Elsasischen Juden stehe?

H[err] Jacobi hatte seine Schrift Ihnen bestimmt, daher sie wieder beykömmt. Da er durchaus Wahrheit und strengen Tadel haben wollte, so werden ihm Ihre Anmerkungen wohl recht seyn, die mir ungemein treffend scheinen.

Dohm
d[en] 25ten Nov. 81.

The first question which Dohm wants to be answered presupposes that he had sent a large consignment of the German edition of his treatise — the French had not yet appeared — to Cerf Berr who had commissioned the writing of the *Mémoire* and was interested in the circulation of the treatise in France, especially since it contained the *Mémoire* as an appendix in French. The second question shows that Cerf Berr had undertaken to secure a licence for the sale of the book and to arrange terms with booksellers. From a letter which Dohm wrote to Nicolai a year later, on November 15, 1782 (Geiger, p. 78 f.), it appears that upon publication of the treatise Dohm had bought 200 copies and it may be safely assumed that he had sought Cerf Berr's cooperation in selling these copies in France. His question stemmed, therefore, from financial considerations and they were rather closely interrelated. In the light of these circumstances his exasperation with Cerf Berr's tardiness in replying is understandable. Fortunately, he took the precaution of pressing for the granting of a licence from the *Chambre syndicale de la Librairie*, and he encountered no difficulty in the sale of the copies. It was to be different with the French edition of which 600 copies were dispatched to Paris only to be confiscated and to be sent to the Bastille *pour être mis au pillon*, viz. to be destroyed. The anguish suffered by Dohm during the prolonged efforts to obtain a licence and his irritation with Cerf Berr's inactivity are vividly expressed in a letter he wrote to Mendelssohn on December 28, 1784, prior to the disclosure that the books had been burnt long ago.[18] Dohm's third question concerning the position of Alsatian Jewry is in accord with the interest expressed in letter 1.

Friedrich Heinrich Jacobi had dedicated a copy of his *Vermischte Schriften* (Breslau, 1781) to Mendelssohn. The inscription read: "Dem Ehrwürdigen Mendelssohn, von desselben vieljährigem Schüler, dem Verfasser. Pempelfort, den 23. Oct. 1781."[19] Mendelssohn must have been puzzled to find that Jacobi described himself as a disciple of his. The volume contained Jacobi's philosophical *Roman* "Woldemar" under the new title "Der Kunstgarten, ein philosophisches Gespräch" and "Eduard Allwills Papiere," both pieces exhibiting the emotionally charged style of the incipient *Sturm und Drang* phase in German literature. In September 1781 Jacobi and Dohm had met for the first time and they had immediately become friends.[20] It appears from the above letter that Jacobi had sent Mendelssohn his book through Dohm, and that Mendelssohn had returned it to Dohm together with a critical note. Thereupon Dohm pointed out that Jacobi had dedicated (*bestimmt*) the copy to Mendelssohn and that, for this reason, it was coming back again (*wieder beykömmt*). He agreed with Mendelssohn's remarks and expressed confidence that Jacobi, being eager for nothing but truth and severe criticism, would welcome them. As

---

[18] The letter has been published by Fritz Bamberger, "Four Unpublished Letters to Moses Mendelssohn," *Living Legacy, Essays in Honor of Hugo Hahn* (New York, 1963), p. 93 f. On the fate of the books, see Gronau, op. cit., pp. 89 f.

[19] See Ludwig Geiger's note in *ZGJD*, IV (1890), 304.

[20] See Gronau, op. cit., pp. 74, 263; *Friedrich Heinrich Jacobi's auserlesener Briefwechsel*, I (Leipzig, 1825), 325–328.

the course of events showed, Jacobi did not take kindly to Mendelssohn's rebuke, which was in sharp contrast to Lessing's reaction to his "Woldemar" as expressed in a letter of May 18, 1779.[21] It is somewhat strange to come across the shadow of Jacobi, who was destined to play so sinister a role in Mendelssohn's closing years, in a letter from Dohm, his close collaborator and friend, who by a twist of fortune happened to be also Jacobi's friend.

Letter 6

(DRvM, C I, Nr. 11)

P. P.

Ich möchte in die französische Uebersetzung meiner Schrift anliegenden kleinen Zusatz über den *Punct des Banns* bringen, und wünsche nur zu wissen, ob Sie denselben billigen, theuerster Herr Moses. Ich glaube dieser Zusatz reicht hin, um allen Missverstand dessen, was über das Ausschliessungsrecht (das ich unschicklich Bannrecht genannt hatte, weil *Bann* nach Ihren Grundsätzen weit Mehreres andeutet) gesagt ist, zu verhindern. Die ausführlichere Erörterung erwarte ich von H[errn] Wessely und werde sie bey einer 2*ten* Ausg[abe] gewiss nutzen. Das von H[errn] *Cranzen* in einer Schrift über die *weltl[iche] Macht in Glaubenssachen* angeführte Beyspiel von Altona habe ich nicht citiren mögen, weil ich nicht glauben kann, dass das Factum richtig erzählt ist.

Dohm

d[en] 14*ten* Dec. 81

Knowing that Mendelssohn had strong misgivings about the advocacy of the *Bannrecht* in the treatise (p. 124), Dohm now wishes to add a clarification of the point at issue in the French edition and submits the proposed text of the *addendum* to Mendelssohn for his approval. He admits that the term *Bannrecht* had been ill chosen since according to Jewish law ("nach Ihren Grundsätzen") the imposition of a ban (ḥerem) implied not merely exclusion from certain religious privileges but also social ostracism.

---

[21] See my *Moses Mendelssohn: A Biographical Study*, pp. 596–598.

The paragraph to be added was to take care of this point. It seems that Mendelssohn agreed to its insertion, although he was not entirely satisfied and was to refer to it obliquely in his *Vorrede* to Manasseh Ben Israel as utterly unrealistic. The insertion is found in the French edition on p. 165, line 18 — p. 166, line 17, and the revised edition of the treatise (*Ueber die bürgerliche Verbesserung der Juden*, Erster Theil, 1783) carries the identical text in German, where it reads:

Nach demselben [viz. the *Grundsatz* of the separation of church membership and citizenship] dürfte die Obrigkeit aber einem Rabbi nie gestatten, einen solchen *Bann* über ein Glied seiner Gemeine auszusprechen, der dasselbe von allem Umgange mit seinen übrigen Glaubensgenossen auserhalb der Synagoge ausschliesst, ihn bey denselben herabsetzt, seine Geschäfte unterbricht oder ihn gar der Verfolgung des Pöbels überliefert. Auch Geldstrafen scheinen bey Uebertretung der vermeynten Gebote des Himmels nicht schicklich zu seyn. Der Missbrauch der von der Gewalt des Rabbi bey Auflegung dieser Strafen gemacht werden kann und auch wirklich oft gemacht ist, macht die beständige Aufsicht der Regierung über die Ausübung dieser Gewalt nothwendig. Nie darf diese in dem übertretenden *Juden* den *Menschen* und den *Bürger* strafen, nur Ausschliessung von der kirchlichen Gesellschaft und den Wohlthaten derselben darf die Folge einer Verletzung ihrer Vorschriften seyn (p. 133, line 14 — p. 134, line 7).

It is precisely this *caveat* which in his *Vorrede* Mendelssohn characterized with the words: "Kirchenzucht einführen, und die bürgerliche Glückseligkeit ungekränkt erhalten, scheint mir ein Problem zu sein, das in der Politik noch aufgelöset werden soll. Es ist der Bescheid des allerhöchsten Richters an den Ankläger: Er sei in deiner Hand, doch schone seines Lebens! Zerbrich das Fass, wie die Ausleger hinzuthun, und lass den Wein nicht auslaufen!"[22]
    Dohm's letter promises to make use of the more elaborate dis-

---

[22] GS III, 201, quoting Job 2:6; b. Baba Bathra 16a.

cussion of the question in Moses Wessely's forthcoming pamphlet,[23] should a second edition of the treatise be published. This promise was redeemed in the form of a footnote to the passage that had been added.[24] It refers to the incident in Altona as reported in [August Friedrich] Cranz' tract *Ueber den Missbrauch der geistlichen Macht und der weltlichen Herrschaft in Glaubenssachen* [*durch Beispiele aus dem jetzigen Jahrhundert ins Licht gesetzt*], Berlin 1781.[25] In the present letter Dohm discounts the reliability of Cranz' report concerning the "example" of the Altona case. His distrust of Cranz stems from the unpleasant experience he had had in his dealings with him as officially appointed censor of his writings.[26] The facts recorded by Cranz had been adduced, however, in Wessely's *Anmerkungen* (pp. 24–25) as evidence of rabbinic abuse of power, and Dohm felt, therefore, justified in referring to the matter in order to clinch his argument.[27]

Letter 7

(DRvM, C I, Nr. 12)

P. P.

Sehn Sie hier meinen ersten Gegner, dessen Äusserungen Sie wohl so wenig befremden werden, als mich. Nur wegen des ersten Eindrucks können sie der guten Sache nachtheilig seyn. Sollte das, was von Eisenmenger gesagt wird, gegründet seyn? Ich werde im Archiv nachsehn, wo sich das, was K[önig] Friedr[ich] I deshalb gethan haben soll, finden muss. Ich höre, dass auch mehrere unserer Theologen nicht mit meiner Schrift zufrieden sind; aber ihr Beyfall war auch nicht das Ziel, das ich zu erreichen strebte.

Dohm

[undated]

---

[23] See also letter 1.

[24] P. 134 (not in the French edition).

[25] Dohm gives mistakenly 1782 as the year of publication.

[26] See Gronau, op. cit., pp. 90 ff.

[27] On the case of Samuel Marcus jun. in Altona see Kayserling, op. cit., pp. 298 ff.

The earliest known review of a severely critical nature was written by Michael Hissmann[28] and published in the *Zugabe zu den Göttingischen gelehrten Anzeigen*, 48stes Stück, December 1, 1781. Dohm mentions it in the introduction to the Second Part of his treatise (1783), pp. 22–24 as hardly worthy of serious refutation.[29] The letter cannot be said to refer to this review, since nothing is found there about Eisenmenger and/or Friedrich I. The possibility is not excluded that prior to the appearance of Hissmann's critique on December 1 some other review answering to the description in the letter had come out and that Dohm refers to its author as his "first opponent."[30] It is also possible that the critic referred to is Johann David Michaelis, the famous orientalist and Biblical scholar, whose critical review of Dohm's treatise appeared in his *Orientalische und Exegetische Bibliothek*, Frankfurt a. Main, 1782, 19. Theil, No. 281, pp. 1–40. In this review Eisenmenger is mentioned. Though calling his *Entdecktes Judentum* (1700) a "Lästerschrift" (p. 9), Michaelis did not entirely discredit the author. He wrote: "Denn dass man bey dem viel Zweifel haben kann, ob der Jude das, was in unsern Augen Eid ist, für Eid hält oder nicht, ist keine von den ungerechten Klagen Eisenmengers" (p. 21). We know that Dohm was perturbed by Michaelis' moral support for the slur cast by Eisenmenger on the trustworthiness of oaths taken by the Jews. In the second part of his treatise (1783) he reproduced the entire text of Michaelis' review (pp. 31–71) and devoted a long section (pp. 300–346) to a refutation of Michaelis' charge. The letter might be considered as his first reaction to that charge. Two difficulties remain: Michaelis was not his first opponent and no mention of Friedrich I occurs in his review. One has the distinct impression that in speaking of his *ersten Gegner* who could harm the good cause merely on account of creating the *ersten Eindruck* Michaelis refers to the very earliest critical review. It seems also clear from the tenor of the letter that the mention of

---

[28] He became professor of philosophy at Göttingen in 1782.
[29] Hissmann characterized the Jews as an incorrigible race.
[30] Eichstädt, op. cit., p. 8, Nr. 90 records no such review in his list.

Friedrich I was definitely in the review. Since Michaelis' *Recension*, though critical and containing a highly irritating reference to Eisenmenger, is not the first of its kind and is silent on Friedrich I, the likelihood that Dohm's letter is referring to it must be considered remote. In order to uphold it, one would have to argue that Dohm meant to describe Michaelis as his first serious opponent; that the clause, "dessen Äusserungen Sie wohl so wenig befremden werden, als mich" does fit Michaelis because of his known antipathy to Judaism and Jews; and that Dohm's intention to consult the files of the state archive about Friedrich's action was prompted by a piece of information communicated to him by someone who had read the review and remarked on the action taken by king Friedrich I of Prussia in support of Eisenmenger.[31] In case the letter is assumed to refer to Michaelis, its date would be March 1782, for from two letters written by Dohm to Nicolai it appears that Michaelis' review was published early in March. On March 13 Dohm sent Nicolai "Michaelis' Rec[ension] meiner Judenschrift," and on March 27 he expressed his intention "H[errn] R[itter] Michaelis zu antworten, auch ihm unsern R[abbi] Ben Manasseh [sic] zu schicken."[32]

The theologians' discontent[33] was in some measure due to the extremely liberal and neutral stance of Dohm's plea as expressed in the assertion that every religion inculcates in its adherents a kind of distaste for members of other faiths, which may border on hatred or contempt (p. 23 f.).

[31] The king intervened in the trial concerning the sale of Eisenmenger's work by pleading with Emperor Leopold I in a personal letter to lift the prohibition. See Gerson Wolf, "Der Prozess Eisenmenger," *Monatsschrift für Geschichte und Wissenschaft des Judentums*, Vol. XIX (1869), 430, where the text of the letter is published.

[32] See Geiger, p. 77, where the sentence in its entirety is said to read: "Schreiben Sie wohl bald nach Göttingen und erlauben mir bei der Gelegenheit Herrn Ritter Michaelis zu antworten, auch ihm unsern R. Ben Manasseh zuzuschicken, damit er *einsehe*, was Michaelisschen *Rechtes* ist." The two words italicized by us are not found in the original text (Nachlass Nicolai, Vol. 15, Staatsbibliothek Preussischer Kulturbesitz, Berlin) but were supplied by Geiger in lieu of two illegible words.

Letter 8
(GB 29/3)

Wenn Sie, theuerster Herr Moses, diesen Nachmittag in Ihrem
Garten sind, so werde ich mit meinem Schwager sie daselbst besuchen. Es muss Sie aber auf keine Weise genieren, da wir der
schönen Sommertage hoffentlich noch viele haben. Wenn Ihnen
unser Besuch lieb ist, so bitte es hierunten zu bemerken, und
Ueberbringern damit an H[errn] Leuchsenring zu schicken, welchen
ich alsdann ersuche, um 5 Uhr uns bey mir abzuholen.

                                                    Dohm
Recht herzlich lieb! also mein   d[en] 19*ten* Juni. 82
theuerster Herr Hofrath! um 5 Uhr
holen Sie den H[errn] Kriegsrath ab.
    [Moses Mendelssohn]
    Dohm's note and Mendelssohn's reply written in his own hand
at the bottom[34] testify to the happy relationship between the two
men. Franz Michael Leuchsenring — Dohm misspells the name
"Leutschenring" — had come to Berlin in 1782, and he had joined
the circle of Mendelssohn. The title *Hofrath* had been awarded to
him by the Prince of Hesse-Darmstadt. In his letter to Herz
Homberg dated July 1, 1782 (GS V, p. 657 f.) Mendelssohn
mentions both Leuchsenring and Dohm. On November 2, 1782
Mendelssohn sent the following note to Leuchsenring: "Bester
Freund! Ich konnte gestern Ihr *Billet* nicht beantworten, weil der
Sabbath schon angegangen war. Die 20 *Louisd'ors* stehn auf den
ersten Wink zu Dienst, wenn es Ihnen gefällig ist zu mir ins *Comtoir*
zu schicken. Ich bin der Ihrige Moses Mendelssohn."[35] On February 23, 1785 Mendelssohn wrote Leuchsenring a note full of

---

[33] See Gronau, op. cit., p. 87, where Spalding is mentioned.

[34] The signature "Moses Mendelssohn" (twice underlined) was added by
a later hand.

[35] See *Inedita Mendelssohniana* published in 20 copies by Gotthilf Weisstein
in Honor of Sanitätsrath Dr. S. Neumann, Berlin, October 22, 1889 (ext^{ant}
at the Widener Library, Cambridge, Mass.).

indignation in which he declared his intention to leave any letter
from him unopened in future (DRvM, B I, Nr. 5).[36]

Letter 9
(DRvM, C I, Nr. 13)

Der Druck meines zweiten Theils ist nun wieder angefangen.
H[err] Prof[essor] Poppe besorgt die 2te Correctur und da er in
Ihrer Nachbarschaft wohnt, habe ich ihm aufgetragen, Ihnen die
Bogen immer zuzuschicken. Da der Drucker treibt, so bitte ich
sie, sobald es Ihre Geschäfte erlauben, an H[errn] Poppe zu remit-
tieren; alle Erinnerungen aber, die Sie haben möchten, besonders
zu schreiben und mir discrete zu schicken, damit ich bey der 3ten
Correctur davon Gebrauch machen könne.

Dürfte ich auch um das genaue Verzeichniss aller Ihrer Festtage
und wiefern sie die Arbeit unterbrechen, baldigst bitten? Verzeihen
Sie, dass ich Ihnen so oft beschwerlich werde, aber ich weiss, dass
Sie, wie bisher, noch immer gerne dazu beytragen, mein kleines
Werk vollkommener zu machen. Wollten Sie sowohl Fehler im
Styl als auch etwa noch übrig gebliebene Druckfehler, davon in
der ersten Correctur eine ausserordentliche Menge waren, sogleich
verbessern, so würden Sie mir einen neuen Gefallen erweisen.

Dohm
d[en] 16ten Juni. 83.

From Dohm's correspondence with Nicolai (Geiger, 77–79) we
know that he had planned to have the second part of his treatise
ready for the Easter Book Fair 1783. The above letter shows that
some hitch had occurred, causing a temporary halt in the printing.
The disagreement over the amount of the author's fee voiced in
Dohm's letter of November 15, 1782 may have been the reason
for the delay. Now, the printer urged Dohm to return the corrected

---

36 On Leuchsenring's chequered career and Mendelssohn's break with him,
see K. A. Varnhagen von Ense's Memoirs (extracts quoted by the editor,
GS V, 657 ff.) and the article "Leuchsenring" in *Allgemeine Deutsche Biographie*, Vol. XVIII, 473 f. Dohm's friendly relations with Leuchsenring during
the years 1782–83 are mentioned by Gronau, op. cit., p. 125.

proofs as quickly as possible. The second galleys were read by
Johann Friedrich Poppe (1753–1843), who had just been appointed
professor at the Königlich Joachimsthalersches Gymnasium in
Berlin.[37] Dohm asked Mendelssohn to check, in the first place,
Poppe's proof-reading and to correct both printer's errors and
the style. In addition, he asked him to write critical notes (*Erinnerungen*) which could be used at the third stage of proof-reading.
The main part of the volume was devoted to an examination of
the reasons advanced against the plea for Jewish equality, and it
was largely argumentative, marshaling a considerable array of
historical material. Mendelssohn had, no doubt, supplied many
data, and it is understandable that Dohm wanted him to look
critically at the manner in which the material had been elaborated.
Interestingly enough, he wished to receive the critical notes con-
fidentially, without Poppe's knowledge. His request for a list of
the Jewish festivals on which Mendelssohn was prevented from
writing shows the pace at which he now worked in order to hasten
the publication of the volume.

Some comment on his remark, *ich weiss, dass Sie, wie bisher,
noch immer gerne dazu beytragen, mein kleines Werk vollkommener
zu machen*, would seem to be in place. It clearly shows that the
treatise as a whole (viz. parts one and two), although owing a
great deal to Mendelssohn, was felt by Dohm to be — and in fact
was — his own work. Mendelssohn's role was certainly not confined to that of a "godfather" (*Pate*),[38] but it was less than that
of a co-author. His function was, in Dohm's words, "to make the
treatise more perfect." A few evidences of his cooperation may be
cited. The *grosse jüdische Gelehrte* whose opinion concerning Jewish

---

[37] Poppe had served in the same capacity at the Friedrichswerder Gymnasium in Berlin from 1780–83. He was a philologist and popular historian.
His works include: *Esprit de Leibniz, ou Pensées choisies de ses ouvrages* aus
dem Französischen übersetzt (Wittenberg, 1775) (4 vls.); *Geschichte der Euro-
päischen Staaten, In Verbindung der Erdbeschreibung und Staatskunde*, I (Halle,
1783); II (Halle, 1784). See (*Michaud*) *Biographie Universelle*, Nouvelle Edition,
XXXIV, 101.
[38] See H. Graetz, *Geschichte der Juden*, XI, 74.

military service on the Sabbath is quoted (I, 144) is obviously none other than Mendelssohn. The passages dealing with Eisenmenger (I, 17 f.; 22 f.; II, 301–346) clearly use notes written by Mendelssohn.[39] The same may be true of the passages referring to Josephus (I, 42; 139–141). The cooperation between Dohm and Mendelssohn is particularly evident in passages discussing conditions obtaining within the Jewish community, or venturing to make predictions about the development of Judaism (e.g. II, 178 ff.). Dohm adopts Mendelssohn's conception of Judaism as congruous with *Religion der Vernunft* (II, 180).

The close collaboration between the two men was, however, no one-way-street. Mendelssohn enjoyed the benefit of Dohm's help when writing his *Vorrede* to the German translation of Manasseh ben Israel's *Vindiciae Judaeorum*. This particular cooperation is attested by a hitherto unpublished letter which Mendelssohn wrote to Nicolai on February 8, 1782.[40] The letter reads:

Bester Freund! Sie erhalten hierbey einen Theil des Mst. [Manuscripts] das Sie gütigst zum Drucke zu befördern versprochen, nebst dem Schreiben des HE.K.R. [Herrn Kriegsraths] *Dohms*, in welchem er anzeigt wie er es mit der Correctur zu halten wünscht. Ich bitte diese Brochure, sobald als möglich abdrucken zu lassen. Ich denke man sollte itzt beständig das Publikum über diese Materie en haleine halten, und immer für und wider die Sachen streiten.

Ich schicke Ihnen auch zugleich das Wiener Patent in extenso mit. Was HE. Dohm davon sagt, habe ich sehr gefühlt. Wollen wir nicht Gelegenheit nehmen, am Ende unserer Brochure, das ganze Patent mit abdrucken zu lassen? Man hat in den Zeitungen einen gar zu windschiefen Auszug davon gemacht. Jedoch mag es lieber noch bleiben! Ich kan doch meine Meinung dar-

---

[39] See Graetz' conjecture, *ibid.*, note.

[40] Now published in *Neuerschlossene Briefe Moses Mendelssohns an Friedrich Nicolai*, ed. Alexander Altmann jointly with Werner Vogel (Stuttgart, 1973), No. 49, pp. 64–66.

über nicht so rund und so frey heraus sagen, als ich thun zu können wünschte. Mithin schweige ich lieber ganz davon.

....

Das Wiener Paket bitte ich mir noch heute wieder aus.

The *Brochure* which Nicolai had promised to publish and which Dohm had agreed to read in proof was *Manasseh ben Israel | Rettung der Juden | Aus dem Englischen übersetzt | Nebst einer Vorrede von Moses Mendelssohn | Als ein Anhang zu des Hrn. Kriegsraths Dohm Abhandlung: Ueber die bürgerliche Verbesserung der Juden* (1782). What the specific wishes were which Dohm expressed concerning procedure in proof-reading we do not know since the letter indicating them is lost. From Mendelssohn's other references to the letter we are able to infer, however, that Dohm was not at all happy with the *Wiener Patent* and that Mendelssohn shared his feelings. The *Wiener Patent* is, of course, the Austrian *Toleranzpatent* of Joseph II which was published on January 2, 1782.[41] A clue to the reason of the disappointment felt by both Dohm and Mendelssohn may be seen in the sentiments expressed in a letter dated also February 1782 which Dohm reprinted in Part Two of his Treatise (p. 137 f.):

Des Kaisers Edikt für die Juden, welches Sie nun auch gesehen haben werden, wird wohl Ihre Erwartung nicht ganz erfüllen. Es ist wohl eigentlich ein *politischer Versuch zu religiöser Verbesserung* der Juden, und hat die natürliche Tendenz sie in 20 oder höchstens zweymal 20 Jahren, also mit Ablauf dieses Menschenalters, zu Christen zu machen. Ich zweifle aber, ob es seinen Zweck erreicht, ein grosser Theil der Juden könnte wohl gar bey einem solchen Toleranz-Edict Lust bekommen, aus dem Lande zu gehen. G. den 23. Febr. 1782. M.

This letter provides clear evidence of the fact that as early as

---

41 The edict of tolerance for Bohemia had already been promulgated on October 19, 1781. See Jacob Katz' article in *Zion*, XXIX (1964), pp. 127 f., where the relevant bibliography is given; cf. Eichstädt, op. cit., p. 15, Nr. 185.

February 1782 the *Toleranzpatent* had aroused the entirely justified suspicion that its ultimate object was the conversion of the Jews. This suspicion was due, in particular, to the passage in the edict for Bohemia which stipulated that estates leased to Jews could become their property in case the leaseholder converted to Christianity.[42] The author of the letter was none other than Michaelis in Göttingen. In his review of Dohm's treatise he had remarked that the imperial edict had wisely stipulated a twenty years' limit to the leasing of real estate to Jews and had permitted an extension "for ever" only if and when the tenant adopted the Christian religion.[43] It was clearly for this reason that in the letter to Dohm he spoke of the tendency to make the Jews into Christians after 20 or twice 20 years. One should not be surprised, therefore, to find that Dohm and Mendelssohn had serious misgivings about the Edict of Tolerance as soon as its text became known. As Mendelssohn's letter to Nicolai shows, he had intended to reprint the text as an appendix to his edition of Manasseh Ben Israel but he had changed his mind because he could not express his view as candidly as he wished to. He suppressed his misgivings and even joined the chorus of universal praise of the tolerant Emperor in the first paragraph of his *Vorrede*. Only in a footnote to Manasseh ben Israel's treatise (GS III, 235) did he permit himself to deplore the *sogenannte Glaubensvereinigung* as a road leading to *gehässige Intoleranz*. He was to expand his treatment of the subject in his *Jerusalem* (GS III, 357–361). His doubts about the "tolerance" of Joseph II were revived when a deistic sect of Bohemian peasants was expelled and deported to the Turkish border by an imperial edict. The reports of this event in the press caused Dohm in March 1783 to insert a note expressing utter consternation in Part Two of his treatise in the writing of which he was then engaged.[44] Mendelssohn's reaction to the "totally

[42] See S. Dubnow, *Weltgeschichte des jüdischen Volkes*, VII, 374 f.; Katz, op. cit., p. 127.

[43] *Orientalische und Exegetische Bibliothek*, 19. Theil (1782), p. 28; Dohm II, 57.

[44] Dohm II, 182–185 and 363–376.

confusing and not a little disquieting" news can be seen in his letter of April 4, 1783 to Carl Julius Redlich in Vienna (GS V, 613).[45] Dohm and Mendelssohn were in complete accord in their reactions to the Emperor's strange mixture of tolerance and bigotry. Both were in agreement too about the need for keeping the public debate on the issue of civil equality going. As Mendelssohn put it in his letter to Nicolai: "Ich denke man sollte itzt beständig das Publikum über diese Materie en haleine halten, und immer für und wider die Sachen streiten." The *Brochure* on Manasseh Ben Israel was meant to serve this purpose. As early as March 19, 1782 Mendelssohn could put his signature under the *Vorrede* and shortly afterwards the book appeared.[46] Its designation on the title page as an *Anhang* to Dohm's treatise fitly expresses the close bond between the two men whom destiny had thrown together in a great and noble enterprise of historic significance.

---

[45] On the persecution of the deists, see Peter Philipp Wolf, *Geschichte der Veränderungen ... unter der Regierung Joseph II.*, Germanien 1795: Achtes Kapitel. Verbesserung des bürgerlichen Zustandes der Juden. Misshandlung der Deisten (p. 234 ff.).

[46] The book was published in mid-April, for on April 27, 1782 August Hennings thanked Mendelssohn for the copy he had received (see Nachlass August Hennings, Hamburg, Nr. 22, Letter 25, p. 50; reproduced by Ludwig Geiger, *ZGJD*, I (1887), p. 119).

FROM *ZUDECHA* TO *YAHUDI MAHALLESI*:
The Jewish Quarter of Candia
in the Seventeenth Century

(A Chapter in the History of Cretan Jewry Under Muslim Rule)*

ZVI ANKORI

I

IN THE PROCESSION of foreign invaders that through the centuries overran the Mediterranean island of Crete, a number of intruder waves were of Muslim persuasion. Of these, only two succeeded in establishing a Muslim dominion that was politically and militarily viable and that lasted uninterruptedly over a period of several generations. One such dominion, generally identified as Arabian, belongs to the medieval story of Crete. The other, that of the

---

* Information on the existence of Turkish archives in Crete and on their potential contribution to the study of Cretan Jewish history was brought for the first time to the attention of Jewish scholars in a paper I delivered at the thirty-fourth annual meeting of the American Academy for Jewish Research (December, 1961). The meeting was chaired by Professor Salo W. Baron, the President of the Academy and my revered teacher, mentor, and friend. It is a source of special gratification to me to present here to him some results of a study based on these archives.

For full documentation the reader is referred to the appropriate chapters of my forthcoming *Cretan Jewry through the Ages.* The Turkish texts are edited in my *Creta Judaica: Documents and Regesta,* to be published by The Israel Academy of Sciences and Humanities. Cf. also my "Jewish Life in Crete under Muslim Rule as Reflected in the Ottoman Turkish Sicillat," presented to the XXVI International Congress of Orientalists in New Delhi (January, 1964); my "Jews and the Jewish Community in the History of Mediaeval Crete," *Proceedings of the Second International Congress of Cretan Studies,* III (Athens, 1968), 312–367; as well as my *The Living and the Dead: The Story of Hebrew Inscriptions in Crete.*

While the Turkish documents utilized in the present essay were originally written in Arabic script (see, e.g., Figs. 4 and 5), all Turkish names, terms, and quotations are transcribed here in Latin characters and in keeping with modern

Ottoman Turks, already forms part of modern history; it came
to an end on the threshold of our own century, with the ultimate
restoration of the island to her Greek Mother-country.

THE ARAB MUSLIM BACKGROUND

Arab inroads into the coast and territory of Byzantine Crete began
as early as the middle of the seventh century. Inextricably inter-
twined with the Caliphate's military designs aimed at Constantinople and at the Byzantine Empire in general, the Muslim raids
were pressed forward unrelentingly throughout the latter half of the
seventh century as well as during the entire century thereafter.
Considering this persistence of Muslim efforts to secure a permanent beachhead on Cretan soil, the eventual victory of Islam,
culminating in a protracted Arab occupation of the island from
the 820s on, was relatively late in coming. Moreover, it did not
materialize as the predicted outgrowth of the classical phase of
Muslim conquests nor was it masterminded, like the major conquests, by the expanding Caliphate itself or by freebooters loyal
to the caliphal flag. Rather, emerging quite unexpectedly under
circumstances which in themselves could in no way have been fore-
seen, the Arab-sponsored First Islamic regime in Crete was carried
on the shoulders of Muslim separatists whose previous background
and interests were entirely unrelated to the Arab-Byzantine contest
in the East Mediterranean. True, once drawn into that contest
after having formed on the island an Arab State of their own,
these separatists, too, continued the age-old tug of war with the
Byzantine Empire.

The story of the Arab conquest of Crete has often been related.
Exiled from their native Andalusia and subsequently threatened
with eviction from their boldly usurped location in Egypt, a band
of desperate Muslim expatriates descended in force on Byzantine-
held Crete to make her their own. In doing so, the Spanish Arab

---

Turkish orthography. For the period of Venetian domination in Crete the
terms "Candia" and "Candiote" are used. The same terms are replaced by
"Kandiye" and "Kandiyote" as we advance into the Turkish period.

adventurers were not motivated by the island's potential usefulness to Islam's traditional drive for supremacy in the region. Similar to other expansionist Muslim movements of those later days, the invaders represented an Islamic force independent of — in a sense, rebellious to — the caliphal Establishment. Their objective was acquisition of land — land on which the participating warriors would themselves settle and live.

Unlike the story of the *conquest*, the story of Arab *rule* in Crete is still to be told dispassionately and in detail. European-centered historians vie with each other in berating Arab Crete as a nest of blood-thirsty corsairs. Now, piracy in that period of time was undoubtedly a way of life to many individuals and groups roaming the East Mediterranean waters; Cretan Arabs may very likely have excelled in it. Yet, no matter how accurate per se, descriptions of piratical raids hardly offer the true measure of the government established on the island after the conquest — a government which, except for a very brief interval of Byzantine recovery in the 830s, lasted a full five or six generations. What really counts is the fact that, after having settled in the newly acquired territory and after having intermarried with the local population, the Arab rulers swiftly proceeded to found a regular Cretan dynasty and set in motion a well-functioning administrative machinery with all the trappings of independent statehood. The trends and processes they initiated within Cretan society far transcended in intrinsic significance and in consequent impact the actual duration of the Arab regime; indeed, their imprint on the islanders' life remains to this day indelible.

Especially prominent was, and still is, the effect of the First Islamic administration on the direction of Crete's urban growth and economic development. Turning their backs on the African coast (whence they had launched their original attack) and opening a window to Europe and the European civilization, the new rulers removed the hub of governmental and economic activities from the Roman and Byzantine provincial capital of Gortys, in the southern tier guarding the rich Plain of Messarà, and addressed themselves to the challenge and potential of the island's northern

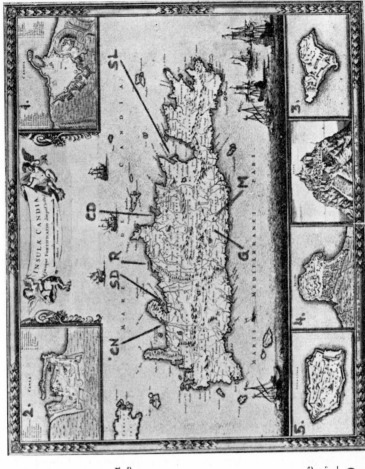

CRETE

1 & CD — Candia
2 & CN — Canea
3 & SD — Suda
4 & R — Retimo
5 & SL — Spinalonga
G — Gortys
M — Plain of Messarà

(The numbers and letters, nonexistent on the original map, are added here for the reader's easier orientation)

FIG. 1. Venetian Crete on the eve of the Ottoman conquest, as depicted in F. de Wit's *Atlas Major* (Amsterdam, 1670) on the basis of earlier sketches.

(Reproduced from original etching in the author's possession)

shore. On that shore, harbors and forts were built or restored and a brand-new capital founded (close to the maritime outlet of ancient Knossos) which, because of the moat adjacent to its citadel, acquired the Arabic name *Khandaq*. Thus, while the fertile south-central hinterland kept on distinguishing itself as the island's granary, the way it did since antiquity, the center of Cretan life and history irreversibly shifted under the Arabs to the northern coast. There it remains to this day (Fig. 1).

Cretan Jews, too, their settlement on the island reaching way back into Hellenistic-Roman times, could not help being deeply affected by these overall changes. Should my historical reconstruction (suggested elsewhere) prove correct, it was during that short, yet crucial, First Islamic period, ending with the Byzantine Restoration in 961 A.D., that elements of local Jewry, until then centered in and around the ancient provincial capital in the south as well as in adjoining *rural* areas, began gravitating northwards, towards the newly built coastal city. Thus commenced also a new trend in the story of the development of the Cretan Jewish community, a trend that continued long after the last Arab survivor assimilated in Cretan society or left the island. Enhanced by fresh waves of Jewish immigrants from abroad, Cretan Jewish life and economy were evermore intensively linked, under later masters, to the burgeoning *urban* centers on the northern coast.

THE ARRIVAL OF OTTOMAN ISLAM

Not until early modern times — beginning with the year 1645, to be exact — was the Cretan population once more subjected to an Islamic experience: the rule of Ottoman Turkey. By then, the remote and fairly brief history of Arab Islam on the island was to all intents and purposes dead, long since buried under not one but two layers of subsequent non-Muslim civilizations: the Second Byzantine, built up during the 250 years that followed the Arab defeat of 961, and the Venetian, a sorry legacy of the Fourth Crusade (1204). It was the consequence of the latter, really, i.e., the protracted period of the rule of Venice, spanning almost one half of a millennium and ending with the arrival of the Turks, that left the lives and minds of the Cretans scarred forever. The Turkish invasion got off to a fast start. Within an interval of fifteen months, both Canea (later renamed *Hanya*) and Retimo (in Turkish: *Resmo*), the northwestern harbor towns second only to the capital itself in size and importance, fell into the hands of the Turks. Still, almost a quarter of a century was to pass before the island's capital, Candia, became the seat of the new Islamic administration. In 1669, worn out by a long and bloody siege, this seemingly impregnable citadel-city, a Byzantine-Venetian out-growth of Arab Khandaq and a marvel of Venice's art of forti-fication, also threw its gates open to the Ottoman invader. The few maritime bastions that remained under the Venetian flag, notably Suda and Spinalonga, were finally ceded to Turkey in 1715 (Fig. 1).

Once in Turkish hands, Crete and her history mirrored the pecul-iar interplay of peace and war, of development and stagnation, that was characteristic of the changing fortunes of Ottoman his-tory in general. Ushered in when the Turkish Empire was about to scale the last peak of her greatness, the Cretan Ottoman regime could at first justly boast of a century-long record of positive action and rehabilitation. At a later stage, however, the very same regime found itself irreversibly embarked on a collision course with awakened native Greek nationalism. The trouble, certainly, was not limited to Crete alone; the mighty Sultanate as a whole was rapidly sliding down the path of disintegration and disaster. When, at last, a mere seven and a half decades ago, Ottoman dominion in Crete came to an end altogether (1898), the entire political order established by past sultans throughout the Balkans, the Aegean, and the Near East was already in a state of virtual collapse.

Even though Turkish Islam meticulously applied to Crete the classical procedures of Muslim conquests, it claimed no roots in the distant Arab period. Indeed, not until the inconsequential Veneto-Turkish peace talks of 1656—i.e., a full decade after the initial Ottoman successes on Cretan soil—did the Sublime Porte care to invoke history and argue to be regaining a once-Muslim possession. Even so, while imposing on the conquered territory the conventional framework of Islamic state institutions, the seventeenth-century Turkish leaders hardly followed the early Arab chroniclers in hailing the island as *Iqritish*; rather, they preferred the Graeco-Roman appellation which, after their own fashion, they modified into *Girit*.

Nor did they revert to the erstwhile form and meaning of the name given to the capital by its original Muslim founders. Characteristically, notwithstanding the unmistakable Arabic ring lingering on in the successive Byzantine and Venetian variants of that name, *Khandax* 〉 *Khandaka* 〉 (*Candiga*) 〉 *Candida* 〉 *Candia*, the new rulers ignored the readily available equivalent *Hendek*, a direct Turkish borrowing from the Arabic *Khandaq*. Muslims of non-Arab stock, they preferred instead a variation on the Venetian theme and coined, accordingly, the turkicized (yet meaningless) name-form *Kandiye*.

THE SHADOW OF VENICE

This indifference of the Ottoman newcomers towards Crete's Muslim past (as partly exemplified by the later vicissitudes of some Arab-originated Cretan toponymics) was not merely reflecting the broader seventeenth-century political realities; it went hand in hand with the attitudes of the islanders as well. To the latter, Venice, not Turkey, was the villain in the drama played out on the stage of Cretan history; Latinity, rather than Islam, loomed as the menace. For, as the islanders saw it, the political overlordship of Venice which unseated the rule of Byzantium in Crete in the early thirteenth century entailed more than national bondage; it had religious implications as well. Venetian control, descending upon Crete in a twisted aftermath of the partition of the Byzantine Empire by her West Christian brethren, brought the Latin rite to bear heavily on the island's Greek Orthodox majority. This situation was bound to overshadow all earlier experiences; it easily made the memory of a short-lived Arab Muslim administration preceding both the Byzantine Restoration and the Venetian rule fade altogether from the historical consciousness of the Cretan people. Certainly, the constructive development stemming from the Arab era — to wit, the north-coastal reorientation of Crete's urban settlement, economy, and politics — continued as a matter of course under the regimes that supplanted its ninth-to-tenth-century initiators. Yet, precisely because this development was in later years taken for granted by subjects and rulers alike, one hardly would expect its beginnings to have been remembered from a distance of seven centuries as an Arab contribution.

On the other hand, the international background of the Ottoman conquest of Crete differed immeasurably from the erstwhile Arab-Byzantine tug of war for possession of the island. While in those earlier years it was the Greeks' own empire that faced the Arab State (or States) in a perennial contest for control of East Mediterranean waters, by the seventeenth century neither of these two traditional antagonists was free any longer to control even its own home-territory. Subdued by the overriding might of the Turkish military machine, both the Greek and the Arab areas had forcibly been merged into a single political framework — that of the Ottoman Empire — which, except for Crete, encompassed the whole East Mediterranean basin and the Aegean and Black Seas as well.

Seen in the context of these historical changes, the Turkish campaign for the strategically invaluable Greek island presented a totally different image — different, that is, from the image conjured by the voluminous literature of the time. That literature, weighing the Turkish expedition against Crete concurrently with the latter-day thrust of the Sultanate into the heart of Europe, viewed the "War of Candia" and its aftermath from a decidedly West European vantage-point. Not so the autochthonous population of the island. The latter hardly felt threatened by the Ottoman action. The Turks' adversary was, in reality, the adversary of the Cretans as well. True, as theater of war, the island had suffered heavy losses in life and property. Yet, priceless asset though she obviously was, it is not Crete herself that served as the final target of the Turkish assault, but the Western Christian power occupying her. Always resentful of that power and decrying it as foreign and exploitative, the islanders surely found it difficult to identify with that power's bloody effort to maintain control over their homeland.

By contrast, the prospect of coming under the dominion of the Sublime Porte seemed to have had at the time an utterly different connotation. Subjection to Ottoman rule had by then become a political pattern common to *all* national, ethnic, and religious groups in Southeast Europe and the Eastern Mediterranean, including the Greeks of both the mainland and the islands. Given this basic situation, the extension of Turkish supremacy to Crete not only was devoid of much of the pointed bitterness accompanying earlier conquests, but could, under the circumstances, offer clearly discernible advantages. As an Ottoman domain Cretan Greekdom would no longer remain cut off from the main body of the Greek people and culture or from the national Greek church, as it was during the extended and burdensome period of Venetian occupation. Rather, within the all-embracing framework of Ottoman suzerainty, it would rejoin (so to speak) the Greek world, and share, for better or worse, in its faith and fate.

Irony of history! By having defeated Venice on the Candiote battlefield and by having finally wrested from the Republic's hands her most precious Greek possession, the Muslim Sultanate unwittingly became Greekdom's great avenger — an avenger not of Cretan Greekdom alone, but of the Byzantine Empire at large. Even the fact that it was this very Sultanate that acted as the Empire's gravedigger and heir two centuries earlier had lost some of its painful sting in the course of the historical reappraisal. After all, Constantinople's final tragedy was but the inevitable consequence of an earlier debacle. Was it not the shattering blow by Venice and Venice's Frankish allies in the Fourth Crusade — a blow never forgotten or forgiven — that irreparably weakened Byzantium and precipitated her eventual downfall in 1453 at the hand of the Turks? And, yes, was it not this very same blow that originally severed Crete from the Greek Orthodox Empire, subjecting the island to long centuries of Latin domination? No matter, then, how violent the arrival of Ottoman Islam on the Cretan scene, for the greater part of the Cretan people that event, paradoxically, bore the prospect of recovery and reassertion: recovery of ethnic and cultural identity within the broader framework of Greek unity (albeit in bondage) and reassertion of religious self-determination by checking the encroachments of Crete's Latin masters upon the Greek Orthodoxy of the majority population on the island.

CRETAN JEWRY AND THE TURKS

The feelings of the Jewish minority in Crete ran very much along parallel lines. True, a few italianized Jewish families preferred to gear their own fate to the shifting fortunes of the Venetian Republic and chose to leave the island altogether rather than be subjected to Ottoman rule. Guided by ties of kinship, by vested economic interests, by cultural affinity, and, very likely, by personal considerations of a kind that cannot easily be documented, they fled to Venice and her mainland dependencies or to one of Venice's still unaffected insular possessions, as did also some of their equally italianized Greek compatriots.

This, however, was hardly the attitude of most Cretan Jews. Despite the obvious hardships of siege and war (of which more later), the wider Jewish circles had little cause for viewing with apprehension the waning of Venetian power on the island — the less cause, indeed, considering how irritatingly hostile that power had been toward them in recent generations. Nor did they have reason to fear the eventual replacement of Venetian dominion in Crete by a Muslim administration whose policies vis-à-vis the Jews were traditionally favorable. On the contrary: while in the case of Cretan Greekdom subjection to the Sublime Porte promised to be a blessing in disguise, to the Jews it was an open boon. To begin with, it cleared the way for Cretan Jewry to rejoin the "Romaniote" Jewish world, i.e., the network of Greek-speaking Jewish communities that since remote antiquity dotted the East Roman landscape. Rent asunder by the Frankish dismemberment of the Byzantine Empire and by subsequent inroads of Turkish forces into the Empire's territory, these communities found themselves reintegrated anew by the all-encompassing bonds of the victorious Sultanate.

More, such Romaniote reunion was but one element in a broader unifying process made possible by the coincidence of Turkey's ter-

ritorial expansion and her generous (and profitable) absorption
of growing numbers of Jewish refugees from West Christian lands,
especially from Spain and Portugal. For the first time in history, the
ancient communities of the former imperial provinces were brought
under one roof together with the evergrowing congregations of
Sephardi newcomers and with the age-old Arabic-speaking Jewries
of territories conquered by Turkey in the early sixteenth century;
a sprinkling of Ashkenazi groups lent an added ingredient to this
East Mediterranean Jewish melting pot. Under the panoply of
Ottoman Islam, thus, Cretan Jewry integrated into what by then
had grown to be very likely the world's largest concentration of
Jews and the richest reservoir of Jewish power and creativity!

To be sure, the Jews of Crete did not have to wait for the arrival
of Turkish soldiers before taking their first plunge into the Ottoman melting pot. Their contacts with Turkish Jewry dated back
many generations prior to the ouster of the Venetians from Crete.
Such contacts covered a manifold variety of fields and were by no
means unilateral. Thus, on the one hand, allegiance to Venice notwithstanding, Jewish life on the island was profoundly affected by
all that was happening within the Turkish Jewish world. Rabbinic
and literary exchanges of those times amply demonstrate the extent
of the influence exerted on Cretan Jewry by the economic, the
institutional, and the cultural Jewish advances in Turkey and, especially, by the impressive rise in stature of Ottoman Jewish Palestine. Conversely, the quality of Jewish life in the Turkish centers
themselves was greatly enhanced (in terms of religious observances
and institutions, that is) by both the flow of Jewish-supervised
goods from Venetian Crete and the steady influx of Cretan Jewish
manpower. Ever since early Venetian days Cretan Jews were engaged in financing and exporting part of the island's agricultural
yield. Since the markets they would cater to in the East Mediterranean centers of commerce were primarily Jewish markets, special
steps had to be taken in order to satisfy the religious sensibilities
of the Jewish clientèle abroad. Especially such items as wines and
cheeses had to be reliably made to conform to Jewish dietary
scruples before they could be declared ritually acceptable not only

by local Jewish standards (sometimes decried as inadequate) but also by leading Jewish jurists in Constantinople, Salonica, Safed, or Alexandria. The Cretan Jewish exporters duly organized and supervised this production process.

In addition to goods, men, too, were on the move. This is true of the Jewish as much as the Greek islanders. Striving to break out of the physical confines of Cretan insularity and making up in quality and diligence for what they lacked in terms of numbers, some Cretan Jews would abandon their native territory in search of new economic opportunities or greater intellectual challenges. In time, a veritable "Cretan Diaspora" arose in the major centers of commerce and learning, exerting, in turn, evergrowing influence on diverse areas of communal activity abroad. Thus, prominent Jewish emigrés from Venetian Crete actually helped mold in late-Byzantine and early-Turkish times the supreme institution of Jewish self-government in Constantinople: the first *haham başı*, or Chief Rabbi, under Mehmet the Conqueror, Moses Capsali, was a Cretan. Similarly of Cretan origin were the Candiottis, the Khoúlis, the Delmedigos, and a host of other Jewish families that distinguished themselves in Ottoman and other territories throughout the fifteenth, the sixteenth, the seventeenth, and the eighteenth centuries.

In short: while the final annexation of Crete by Turkey undeniably played havoc with the economic and cultural bonds that linked *some* Cretan Jews with Venice and with the Italian mainland, other bonds, of equally long standing and possibly more vital to *many*, did, as events unfolded, acquire new meaning and depth. These bonds, uniting the Jews of Crete with the Jews of the Balkans and the Near East who long since experienced the broader horizons of the Turkish Sultanate, proved extremely helpful; they made Cretan Jewry's own transition from the tutelage of Venice to that of Turkey a smooth and painless process.

THE TURKISH SICILLAT

Regrettably, this exciting story of both the background and the early years of cooperation between the Ottoman conquerors and broad segments of Crete's native population is rarely ever told. History books prefer stories of conflict and war. Invariably, then, after describing the stormy years of the Ottoman invasion, historians are prone to dispose of the first century of *peaceful* Turkish rule on the island (till the Daskaloiánnis uprising of 1770) in a short paragraph or two of meaningless generalities, to make way for the great saga of modern Cretan Greekdom: the dramatic rebellions against the liberator-turned-oppressor. These rebellions galvanized public opinion in the nineteenth century and drew the attention of the Western world to Turkish-occupied Crete and her brave and freedom-loving people.

Indeed, it is the preoccupation with these late developments — extremely important developments, to be sure — that lies at the root of the inexcusable imbalance between the way our histories are treating the early post-conquest story and the way they narrate the details of later revolutionary days. Militant Greek nationalism, reawakened some hundred years after the "War of Candia," contributed significantly to furthering this imbalance. Exacerbated by the progressive deterioration of Turkish-Greek relations in the nineteenth century, the nationalist attitudes tended to erase, as it were, from the islanders' collective memory the recollection of the one-time assistance which the Ottoman invader had received from the Greek Orthodox majority no less than from kindred segments of the island's minorities. Instead, the historical record of collaboration and understanding was readily tainted by the facile, Venetian-inspired canard of "treason" (including "Jewish treason," of course), reminiscent of the medieval Christian rumors concerning earlier Islamic conquests in Christian lands.

This historiographic gap that separates at present the dramatic entry of the Ottoman regime onto the Cretan scene from the even more dramatic events that eventually precipitated that regime's overthrow, need not persist any longer; the gap can, and should, be filled now by solid documentary testimony. To recover that testimony — the testimony, that is, of peaceful development and reconstruction during the first hundred years of Ottoman rule on the island — one must turn to a hitherto almost untapped and

virtually unknown source: the Turkish Archives of Crete. Unlike
the Venetians who successfully transferred to the Mother-city the
Duca di Candia records of most of the 450 years of their Cretan
administration (that marvelous collection forms now part of the
State Archives of Venice), the Turks left their papers behind. About
400 *defters*, i.e., registers, of cadastral, notarial, and *Vakıf* records,
as well as some 500 volumes of *mahkeme sicillati*, or court-registers,
of the Kandiyote kadis gather dust to this day in the Municipal
Library of Iraklion (the former Turkish Kandiye). They cover the
entire period of Turkish domination on the island, from the very
first year following the conquest till 1898. In addition, rows upon
rows of Turkish registers fill the shelves of the Cretan Historical
Archives in present-day Khanià (the Canea-Hanya of Venetian
and Turkish times). Since the latter deal exclusively with the latest
stages of Ottoman rule — the early *sicillat* of the Hanyote kadis
perished in the fire that ravaged the city in 1897 — the only documents that hold special interest for the present study are those
contained in the *defters* of Kandiye-Iraklion. These are stored
under the lonely care of the erudite Kyrios Nikos Stavrinidis,
and it is to Mr. Stavrinidis that I owe a debt of gratitude for
introducing me to this hoard of archival material.

CENTRAL AND PROVINCIAL ARCHIVES

Now, the existence in the *Central* Ottoman Archives in Istanbul
of documents pertaining to Turkish rule in Crete (including its
early period) did not pass unnoticed by students in the field. Two
such documents — the *kanunname*, or imperial regulations, governing the relations of subjects and rulers in the cities of Hanya and
Kandiye, respectively — were actually published; a handful of
other archival entries is merely listed by reference-number in one
bibliography or another. None had ever been really integrated into
the life story of Ottoman Crete. In many ways, however, the
local source-materials stemming from the office of the Kandiyote
kadis may prove even more revealing than the Istanbul documents.
For, in the bureaucratic structure of provincial governments in the
Ottoman Empire, the role of the kadi far transcended his traditional

function as Muslim judge. The religious and moral prestige of his person extended into the administrative domain as well, manifesting itself in the actual performance by the kadi of certain bureaucratic duties. He, thus, was registrar, notary public, and keeper of *sicillat* and he supervised in a general way the conduct and performance of officials entrusted with the maintenance of governmental affairs in his *kaza*, or district.

This two-fold character of the kadi's business — i.e., his supervision cf both the *general*-governmental and the *local* actions of the provincial administration — is well mirrored in the variety of *sicillat* he entered into the *defters*. That is why, broadly speaking, the *defters* also fall into two categories. They feature, in the first place, copies of governmental ordinances, instructions, and correspondence that were issued by agencies of the *central* Ottoman administration in Constantinople. Such documents would be conveyed to local officials either through direct channels or, in keeping with Ottoman usage, by the hand of plaintiffs seeking redress or action. In addition, the *defters* include materials that pertained to *local* affairs or litigations and were entered exclusively into locally-kept records: court-minutes, testimonies, statements, and copies of legal papers filed locally with the kadi's office. In this sense, the *sicil*-records can be expected to both corroborate the documentary material stored in the Istanbul Archives (no such comparative study has as yet been undertaken) and supplement that material considerably by introducing information of purely local color.

As already emphasized, the Turkish *sicillat* of Iraklion deal with the better-known nineteenth-century chapter of Cretan history, too. But, more important still, they bring to life also the earlier and by far most neglected half of the story of Turkish dominion in Crete — the story, that is, in which the constructive determination of the rulers to rehabilitate the war-ravaged island is translated into the language of daily actions on the local level. Thus, the *sicils* tell us how, following the conquest, a new land-system was imposed and an ambitious urban development was initiated, ultimately re-fashioning Kandiye into the city we know as Iraklion today. They show the variety of public works that were continuously organized:

the strengthening of city walls and ramparts, the repeated dredging of the harbor of silt, and the keeping of the watersupply lines in good repair. They introduce us to the way taxes were apportioned and collected, the way deeds of sale and other civil contracts were entered into the books, and the way trade guilds and industry were regulated and controlled. Finally, they allow a step-by-step reconstruction of the manner in which justice was administered and grievances were investigated against the greed of governors and the abuse of lower officials.

By the same token, the *sicillat* show us the other side of the coin as well. They indicate the extent to which the life of the *râya*, i.e., of the non-Turkish subjects, was kept under supervision and, occasionally, placed under constraint, in line with Islamic usage. They depict churches being consecrated into mosques (no record is available to suggest the parallel islamization of synagogues), intermarriage and conversion to Islam being encouraged, and rental fees being imposed on whole non-Muslim neighborhoods for the sake of funding pious Muslim institutions. Finally, as years went by, the *sicillat* implacably begin reflecting the changing spirit of the time, showing how things got gradually out of hand and drifted into the state of anarchy and decline which brought about, in 1770, the first revolutionary response on the part of the Greek Orthodox majority — the very same majority that initially looked upon the Turkish conquest as a welcome respite from Latin oppression.

CRETAN JEWRY AS REFLECTED IN THE SICILLAT

Culled out of the *defters* pertaining to the first century of Ottoman rule, some sixty-odd *sicillat* can also be enlisted in the service of Jewish historiography. This will be welcome news particularly to students of Mediterranean Jewish history who long were baffled by the conspicuous paucity of meaningful references to Cretan Jewry during the seventeenth and eighteenth centuries. Elsewhere I have raised a number of questions concerning this silence of outside Jewish sources and the absence of literary testimonies stemming from the Jews themselves who resided in Ottoman Kandiye. The Turkish *sicils* do not answer all these questions, of course, nor can they be expected to. But they go a long way in dispelling much of the darkness which surrounds the Cretan Jewish community in the wake of the establishment of the new regime. Especially the day-to-day realities of Cretan Jewish life at the time — the problems connected with the *physical* rehabilitation of the Jewish settlement, for one thing — reëmerge from these documents full of detail and color.

Thus, the *sicils* introduce us into the changing topography of the Kandiyote Jewish Quarter, into the efforts invested in the repair of the local synagogues, and into the procedures governing the purchase of real estate in and outside the Jews' Quarter. They further contain official tax-figures which, besides their intrinsic interest, provide reliable clues to estimating the size of the Jewish population. Also valuable are the economic details scattered throughout the *sicillat*: they give us direct and indirect information on the economic pursuits of Cretan Jews in the Ottoman period, including the activities of those who, as brokers or dragomans, were in the employ of foreign powers. Finally, the documents throw open unexpected channels for the understanding of the Jews' relations with their neighbors, be they Greek Orthodox, Armenian, or Muslim, and of the alignments and tensions within and outside the Jewish community. Surprisingly or not, some of the alliances were often based on social class-consciousness and on affinities stemming from common economic standing rather than on ethnic ties and conventional religious allegiances.

On the reverse side of the picture, the *sicillat* afford a glimpse into the precarious security conditions prevailing in the early decades of Ottoman rule, when some of the naval bases of Crete still remained in the hands of the Venetians. Such bases easily lent themselves to be used as refuge for outlaws, as was indeed the case with Spinalonga, the Venetian sea-fort off the northeastern coast of Crete (Fig. 1); in the early days of Turkish rule (so we learn from a number of *sicillat*) this base extended protection to Greek villagers who were involved in the murder of some travelling Jewish salesmen. Other *sicils* record acts of conversion to Islam by a few Cretan Jews and mirror the complications, personal as well as social and economic, that acts of this kind were bound to produce in the small and well-knit community. Still other entries give details of grievances which local Jews, along with other segments of the population, would lodge occasionally with the central authorities against blackmail and extortion by rapacious administrators.

RURAL SETTLEMENTS

Last but not least, by their eloquent silence the *sicils* raise crucial questions concerning one of the most interesting features of Cretan Jewish life — the existence of rural Jewish settlements in south-central Crete. We have already referred to the fact that, since early Venetian days, the Jews of Candia were active in financing and exporting some of the island's agricultural produce. This they did either directly, through anticipatory contracts with Greek farmers (a great number of such contracts are preserved in the logbooks of Veneto-Cretan notaries), or through the agency of Jews who themselves lived in villages. To be sure, the village Jews engaged in ramified enterprises and services, from meat production to medicine and surgery. By reason of their residence and contacts in the villages, however, they would also, irrespective of profession, serve as intermediaries between the Greek tiller of the soil and the northern harbor cities marketing the fruit of the tiller's labor. To a large extent, then, on the continuity of Jewish presence in the rural areas hinged not only the livelihood of many Cretan Jews themselves but the special role which the Jews played in Cretan economy in general — an economy that was then, as it still is today, agrarian-oriented.

The advent of the Turks, so we learn from the *defters*, did not change that role. Throughout the first century of Ottoman domination instances of continuous existence of Jewish landownership and of Jewish settlement in rural areas are well attested to in the *sicillat*. The fact is, however, that from the second half of the eighteenth century on, not a single document concerning rural Jewry or rural Jewish possession turns up in the registers. No matter how diffident one is to adduce an *argumentum ex silentio*, the cut-off date at hand seems too conspicuous to be taken as purely coincidental. Coupled with other evidence, one cannot help linking the disappearance of the rural Jew from the human and socioeconomic landscape of Crete to the broader developments which began evolving precisely at that time: the awakened Greek-Turkish animosity that was to erupt in 1770 and was to culminate eventually in the revolutionary upheavals of the nineteenth century. The Jew was but a marginal factor in these developments, of course, and had no power to influence one way or another their pace or direction. Yet, the intensification of *ethnic-Greek* mindedness and *Orthodox-Greek* mindedness (or the combination of both) could not but adversely affect the Jew's personal fate and security, especially in the less-controllable inland rural regions. The inevitable polarization of loyalties left little room, indeed, for the safe presence of people who were neither Greek nor Orthodox, nor really identified in either of these two ways with the Greeks' national struggle.

*   *   *

Many aspects of Jewish life in Crete during the first century of Ottoman rule are thus elucidated for the first time by the Turkish *sicillat*. Of that variety of aspects our paper selects only one upon which to concentrate: the topography of the Jewish Quarter of Kandiye in the aftermath of the Turkish conquest as compared with the state of that Quarter under the Venetians. The *sicils* at hand are of different categories. Some register the purchase of houses by Jews and their neighbors in and around the Jews' Quarter. Others contain minutes of court-proceedings initiated by the kadis for the sake of establishing the legal ownership of real estate and issuance of the necessary title-deeds. Still another group of documents includes tax-rolls and rent-lists of the *Vakıf* administration. The cumulative testimony of these *sicillat* is extremely revealing. It not only indicates the mere fact that a crucial change in the character of the Jews' Quarter had set in with the advent of the Turks, but also documents in detail the three major directions of that change: in the territorial extent of the Jewish neighborhood, in its socioeconomic basis, and, finally, in its demographic make-up. To these new data we shall turn our attention now.

II

THE ZUDECHA

The Jewish Quarter of Venetian Candia which the victorious Turks had entered in 1669 upon the city's final capitulation dated back many generations prior to the arrival of the Venetians. In the beginning section of this study I repeated my earlier suggestion that native Jewish settlers from the rural areas may have begun moving into Arab Khandaq as early as the ninth century, i.e., soon after the city was founded. It is, however, to the tenth-century Byzantine reconquerors that one must ascribe most likely the establishment of a regular Ἰουδαία or Ἰουδαϊκή (in popular parlance: Ἑβραϊκή or Ὀβρηακή) on the presently-known location.

After having resolved to restore the half-desolate former Arab capital of the island rather than designate a different site for that purpose, the returning Byzantines allowed the Jews to settle again in Khandaq (now renamed *Khandax*) but made them occupy exclusively the northwestern edge of the city's seaboard overlooking Dermatà Bay (of which more later). When, in the subsequent century, the entire Arab-Byzantine urban development was girded with a belt of protective sea and land fortifications, the Jews' Quarter, too, grown stronger through influx of immigrants from other imperial provinces and the Near East, was included within the Byzantine walls; a "Jewish Gate" ushered into the Bay area. Thus, entering the Cretan scene in the early 1200s, the Venetians merely confirmed Khandakite Jewry on its already-established location and took over, as elsewhere, the Greek appellation of the Jewish Quarter, latinizing or italianizing it to *Iudaica* — variously spelled *Judayca* > *Giudaicha* > *Judecca* > *Giudecca* > *Zudecca* > *Zudecha* — or to *Hebraica* and *Hebraca*. The Venetian government did, however, a hundred years later, move to define the physical boundaries of the *Zudecha*, articulating into law the prohibition of Jewish residence and business in other parts of the city (Fig. 2).

On another occasion I have discussed both the Byzantine motive in selecting, of all places, the city corner adjacent to Dermatà Bay as the site of the Jews' Quarter and the reasons for the perpetuation

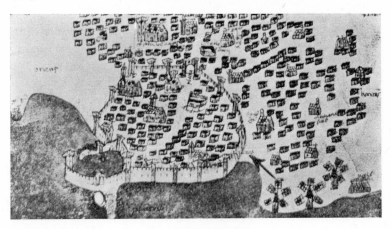

FIG. 2. Oldest representation of Venetian Candia within its former Byzantine walls, as viewed from the sea (north to south) in 1429 by C. Buondelmonti [*MS Bibl. Laurenziana, Florence*]. Note the 'Main Street' bisecting the walled area, from the fortified port (*bottom left*) up to the central square. Midway, on the left, is the Church of Ayos Titos, later converted into the Vizier Mosque. Flanking the main square on the north are the Ducal Palace (*right*) and the Church of San Marco (*left*); the southern end is dominated by the high gate of 'Voltone'. Beyond the southern wall (*left of center*) stands the Church of San Salvador, the latter-day Valide Sultan Mosque. The northwestern corner of the walled city (*center foreground — see arrow*) is clearly marked 'Zudeca'. Touching it on the left is the Church of San Pietro, the Sultan Ibrahim Mosque of Turkish times. Dermatà Bay and its mills, on the *Zudecha's* righthand flank, are outside the Byzantine walls. They will later be included in the new Venetian perimeter (cf. Fig. 6).

FIG. 3 (below). Present-day view of the former Jewish Quarter of Candia from across Dermatà Bay. The right-angle corner of the *Zudecha* is shown exposed to the open sea in the north (*left*) and to the Bay in the west (*center foreground*).

of the Quarter there down to modern times. I shall return to that problem in the last chapter of this study. For the purpose of the present analysis the topography of the site itself is of special interest. A glance at the medieval and early modern charts suffices to make us understand how extremely vulnerable, security-wise, the Zudecha's location used to be in the more distant past. To begin with, the Quarter was exposed to the sea on two sides. With the right-angle point of its northwestern corner jutting out into the water, the Jewish neighborhood touched the sea both alongside a sizable strip of the city's coastline in the north and along the abrupt southward indentation of the coast in the west which forms Dermatà Bay (Fig. 3). The neighborhood was thus susceptible to simultaneous *naval* assault on two fronts, by some light craft from the west and by heavier men-of-war from the north. In addition, with Dermatà Bay remaining just outside the wall, the Quarter constituted in the early days the western limit of the city on *land*, too; hence, its western flank was exposed not only to hostile vessels venturing into the Bay but to attack by *land* troops as well. A precarious position indeed!

For objective reasons, however, later generations of Candiote Jews began experiencing a steadily rising sense of safety on their *Zudecha* homeground. The persistent extension of Venetian Candia (though scarcely of the Jews' Quarter itself) westwards and southwards moved the city limits far beyond the original Byzantine walls. Coupled with the ever-present need for being on guard against Turkish aggression, such urban growth did ultimately call for throwing a new defensive ring around the whole settled area of Candia in order to extend protection also to the recently built *borghi*. The net result of this urban expansion and of the consequent build-up of Venetian walls and ramparts was a pronounced change in the relative position of the Jews' Quarter. The original Khandakite nucleus of the capital (now marked on Venetian maps as *Città Vecchia*), and for that matter the adjoining Dermatà Bay as well, found themselves, as of a sudden, centrally located. Inevitably, the Jewish section, leaning from within against the Bay corner of the Old City, felt even better protected than many a latter-day neighborhood (Fig. 6).

IMPROVED IMAGE

The added sense of security was but one of a number of ways in which the impressive growth of Candia under Venice favorably affected the life and fate of the *Zudecha*. The changing scene eventually contributed also to the upgrading of the *Zudecha*'s image and real estate value — so much so in fact that, less than a hundred years prior to the Ottoman conquest, the Quarter could aptly be described by the Venetian administrator Lorenzo da Mula as situated "in the prettiest part of town, above the sea, with very handsome homes and buildings." To be sure, even at the time of its pronouncement in 1571 this flattering (or envious) testimony did, at best, fit a handful of residences in the Jews' Quarter. Some of these mansions, the property of noble italianized Jewish families, answered the description well, just as they would also in Turkish times. An empty shell of one such building, sadly bespeaking the faded glory of yesteryear, is still extant these days in what used to be the *Zudecha*. Yet, no matter how accurate the Venetian official was in his appraisal of some exceptional examples of Veneto-Cretan Jewish architecture, he could not have intended his remark to serve as a basis for unqualified generalization. Rather, having had the economic, the fiscal, and the political objectives of the Republic paramount in mind, Lorenzo was pointing to the high standard of living of those only among the inhabitants of the *Zudecha* who "really counted," being the proud owners of "very handsome homes and buildings." Moreover, in taking notice of the elegant mansions overlooking the waterfront of the *Zudecha*, the reporting aristocrat displayed a natural enthusiasm for things that remained throughout in accord with his own station and social concepts. The slum section was outside his interest; at any rate, one hardly can expect him to have ventured into it.

The truth of the matter is, however, that, *viewed from within*, the *Zudecha* presented an entirely different picture. Despite its latter-day distance from the western approaches of the city and the resultant feeling of greater safety and protection and, yes, notwithstanding the conspicuous (perhaps too conspicuous) beauty of the homes of *the few*, the Jews' Quarter *in general* could not have by any standard been considered a comfortable place to live in. Indeed, it was getting less and less comfortable with the years, even for the rich. With accommodations for 800 to 1000 souls squeezed into a few lanes and alleys, of which the main one was quite appropriately nicknamed *Stenón* ('The *Narrow* [Street]'), and with stalls and workshops and as many as four synagogues (and the usual annexes for school, court, etc.) crowding a short stretch of the public thoroughfare, the Quarter began developing from the early decades of the fourteenth century many of the known traits of a compulsory ghetto; as time went on, it grew increasingly inadequate in space and facilities.

Limited by Venetian law to the choking bounds of *confinia determinata*, yet serving through the years as the goal of considerable Jewish immigration from abroad as well as from Crete's inland rural communities, the little Quarter suffered from evergrowing congestion and from steadily declining sanitary conditions. Now, Candia as a whole never earned the reputation of a clean city. *Strade da porci e case da cavalli*, some contemporaries described it. The garbage strewn in its streets dismayed visitors and exasperated generations of administrators. Chances are that the situation in the *Zudecha* was even worse than in other neighborhoods. At any rate, it is a fact that as early as a hundred and twenty years before the Turkish conquest, the Jewish leadership of Candia saw fit to abolish the traditional practice of conducting religious services in the private home of mourners, "because nowadays the homes in the Jews' Quarter are small and are not truly clean for prayer" (*Takkanoth Kandiya* [Statuta Iudaeorum Candiae], no. 81, of 1549).

This picture of Candiote *Zudecha* as a jumble of small, dreary homes huddled together behind the façade of a few large mansions, themselves in a state of progressive deterioration, is confirmed by the seventeenth-century Turkish traveler Evliya Çelebi. Since the latter visited Candia twice, both before and after the entry of Ottoman soldiers into the city, his *Itinerary* is of great relevance to our topic; we discuss it again at some length in the last chapter of the present study. "It is so," Evliya tersely reports, "that they all [i.e., the Jews of Candia] have small as well as large decrepit houses, three hundred hopeless dwellings" (*Öyledir kim cümlenin sağır ü kebir dâr-i menhus haneleri, üç yüz adet dâr-i naçarları vardır*). As a somewhat disconnected afterthought, however, or perhaps sensing the paradox of the situation, Evliya makes an added observation at the very end of his brief paragraph devoted to Candia's Jewry: "All together there were three hundred fenced-in vegetable gardens, ponds, rose gardens, and in each of them one or two wells of water of life" (*Ve cümle üç yüz adet müşebbek bostan, göl, gülistanlar var kim, her birinde birer ikişer adet ab-i hayat çah-ı malar vardır*). Now, on first reading, this detail seems incongruous. In reality, however, the sight of three hundred Jewish families clinging pathetically to a patch of greenery of sorts in their dismally undersized and inadequate Quarter helps emphasize, rather than obviate, the impression of crowded drabness in that "prettiest part of town" on the eve of the Ottoman conquest. It was only natural, then, for Candiote Jews to pin their hopes on the defeat of the power dedicated to their ghettoization and to view such defeat as an opportunity for breaking out of the ghetto confines and expanding outwards.

ON THE EVE OF THE CONQUEST

The objective conditions in Candia on the eve of the entry of the Ottoman armies tended to encourage these hopes. The evacuation of the Venetians and of some of their Greek allies and the ravages of the 23-year-long siege and war had depleted the population of the neighborhoods adjoining the *Zudecha* and had left a goodly number of Christian homes emptied of their former occupants. The resulting vacuum could hardly be maintained for long in the face of the housing shortage that was plaguing Candiote Jewry for years on end.

That shortage of accommodations inside the *Zudecha* did, on the other hand, grow even more acute under the onslaught of the Ottoman offensive. Indeed, sympathies and expectations notwithstanding, by no means should the impression be gained that Venetian-Turkish hostilities had left the body of the *Zudecha* unscathed. The contrary rather is true. The scars were deep and many and would not heal for a long time. With Turkish pressure mounting against the city's western fortifications and with the invaders marshalling their forces for a final breakthrough along the road leading from the west to the Dermatà and the Jews' Quarter, the whole area comprising the *Zudecha* had paid an extremely heavy toll. The *Zudecha* itself, however, had more than its share in the overall balance of destruction suffered by the besieged city. A study of the war maps and diaries of the time reveals that during the siege the Venetians actually mounted their batteries on the protruding walled corner of the *Zudecha* in order to control the Dermatà waters and the land approaches to the citadel. In return, the *Zudecha* itself became a military target of prime importance. No wonder that, as late as a decade after the conquest, the Jewish neighborhood was still described by a visitor as "a quarter in ruin." Adding to the plight was the sheer deterioration of the *Zudecha*'s long overused ancient buildings, whether private or public. Obviously, their maintenance — an almost impossible undertaking even in normal times — had come to a complete standstill during the protracted campaign and could not immediately be embarked upon on the morrow of the Ottoman victory.

Gauging the extent of physical disrepair in the Jews' Quarter on the eve of, and subsequent to, the Ottoman takeover is no easy task. True, the already-mentioned "War of Candia" literature that sprang up in Europe during and after the Venetian-Ottoman conflict abounds in references to the general state of destruction prevailing in the city. Contemporary reporters and travelers — and, in their wake, modern historians, too — seem to have been deriving strange delight out of the count of mines exploded, cannon balls fired, and warriors felled by the enemy's blows. Yet, their description of the damage inflicted on the non-fighting population and its less glamorous dwellings seldom is couched in other than the most general terms. In that respect, the incidental scraps of information scattered throughout our post-conquest *sicillat* often prove far more illuminating than the literary works. Their stereotyped legalistic phraseology does not make exciting reading, to be sure; but the picture they present is trustworthy and accurate.

RECORD OF DEVASTATION

The legally required detailed descriptions of houses involved in real estate deals are a case in point. Thus, for instance, when, soon after the establishment of the Ottoman administration, a settlement was recorded between two Kandiyote Jewish partners concerning a house they owned jointly in the *Zudecha*, the formal Turkish *sicil* — one of our earliest — containing such routine description divulged the fact that two shops, out of a total of three, on the ground floor of the building were nothing but heaps of debris (*Defter* no. 2, p. 34; we shall return to discuss this document at a later stage of our study). Similarly revealing are other legal instruments that were drawn up on the conclusion of real estate transactions in the Jews' Quarter. Required by law to list the estates bordering on the purchased property, some of the documents remark cryptically that one or more of the neighboring plots had "ruined houses on them." In fact, details like this keep recurring as late as forty years after the conquest!

Regrettably, the *sicillat* do not pause to differentiate between types and causes of destruction. Perhaps as a matter of deliberate policy, they fail to indicate which damage was geared directly to the war action of the 1660s and which was a mere case of physical dilapidation, unchecked (if not indeed accelerated) by the war and by post-war conditions. Such differentiation is missing even where the *sicils* are specifically concerned with the problem of repairs, as, for instance, in the case of the repair of synagogues. Accomplishing the latter, even under normal circumstances, was no simple matter in a country governed by Muslim law: exact specifications had to be entered into the *defters* to satisfy the Islamic provision that the contemplated repairs would not make the non-Muslim prayerhouse "higher or larger" than it was "before the [Muslim] conquest." Nevertheless, even in these extremely sensitive instances the *sicillat* refrain from pinning down the reasons for the damage.

By way of illustration the *sicils* from the 1690s concerning the reconstruction of one of the ancient synagogues in the Jews' Quarter may be invoked here. The documents simply inform us that the said synagogue (to be mentioned yet further in this study) remained in a state of disrepair for a number of years; neither the time when the damage occurred nor the cause of the damage is given. It so happens that in this particular case we are able to deduce from the narrative that the sorry state of the building went back to the period of the siege. Indeed, encouraged by the Turkish takeover, a hasty attempt was made in the years following the conquest to remedy the situation. The community's undisguised zeal, however, so we learn fiom the *sicillat,* proved unwise and extremely costly. Readily exploited by a rapacious Turkish governor, the Jewish display of overeagerness not only failed to speed up the rebuilding of the shrine but left for a number of years the Kandiyote community open to a campaign of ugly extortion (*Defter* no. 8, pp. 16, 82, 136). Not before the greedy pasha had lost his job and, literally, his... head, in punishment for this and many other acts of oppression, was full-fledged reconstruction work finally performed on the site, backed by the prerequisite authorization of the Muslim religious court (*Defter* no. 8, p. 80).

While the state of disrepair of synagogues may have posed special problems, the general housing situation obtaining in the former *Zudecha* after 1669 can be summed up rather simply. With the advent of the Turks, two mutually complementary physical developments bearing on the future of the Kandiyote Jewish Quarter confronted each other across the ghetto border. On the one side of the Venetian-decreed demarcation line was the *Zudecha*'s perennial want of adequate living space, a want compounded by the miseries of the prolonged siege and grown evermore poignant during the difficult years that followed the conquest. Facing it, on the other side, was a territorial void (of sorts), created in some Christian sections adjoining the *Zudecha* by the exodus of individuals and families too closely linked with Venetian interests. Combined, the two developments held out unprecedented prospects for effectively improving the living conditions of Kandiyote Jews, once the *Zudecha* walls had been (literally and figuratively) abolished. The extension of Jewish domicile into the vacated neighboring areas could not be delayed much longer.

JEWISH VS. STATE INTERESTS

This twin set of physical factors favoring the expansion of the Jews' Quarter in the conquered city was paralleled by a twin set of State interests which made the conquering power move in the same direction. To begin with, there was the new administration's short-range need for balancing the enormous war expenditure by tapping local sources of revenue over and above routine taxation. Simultaneously, foundations had to be laid for the upkeep of a regular administrative machine and permanent revenues had to be lined up for funding the Evkâf (plur. of Vakıf), i.e., the pious Muslim institutions established in the city. Welded together and, more important, enhanced by the conquerors' basic philosophy of government which remained unhampered by segregationist concepts of the type that beclouded medieval Christian legislation, these two sets of factors produced a situation for which the earlier centuries of Christian domination on the island had no precedent: the readiness of the Turkish Provincial Treasury to dispose of abandoned (hence State-owned) real estate property by posting it for auction to private bidders, *any* bidders, Jews included. The Jews' movement outwards, across and beyond the former ghetto boundaries, was thus an objective in which both the self-interest of the new subjects and the self-interest of the new rulers coincided.

With the concurrent initiation of a new cadastral survey by the Ottoman authorities, the changes in real estate ownership were now placed on firm legal basis. This involved both the extraordinary changes produced by war and siege and those resulting from transfers of government-owned and other property in the aftermath of the conquest. Entered into the *sicil-defters*, their registry generated a welcome air of permanency and order. No wonder the earliest post-conquest *sicillat* concerning the Jewish population in Ottoman Kandiye deal with such transactions. In no time at all, the residential area that was traditionally identified as Jewish underwent considerable transformation. No longer geared to the topographic and legal limitations of the Venetian era, it still centered around the nucleus of former *Zudecha*, of course, but did not stop at the *Zudecha* gates.

The process of change that promised to reshape the character of the neighborhood as a result of the above-described developments was given an added twist through deliberate government action; that action also affected the terminology applied to the place. As with some other major churches in the city, the basilica of the Dominican Monastery of San Pietro, closely adjoining the eastern boundary of former *Zudecha*, was seized and converted into a mosque. Commemorating Sultan Ibrahim (1640–48), the Ottoman ruler who first ordered the invasion of Crete, this newly instituted Muslim prayerhouse soon became the center of the whole neighborhood "above the sea." Indeed, in line with common practice whereby the mosque would lend its name to the broader area surrounding it, the neighborhood at large, including the Jews' Quarter, was to be known hence, in both popular parlance and official phraseology, as *Sultan Ibrahim Mahallesi*. Nevertheless, a still predominantly Jewish *subsection* around the Old Venetian Synagogue, while no longer a ghetto in the technical sense, continued to be easily distinguishable within the broader boundaries of the Sultan Ibrahim Quarter and did at no time lose its separate Jewish identity and label. Certainly, its *Venetian* name, no longer justified on objective grounds, soon was consigned to oblivion. Not so the other terms. The new appellation *Yahudi Mahallesi*, as the *Turkish*-speaking neighbors and the Turkish documents would have it, or the old designation *Evraïki* (or *Ovraki*), as preferred by the *Greek* neighbors, perpetuated the separateness of the "Jews' Quarter" down to modern times (Figs. 2 and 6).

III

EXPANDING THE YAHUDI MAHALLESI

But let the documents tell the story. Of the many *sicils* available, we shall select here only a few that illustrate the new trends; the presentation of additional material will have to await the full-scale monograph on the subject as well as the publication of the complete collection of documents and regesta in my *Creta Judaica*.

Barely eleven months after the establishment of Ottoman regime in Kandiye — so we learn from the earliest-available *sicil* mentioning Kandiyote Jews (*Defter* no. 2, p. 137, of August 27, 1670; Fig. 4) — abandoned Christian houses were auctioned off to Jews in *Hιristo Iskuludi Mahallesi* (Χριστὸ Σκουλούδη), a Greek Orthodox Quarter adjacent to former *Zudecha*. The sale, effected by Abu Bakr Effendi, the *defterdar* (or State Treasurer) of Kandiye, transferred to Jews hailing from the old Jewish *mahalle* as many as four houses and yards in one major transaction. The home of an absentee Greek priest was part of the package deal, whereas the adjoining church building remained excluded from the negotiations (Fig. 6).

The payment procedure consisted of two components: remittance of a basic price to the Treasury purse and the obligation to pay in perpetuity a rental fee (by the day, the month, or the year) for the benefit of one of the newly instituted Kandiyote *Evkâf*. In the case recorded in our first *sicil*, the basic price destined for the Treasury coffers was a lump sum of 100 *kuruş arslanı* (or *esedi* = "Löwenthaler") for the four pieces of real estate, whereas a daily rent (*yevmi icare*) of 4 *akçe* was allotted to Crete's largest Muslim foundation, the *Valide Sultan Cami*, i.e., the Mosque of the Queen Mother, formerly a major church in the upper part of town (Figs. 2 and 6).

A similar method of payment was used in the case recorded in a *sicil* of January 26, 1671 (*Defter* no. 2, p. 97), involving again the transfer into Jewish hands of an abandoned Christian house in the *Hιristo Iskuludi Mahallesi*. The operation was sanctioned by the same Ottoman official, the *defterdar*, and the procedure throughout resembled in all details the one recorded in the earlier-cited *sicil*. The house itself, however, seems to have been considerably larger than the buildings sold in the former auction. Also, the swift recovery of the Jewish community when life in Kandiye returned to normalcy may have made the demand for housing evermore urgent and may have caused a marked rise in prices. At any rate, the basic price as well as the rate of the *Vakıf*-rent were in the latter case twice the amount averaged by one building in the first transaction: the buyers were to pay directly to the Treasury as much as 55 *kuruş esedi* plus a daily rent of 2 *akçe*

FIG. 4. Earliest-available Turkish document pertaining to Jews of Kandiye:
a title-deed of 1670 recording the acquisition by Kandiyote Jews of four
houses outside the traditional Jewish Quarter.
(Defter no. 2, p. 137 — *Turkish Archives of Iraklion, Crete*)

which was the Valide Mosque's perpetual share in the deal.

The dual payment method was not the only fixed characteristic
of the real estate transfers transacted between the Cretan Turkish
Treasury and the space-hungry Jews of Kandiye. Also the legal
procedure repeated itself unchangingly. In that respect, again, our
first *sicil* (recorded, we remember, in the latter part of the very

first year of Turkish rule) serves as an instructive prototype for all later documents of the kind. Step by step, it takes us through the four stages that followed the actual auction and purchase of the property and that culminated in the registration of the title, as required by law.

First, a patent, the *berat*, was issued, stating the details of the sale, specifying the size of the plot, and recording the payment of the agreed price. This opened the way for court action intended to notarize the transfer of ownership rights. The second step, therefore, was up to the buyers. They would deposit in the Muslim court, the *Meclis-i Şer'î*, a *takrir*, i.e., a formal notification of transference of real estate. They would, further, petition the court to lend validity to the *berat* by issuing the proper *hüccet*, that is, the canonically prescribed title-deed.

Responding to the plea, the kadi, in turn, would initiate the third step. The latter was a three-stage operation: a) a *mevlâna*, i.e., a pious and respected person representing the kadi, along with a *mimar* (architect) and the *mütevelli*, or administrator, of the interested *Vakıf* would be sent to survey the plot(s) and/or the building(s) and perform the necessary measurements on the spot; b) consequently, on location, the *mevlâna* would confirm the details specified in the *berat* and describe the boundaries of the sold plot, listing the adjacent pieces of property along with the names of their owners. He then would record his confirmation in writing; ultimately — c) he would appear before the court and testify as to the veracity and accuracy of the recorded data. Thereupon, the fourth and final step, the act of issuing the desired *hüccet*, would be performed by the *Meclis-i Şer'î*. The minutes of the court-proceedings would then be duly entered into the *defter*, thus sealing the transfer of the property and affirming the newly acquired rights of legal ownership.

CLIENTS OF THE VALIDE SULTAN

It will be remembered that, in addition to the purchase price flowing into the Treasury chest, a daily rental was collected by the *Vakıf* from Jews acquiring abandoned property in adjoining neighborhoods. By no means, however, were the *Vakıf* payments accompanying such property transfers the only type of profit accruing to local Muslim foundations from Jewish sources. Rather, they formed part of a general policy governing the funding of Muslim religious establishments under the new administration. For the purpose of such funding, the Kandiyote Jewish Quarter in its entirety — the original *Zudecha*, that is, no less than its newly occupied annexes — was declared a revenue-bearing *Vakıf* endowment, with the Valide Sultan Mosque acting as its principal beneficiary.

Included in the *Vakıf*-earmarked income were even payments of rental by Jewish prayerhouses. Thus, besides the prayerhouse already mentioned briefly in this study, another one (out of the original four Jewish houses of worship that existed in the Venetian-dominated ghetto) was reopened in later days. Both institutions, usually described as *Yahudilerin kadim havraları,* "the Jews' ancient synagogues," are specifically listed for their rent-paying capacity in the extant nineteenth-century *defters* of *Evkâf* (cf., e.g., *Valide Sultan Cami Şerifi* [Atik], *Defter* no. 87, p. 42). One, so the documents inform us, the so-called Upper Synagogue (*yukarıki havra*), was to pay 3 *akçe* daily *icare* to the Valide Sultan *Vakıf.* The other, registered as the Lower Synagogue (*aşağı havra*), had to pay an appreciably higher fee to the same *Vakıf.* That fee amounted to a *per diem* payment of 5 *akçe*, almost twice the rental collected from the Upper Synagogue. It is to this synagogue indeed that we referred earlier in connection with the damage it sustained during the siege and the post-war efforts to rebuild it; its restoration was formally authorized by the Muslim court in 1694 (*Defter* no. 8, p. 80).

As we shall suggest later, the difference in rent between the two synagogues was no mere whim of meek or unscrupulous pashas. Rather, it reflected a very real socioeconomic disparity between two Jewish population groups centered around their respective shrines. Predictably, that disparity manifested itself also in the architectural quality and durability of the respective buildings. While no trace remains of the poorer Upper Synagogue, the impressive three-nave basilica known as the Lower Synagogue con-

stituted all through Turkish and modern Greek times the hub of
the Jewish Quarter, as it did also under Venetian domination. Alas,
almost deserted in the years of Cretan Jewry's decline prior to
World War II and severely damaged by Allied air raids during
the initial stages of German occupation, it finally was turned over
to the demolition squads in autumn, 1942. Like the people it served
for hundreds of years, it did not survive the Nazi Holocaust.

REGISTERING JEWISH PROPERTY

On April 21, 1671, some three months after the above-discussed
second title-deed was issued to Jews outside their traditional Quarter, another *sicil* concerning Jewish real estate ownership in Kandiye
was entered into the books. This entry (*Defter* no. 2, p. 34, already
invoked above for its description of partially destroyed shops on
its ground floor) did not involve real estate *outside* the former
Zudecha, nor for that matter did an act of new acquisition take
place at all. The *sicil* was merely recording a settlement reached
by two *Jewish* partners with respect to a house they already owned
inside the Jews' Quarter. Having divided the property between them,
the partners declared their joint ownership of the house terminated
and asked the Muslim court to provide them with a *hüccet* that
would canonically confirm each partner's title to his respective
share.

Admittedly, the very occurrence of such a petition runs counter
to the legal philosophy of medieval Jewry. Surely, here, if ever, was
a typical case of *intra-Jewish* litigation and agreement; thousands
like it fill the pages of rabbinic literature throughout the Middle
Ages. Filing the resultant document with the office of a Muslim
kadi was hardly the medieval Jewish jurist's idea of what com-
munity-minded Jews were supposed to do.

Nevertheless, the appearance of the two Jewish litigants before
a Muslim judge should come as no surprise to the student familiar
with the contradictions and paradoxes of the medieval Jewish scene.
The tedious repetition of rabbinic exhortations in many a communal Jewish statute or legalistic treatise, calling on Jewish defendants
to have sole recourse to Jewish courts, proves that the principle of

Jewish reliance on their own judiciary was very frequently honored
in its breach. Obviously, the extent of that breach varied with time
and region. In the Cretan milieu, at any rate, letting the State court
adjudicate intra-Jewish problems must have become the prevailing
trend rather than the exception. This trend is amply documented
by the abundant material from the archives of the Dukes of Candia
and of Candiote notaries stored in Venice. It can also be demonstrated in an indirect way by the conspicuous paucity of local
rabbinic literature of this genre, despite the highly developed communal and intellectual Jewish activity on the island. Last but not
least, it can (in a sense) be seen written into the Hebrew Statutes
of the Candiote communities. Far from fighting the trend, these
Statutes, repeatedly reëdited since 1228, merely try to regulate the
Jews' appearance before the Venetian courts so as to prevent the
desecration of the Sabbath; the appearance itself is apparently
taken for granted. In brief, the Kandiyote Jews' action of resorting
to the kadi's office clearly *continued* a local practice of long standing; it automatically substituted the freshly established Turkish
court for its defunct Venetian predecessor.

Moreover, the *sicil* in question becomes perfectly understandable
when viewed against the background of the early post-conquest
years and the *novel* exigencies stemming from the new situation.
The partners' move, undoubtedly, was designed to meet possible
difficulties arising from the cadastral survey which the new regime
embarked upon at the time. Evidently, clear title to one's property
and, more important still, official notarization of such title by the
Turkish court seemed imperative. Besides, with the Jewish *mahalle*
becoming a rent-paying domain of the *Vakıf*, a court-*hüccet* stating
the separate shares in the registered property was necessary to ensure each partner's fair allotment of the *Vakıf*-rent burden. Neither
of these actions could be initiated without regular proceedings of
the Muslim court.

MUSLIMS MOVE IN

The above-described open housing trend, which made the *Yahudi
Mahallesi* a different place to live in than was the former *Zudecha*,

could not be a one-way street, of course. While Jews expanded into the outlying neighborhoods after having been pent up for generations within the tightly circumscribed confines of their Quarter, Muslims began moving in. The nucleus of the Quarter, to be sure, remained Jewish and continued to be known as such throughout; this point was stressed already earlier in our discussion and will be reiterated again at a later stage, when the economic factor behind the limitations of the Jewish residential expansion is revealed in our examination of tax-rolls and of taxpayer categories. Conversely, however, the area at large did absorb, in time, a counterflow of non-Jewish population, large enough to alter considerably the general physiognomy of the Quarter.

Thus, the size and quality of some of the houses in the Jewish section proper and in the Greater Sultan Ibrahim Quarter—this can be gathered from the descriptions in the *sicils*—as well as the relative proximity of these houses to the harbor and to the port citadel (the so-called *Büyük Kule*) made it convenient, say, for an *ağa* of the Janissary Corps or for the *dizdar* (commander) of the citadel to actually settle in the *mahalle*. Such instances are attested to, among others, by documents of the years 1686 and 1708 (*Defters* no. 6, p. 106; and no. 11, pp. 218, 218–219). Evidently, the old Venetian appreciation of the town section "above the sea" as one comprising "very handsome homes and buildings" was fully concurred with by the Venetians' successors. Prices went up, as can easily be gauged from a comparison of the very early documents with the later ones, and the rise seems real enough even after the fluctuation of the exchange rate had properly been taken into account.

Gradually, a rather glamorous circle of residences emerged within the broader bounds of the Quarter. Indeed, the detailed listing of the neighboring plots and their owners (which, we recall, was required by law whenever a house was sold) affords a glimpse into the social and financial élite of the district: some Jewish owners of a *sabunhane*, or soap factory — "*Kandiye sabunu*," i.e., Kandiyote soap, was an export article enjoying great popularity in the major trade centers of the time —, a banker or two, a few Jewish doctors, a military commander of rank, a Bosnian Jew of extreme wealth, a French dragoman, and the like. Any deed of sale filed with the kadi's office becomes, so to speak, a "Who's Who" of the buyer's future neighbors. While for obvious reasons the documents themselves are not explicit in the matter, it will not be too far-fetched to assume that some kind of neighborly relations began developing among the wealthy dwellers of the Quarter, relations which cut across religious and ethnic lines. Based on community of human interest, of class-consciousness and of taste, such person-to-person relations may have also been used, at times, for causes other than personal. Very likely, a powerful Jewish member of the Quarter (though not necessarily a communal leader in the formal sense) would intercede, on occasion, with a Turkish neighbor of high station on behalf of an individual coreligionist in need or even in favor of the Jewish community at large. These unprecedented neighborly contacts between prominent figures of the ruling circles and prominent members of the Jewish minority may have, indeed, become immeasurably more meaningful and binding than those made in the course of formal encounters between the communal leadership and the Turkish administration.

No matter how correct and fair such relationships, cases of *illegal* action vis-à-vis Jewish property in the *mahalle*, even forcible seizure thereof, did occur sometimes. Witness, for instance, the extortion case discussed earlier in connection with the repair of the Jewish synagogue. In another case recorded by our *sicils* (*Defter* no. 12, p. 335), the heirs of a deceased Jewish homeowner asked the court to evict a Turkish woman who occupied the Jew's house unlawfully; they were, indeed, granted a formal writ against her. Whether this was an isolated incident or one that reflected a somewhat anarchical situation in real estate ownership during the post-war years is a matter for further study. Surely, by ultimately remedying the inequities, the new regime manifested a genuine resolve to curb lawlessness from whatever quarter. Yet, no matter whether our documents report lawful purchases or occasionally reveal illegal acquisitions, they cumulatively bear witness to the degree of attraction, practical as well as psychological, that settlement in the

Jewish *mahalle* and its vicinity had held for Kandiyote non-Jews in the early years following the conquest.

RESIDENCE AND BUSINESS

The extension of Jewish residence into city areas that were formerly closed to Jews paved the way for Jewish businesses as well. Or, was it business that preceded actual Jewish settlement in certain neighborhoods? The latter seems to have been the case at least in those sections that were not merely outside the broader boundaries of *Sultan Ibrahim Mahallesi* but at an appreciable distance from it. Conversely, while some non-Jews chose to make their *home* in the *Yahudi Mahallesi*, others apparently found it advantageous to merely open *businesses* in it.

To begin with the Jewish part of the business expansion, a document of 1693 (*Defter* no. 8, p. 129) reports the presence of a Jewish store up 'Main Street', in the nowadays no longer existing *Kemer Altı* Bazaar. Set within the southernmost link of the former Byzantine fortification belt of Khandax, this *fontego*, contiguous with the high gate of 'Voltone', was definitely "off limits" to Jewish merchants in Venetian times. It faced the central square and its most noteworthy landmarks — the Morosini Fountain, the Ducal Palace, and the San Marco Church (subsequently converted into a mosque) — and was within a distance of a mere two hundred yards or so from the then-fashionable residential section of the city (of which more will be said later; Figs. 2 and 6).

Regrettably, the 1693 Turkish *sicil* informs us neither of the nature of the Jew's business on this formerly forbidden location nor whether there were any other Jews who, following the change of regime, succeeded in opening stores in the same bazaar or its vicinity. Whatever the case, our merchant appears to have been a man of means and of variegated financial interests. To cite the *sicil* again, he did also purchase in public auction from another Jew a piece of *rural* property to the impressive tune of 150 *kuruş arslanı* — an impressive amount indeed, compared with the earlier-quoted prices for *urban* (hence, as a rule, more expensive) items of real estate. Now, the *Kemer Altı* businessman was by no means the sole Jewish owner of rural land recorded by our *defters* during the first century of Ottoman domination in Crete. Not before the second half of the eighteenth century, we recall, do Jews retreat from the rural regions. Nevertheless, the contribution of this *sicil* goes beyond the mere addition of another name to our list of Cretan Jewish landowners; it is instructive in general economic terms as well. The handsome sum paid for the land in the present case indicates that Jews, even as late as the 1690s, continued to consider participation in agrarian ventures a sound and profitable investment.

Of an entirely different type were the business enterprises of non-Jews in the *Yahudi Mahallesi*. This we learn from two documents entered into the registers in 1684 and 1697 (*Defters* no. 4, p. 481; and no. 10, p. 21). Recording the regulations that were agreed upon by members of the bakers' guild as to weight, quality, and price of their product, the *sicils* give detailed lists of the bakers' shops of Kandiye. The shops were owned and operated by fifteen bakers headed by an *etmekçi başı*, or Chief Breadmaker, who signed the documents in the presence of the governor of Kandiye. Out of the total number of fifteen, two bakers — one Muslim and one Greek (to judge by their names) — are reported owning and operating shops in the Jews' Quarter; no Jewish-owned bakery is mentioned.

Now, true, the absence of facilities inside the Jews' Quarter for baking bread and pastry by and for the local Jewish population does indeed seem strange, considering the stringency of dietary laws in Judaism. It was no novelty, though. Rather, it constituted the perpetuation of a situation already deplored by local Jewish leaders, notably Rabbi Elijah Capsali, as far back as the first half of the sixteenth century, at the height, that is, of Jewish communal development in Venetian Candia. Some steps to remedy the situation were in fact taken then, a Hebrew text informs us, and communal ovens were built at Capsali's personal expense. These ovens may have been destroyed or no longer usable in the 1680s.

Nevertheless, if I read the texts correctly, the state of affairs recorded by the 1684 and 1697 Turkish documents marks a distinct departure from that described in, and bitterly criticized by, the earlier Hebrew document. The sixteenth-century practice consisted of having home-made dough brought by Jewish customers to be baked in Gentile-owned and Gentile-operated ovens *outside* the *Zudecha*. There is no evidence of actual existence of non-Jewish bakeries *inside* the Jews' Quarter in the Venetian period. Such bakeries, however, the *sicillat* tell us, did exist under the Turks. It stands to reason, then, that the Muslim and Greek bakers of the *Yahudi Mahallesi* adapted themselves to the dietary requirements of the local Jewish clientèle, possibly employing some Jewish supervision. For this, we recall, they had ample precedents from centuries past, when Christian producers in Crete learned to deliver ritually acceptable "good and pure *Jewish* wine" (*vinum bonum purum Judaicum*) and "good *Jewish* cheeses" (*boni casei iudaici*) to local Jewish contractors for marketing in Jewish centers abroad. Precedent or not, the bakers could soon have found themselves out of business, after all, if their insensitivity to Jewish religious scruples would cause the Jewish customers to desist from patronizing their shops; these customers, we remember, did at all times constitute the majority of the Quarter's population.

IV

THE "OTHER SIDE" OF MAIN STREET

So far we have concentrated on the steady upgrading of the Jews' Quarter of Kandiye in the aftermath of the Ottoman conquest, a process stimulated by the opening up of that Quarter and of adjoining neighborhoods to a two-way population movement. It will be a fallacy, however, to think that our findings regarding the Jews' greater freedom of residence apply in equal degree to other parts of the city.

Though, as apparent from our *sicillat*, the Jewish *mahalle* became socially acceptable and in many ways attractive even to non-Jews, it lagged behind at least one residential section that was truly exclusive. That section, while facing the *Sultan Ibrahim Mahallesi* on the east and southeast, was neatly separated from the latter

by the *ruga maïstra* of Venetian times, i.e., the already-mentioned
'Main Street' which bisected the *Città Vecchia*, descending from
the center of the city down to the port basin. The neighborhood
across that street fanned out as far as the seashore from a near-
by square, northeast of the Morosini Fountain and within negligible
distance from the *Kemer Altı* Bazaar (referred-to above). On that
square, where at present the Church of St. Titus is located, stood
at the time the elegant *Vezir Cami*, or Mosque of the Vizier, commemorating the final victory of 1669 and the triumphal entry into
Candia of the Turkish Grand Vizier Ahmet Köprülü; as customary,
the neighborhood as a whole was also named after the Grand
Vizier (Figs. 2 and 6).

Real estate prices were markedly higher in the Vizier Quarter
than in the *Sultan Ibrahim Mahallesi*, a comparison of our documents shows, and the settlement there was far from open. True,
in one entry regarding the Quarter (*Defter* no. 11, p. 234), the
legally required description of adjacent plots lists also a piece of
Jewish-owned property. That entry, of the year 1708, is contained
in a *sicil* notarizing on behalf of the kadi's office the transfer of
a house in the Vizier Quarter from the hands of an Englishman
to a Frenchman (both buyer and seller were staying in Kandiye
merely as temporary residents). It seems, however, that the particular property in question was, literally, a border-case. Otherwise,
not counting foreign notables, the *Vezir Cami* neighborhood was
entirely out of the reach of non-Muslim mortals.

This is not to say that Kandiyotes of Jewish origin — the financially well-off and the socially prominent, that is — gave up all
attempt to penetrate this towering citadel of social status and ethnic
exclusiveness. The contrary rather was true, if I interpret correctly
a somewhat puzzling document of 1693 (*Defter* no. 8, p. 9). It tells
of a group of Jews who on one occasion ventured into the Vizier
Quarter and, of all things, were promptly charged with larceny by
a local Turkish resident; were it not for the appearance of trustworthy witnesses on their behalf, the accused may have paid dearly
for their intrusion.

Now, if we insist on accepting the story at face value — that is, as a mere item in the local police chronicle — there is very little that it can add to our discussion. But the story is too incredible to be accepted on the face of it, both as a whole and where specific details are concerned. Nor was it accepted at the time by the Muslim court. The favorable testimony of the witnesses (Muslim witnesses, to be sure), extolling the defendants' irreproachable character and their social respectability, suffices to make us realize that it was a trumped-up charge altogether. What those intervening Muslims — the defendants' peers and neighbors from the Sultan Ibrahim Quarter, one might presume — were implying was that, while a verdict was sought on a case of law and of a supposed transgression of law, the court would really be passing judgment on matters of social convention and of a challenge to that convention. It is obvious that, by implication again, the court concurred with the witnesses' appraisal of the problem and, while exonerating the defendants from the specific charge, felt neither competent nor called upon to act on the broader issue of segregation. Thus, the Vizier Quarter remained closed to Jews in subsequent generations as well.

Evidently, only a foreign passport (as we have seen in the aforecited case involving the Englishman and the Frenchman) or, better still, conversion to Islam could provide the status-seeking *râya* with the key to the coveted neighborhood that bore the name of Candia's illustrious conqueror. Interesting insights into the latter manifestation of our problem are offered by the Cretan Turkish *sicillat*.

THE ENTRANCE KEY

The many conversions to Islam that were duly registered in the *sicil-defters* by the Kandiyote kadis during the first generation of Ottoman rule on the island involved only a negligible number of Jewish families, utterly negligible indeed — four in all (*Defters* no. 7, p. 74; no. 8, pp. 62, 64, and no. 11, pp. 120, 121; no. 9, p. 119; no. 20, p. 170). Significantly, two of the Jewish converts have also made the grade socially and have eventually established themselves in the Vizier Quarter along with some of their dependents. The subsequent vicissitudes of these two families are not devoid of interest, even drama, and should briefly be related here.

In the aftermath of the Ottoman conquest, apparently, a Cretan
Jew had entered the Muslim fold together with his father; they
both are mentioned in the *sicillat* by their Muslim names (*Defters*
no. 8, pp. 62, 64; no. 11, pp. 120, 121). The convert's son, however, as well as daughter-in-law and widowed son-in-law remained
Jews. A family rift ensued along religious lines, giving rise to a
series of legal wrangles that are reflected in the *sicillat* of 1695–
1696. There were, first and foremost, the inevitable economic after-
effects. The convert found it difficult to maintain his business association with his Jewish son — or was it the son who could no
longer bear the partnership? In addition, the changed legal status
enabled the new Muslim to dispute his Jewish son-in-law's claim
regarding the dowry of the deceased daughter.

There was, however, more to the case than a mere family squab-
ble over money. Characteristically or not, it is precisely the younger
generation that appears to have been tenaciously clinging to Judaism, while father and grandfather chose to join the ruling religion.
One wonders whether the somewhat mysterious daughter and her
unexplained death had anything to do with the opposing decisions
of either side. Be that as it may, the documents allow us to follow
the accompanying real estate aspect of the rift. Thus, in the last
stage, the convert is reported to have sold the house he owned
in the *Yahudi Mahallesi* to his Jewish daughter-in-law (characteristically, not to her husband, the convert's own unconverted son!),
while he himself, the honorific title *ağa* securely pinned to his
name, settled comfortably in the Vizier Quarter to savor its exclusive glamor. Entrance into the ruling religious Establishment
and residential eligibility for the Vizier Quarter had apparently to
be coupled with the convert's unequivocal separation from his former family, community, and neighborhood.

Quite different was the fate of the other Kandiyote Jew who,
together with his wife, decided to join the Muslim faith and... the
Vizier Quarter. It seems that, profession of Islamic creed notwithstanding, the newcomer's social aspirations clashed dismally with
his newly adopted milieu. Registering indignation, supposedly on
moral grounds, the residents of *Vezir Mahallesi* joined hands with

the imam of the Vizier Mosque to ward off the intrusion of the ambitious upstart: his own behavior, so they are reported to have claimed in a *sicil* dated 1691 (*Defter* no. 7, p. 74), as well as the behavior of his wife were incompatible with the standard of morality expected of people living in so distinguished a neighborhood. Recurrent complaints (or, possibly, allegations) did finally bear fruit and made the law catch up with the villain. He was sentenced to a Sultan's punitive galley, with ample time at the oars to reconsider his ways. There is little room for doubt that his fun-loving wife, too, was forced to leave the Vizier Quarter. Gallantly, the kadi's *sicil* remains silent on her further doings, nor is there a record of where she settled thereafter.

THE LESSON OF TAX-ROLLS

In closing this part of our survey of the housing data provided by the Ottoman Cretan *defters* — data that indicate the emergence of a new housing pattern in and around Kandiye's Jewish Quarter — a word of caution seems imperative. For, no matter how accurate in every *detail*, the information culled out of the *sicillat* and presented above cannot but lead to distorted conclusions if believed to be reflecting the situation in the Jewish community *as a whole* during the first generation or so following the conquest of Candia by the Turks. Just as in earlier days a handful of splendid Jewish mansions did not warrant picturing all the streets of Veneto-Cretan *Zudecha* as lined with "very handsome homes and buildings," so one must refrain from similarly groundless generalizations regarding the post-Venetian Jewish Quarter. The aforecited *sicillat* — be that stated as emphatically as possible — deal only with those homeowners and merchants who formed the upper crust of Kandiyote Jewish society; these rich individuals accounted merely for a fraction of the total number of Jews residing in the island's principal city.

　How absurdly small was the group of wealthy Jewish notables in Ottoman Kandiye or, for that matter, in the much better known Candia of Venetian days! How small it was, indeed, both in relation to other population groups in town, Jewish or non-Jewish, and when counted in absolute figures! At no period in the history of the city did the Jewish upper class amount to more than twenty percent of the total number of local Jewish inhabitants, while that Jewish total itself constituted but a ridiculous 5 to 10 percent of the city's general population!

The *relative* numerical insignificance of the rich stands out even more poignantly when expressed in *absolute* figures. Such figures are available, to be sure, for both the Venetian and the Turkish periods. True, the materials invoked so far in Veneto-Cretan statistics — e.g., the successive *Relazioni* of Venetian administrators and kindred reports — usually offer one single figure for the totality of the Jewish population in the city. However, with the magnifying glass of Jewish tax-rolls which this writer has discovered recently in the State Archives of Venice among the papers of the Cretan chancery we now are afforded a close-up view of the anatomy of such general statistical entries. Featuring actual name-lists of Candiote Jewish taxpayers along with their respective tax assessments, these hitherto-unpublished documents open the way for charting the socioeconomic diversity *within* Cretan Jewry, a diversity deliberately ignored by the biased contemporaneous sources which preferred to lump all Jews together under the common denominator of *divites* and *potentes*. Even more eloquent is the post-conquest information provided by the available Cretan Turkish *sicillat* dealing with payments of poll-tax (*cizye*) to the Ottoman Treasury. Of course, a standard multiplication formula easily converts such tax information into general population estimates as well. More importantly, however, by *a priori* dividing the annual census of taxpayers into the classical-Islamic three categories of capitation impost — the high rate (*âlâ*), the mean rate (*evsat*), and the low rate (*edna*) — the Turkish tax-lists carry, so to speak, a built-in measuring rod, enabling us to gauge, year by year, the basic class-distinctions within the taxpaying subject-group.

Elsewhere I expect to discuss at length the problems of Cretan Jewish taxation and establish the criteria for enlisting the available tax documents in the service of Cretan Jewish population studies. At the present juncture, a few salient data from the Turkish tax-*sicils* will suffice. Our task is fairly simple. Given the fact that not the actual population total but the basic picture of socio-economic stratification is the object of our quest, we shall dispense here with converting the taxpayer figures into population statistics. Rather, we shall present the figures themselves as they appear in the archival documents; the separate listing by taxpayer categories to which our *sicils* adhere will keep our post-conquest real estate information in proper perspective.

THE "UPPER CLASS"

It follows from the tax-lists compiled in Kandiye in the early 1690s in the context of Mustafa Pasha's *Nizam-i Cedid*, or 'New [Fiscal] Order' (cf., e.g., *Defters* no. 8, pp. 5–6, 95, 103–104, 105; no. 11, pp. 44–46; no. 16, p. 41; no. 17, pp. 54–56), that, by one count, 17, i.e., twenty percent, of a total of 85 Jewish taxpayers were required to pay the *cizye* at the highest, i.e., *âlâ* rate. Should we rely on another count, no more than 8 — yes, a grand total of 8! — i.e., somewhat less than five-and-a-half percent of 151 taxpaying Jews, were in the highest tax-bracket. The preponderant majority of local Jewry, according to the first set of documents, belonged to the second category — in present-day jargon we might call them the middle-middle class — with 51 out of 85 (= 60%) paying the *evsat*, or mean rate. Differing figures, however, are offered by the other set of documents. According to that other count, most of Kandiyote Jews might sociologically be classified as lower-middle class or even poor, with as many as 112, out of a total of 151, paying the *edna*, i.e., the lowest rate. It is proper to note, though, that the latter computation was under heavy suspicion at the time; our documents report it to have repeatedly been the subject of official investigation by the central Ottoman authorities. No matter which count proves to be accurate in absolute figures, the main thrust of our statistical findings, weighing the ratio of the upper-class group against the totality of Kandiyote Jewish taxpayers, remains substantially the same. Obviously, this top-bracket group, whose members were the only ones to afford acquisition of abandoned houses in the better residential sections adjoining former *Zudecha*, constituted but a minority of the city's Jews. As already stated, never, not even under the most propitious conditions, did the size of the group exceed one fifth of the overall Jewish population; the chances are that the ratio may have been considerably lower at times, though it hardly dropped to the unbelievable level claimed by the other tax-count.

Now, *statistical* realities must not, of course, detract from the *intrinsic* importance of those upper-class individuals within Kandiyote Jewry whose drive to break out of the legal, social, and territorial confines of the Venetian-bequeathed ghetto transpires through the early Turkish data of real estate registry. Here was a group of people whose impact on the life of their own community far exceeded their actual numerical weight. We have already stressed earlier in this discussion that topography alone — the contiguity, that is, of their own homes with the homes of high-ranking administration officials — may have given these prominent Jewish individuals unprecedented leverage. Being, literally, neighbors of the Turkish officials across the fence, they may have been in a position to more effectively influence governmental decisions in Jewish affairs, irrespective of whether they were formally recognized as leaders of local Jewry. Conversely — again not by formally serving as lay leaders or rabbis, but through sheer capacity to generate employment, bestow patronage, and dispense charity to needy coreligionists — these wealthy notables could virtually dictate from within the pace and way of life of the whole Jewish community.

And yet, it is precisely this undisputed financial and communal prominence of the few that must make us doubly mindful of the plain arithmetics of our population figures in relation to both the tax data and the information concerning the expansion of Jewish settlement in Kandiye. The few who did succeed in extending their residence under the Turks to *Hıristo Iskuludi* and the Greater Sultan Ibrahim Quarter bring into even sharper relief the state of the many who did not. Indeed, more than once at an earlier stage of our discussion we pointed out that, notwithstanding the unbearable squalor of the *Zudecha* and despite the eventual obsolescence of the *Zudecha* boundaries following the departure of the Venetians, the nucleus of the Jews' Quarter in Ottoman Kandiye remained on its historical location and basically within its original bounds. A variety of reasons combined to perpetuate as late as the twentieth century the center of gravity of Kandiyote Jewish life inside the confines of former *Zudecha*. Most of the reasons are self-evident and need only briefly to be mentioned here.

There was, among other things, the inherent conservatism of certain segments of the Jewish community and the emotional attachment of individuals and families to the site which harbored their ancestral roots for generations on end. There further was the concrete physical factor that the community's ancient synagogues were all located in the old Quarter. The difficulty under Islamic law of building new ones outside that Quarter was almost impossible to overcome; even the repair of the old structures, we recall, was a formidable task. The added legal twist, resulting from the fact that all Jewish buildings, including the synagogues, were now rent-paying clients of the Muslim *Vakıf*, contributed to the difficulty of the situation. No less decisive were the economic interests — ties of long standing, geared to businesses and workshops that served the residents of the area. Also, very likely, there was the feeling of alienness, more acutely sensed in the outlying Muslim and Greek districts than in the relative security of the familiar, predominantly Jewish neighborhood. However — this we learned from our tax-*sicils* — not the least of the factors hindering a wider movement out of the *Zudecha* was sheer poverty: only a few handfuls of people in the Jewish community could financially afford to avail themselves of the real estate opportunities in the better residential sections of the city. In brief: if, in spite of the stimulating examples of successful penetration into adjacent neighborhoods, the former *Zudecha* continued on the whole to be a *Yahudi Mahallesi*, it was so largely because not too many of its members had the means to buy their way out of it.

This is not to say that the broadened horizons of the Turkish era revealed themselves only to the wealthy. The Ottoman conquest introduced crucial changes in the living conditions of the less affluent Jewish classes as well. These changes, affecting considerable numbers of Kandiyote Jews, must also be charted. Admittedly, the task is not easy. Matters originating with the upper-crust Jewish notables or involving them in one way or another would, predictably, tend to monopolize (as it were) the documentary record and make a handful of prominent names recur in the notarial books, in the real estate registry, and in the minutes of court-proceedings far more frequently than the names of these notables' plebeian brethren. Nevertheless, documents dealing with other strata of the Jewish population are not altogether lacking and, though few in numbers, they afford a glimpse into an area heretofore utterly unknown.

V

ALONG DERMATA BAY

Indeed, complementing the above information about the upper echelon of Kandiyote Jewry, the Cretan Turkish *defters* reveal the existence in Ottoman Kandiye of yet another extension of the Jews' Quarter beyond the former *Zudecha* boundaries. That other extension, no doubt, was motivated by the same housing shortage and was made possible by the same objective factors that governed the residential expansion discussed above. Nevertheless, its direction and sociological make-up were so different as to warrant a separate discussion.

The heretofore analyzed expansion of Jewish residence in Kandiye had as its target the more comfortable neighborhoods that were historically out of bounds to Jews. These coveted neighborhoods, we recall, either touched the *Zudecha* directly or faced it across the street on the east, the south and the southeast. Not so the housing thrust to be discussed presently. That other drive, so the *sicil* at hand shows us, was oriented westwards, past the one-time line of land fortifications protecting the western flank of Byzantine Khandax and its Jewish Quarter and on into the area washed by the waters of Dermatà Bay. Unlike the Jews' Quarter — we stressed it repeatedly — that area remained outside the Byzantine walls.

In discussing the site we shall dispense with its latter-day Turkish appellation, *Kum Kapı* ('The Sand Gate'), for it has no bearing on our topic. Instead, we shall refer to it by its Greek name, going back no doubt to Byzantine times ; that name, as we shall see, provides some guidance to the character of the area and its inhabitants (Figs. 2 and 6).

Dermatà (Δερματᾶ), i.e., 'The [Bay of] Hides', was, and still is, the Greek name of the place, for it was there, through the centuries, that the refuse and dirty liquids of local tanneries were swept into the sea. Now, at the beginning of our topographic survey of the *Zudecha* I had the opportunity to refer briefly to an earlier study of mine in which I discussed the motives for the characteristical contiguity of the Jews' Quarter with the tanners' district. In that other study I suggested that this contiguity be viewed in the context of the anti-Jewish policies of tenth-century Byzantine emperors preceding — and then coinciding with — the restoration of Byzantine rule in Crete. These discriminatory policies would, among other things, condemn the Jews to settling on the waterfront and eking out a meager living as tanners of hides. The situation was changing at a fast pace, however, under the impact of Byzantium's great territorial expansion (of which the reconquest of Crete was just the beginning) and thanks to the ensuing economic prosperity. This changed atmosphere as well as the changing status and economic role of the Jews in the Byzantine Empire are reflected, in a sense, in the very fact that the Jews' Quarter was included *within* the Byzantine city walls, while the Dermatà Bay tanneries were left outside; these walls, we now know it, were built in the already different climate of the eleventh century. Be that as it may, the "Jews' Gate" still opened, as we remember, into the Dermatà and the link between the Jews' Quarter and the tanners' district has never really been broken.

Whether under Venetian rule Jews actually crossed the line westwards to *settle* in the Dermatà district is a moot question. I, for one, am persuaded that some did. After all, the *Zudecha*'s *confinia determinata* laid down by Venice were designed to keep the Jews out of the *better* residential parts of the city, not the Dermatà slums.

Moreover, gravitating into the Bay area must have become a rather
simple matter in later centuries, when the old Byzantine landwall in
the west fell into disuse and the newly built western *borghi* began
blending evermore naturally with the Old City. It is perhaps no
coincidence that, while late Venetian maps still chart sizable sections of the Byzantine wall at the southern (i.e., non-Jewish) end
of the *Città Vecchia*, they show very few vestiges, if any, of that
wall along the *Zudecha*'s western flank. Apparently, the areas on
either side of that part of the former wall have by then noticeably
grown together (though, due to physical peculiarities of the terrain,
never fully coalesced).

   More, in the sixteenth century Jews of the *Zudecha* are reported to
have actually spent over a thousand ducats on installing a fountain
in the Dermatà district. To be sure, not much is known about this
no longer existing fountain, its exact location, shape, watersupply
system, and the people it was designed to serve. Jewish sources
fail to mention it altogether, but, then, Jewish sources fail to describe important landmarks of the *Zudecha* as well. Of the texts
preserved in the State Archives of Venice (which usually are more
articulate) only two official *Relazioni* by Veneto-Cretan administrators have so far been found referring to the "Jewish Fountain."
One report was submitted to the Venetian Senate in 1594 by Pasqua-
ligo; the other, of 1628, was compiled by Morosini, himself a master
fountain-builder and the creator of Candia's most famous "Fontana
di Piazza" on the main square. The authors of both reports were,
of course, men in a position to know. They both identify the location
of the "Jewish Fountain" *vicino al Dermata appresso il quartier
degli hebrei* and praise the artistic quality of the structure as *bellis-
sima et con molte figure di rilievo*. However, no detailed description
is offered nor have I encountered in any other archival record,
manuscript, map, or drawing a graphic representation of the
fountain — except perhaps for the fresco discovered a few years ago
in the remains of an eighteenth-century Kandiyote Turkish villa
and put on display now at the Historical Museum of Iraklion. This
mural features, among other things, a fountain in the Dermatà
area; chances are that what we see is a stylized likeness of the "Jew-

ish Fountain." True, in 1666 the Dermatà neighborhood was endowed with still another monumental fountain, the "Fontana Priuli," which survived till our own time. It seems doubtful, however, that the artist intended to depict this younger monument; had this been his objective, he would not have failed to outline the temple-like classical Corinthian façade, characteristic of the Priuli fountain as we know it today. Since the form sketched in the fresco is of an entirely different style, the assumption remains plausible that it is the older and more venerated "Jewish Fountain" that is being shown in the mural.

Whatever the case, the existence since the sixteenth century of a "Fontana degli Ebrei" in the Dermatà region is an undeniable fact. The question arises, then, why would Candiote Jews spend of their own volition the enormous sum of over one thousand goldpieces on an undertaking outside the *Zudecha* proper. Of course, for all we know they may have been engaging in a neighborhood improvement project, generously dispensing Jewish funds for the benefit of the non-Jewish dwellers of the adjacent slum. One might be pardoned, however, for entertaining doubts as to the purely altruistic motive of such an act of philanthropy. Things simply were not done that way in Crete in the sixteenth century, if ever. With the tremendous fiscal burden imposed at the time on Jews and other residents in connection with the new Venetian ring of walls and ramparts that was under construction then around Greater Candia (including the Dermatà), one finds it difficult to visualize a voluntary assumption of an added expenditure without actual Jewish needs being urgently involved. Rather, it is more realistic to presume that concrete Jewish interests were at stake and that the project mirrored a sufficiently conspicuous *Jewish physical presence in the Dermatà district* and answered the *practical needs* of new Jewish inhabitants who entered the area. At some juncture even a synagogue may have been built close by; thus, also the *spiritual needs* of the settlers could be satisfied in the Dermatà proper, though (as we shall suggest later on) many Dermatà Jews would continue their attachment to one of the ancient synagogues in the original *Zudecha* (Fig. 6).

THE DERMATA JEWS

Who could have been the Jews that settled in the Dermatà? For lack of sources we cannot but speculate on the matter. In all likelihood they came from three groups. First, there were the *immigrants* from abroad. It stands to reason that the thrice-mentioned constant flow of Jewish immigration to Crete could not have but forced some of the poorer elements among the newcomers into settling along Dermatà Bay. The other group may have included destitute *native* Jews leaving the villages. Indeed, these Greek-speaking Jews from the rural areas would be even more prone than the immigrants from outside the island to seek shelter in the working-class quarters of the Bay district. Finally, there were the *Karaites*. The presence of the latter, especially, merits closer examination.

The interest in Karaism and the Karaites shown by Candiote Jewry's most illustrious son, the seventeenth-century Joseph Solomon Delmedigo, has long been a puzzle to scholars. Since our Cretan Hebrew writings failed to produce so far any hint as to the possible physical presence of Karaites in Candia, Delmedigo's interest was variously attributed to his own rebellious nature or to encounters with Karaites in the course of his wanderings outside Crete. The doubts regarding the actual existence of a Karaite population on the island can no longer be sustained, notwithstanding the silence of "official" Jewish sources. Such existence is known now to have been a fact, conspicuous enough to have been recorded by a sharp-sighted observer. It thus clearly is attested to by the earlier-cited Turkish traveler Evliya Çelebi who, we recall, toured Crete twice, during as well as after the "War of Candia," and, though not a Jew himself, appears to have been quite familiar with intra-Jewish divisions and organization. If I read his *Seyahatname* report from the conquered Cretan capital correctly, Evliya was satisfied that "the totality of the Jews' Quarter is but one quarter, yet comprising seven congregations" (*Ve cümle mahalle-i yahudan bir mahalledir amma, yedi adet cemaattır*). He noted, however, that "the Karaite Jews live in a different quarter, separated from the Israelite [i.e., Rabbanite] Jews" (*karayi yahudileri israilî yahudilerinden ayrı başka bir mahallede*).

Now, copyists have encountered difficulties in tackling Evliya's text; hence, several sections of the printed *Itinerary*, including the passage on Karaites, are marred by variant readings. I have it, however, on good authority — the considered judgment of Professor Pierre MacKay who is preparing a critical edition of the book — that the manuscript underlying the projected publication, Cod. Bagdat Köşkü 308, "is the archetype of the entire manuscript tradition of the *Seyahatname*." In that manuscript, the pertinent passage (a facsimile of which the editor kindly placed at my disposal) is perfectly legible and the reference to Karaites within it, though arbitrarily stripped of diacritical marks, can under no circumstances be considered equivocal or in doubt. Moreover, not only the Turkish author himself but the compiler of the manuscript as well — a Cairo Egyptian, the editor assures me — hailed from an environment in which Karaism and the Karaites were very much in evidence; he hardly could have misunderstood, then, Evliya's mention of Karaites in the Cretan context.

The import of the above confirmation of the physical presence of Karaites in Candia goes, of course, beyond the historical detail per se; it is extremely instructive both for Karaite history and for the story of Cretan Jewry at large. Thus, on the one hand, the account bears added proof of the long-noted propensity of Karaism and the Karaite Diaspora to spread into areas which were within the sphere of influence of Greek Orthodoxy or Islam. Simultaneously, it presents the Jewry of Crete in general as a society that was intellectually and communally even more diversified than we knew all along. It also reopens a number of questions pertaining to the formative years of Joseph Solomon Delmedigo and his special attitude toward Karaite learning and toward living Karaites of his generation. Last but not least, it demands a fresh look at Cretan Jewish onomastics as a way of discerning hitherto unsuspected possible Karaite origins of certain Cretan Jewish personalities and families.

For the purpose of our present discussion, however, it is the other piece of information offered by Evliya Çelebi that is of greater relevance — the information, that is, regarding the Candiote Karaites' geographic separation from the local Rabbanites and their settlement "in a different quarter," i.e., outside the confines of the traditional *Zudecha*. Such a separation, whether forced or voluntary, whether legally confirmed or merely condoned by the authorities, could have been, so I submit, effectively achieved in one way only: through settling in the Dermatà district. No other direction was open to Jews of whatever denomination in Venetian times. Indeed, it is this geographic, and not merely communal and institutional, separateness that may have been responsible for the total lack of references to Karaites in Cretan Hebrew literature.

Conversely, there is neither a known legal reason nor a historical precedent to suggest that residence in the Dermatà was limited solely to the Karaite segment of Candiote Jewry. The contrary rather must have been true. Since the authorities would make no formal distinction between Karaite and Rabbanite and would extend to both the general designation *Judeus* (which, incidentally, explains the absence of specific references to Karaites in the chancery records), the physical presence of Karaite settlers in the Dermatà prior to the advent of the Turks does *ipso facto* confirm the assumption that the option of spreading into the Dermatà area was open to *all* Jews in Venetian times. The fact that no substantial numbers of Rabbanites availed themselves of that option at first was a result of their own reticence rather than of legal limitations imposed by the Venetian government. As time went on, however, pressing needs may have made a broader movement westwards simply inevitable. Thus, in spite of the social stigma attached to the site, the Dermatà periphery ceased to be limited to Jews of Karaite persuasion alone. Chances are, in fact (as we have already observed a while ago), that even a synagogue was in existence in the district, in the general area of the "Jewish Fountain," close to the latter-day *Çiçek Hamami* (the Turkish 'Bath of Flowers'); there is no way of ascertaining, though, whether it possibly was the original and sole house of worship established by the Karaites or a later shrine, built, in time, to serve the incoming Rabbanite settlers in the Dermatà periphery (Fig. 6).

While the sheer fact of the existence of a Jewish settlement in

Venetian Dermatà is beyond doubt now, the character and history of that settlement under the Venetians are far from clear, to say the least. Any further statement on the subject must therefore await the uncovering of additional source-material. Such material, if at all existent, will hopefully turn up in the inexhaustible Cretan archives of Venice (the sifting of which had been my daily bread for the past several years) or in some forgotten or not yet fully edited traveler's account. Less likely, it may surface one day when a few still-unpublished Hebrew writings from Crete are brought to press. Less likely, I say, for, on the basis of the known texts, one hardly can expect the Hebrew sources to come forward with a tale of Jewish squatters clinging to lodgings of sorts in the tanners' district. These sources, stemming as they usually do from highbrow intellectuals who, in alliance with the wealthy notables, constituted the recognized leadership of the Jewish community, would have little in common with this sorry periphery of the already over-crowded original Jewish Quarter.

THE "LOWER CLASS"

By contrast, the Turkish *sicillat* appear to be refreshingly clear on the subject. Thus, a document filed in the year 1719 (but surely reflecting conditions that prevailed already during the earlier decades of Turkish rule) catalogues the rent-payments due to the *Vakıf* from the inhabitants of the Dermatà Quarter (*Defter* no. 15, pp. 254–256—Fig. 5). Among those listed as paying their *Vakıf*-dues for the usage of "a house" (*hane*) or "shop and house" (*dükkân ve hane*) are some thirteen Jewish households. This, as far as I know, is our first unequivocal testimony concerning the existence of Jewish homes and shops in the Dermatà neighborhood. As such, the information in itself is extremely significant.

There are, however, a number of additional features to this information that warrant a closer examination. To wit: the citing of the basic rent-unit as "shop and house" suggests that the document deals with *craftsmen's* homes — with homes, that is, which served both as a *dwelling* for the craftsman and his family and as a *workshop* in which he produced as well as sold his product or

FIG. 5. Partial list of *Vakif*-dues collected from houses and shops in the Dermatà neighborhood in 1719, including those belonging to Jews. The first two Jewish entries, on p. 254 (*box, bottom row on right*), show a rather high rate of daily *Vakıf*-payments (12 *akçe*). Ten Jewish households are listed on p. 255 (*box, top four rows on left*). Nine of them were paying 1 *akçe* a day. The tenth rentpayer (*fourth row, center*), "the Jew the tanner," had apparently his rate corrected from 1 to 2 *akçe*. The thirteenth entry, on p. 256 (*top row*), is not reproduced here. It features the lowest Jewish payment to the *Vakıf* (20 *akçe* per year).

(Defter no. 15, pp. 254-5 — *Turkish Archives of Iraklion, Crete*)

service. Other data, too, besides the *dükkân ve hane* character of
the rent-units involved, point to the lowly status of the Quarter —
'lowly', when compared with the upgraded status of the Jewish
mahalle discussed before. Thus, it is no longer the distinguished
Mosque of the Queen Mother that appears as the beneficiary of
the rent due from the Dermatà buildings, but a secondary Muslim
prayerhouse commemorating Balta Ahmet Ağa, a military commander (*turnaci başı*) of the early post-conquest days. Further, the
rate of the rent itself is remarkably low. In ten of the thirteen cases
it does not exceed one *akçe* of daily fee (*yevmi icare*) and in one
case it actually amounts to a mere 20 *akçe* for a whole year (*senevi
icare*)! Obviously, the quality, the size, and the state of repair of
the housing units in question left much to be desired. Finally, included among the tenants is also a man whom the document fails
even to list by his proper name; he is identified simply as *tabak
yahudi*, "the Jew the tanner." In the context of the social concepts
of the time, this detail suffices to give us an idea of the socio-
economic stratum to which this tenant and probably also many
other Jewish settlers of the Dermatà Quarter belonged.

It is only natural to assume that the plebeian quality of the
Dermatà dwellings would be reflected also in the quality and size
of the prayerhouse that served the religious needs of the Dermatà-
based segment of Kandiyote Jewry. To rephrase this assumption
in terms familiar to us from the Cretan *sicillat*: the low rate of
Vakıf-rental, set for the individual home-and-workshop in the Dermatà Quarter, may be expected to be paralleled by a low-rate rental
fee imposed on the synagogue which Dermatà Jews considered
their own. Indeed, earlier in this paper we discussed the only two
synagogues that were entered into the *Evkâf*-lists of Kandiye.
They both dated back to Venetian times and both became under
the Turks rent-paying clients of the Valide Sultan Mosque. Yet,
this is where the similarity ends. Unlike the case of the Lower
Synagogue — the noble basilica which, we remember, outlived the
Turkish regime and survived till 1942 — no remains are left of
the *Zudecha*'s Upper Synagogue. Also, there was a conspicuous
disparity between the rental fees imposed on each of these prayer-

houses: the Lower Synagogue paid almost twice the rate accrued from the Upper Synagogue. That disparity was not without reason.

True, the Turkish *sicillat* cannot be expected to give us information on who in the Kandiyote Jewish community frequented which synagogue. It seems, however, fair to assume (and we stressed this point earlier in the study) that the assessment of rental to be paid on a property did mirror the financial potential and the general socioeconomic standing of the group expected to make the payment. The imposition of a low *Vakıf*-rent on the Upper Synagogue was thus neither a caprice nor an act of exceptional generosity on the part of one Ottoman official or another, but a fairly accurate reflection of the social and economic status of the people served by this particular synagogue. Indeed, no *Vakıf*-rent altogether was collected from the Jewish prayerhouse which was located *inside* the Dermatà Quarter proper. Whether the worshippers there were too poor to build a respectable structure or too poor to overcome the difficulties of obtaining a permit under Islamic law for establishing a new synagogue, theirs was a prayerhouse so negligibly small, apparently, and so inconspicuous (or perhaps even located in a private home) that we have only an oral testimony to account for its one-time existence in the vicinity of *Çiçek Hamami* (Fig. 6).

To be sure, Dermatà Jewry was not the only group that considered the Upper Synagogue its own. After all, the synagogue was located in the original *Zudecha* and the majority of *Zudecha* Jews belonged to the middle-middle or lower-middle class. How large, then, in relation to these other groups, was the *poorest* segment of Kandiyote Jewry, the one, that is, that settled in the Dermatà area, on the periphery of the Jews' Quarter? Again, for the purpose of our present investigation, no computation of the absolute population figures is required. From our earlier discussion of population numbers it will be remembered that the tax-rolls and the *Vakıf*-lists we have are dealing with *taxpayers* and *buildings* rather than with the actual number of *inhabitants*. The raw taxpayer figures give us a clear idea of the relative strength of each group within the Jewish society as a whole.

Returning, then, to the same tax-rolls we used before and com-

paring the taxpayer figures of the three classes as they are given
in the *sicils*, we witness an unusually interesting phenomenon: according to one set of documents (the more trustworthy one, that
is), the number of Jewish families whom the government considered
poor enough to place in the lowest, i.e., *edna* class, equals exactly
the earlier-adduced number of families listed in the first-class (or
âlâ) rubric of the poll-tax: 17! Either of these two groups counted
twenty percent of the total Jewish population of Kandiye, leaving
the bulk of the Jewish inhabitants in the intermediate class (*evsat*).
The latter, amounting, as we have seen, to sixty percent of Kandiyote
Jewry, was exactly three times the size of either the top or the bottom
tax group:

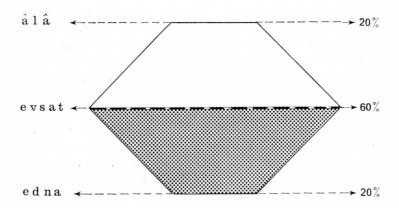

The overall picture emerging from such comparative examination
can thus be reproduced here by way of a perfectly symmetrical
diagram — a flattened hexagon, if you will, or, better still, a mirror
picture of a truncated pyramid, with the majority class serving as
the pyramid's base while the two other groups are represented by
the flattened top of the pyramid or its reflection.

THE KARAITES

It will be noted that in our handling of Kandiyote Jewish statistics
no separate figures were quoted with reference to Karaites. This

by no means was accidental. While the physical *presence* of a Karaite population in Candia-Kandiye has now been established beyond reasonable doubt, the *size* of that population cannot as yet be estimated on the basis of the available documents.

No less difficult than gauging the share of the Karaite element in the Cretan Jewish population totals is the analysis of the *socio-economic composition* of the Karaite settlement on the island. Though Dermatà-based, that settlement must under no circumstances be visualized as cast in a mold identical with that of the Rabbanite extension in Dermatà. After all, Dermatà Rabbanism was of one piece, as it were, the lowest-income group in the greater Rabbanite society of all Candia whose more affluent classes lived in the original *Zudecha* or spread (under the Turks) into adjacent sections of the Old City. By contrast, the entirety of the Karaite population of Crete, poor and rich alike, was concentrated in the Dermatà Quarter; as such, it was anything but homogeneous.

Indeed, in sociological and economic terms, Karaite Dermatà was the counterpart not of Rabbanite Dermatà but of Rabbanite *Zudecha* and its annexes. Just as there were, we remember, "handsome homes and buildings" in the ghetto-squalor of the *Zudecha*, because Venetian segregationist policies prevented rich Rabbanites from moving out of the Quarter and settling in better neighborhoods, so there must have been a few mansions in the Dermatà as well; they belonged to Karaites whom Rabbanite bias forced to reside in the slum. It is tempting to suggest, for instance, that the first two Jewish entries in the aforecited *Vakıf*-list from the Dermatà did, in fact, deal with such wealthy Karaite homeowners (cf. Fig. 5). Unlike the conspicuously *low* rental collected from the eleven shops-and-houses discussed above, the *high* rate of rent imposed on the remaining two (in that list of thirteen) was even more conspicuous: 12 *akçe* a day!

Last but not least, there is the problem of the topography of the Karaite Quarter in the Dermatà and, more particularly, of the location and identity of the synagogue frequented by the sectaries. Was the Dermatà prayerhouse (briefly alluded to earlier in this essay) a Karaite place of worship originally? This and related questions call for comprehensive treatment which, however, will have to be deferred to a separate study.

*   *   *

Some 300 years have passed since Turkish troops entered the Jews' Quarter of Venetian Candia. Among the processes generated by that event was expansion of the city's hitherto ghettoized *Zudecha* into a broader and more open *Yahudi Mahallesi*; this is summed up clearly in the map closing our essay (Fig. 6). The process lasted all through the first century of Ottoman rule. When, subsequently, developments over which Jews had no control and in which they could play no role whatsoever caused Cretan history to take an entirely different direction, the history of the island's Jewry had run its course. That last chapter of Cretan Jewry's decline and death is outside the scope of the present essay.

Wandering nowadays through the streets and alleys of what used to be Turkish Kandiye and became Greek Iraklion, the researcher experiences an eerie feeling. Accompanied by the ghosts of private residences and of historic houses of worship, Jewish and non-Jewish, which for a fleeting moment were brought back to life through the study of centuries-old *defters*, he cannot help pondering over the strange whims of history. Gone are the Venetian churches, the Turkish mosques, and the Jews' synagogues! Of the Sultan Ibrahim Mosque — the commanding edifice which forced its name and form on the whole neighborhood "above the sea," including the Jews' Quarter — no more than a ruined shell remains. The structure is impressive enough, though, even at the present, to conjure up images of ages past, and work is under way to restore the building to its erstwhile shape — its pre-Ottoman shape, that is, dating back to the days when the shrine served the Dominican Order as the Church of St. Peter the Martyr. Up the hill from the harbor, across 'Main Street', on the square below the Morosini Fountain, the once-fashionable Vizier Mosque reverted to Greek Orthodoxy again and is once more dedicated to St. Titus, Crete's First Bishop and Patron Saint; characteristically, it still remains as fashionable as ever.

But the mighty Valide Sultan is no more. For almost ten generations it usurped the place of Crete's largest Catholic shrine, the
Church of the Holy Saviour. Its minaret cut down already by the
turn of the century and its function de-islamicized then and there,
the building recently fell victim to our era's most potent weapon —
the ubiquitous bulldozer — and was razed to the ground. So was
the whole Jewish Quarter — synagogue, *Stenón*, and all — which
used to pay rent to that mosque. Incongruously left standing on
the southern edge of the former *Stenón*, an abandoned skeleton of a
one-time Jewish mansion is the sole survivor of Venetian *Zudecha*;
it hardly helps recall the Quarter's rich history and the identity of
the people who populated that Quarter in bygone days. Opposite,
perched atop the Jewish Quarter's northwestern corner, the "Glass-
house" reverberates each evening with the haunting strains of the
bouzouki and the rythmic sound of dancing Cretan boots, to the
tourists' undeniable enjoyment: it evokes no memory of the historic
"Jewish Gate" which occupied that very spot for over half a millennium. Nor is there anything left to remind those residing in the
near-by modern hotel that beneath the shining frame of concrete
and glass, entombed forever, lie the debris of the demolished Lower
Synagogue of Candia.

Only the dark waters of Dermatà Bay provide the unbroken link
between past and present. Dirty since the times of Byzantine tanneries and even more pclluted nowadays from the discharge of a
modern power plant, they unperturbedly beat against the curved
Cretan coast, as they have for ever and ever...

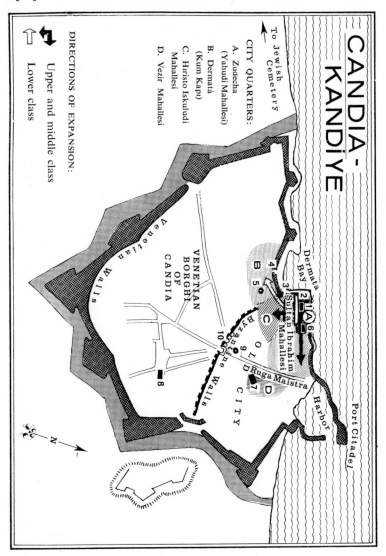

CITY LANDMARKS: 1. Lower Synagogue.   2. Stenón.   3. Jewish Gate.   4. Dermatà
Gate.   5. Jewish Fountain & Dermatà Synagogue (Çiçek Hamami).   6. Sultan Ibrahim
Mosque *(San Pietro)*.   7. Vizier Mosque *(Ayos Titos)*.   8. Valide Sultan Mosque *(San
Salvador)*.   9. Morosini Fountain.   10. Voltone & Kemer Altı Bazaar.

FIG. 6. Map showing expansion of the Jewish residential area in the Cretan
capital following the Turkish conquest.

(Prepared by the author on the basis of 17-cent. charts)

ROBERT OWEN AND HIS
NEW VIEW OF SOCIETY

HERMAN AUSUBEL

ROBERT OWEN was in his early forties when he brought out the four essays that were to make up his *A New View of Society* (1813–1816). Although Owen was middle-aged, there was nothing middle-aged about his book. Quite the contrary; it had all the ebullience and enthusiasm of a young reformer who has discovered certain basic truths and can hardly wait to communicate them to others. It disclosed the same kind of spirit that the French Revolutionary Republicans had revealed recently when they separated themselves from a past they deplored by adopting a calendar that made the first day of the Republic, September 22, 1792, the first day of the first month of the Year I. Like the French Republicans, Owen believed that he was inaugurating a new era in human affairs. Indeed, through thick and thin and despite countless frustrations, he managed to preserve this belief until his death at eighty-seven in 1858.

The Robert Owen of *A New View of Society* is best understood as he understood himself. This was in the role of an experienced doctor ministering to a very sick society, but with the profound confidence that he had the cure that would not only drive the illness away but prevent it from recurring. Owen's self-confidence is both striking and refreshing. He knew beyond a doubt what was wrong. He knew beyond a doubt what should be done about it. And without waiting for others to hail him as a pioneer in the study of human nature, he proceeded to do so himself. He may have suffered from many things, but low self-esteem was not one of them.

Owen was aware that as a reformer he had several marked disadvantages to overcome. He knew that his critics would insist that he was simply speculating — that he was merely setting forth a number of fanciful hypotheses and theories. He knew that some critics would dismiss him as an enthusiast; others would cast him aside as a visionary; still others would regard him as a wild man even as they conceded that he was doubtless kindhearted and well-intentioned. Even more important, he recognized that the traditional churches and denominational schools would not approve of his attributing to them responsibility for a great part of the misery in the world. And there is no question that he anticipated correctly the kinds of attacks to which he was to be subjected.[1]

At the same time, however, Owen was acutely conscious of the immense advantages he enjoyed as a publicist and reformer, and again he proved to be correct in his anticipations.[2] First of all, he was a successful business man with an enviable reputation for being what he called "a manufacturer for pecuniary profit" — an expression that would have delighted Thorstein Veblen. Secondly, his principles were not simply talk; they were action, too, and on an impressive scale, for they had been in effect for sixteen years in New Lanark, Scotland. In the third place, he knew that his principles were true; and so they had to triumph for the reason that truth ultimately had to prevail over error. Fourthly, the changes he was proposing, unlike those associated with the Revolutionary French, were to be put into effect gradually and temperately and with a minimum of disruption and inconvenience and certainly without bloodshed and public disorder, much less revolution or war. Fifthly, there was no danger whatever in applying his principles, and their results were guaranteed to be of a "value permanent and substantial beyond any of the discoveries which have

---

[1] See, for example, *Antijacobin Review*, LII (1817), 541–542; LVIII (1820), 121; LX (1821), 130–155; *Blackwood's Edinburgh Magazine*, IX (1821), 85; XIII (1823), 338, 341; *British Critic*, VIII (1817), 365; *Edinburgh Review*, XXXII (1819), 454, 464, 467.

[2] See *Report of the Proceedings of the Festival in Commemoration of the Centenary Birthday of Robert Owen, the Philanthropist, Held at Freemasons' Hall, London, May 16, 1871* (London, 1871).

hitherto been made." Furthermore, there was nothing hasty or precipitate about his principles. On the contrary, they were based on more than twenty years of patient observation of human nature in action, and those principles had been subject to close examination by a host of learned people. Finally, Owen's principles would at last give the kind of attention and recognition to human beings — to "living machines" — that only inanimate machines were receiving in the incipient industrial society of the early nineteenth century. The result would be good business. Employers would increase their profits and prosperity as they raised the morale of their workers.

In short, Robert Owen was a man with a mission. He looked about him, and everywhere he saw evils that needed to be remedied. All the while, however, politicians were preoccupied with trivial questions, and for all practical purposes they left untouched the suffering, misery, wretchedness, discontent, folly, absurdity, inconsistency, insincerity, hypocrisy, injustice, superstition, bigotry, irrationality, selfishness, crime, vice, immorality, idleness, poverty, drunkenness, lying, cheating, stealing, distrust, dissension, jealousy, vengefulness, and fanaticism that marked the human condition.

As far as Owen was concerned, what mattered was to understand how these evils came about. The answer was plain and unmistakable. They were the products of ignorance. Indeed, human history in all ages and countries was one long and pervasive conspiracy against man's happiness, and although there was an untold number of books in the world, the steps necessary to achieve happiness were either unknown or disregarded. Not that Owen was bitter; far from it. His point was that the uninterrupted reign of ignorance in human history rested on one fundamental error — the notion that each individual formed his own character and was therefore accountable for his sentiments and habits. Owen insisted that the will of man had no power whatever over his opinions. Men simply believed what he had been taught. Since he was taught from infancy to believe all kinds of nonsense, the world was a mess and the people in it wretched.

Owen was not harsh in his treatment of earlier generations. He recognized their errors and failings, but he contended that they were warped inevitably because of having been educated upon faulty and misguided principles of human nature. As a matter of fact, Owen saw no reason ever to be irritated or angry with anyone, arguing that there was "no conceivable foundation for private displeasure or public enmity." After all, children had the sentiments and habits of the adults who surrounded them. They themselves were passive, plastic, malleable, capable of being trained to acquire any character. Owen insisted, therefore, on the importance of making allowances for the unpleasant features of human behavior. People were taught to behave unpleasantly, and so they behaved unpleasantly. Since churches, sects, and parties were constantly inculcating "a total want of mental charity among men," it was no surprise that people proved themselves to be apt learners as they demonstrated this lack of charity.

The good society, according to Owen, presupposed the recognition of the great truth that human nature was one and the same in all people everywhere. And the central feature of human nature had always been and would always be its pliability. It was essential, therefore, to train children from their earliest infancy in good habits, and Owen never doubted for a moment that through what he called "persevering kindness" children would become eminently rational human beings. As for damaged adults, they, too, could be taught to unlearn and change old and vicious habits. Both for children and adults, in short, Owen saw his philosophy of kindness achieving extraordinary results. Always, however, people had to remember and act on the principle that, without exception, man's character was formed for him, that it was created by his predecessors who gave him both the ideas and habits that shaped his behavior.

Nor was this all. Owen also argued that the nature of happiness was almost always misunderstood. Indeed, he saw every individual's happiness as utterly inseparable from the happiness of those with whom he interacted; everyone's happiness depended on the happiness of others. It was imperative, therefore, to teach people to promote their own happiness by promoting the happiness of others and this without reference to sect, party, or country. This principle of the indivisibility of private and community happiness, Owen emphasized, applied to all places, periods, people, and circumstances. It was an eternal truth of the greatest importance in the history of mankind.

Filled with his principles, Robert Owen could hardly wait to convince others of their validity. Small wonder, therefore, that he found the early nineteenth century an exciting time to live. At long last the world was prepared for the emancipation of the human mind, and momentous changes were, therefore, impending. And what an inspiring future Owen envisaged as people developed — through the right kind of education — into the right kinds of human beings, rational, confident, harmonious, industrious, temperate, faithful, loyal, generous, kind, just, benevolent, sincere, open.

Owen regarded his essays as an explicit invitation to debate and discussion. From the clarification that would ensue he hoped that he would win the backing of the very sects and parties that in the past had helped to misshape man's character. Once these sects and parties learned the vital principles that Owen set forth, they could use their influence in government circles to undertake the first and most important duty of every state: to create rational and happy citizens and human beings.

Owen was a great and wonderful oversimplifier, to be sure: human beings were far more complicated and mysterious than he ever gave them credit for being. Yet much of what he pointed out in the early part of the nineteenth century is still embarrasingly pertinent in the latter part of the twentieth century. Some strong applications of Owenite good will and kindness may be precisely what the world of the post-nuclear age requires.

SELECT BIBLIOGRAPHY

Arthur Eugene Bestor, Jr. *Backwoods Utopias: The Sectarian and Owenite Phases of Communitarian Socialism in America: 1663–1829.* Philadelphia, 1950. An example of meticulous scholarship at its best in a field not notable for accuracy and soundness.

G. D. H. Cole. *The Life of Robert Owen*. Third edition. Hamden, Conn., 1966. A warm, sympathetic, and vigorous biography by a leading twentieth-century British socialist.

Margaret (Mrs. G. D. H.) Cole. *Robert Owen of New Lanark*. London, 1953. The best brief life available. Spirited and sympathetic yet fairminded.

Sir Alexander Gray. *The Socialist Tradition, Moses to Lenin*. London, 1946. Easily the finest short history of socialist thought. The author is a tough-minded, witty, and literate scholar.

John F. C. Harrison. "The Steam Engine of the New Moral World': Owenism and Education, 1817–1829," *Journal of British Studies*, VI (1967), 76–98. A perceptive essay on the importance of education in the Owenite scheme of things.

Rowland Hill Harvey. *Robert Owen, Social Idealist*. Berkeley and Los Angeles, 1949. A posthumously published monograph which because of its thoughtfulness deserves to be better known than it is.

Richard William Leopold. *Robert Dale Owen, A Biography*. Cambridge, U.S., 1940. A solid and balanced study of Owen's oldest son.

A. L. Morton. *The Life and Ideas of Robert Owen*. London, 1962. An unsophisticated Marxist presentation that praises Owen for helping to develop working-class self-confidence and criticizes him for not understanding the nature of class struggle.

Robert Dale Owen. *Twenty-Seven Years of Autobiography: Threading My Way*. New York, 1874. An invaluable as well as a heartwarming book of reminiscences.

Frank Podmore. *Robert Owen. A Biography*. Two volumes. London, 1906. The richness of detail keeps this account immensely useful two generations after its original publication.

Sir Leslie Stephen. "Owen, Robert," *Dictionary of National Biography*. London, 1895, XLII, 444–452. Certainly not one of the author's best biographical essays but one that reveals his capacity for condescension and waspishness.

FINALIZING AN ISSUE: MODENA'S AUTHORSHIP OF THE *QOL SAKHAL*

ISAAC E. BARZILAY

A FEW YEARS AFTER REGGIO'S PUBLICATION of the *Qol Sakhal*,[1] Abraham Geiger published the *Magen v'Şinnah* which contained the eleven questions of the "fool of Hamburg" and replies to them.[2] In his German introduction to this publication, Geiger agreed with Reggio that Modena was the author of the *Qol Sakhal*, and expressed the further view that Modena was also the author of both the questions and the answers of *Magen v'Şinnah*.[3] The validity of Geiger's view regarding the questions of *Magen v'Şinnah* was first questioned by Ludwig Blau who published, among the writings of Modena, the letter Modena had written, in 1616, to the *parnasim* of Hamburg on behalf of the Sephardi community of Venice. In this letter Modena referred to anti-traditional writings by a member of the Hamburg community and to replies that were given to them.[4] It was, I believe, Porges who first undertook to prove that the questions of the "fool of Hamburg" were those of da Costa, indicating the similarity between them and the criticisms leveled against them by da Silva.[5] The issue was finally resolved by Gebhardt's

---

[1] *Beḥinat ha-Qabbalah, Ḥibbur Kolel Sefer Qol Sakhal v'Sefer Sha'agath Aryeh l'Morenu ha-Rav R' Yehudah Aryeh mi-Modena*, with notes and inquiries by Isaac Shmuel Reggio (Gorizia, 1852; Jerusalem, 1968).

[2] Abraham Geiger, ed., *Magen v'Şinnah l'ha-Rav Yehudah Aryeh mi-Modena v'nosaf 'alav shnei Ḥibburav Magen va-Ḥerev 'im Ḥayyei Yehudah* (Breslau, 1856).

[3] Geiger wrote: "Trotzdem aber kann es keinen Augenblick zweifelhaft bleiben, dass die Fragen, nicht minder als die Antworten von Leon selbst ausgehen und dass seine eigentliche Absicht eben die Fragen sind", ibid., p. 27.

[4] Ludwig Blau, *Leo Modenas Briefe und Schriftstücke* (Budapest, 1905), par. 156, p. 146.

[5] N. Porges, "Zur Lebensgeschichte Uriel da Costas," *MGWJ*, LXII (1918), *NF*, XXVI, 37–48, 108–124.

publication of the original Portuguese text of da Costa's *Propostas Contra A Tradiçaõ*. His comparison of the original with the Hebrew version of the questions of *Magen v'Şinnah* left little doubt as to the validity of Porges' assumption and the untenability of Geiger's view.[6]

Once a connection was established between the *Magen v'Şinnah* and da Costa, the way was open for new assumptions regarding the *Qol Sakhal*. Blau was the first to remark that the *Magen v'Şinnah* contained *in nuce* the *Qol Sakhal*.[7] It was, however, Isaiah Sonne who proposed the new hypothesis that the author of the *Qol Sakhal* was no other than Uriel da Costa. Sonne arrived at this conclusion in the late twenties, and twenty years later he still held to it.[8]

A Critique of Sonne's Hypothesis

What is Sonne's hypothesis? He believes that the *Qol Sakhal* is da Costa's lost work, *Examen dos Tradiçones Phariseos*, some excerpts of which have been preserved in Samuel da Silva's *Tratado da Immortalidade*.[9] It was written in 1622 and, as indicated by Modena in the brief preface to the *Qol Sakhal*, had reached him in the same year. Sonne surmises that it might have been through the instrumentality of his good friend from Amsterdam, Dr. David Farrar, that Modena obtained the manuscript.[10] In its present form, as translated by Modena, the *Qol Sakhal* constitutes a first version of da Costa's work, in which the belief in immortality is still retained; in the subsequent revised text, however, da Costa retreated from this position.

What is the evidence in support of this theory? First of all,

---

[6] Carl Gebhardt, *Die Schriften des Uriel da Costa* (Amsterdam, 1922), pp. 1–32.

[7] Blau, op. cit., "Einleitung", p. 90.

[8] I. Sonne, "Da Costa Studies," *JQR*, NS, XXII (1931–1932), 247–293; idem, "Modena and the Da Costa Circle in Amsterdam," *HUCA*, XXI (1948), 1–28.

[9] Gebhardt, op. cit., pp. 158–181.

[10] On the relations between Modena and Farrar, see Sonne, in *HUCA*, XXI, 10 ff.

Sonne detects a direct relationship between the *Magen v'Ṣinnah*
and the *Qol Sakhal*. He believes that Modena's reply to da Costa's
Propostas of 1616 directly influenced the structure of the *Qol
Sakhal*. In his reply to question seven regarding the Oral Tradiion
in general, Modena observed that without such a tradition we would
be at a loss not only in regard to the particulars of the commandments, but also with regard to the articles of faith. He wrote:
"Where may we find clearly in the Torah the immortality of the
soul, its reward and punishment... the resurrection of the dead,
etc?"[11] It was in reaction to these words, Sonne believes, that da
Costa began his new work, i.e., the *Qol Sakhal*, with a treatise
concerning the articles of faith. He also thinks that the second
treatise, which begins with a general assault on the Oral Tradition,
was influenced by Modena's reply in which he treated da Costa's
seventh question first.[12] As for the third essay, it is, in Sonne's
view, a mere expansion of the *Propostas*.

Before going any further, it should be pointed out that these
very arguments which Sonne is using in support of his hypothesis
may be turned against it. It may be argued that, since it was
Modena who, in his replies to the *Propostas*, pointed out the necessity of an Oral Tradition not only in legal matters but also in
matters of faith, and since it was he who thought it methodically
preferable to deal with the general conception of an Oral Law
first and only then with its particulars, why not assume that in
the *Qol Sakhal* he was actually following his own views, and that
the structure of the work, therefore, points to his, rather than da
Costa's, authorship?

The same reasoning may also be used with regard to the alleged
textual similarities which Sonne believes he has discovered between
the *Qol Sakhal* and *Magen v'Ṣinnah*. Assuming, with Sonne, that
the passage of the *Qol Sakhal* (p. 26) emphasizing the necessity of
an Oral Tradition, is similar to a passage of *Magen v'Ṣinnah* (p. 4a)
emphasizing the same opinion, and that there is also a similarity

---

11 Geiger, op. cit., p. 4a.
12 Ibid., p. 3b.

between the two texts with regard to the argument of the Qaraites against the rabbinic Oral Tradition, what does it prove? That Modena who wrote those passages in *Magen v'Şinnah* also wrote them in *Qol Sakhal*.

More pertinent to Sonne's hypothesis, though, as we shall presently see, equally untenable, are the alleged similarities he adduces between the *Qol Sakhal* and the writings of da Costa, i.e., his *Sobre a Mortalidade da Alma do Homen* and *Exemplar Humanae Vitae*.[13]

In an invective-ridden passage of his *Exemplar*, which smacks of both Classical and Medieval anti-Jewish prejudices, da Costa labels the Jews enemies of the human race who hold all peoples in great contempt, on a par with animals, and think highly only of themselves. Addressing himself to the Jews, he concludes: "You can boast of no greater glory... than being despised and hated by all on account of your ridiculous and affected customs, by which you wish to separate yourselves from all other people."[14] Sonne finds this conclusion similar to the following passage of the *Qol Sakhal*: "For thus they [the nations] deride our superfluous regulations as puerilities... suppress us like enemies, make us slaves, so that everywhere we are treated with contempt and mockery."[15] Supposing with Sonne that contentwise there is a certain similarity between these two passages, this similarity dwindles to insignificance, when the fuller contexts of these two passages are compared. It becomes rather obvious then that there is almost no room for comparison. Whereas da Costa writes as a Christian, pointing an accusing finger at the Jews for their alleged contempt and hate of all the world, the author of the *Qol Sakhal* writes as a loyal Jew, deeply grieved by Jewish misery and degradation. To be sure, the author of the *Qol Sakhal* does share da Costa's view that the excessive load of legal prohibitions and restrictions has contributed to the worsening of the Jewish situation among the nations. Such a view, however, is implicitly encountered in some of the writings

---

13 Gebhardt, op. cit., pp. 33–145.

14 Ibid., p. 115, lines 20–27; German transl. p. 136, lines 23–33.

15 *Qol Sakhal*, p. 33.

of both Modena and his younger contemporary, Joseph Solomon Delmedigo. More significant, however, is the basic difference between the two texts. Whereas the author of the *Qol Sakhal* displays an identification with the lot of suffering Jewry and a sharing of its hopes and aspirations, these elements are entirely missing in the *Exemplar*.

Equally unconvincing is another similarity Sonne adduces between the two texts with regard to the commandment to honor one's father and mother.[16] The *Exemplar* cites this injunction, together with the injunction to respect private property, as the best part of the Mosaic law, constituting, in his view, the mainstay of society. However, he attacks, in the name of natural law, the belief in the revealed origin of these injunctions, thus giving expression to his early deistic orientation. No trace of this tendency is noticeable in the *Qol Sakhal*. To be sure, its author also labels that injunction "a foundation of natural law;"[17] this must not be interpreted, however, in deistic terms, implying a rejection of revelation, but rather as emphasizing the naturalness of that law, making an extensive elaboration of it utterly superfluous. Respect for parents being natural to man, the *Qol Sakhal* is critical of the rabbis for having wasted so much time and energy on defining all the laws and regulations pertaining to a "stubborn and rebelious son."[18] Cases of such a nature, he feels, ought rather to be left to the discretion of the judge, and adjudicated in accordance with local custom. Thus, while da Costa criticizes that injunction as part of his onslaught on revealed religion, the author of the *Qol Sakhal* criticizes it as part of his struggle against the excesses of the Oral Law.[19]

Entirely speculative is Sonne's reply to the argument on behalf of Modena's authorship of the *Qol Sakhal* based on the almost

---

16 Ibid., p. 58; Gebhardt, op. cit., pp. 118, 140.

17 ״כיבוד אב ואם הוא ליסוד מן הדת הטבעית״.

18 בן סורר ומורה.

19 In view of the fact that in the first treatise the author of *Qol Sakhal* accepts revelation as an integral part of his philosophy (see chap. 6, pp. 12–13), the expression "natural law" here cannot be interpreted in deistic terms.

complete identity of the prayer "kelilat yofi" of his *Tefillat Yesharim* and the short prayer suggested for daily recitation in the *Qol Sakhal*.[20] Since Sonne claims to have discovered in that collection of prayers by Modena a prayer from Joseph Karmi's *Kenaf Renanim* (1626), without acknowledgement of source, he feels justified in assuming that the prayer "kelilat yofi" may be a Hebrew translation of a prayer by da Costa, written in Portuguese.[21]

More central and crucial in Sonne's hypothesis is his theory regarding the redaction of the *Qol Sakhal*, alluded to earlier. Aware of the contradiction in views between da Costa and the *Qol Sakhal* with regard to immortality, Sonne realized that the burden of his hypothesis must be an explanation of this contradiction. He thought he found a clue to it in a statement by Samuel da Silva.

At the end of his *Tratado da Immortalidade*, a polemical pamphlet against da Costa's writing on this subject, da Silva points out that the "root of all that befell him [i.e. da Costa]" was his denial of the Oral Tradition, "a thesis he claims to have demonstrated and launched in the seventh chapter of his book."[22] Starting out from the assumption that the book alluded to is the *Qol Sakhal*, Sonne ingenuously develops a sophisticated theory, identifying that chapter seven with chapter one of the second treatise of the *Qol Sakhal*, and thereby allegedly also solving the problem of the above mentioned contradiction regarding immortality. Here are his words:

> Da Costa says that in the seventh chapter of his book he described and proved the first and chief foundation of his theses, that 'tradition is false and has departed from truth and the right way of the Law'. Now this thesis forms the subject of the first chapter of the second treatise of the *Qol Sakhal*, which apparently is a counter-argument. However, if we consider that the first treatise is composed of the following

---

[20] Cf. N. S. Libowitz, *Rabbi Yehudah Aryeh Modena* (New York, 1901), p. 30; B. Klar, "Sha'agath Aryeh 'al Qol Sakhal," *Tarbiz*, XIII (1942), 135–149.

[21] Sonne, in *JQR*, NS, XXII (1931–32), 278–279.

[22] Gebhardt, op. cit., pp. 167–168, 180.

ten chapters: (1) God's existence, (2) creation of the world, (3) purpose of creation, (4) providence, (5) reward, (6) revelation, (7) immortality of the soul, (8) that the righteous are not well off in this world, (9) the essence of reward and punishment (in the other world), (10) summary chiefly of the last three chapters, it becomes clear that in the later redaction, after da Costa reached the negation of the immortality of the soul, the last three chapters of the first treatise had to be excluded, and thus the first chapter of the second treatise came to follow the sixth chapter of the first treatise, forming the seventh chapter. Only thus can we explain how it came about that the first and chief foundation of his theses formed the seventh chapter.[23]

This hypothesis thus assumes that da Costa's work, i.e., the *Qol Sakhal*, went through a process of redaction, in consequence of which there were at least two versions of it, an earlier one, in which the belief in immortality was still retained, and a subsequent one in which it was renounced. The version that reached Modena in the spring of 1622 was the earlier one. In the later version, the last four chapters of the first treatise were eliminated and chapter one of the second treatise thus became the seventh chapter.

This theory appears artificial and without any foundation in fact. The assumption of an earlier and later version of the *Qol Sakhal* has no evidence whatsoever to support it, either in the writings of da Costa or of da Silva. To be sure, da Costa does write that, after he began his work (*Post caeptum opus accidit etiam*), he reached the conclusion that the Bible speaks of reward and punishment only in temporal terms and knows nothing of an after-life and immortality of the soul;[24] never does he say, however, that there was an earlier version of his writing in which he had embraced that view. Moreover, even before da Costa had time to publish his work, part of it came into the possession of da Silva, and in that part da Costa, according to da Silva, maintained his

[23] Sonne, in *JQR*, NS, XXII, 274–275.
[24] Gebhardt, op. cit., pp. 108, 128.

denial of immortality. Eager as da Silva was to put his hands on
da Costa's writings, is it possible, if there were an earlier version
of the work, that it reached Modena in Venice before it even came
to the notice of da Silva in Amsterdam?[25] Besides, were the *Qol
Sakhal* the lost *Examen* of da Costa, where does one find in it
the quotations from the works of the *romanticistas* for which da
Silva rebukes him,[26] and the passages from Ecclesiastes and Job
which da Silva also mentions as having filled that work?

There are, however, stronger reasons against the acceptance of
Sonne's thesis. In order to prove that chapter seven of da Costa's
lost work is actually chapter one of the second treatise of the
Qol Sakhal, Sonne truncated the last four chapters of the first
treatise as belonging to an alleged first version of the work, which
were excised from the second version. By doing so, he apparently
intended not only to solve the problem of the identification of
chapter seven, but, as indicated, also to solve the more serious
problem regarding the contradiction between the *Qol Sakhal*'s
acceptance of immortality and the rejection of this belief by da
Costa. However, this solution is no solution, since da Costa rejects
not only immortality, but also the beliefs in reward and punishment and revelation — beliefs embraced by the *Qol Sakhal*.[27]
In order to make his theory plausible, Sonne's excision is thus
insufficient; he should also have excised chapters five and six of
the first treatise. However, even this would not have solved the
problem. A cursory reading of this treatise makes it perfectly clear
that all of it, from chapter one to nine, is a coherent whole from
which no part can be removed without destroying the whole.
Indeed, this is what the author himself emphasizes.[28]

25 Ibid., pp. 162–163, 174.
26 Ibid., pp. 164, 175.
27 Ibid., pp. 109–110, 129–130; *Qol Sakhal*, I, 5, 6.
28 ״חשוב על מאמר זה מראשו לסופו תראה איך נתאמת לי מציאות ה׳, ברא וחדש
העולם מרצונו, משגיח ומביט על כל מעשי בני אדם, נותן שכר טוב לטובים ועונש
לרעים, אשר למען נדע נדע מהו טוב ורע נתן לנו תורה, והיא אותה שקבל משה בן עמרם
על הר סיני ונתנה לישראל אשר על קיומה אנו או ביטולה נקבל שכר או עונש בנפשנו
הנשארת אחר המות...״. *Qol Sakhal*, I, 10, p. 19.

Analysis of the First Treatise of the Qol Sakhal

Having argued against Sonne's hypothesis, we may now turn to the second, positive, part of this essay, an analysis of the first treatise of the *Qol Sakhal*, through which we shall attempt to prove that its author was no other than Judah Aryeh Modena.

It was, in all likelihood, the somewhat "strange" character of the views of the first treatise which kept scholars away from a thorough investigation of it. Whereas it seemed relatively easy to discover in Modena's writings parallels to the legal aspects of the *Qol Sakhal*, it appeared much harder to find parallels to the philosophical views of that treatise. However, such parallels do exist and we shall presently indicate them. We shall follow in our analysis the order of the *Qol Sakhal*.

The author of the *Qol Sakhal* opens his first treatise with the assertion that he is thoroughly acquainted with all kinds of speculations concerning religion. He claims not only that he was well-read in the literature of the various faiths, but also that he had been living in the midst of and in contact with "various people of different religions." That such assertions well suit Modena can amply be substantiated from his writings.[29]

His subsequent statement that he imagines himself as if he were detached from the present, born and raised in a society with no religion or ethical code, is typical of the Cartesian age of methodical doubt and of an age that witnessed the mass phenomenon of Marranism. It is also, no doubt, characteristic of a man like Modena who, in a number of his works, displayed a remarkable talent for detachment and objective analysis. As early as his *Sur*

---

[29] Cf. Geiger, op. cit., Hebr. sec. pp. 11b, 13b; R' Yehudah Aryeh Modena, *She'eloth u'Teshuvot Ziqnei Yehudah*, ed. Shlomo Simonsohn (Jerusalem, 1956), par. 77, p. 99; idem. *Ari Nohem*, ed., N. Libowitz (Jerusalem, 1929), chap. II, p. 7, and last chap; L. Blau, op. cit., p. 69; S. Bernstein, ed., *Diwan l'R' Yehudah, Aryeh mi-Modena* (Philadelphia, 1932), III, "Shirei Tehillah l'Noṣerim Ḥashuvim;" *Ḥayyei Yehudah* in Y. A. Modena, *Leqet Ketavim*, ed., Peninah Navah (Jerusalem, 1968), pp. 71, 83, 86–87, 92; C. Roth, "Leone da Modena and the Christian Hebraists of his Age," *Jewish Studies in Memory of Israel Abrahams* (New York, 1927), pp. 384–401.

me-Ra', a youthful defense of gambling,[30] he illustrated his mastery
of the actor's art by assuming two opposite roles and carrying
out each of them with equal skill and conviction. His *Riti* is also
a superb example of detached description and analysis.[31] Again,
in his anti-Christian polemical work, *Magen va-Ḥerev*, he writes
that he tried several times to investigate the beginnings of Christianity and to understand the acts and thoughts of Jesus, especially
how he came to consider himself the "son of God". Finally,

> in consequence of reading our own and their books, I formed
> a view on the matter, which, in my view, is both true and
> valid as if I had lived in his generation and as if I were sitting
> next to him.[32]

In chapters one and two of the first treatise the author briefly
expresses his belief in the existence of God and His creation of
the world. The wisdom and orderliness of the universe, he explains,
indicate the purposefulness of a supreme order. Moreover, no
thing can make itself but must have its cause, and this cause
another cause, until a first cause is reached, the existence of which
is absolute and dependent on no other cause.[33]

Regarding the relationship between God and the world, the
author writes, one may accept either of two alternatives, that of
eternity or creation. Were the world eternal, he reasons, God and
the world would be one, like body and soul. Such a view he finds
unacceptable on two counts: first, it leaves no room for change,
and, second, man, by virtue of his freedom, would be superior
to God.[34]

[30] First edition, Venice, 1596.

[31] Cf. Introduction.

[32] Yehudah Aryeh Modena, *Magen va-Ḥerev*, ed. S. Simonsohn (Jerusalem,
1960), p. 43.

[33] *Qol Sakhal*, p. 6.

[34] It was this reference to pantheism, the source of which Yiṣḥaq Einhorn
thought to be in Spinoza, from which he drew, *inter alia*, his conclusion regarding the late date of the *Qol Sakhal*, see *Tarbiz*, XIII (1941–42), 60. That
such an assumption is incorrect has been pointed out by Benjamin Klar and
needs no further elaboration, ibid., pp. 141–142. Regarding this subject, W.

More interesting and more relevant to the problem of the authorship of the *Qol Sakhal* is chapter three, dealing with the purpose of creation. The author writes:

My investigation led me to the notion that God's purpose in creating this world is to derive some pleasure from His creatures, by having some of them acknowledge Him and others serving those who acknowledge Him and filling their needs. The knowledge of the Divine differs markedly: it is abundant with some, less abundant with others, or very little with others. Equally, the worshippers differ: some being important, others less important, still others utterly despicable. It is the perpetuation of this order of things that causes Him pleasure... God is like a king who, having built himself a palace, populated it with servants and with all kinds of servants, dishes, and beasts to serve those servants. In addition, he also filled it with puppies, monkeys, and animals, birds, horses and the like, solely for his own delight.... It is my opinion that man is the most excellent of creatures, and all the world, above and below, was created for his sake. This is the reason why man was created last.... Although all creatures were created for God's delight, none delights Him more than man, because none is more excellent. Like human servants of a king, dignitaries of some sort though they may be, do not consider it degrading to themselves to serve a monkey or an exquisite bird that is dear to the king, equally the heavenly stars with their leading intellects serve man, and so certainly do all other creatures, because the Creator is most fond of him.... The reason why God derives greater pleasure from man than from other creatures is obvious. Even assuming the existence of de-

Windelband writes: "This identification of the essence of God and the world is a general doctrine of the natural philosophy of the Renaissance. It is found likewise in Paracelsus, in Sebastian Franck, in Boehme, and finally also with the whole body of Platonists" (*A History of Philosophy*, New York, II 1958, 368–369). In his *Novlot Ḥokhmah*, Yashar of Candia attributes pantheistic ideas to Abraham Ibn Ezra, see *Sefer Novlot Ḥokhmah* in *Ta'alumot Ḥokhmah* (Basel, 1631), pp. 136–137.

tached intellects, there is never anything new in their motions, knowledge or perfection, as there is never anything new in those of the heavenly hosts. Nor is there ever any change in the lower creatures, in animals, vegetables and inanimates. Only man forms an exception, going up and down, up and down... constantly changing in his knowledge, inquisitiveness, will, desire, deeds and the choices he makes, as a result of the freedom that was given to him and by virtue of which it is said of him 'in our image, after our likeness.' Moreover, the species of man is unique among all other species [by its great versatility]. Among its individuals you see people both wise and foolish, moral and immoral, rich and poor, kings and peasants; some pursuing one trade, others another; some inventing... one invention, others another, an even greater one; some boasting to know their Creator and clinging unto Him by one religion, others sacrificing their lives to uphold another religion. God in heaven laughs at all that. Like a king of flesh and blood, who derives no pleasure from his trusted servants... but from a puppy, a monkey, a bird or a horse.... God created the world to be entertained by man.[35]

We have quoted the above passage at great length because its ideas are central in the philosophy of the *Qol Sakhal*, and because we believe that it contains strong indications of Modena's authorship. Basic in it is, first, the concept of man's uniqueness, deriving from his freedom of choice, and, second, the divine pleasure this causes. We shall analyze these two notions closely, attempting to indicate their sources.

Ancient as the notion of man's freedom is, encountered both in the Bible and classical literature,[36] it suffered a setback in Christian thought, dominated to a great extent by the fatalistic notion of man's innate depravity. It reemerged with great vigour during the Renaissance and became a leading idea among the Neo-Platonists.

---

[35] *Qol Sakhal*, I, 3, pp. 8–9.
[36] For just a few references see, Lev. 26, Deut. 25, 30:11 ff., Jer. 18:5–11, Ez. 18; W. Windelband, *A History of Philosophy*, pp. 190 ff.; 251 ff; 282 ff; 329 ff.

It is central in Marsiglio Ficino's *Theologia Platonica* (Florence, 1482),[37] and was given a most solemn and eloquent expression by Pico della Mirandola (1463–1494) in his famous *Oration on the Dignity of Man*, intended as an introductory speech for a disputation that was to be held in the spring of 1487. In it Pico writes:

> Having completed all the work of creation, the Supreme Maker set man in the middle of the world and thus spoke to him: 'We have given you, oh Adam, no visage proper to yourself, nor any endowment properly your own, in order that whatever place, whatever form, whatever gifts you may, with premeditation, select, these same you may have and possess through your own judgement and decision. The nature of all other creatures is defined and restricted within laws which We have laid down; you, by contrast, impeded by no such restrictions, may, by your own free will, to whose custody We have assigned you, trace for yourself the lineaments of your own nature.... We have made you a creature 'neither of heaven nor of earth, neither mortal nor immortal, in order that you may, as the free and proud shaper of your own being, fashion yourself in the form you may prefer. It will be in your power to descend to the lower, brutish forms of life; you will be able, through your own decision, to rise again to the superior orders whose life is divine.[38]

The emphasis of the *Oration*, like that of the *Qol Sakhal*, is primarily on man's freedom of choice. Man is the only creature in the universe whose destiny, for good or for bad, is entirely entrusted to himself. He alone is free to choose, whereas all other creatures are constrained to follow the predestined course of their unchangeable natures. The two texts are not only similar in their basic concept of man's uniqueness, but even in their formulation of it. Modena was well acquainted with the writings of Pico, and may have

[37] For some excerpts translated by Josephine L. Burroughs, see *Journal for the History of Ideas*, V (1944), pp. 227 ff.

[38] Giovani Pico della Mirandola, *Oration on the Dignity of Man* trans. A. Robert Caponigri, introduction by Russel Kirk (Chicago, 1956), pp. 6–8.

borrowed this idea directly from them.[39] On the other hand, it is more probable to assume that he may have drawn it from Hebrew sources which were closer to him and with which he was more familiar.

Man's supremacy and uniqueness is a leading idea in the writings of Isaac Abravanel. Against Maimonides' rejection of the homocentric conception of the universe, on account of the alleged superior nature of the heavenly bodies and their leading intellects,[40] he asserts man's supremacy not only in the sublunar region, but throughout the universe. The fact that man appears last in the order of creation points, in his view, to his being the highest stage of it and its final goal.[41]

The idea of man's uniqueness and supremacy is even more prominently displayed in the sermons of the famous scholar and preacher of Mantua, Yehudah Moscato (1532–1590). Indeed, in a sermon entitled "Glory of Man,"[42] he not only extolled the uniqueness of the human spirit, but also emphasized the contribution man makes to his own perfection, because he possesses freedom of choice.[43] In another of his sermons, Moscato wrote:

> There is a tremendous difference between the essence and destiny of man and those of other natural creatures.... His .... are the result of his own choice... whereas those of other creatures are fixed and in accordance with their immutable natures... What is unique in man is his tendency to succumb to extreme opposites. Being free, he can soar to the heavens; however, he can also descend to the lowest pit. When corrupt, he is the worst of all creatures; when good and acting in accordance with the will of his Creator, his

---

[39] Cf. *Ari Nohem*, ed. Libowitz, chaps. II, XIII, XXXI, pp. 9, 44, 96.

[40] Cf. mainly *Moreh*, III, 13.

[41] Cf. Comm. Gen. 1:1, 1:26; I. Barzilay *Between Reason and Faith Anti Rationalism in Italian Jewish Thought (1250–1650)* (The Hague, 1967), pp. 87 ff.

[42] Sermon 34, "Tifereth Adam," *Sefer Nefuṣoth Yehudah* (Lwow, 1859), pp. 99 ff.

[43] Ibid., p. 100b, bottom of left column.

essence is elevated to heights unattainable by any other species.[44]

Moscato was one of the eminent scholars and preachers of his day, and it may be assumed that Modena, who himself spent a lifetime in sermonizing and preaching, was no doubt acquainted with his work. Indeed, in one of his sermons, Modena uses a theme and midrashic interpretation which is directly drawn from the sermons of Moscato.[45] It may be assumed that a closer scrutiny of *Midbar Yehudah* would show greater indebtedness on the part of Modena to Moscato. Moscato's sermons, as well as his commentary on the *Kuzari*, the *Qol Yehudah*, indicate his close acquaintance with the philosophical, notably the Neo-Platonic, trends of his time. He was also familiar with the work of Pico.[46] It is therefore safe to assume that it might have been through him, rather than directly from Pico, that the idea of man's freedom of choice, as the unique and essential in man, may have reached Modena.

Having indicated the possible sources of the *Qol Sakhal*'s views on man, we shall now attempt to strengthen our contention regarding Modena's authorship of this work by adducing passages from his works, in which these very ideas are amply displayed. Above all, we have in mind his collection of sermons, *Midbar Yehudah*. To the discussion of man's supremacy he dedicated his sermon on Sukkoth, especially the first part thereof. Taking for his exordium the text of Ps. 8, he expounds the idea of man's uniqueness and freedom of choice. In doing so, he not only follows the same train of thought as the *Qol Sakhal*, but also uses the same Biblical references in its substantiation. Isaiah 43:7 and excerpts from Psalm 8 are to be found in both texts.[47] As in the *Qol Sakhal*, Modena points out here that man is not only superior to all sub-

---

[44] Ibid., sermon 31, p. 85b.

[45] Ibid., left column, "מה רב טוב אשר צפנת ליראיך" and Modena's "Drush li-Teshuvah, Shabbath shelifnei Rosh ha-Shanah," *Midbar Yehudah* (Venice, 1602), p. 16a.

[46] Sermon 8, p. 23a; see also Barzilay, op. cit., pp. 172 ff.

[47] Cf. "Drush l'Sukkoth," *Midbar Yehudah* pp. 29b, 30a.

lunar creatures but to the heavenly hosts as well. Their divine glory notwithstanding, they still "serve earth."

A comparison of chapter three of the first treatise of the *Qol Sakhal* and this sermon leaves little doubt as to the common authorship of both. Indeed, it is, no doubt, to this sermon that the author of *Qol Sakhal* is referring when he writes:

> Somewhere else I have already adduced proofs and Biblical references against one who has written in opposition to this [homocentric] view, asserting that one must not ascribe to the Creator the subservience of the superior to the inferior.[48]

It may be assumed that these words are directed against no other than Maimonides who, as mentioned earlier, in *Guide*, III, 13, rejected the homocentric view, arguing that "man is more perfect and of greater dignity than all sublunar creatures, but not beyond it. Indeed, if compared with the spheres, especially the intellects, he is much inferior."[49] Be this as it may, more essential to our argument is the fact that both texts, the *Qol Sakhal* and *Midbar Yehudah*, share not only the same ideas and Biblical references, but also the specific expression "subserving the superior to the inferior." It is above all man's uniqueness, grounded in his freedom of choice, which is central in both of them. Like the *Qol Sakhal*, Modena the preacher also asserts: "None of the other creatures, besides man, acts voluntarily... whereas many serve him, he serves no one but God alone."[50]

More puzzling is the other aspect of the *Qol Sakhal's* philosophy, namely, the view that the purpose of creation, notably of man, is to delight the Creator. True, at the beginning of chapter three (of the first treatise), the author does suggest a rather refined and spiritual interpretation of divine delight, its source being man's "acknowledgement of Him," an idea expressed by Isaac Abra-

---

[48] ״וכבר הבאתי ראיות ופסוקי תורה במקום אחר נגד מי שכתב נגד זה כאומרו חלילה ליוצרנו מהכניע היקר לזולל״, *Qol Sakhal* p. 8.

[49] ״שהאדם הוא יותר שלם ונכבד מכל מה שיהיה מזה החמר לא זולת זה. וכשתעריך מציאותו למציאות הגלגלים כ״ש למציאות השכלים הנפרדים יהיה פחות מאד מאד.״

[50] *Midbar Yehudah*, p. 30b.

vanel;[51] however, in the remainder of that chapter this meaning
is abandoned, and the view yields to the interpretation of man as
actor on the world scene, created for the entertainment of his
master-spectator, God, not necessarily by his moral and speculative
attainments, but by his general versatility and unpredictability.

For this task man is uniquely endowed. Being free to choose,
his deeds and thoughts are of the widest possible range. They are
equally unpredictable, having always an element of novelty in
them. It is these two characteristics which are the source of divine
delight. Interesting in this view is not only the author's marvel
at man's initiative and inexhaustible potentialities, but his conception of God as restless and desirous of ever new impressions
and new situations, a conception so typical of modern man. How
far is such a notion of God removed from that of the self-contem-
plating being of previous centuries! Inescapable in this view is also
its worldliness and both the optimistic and pessimistic strains
which permeate it. Noteworthy, since heralding the advent of the
new age with its growing religious skepticism, is the fact that
among the examples of man's versatility entertaining the Lord,
the author cites man's variety of religious creeds. One, he writes,
worships God in one way, another in another way, with each one
ready to sacrifice his life in defense of his faith. And this is cited
as a source of entertainment for God! How wordly and skeptical
a view!

As we shall presently attempt to show, all the elements of this
conception are present in the writings of Modena. Before doing
this, however, we must first try to discover its possible sources.
Strange as it may seem, an allusion to this view, in a negative way,
refuting it, is found in Maimonides' *Guide*. In discussing the purpose
of natural things, Maimonides asserts that whatever that may be,
it definitely is not mere play or entertainment. He writes: "Do not
give heed to the crazy notion of those who think that the monkey
was created for man to make fun of."[52] In Classical literature this

---

51 I. Barzilay, op. cit., pp. 88–90.
52 *Moreh*, III, 25: "ולא תביט לשגעון מי שחשב שהקוף נברא לשחוק ממנו בני אדם".

view is found in the writings of Marcus Aurelius, Epictetus, and the Neo-Platonists.[53] It reappeared during the Renaissance as part of a broader conception emphasizing the uniqueness of man.

Worth mentioning in this connection is "A Fable about Man" by the Spanish humanist, Ludovicus Vives (1492–1540). Its setting is a birthday party for Juno, the spouse of Jupiter, during which the gods are entertained by all kinds of performers. They derive, however, their greatest pleasure from the spectacle of man. "Embracing all things in his might, is all things, they saw man, Jupiter's mime, be all things also." One after another he assumed various forms, of a plant, of a moral satirist, in the shape of a "thousand wild beasts," and finally of man:

> Prudent, just, faithful, human, kindly and friendly, who went about the cities with the others, held the authority and obeyed in turn, cared for the public interest and welfare, and was finally in every way a political and social being.

However, they were struck with the greatest amazement and experienced the height of delight upon watching him "surpassing the nature of man and relying entirely upon a very wise mind." In this performance man so closely personified Jupiter, that the gods mistook him for Jupiter himself. They finally prevailed upon Jupiter that man be seated among the gods, and it was their greatest pleasure to study him and his manifold endowments.[54]

Although the theme and motifs of the "Fable" are similar to those of the *Qol Sakhal*, it is not necessary to infer a direct indebtedness of the latter to the former. Ideas of this sort must have been common in the writings of other humanists as well, and it may be assumed that the author of *Qol Sakhal* was acquainted with them.

The closest expression of these ideas in the writings of Modena is to be found in his *Sur me-Ra*ʿ[55] which, according to Modena

---

[53] Cf. Nancy Lenkeith, "Introduction," in E. Cassirer, P. O. Kristeller, J. H. Randall, *The Renaissance Philosophy of Man* (University of Chicago Press, 1948), p. 385.

[54] Ibid., pp. 387–393.   [55] (Wilno, 1903).

himself, he composed at the age of thirteen and which was first printed in 1596.[56] The pamphlet has the form of a dialogue between Eldad and Medad, the former condemning gambling and the latter defending it. Medad defends gambling from both a sociological and religious point of view. There is nothing wrong in it, he argues. God made men sociable, mutually complementing each other's needs: "One is a tanner, the other a taylor, the third a scribe, a cattlemen, a shepherd," etc., so that by helping each other they make human life easier and more comfortable. It is the Creator's will that men be bound together, "to buy and sell, to give and take, to change and exchange, to profit and gain from each other." Since it has been decreed by heaven that "the flow of money from hand to hand, by whatever means and causes, be the mainstay of human existence on earth," why should gamblers be considered less respectable than merchants? Indeed, they ought rather to be considered better than they, "since all their actions are directed in accordance with the heavenly indications."[57]

It is above all the heavenly emdorsement of gambling that deserves attention. This may, of course, be interpreted in the framework of Modena's strong astrological convictions as indicative of the view that the gambler's fate depends on the heavenly constellations. However, the text contains ample allusions and Biblical references supporting a somewhat different interpretation, one that would bring its train of thought closer to that of the *Qol Sakhal.* Gambling, Medad argues, is not only socially useful; it also has the Creator's approval. "God loves His creatures. He investigated and provided for all their needs, and from His abode He is watching."[58] What seems to be missing in this statement is a word or phrase pointing to God's delight with man's gambling. Otherwise we would have here the exact same philosophy of God and man as in Vives' "Fable" and in the *Qol Sakhal.* Nor may it be farfetched to interpret in this spirit the Biblical passages adduced

---

[56] Cf. *Ḥayyei Yehudah* in *Leqet Ketavim*, p. 66.

[57] *Sur me-Ra‘*, pp. 16–18.

[58] Ibid., p. 16: "...והנה חבה יתרה חמל על יצוריו, אזן חקר ותקן כל צרכיהם וממכון שבתו השגיח".

here in support of gambling. It was in accordance with God's will, he writes, that the lot[59] decided on the Day of Atonement the fate of the two goats (Lev. 16:18). According to the lot the Land of Canaan was ordered to be divided (Num. 26:56). King David declared that God maintains his lot (Ps. 16:5), and "his wise son, Solomon," that "the lot causes contentions to cease" (Prov. 18:18). If "dice" be substituted for "lot", since it is in this sense that "lot" is used in all above examples, the references adduced give ample support to divine endorsement of gambling, a contention the young author so cleverly attempted to prove. Moreover, it is quite possible that the phrase "one lot for God"[60] was inserted here with the frivolous intention of alluding to the notion of a gambling God.[61] Even excluding such an interpretation, the notion of a God benevolently disposed toward man and approvingly watching from above his playful ways on earth, a notion so emphatically brought forth here, is so close to that of the *Qol Sakhal* that it leaves little doubt as to the common origin of both texts. True, the *Sur me-Ra'* does not explicitly contain the view of the *Qol Sakhal* that the purpose of man is to delight the Creator; it strongly adumbrates it, however, or, more precisely, anticipates it both by its emphasis on man's versatility and its divine justification of gambling. In view of the great lapse of time that separates these two writings, the *Qol Sakhal* may be seen as a mature formulation of ideas the origin of which may already be detected in the young Modena.

Having asserted in chapter three his belief in man's freedom of choice as the source of God's delight, the author of *Qol Sakhal* proceeds in chapter four to expound his belief in divine providence. Inasmuch as that delight stems from man's versatility, he conceives of providence as encompassing the full range of man's deeds and thoughts, to their minutest detail. That such a conception is not unreasonable — the author assures us — may be inferred from

---

[59] הגורל.

[60] גורל אחד לה׳.

[61] Noteworthy is the statement of the *Qol Sakhal* that there is no difference between the heavenly and the earthly kingdoms: שלא יבצר מלכותא דרקיעא "ממלכותא דארעא" (p. 11).

watching the chess game, in which each player must keep his eyes
on thirty-two pieces with their numerous possible moves. He further
illustrates God's synoptic knowledge by comparing it with a
mirror in which are reflected the images of all objects in front
of it. Without elaborating he also asserts that there is no contradiction between divine omniscience and man's freedom of choice.[62]
In support of such a conception of providence he quotes Ps. 33,
notably: "The Lord looketh from heaven, he beholdeth all the
sons of man. From the place of His habitation He looketh upon
all the inhabitants of the earth. He fashioneth their hearts alike;
He considereth all their works."

All these ideas, Scriptural substantiation included, clearly point
to Modena as their author. It is almost certain that he was acquainted with the chess game.[63] The simile of "a clear mirror"[64] is
strongly reminiscent of the "polished mirror" in *Sur me-Raʿ*.[65]
There also appears in the latter text the above reference to Ps. 33:
"From the place of His habitation He looketh upon all the inhabitants of the earth".[66] The statement that there is no contradiction
between divine providence and human freedom is also found in
Modena's sermons, *Midbar Yehudah*.[67] Finally, it has already
been pointed out by Reggio that indicative of Modena is the
phrase: "I am not going to be a preacher here."[68]

In chapter five, the author of *Qol Sakhal* asserts his belief in
reward and punishment. Since he will deal with this subject more
extensively in chapter eight, the discussion here is rather brief.
Were there no reward or punishment, he argues, there would be
no purpose to the creation of man; nor would there be any sense

---

[62] *Qol Sakhal*, pp. 9–10.

[63] Cf. *Ziqnei Yehudah*, p. 104, n. 17; N. Libowitz, *Leon Modena* (1901), p. 23·

[64] כמראה בהיר, מראה זך, *Qol Sakhal*, pp. 10, 11.

[65] מראה מלוטש, p. 15.

[66] *Sur me-Raʿ*, p. 16.

[67] In *Qol Sakhal*, p. 10, it is stated: יעמדו יחד ידיעתו ית׳ ובחירת האדם ולא״
תכריח זו את זו.״; in *Midbar Yehudah*, p. 42a, it is stated: וידיעתו לא תבטל״
הבחירה...וזה אינו סותר לזה״. See also, Modena, *Ma'amar Magen v'Ṣinnah*,
ed. A. Geiger (Breslau, 1866), Hebr. sec., bottom of p. 6b.

[68] *Qol Sakhal*, p. 10; *Beḥinath ha-Qabbalah* p. 78.

in man's striving for perfection. He would be equal then to all other creatures, whose actions are predetermined by their unchangeable natures. Man's freedom, however, and the Creator's justice preclude such an assumption.[69]

If the views of the preceding chapters were unique to some extent, this uniqueness subsides in the following chapters, and the views expressed in them are rather conventional and traditional. In chapter six, the author wholeheartedly embraces the belief in the revealed nature of the Torah. Noteworthy is the argument he adduces in its support, reiterating the views of Saʿadyah, Maimonides, Albo and his own older contemporary, Moscato. Dependent as man's destiny is on proper deeds and thoughts and inadequate as his own faculties are in defining them, it was necessary for a divine revelation to take place and furnish man with the means of attaining that goal.[70] Also the conception of the Torah as implicitly containing all human knowledge and the answers to all the problems and situations facing man,[71] seems indebted to the above sources, notably Albo and Moscato.[72]

The *Qol Sakhal*'s chain of reasoning reaches its final links in chapters seven and eight, in which the belief in immortality of the soul and in reward and punishment in the hereafter is expounded. They also offer additional convincing proofs of Modena's authorship of the work.

The problem of the soul, whether mortal or eternal, a mere capacity or a substance, was a central issue in the speculations of the Renaissance. It was usually the Aristotelians who, defining it either as form or capacity, denied immortality; whereas the Platoists and spiritualists, who defining it in terms of a substance with

[69] *Qol Sakhal* pp. 11–12.

[70] Cf. *Qol Sakhal*, chap. 6; Saʿadyah, *Emunot v'Deʿot* (Tel Aviv, 1959), preface, p. 27, III p. 101; Saʿadyah Ga'on, *The Book of Beliefs and Opinions*, trans. Samuel Rosenblatt (Yale University Press, 1948), pp. 31, 145–147; *Moreh* (Sabionetta, 1553), III, 13, p. 137b; J. Albo, *Sefer ha-ʿIqqarim* (Tel Aviv, 1951) preface, p. 5; Yehudah Moscato, *Sefer Nefuṣot Yehudah* (Lemberg, 1859), sermon 14, p. 42; sermon 34, p. 100b, and passim.

[71] *Qol Sakhal*, pp. 12–13.

[72] *ʿIqqarim*, I, 8; *Nefuṣot Yehudah*, sermon 14 and *passim*.

an existence both preceding and surviving that of the body, upheld it.[73]

The arguments of the *Qol Sakhal* on behalf of immortality indicate indebtedness to the thinking of the Neo-Platonists of the
Renaissance. To be sure, before adducing these arguments, the
author first expresses his doubts as to immortality, doubts that
were rather common in the speculations of the sixteenth century.[74]
He writes:

> Since the appearance of man on earth no clear evidence in
> support of immortality has ever been adduced. One who does
> not want to delude himself must admit that so far no decisive
> proof regarding this matter has ever been suggested by any
> scholar, either Jew or Gentile. On the contrary, almost all
> irrefutable proofs are on the side of those who deny it.... Most
> disturbing, indeed frightening, to any Jew is the fact that in
> all books of the Torah there is not one single word to indicate
> a belief in immortality and in an hereafter. Although the Torah
> speaks on several occasions of reward and punishment, it is
> always in material and this-worldly terms.[75]

Having given expression to his doubts, the author goes on to assert
his belief in immortality. Of course, he can offer no conclusive
evidence; he thinks, however, that contemplation on man's essence
and destiny tends to uphold this belief. He suggests three reasons
in its behalf. First, nature, which does not do things in vain,
implanted in man a desire, unattainable in this life, to live forever.
Second, there exists in man an inverse relationship between mind
and body: in old age, as the body grows weaker, the faculties of
the mind grow stronger. Were mind a mere function of the body,
the opposite should rather take place, i.e., with the weakening of
the body, the mind ought to weaken too.[76] Strongest, however, in
his view, is the third reason, derived from man's uniqueness:

73 Cf. I. Barzilay, op. cit., p. 91, n. 93.
74 Cf. E. Renan, *Averroes et l'Averroism* (Paris, 1866), pp. 358 ff.
75 *Qol Sakhal*, p. 14.
76 The Hebrew is rather awkward and possibly distorted : "...והנראה

How is it conceivable that man, who by his mind builds cities, moves mountains, changes the course of rivers, knows the paths of the high heavens and acknowledges God, should in the end perish and disintegrate like a horse, a dog, or fly?

Were this so, man's lot would be worse than that of any other creature, since in addition to being mortal like them, he, in contrast to them, is also conscious of it.[77]

As for the first argument, inferring immortality from the notion or desire of it, or making a state of mind warrant ontology, this is reminiscent of Descartes' method, deriving the existence of God from man's notion of God. It approximates perhaps more, however, the thinking of Marsiglio Ficino, the greatest Italian Neo-Platonist of the second half of the fifteenth century, who made "the general ontological principle that no natural desire can be in vain" warrant the validity of the belief that "the human soul must attain knowledge and enjoyment of God, if not in this life, then in the after-life."[78] Or, more incisively:

As... intelligence and will proceed beyond the ends of mobile things to those things which are stable and eternal, so life itself certainly reaches beyond any temporal change to its end and good in eternity; indeed, the soul could never pass beyond the limits of mobile things either by understanding or by willing, unless it could transcend them by living.[79]

We also find in Ficino the second argument of the *Qol Sakhal* on behalf of immortality. He writes:

It goes without saying that intellect... is perfectly employed much later in life... Indeed, as if it were an end it is granted

---

מתגבורת כחות השכל לעת הזקנה וחולשת הגוף. שאם היה בו הקשר החלק השכלי
הקשר עכוב לא הקשר מציאות היה הדבר בהיפך, ובהחלש כחות הגוף יחלש גם הוא"
Qol Sakhal, p. 14.

[77] Ibid., pp. 14–15.

[78] Josephine Burroughs, "Introduction" to excerpts from Ficino in *Renaissance Philosophy of Man.* pp. 191–192.

[79] Ibid., pp. 198–199.

only after the vegetable powers and senses have been exercised
...Moreover, sense seems to be dulled in a certain manner by
advancing age, whereas intellect is certainly by no means
dulled.[80]

More direct and substantial is the evidence regarding Modena's
authorship of the *Qol Sakhal* which one may derive from chapter
eight. In it, as mentioned, the author rounds out his "system."
He reiterates the basic ideas he had expressed earlier: man's freedom of choice, the versatile and unpredictable nature of his actions,
and the Creator's delight with them. He devotes most of the chapter,
however, to the problem of reward and punishment. As may be
recalled, he had already expressed his general belief in this principle
in chapter five. He now elaborates upon it, explaining why reward
and punishment cannot take place during man's temporal existence
and must be reserved for the hereafter.

As a composite of body and soul, two elements so diametrically
opposed to each other, man is a constant battleground of contradictory inclinations, the subject of ceaseless struggles within himself. Man's tragedy, however, stems less from the struggle itself
than from the fact that its outcome, at least as far as his temporal
existence is concerned, is entirely independent of himself and his
behavior. Everything pertaining to the temporal aspects of his
existence, such as family, wealth, honor, power, etc., is predetermined by the astral constellations under which he is born, and
cannot in the least be changed. There is thus no relationship between his morality or immorality and his temporal success or
failure. As a result, man's existence in this life is not only frequently
miserable but also confusing, as he is at a loss to choose between
good and evil. Yet, this fatalism notwithstanding, man remains
free in his choices and decisions, but it is only in after-life that the
direct relationship between deeds and consequences prevails, and
it is only there that the injustices of fate are rectified, with the
pious reaping the reward for his piety and the wicked undergoing
punishment for his wickedness. This is the divine scheme of things,

[80] Ibid., p. 205.

and it cannot be any different. Were man to be rewarded or punished in this life,

> all people would be following the same path and law; they would all be striving for one and the same goal, the result of which would be that the multiplicity and versatility of man's deeds, thoughts, religious creeds, etc. would all disappear, and with it divine delight and entertainment, the foundation of all creation.[81]

There is almost no idea in this chapter which does not have a parallel in the writings of Modena. The astrological convictions, to begin with, so strongly displayed here, appear in almost all of his writings, beginning with his *Sur me-Ra'* and ending with his autobiography.[82] Moreover, they are even expressed in terms that are very similar to and frequently identical with those of the *Qol Sakhal.*[83]

As for man's versatility, we saw it strongly stressed in *Sur me-Ra'* as the mainstay of human society. Indeed, he even expressed it there in terms that are very similar to those he was to use, so many years later, in the *Qol Sakhal.*[84]

---

[81] *Qol Sakhal*, p. 16.

[82] Cf. *Sur me-Ra'*, chap. 6; *Midbar Yehudah* (1602), p. 4, *Drush l'Purim*, esp. pp. 39b, 40a; "Sefer Ben David," in E. Ashkenazi ed., *Ta'am Zeqenim* (Frankfurt am Main, 1854), p. 61; L. Blau, *Modenas Briefe*, Hebr. sec., par 45; *Diwan*, ed. S. Bernstein, pars. 59, 62, 91 (p. 134), 110 (p. 144); *Ḥayyei Yehudah*, ed. A. Kahana (Kiev, 1911), pp. 16, 19, 20, 35, 50 and passim: "Tefillat Yesharim," in *Leqet Ketavim*, p. 105.

[83] Thus: "בסבות שניות ימשלו", *Qol Sakhal*, p. 16, also appears in "Tefillat Yesharim," *Leqet Ketavim*, p. 105; "יטו ולא יכריחו", *Qol Sakhal*, p. 16, is also found in the autobiography, *Leqet Ketavim*, p. 76; the view that fateful to man is the constellation at his birth: "והשפעתם על האיש ההוא בעת הריונו ולדתו", *Qol Sakhal*, p. 16, is similar to "בלידת האשה יש מכלם", *Midbar Yehudah*, p. 40a.

[84] Were man to be rewarded or punished in this life, he writes in the *Qol Sakhal*, "ולא היה כי אם דרך אחד ודת אחת לכל האנשים ותכלית אחד לכולם ובטל וסר העונג הנמשך לה׳ מפעולות בני איש בבחירה...שהוא יסוד כל הבריאה" (p. 16), and in *Sur me-Ra'*, p. 16: "כי אם פועל אחד יהיה לכל האנשים תשחת הארץ ויושביה". As indicated above, the only difference between the two texts is

It remains for us now to find in the writings of Modena parallels to the crowning notion of the *Qol Sakhal* regarding reward and punishment in the hereafter and why this must be so. Such parallels are amply displayed in Modena's sermons and it is puzzling, indeed, how they escaped the notice of scholars dealing with Modena. He writes in one of them:

> Were man like God to know the good or evil in store for him and the results of his actions, there would not be even one single individual who would have to regret anything he did. Everyone would then be acting in such a way as never to have any regrets.[85]

Or again, in somewhat different terms:

> God wanted to reward His creatures. He therefore concealed the future from them, so that everyone, by exerting his mental faculties, would be rewarded in accordance with his achievements.... Were everything revealed and known, and the good openly displayed, there would then be no room for any reward.[86]

The notion of man as a battleground between opposite tendencies and passions, his great difficulty in making wise choices and decisions in the face of the hidden nature of the future, and the reward and punishment in store for him in the hereafter, are the major themes of Modena's sermons for *Shabbat Naḥamu* as well as for the *Shabbat* preceding *Rosh ha-Shanah*.[87]

Our analysis of the first treatise of the *Qol Sakhal* thus leads to only one conclusion, namely, that it is wholly the work of Modena. All its ideas and emphases: the uniqueness of man, his freedom of

---

that the earlier one does not cite the divine delight as the reason of man's versatility. However, being a youthful work, Modena had not yet reached such a sophisticated and skeptical conclusion, though, as pointed out, it is already strongly adumbrated.

85 *Midbar Yehudah*, sermon for *Shabbat Naḥamu*, p. 7b.

86 Ibid., pp. 8b, 9a.

87 Ibid., pp. 14b ff.

choice and versatility, on the one hand, and his being dominated by the stars, on the other, both its denial and affirmation of immortality, its optimism and pessimism, and, finally, its unique conception of the Deity in its relationship to man, are not only for the most part explicitly stated in the writings of Modena, but are also most naturally attributable to him and in full harmony with his personality, as it so clearly emerges from his writings and activities.

Typical of Modena, indeed a reflection of his restless and dynamic personality, is above all his conception of God, bored in His heavenly abode and in need of man's versatility and unpredictability for His entertainment. He himself, throughout most of his life, was leading a very restless existence, constantly changing his occupations and busying himself with numerous projects. Scholarly solitude and detachment were never his ideals. He lived in the open, in communication with all kinds of people, Jews and Gentiles, scholars and laymen, preaching and teaching, writing books and endorsements of books of others, gambling and arguing, at times grieved and at times entertained, and so on and so forth. He wrote a great deal on a variety of subjects, but always in haste, as if unable to concentrate too long on any one subject.

God, he thought, loves man, singling him out from all His creatures. But so did Modena. He was a humanist not only by his artistic pursuits and refined taste, but, in the deeper sense of the term, by his love of man and his marvel at him. Like Socrates of old, he had no interest in nature, but in man. When a youngster of sixteen, in the provincial Montaghana, and rebuked by his step-brother from Ancona for not writing more frequently, he replied:

> Were I like you, in a big city of scholars and writers, the destination of ships and people from distant lands, of merchants bringing news from all over the world, and where the deeds of the mighty become known every hour and minute, I would write to you so much that the carriers would not be able to carry.... Unfortunately, I live in the province, a place of cattle, fields and vineyards, with no traffic or news. What should I

write to you about? The chirping of the birds? The bellowing
of the oxen, or the harvest time, whether it has arrived or
not?[88]

Modena thought that God was entertained by man, and that
pleasure was the purpose of creation. I know of no other Jew
of the Renaissance period to whom such notions can be more
naturally attributed than to Modena. They seem least of all asso-
ciable with so serious and gloomy a person as da Costa. Let us
only recall how attracted Modena was by the lighter and esthetic
aspects of human existence and how frequently and strongly he
emphasized pleasure as their justification. He could see nothing
wrong in playing ball on the Sabbath, in as much as "it causes
pleasure to the young."[89] He regretted that the forthcoming water
games were to take place during the "three weeks, when we are
to mourn the destruction of our Temple and the Holy City;"
nevertheless, he asked his friend to keep him informed as regards
the day set for those games and also reserve a seat for him, since
"everything new is desirable."[90] He pleaded that choir singing be
permitted in the synagogue to make the service more elevated and
attractive.[91] It is possible that he himself conducted a choir and
for a time was the head of a musical academy in the ghetto of
Venice.[92] Indicative of his great appreciation of music is the fact
that when his middle son, Zebulun, was murdered, and he was
stricken with grief and pain, he eulogized him above all for his
"sweet angelic voice... his love of poetry" and his great courage
in defending Jews.[93]

It was the company of men, the exchange of wits and ideas,
the observation of man at play and game, the contemplation of
the beautiful and entertaining that he craved for and which satisfied

---

[88] *Ḥayyei Yehudah* in *Leqet Ketavim*, p. 29.

[89] *Ziqnei Yehudah*, par. 22, p. 40.

[90] "כי כל דבר חדש נכסף," Blau, op. cit., par. 122.

[91] *Ziqnei Yehudah*, par. 6, pp. 15 ff.

[92] *Diwan*, n. 86, p. 131; *Ziqnei Yehudah, mavo*, p. 25.

[93] *Ḥayyei Yehudah* in *Leqet Ketavim*, p. 65.

him most.[94] If he may be labeled an hedonist, his was an hedonism of an esthetic and spiritual, rather than a physical and materialist, kind. He loved the beautiful and intellectual in man, and detested the low and beastly in him. Moreover, it was an hedonism strongly permeated with an element of grief and resignation, clinging to the enjoyable not only for satisfaction, but perhaps even more as a refuge from the dreary and tragic in life. Convinced of the inescapable power of the stars on man, human life appeared to him a sad and tragic affair. Hence he felt that whatever helps to make life more bearable and enjoyable ought to be permitted and encouraged.

It is these attitudes and psychological elements that must be kept in mind in order to realize the background of Modena's unique ideas about God and man. The notion that man was created for the purpose of delighting his Creator may, of course, be interpreted in rather pessimistic and fatalistic terms, as a mere puppy or monkey entertaining its master, but otherwise of no value or purpose in itself. On the other hand, it also yields a more optimist and idealist interpretation, one that emphasizes the uniqueness of man's spirit, and the intellectual heights he is able to reach. It is this dualistic attitude for which support can be gleaned from the writings of Modena.

As far as the other two treatises of the *Qol Sakhal* are concerned, their analysis leads one to the same conclusion, namely, Modena's authorship. The many similarities between these two treatises and the works of Modena, indicated by Reggio, Geiger, Libowitz, Klar, Shmueli and others,[95] cannot be explained in any other way. The attempt of Professor Ellis Rivkin[96] to refute these similarities by pointing out the alleged many differences between the *Qol Sakhal* and the works of Modena, suffers from two major inadequacies:

---

[94] It is interesting to note that among the advantages of gambling he cites the insight its observation offers into the nature of man, *Sur me-Ra'*, chap. 4, pp. 32–33.

[95] B. Klar, "Sha'agath Aryeh 'al Qol Sakhal," *Tarbiz*, XIII (1941–1942), pp. 135–147; E. Shmueli, *Bein Emunah li-Kefirah* (Tel Aviv, 1962), passim.

[96] *Leon da Modena and the Kol Sakhal* (Cincinnati, 1952).

first, he fails to take into account the unique character of the works of Modena with which he compares the *Qol Sakhal*, notably the *Riti*, and, second, he totally ignores the tactics of concealment and camouflage that were prevalent in the writings of the age. Such tactics are typical of almost everything that came from the pen of Yashar of Candia (1591–1655), a younger contemporary of Modena and a kindred spirit. It is equally typical of parts o Modena's *Ha-Boneh*, as indicated by Geiger,[97] and of his *Midbar Yehudah*. Hence, it is an unrealistic approach to attempt to show that Modena could not have been the author of the *Qol Sakhal* since some of its views are in contradiction to those he maintained in his other works. It is not the contradictions that are decisive, but rather the similarities. Taking into consideration the nature of the time and Modena's official status as rabbi and preacher, no other approach would have been conceivable without exposing himself to many dangers. Besides, many of the alleged contradictions Rivkin cites in support of his views, can either be explained or refuted.[98]

Finally, in support of Modena's authorship of the *Qol Sakhal*, two basic characteristics of this work must be pointed out: first, the great Jewish erudition displayed in it, and, second, the deep Jewish nationalism that permeates it. Its author's knowledge of the wide field of Judaica, history, philosophy, literature, but above all Halakhah, is very impressive, and can by no means be ascribed to a man of da Costa's type. Sonne's attribution to da Costa of a knowledge of post-Biblical Judaism has no foundation whatsoever in the primary sources of da Costa's time, and is, indeed, in violation of them.[99] Also disproving Sonne's theory is the deep love of Jews and Judaism that permeates the *Qol Sakhal*, a trait completely alien

[97] A. Geiger, *Leon da Modena* (Breslau, 1856), pp. 17–22.

[98] The present writer has written a more extended analysis of Professor Rivkin's thesis; due to space limitations, however, it could not be included in this essay.

[99] Cf. Gebhardt, op. cit., "Einleitung", p. XXVII: in text, pp. 162, 163, 164, 165, 166: Germ. transl. 173, 174, 176. 177, 178.

to da Costa, but strongly characteristic of all the writings and activities of Judah Aryeh Modena.[100]

We may conclude by noting that, Modena's authorship of the *Qol Sakhal* notwithstanding, it would be wrong to suspect him of duplicity and hypocrisy. We believe that the assertion he made in his last will (written fourteen years before he passed away) to the effect that he was not a hypocrite and that he was 'more fearful of God in secret than in the open"[101] is genuine. Indeed, he was a truthful and honest man; moreover, he also was a devout, religious Jew. Of course, he had his doubts and critical views; however, it is only to the claimants upon a monopoly of absolute piety and truth that such doubts and views may appear heretical.

---

[100] Cf. Blau, op. cit., pars. 14, 19, 123, 139, esp. 147, 151; *Diwan*, pp. 81, 82–83, 90, 118, 120, 200, 201, 204, 212; *Midbar Yehudah*, pp. 9, 10, 11, 33, 35, 36, 37, 46, 82; *Sur me-Ra'*, p. 39; M. A. Schulvass, *Roma vi-Yerushalayim* (Jerusalem, 1944), p. 92.

[101] *Ḥayyei Yehudah* in *Leqet Ketavim*, p. 79.

SCHOLARS' "OPINIONS":
DOCUMENTS IN THE HISTORY OF
THE DROPSIE UNIVERSITY

MEIR BEN-HORIN

AMONG THE PUZZLES which my study of the Solomon Schechter —
Mayer Sulzberger correspondence left unsolved was the meaning
of the following line in Schechter's letter of 23 March 1906: "I
enclose here the 'Opinion'."[1] Nothing, unfortunately, was attached
to the original document before me. It was not until nearly two
years after the rediscovery of Schechter's letters to Judge Sulzberger[2] that I happened to find not only his own "Opinion" but also
the "Opinions" of twenty other persons.

These documents turned out to be responses, by some of America's leading scholars in certain fields, by topflight academic administrators, and by religious and lay leaders, to a confidential circular
letter which had been addressed to them and several others by the
Judge. The "Opinions" returned by the scholars in the group are
presented in the following pages. I have in mind publishing the
equally valuable remainder in the not too distant future.

The polling of opinions had been decided by the Governors' first
meeting, held in the home of the Judge on 7 November 1905. At
this meeting there were present Cyrus Adler,[3] William B. Hackenburg,[4] and the Judge — three of the five Governors appointed in

1 See note 67 in my "Solomon Schechter to Judge Mayer Sulzberger: Part II.
Letters from the Seminary Period (1902–1915)," *Jewish Social Studies*, XXVII
(1965), 90.

2 "Solomon Schechter to Judge Mayer Sulzberger: Part I. Letters from the
Pre-Seminary Period (1895–1901)," *Jewish Social Studies*, XXV (1963), 249–86.

3 Adler (1863–1940) served as president of Dropsie College for Hebrew and
Cognate Learning from 1908 until his death. The name of the College was
changed to The Dropsie University on 1 September 1969.

4 Hackenburg (1837–1918) was a founder of The Jewish Publication Society
of America, the first president of the Jewish Chautauqua Society, a founder

Moses Aaron Dropsie's Testament of 17 September 1895 for the management of the college whose establishment was "ordered and directed" in that Testament.[5] While the Judge, who chaired the first meeting of the Governors and appeared in the Dropsie Testament as an executor, had signed the circular letter, Dr. Adler, "Clerk pro tem" of the meeting, had prepared the draft of the minutes and of the letter.[6]

The minutes refer to the understanding "that the Chairman might in his discretion increase the number" and list the following as possible recipients of the circular letter: "Andrew D. White,[7] Daniel C. Gilman,[8] Solomon Schechter,[9] Kauffman [sic] Kohler,[10] Henry

of the Federation of Jewish Charities in Philadelphia, and a leader of Reform Judaism who presided over the early conferences of the Union of American Hebrew Congregations. Under his presidency, the Jewish Hospital in Philadelphia became "one of the best equipped, one of the best managed" in Pennsylvania. Cf. Mayer Sulzberger in *Publications of the American Jewish Historical Society*, XXVIII, 282–284; Joseph Krauskopf in Grand Lodge of Free and Accepted Masons of Pennsylvania, *In Memoriam... William B. Hackenburg* (1918); Herbert Parzen, "New Data on the Formation of Dropsie College," *Jewish Social Studies*, XXVIII (1966), 140. Cf. also Maxwell Whiteman, *Mankind and Medicine: A History of Philadelphia's Albert Einstein Medical Center* (Philadelphia, 1966), passim.

[5] According to Adler's draft of the minutes of this meeting, one of those named in the Testament, Oscar S. Straus, "was unavoidably prevented from being present" and the other, Dr. Aaron Friedenwald of Baltimore, predeceased Dropsie in 1902.

[6] The late Abraham A. Neuman (1890–1970), who served as president of Dropsie College from 1941 to 1965, writes in his *Cyrus Adler: A Biographical Sketch* (New York, 1942), pp. 103f., that the publication of the Dropsie Testament "brought in its wake a flood of comment in the Jewish press, and... innumerable suggestions were visited upon the governors from persons who had their own pet schemes to promote or interests of their own institutions to advance." But the Sulzberger-Adler circular makes it clear that at least a portion of the suggestions offered had been solicited by the Governors.

[7] White (1832–1918) was president of Cornell University.

[8] Gilman (1831–1908) was first president of Johns Hopkins University.

[9] Schechter (1848[?]–1915) was president of The Jewish Theological Seminary of America from 1902 to his death.

[10] Kaufmann Kohler (1843–1926) was president of the Hebrew Union College 1904–1922.

M. Speaker,[11] Dr. Sachs,[12] Francis Brown,[13] Francis L. Patten [sic],[14] S. P. Langley,[15] Arthur T. Hadley,[16] George F. Moore,[17] C. H. Toy,[18] B. L. Gildersleeve,[19] Henry Hyvernat,[20] Charles P.

[11] Speaker (1868–1935), principal of Gratz College in Philadelphia, served as instructor in Bible and Talmud at The Jewish Theological Seminary of America and as first president of the Seminary's alumni association. He contributed entries to the *Jewish Encyclopedia.*

[12] Julius Sachs (1849–1934) was professor of secondary education at Teachers College, Columbia University. He served as president of the American Philological Association and of the Association of Colleges and Secondary Schools of the Middle Atlantic States.

[13] Brown (1849–1916) was professor of Hebrew from 1890 and president from 1908 of the Union Theological Seminary in New York City. Adler in his *Lectures, Selected Papers, Addresses* (Philadelphia, 1933), pp. 284 f., writes that we owe him "the first regular teaching in Assyriology" offered in America.

[14] Francis Landey Patton (1843–1932) was president of Princeton University. He served as professor of the relations of philosophy and science to the Christian religion. Among his books is *Fundamental Christianity* (New York, 1926).

[15] Samuel Pierpont Langley (1834–1906) died 20 days after the date of Sulzberger's circular. He was secretary of the Smithsonian Institution from 1887, a noted physicist and designer of airplanes. See Adler, op. cit., pp. 1–26; also id., *I Have Considered the Days* (Philadelphia, 1941), p. 251: "I had become a sort of immediate unofficial aide to Mr. Langley."

[16] Arthur Twining Hadley (1856–1930) was professor of political science and from 1899 to 1929 president of Yale University.

[17] George Foot Moore (1951–1931) was Frothingham professor of the history of religions at Harvard. He delivered a ten-lecture course at Dropsie early in 1911 on "Judaism at the Beginning of the Christian Era." These lectures he later incorporated in his *Judaism,* published in two volumes in 1927. Cf. my "Cyrus Adler and Adolf Büchler Correspondence (1910–1938)," *American Jewish Historical Quarterly,* LVI (1966), 210.

[18] Crawford Howell Toy (1836–1919) was professor of Hebrew and Oriental languages at Harvard University. A bibliography of his writings, prepared by Harry Wolfson, appears in David Gordon Lyon and George Foot Moore, eds., *Studies in the History of Religious,* Presented to C. H. Toy by Pupils, Colleagues, and Friends (New York, 1912).

[19] Basil Lanneau Gildersleeve (1831–1924) was professor of Greek at Johns Hopkins University from 1876. He edited *The Apologies of Justin Martyr* (New York, 1877) and published such works as *Hellas and Hesperia, or The Vitality of Greek Studies in America* (New York, 1909). Adler, *I Have Considered,* p. 50, reports that he enjoyed Gildersleeve's friendship.

[20] Henri Hyvernat (1858–1941) was professor of Biblical archaeology and

Grannan,[21] C. C. Torrey,[22] Morris [sic] Bloomfield,[23] Jacob Voorsanger,[24] Jacob H. Schiff,[25] Bernard Bettman,[26] Richard Gottheil,[27]
Morris Jastrow,[28] Paul Haupt,[29] Marx Margolis,[30] Rabbi Leventhal

Semitic and Egyptian languages and literatures at the Catholic University in
Washington, D.C. He served as consulting editor of the *Jewish Encyclopedia*.
Adler, op. cit., p. 54 says he formed "a close friendship" with him.

[21] Charles P. Grannan (1846–1924), professor of sacred scripture, Catholic
University of America, since 1892, was appointed vice-rector of the same ins-
titution in 1905/6. Pope Leo XIII appointed him American member of the
International Pontifical Commission on Biblical Studies, and Pope Pius X made
him domestic prelate in 1911. His major work is *A General Introduction to the
Bible*, 4 vols. (St. Louis, Miss., 1921).

[22] Charles Cutler Torrey (1863–1956) was professor of Semitic languages at
Yale University. His *The Jewish Foundations of Islam* (New York, 1933) was
republished, with a critical Introduction by Franz Rosenthal, by Ktav Publishing House (New York, 1967). In 1970, Ktav republished Torrey's *Ezra Studies*
and *Pseudo-Ezekiel and the Original Prophecy*, with prolegomena by W. F.
Stinespring and Moshe Greenberg, respectively.

[23] Bloomfield (1855–1928) was professor of Sanskrit and comparative philology at Johns Hopkins University, 1881–1926. See Adler, op. cit., p. 166
and *Who Is Who in American Jewry* 1926, q.v. He translated *Hymns of the
Atharva-veda* (Oxford University Press, 1897) and wrote *The Religion of the
Veda* (New York, 1908).

[24] Voorsanger (1852–1908) was a Reform rabbi at Philadelphia and, chiefly,
at San Francisco, California. He served as professor of Semitic languages and
literatures at the University of California from 1894 to 1908.

[25] Schiff (1847–1920) was a noted financier and philanthropist and a founder
of the American Jewish Committee.

[26] Bernhard Bettman (1834–1915) was a founder of the Hebrew Union College and president of its Board of Governors 1875–1910.

[27] Gottheil (1862–1936), professor of Semitic languages at Columbia Uni-
versity, was one of the founders of the Jewish Institute of Religion in New
York City. See Louis I. Newman, "Richard J. H. Gottheil," *American Jewish
Year Book*, XXXIX (1937), 29–46.

[28] Jastrow (1861–1921) was professor of Semitic languages at the University of Pennsylvania. His brother Joseph married Henrietta Szold's sister Rachel.
Adler was a close friend of the Jastrows.

[29] Haupt (1858–1926), director of the Oriental Seminar at Johns Hopkins
University and, in Adler's words, "one of the most distinguished Orientalists
of his time," was Adler's teacher (Adler, *I Have Considered*, passim).

[30] Max Leopold Margolis (1866–1932) served on the Hebrew Union College faculty and, for 24 years, was professor of Biblical philology at Dropsie

[sic],[31] Dr. Benderly,[32] Dr. B. Felsenthal,[33] Joseph Jacobs,[34] Prof. Morris Loeb."[35]

College. Although Adler was opposed to Zionism, he invited Margolis (and Henry Malter) to Dropsie: "This action was a measure of Dr. Adler's liberalism which... enhanced academic freedom in Jewish institutions of higher learning" (Herbert Parzen, *Architects of Conservative Judaism* [New York, 1964], pp. 97 f.).

[31] Bernard Louis Levinthal (1864–1952) was the leading orthodox rabbi of Philadelphia and, in Adler's words, "a great power, not only in the City of Philadelphia... but throughout the entire country" (*Sefer Kevod Ḥakhamim* in Honor of Rabbi Levinthal's Seventieth Birthday [Philadelphia, 1935], p. 5).

[32] Samson Benderly (1876–1944), often identified as "the father of modern Jewish education in America," was director of the Bureau of Jewish Education of the New York Kehillah. Cf. my "From the Turn of the Century to the Late Thirties" in Judah Pilch, ed., *A History of Jewish Education in America* (New York, 1969), pp. 70–76. There can be no doubt that a Benderly "Opinion" *was* received by Judge Sulzberger. In a letter of 1 October 1906 to him, Adler explicitly referred to "Dr. Benderly's scheme," "Benderly's method," and "the proposed plan of Dr. Benderly's." The entire letter dealt with the Dropsie Bequest and the purposes of its implementation. According to Professor Solomon Grayzel of The Dropsie University, Benderly sought to create an experimental school of Jewish education and tried to persuade the executors of the Dropsie Will to establish such an institution with Dropsie's Bequest. Adler was opposed to the idea, Harry Friedenwald favored it. As a consequence of this controversy, Adler and Friedenwald ceased to be on speaking terms. — For a characterization of Benderly by probably the most important of the "Benderly boys" see Alexander M. Dushkin, "Antaeus — Autobiographical Reflections," *American Jewish Archives*, XXI (1969), 113–139.

[33] Bernhard Felsenthal (1822–1908) was a Reform rabbi in Chicago. As early as 1888 he recommended to Adler the formation of a Jewish Historical Society (Adler, *Lectures*, p. 189). On his interest in Jewish education see Aaron Soviv, "Bernhard Felsenthal, A Great American Jewish Educator," *Jewish Education*, XXV (1954), 35–41, 64. Mordecai M. Kaplan's *Judaism as a Civilization* (New York, 1934) opens with a Felsenthal quotation in which Judaism is defined as "the composite of the collected thoughts, sentiments and efforts of the Jewish people."

[34] Jacobs (1854–1916) served as professor of English and rhetoric at The Jewish Theological Seminary of America. He was a close friend of Solomon Schechter.

[35] Loeb (1867–1912), professor of chemistry at New York University, was a trustee of The Jewish Theological Seminary of America from its foundation, a founder of the American Jewish Committee and of the Educational Alliance

Two additional men were considered but apparently dropped: Professor William James and Professor Hugo Münsterberg, both of Harvard University. Their names are deleted, in ink, by Adler.

The "Opinions" are of considerable interest for a number of reasons. To begin with, most of the respondents played important roles in the development of American higher education, of American scholarship in Near Eastern linguistic and historical research, of the American version of *Wissenschaft des Judentums*. Their views on what today would be called meaningful graduate education may be of practical as well as historical significance. Many a recommendation made in 1906 remains a desideratum today.

Secondly, the responses themselves are often carefully formulated statements reflecting their authors' views on such topics as professional as contrasted with academic education; faculty qualifications; subject matter priorities and desirabilities; graduate school requirements for efficient operation and high-standard performance; relations between smaller colleges and large universities; and inter-institutional competition and cooperation.

In the third place, even though more than six decades separate us from these documents, the persistence of most of the problems to which they refer assures them a topical and an historical importance. Their publication may reopen the discussion of issues whose wider range was not yet visible in 1906 but whose solution should not be postponed to the end of the century. An example may be the question of the proper relationship between, on the one hand, academic institutions concerned with scholarly excellence and intellectual independence or academic freedom and, on the other, theological schools which must prepare spokesmen for particular faiths, movements, denominations, or versions within larger persuasions. Behind this issue looms that of the partisanship of evidence-bound or scientific scholarship as against the partisanship or "commitment" of, say, orthodox, conservative, or reform schools and interpretations of Judaism, its history, literature, and institutions.

as well as a member of the New York Board of Education (cf. Cyrus L. Sulzberger, "Morris Loeb," *PAJHS*, XXII [1914], 225–227).

Another example would be the very meaning of *Wissenschaft des Judentums*. In the Dropsie College Founder's Day address of 2 June 1940, the first after the death of Cyrus Adler, Abraham A. Neuman, who was to serve as Dropsie's president from 1941 to 1965, declared that "the faith which inspired the founders of *Jüdische Wissenschaft* is the basic philosophy of the work of the Dropsie College. This College is dedicated to the principles of the science of Judaism."[36] And the science of Judaism "means simply the application of scientific method to the study of the Jewish past,"[37] i.e., the eliciting of new knowledge about the Jewish people of old. Such knowledge, Neuman asserted, "gave heart to a wavering generation. It restored their faith in Judaism and therefore in themselves."[38] In 1967, Neuman repeated this position as he looked back on a quarter of a century in the life of the College: "...ideologically, the Dropsie College is the offspring of... *Jüdische Wissenschaft* or *Die Wissenschaft des Judenthums*....[39] A direct line of scholarly succession may be drawn from Leopold Zunz, the father of the *Jüdische Wissenschaft*, to the scholars and schoolmen who directed and elaborated the program of the College from its earliest beginnings to this day."[40] To be sure, Jewish scholarship will always

[36] Neuman, *Landmarks and Goals* (Philadelphia, 1953), p. 284.

[37] Ibid., p. 283.

[38] Ibid., p. 284.

[39] Neuman "The Dropsie College for Hebrew and Cognate Learning — Basic Principles and Objectives," *The Seventy-fifth Anniversary Volume of the Jewish Quarterly Review* (Philadelphia, 1967), p. 19.

[40] Ibid., p. 20. Cf. also Solomon Zeitlin, "Seventy-five Years of the *Jewish Quarterly Review*," ibid., p. 67: The *JQR* editorship "strongly believed that history — *magistra vitae* — is the teacher of life." On the history of *Jüdische Wissenschaft* see Julius Guttmann, "Jüdische Wissenschaft — Die Akademie für die Wissenschaft des Judentums," *Der Jude*, 7. Jhrg. (Berlin, 1923), pp. 489–492; id., "Die Akademie für die Wissenschaft des Judentums — Zu ihrem zehnjährigen Bestehen," *Festgabe zum zehnjährigen Bestehen der Akademie 1919–1929* etc. (Berlin, n.d.), pp. 3–17; Heinz Mosche Graupe, *Die Entstehung des modernen Judentums — Geistesgeschichte der deutschen Juden, 1650–1942* (Hamburg, 1969), ch. 14, "Die Wissenschaft des Judentums," pp. 183–203. The latter, I note, refers to various sources which warn against a "theologization" of Jewish scholarship.

play an important role amidst Jewish intellectual activity. But today questions such as the following keep calling for new answers: Shall scholars of Judaism continue working essentially along the lines of their nineteenth and early twentieth century predecessors? Must they, in the main, be past-oriented? Is their chief obligation indeed the recovery and restoration of Jewish antiquity and the Jewish Middle Ages? Does such a science of Judaism in fact restore the faith of late twentieth century Jews? Does it give heart, as Neuman put it, to our generation and to our children?

Three master questions, I believe, are of vital concern for every member of the Jewish community and the Jewish people: What kind of a people are we? How did we come to be what we are? Where, as a people, do we want to go?[41] If this is so, the question before Jewish scholarship is whether it should address itself solely to the second but hardly to the first and not at all to the third of these central or focal directions of inquiry. Stated differently, must the determination of the Jewish future be left entirely to non-scholars — to the uninformed, the misinformed, and to those of nonscholarly partisanships? Is there, indeed, no escape from the conception of scholarly activity as one belonging to the self-decorative arts, providing enviable careers for those engaged in it, but furnishing little of applicatory value to the rest of society which must grope its way through current crises toward a better life vaguely perceived? Or can we reconstruct the very idea of "Jewish science" so that its major questions may come to refer to current realities and future conditions[42] and that its answers speak of alternative

[41] See my *Common Faith — Uncommon People* (New York, 1970), p. 163.

[42] Writing in *Essays on Jewish Life and Thought* — Presented in Honor of Salo Wittmayer Baron, edited by Joseph L. Blau et al. (New York, 1959), Shelomo M. Gelber asked, "Does the Jewish Past Have a Future?" (pp. 251–264). My question reads: Does the Jewish Future Have a Future in Jewish Scholarship? Dr. Eliezer Rieger (1896–1954) of the Hebrew University's Department of Education put it this way in an address on "The Hebrew University and the Future of the Jewish People," given in South Africa in 1942: "...we therefore... expect that our Hebrew University will perform the same function in the twentieth century as the *Yeshiva* of Yavneh did in the second, — but with this difference: Yavneh taught the Jewish people how

possibilities and the best defensible courses of action for the Jewish people in its local and regional communities the world over and in the State of Israel, the major laboratory of its genius?[43]

A third unsolved problem on which the "Opinions" touch and which merits fuller consideration is that of the range of studies properly offered in an institution of higher Jewish learning. Some of the respondents recommend that Greek and Latin be included among the courses offered by the new Dropsie College, while others speak of archaeology and bibliography. But what of other languages, other disciplines? What of Jewish sociology, Polish, Russian, Rumanian, Hungarian, German? Jewish life and culture in the lands in which these tongues predominate match those in the Arabic-speaking countries and ages and those of antiquity. What of the arts? Is there no record to be uncovered here, no new record to be established? Modern schools of higher learning cultivate the practice of all the arts — why not schools of higher Jewish learning also? The question that is being raised is whether the Jewish people's return to whole-life existence in *Eretz Yisra'el* can be followed by the Jewish scholar's return to whole-life concerns instead of a continuation of self-immurement in the pre-emancipation and post-emancipation subject matter to the exclusion of inquiry into the question of how to ensure not only the life of study but studies of ongoing life. Little wonder, then, that the idea of a "Jewish University of America" is made explicit in at least one of our documents.

****

The documents are presented without substantial changes. I have usually omitted routine addresses of respondent and recipient, open-

to live after the destruction of the Second Temple; the Hebrew University will lead the way to Jewish life in the Third Commonwealth" (quoted from the doctoral dissertation on Eliezer Rieger by Alvin Mars, submitted at The Dropsie University, Division of Education, 1970, ch. 6, note 23). — Cf. also Mordecai M. Kaplan, *Judaism as a Civilization* (New York, 1867 [1934]), p. 44.

43 Relevant to these comments is Solomon B. Freehof, "American Jewish Scholarship," in Theodore Friedman and Robert Gordis, eds., *Jewish Life in America* (New York, 1955), pp. 155–169. See esp. Zalman Shazar, אורי דורות (Jerusalem, 1971), pp. 389–394.

ing salutations and complimentary closings, references at the beginning of the response to receipt of the Judge's confidential circular.
Also omitted are sub-headings and lengthy statements which repeat
what other respondents have already said equally well or which
have lost all topical interest (e.g., suggested salaries). Omissions are
indicated by [...]. The "Opinions" are presented in alphabetical
order; identification of the respondents is given in the notes to the
list of names appearing in the document cited on p. 168 ff. above.

I am glad to contribute this modest study to the Jubilee Volume
honoring Professor Salo W. Baron on his seventy-fifth birthday.
For over a quarter of a century he has been my teacher, mentor,
and friend. I count among my prized possessions the personal portion I own of the vast indebtedness of the Jewish people to this
Master Reader and Caller of the Generations. To the reality of
Dropsie College anticipated in the "Opinions" he added the luster
of his name when in 1962 he became its honorary alumnus. May
he be granted ample time to continue his monumental work and
to enjoy its fruition.

1.

February 2, 1906.
... The highest kind of study of language, and literature, and religion, in any form, bearing upon any people of the human race,
is an aim that must from the beginning hold the sympathy of enlightened men. I am not at all an expert, or even a student of these
matters in the special domain of the Semites: I can speak only
as one who is interested in precisely the same matters from other
ethnical point of view [sic].

If I can make a recommendation at all it is this: Make the school
a seat of enlightened Jewish learning; let it live its life divorced
from dogmatic assumptions and prejudices; treat Jewish learning
precisely in the same way as you should wish to see treated the
knowledge about similar matters in Babylonia, or Greece, or India.
What ultimate gain can there be in disguisement, sententialism, or
mystification?

As regards the teachers: the College will be no more and no less than the sum of the intellectual accomplishments of its teachers. I should not choose teachers but thinkers; I should not choose those that speak glibly to the gallery, but profound scholars that look for the truth first, last, and all the time.

Now I believe that is all I can say to you, standing, as I do, very much on the outside. Your board is a body of enlightened men: I believe that the foundation is in the best hands; I hope to hear in due time of an institution of true, liberal learning. [...]

MAURICE BLOOMFIELD.

2.

New York, February 10, 1906.

... It seems a pity that the intention of Mr. Dropsie was not known prior to the establishment of the Jewish Theological Seminary of America, in New York. A theological seminary must, from the nature of its work, be carefully distinguished from a college, the object of which is learning and investigation. A seminary has to turn out men who will be engaged for the greater part of their lives in pastoral, pulpit, and economic work. In this country, the calls upon the minister's time and effort are so numerous and so many-sided, that it becomes practically impossible for him to think of serious scientific work when once he had entered upon his active duties. This is not so true of the rabbinical position in Europe. There the church and the synagogue do not take part in the public life around them in any such manner or to any such degree as they do in the United States. I have, therefore, for a long time been of the opinion that two separate and distinct courses ought to be established even at our seminaries — one leading to the practical ministry, the other to scientific investigation and research. The Christian seminaries turn out almost exclusively pastors and preachers; and they have this sole object in view. An exception may be made of two or three, as the Union Theological Seminary in New York, and the Harvard Divinity School, which, on account of their intimate connection with a large university, are able to offer courses in co-relation with courses at the University, and which are expressly intended for men who desire to devote their life to such investigation and research. I have, therefore, fully expected to see the Jewish Seminary of America develop such parallel courses. The foundation of the college provided for by Mr. Dropsie, renders one of these courses unnecessary; and I venture to say (though this does not belong within the terms of the reference), that the seminary will have to devote all its energies to the task simply of providing future occupants for synagogue pulpits. A student for the rabbinate naturally must make more extensive studies than must a student for a Christian church pulpit; but it is not at all necessary for him to go into all the minutiae of literary, historical and bibliographic study with which most of our seminary curricula are weighted down.

I feel quite certain that if the new institution is laid down upon the lines that I have in mind, even the eventual $800,000 with which it will be endowed will prove insufficient. [...]

A further question that I think arises naturally in one's mind, is in regard to the future positions of those who pass through the seminary. They are evidently not to go into the ministry. Where then are they to do their work in the future? There are not enough positions in American universities that are open to Jews, to take up the supply which the new institution will put forth. Only a limited number will find work in our universities. A few more will get teaching positions in the two or more seminaries that may exist in the future. Some place will have to be found for the rest; and I can only imagine that the custom somewhat in vogue in Germany will be found the best — to give to learned men positions at the head of orphan asylums, homes, and the like, where their active duties will be at a minimum and the greater part of their free time for research. [...]

From the provisions of Mr. Dropsie's will I see that he has dedicated for the purposes of the foundation, the premises at the southeast corner of Broad and Somerset Streets in the City of Philadelphia. Mr. Dropsie, however, very wisely has not bound his trustees to a definite course of procedure in this matter. I am very strongly of opinion that such a college for Jewish learning in the City of Philadelphia, ought to be situated as near as possible to the University of Pennsylvania. The college will never be able to give instruction in all branches which are co-related to its work; it ought to make every possible use of the University, and try to enter into as cordial relations as possible with it. I am thinking of relations such as exist between the Union Theological Seminary and Columbia University; which relations permit of regularly matriculated students in either institution taking courses in the other. Each institution ought then to recognize the degrees of the other. Such a contiguity would also make the library of the University of Pennsylvania available to the students of the new college. Without such a general library close at hand, the library of the college will have to be enlarged entirely beyond its means, and entirely beyond the space which its buildings can give to such a purpose. [...]

Candidates for a degree at the new college ought to be required to show the degree of Bachelor of Arts from some college in good standing; and in addition they should be able to pass an examination in Biblical Hebrew and in general Jewish history. [...]

There ought to be three sessions, a Spring, a Summer and a Winter Session; and the work of the students ought to be arranged in some such manner as in the University of Chicago, where special attention is given to a certain definite subject for a number of consecutive weeks. This produces concentration on the one subject, and works against the dissipation of the student's forces. I am rather insistent upon the summer session, as it will enable students to attend who are engaged in other work during the spring and winter months. [...]

The regular course leading to the degree of Doctor of Philosophy [...] should, in my opinion, last for nine sessions. A student working continuously at the college would accomplish this result in three years; while a student who was only able to attend during two of the sessions would take naturally a longer time in acquiring his degree. [...]

The degree of Doctor of Philosophy ought to be conferred upon students who have been in good standing during the nine sessions, who have passed an examination at the end of the course before the faculty or a committee of the faculty, and who have written a thesis approved by the professor in charge of their major subject. Such a thesis must be presented in print to the council of the college.

The only degree that will be conferred is that of Doctor of Philosophy. The examination for this degree may be held at any time at which the institution is in session and shall cover only such subjects as have been selected as major and minors by the candidate. The degrees shall be conferred in public session, on one stated occasion during the year.

The thesis which is written in part[ial] fulfillment of the requirements for the degree of Ph.D. must contain evidence of some original investigation in some branch of the work taught at the college. When accepted it is to be published by the college from the proceeds of a sum of money set apart for that purpose. All theses and all publications of the college are to be a uniform size, so as to present to the world a compact series of the work done in the institution. [...]

The following departments of instruction ought to be established: [...]

Department of Bibliography and the History of Jewish Literature.

The courses to be given in this department should comprise the following:

   a. The history and practice of Hebrew Bibliography.

   b. The history of Hebrew book-making and typography.

   c. The history of Jewish literature. This course is intended to be a general introduction covering the various fields of Jewish science. Special courses, dealing with each individual subject will naturally be given in the respective departments to which they belong.

   d. Seminar in reading and classification of Hebrew mss., with a view to a study of the peculiarities of the script and of the methods of determining the age and provenance of the mss.

Department of Hebrew Philology and Bible Exegesis.

   a. Comparative Hebrew Philology.

   b. A study of Hebrew as a written and spoken language. The instruction in this class to be given in Hebrew.

c. The History of Jewish Bible exegesis, and introduction to the study of the Bible.

d. History of the canon.

e. Exegesis of some particular portion of the Bible.

f. Seminar in Biblical exegesis.

Department of History.

a. Methods of research in Jewish history; study of the original works from which this history is derived with readings in the original.

b. The Biblical period in connection with a study of the geography of Palestine, of Mesopotamia and of Babylonia; the position of Judea in the ancient Semitic world.

c. Biblical archaeology or the results of archaeological research in Palestine and neighboring lands as far as they are connected with the Bible.

d. The post Biblical period down to the destruction of the temple by Titus.

e. History of the Jews from the destruction of the Temple to 1492, with a special excursus on the Jews in Egypt.

f. History of the Jews from 1492 to Mendelssohn.

g. History of the Jews to the 19th century.

h. Seminar in Jewish archaeology.

j. Seminar in some one period of Jewish history.

Department of Philosophy.

a. A general view of the history of Jewish Philosophy in its connection with other systems and its dependence upon them.

b. Theology of the Bible.

c. The Greco-Alexandrian period.

d. The philosophy of the Jews in the Middle Ages, with a special reference to Aristotle and Plato, and the Mohammedan philosophers.

e. The history of the religious and philosophical conflicts within Judaism; Karaism and other sects; the Samaritans; the history of the reform movement.

f. Readings from selected philosophical writers.

g. Jewish ethics in their historical development from Bible times to the present day.

h. Seminar in the study of individual topics, e.g., dogmas, free will, predestination, immortality.

i. Seminar in ethics.

The Department of Rabbinial Literature.

a. History of the development of the Halakah from Biblical times, through the Talmudic and Middle Age period down to our own day.

b. Readings of selected portions from the Mishnah.

c. Readings of selected portions from Talmudim.

d. Readings of selected portions from the Codes.

e. The history of the responsa literature, with illustrative readings from the original.

f. History of the Midrashim.

g. Selected readings from the Midrashim, showing their historical development.

h. Seminar in selected Talmudic topics.

i. Seminary in the study of selected Midrashic topics.

Department of Belles Lettres.

a. Historical development of Hebrew Belles Lettres.

b. Hebrew poetry, its form, its metres, illustrated by selected readings from the various authors.

c. Contes, fables, tales and the like in Hebrew, with illustrative readings from the chief works.

d. Hebrew literature in the 19th century, with special reference to the development of the language as a living tongue.

e. Judaeo-German literature with a grammatical study of the dialect.

f. Judaeo-Spanish literature, with a grammatical study of the dialect.

g. Seminar. Some selected topics of Hebrew Belles Lettres.

Department of Cognate Languages.

a. The Arabic language spoken and written by the Jews in various parts of the Mohammedan world. With selected readings from various authors.

b. Comparative grammar of the Aramaic languages.

c. Readings of selections from the various Targumim, from the Aramaic portions of the Talmudim, and from later works written in Aramaic.

d. Seminar for the study of early Judaeo-Arabic documents.

e. Seminar for the study of Middle Age Judaeo-Arabic literature.

[...] The teaching staff of the institution shall consist of a Dean, full professors, adjunct professors, instructors and lecturers. The salary of a full professor shall be $5,000 a year;[44] that of an adjunct professor $3,000 a year; that of an instructor $1,500 a year; and that of a lecturer $500 a year. No one giving instruction shall be called upon to do more than eight hours of class and lecture work per week. Professors and instructors shall have the right of selecting one term during the year as their period of vacation. Every seven years any professor or instructor may have leave of absence with full pay for any two successive terms which he may choose — providing always that the necessary arrangements can be made so that his work is carried on during his absence.[45] A fund shall be collected for the pensioning of the professors when they shall have reached the age of sixty years and shall have been doing work in the institution for twenty consecutive years.[46]

The faculty, subject to confirmation by the Board of Trustees, shall have charge of all the arrangements connected with the internal working of the institution, and shall have disciplinary power over the students. The dean shall be an ex officio member of the Board of Trustees.

---

[44] These are respectable figures. In his letter of 5 March 1900, Schechter indicated he had agreed to $4,000.00 and "I ought not to bargain now. But," he added, "why should not the thing be done בעין יפה!" (my "Solomon Schechter" etc., Part I, Letter No. 31). A cable, dated 28 October 1901, from Sulzberger to Schechter — I hope to publish Sulzberger-Schechter correspondence — speaks of $5,000 as Schechter's annual salary. Prof. Samuel A. Poznansky asked for a $4,000 salary in 1903 (see my "Cyrus Adler and Ahad Ha-Am Correspondence [1910–1913]," *The Seventy-fifth Anniversary Volume of the Jewish Quarterly Review*, p. 59, n. 6).

[45] Still a desideratum today.

[46] In 1972 a satisfactory pension plan for professors remains to be worked out.

[...] Each student entering as a candidate for a degree of Doctor of Philosophy shall, after his first two terms, select as his work for the degree one major subject and two minor ones. He shall be under the direction of the professor in charge of his major subject, and his thesis for the degree must be written on some point connected with that subject. As one of his minor subjects, he may be allowed to take one of those in the University of Pennsylvania designated as co-related subjects. One year prior to his coming up for his degree, the candidate shall pass an examination in Latin, German and French, in order to convince the faculty of his fitness to use these languages in his research work. A certificate to that effect from the professor in charge of the respective work at the University of Pennsylvania, will be received in lieu of a special examination. [...]

No restrictions are placed upon the student's choice, with the exception of the following:

Every student must take a course in bibliography and in the History of Jewish Literature; every student selecting history as his major must take a course in the methods of historical research at the University of Pennsylvania (if such is given). Every student who selects philosophy as his major must take a course in the University of Pennsylvania on the general history of philosophy. Every student who selects Belles Lettres as his major must take a course in comparative literature, or in literary criticism at the University of Pennsylvania. [...]

There shall be a number of fellowships established, called by appropriate titles such as the Maimonides Fellowship, the Rashi Fellowship; each one of these shall be of the value of $500, and shall not be tenable by one and the same holder for more than two years. [...] One or more traveling fellowships of $750 each shall be established in order to enable the holder to work in the libraries and collections of Europe or to make investigations in any part of the world to which he may be sent.[47]

---

[47] Cf. Jacob Neusner, "Graduate Education in Judaica: Problems and Prospects," *Journal of the American Academy of Religion*, XXXVII (1969), 329.

[...] The institution shall become a regular member of the School of Oriental Research at Jerusalem established by the Archaeological Society of America in conjunction with the American Oriental Society and the Society of Biblical Literature. It shall found a special fellowship in connection with that school in order to enable it at all times to have one of its students studying archaeology in Palestine.

... The library will be the workshop of the new institution; and it ought to contain from 40 to 50,000 volumes.[48] A theological school requires a much smaller collection; and I think it might be possible for the seminary in New York to place at the disposal of the new institution a large part of its own collection for which it evidently has little use. All manuscripts, rare books, collections of periodicals, newspapers and the like, ought to be at the immediate disposition of the professors and students of the Institution in Philadelphia. I doubt whether sufficient money will be forthcoming to enable the institution to make the necessary purchases. I am thinking of some such arrangement as that made by the Montefiore College in Ramsgate, London, with the Jews' College in London. Every effort should be made to collect in the library of the institution a large series of original manuscripts and of other material which may be for sale with which the students are to do their work. For all other books, outside of the most necessary reference works, the institution should depend upon the University of Pennsylvania and should secure from the University all the necessary privileges for the full use of its collection. It must be remembered that the City of New York already possesses two good Hebrew collections, the one at the New York Public Library, the other at Columbia University. The transference of a great part of the library belonging to the Jewish Theological Seminary of America to Philadelphia would therefore not deprive Jewish scholars in New York of the means to prosecute their work.

---

[48] This figure was actually reached some forty years later. See Adolph S. Oko, "Jewish Book Collections in the United States — In Commemoration of the Centenary of Mayer Sulzberger," *American Jewish Year Book*, XLIV (1943), p. 88.

[...] A publication fund ought to be set aside at once, in order to secure a definite income every year for the printing of a quarterly review devoted to Jewish science, the theses of the graduates of the institution, and such other learned works as the publication committee may think desirable.

[...] A special fund is to be set aside for the purpose of aiding research work in any of the departments of which the institution is composed. Such research work need not necessarily be done by the students themselves; but the committee having this fund in charge shall be allowed to subvention such work when it is done by scholars in any part of the world. It should, however, have the right of publishing any and all the results produced by such research. [...]

I am well aware that such a comprehensive plan calls for a much larger endowment than the $800,000 which will eventually become the property of the institution. We shall need some Jewish Carnegie who will be willing to add at least a like sum to the present endowment. [...]

RICHARD GOTTHEIL.

3.

Baltimore, Md. Feb. 3, 1906.

[...] If this institution is to make adequate provision for advanced instruction and original investigation in Hebrew and the cognate languages, the Hebrew Bible and post-Biblical Hebrew Literature, it will be necessary

(1)   To appoint as President of the Institution a competent Talmudic scholar with executive ability. This President, who should be a native of this country if possible, might conduct courses in post-Biblical Hebrew Literature and in Hebrew Conversation. He might also interpret the Targums (see #4). [...]

(4)   The Hebrew Bible cannot be studied in a scientific manner, unless the students are able to compare the Ancient Versions, especially the Septuagint, Targums, Peshita, and Vulgate. The Targums may be interpreted by the President (see #1); but the critical interpretation of the Septuagint and the Vulgate would require the appointment of

(5) A lecturer of Hellenistic Greek and Patristic Latin. [...]

(6) For students who have no knowledge of Greek and Latin it will be necessary to appoint a Philadelphia classical scholar to give elementary instruction in Greek and Latin.

(7) The regular students of the Institution should be college graduates; but other students may be admitted as special students.

(8) Instruction should be provided in Comparative Hebrew Grammar; Comparative History of Religions; History, Geography, and Archaeology of the Ancient East[sic]; Assyriology, Egyptology, Syriac, Arabic, Ethiopic &c. Professor Jastrow[49] and Professor W. Max Muller[50] of Philadelphia might conduct some of these courses; and Professor Gottheil of New York would perhaps be willing to come to Philadelphia once a week to interpret the Peshita and other Syriac texts, or to give some courses in Arabic, &c.

(9) Of special importance would be the establishment of an Old Testament Seminary [sic] for the advanced study of the Hebrew Bible, under the guidance of a competent Old Testament critic, with special reference to textual and literary criticism, metrical and historical questions, &c. Perhaps Professor Brown[51] of the Union Theological Seminary, New York, would be willing to come to Philadelphia once a week for this purpose, although it would be more advisable to appoint a philologian instead of a Christian theologian. It will be hard to find a competent Jewish scholar; men like Geiger and Graetz, D. H. Muller[52] and Perles[53] are scarce;

---

[49] See Documents Nos. 6 and 6 (a) below.

[50] Wilhelm Max Muller (1862–1919), professor of Bible exegesis in the Reformed Episcopal Seminary at Philadelphia and assistant professor of Egyptology at the University of Pennsylvania, was a contributor to the *Encyclopaedia Biblica*, the *Jewish Encyclopedia*, and joint editor of *Gesenius Hebrew Dictionary*.

[51] Note 13 above.

[52] David Heinrich Müller (1846–1912) was professor of Oriental languages at the University of Vienna and professor of Hebrew and Religious philosophy at the Israelitisch-theologische Lehranstalt, Vienna.

[53] Felix Perles (1874–1933), rabbi in Königsberg in Prussia, was a noted Bible scholar.

but it may be possible to train some Jewish scholars at the Dropsie Institute for this purpose.

(10) The appointment of a number of non-resident lecturers would add to the prestige of the institution and would secure the co-operation of distinguished investigators whose services would otherwise not be available. [...]

(12) The President of the College should publish an Annual Report containing original investigations by himself and members of the Faculty.

(13) It would also be well to make arrangements for an annual course of public lectures to be given at the College by members of the Faculty, &c. [...]

(17) If the object of the founder of the Dropsie College is not only to provide opportunity for advanced Semitic instruction in Philadelphia, but to promote thorough and systematic education and ripe scholarship in Jewish lore in general, and original investigation and research in the domain of Hebrew Literature, both Biblical and post-Biblical, and the cognate languages, the Dropsie College should be a "Jewish Carnegie Institution," i.e., it should provide special grants for fellows and research assistants in the Semitic departments of some of our leading institutions, traveling fellowships, Semitic publications (e.g. Ph.D. dissertations of Students of Semitic [sic]) &c. These fellowships need not be assigned to any institution as a permanent subvention: they should rather be awarded to individual students for limited periods, on the recommendation of competent Semitic scholars. Dispersion is a characteristic feature of Judaism, and it would be better to diffuse the benefits of the Dropsie Institution instead of confining them to Philadelphia.

[...]   PAUL HAUPT.

4.

The Catholic University of America
Washington, D.C.

March 29th, 1906.

[...] The founder seems to have realized that between the Jewish Theological Seminary, where Biblical and Rabbinical literatures are taught from a more professional standpoint, and the University Oriental department on the program of which Jewish post-Biblical literature is at best only insufficiently represented, there was room and need for an institution of the type we have described, a kind of "Ecole des Hautes Etudes Juives," where, without distinction of creed or race, young students could be initiated to, ripe scholars carry on, research work in all the branches of Biblical or Jewish post-Biblical literature, with no other end in view than knowledge and truth. Such, I think, ought to be the general scope of the contemplated Institution.

As for the branches to be taught, the program, to attain the primary object of the founder, ought to include:–

(1)   Hebrew in all its stages, viz., Biblical, post Biblical, so-called Rabbinical and modern Hebrew, the last two classes from a practical point of view, the first two from a strictly philological point of view.

(2)   Aramaic, particularly Jewish Aramaic both Palestinian and Babylonian.

(3)   History of the Text and Versions of the Bible, inclusive of the Massorah in its widest acceptation.

(4)   Jewish Hermeneutics.

(5)   History of the Jewish People.

(6)   History of the Jewish Institutions.

(7)   History of Jewish Literature.

[...] I should suggest to the Trustees to get the best men that money can procure, all *University trained men*, not only good teachers but also and above all original thinkers, capable of inspiring and directing research work. Better have few men, but good and well paid, so that they *have not* to do something else *for a living*. Do not, as a rule, ask a professor to teach more than four times a week, as he must devote considerable time to advanced students engaged in research, and moreover, must attend to his own personal studies and publications.

Let every professor in charge of a chair permanently established, have an assistant, to relieve him of the drudgery and routine work.

That assistant must not be of an inferior kind, but such as may, in the future, develop into an original thinker and master.

In the course of time, it may be found advisable to give public lectures of a popular character. Those ought to be given, as a rule, by special men, not by your own professors, as an excellent professor may be a very poor lecturer, and vice versa. [...] Do not count the number but the quality. Beware of the dangers of red tape in the requirements of admission. Let your idea be to turn out scholars, perfect scholars. The publications of your professors and students will give you, in course of time, all the advertising you need, and you will soon have your hands full.

As for the kind of man to be chosen as President, his attributions, his relations to the Board of Trustees on the one side, and to the Faculty and Students on the other side, I beg to refer you to a recent article by Benjamin Andrews in the Educational Review, March 1906, *University Administration*.[54]

I should insist on the necessity of having a good, complete working library, before even thinking of throwing the doors of the institution open to the public. There is no exaggeration in saying that the efficiency of all the other factors of the Institution will [be] in proportion with the excellence of the library. [...]

I hope the above suggestions may prove not entirely useless to you, and, at all events, I beg you to consider them as a token of the good will and kind feeling I entertain toward the Jewish race. [...]

H. HYVERNAT.

5.

New York, March 23rd, 1906.

[...] I have found some difficulty in getting a clear view of the main object aimed at by the testator Mr. Dropsie. From his direction that students should not suffer any distinction on account of creed, color or sex, and his reference to the general utility of Jewish

---

[54] E. Benjamin Andrews, "University Administration," *Educational Review*, ed. by Nicholas Murray Butler, March 1906, pp. 217–15. Much in the essay remains valid to this day, particularly the statement on the qualifications of a university president.

learning, it would appear that he had in mind a secular institution, which would exhibit the highest standing of Jewish learning and thus give it academic rank. Yet, by his reference to the "religion of their ancestors," in the introductory paragraph, to me it would appear that Mr. Dropsie had some theological advantage in view in founding the college.

I do certainly agree that if Jewish learning could be in some way incorporated with the general body of knowledge, regarded as academic by the universities of this great country, advantage would indirectly accrue to the estimate in which the Jewish religion is held.

[...] Indeed it is obvious that any theological color given to the institution would cause it mainly to duplicate Jewish places of learning already existing, before Mr. Dropsie's demise. [...]

Mr. Dropsie had probably in mind Jewish Biblical study, that is, the development of Biblical exegesis among Jewish teachers of all ages from Biblical times. This could not be dissociated from the development of Biblical Law and Legend in the Talmud, or from the Biblical Commentaries of the Middle Ages, subjects which would come under Talmudics and Rabbinics, rather than pure Biblical study. [...]

I should recommend confining the purview of the Trustees to the sides of [the scientific study of Hebrew] not elsewhere represented. Jewish[55] grammar of Hebrew, that is, historical Hebrew grammar, middle and modern Hebrew with a study of dialects Ladino and Yiddish of Cognate languages; I would suggest special attention be paid to Aramaic.

Further, a study of Jewish history in its secular phases should be encouraged by such an institution. This I consider of great importance, since Jewish history touches upon all other modern histories and it is by supplementing other branches of knowledge that special subjects obtain academic recognition. In particular, Jewish history is one long lesson on religious liberty and upon the iniquitous results of the identification of Church and State. If persons

---

[55] The text is probably incomplete here.

interested in Japan find it desirable to have a Professor of Japanese history at Yale, it should surely be worth while of the Jewish people to have Jewish history academically represented. With it might be associated sociological studies on aspects of Jewish life which contrasts with that of the general population and may thus throw light upon general economic and other problems.

Finally the study of Jewish literature as a whole, should form one of the topics of Mr. Dropsie's college, including as subsidiary portions Hellenistic, Judeo-Arabic, Judeo-Persian, Yiddish and Ladino. [...]

If the college is not to be Theological, not to train Rabbis — which would clash with already existing institutions, the object of students could only be either disinterested love of Jewish learning in itself, or the selection of it as an elective topic in one of the university courses; or possibly a few students would care to have what might be termed secular training in Hebrew learning, before proceeding to the Theological Seminaries for a Rabbi's degree. As regards the former, it would be idle to expect more than a few isolated individuals, who like Miss Szold[56] would undergo a severe course of training from pure love of the subject. Jewish learning as an elective course at the university would involve the association of the Dropsie institute with such bodies, an alternative to be considered later. There remains only the previous training of Jewish theological students before they proceed to their special work as Theologians, which would reduce the Dropsie institute to a mere preparatory school for Rabbis and scarcely carry out the high aims indicated in the Will.

There remains, however, one other view of the term student which seems more in constance with the Will, that is, persons studying a subject with a view to original research in it. If the Dropsie institute could be so constructed as to encourage students

---

[56] Henrietta Szold (1860–1945) was admitted to The Jewish Theological Seminary of America in 1902 as a student whose "object was not a rabbinic diploma [but] ...wider knowledge" (Alexander Lee Levin, *The Szolds of Lombard Street* [Philadelphia, 1960], p. 366).

of this type, it would indeed carry out all that its founder could have desired.

[...] Having this last kind of student in mind, it becomes a question whether it would be necessary or desirable to have a definite college with location and faculty for the encouragement of higher Jewish learning. If a separate college were established the cost of equipment, allowing for an adequate library and museum, could not be much less than $200,000 if the requisite dignity and importance is to be given to the subject. This would cripple the resources of the college very greatly in the early years and reduce its efficiency later, and as has been seen above, it would be doubtful whether any definite class of students would attend. The total result, I cannot help thinking, would be a number of "soft snaps" for the faculty and administration. Even if the college was affiliated with the University of Pennsylvania, this could only appeal to the somewhat small circle of Jewish and other students at the University who would be attracted to the subject sufficiently to take post-graduate or elective courses in it.

If the idea of a separate college at Philadelphia be given up, there appeared to me to remain two courses that might be adopted; either an establishment of the Dropsie Professorships in all or some of the subjects indicated above at the seven great American universities. This would indeed give academic standing to the subject, and enable students throughout the country to attend high class lectures upon it, thus carrying out part of Mr. Dropsie's intentions, but on the whole, I am inclined to recommend the Trustees to form a Dropsie Institute for the promotion of higher Jewish learning with their local office at Philadelphia, but with a watching brief to encourage the higher sides of Jewish learning throughout the country by founding professorships at the Universities when the appropriate men appear, by establishing fellowships for special research on subjects in connection with the Universities and theological Seminaries, by subventioning the production of works of original research on Jewish learning, by aiding in the purchase of important books or manuscripts for the great Jewish libraries of this country, by founding prizes for the study of special problems, and in general doing for Jewish learning what the Carnegie Institute is trying to do for the higher science of the country. One advantage of this suggested institute would be the limitation of administrative expenses to a minimum, the avoidance of duplication with existing institutions, and the possibility of crystalizing the work in a more definite form as wider experience is gained in the future. Much of course would depend upon the initiative of the Director of such an institute; but whatever form the Dropsie bequest takes, its success would depend upon the leading mind. [...]

JOSEPH JACOBS.

6.

Philadelphia, Pa., February 13, 1906.
[...] The purpose of the proposed institution is to train scholars without reference to their religious affiliations or their religious bias, and since the will also specifies original investigation and research as one of the purposes of the institution, the opportunity, it seems to me, is afforded to the Board of Governors named in the will to establish in this country a seat of learning of unique character, to-wit: A School, College or Institute (whatever the chosen designation may be), for Semitic Research, in the broadest sense of the term. The full scope of such an Institute would embrace the following sub-divisions:

First: Instruction
Second: Aid to students capable of conducting original investi-
             gations.
Third: Publication of researches. [...]

The following three chairs might suffice, at least for the present, as the permanent section of the faculty, namely:

(a)   A Chair for Hebrew and Biblical Literature.
(b)   A Chair for Rabbinical Literature.
(c)   A Chair for Semitic Languages. [...]

An institute, as here outlined, will naturally appeal to a limited number only, but in addition to those pursuing a systematic course of study, provision might be made for "auditors" or special students interested merely in certain of the courses offered. [...]

Coming to the second division, the encouragement of original investigation, provision should be made for the appointment of Fellows prepared to undertake investigation of some special theme, and also a limited number of Research Fellowships to be offered to such students as have already shown their ability in original investigations and who require aid in carrying out some larger project. While the Fellows of the Institute would naturally be expected to do their work under the direction of the Faculty, the Research Fellows should not be limited in their residence to the city in which the Institute is situated. The opportunity should be afforded the Research Fellows to proceed to centers where the material needed by them would be available, or to undertake explorations or excavations. [...]

The third division will naturally include, primarily, the publication of investigations and researches conducted by members of the Faculty, the Research Fellows and the Fellows, but it should also so far as possible include publications of monographs in the field of Semitic studies offered for publication by those not directly connected with the Institute. The publication of the Researches, representing, as it were, the flower of the entire scheme, should be conducted on the broadest possible basis, so that in addition to direct publication, subventions for works of research, which are too expensive to be published through the ordinary channels, should also be included in this division. [...]

For the carrying out of the first and second divisions of the scheme above outlined, — instruction and encouragement of investigation, an extensive Library and a liberal amount of original material is indispensable. The principle of economy, which applies in the realm of learning, as elsewhere, suggests the avoidance of duplication and the desirability of co-operation. Approached from this point of view, the affiliation between the proposed Institute and the University of the city in which it is situated ought to be as close as possible, so that the students of the institution may keat part of their courses at the University and avail themselves of material there found, while in return the course of the Institute would be open to the students registered at the University.

Assuming that your institution is to be established in Philadelphia, the affiliating or the affiliated Institute would naturally be the University of Pennsylvania, and, while I am not authorized to speak officially, I have reason to believe that the Trustees of the University of Pennsylvania would welcome with interest and sympathy the consideration of such a plan.

[...]   MORRIS JASTROW, JR.

6a.

Philadelphia, Pa., March 8th, 1906.

[...] Will you permit me, if there is still time, to add a brief supplement to my letter to you of February 13th. [...]

It occurs to me that of the three divisions of the scheme for the proposed institution indicated in my letter [...], it might be wiser to lay the *chief* stress upon Research and Publication. This suggestion occurs to me in view of the circumstance, which I had not taken up in my letter, that instruction in the Semitic languages is offered at all of our leading Universities and that, in the nature of things, the majority of students interested in Rabbinical literature will go to one or the other of the two Jewish Theological Seminaries now established in this country.

My thought, therefore, is that the Dropsie Institute of Semitic Research might assume relationship to the Semitic Departments of our Universities and to the Theological Seminaries in question, as that of a post-graduate school in Semitics to that of a graduate department. The Institute would in that case occupy a position somewhat like the Rockefeller Institute of Pathological Research established in New York, the Wistar Institute of Anatomy in this city,[57] or The Johns Hopkins School of Medicine, namely: as offering an opportunity for advanced and already-trained students to take up special lines of research with a view to publication.

---

[57] The Wistar Institute of Anatomy and Biology at the University of Pennsylvania was named in honor of Caspar Wistar, professor of anatomy at the university and successor to Thomas Jefferson as presidento f the American Philosophical Society.

Such a plan would, of course, limit the Fellowships to those intended for *research*, while the time of the members of the faculty would be given over wholly to researches of their own and to the superintendence of work done at the Institute by the advanced students I have in mind. [...]

MORRIS JASTROW, JR.

7.

Hebrew Union College
Department of Biblical Exegesis
Cincinnati, O., February 8, 1906.

[...] I am glad that my connection during the last thirteen years with a Jewish theological school and an American University has furnished me with the experience requisite for forming an opinion with reference to the present educational needs of the American Jewish community.

The theological seminary is necessarily a professional school. The divinity schools forming a part of some of our Universities are everywhere on a level with the schools of applied science, as the schools of medicine, civil engineering, electricity, chemistry, etc. The law school is equally a professional school. The entrance requirements in all such schools vary in different institutions. In the majority of cases the Bachelor's degree is not required for entrance. Even in the Universities of higher standing, the system of electives makes it possible for a student to enter upon his professional preparation in his junior year. The Hebrew Union College admits to its First Collegiate Class University Freshmen. It is true, of recent years an additional (fifth) year has been imposed upon the students of the College; it is equally true that many of its students have brought with them a University training. With all that, the character of the institution, and rightly so, has remained unchanged. It is a school for the training of rabbis, a professional school. The crowning effort of the student is his sermon preached before Faculty and students. The student's mind is concentrated upon that effort. No wonder that frequently he loses interest in his ordinary college work which to him seems to be remotely connected with his ultimate ambition. A minute point of exegesis or criticism, a talmudic sakla [sic] we-taria,[58] a gaonic responsum, — can such things be preached? and if not, then of what use? Moreover, the system of instruction must necessarily be that of lecture and recitation followed by periodical examinations. The student is expected to cover much ground and to be saturated with thoughts very few of which are of his own thinking. He may carry away with himself much or little Jewish knowledge; but he adds nothing thereto of his own. He is reproductive, but is in no way productive.[59]

The professional seminary serves a definite purpose and we can not expect that it will swerve from it. It will train more or less well informed rabbis; it will not and cannot train scientific workers. The sermon and the scientific effort are antipodal. A good preacher is unfitted for painstaking scientific labor, and the specialist-investigator is rarely a good preacher. Scientific work may and may not lead to a professional calling; it must be pursued without reference thereto, li-smah. The only possible avocation it might lead to is that of the College or Seminary instructor who, if of the right kind, is reproductive and productive at the same time, transmitting knowledge and searching out new information.

I believe it to be a very fortunate circumstance that Mr. Dropsie's will lays particular stress on "original investigation and research." [...] Accordingly the Dropsie College should exist for the purpose of training original workers in the fields of Biblical and post-Biblical Jewish literature. The students should be preferably graduates from Universities or theological schools possessing a certain amount of Semitic and Jewish knowledge and the capacity for research. The students should be designated as Fellows in the particular subjects chosen by them. [...] The faculty should consist

---

[58] Argument, debate, consideration of pros and cons.

[59] For a current critique of courses of study in American rabbinical schools see Charles S. Liebman, "The Training of American Rabbis," *American Jewish Year Book*, LXIX (1968), 3–112. A proposal for a radical reorganization of rabbinical school curricula appears in my "Toward a New Generation of American Rabbis," *Reconstructionist*, XXV, 9 (September 19, 1969). Cf. also Arnold Jacob Wolf et al., "The Future of Rabbinic Training in America: A Symposium," *Judaism*, XVIII (1969), 387–420.

of men chosen for their ability to do research work of their own as well as fructify the minds of younger men and to inspire them with a love of painstaking and accurate investigation. The Dropsie College may well co-operate with institutions in the city of Philadelphia to which it may leave the task of preparing candidates for its Fellowships and even of furnishing its students part of the education they may require. The work, e.g., of the Semitic department in the University of Pennsylvania need not be duplicated. There should be created immediately the following three departments: (1) The department of Hebrew and cognate languages and Biblical exegesis (this department may subsequently be split up into two or more; (2) that of Talmud and cognate literature; (3) that of history of the Jewish people and of Jewish literature (this department again may subsequently be split up). [...] The College should also maintain a College press for the publication of the works of its staff of professors and investigators.

We have two rabbinic training schools. We have in the city of Philadelphia also a smaller College for elementary instruction. We are surely in need of a College for research in Jewish history and literature. Tasks without number await such an institution. To mention but one, we need a Thesaurus of the Hebrew Language covering our entire literature from the Bible down to the latest essayist. It is a stupendous task requiring the co-operation of a goodly number of workers. The necessity for establishing with accuracy the Hebrew-Aramaic equivalents of the Greek words in the Septuagint and the other Greek versions has recently been pointed out by me. Most of the Midrashic texts are unreadable awaiting critical editions based on manuscripts and parallel references. Numerous obscure points in Jewish history await elucidation through special treatment. Let the Dropsie College undertake as many of these tasks as it may have means or facilities for. [...]

Max Margolis.

8.

Harvard University
Cambridge

March 12, 1906.

[...] I assume that it was not the testator's intention that his college should be exclusively, or perhaps primarily, devoted to the education of men for the Jewish ministry; but that he wished rather to give opportunity and offer inducements to the Jewish young men, whatever their plans in life might be, to acquire thorough acquaintance with Biblical and Rabbinical literature and the languages in which this literature is written. Doubtless some students would proceed from the college to the schools which offer more strictly professional training to candidates for the Rabbinate. It would seem, therefore, that the first thing was to establish chairs of instruction in Biblical and Rabbinical Hebrew and the Aramaic of the Targums and Talmud. For the other Semitic languages, I should think that the college might enter into such an arrangement with the University of Pennsylvania as would admit its students to such courses in those languages as they were prepared to take. [...] I should think that provision should be made for instruction in Greek, with especial reference to the study of the Greek versions of the Bible, which are of so much importance both for the history of the text and early interpretation. In this I suppose the University, like most of our institutions of the kind, makes no sufficient provision. Whether preparatory classes giving elementary instruction in Hebrew should be established would depend, doubtless, upon the opportunities which already exist in Philadelphia for boys to pursue this subject while they are attending, as I suppose most of them do, the public schools.

I am glad to see that Mr. Dropsie included [...] original investigation and research. [...]

I shall look with great interest upon the plans which may be formed for this somewhat unique institution, and hope that it may fulfil in the fullest measure the wishes of its founder and its governors.

[...] GEORGE F. MOORE.

9.
New York, March 23, 1906.

[...] The following subjects are to be considered:

1. BIBLE   (a) Exegesis
            (b) Introduction
            (c) Biblical History & Archaeology
2. TALMUD
    HALACHA (a) Talmud of Babylon and Talmud of Jerusalem,
            including also other Halachic matter, scattered
            over the various ancient Rabbinic interpreta-
            tions of the Pentateuch;
            (b) Introduction to the Talmud
            (c) Codes and Responsa
            (d) Introduction to the Rabbinic Law;
    HAGGADAH (a) The two Talmuds and the Midrashim, and other
            Haggadic matter embodied in the various col-
            lective works, and in the devotional literature;
            (b) Introduction to the Midrashim.
3. HELLENISTIC LITERATURE. The various Apocryphal and Apoca-
   lyptical works, and Philo's writings;
4. HISTORY, from the earliest Biblical times reaching down to our
   age
            (a) Political History
            (b) History of the Sects
            (c) History of Jewish Literature
5. THEOLOGY, prepared after Jewish sources
            (a) Jewish liturgy
6. PHILOSOPHY AND MYSTICISM, beginning with the earliest times
   and going down as late, at least, as Mendelssohn;
7. JEWISH POETRY, sacred and secular.

The ideal would be that these seven subjects should be taught
by men, each of whom shall be a specialist in his own subject. In
case of necessity, however, Halacha and Haggadah might be confined to one Professor; and Philosophy and Theology, but in this
point is the difficulty that it is practically impossible to have a

proper knowledge of Jewish Philosophy without being at the same time an expert in the Arabic language, to the acquirement of which a good deal of time has to be devoted, and thus his Arabic studies may impair his efficiency as an exponent of Jewish theology, which has to be drawn chiefly from Rabbinic sources and the Hebrew devotional literature. On the other hand, the subject of Hellenistic literature might be taught by the same professor, who would lecture either on the Bible, or on the History of Jewish sects. The subjects of Poetry, again might be taught by the Professor of the History of Literature. [...]

The course should extend over a period of four or five years, to enable the student to acquire something of "ripe scholarship."

The testator, I note, further wishes that with the "ripe scholar-ship" in Hebrew, Bible and Rabbinic Literature, should be con-nected "original investigation and research." This could only be ac-complished by the creation of a number of Fellowships, thus giving the opportunity to those who distinguish themselves by special bril-liancy in their examinations to pursue those branches of study for which they have shown particular aptitude. For this purpose the Fellows should have three years in which to pursue their special subjects, under the guidance and assistance of the Professors, at the end of which they should be obliged to sum up their researches in scientific form.

I am inclined to think that it would be proper to enlist all the learned forces in this country that have some scholarly message to the world, in connection with Judaism. The Trustees should, for instance, invite men whose specialty is Oriental Languages, to give courses of philological lectures on the affinities of the Semitic lan-gu ages. A course of lectures on Assyriology and its relation to the Bible and post-exilic literature by a real specialist would also prove helpful.

Invitations should also be extended to such men as Professor George Moore,[60] of Harvard, for a course (or courses) of lectures on the influence of the Jewish commentators of the Bible, on their Christian fellow-workers in the same field, as well as the influence

[60] Note 17 above.

of the Haggadic literature on the Fathers who wrote in Greek and Syriac. A course of lectures on Jewish folk-lore, and its influence on the legend and myth of the world at large, by an expert, is also desirable.

From time to time, invitations might also be extended to European scholars, such as Professor Goldziher,[61] of Budapest, on Jewish Philosophy; Professor Cohen [sic],[62] of Breslau, the editor of "Philo", on Hellenistic Literature; Professor Cohen,[63] of Marburg, on the Relation of Judaism to Modern Philosophy, Kant, Hegel, etc.; Doctor Jacob,[64] of Göttingen, on his method of Bible Criticism; Doctor Poznanski, of Warsaw, on the History of the Sects, and so on.

I hardly need say that such a College would be entirely impossible without having attached to it a great Library, consisting both of printed works and manuscripts, and representing Jewish Literature in all its various branches. To this will have to be added thousands of volumes, included under the name of Judaica, treating also of Jewish subjects.

As will be seen, the above is a sketch of the outlines of a College, as I judge was in the mind of the late Mr. Dropsie. To bring in

---

[61] On Schechter's effort to bring Ignaz Goldziher (1850–1921) to America see my "Solomon Schechter" etc., Part II, Letter No. 64. — I note that Goldziher's *Mythology among the Hebrews and Its Historical Development* has been republished in 1967 in New York. The original German appeared in 1876 and the English translation in 1877.

[62] Leopold Cohn (1856–1916) was professor at the University of Breslau, author of numerous works on Greek literature and editor of works by Philo. Schechter met him in Florence in 1893 (Bentwich, op. cit., p. 121).

[63] Hermann Cohen (1842–1918) was leader of the Marburg School of neo-Kantian philosophy. By 1906 he had published a number of papers on Jewish topics, but his major work on Judaism, *Religion of Reason out of the Sources of Judaism* appeared only in 1919. For recent discussions see Mordecai M. Kaplan, *The Purpose and Meaning of Jewish Existence* (Philadelphia, 1964) and Nathan Rotenstreich, *Jewish Philosophy in Modern Times: From Mendelssohn to Rosenzweig* (New York, 1968), ch. 4.

[64] Benno Jacob (1862–1945), rabbi in Göttingen and Dortmund, was a Bible scholar. Rabbi J. H. Hertz used his commentaries in *The Pentateuch and Haftorahs* (London, 1961 [1936]).

secular subjects, in such a College, or to create any fancy need, would be certainly, in my judgment, not in the compliance with the wish of the testator.

It is, however, to be noticed, that, except as regards the institution of Fellowships and the various courses of occasional lectures, the above scheme duplicates that of the Jewish Theological Seminary of America, and it would be a serious misfortune if two similar institutions were established in such close proximity, considering the fact that the number of competent instructors is so few, while the number of students is also comparatively small.[65] There is also to be considered the fact that such an institution as outlined, together with an equipment of a library, and a suitable building, could scarcely be adequately supported on an endowment, such as that indicated in your letter. I am, therefore, of opinion, that the best way to carry out the will of the testator, would be to adopt means to combine it with the existing institution, the curriculum of which could be easily adapted, so as to render the lectures accessible to persons of any creed, color, or sex.

The increase of funds would enable the trustees of the combined institutions to create the Fellowships and the courses of lectures outlined above. In the course of time, a scientific periodical (a monthly or quarterly), could also be established, which would greatly promote the cause of Jewish science in this country, and make America a real center of Jewish learning.

[...]   SOLOMON SCHECHTER.

---

[65] Schechter was seriously disturbed over the Dropsie Bequest. He regarded it as a real danger. He concluded a lengthy memorandum of 8 November 1906 to Jacob H. Schiff with this last plea: "I am not a young man any more. My life is devoted to this institution [The Jewish Theological Seminary of America], and it will be very hard for me to have the few years God may grant me still, connected with an institution whose failure will be unavoidable under the circumstances." In a letter of 21 November 1906 he told Adler quite bluntly: "But when it transpired in the papers that practically the necessary steps had been taken to establish a separate institution in Philadelphia, which... must cripple the Seminary for ever, I thought it my duty to approach such of our Trustees as would not consider a discussion of the subject indiscreet and intrusive."

10.

March 3, 1906.

[...] As for the character of the institution:

I should think that it would be most desirable to have an institution of the same general nature as the Jewish Theological Seminary in New York, or the Hebrew Union College in Cincinnati. There is certainly abundant room for another such institution, and I should think that Philadelphia would be a very favorable city in which to establish it.

As to the prime object of the college:

It should aim, first of all, to raise up learned men, rather than to train practical workers; to turn out thorough and productive scholars in the field of Hebrew and Jewish learning; to provide a place where "original investigation and research" of the highest class shall be encouraged and made possible. This seems to have been the purpose of the Testator in establishing this foundation.

The subjects taught:

According to my idea the main subjects to be taught would be the following:

1. Biblical Literature and Exegesis.
2. Hebrew and the cognate Semitic languages.
3. Talmud.
4. History and Archaeology.
5. Jewish Literature.
6. The History of Religion. [...]

The Faculty:

I should advise, first, a very few regular professors at as high a salary as it practicable; second, a few assistant professors at a considerably lower salary; third, as many instructors as the funds can comfortably maintain. The institution ought to be able to command a few of the very best scholars in the world. The regular professorships in the institution should be prized to be eagerly sought. There is no greater incentive to the younger scholars in the pursuit of their studies, than the possibility of ultimately gaining places where the salary offered would be large enough to relieve them of care, and where every opportunity would be given them of carrying on their work unhampered. I would suggest, for example, that the institution begin with the appointment of regular professors in these subjects: Biblical Literature and Exegesis; Hebrew and cognate Semitic Languages; Talmud; Jewish Literature. The rank of assistant professor might well be the same as in the most of our principal universities. The place might either be a stepping-stone to the higher position of regular professor, or occupied by those who, while excellent scholars and teachers, could hardly attain to the first rank. I should recommend that the instructors be given very small salaries, and as few hours of instruction as is practicable. You should always get first-rate men, fresh from American or German universities, without families to support, to whom it would be much more important to spend a few years in an atmosphere of high class work and in company with scholars of international reputation, even at a very small salary, than to teach for good pay at an inferior institution. The instructors ought to be encouraged in every way to pursue original investigations. If care is taken in the selection of the men, and they are not hampered by too much teaching, your college might very soon get the reputation of the very best place in the country for a young scholar to win his spurs; and if the institution really gained this reputation, any young man of the right sort would much rather begin work there than to teach at double or treble the salary, in some place where reputations are not easily made.

The students:

I should say that it would be well to adopt, from the first, the policy of admitting only students of real promise, such as have shown that they are both earnest and able. It would be easy, no doubt, to bring together within a very short time, a large number of poorly equipped and mediocre men, but such a student personnel would hamper and discourage the instructors and hurt the reputation of the college from the start. If the institution is to have for its prime object the encouragement of thorough training and advanced research, as its founder seems to have wished, then it ought to be careful to begin with high standards of admission, and to keep them as high as practicable.

I shall wait with great interest to see what your Board of Governors decides in regard to these matters. I wish you all success in your important task, and hope to see an institution founded, in Philadelphia, which will be an honor to this country and a great help to the cause of Hebrew and Semitic learning in the world. [...]

CHARLES C. TORREY.

11.

February 9, 1906.

[...] As instruction in Semitic languages, Bible and Talmud, and Rabbinical literature is now given in the Hebrew Union College and the New York Theological School as well as in other institutions in this country, I am of opinion that the proposed college should be of the nature of a Graduate School.

The subjects taught should be: all Semitic languages, including Hebrew (Biblical, Mishnaic, mediaeval), Aramaic (Biblical, Samaritan, Syriac, Mandean and modern dialectical), Babylonian and Assyrian, Arabic (with dialects), Sabean, Ethiopic (with dialects); Old Testament and Apocrypha, textual and historical criticism; New Testament &c. (this is important for the history of Jewish thought), Talmudic and Rabbinical, &c (stress should be laid on scientific exegesis in accordance with modern principles).

Professors and other instructors should be chosen for scholarly ability without regard to creed, the great majority will naturally be Jews.

The salaries of the instructors should be high — so high, relatively to expense of living, as any in the country; it is important to be able to command the best talents. Better one or two men of eminent ability than many of inferior stamp. [...]

As to requirements for admission: The applicant should already have the degree of A. B. or its equivalent, and should have some knowledge of Hebrew, Aramaic, Greek, Latin, French, German. The College should stand for scholarship. It will be wiser to insist on a high grade for entering students even if the College should begin with one student. Elementary instruction is given elsewhere —

here should be something different. — A working knowledge of Greek and Latin, French and German is essential. [...]

It seems to me of prime importance to insist from the start on a high standard and strictly scientific work. All other points can then be arranged.

Entrance examinations will be necessary. [...]

C. H. Toy.

Addendum to note 8

Prof. Woodrow Wilson compared Gilman's achievement at Baltimore to Jefferson's at the University of Virginia (cf. Abraham Flexner, *Daniel Coit Gilman: Creator of the American Type of University* [New York, 1946], pp. 105 f.)

AYALTA

FROM THE DOE IN THE FIELD
TO THE MOTHER OF THE MESSIAHS

ABRAHAM BERGER

THE AGADA CONTAINS many stories, in various versions, about the *ayala* (hind, or more generally, doe) and the *yaala* (the doe of the wild goat).

This essay will trace some of the steps by which such stories became part of a great kabbalistic symbol of Divine Providence and the Birth of Redemption amidst suffering. It will also explore the possible origin of these stories.

The *ayala* (in Aramaic *ayalta*) is the *hasida* (selflessly devoted) among the animals. When the animals are in search of water, they gather round her. She digs a hole in the ground, places her horns in it and cries out to God. God hearkens to her prayer and sends up the *Tehom* (Primordial waters)[1] or, according to another version preserved in the *Yalkut Shimeoni*, God rends the *Tehom* asunder for her.[2]

The *ayala* has a narrow womb and therefore suffers great difficulties and acute pains in giving birth. God provides a dragon who bites her at the opening of the womb. so that her tightness is loosened and the kid is released.[3]

---

[1] *Midrash Tehillim*, ed. Buber, 42,1 and 22,14.

[2] *Yalkut Shimeoni* on Ps. 42:2.

[3] *Baba Bathra*, 16b; *Midrash Shemuel*, ed. Buber, 9,2. Here the expression is: "her organs are tight"; Louis Ginzberg, *Legends*, II, 228; *Sefer ha-Peliah* (Kolemea, 1883), f. 67c; Abraham ben Azriel, *Arugat ha-bosem*, III, 58, ed. E. E. Urbach (Jerusalem, 1947–1963), II, 123. This great treasury of reflection on Aggada and Piyyut divides the chores by having the stag (*ayyal*), as the *hasid*, do all the praying and leaving the birthpangs to the *ayala*. The author shows awareness of philological problems (Psalm 42 reads: *ke-ayyal*/masculine/

The *yaala* expresses her fury over her birth pangs by dropping her offspring over the cliff. God sends an eagle who, at that split second, catches the kid in his wings and places it safely before its mother.[4]

The scarcity of water, the cliffs and the animals themselves, suggest the Palestinian landscape.[5] Many of these stories served a didactic purpose as interpretations of biblical verses. The first story is a comment on Psalm 22:1: "according to the Hind of the Dawn" and on Psalm 42:2: "as the hind cries aloud at the *afiqe mayim*" (usually translated running streams, springs of water, etc.). The second and third stories elucidate Job 39:1: "Do you know how mountain goats give birth, or have you watched the hinds in labor?"

These stories must have been widely diffused especially in connection with prayers for women in childbirth. In some ancient paradigm prayers the following is included: "He Who answers the hinds in the mountains, may He answer us."[6]

Eventually, these stories even reached Yiddish folklore. A jingle apparently intended as a birth-easing spell reads as follows:

---

ta'arog/feminine/) and zoological problems (the hind has no horns). He misses the point, however. In the aggada, the *ayyal* (in contrast to the *zevi*) has a predominantly negative character. Ayala does not necessarily mean "hind."

[4] *Baba Bathra*, 16b; *Midrash Shemuel*, 9,2; Louis Ginzberg, *Legends*, II, 228; L. Lewysohn, *Zoologie des Talmuds* (Frankfurt a. M., 1858), p. 115; *Midrash Iyob* in *Bate Midrashot*, ed. S. A. Wertheimer (Jerusalem, 1953), p. 186.

[5] In *Baba Bathra*, 16b, the stories are told by the Babylonian Rabbah (Rava) in a lengthy discourse on God's answer to Job's challenge. However, in the midrashic sources, the transmitters of the aggadot are Palestinian amoraim (Simon ben Lakish, Yudan, Judah ben Simon). On the fauna of Palestine in general, see F. S. Bodenheimer, *Ha-hay be-artsot ha-Mikra* (Jerusalem, 1949–1956) (in English, Vol. I, *Animal and Man in Bible Lands*, Leiden, 1960). However, as a cultural history which the book purports to be, it is a grand failure. Although Bodenheimer cites works dealing with animal folklore from Egyptian, Canaanite, Syrian, Greek and Arabic sources, he utterly ignores the Midrash.

[6] Cf. Saul Lieberman in *Jewish Quarterly Review*, N. S., XXXII (1946), 320, where further references are cited.

"Oif den barg Karmel shtayt eyn hindin un shrayt... ikh bin eyne gevinerin... Got virt dir un ale menshen helfin."[7]

The author of the *Tana debe Eliahu*, in the course of his meditations on the fate of Israel, is moved to exclaim: "To whom is Israel likened before their Father in Heaven? To this *ayala* who conceives in anguish and gives birth in pain, for all beginnings are difficult, as it is said: 'The voice of the Lord causes hinds to calve,'" (Psalm 29:9).[8] This is in line with the language of Jewish tradition which since the days of Isaiah and Micah has portrayed Israel's crises as painful births.[9]

In the *Hodayot* (Thanksgiving Hymns) of the Qumran sect, the community, heir of the prophetic Remnant, is portrayed as a mother giving birth to the prophetically promised Redeemer amidst great tribulations.[10]

Israel is represented as a Mother, called Zion, Jerusalem or Mother Rachel,[11] and since Hosea as the Bride of God.[12] According to the *Pesikta Rabbati*, Jeremiah at the time of the destruction of the Temple saw Mother Zion as a woman in mourning,[13] a motif carried down to the Lurianic kabbalah and hasidic legend.[14]

---

[7] Eleazar Shulman, *Sefat Yehudit-Ashkenazit* (Riga, 1913), pp. 202 ff.

[8] *Seder Eliahu Rabba*, ed. Friedmann, near the end of chapter 2. Rashi on Ps. 68:11, speaks of the Jewish Community as God's animal.

[9] Isaiah 66:8; Micah, 4:10; Cf. Gershom G. Scholem in *Eranos Jahrbuch*, XXI (1952), 50–51.

[10] *Megillat ha-Hodayot*, ed. Jacob Licht (Jerusalem, 1957), ch. 5.

[11] B. Z. Dinaburg in *Zion*, VI (1951), 1 ff.; *Berakot*, 35b, commenting on Proverbs 28:24, speaks of God as Father and the *Ecclesia Israel* as Mother. Cf. Scholem, *Eranos Jahrbuch*, VII (1952), 51.

[12] Cf. the various commentaries on Hosea and on the Song of Songs; Gerson D. Cohen, "The Song of Songs and the Jewish Religious Mentality," *The Samuel Friedland Lectures* (New York, 1966), pp. 1–21.

[13] *Pesikta Rabbati*, ed. Friedmann, f. 131b–132a; Victor Aptowitzer in *Hebrew Union College Annual*, pp. 403–407.

[14] *Hemdat Yamim* (Livorno, 1763), II, Chap. 1, f. 4ab, tells the story of Abraham ha-Levi, the Lurianic ascetic who had a vision of Mother Zion. The last such vision is recorded by Isaac Judah Yehiel Safrin. Cf. his *Megillat Setarim* (Jerusalem, 1944), p. 19.

In the earlier Apocalypse of Ezra (IV Ezra) a mourning woman turns into the beautiful city of Jerusalem.[15]

In the *Sefer Zerubabel*, which reflects the last struggle of Israel against the Byzantine Empire, the fighting and sorrowing Mother of the Messiah ben David is called *Hefzibah*, a name given by Isaiah to the future redeemed Jerusalem.[16]

Out of all of these strands, the Zohar weaves a grandiose and, to our sensibilities, bizarre pattern of the birth of redemption. It uses the story of the *ayala* as an allegory of the redeeming activity of the *Ecclesia Israel* (*Kenesset Yisrael*) which already had become identified with the Shekhinah.[17] One version (*Zohar*, II, 52 b) is essentially the *ayala* story as told in the Midrash.

A fuller version of the myth is given in another section of the *Zohar* (presented here in abridged form). By combining the image of the Doe of the Dawn (Psalm 22) and the image of the Woman of Valor (Proberbs 31) with that of the *ayalta*, it depicts the Shekhinah-Ecclesia as *ayalta*, rising before dawn to provide food for all creatures. In the mountains of darkness she encounters an adversary in the form of a winding serpent. She escapes to the mountains of light where another serpent engages the first one in combat and the doe is thus saved. When the world is in need of rain, the animals gather about her; she climbs to the top of the mountain, places

[15] IV Ezra 8:27.

[16] *Sefer Zerubabel*, in Yehuda Ibn Shmuel (Kaufman), *Midreshe Geulah* (Tel-Aviv, 1954), pp. 55–83. On the legendary-historical aspects of Hefzibah, see S. W. Baron, *Social and Religious History*, V, 140–141 and 354–355. The Zohar is one of the few Midrashim which refer to this legendary Hefzibah, but eventually it allegorizes her, so that she becomes another name of the many-named Shekhinah-Ecclesia.

[17] Gershom G. Scholem in *Eranos Jahrbuch*, XVII (1949), 315 ff; ibid. XXI (1952), 67–68.

[18] *Zohar*, II, p. 52b.

[19] In the Midrash, "the Ayelet ha-Shahar" (the Doe of the Dawn) whose horns are the first rays of the sun breaking through the darkness, is a popular symbol of the coming Redemption. Cf. e.g. *Shir ha-shirim rabba* on Song of Songs 6:10. *Zohar*, III, 21b, especially identifies the Doe of the Dawn with *Ecclesia Israel* and the Woman of Valor of Proverbs 31 with the Shekhinah (*Zohar*, III, f. 178b).

her head between her knees and emits wail after wail. God hears her voice and has mercy upon the world. She comes running down the mountain and the other animals run after her but cannot overtake her. After she conceives, her organs become closed up and when the time comes for parturition, she sends forth ninety wails of agony, the number of letters in Psalm 20:2 ("The Lord will answer you in the day of trouble..."). God sends a powerful snake who bites at her womb twice. At the first bite, blood spurts forth which the snake licks up; at the second bite, water gushes forth and she gives birth. The Zohar then quotes: "And he smote the rock with the rod twice" (Numbers 20:11).

Finally, the *Raya Mehemna* adds: "And through the seventy wails, the two parts of her womb open up to give birth to the two Messiahs (Messiah ben Joseph and Messiah ben David)."[21]

Many more allusions to *ayalta* as the combined Shekhinah-Ecclesia may be found in various parts of the *Zohar*, *Tikkune Zohar*, and *Zohar Hadash*.[22] The Zoharic myth found ready acceptance among Kabbalists, in discourse and ritual, although the commentators tried to spiritualize its "natural" language.[23]

The Zohar calls the *ayalta* myth a mystery and connects it with the emergence of Israel from the womb of Egypt and the splitting

---

[20] *Zohar*, III, f. 249 ab. The motif of Moses striking the rock twice, with blood first gushing forth and then water, is already found in the Targum (Targum Jonathan on Numbers 20:11). On the parallel to the *Ayalta* story, see the various commentaries and especially Moses Zacuto in Shalom Buzaglio, *Mikdash Melekh* (Premysl, 1871). Cf. e.g., his remarks on *Zohar*, I, 6b.

[21] *Zohar*, III, f. 68a; f. 249a.

[22] *Zohar hadash* (Balak), f. 44d–45b which one might characterize as a little *Ayalta* apocalypse.

[23] Hayyim Vital, *Peri Ets Hayyim, Shaar Hag ha-Matsot*, chapter 8; *Shaar Hag ha-shevuot*, chapter 1. Cf. G. Scholem, *On the Kabbalah and its Symbolism*, chapter 4. Kurt Wilhelm in *Ale Ayyin* in honor of Zalman Schocken (Jerusalem, 1951/52), pp. 143–145. The most prominent of the spiritualizers is of course Moses Cordovero in his great commentary on the *Zohar* in Abraham Azulai, *Or ha-hamah*. This tendency continues to our very days although we also find cases where, as Scholem puts it, "the images rebelled" and produced new offspring, e.g. in Safrin's *Zohar hay*, 3 vols. (Przemysl, 1878–1881), and his commentary on the Pentateuch.

of the Sea of Reeds.[24] Abraham Galante relates that Luria expounded the mystery of the *ayalta* at the insistence of his pupils, against his own better judgement; for this he was punished by the death of his son.[25] Galante adds a folkloristic note that "one should resist the temptation of housing a pregnant hind and watching a snake bite her, for this would surely be tempting the Lord."[26] Apparently, after all the allegorizations, the animal aroma still clung to the *ayala*.

Lurianic and pseudo-Lurianic texts see the *ayalta* myth as a parallel of the story of Eve and the Serpent, Cain being considered as really the son of the Serpent.[27]

Menahem Azariah da Fano in his *Asarah Ma'amarot* (Ten Kabbalistic Essays) refers to the Messiah [ben Joseph] as "our darling... born through the bite of the snake."[28] Baruch Ibn Yaish speaks of the Messiah as the son of the Shekhinah and the *Ecclesia Israel* and as the young Stag, son of the Doe of the Dawn.[29] This, however, touches on another symbolic complex, that of the *zevi* (buck of the gazelle) in the Song of Songs which is not within the scope of this essay.

We have thus far traced some of the steps in the career of the *ayala*. On its face, the story appears to resemble the folklore of the type of the *Physiologus* which combines animal stories with a verse from Scriptures for didactic entertainment purposes. Actually, this is only the beginning of our problem: Are these *ayala* stories merely an exegesis of the Bible combined with keen observation of nature? Do they contain "faded fragments of old myths?"[30]

[24] *Zohar*, II, f. 52b. The mystery of the splitting of the Sea of Reeds together with the *ayalta* mystery were the subject of cabbalistic rites and meditations for the 7th day of Passover and Shevuot.

[25] Abraham Galante in Abraham Azulai, *Or ha-Hamah* on *Zohar*, II, f. 52b.

[26] A. Galante, ibid. refers to a tradition that a "king" once tried to effect such an experiment.

[27] *Arba meah shekel kesef* (Koretz, 1804?), f. 16c.

[28] [*Asarah Ma'amarot*] Maamar ha-hamishi... (Hamburg, n.d.), f. 2b.

[29] Baruch Ibn Yaish, *Mekor Barukh* (Constantinople, 1576), f. 9b; f. 11b.

[30] Louis Ginzberg, *On Jewish Law and Lore* (New York, 1955), p. 63, thus characterizes the agadic accounts of Creation, Tehom, Leviathan, etc.

Do they possibly go back to a remembered nomadic "patriarchal" era? Biblical puritanism suppressed all references to "goddesses" active in nature. Is it possible that after the goddesses had been banned, the animals symbolizing them have been retained? In the Song of Songs the maidens are adjured by the gazelles and the does of the field.

We always find that archaic thought clings to the prime elements of the human condition; life and death; aggression and procreation; water and rock. Let us now examine the story of the hind at the *afiqe mayim.*

In *Pirke Rabbi Eliezer* we read that the Big Fish, which swallowed Jonah, showed him the place where the Sons of Korah (who were swallowed up alive by the earth) are standing in prayer on the *Even Shetiya* over the *Tehom* underneath the Temple, Navel of the Cosmos, the very spot where one's prayers are especially heard.[31] As part of the *ayalta* aggada we are told that just as the *ayalta*'s prayer is heard, so will the prayer of the "Sons of Korah."[32]

David Feuchtwang has shown in a series of articles that the water-drawing ceremonies in the Temple on the Sukkot Festival (*Simhat Beth Ha-shoevah*) in which the Tehom plays an important role is paralleled by the water rites of Atargatis at Bambyke (Hieropolis), as described by Lucian in his *De dea Syria*.[33] In the Ugaritic mythological texts, the abode of the god El is at the *afiqe Tehomot* (*apk thmtm*).[34] And, of course, the pagan fairs of Acco, Askalon and Caesarea were right in the very heart of Jewish Palestine.

---

[31] *Pirke de Rabbi Eliezer,* chap. 10.

[32] *Midrash Tehillim,* ed. Buber, 42,1.

[33] *Monatsschrift für die Geschichte und Wissenschaft des Judentums,* L (1910–1911), 534–552; 713–729; LV, 43–63.

[34] W. F. Albright, *Archaeology and the Religion of Israel,* 5th ed. (Baltimore, 1968), p. 71 and p. 191, note 7; Marvin H. Pope, *El in the Ugaritic Texts* (Leiden, 1955), pp. 61 ff. On the navel of the Cosmos and the Tehom, cf. Joachim Jeremias, *Golgotha* (Leipzig, 1926). There is now a wealth of literature on this universal topic, awaiting coordination and analysis.

The *ayalta*'s placing her head between her knees and then running down the mountainside may perhaps throw light on a similar act performed by Elijah as part of the rain rite on Mount Carmel.[35]

The story of the eagle retrieving the newborn kid of the wild goat is of course primarily a folklore motif. The infant Gilgamesh was dropped from a tower but picked up by an eagle in flight and saved.[36]

The theme of the difficult birth and the bite of the snake is both folkloristic and mythological. Alkmene who had difficulties in giving birth to Herakles is bitten by a marten, loosening "the bonds of her womb," thus quickening his birth.[37] The snake is also a phallic symbol and is generally considered an aid to fertility. The theme may also be obscurely related to a Canaanite myth recorded in a fragment from Egyptian literature, that Anat and Astarte become pregnant but cannot give birth. "They are closed up by Horus (Horon) and opened up by Seth (Baal)."[38] However, scholars have not as yet developed any uniform interpretation of this enigmatic statement. Some claim that "closing" meant not hindering but rather protecting it while "opening" was not facilitating but destroying the offspring by an abortion.[39]

It seems very likely that the story of the *ayala* at the *Tehom* and the story of her difficulties in giving birth are fragments of a single fertility myth which also included an item (no longer extant today by itself) about her impregnation. This may be deduced from the

---

[35] Cf. Raphael Patai in *Hebrew Union College Annual*, XIV (1939), 254–258.

[36] Aelianus, *Hist. anim.*, XII, 21.

[37] Ibid., XII, 5.

[38] *Papyrus Harris*, ed. H. O. Lange (Copenhagen, 1927). W. F. Albright, *Yahweh and the gods of Canaan* (New York, 1968), p. 129–130; H. P. Blok, *Acta Orientalia*, VIII, 185–186; Wolfgang Helck, *Die Beziehungen Ägyptens zu Vorderasien* (Wiesbaden, 1962), p. 495–496.

[93] Cf. A. A. Barb in *Journal of the Warburg Institute*, London, XVI (1953), 241, note 23; Wolfert Westendorf in *Zeitschrift für die ägyptische Sprache*, XCII (1966), 144 ff.

Tana debe Eliahu's reference to the *ayala* conceiving in anguish as well as to allusions in the *Zohar*.[40]

The possible connection between the *ayala* stories and ancient myths shows that the changeover from folklore to sacred myth is preceded by the transformation of sacred myth into folklore. However, these speculations are merely probings. The subject awaits fuller exploration.

[40] *Zohar*, II, 219 b.

ON THE SUPPOSEDLY ARISTOTELIAN CHARACTER OF GABIROL'S *KETER MALKUT*

JOSEPH L. BLAU

IN THE MAJOR PHILOSOPHIC WORK of Solomon ibn Gabirol (Avicebron), *The Fountain of Life* (*Fons Vitae*; *Meḳor Ḥayyim*), the only previous author referred to by name is Plato. Even the references to Plato are unspecific; Gabirol does not cite particular passages, or even particular dialogues of Plato, but merely mentions the name of the great Greek philosopher in connection with his discussion of certain ideas. If, on the other hand, we examine with critical care those passages in which Gabirol indicates dependence upon his predecessors without reference to any individual,[1] we find that these references point to his knowledge and acceptance of the form of neo-Platonism that was current among the Muslim philosophers of the tenth century and after. This was a syncretistic and eclectic development that included elements derived from virtually all of the Greek philosophic schools. For the most part, the key concepts of these schools of thought were used in later, Hellenistic versions rather than in the original "classical" versions.[2] There is no indication in Gabirol's philosophic treatise that he had any knowledge directly of any of the works of Aristotle, although it is quite conceivable, perhaps even probable, that he knew the brief pseudepigraphon widely circulated in the Middle Ages under the title "The Theology of Aristotle," which was actually a para-

---

[1] As, for example, "Philosophers are accustomed to say..."

[2] Gabirol's use of source references is discussed by Theodore E. James in his "Introduction" to Harry E. Wedeck's English translation of a part of Book III of *The Fountain of Life* (New York, 1962). See also the discussion in Chap. V of Isaac Husik, *A History of Mediaeval Jewish Philosophy* (Philadelphia, 1916).

phrase of one of the *Enneads* of the third century anti-rational neo-Platonist, Plotinus.

It is also worthy of note that Gabirol does not quote any biblical or rabbinic sources in *The Fountain of Life*, and in his other philosophic work, *The Improvement of the Moral Qualities*, he uses some biblical material but eschews the use of rabbinic materials, even though, as Stephen S. Wise pointed out in his scholarly edition and translation of Gabirol's ethical treatise, there are many apt passages in the Talmudim that Gabirol might have cited.[3] The absence of reference to the rabbis and the scarcity of references to the Bible accounts for both the supreme disregard of Gabirol's philosophic work among the Jews of the Middle Ages and its wide acceptance by Christians as a basic text in philosophic education. As Husik points out, Gabirol was a primary source of the Franciscan acceptance of the concept of "a universal matter underlying all existence outside of God". Duns Scotus, for example, in discussing the principle of matter, uses the formula, "Ego autem redeo ad sententiam Avicembronis."[4] In Maimonides' letters to Samuel ibn Tibbon, of which unfortunately only fragments survive, there is no mention of Gabirol, an omission that suggests either that Maimonides was unaware that Gabirol had done any philosophic writing or that Maimonides did not consider what he knew worthy of mention. This possibility, in turn, suggests that Maimonides implicitly rejected Gabirol because of his neo-Platonism, as he explicitly rejected other Jewish neo-Platonists like Joseph ibn Zaddik. Not until the latter part of the thirteenth century was an abridged translation of Gabirol's *Meḳor Ḥayyim* into Hebrew produced by Shem Tob ibn Palquera. It was Palquera's epitomized translation that made possible Salomon Munk's mid-nineteenth-century identification of the identity of Solomon ibn Gabirol and the author of *Fons Vitae*, known as Avicebron.[5]

---

[3] Stephen S. Wise, *The Improvement of the Moral Qualities... by Solomon ibn Gabirol...* (New York, 1902), esp. p. 11.

[4] Husik, *History*, p. 61.

[5] Ibid., p. 63, retells the romantic story in a matter-of-fact tone.

Palquera's introduction to his Hebrew epitome suggests a further source for Gabirol's work, "the views of the ancient philosophers as we find them in a book composed by Empedocles concerning the 'Five Substances'."[6] Indeed, it is to this "Empedoclean" work that Palquera attributes the most influential of Gabirol's ideas, that of universal matter. This work on the five substances was, however, another pseudepigraphical writing of the Hellenistic period, and bears no relation to the thought of Empedocles himself. Palquera's suggestion merely reinforces the conclusion that Gabirol's work was grounded in the eclectic neo-Platonism so common in the Muslim world.

Gabirol, however, was known and celebrated in the Jewish world of the European Middle Ages as a poet, one of the very greatest of the age. Of all his poems, it was the *Keter Malkut* that came closest to immortality by its incorporation into the evening service for the Day of Atonement. A poem is evidently not a philosophic treatise; yet every language has seen the production of poems that have a profoundly philosophical character. Certainly one would anticipate no radical difference between the thought expressed in the poetry and in the philosophy of a poet-philosopher like Gabirol.

It comes, therefore, as something of a shock to read in Steinschneider's *Jewish Literature*, that "the celebrated *Keter Malkut* of SALOMO IBN GABIROL, now to be found in the evening service of the Day of Atonement, is, in fact, a versification of Aristotle's book *De mundo*."[7] *Prima facie*, if there is any attribution of influence on Gabirol's poetry that should not be made, it is an attribution of Aristotelian influence. Steinschneider must have been wrong. Yet this *prima facie* argument is not as strong as it seems, for the consensus of scholarship in the twentieth century is that the short treatise *De mundo*, long included in the Aristotelian corpus, is not to be regarded as a genuine work by Aristotle.[8] Capelle,

---

6 Ibid., pp. 63–4, citing Munk's edition of Maimonides, *Guide of the Perplexed*, II, 25, note 1.

7 M. Steinschneider, *Jewish Literature* (New York, 1965), p. 160.

8 See, e.g., Wilhelm Capelle, in *Neue Jahrbücher*, XV (1905), 529–568.

who gave the work thorough study, considered it to be a popu-
larized version of two works by Posidonius, composed in the first
half of the second century of the common era.[9] Other scholars,
basing their conclusion on the dedication to one "Alexander,"
whom they identify with Tiberius Claudius Alexander, nephew of
Philo Judaeus, date the work early in the second half of the first
century of the common era.[10] Whichever of these attempts at
dating *De mundo* we accept, it is clear that it is merely another of
the many pseudepigrapha of the Hellenistic age of philosophic
eclecticism, and only in part a work preserving aspects of the
Aristotelian tradition.

The standard English version of the Aristotelian corpus is that
of the Oxford edition. E. S. Forster of Sheffield University, who
was assigned the responsibility for preparing the Oxford translation
of *De mundo* wrote: "The description of the natural phenomena of
the universe is the most Aristotelian portion of the work."[11] I take
this to mean that any interpretive or speculative passages in the
treatise are not significantly Aristotelian. Further, considering the
presumed date of composition, there is no reason for regarding
interpretive and speculative passages as either based directly upon
an oral (esoteric) tradition deriving ultimately from Aristotle himself or as founded upon authentic developments within the post-
Aristotelian peripatetic tradition.

If this line of argument is sound, then Steinschneider, though
still in error, was less egregiously so than seemed likely at first

---

[9] Elements of Meteorology (Μετεωρολογικὴ στοιχειώσις) and Concerning the Cosmos (περί κόσμου). Posidonius of Apamea was a Middle Stoic
of the late second century (d. ca. 91 B.C.E.) before the common era; no dog-
matist, he intermingled Platonic and Aristotelian elements with his Stoic teachings. See Ueberweg-Heinze, *Geschichte der Philosophie*, 9th ed. (1903), I,
336.

[10] Rather a remarkable piece of scholarly labor, since the only justification
is the author's use of the phrase ἡγεμόνων ἄριστος (noblest of rulers) at
391b6, a phrase that any author might have used of almost any dedicatee and
potential patron.

[11] "Preface" to Forster's translation of *De mundo* in *The Works of Aristotle*,
translated into English, ed. W. D. Ross, vol. III (Oxford, 1931).

glance. It would, indeed, be possible for Gabirol's *Keter Malkut* to be a versification of *De mundo*; Steinschneider's venial error would have been merely his assuming the correctness of the traditional attribution of *De mundo* to Aristotle himself. Gabirol, as his major philosophic work attests, was certainly not an Aristotelian in his speculative, metaphysical and theological discussions; but then, as we have seen, no more so is the treatise *De mundo*. Physical or descriptive science, however, had not advanced in Gabirol's time significantly beyond the observations and conclusions of Aristotle and his followers, so there would have been no reason for Gabirol to have rejected the descriptive elements in this pseudo-Aristotelian text. Nor, since the falseness of the attribution to Aristotle was not suspected until the latter part of the nineteenth century, could Gabirol have had any occasion to suspect the genuineness of the work.

The source cited by Steinschneider for his categorical assertion of Gabirol's dependence upon what we may now refer to as pseudo-Aristotle's *De mundo* was Michael Sachs' study of Jewish religious poetry in Spain.[12] Sachs, however, was by no means as decisive in making the attribution of Aristotelian influence as was Steinschneider. Indeed, Israel Abrahams has exaggerated Sachs' attitude while moderating Steinschneider's in his assertion that "It has been said (among others, by Sachs and Steinschneider) that the 'Royal Crown' is substantially a versification of Aristotle's short treatise 'On the World'."[13] Steinschneider did not restrict himself to the declaration that Gabirol's poem was "substantially" based upon *De mundo*; in general, Sachs merely asserted the lesser contention that there are substantial parallels to *De mundo*. Sachs also points to parallels in Zeno (as reported by Diogenes Laertius) and to other Greek, Hebrew, and Arabic writers.[14] Significantly, although Sachs' discussion of Gabirol's poem antedates Munk's use of Palquera's epitome of Gabirol's *Meḳor Ḥayyim* to establish the iden-

---

[12] Michael Sachs, *Die religiöse Poesie der Juden in Spanien* (Berlin, 1845).

[13] Israel Abrahams, *By-paths in Hebraic Bookland* (Philadelphia, 1920), p. 78.

[14] See, e.g., Sachs, *Poesie*, p. 226, n. 1.

tity of "Avicebron," Sachs was already aware of the presence of "Empedoclean" elements in Gabirol's *Keter Malkut*.[15] For the most part, then, Sachs is suggesting only that Gabirol was making use of Greek ideas that were widely known in his intellectual *milieu*.

Only with respect to one section of *Keter Malkut*, beginning at verse 107, does Sachs claim greater dependence of Gabirol on *De mundo*. Now he makes the assertion that Steinschneider broadened to include the entire poem:

> Es folgt nun (V. 107 ff.) eine von poetischer Seite geringhalti-gere, zur Kenntniss der mittelalterische Denkweise für die Ge-schichte der Wissenschaft höchst interessante Ausführung, — die Beschreibung der das Universum nach der Vorstellung der Alten constituirenden Theile. Die ganze Partie ist fast nichts weiter, als die poetische Umschreibung des aristotelischen Buches περὶ κόσμου, dem es sich ziemlich genau, sogar in einzelnen sprach-lichen Wendungen anschliesst.[16]

To say that a group of verses in which an ancient cosmological theory was presented is "scarcely more than" or "hardly anything but" a poetical version of *De mundo* may well be a justifiable scholarly assertion. To generalize this limited statement, eliminate its (perhaps self-protective) humility, and apply it to the entire poem of nearly 850 verses, as Steinschneider did, is either arro-gance or irresponsibility.

If, however, the "Aristotelianism" of *Keter Malkut* is limited to its cosmological materials, as presented in a part of the poem, one is led to ask the further question whether it is necessary to postu-late a source in the works of antiquity — even late antiquity — for the Ptolemaic cosmology that was still the prevailing view in Gabirol's own time. A modern poet who wrote on the assumption

---

[15] Ibid., p. 227, n. 1: "Diese Vorstellung vom Sehen hat Empedokles zuerst gehabt." This same note also refers to Plato's *Timaeus*, Aristotle's *De sensu*, Galen, and then to the agency of the "Arabs" in transmitting the idea to the "Jews."

[16] Ibid., p. 229.

that the Sun is the center of our galaxy and that the various pla-
nets, including our Earth, travel around the Sun in elliptical paths
would not necessarily have to have read the works of Sir Isaac
Newton or any of his successors. Only if there were in the poetry
some decisive use, not of Newtonianism in general, but of specific
notions that are present in the work of Newton and not found
elsewhere would it be legitimate to assign Newton as a definite
source. So it is with the cosmology of Aristotle in the age of
Gabirol; it was the common and universally shared picture of the
universe, and the fact of its use in the pseudo-Aristotelian *De
mundo* and in Gabirol's *Keter Malkut* proves nothing more than
that the two works emerge from the same scientific *milieu*.

Sachs and Steinschneider, again, based their judgment that *De
mundo* was the source for, at least, the cosmology of *Keter Malkut*
on the text of *De mundo* presented in the great nineteenth-century
Berlin edition of Immanuel Bekker (1831 and following years).
Later scholars, notably Capelle, have pointed out that the better
manuscripts of *De mundo* express a far more pantheistic interpretation of the universe than does the text printed by Bekker, and
that, indeed, where there is a choice of readings, Bekker invariably
selected the reading that most de-emphasized these pantheistic lean-
ings. If we accept this modern view of the character of the text of
De mundo, then the absence of pantheistic elements in Gabirol's
text would militate against the possibility that *De mundo* was a
direct source for *Keter Malkut*.

What we do find in Gabirol's poem — and might very well
expect to find considering the Platonistic tendencies in his philosophic writings — is a doctrine of emanation. As presented by
Gabirol, this is akin to, but not identical with the doctrine of
emanation as it is found in the earlier Kabbalistic literature.

Thine is the existence, from the emanation of whose light sprang
every existing thing.... Thou are wise; and from thy wisdom
emanated the divine will, which, like a workman and a master,
brought forth at the predestined time the pleasing creation, and
drew forth the thread of existence from non-existence, as the

light issueth from the eye, and is drawn from the fountain of light without bucket.[17]

This theory of light as the vehicle of emanation, as the Reverend D. A. de Sola points out in his notes to the translation of *Keter Malkut* in the Atonement Service of Bevis Marks, the Spanish and Portuguese Synagogue in London, is "agreeable to the ancient theory of light, according to Empedocles and Plato"[18] but it is only so if one interprets this as meaning that "vision was occasioned by particles continually flying off from the surface of bodies, which meet with others proceeding from the eye."[19] To interpret in this fashion seems to me to strain unduly the literal meaning of the text, which can be paralleled in *Sefer Bahir* and other early Kabbalistic writings. I suggest, therefore, that although Gabirol's emanationism does not contravene a generally Platonistic orientation, its actual source lies within the esoteric Jewish tradition to which scholarship has only recently begun to give the attention it deserves.

A similar conclusion can be reached, though with less confidence, about the traces of astrological belief that are revealed in *Keter Malkut*. Astrology is not foreign to esoteric theory within the Jewish tradition, any more than it is to the general European tradition deriving from the Greeks. Perhaps when enough scholarly concern is given to differentiating these two astrological traditions, it will be discovered that in the tradition dervied from the Greeks, the influence exerted by the stars and other heavenly bodies comes into play mechanically, that is, that it is regarded as automatic in its operation; whereas in the Jewish tradition of astrology, while planetary influences are asserted, they are always operative under the hand of God. If this hypothesis, based admittedly on inadequate evidence, should prove to be correct, then it will be possible

---

[17] The translation is that of *The Book of Prayer* of Bevis Marks Synagogue (London, 1934), III, 47–48.

[18] Ibid., p. 264, n. 2.

[19] Ibid.

to assert the Jewish source of Gabirol's astrological tendencies more confidently.[20]

One final question that should be commented upon here is the assertion by Israel Abrahams that, even if the content of *Keter Malkut* is not dependent upon Aristotle (that is, upon the *De mundo*), the over-all structure of the poem does depend upon the Greek original.

> Moreover, Aristotle, in his treatise cited above, anticipated Ibn Gebirol in the motive with which he directed his ancient readers' attention to the elements and the planets. 'What the pilot is in a ship, the driver in a chariot, the coryphaeus in a choir, the general in an army, the lawgiver in a city — that is God in the world' (*De Mundo*, 6). This saying of Aristotle is indeed Ibn Gebirol's text. But the Hebrew poet owes nothing else than the skeleton to his Greek exemplar.[21]

There is, of course, a parallel between the literary structure of *Keter Malkut* and that of *De mundo*. In both, the first section does present the Aristotelian-Ptolemaic system of the universe in reasonably full detail, while the latter part uses the glories thus depicted as a basis for praising the God who ordained the system in all its majesty. It is conceivable, though scarcely provable, that Gabirol did, in fact, have *De mundo* in mind in designing his poem. Yet one has only to read the later sections of *Keter Malkut* to realize that it is not the abstract and philosophic "god" of *De mundo* whose praise is sung by the poet, but the living God of the biblical tradition.

Étienne Gilson, the French medievalist and historian of philosophy, includes a discussion of *Keter Malkut* in his study of medieval philosophy. Gilson comes to a conclusion that is worth recording here:

> Tant qu'il se contente de décrire le *quoi* des choses, Gebirol peut

---

[20] E.g., והוא מעורר מדי חדש בחדשו עולם וקורותיו וטובותיו ורעותיו, ברצון הבורא אותו.

[21] Israel Abrahams, *By-paths*, pp. 78–79, n. 13.

rester fidèle à la tradition grecque; lorsqu'il en vient à poser leur *pourquoi*, la tradition biblique reprend le dessus dans sa pensée, et c'est le Dieu de la Genèse, plus peut-être que celui du *Timée*, qui devient le seul principe concevable d'explication.[22]

This is a valuable suggestion, though perhaps Gilson goes too far in identifying the God of Gabirol's inspiration with the anthropomorphic creator of Genesis. To my mind it is quite clear that Gabirol was celebrating a biblical conception of God, but more the God of the book of Psalms than of Genesis. Many of the biblical phrases and verses that Gabirol ingeniously and beautifully works into the text of *Keter Malkut* are drawn from the book of Psalms. It would not be an exaggeration to describe *Keter Malkut* as an extended poetic rhapsody on the first verse of the nineteenth Psalm, "The heavens declare the glory of God, and the firmament showeth his handiwork."

It is surely important that Jewish scholarship should be more ready than it has been in earlier times to acknowledge the influence of sources external to the Jewish tradition. Such acknowledgments should be made with care, however, and with due attention to all possibilities of internal Jewish sources. On a failure to observe this caution rests the unjustified attribution of Aristotelian influence in the writing of Gabirol's *Keter Malkut*.

---

22 É. Gilson, *La philosophie au moyen âge* (Paris, 1947), p. 371.

PREMIERS TÉMOIGNAGES
ÉPIGRAPHIQUES
SUR LES JUIFS EN FRANCE

BERNHARD BLUMENKRANZ

SI TOUTE INSCRIPTION JUIVE était toujours rédigée — ne serait-ce que partiellement en hébreu, ou bien si, à défaut de cela, elle comportait tout au moins chaque fois un symbole juif (le chandelier à sept branches, *ménorah*, ou la branche de palmier, *lulaf*, ou le cédrat, *etrog*, ou la corne de bélier, *shofar*) il n'y aurait point de difficulté majeure à en dresser le catalogue. Or, on sait bien qu'il n'en est rien pendant les premiers siècles de l'ère commune en Occident.

En Italie, notamment à Rome, la situation est encore relativement aisée. D'abord, en raison de l'existence d'un certain nombre de lieux de sépulture authentiquement juifs. Bien sûr, il est aussi bien établi que toutes les épitaphes qui ont été trouvées en ces endroits n'ont pas toujours primitivement appartenu à ces ensembles. N'empêche que le nombre de celles qui sont encore scellées — ou gravées ou tracées, quand il s'agit de graffiti — dans les parois est déjà assez important. En y ajoutant celles qui par les mots en hébreu ou les symboles juifs ou l'ensemble du contenu sont incontestablement juives, on arrive à un total assez appréciable qui, par les listes onomastiques aussi bien que par les formules qu'il peut livrer, offre un précieux matériel de comparaison et, partant, d'authentification éventuelle pour les inscriptions douteuses.

Toute autre est la situation en France. A ce jour, aucun lieu de sépulture authentiquement juif n'a été trouvée pour les derniers siècles de l'antiquité ou les premiers du moyen âge. Et les inscriptions connues qui par les critères énoncées plus haut sont identifiées comme authentiquement juives sont trop peu nombreux pour livrer, sur un plan géographique autonome, un matériel onomastique de comparaison.

Mais, par ailleurs, nous croyons avoir réussi à prouver, par des produits archéologiques, la présence des Juifs en France dès la fin du Ier siècle, présence attestée à nouveau aux IIIe, IVe et début du Ve siècles. Et à partir de la seconde moitié du Ve siècle, le nombre de documents parfaitement bien connus jusqu'ici déjà sur les Juifs en France est assez considérable pour nous engager à reprendre, si faire se peut, l'examen des inscriptions.

Nous disposons, à ce jour, de trois tentatives de réunir les inscriptions juives de France.

La première est le fait d'Edmond Le Blant, qui se proposait de les insérer dans son ouvrage *Inscriptions chrétiennes de la Gaule antérieures au VIIIe siècle*, deux volumes, Paris 1856 et 1865. Dans la préface (p. CXIV–CXV) il dit quelques mots de la présence des Juifs en Gaule et mentionne déjà l'inscription (funéraire) juive de Narbonne qui, seule, figure dans son ouvrage (no. 621, t. 2, p. 476–480).

On sait bien que cette inscription comporte deux éléments qui, sans conteste possible, affirment son caractère juif: le dessin du chandelier à sept branches en tête du texte, et les trois mots en hébreu שלום על י[שראל, *shalom al Israël*, vers la fin.

Dans le complément qu'Edmond Le Blant a réuni sous le titre de *Nouveau Recueil des Inscriptions Chrétiennes de la Gaule antérieures au VIIIe siècle*, Paris 1892, deux nouvelles inscriptions juives seront inventoriées parce qu'elles comportent soit un symbole juif, soit également un mot en hébreu. Nous y trouvons alors la bague (d'identité) de Bordeaux (no. 284 A, p. 305–307) qui comporte même trois fois le dessin du chandelier à sept branches, et l'inscription (dédicatoire?) d'Auch (no. 292, p. 319–324) qui comporte à sa fin en hébreu le mot שלום, *shalom*, et, en plus du chandelier à sept branches, deux autres symboles juifs que sont la branche de palmier, *lulaf* et la corne de bélier, *shofar*.

Moïse Schwab, dans son *Rapport sur les inscriptions hébraïques de la France*, dans *Nouvelles Archives des Missions scientifiques et litt.*, t. 12, 1904, 143–383, apporte déjà par son titre une discrimination plus grande: pour figurer dans son recueil, il ne suffit pas qu'une inscription soit juive; il faut ou bien qu'elle soit entièrement en hébreu ou au moins qu'elle comporte des mots en hébreu; dans son chapitre Ier consacré au haut moyen-âge (jusqu'au XIe siècle compris) il maintient donc, à ce titre, les inscriptions de Narbonne (§ 1, p. 169–174) et d'Auch (§ 2, p. 174–184).

Il ajoute ensuite deux inscriptions d'Arles (§ 3, 1 et 2, p. 184–186) qu'on a voulu dater du VIIe ou VIIIe siècle mais dont il convient lui-même que la date réelle peut-être plus tardive encore, et une de Vienne dans l'Isère (§ 4, p. 187–189), dont il n'exclut pas — en raison de la rencontre du nom de Justus dans des documents du Xe siècle—une date semblable (nous négligeons son § 5 sur les inscriptions de Hamman-Lif en Tunisie, p. 189–193). C'est donc déjà là, avec les réserves qui s'imposent pour les inscriptions d'Arles et de Vienne, un ensemble de cinq documents.

Enfin, le Père Jean-Baptiste Frey, dans son *Corpus Inscriptionum Iudaicarum* (t. 1, Europe, Cité du Vatican 1936), *Recueil des Inscriptions Juives qui vont du IIIe siècle avant Jésus Christ au VIIe siècle de notre ère*, indique déjà par son titre qu'il veut embrasser l'ensemble des inscriptions juives, quelle que sont leur langue.

Bien mieux, il n'entend pas se limiter à des inscriptions d'origine juive, mais se propose d'englober dans son *Corpus* aussi celles qui concernent les Juifs.

Par contre, en opposition à Moïse Schwab, il entend — comme l'a fait Le Blant — s'arrêter à la fin du VIIe siècle. Cela ne l'empêche pas de reprendre l'ensemble des cinq documents produits par Schwab, auxquels il joint la bague de Bordeaux relevé par Le Blant et omise par Schwab, et ajoute enfin le "sceau carré" d'Avignon (en réalité: matrice rectangulaire), pour arriver ainsi à un total de sept documents (no. 666–672, p. 478–484).

Mais là ne s'arrête point l'enrichissement apporté par le Père Frey. Il donne, en appendice du volume, les "inscriptions considérées à tort comme juives," et alors, nous trouvons sous la rubrique des "Inscriptions probablement païennes," et ensuite sous celle des "inscriptions probablement chrétiennes," six autres documents que lui a procurés en premier lieu un dépouillement attentif du *Corpus Inscriptionum Latinarum* et qui avaient été considérées, soit déjà par l'éditeur du *CIL*, soit par d'autres savants (en particulier par

J. Oehler, dans *MGWJ*, LIII (1909), 292 sqq., 443 sqq. et 525 sqq., comme juives.

Inutile de s'attarder au no. 61* (p. 565), inscription bilingue grecque et latine trouvée à Genay près de Trévoux (Ain) et qui concerne un marchand syrien, originaire de Canatha. C'est par erreur qu'Oehler l'a citée comme juive; car il en doit la connaissance à E. Schürer (*Geschichte des jüdischen Volkes im Zeitalter Jesu Christi*, t. 2, 1898, p. 133) qui l'invoque non pas comme inscription juive, mais comme celle "eines syrischen Kaufmanns," d'un marchand syrien.

Le no. 62* (p. 566) de Lyon, concernant une Aurelia Callistes, est encore une inscription bilingue qui, en vérité, ne comporte aucun élément juif.

Plus délicat est le cas du no. 63* (p. 566) du Trion à Lyon, concernant une Aurelia Sabbatia. Si, en effet, le *D(iis) M(anibus)* en tête de l'inscription interdit de considérer l'enfant concernée comme juive, il n'est point improbable que c'étaient des influences juives qui avaient déterminé le choix de son nom, à moins que la mère (comme l'éditeur du *CIL*, en propose la possibilité) n'ait été juive.

Au no. 94* (p. 588–9), l'épitaphe dédiée aux trois enfants de Vitalinus et de Martina: Sapaudus, Rustica et Rusticula, n'aurait probablement pas été considérée comme juive si elle ne présentait pas le nom de Sapaudus, attesté par ailleurs dans une inscription authentiquement juive, celle de Narbonne. Mais tout d'abord, le rapport de cette inscription avec celle de Narbonne a été suggéré par le fait que toutes deux sont dédiées chaque fois à trois enfants morts en un très court espace de temps; de là on a vite été amené à déduire qu'il a pu s'agir dans les deux cas des victimes d'une persécution antijuive.

Les nos. 95* et 96* (p. 589), concernent le premier une Sabatia, et l'autre un enfant Sabat(ius); tous deux proviennent de Soulosse (Vosges). Comme pour le no. 62*, à défaut d'une appartenance réelle au Judaïsme de ces deux personnes, on peut encore envisager une influence juive qui a présidé au choix de ces noms.

On est d'autant plus en droit de supposer une influence juive présidant au choix des noms de Sabatius ou de Sab(b)atia, que ces noms sont très rares. Le tome XIII du *Corpus Inscriptionum Latinarum* n'en connaît que trois attestations: celles précisément auxquelles nous avons affaire ici. Par contre, ce nom est bien attesté parmi les inscriptions authentiquement juives de Rome. Avec la forme grecque au féminin Sabbatis, l'inscription CII 155 se trouve à la catacombe juive de la Vigna Randani, dans la via Appia; toujours au même endroit et sous la même forme dans les inscriptions CII 156 et 157; CII 263, encore au même endroit, présente la forme latine au masculin Sabatius. De la catacombe juive de Monteverde, dans la via Portuensis, provient CII 470 qui comporte Sabbatis en caractères latins. Si CII 530 est de provenance incertaine, cette inscription nous fournit un Sabbatius dont la qualité de Juif ne peut prêter à aucun doute, lorsqu'on le trouve en compagnie d'un Isacis d'une part, et d'un Felix Tineosus Iudaeus et d'un Cretic(u)s Iudeus d'autre part.

Toute vaste que fût l'information du P. Frey, deux inscriptions de France lui ont échappé. La première, il est vrai, n'aurait été rangée par lui — et à juste titre — que parmi les inscriptions fausses. C'est sous cette rubrique qu'elle figure également dans le tome XII du *Corpus Inscriptionum Latinarum*, no. 146*, p. 15*. Il s'agit de l'inscription de Peyruis (Basses-Alpes) qui y aurait été découverte et transcrite par un Dr. Bérenger, pour être publiée ensuite par Scaliger et par Gruter. Cette inscription relate le meurtre d'un préfet romain, sous Constantin, par des "sicaires et des Juifs." Muratori déjà — suivi en cela par Papon (*Hist. gén. de Provence*) — avait démasqué la supercherie destinée à conférer une très grande ancienneté à cette petite localité sur la Durance. Aux arguments avancés par Muratori, nous sommes aujourd'hui en mesure d'en ajouter un autre qui peut éclairer le mécanisme de cette forgerie: face à Peyruis, de l'autre côté du fleuve, se trouve la commune Les Mées qui possède, depuis le moyen âge, une "rue des Juifs"; c'est là, très probablement, que l'"inventeur"-faussaire du début du XVIIe siècle a trouvé l'idée d'introduire des Juifs dans *son* inscription romaine. Mais, quoiqu'il en soit, l'insertion dans un recueil qui se veut complet de cette inscription, toute fausse qu'elle soit, se recommande d'autant plus qu'elle continue encore, jusqu'à aujourd'hui, à être invoquée quelquefois pour prouver la très haute ancienneté de la présence des Juifs en Haute Provence.

Enfin, une inscription grecque d'Antibes mériterait de figurer au moins parmi les inscriptions juives douteuses. Bien que découverte depuis la fin de l'autre siècle, elle est restée, à ma connaissance, entièrement ignorée par les études juives; il m'est agréable de la relever aujourd'hui, dans cet ensemble d'études juives en l'honneur du Professeur Baron.

Il faut aussitôt ajouter que si j'ai le tout mince mérite d'avoir "redécouvert" cette inscription, je dois le plus substantiel des renseignements à son propos à la courtoisie de M. Dor de La Souchère, Conservateur du Musée Picasso d'Antibes, qui m'en a aussi bien fourni la photo.

Cette inscription se présente sur une petite tablette de marbre blanc, de forme rectangulaire (hauteur: 149 mm; largeur: 170 mm; épaisseur: 24 mm), brisée à l'angle supérieur gauche. Elle a été trouvée, en janvier 1884, aux bords du Fort Carré d'Antibes, au milieu des balayures de la ville. L'original qui se trouvait dans la collection du Dr. Mougins de Roquefort doit être considéré comme perdu; le Musée d'Antibes possède le moule et le moulage (Inv. Gén. no. 100 et 100 bis).

Le texte et la traduction ne présentent point de difficulté majeure. La lacune du début de la première ligne, due à la brisure de la plaque, se laisse aisément combler: ['Io]ῦστος Σεῖλου ἔζησε ἔτεσι $\overline{\text{OB}}$

Traduction: Justus, fils de Silas, a vécu soixante douze ans.

Les deux savants locaux qui, les premiers, se sont intéressés à cette inscription, le Colonel Gazan et le Dr. Mougins de Roquefort (*Une inscription tumulaire grecque à Antibes*, dans *Bulletin de la Société d'études scientifiques et archéologiques de la ville de Draguignan* XVI, 1886–7, 279–84), se sont demandé si elle était païenne ou chrétienne, sans même envisager la troisième solution possible, à savoir qu'elle fût juive. M. Dor de La Souchère, dans ses notes personnelles, s'engage lui résolument dans cette voie: "L'inscription est à mon avis l'épitaphe d'un juif... Il est probable que Justus et Silas étaient des juifs."

S'il est vrai que le nom de Justus — au contraire de ce que nous avons pu dire tout à l'heure à propos de Sabatius ou Sab(b)atia — est généralement très répandu, il est aussi bien vrai que nous possédons de nombreuses attestations formelles où il est porté par des Juifs. Pour nous limiter à la documentation réunie par le P. Frey, nous y trouvons Justus quatorze fois, soit en grec soit en latin. CII 3 est identifiée comme juive par la formule "Qu'en paix soit son sommeil." Avec CII 125, nous avons affaire à une inscription peinte dans la catacombe juive de la Via Nomentana; de la catacombe juive de la Vigna Randanina proviennent les nos. 125, 224, 245 et 252; de celle de Monteverde les nos. 358 et 359. CII 502 nomme avec Justus deux autres personnes qui sont désignées comme "hébreux". Dans le no. 533, Justus est un fonctionnaire de la communauté juive d'Ostie. Le no. 629 (comme également d'autres) comporte l'identification juive par le symbole de la *menorah*; enfin, dans le no. 670, l'inscription incontestablement juive de Narbonne (cf. supra), le nom Justus figure même deux fois.

Les lettres (E et S lunaires ainsi que le zeta) semblent dater l'inscription de la fin du IIe siècle de l'ère commune. Si nous ne sommes pas en droit d'affirmer l'existence d'une communauté juive à Antibes à cette époque, nous possédons toutefois, grâce à cette inscription, de fortes présomptions pour la supposer.

DON "IṢḤAQ BRAUNEL"
(ALGUNAS PRECISIONES BIOGRAFICAS SOBRE SU ESTANCIA EN CASTILLA)

Francisco Cantera Burgos

ENTRE LAS PERSONALIDES JUDÍAS que brillaron en el reinado de los Reyes Católicos así por su actuación en la esfera administrativo-hacendística como en el campo de la exégesis y la filosofía religiosa, pocas hay de la talla y relieve del judío portugués, aunque de abolengo castellano, Don Iṣḥaq Brauanel o Abravanel.

Si bien a tan famosa figura se le han consagrado múltiples estudios, sobre todo con motivo del quinto centenario de su nacimiento,[1] y el Prof. B. Netanyahu ha publicado acerca de él una monografía notable que en 1968 ha alcanzado segunda edición,[2] quedan todavía, como es frecuente en toda obra humana, no pocos extremos que profundizar y susceptibles de nuevos trabajos e investigaciones.

En esta nuestra suscinta aportación al merecido Homenaje dedicado al Prof. Salo W. Baron nos limitamos a ilustrar algunos extremos de la biografía del sabio lusitano en su relación con España. Dejando para otra ocasión lo que atañe a los orígenes españoles de la familia Abravanel y a sus representantes conocidos antes de su partida hacia Portugal — de lo cual sabemos harto poco — concentraremos aquí nuestra atención en los puntos en los que cabe proyectar alguna luz nueva durante la estancia de Don Ishaq en las tierras gobernadas por Isabel I y Fernando V de Castilla.

---

[1] Cf. lo que escribimos en el fasc. 2 de SEFARAD (I, 1941), pp. 404–405.

[2] La primera es de 1953, Philadelphia, The Jewish Publication Society of America.

1. *Entrada y primer asiento de Don Isḥaq en Castilla.*

Con arreglo a los datos que B. Netanyahu, el más completo de los biógrafos de Abravanel, nos ofrece (pp. 31–32), envuelto éste en el complot de los Braganza contra João II de Portugal, el 30 de mayo de 1483 era requerido por el Monarca para que compareciese ante él en Evora. Camino de esta ciudad, cuando proyectaba detenerse en Arrayolos para pernoctar, un amigo, quizá de la casa del Duque, hízole saber la detención de éste el día anterior y le urgió a huir del país, ya que figuraba entre las personas incluídas en la purga proyectada por João II. Sólo "sixteen leagues" separaban entonces a Abravanel de Castilla por la ruta de Badajoz, mas como ésta pasaba por Vila Viçosa, residencia del Duque de Braganza, y suponía el lugar peligroso, como más custodiado por los agentes del Rey, optó al huir por dirigirse hacia el Norte, viajando durante el día por territorio portugués y rehuyendo las rutas de Castilla entre Guadiana y Tajo, que supuso más vigiladas. Al oscurecer alcanzaría el segundo de esos ríos, que cruzó por Vila Velha de Rodão, para seguir todavía "ten leagues" más y, tornando luego hacia el este, cruzar la frontera luso-castellana "only in the middle of the second night", la noche del 31 de mayo.

"*On crossing the Castilian border*-escribe Netanyahu al iniciar el capítulo segundo de su libro — *Abravanel arrived at the small town of Segura de la Orden.* Segura *belonged to the district of Plasencia* and from there to the city of Plasencia was a comparatively short distance. The city had a sizeable Jewish community — *the only considerable community in that region* — and it must have seemed the logical place for Abravanel to go to under the circumstances. There is reason to believe that he did so and that he remained in Plasencia for some time, although a few months later we find him again in Segura. What attraction could *the small frontier town* have held for him in those days? *Only a few Jewish families lived there — perhaps no more than forty or fifty* — and the fact that the town was *so close to the border* would seem to have made it

anything but a desirable spot for a fugitive from an enraged
monarch. Joao, Abravanel knew, would not ordinarily tres-
pass the rights of his powerful neighbor, with whom he was
resolved to live in peace. Still, there was no telling what he
might do to recapture an alleged rebel who was right at his
threshold. Abravanel, it seems, was in hiding the first months
after his escape, and Segura was too small a place to enable
him to keep his identity secret. From the one remark left us
by Abravanel on this point, it appears in fact, that it was not
Segura where he hid; yet he must have gone to Segura from
time to time, and for a reason which can be readily understood.
The proximity of the town to the Portuguese border offered
him obvious advantages. He still had many things to settle
in Portugal. From Segura, it may be safely assumed, he dispatched warnings to his family, advising them to hasten their
departure from Portugal and to take with them whatever property they could save. He must have succeeded in establishing — and maintaining — contact with his family, and perhaps also some of his friends, for he soon received word that
Joao II had confiscated all his possessions."

En la página transcrita (y sus notas correspondientes) hay no
pocas cosas que precisar y aun corregir. Sobre todo mézclanse en
ella diversas poblaciones de nombre *Segura* que conviene no con-
fundir. Una de éstas es la Segura asentada a orillas del Eljas,
afluente del Tajo, en tierra portuguesa de la misma línea fronteriza;
es obvio que en ella, si por allí cruzó frontera Abravanel, no se
detendría lo más mínimo. Adentrada en la provincia de Cáceres
hállase Segura de Toro, aldehuela próxima a Hervás y no alejada
de Plasencia; también juzgamos ha de descartarse, pues ni consta
que hubiera allí judería ni es imaginable ofreciera asilo adecuado
a un extranjero fugitivo. La región extremeña a la que llegaba
Abravanel, contra lo que Netanyahu parece suponer, contaba a
la sazón con múltiples aljamas judaicas, además de Plasencia, para
brindar refugio a un correligionario en peligro. Entre ellas no fi-

guraba, desde luego, la Segura de cuarenta o cincuenta vecinos judíos a que alude Netanyahu; pues tal villorrio, que él aduce a base de F. Baer,[3] hallábase a cientos de kilómetros de distancia, en la provincia vasca de Guipúzcoa.

Para nosotros la Segura en que I. Abravanel encontró cobijo no estaba en tierras de Plasencia sino bastante más al sur en la Extremadura de Badajoz cerca de la raya de Huelva. Es la *Segura de la Orden* que en el repartimiento de servicios y medios servicios de 1474 figura con 6.000 mrs. y sabemos fué una de las comunidades judías extremeñas que vió acrecer su contingente de vecinos hebreos por virtud del decreto de 1 de enero de 1483, que había obligado a disolverse a las aljamas del arzobispado de Sevilla y prohibido a los judíos morar en el territorio de las diócesis de Sevilla, Córdoba y Cádiz. En efecto, los Reyes en documento de 1485, al repartir el tributo extraordinario de castellanos por guerra, señala a Segura de la Orden, además de los 200 que normalmente le hubieran correspondido, otros 60 por ese acrecentamiento que había experimentado con vecinos judíos del arzobispado sevillano.

La población — insistimos — hallábase en comarca de múltiples e importantes juderías y donde actuó y pobló la Orden de los Templarios en tiempo de Alfonso IX de León. Figura en el Nomenclator de Floridablanca como villa de Orden Militar.[4] Después de poseerla dicha Orden pasó a ser villa de Realengo y, al igual que otras de la región, v. gr. Xerez de los Caballeros, tras pertenecer a los caballeros templarios, pasó a los santiaguistas. En esta última etapa se la denominó *Segura de León*, por pertenecer, como otros pueblecitos comarcanos, a la Encomienda mayor de León. En su notable castillo residía el administrador de esa Encomienda. En tiempo de Madoz[5] se le asignan 550 casas. Las circunstancias antes

---

3 *Die Juden im christlichen Spanien* (Berlin, 1936), I/2, p. 369.

4 No ha de ser confundida con *Segura de la Sierra*, en la provincia de Jaén, junto a Orcera y en la Sierra de Segura, la cual perteneció también a la Orden de Santiago. Segura de la Orden o de León está en la Sierra de Tudia (No es claro L. Suárez en sus *Documentos acerca de la expulsión de los judíos*, p. 36, e Indice, s. v.)

5 Cf. en *Diccionario geográfico-estadístico-histórico* t. XIV (Madrid, 1849).

aducidas, su prudente distancia de la frontera portuguesa (menos de 30 kms.) y su relativa proximidad a Lisboa y Evora, así como su fácil conexión con otras juderías de abolengo (como Badajoz, Mérida, Cáceres, Coria, Plasencia, Llerena, etc.) ofrecían, según creemos, lugar muy apropiado de asilo para aquel refugiado portugués, que incluso pudo topar allí parientes de su mismo apellido acogidos a Segura tras la expulsión de Sevilla.

En el agosto siguiente le llegarían noticias de un nuevo enfurecimiento de João II y del asesinato el 23 de agosto de 1484 del Duque de Viseu, de quien era administrador y privado Don Yuçef Abravanel, yerno y sobrino de Don Işḥaq. Huyendo de la muerte y con no escasa fortuna, llegaría poco después a tierras extremeñas con su mujer y su hermano Don Jaco para establecerse en Plasencia, donde años adelante obtendría (en 1488) el cargo de recaudador mayor de la renta del servicio y montazgo del ganado "de nuestros regnos e señoríos" y el de recaudador general de Plasencia.

2. Su actividad de financiero al servicio de los Mendoza.

Son muchas las lagunas que aún ha de colmar una esmerada investigación sobre la década de existencia, muy activa y movida, que Don Işḥaq desarrolló en Castilla. Sus biógrafos, en general, se han cuidado de modo especial de encarecer su puesto excepcional como financiero al servicio de los Reyes Católicos: arrendador de las rentas públicas, asentista del ejército que conquistó Granada; ministro de Hacienda de Doña Isabel y Don Fernando para otros.

Netanyahu señala que, estando en Segura, fue invitado a una audiencia con los Reyes de España hacia mediados de marzo de 1484. La entrevista tendría lugar con ocasión de las cortes de Tarazona. Los graves problemas planteados entonces, no debieron de permitir muy pausado coloquio. Al menos nada traslucen nuestros cronistas.

Según F. Baer la primera prueba documentada del establecimiento de Don Işḥaq en Castilla es de 1488, fecha en que aparece

como arrendador de las alcabalas de Requena "Don Isaque Abravanel, vesino de Alcalá de Henares" en compañia de "Don Yuçe
Abenaex, vesino de Cordoba"; y la misma pareja figura como
arrendadora de las salinas de Atienza.

Sin embargo, ya para 1485 debía de andar por el centro de España e incluso morar en el "mesón pintado" de Alcalá de Henares
a juzgar por un importante documento del Archivo Provincial de
Toledo, cuyo conocimiento debemos a la gentileza amable de su
Director Don Emilio Garcia Rodríguez.

En él se especifican las condiciones en que "don Ysaque Ab-
rauanel el judío, natural del Reyno de Portogal" acepta las "rentas del obispado de Sygüença que pertenecen al Rmo. Señor Cardenal d'España e a su mēsa episcopal de Siguença con las alcaualas
de la dicha çibdad e su tierra, con Val de la rriba e la suya, e con
las terçias que a su señoria pertenesçe e lieua en la dicha çibdad
de Guadalajara, y Santa Maria de la Fuente e con los otros logares
de la tierra dela dicha cibdad e con Alhondiga e Alhoçen, segund
se suelen arrendar los años pasados, por estos dos años venideros
que començaran primero dia de enero del año venidero de 1486
años e fenesçeran el postrimero dia de disienbre del año que verná
de 1487 años."

Primeramente pone dichas rentas, alcabalas y tercias "por los
dos años de 86 e 87 en presçio e contia de 6 cuentos e 4000.000
mrs., a razon de 3 cuentos e 200.000 mrs. cada uno de los dichos
años" con las condiciones y de la manera que se arrendaron el
presente año de 85 a Diego de Villanuño y García Rodrigues
Gallego, vecinos de Sigüenza, y a sus compañeros, a excepción de
lo en dichas condiciones exceptuado. En cuanto al modo de pago
a su Señoría, los 3 cuentos y 200.000 mrs. del año 86 se pagarán
así: el un cuento y 400.000 mrs. de la primera paga en fin de enero
de 87 y 200.000 mrs. en fin del abril siguiente, otro cuento y 400.000
en fin de junio del mismo año y los 200.000 mrs. restantes del
año 86 al finalizar setiembre del 87. De la suma pagaranse a su
Señoría los tres cuentos de las primeras tres pagas puestos en
Sigüenza en poder de la persona o personas que el Sr. Cardenal
mandare; y los 200.000 mrs. restantes de la paga postrimera de

en fin de setiembre puestos en la villa de Alcalá en quien su Señoría mandare, en la moneda corriente al tiempo de las pagas. De igual forma se pagarán en el año 88 al Sr. Cardenal los 3 cuentos y 200.000 mrs. del 87.

Se estipulan, además, las condiciones siguientes: Don Isaque pagará en cada uno de los dos años, demás de lo susodicho, "el pan, triego e çeuada que esta sytuado en las terçias" de Guadalajara y su tierra a Don Hurtado de Mendoza y a la abadesa y monjas del monasterio de San Bernaldo de dicha ciudad.

Dichas rentas del obispado con las alcabalas y las rentas de las tercias que Don Isaque pone en los 6 cuentos y 400.000 mrs. estarán abiertas desde hoy fecha de esta escritura hasta el 10 de octubre del presente año 85 para que las pueda pujar quien los deseare dentro de ese plazo y la puja o pujas hechas las reciba el Sr. Cardenal, "tanto que sean por los dichos dos años e non el uno syn el otro".

Desde la fecha de esta capitulación hasta fines de julio próximo inmediato Don Isaque podrá hacer el repartimiento que desee de los citados 6 cuentos y 400.000 mrs. para que puedan pujar quienes quisieren en cada una de las dichas rentas.

El señor Cardenal mandará dar y dará a Don Isaque "por esta postura que haze" de tales rentas 200 castellanos de oro, cien por cada año, que se le pagarán "luego los 100 castellanos e los otros 100 al tiempo del remate".

Señala por último que, si bien en el arriendo de 1485 se exigía que había de ser receptor de las rentas el referido G. Rodrigues Gallego, ahora "quedo asentado con el dicho Don Ysaque quel... señor Cardenal pueda poner por su reçeptor" de las rentas de los años 86 a 87 a quien su señoría pluguiese, "el qual aya de reçebir las fianças por menudo e sea obligado el tal reçeptor de pagar a su señoria la quantya de mrs. porque fueren arrendadas e afiançadas... por menudo; pero que sy... Don Isaque quesiere la dicha reçeptoria para persona que sea christiano, que la pueda poner de su mano contentado de fianças de los dichos tres cuentos e 200.000 mrs. en cada año e sea obligado de pagar a su señoria a los dichos plasos" en ambos años convenidos y en dineros contados.

La capitulación hízola don Ysaque, en Córdoba, a 6 de junio de 1485, estando presente el Rmo. señor Cardenal, con los requisitos arriba declarados "e con condiçión que [el primero] gane e le ayan de ser pagados los dichos 200 castellanos del prometydo... e obligose por sy e por sus bienes de que, sy non le fueren pujadas las dichas rentas" por los dos años referidos, pagará los 6 cuentos y 200.000 mrs. de los plazos y con las condiciones susodichas so pena del doblo, "sobre lo qual otorgó carta firme e dio poder a las justiçias e sometiose a la juridiçion" del Cardenal "e señalo casa para donde se hagan los proçesos contra él en la villa de Alcala de Henares en el meson pintado". Luego el señor Cardenal dijo que recibía la postura con las condiciones dichas y prometido de los 200 castellanos; "e sy las rentas non le fueren pujadas dentro del dicho termino de suso declarado, que desde agora para estonçes ge las remataua e remato, e prometia e prometio de non ge las quitar por mas nin por menos, ni por al tanto nin por otra rason alguna". Fueron testigos presentes Diego Gonçales de Guadalajara, secretario de su señoría, y Diego Fernandes y Diego de Talavera. Firman la capitulación "El Cardenal" e "Ysaq brauanel".

De otros contactos de orden similar entre I. Abravanel y el cardenal Pedro González de Mendoza tenemos alguna otra referencia menos solemne y es muy de notar esta relación de Don Isaq con el "tercer rey de España" como por su influencia se llamaba al Cardenal. A Abravanel debió de servir grandemente para su medro en la Corte de los Reyes Católicos, no menos que el apoyo del encumbrado Don Abraham Seneor.

Por otra parte hemos de destacar aquí también el cargo que Don Yshaq ejerció de contador mayor de los Duques del Infantado, Don Iñigo López de Mendoza y su esposa Doña María de Luna. Así, v. gr., en 10 de septiembre de 1490 ordenaban en Guadalajara a su contador don Ysaque Abrabanel que consignara en los libros ducales el traslado de una importante carta en que los Duques confirmaban a la villa de San Martín de Valdeiglesias la merced regia de mercado franco que venían disfrutando sus moradores "christianos y judios y moros", de cuyos leales servicios se muestran agradecidos los señores de la Villa.[6]

Al año siguiente sabemos que don Isḥaq Abravanel, vecino de Guadalajara y titulándose "contador mayor del ilustre y muy magnífico señor el duque del Infantazgo", sostenía pleito contra los concejos de San Agustín, Alcobendas y Pedrezuela. Según la demanda presentada por el procurador de Abravanel, Francisco Sánchez de Valladolid, dichos concejos, cada uno por sí e in solidum, habíanse obligado de pagar al referido contador la bonita suma de 408.550 mrs. "por cierto brocado e mercaduria que el dicho mi parte dio a doña Maria de Mendoça." Como no pagasen, Abravanel reclama a los concejos en juicio que quedó "olvidado" en marzo de 1492.[7]

3. *La salida de España.*

No se conocen demasiados testimonios (documentales o historiográficos) sobre la actuación pública de Isḥaq Abravanel en su decenio español. Sin embargo, no faltan algunos documentos, todavía inéditos, que se refieren a sus actividades de arrendador. El Archivo de Simancas conserva, v. gr., además de escrituras ya publicadas por F. Baer y L. Suárez, alguna otra inédita como la carta dirigida desde Ubeda por el Consejo real, en 12 de noviembre de 1489, al corregidor de Moya para que determine acerca de una iguala hecha entre Martín de Perato, habitante en Valencia, y un factor que Abravaniel (!) tenía en aquel puerto.[8] Y en diciembre, el mismo Consejo, también desde Ubeda, remitía carta para que un escribano entregara un traslado de emplazamiento hecho por don Isaac Abravanel a otro del Concejo de la Mesta.[9]

Mas, prescindiendo de datos similares, vamos a referirnos bre-

---

6 Vide cód. 9/832 de la "Colección Salazar" de la Real Academia de la Historia, fol. 150v a 156v. Cf. nuestro trabajo *La judería de San Martín de Valdeiglesias* (Madrid; SEFARAD, XXIX, 1969, p. 223).

7 Arch. Chanc. Vall., escribanía de Zarandona y Vals, olvidados, leg. 166 Cf. N. Alonso Cortés, *Acervo bibliográfico*, "Bol. R. Ac. Esp." XXIX, 1949, p. 279-280.

8 Simancas, R. G. S. 1489 — XI, fol. 209.

9 Simancas, R. G. S. 1489 — XII, fol. 98.

vemente a algunos aspectos de la salida de los judíos de España en 1942. Sabido es el papel destacadísimo que en aquellos días trágicos para el judaísmo español desempeñó Don Isḥaq al frente de los exiliados. Abraham ben Selomoh de Torrutiel lo destacó en *Sefer ha-Qabbalah* con firmes trazos, y recientemente H. H. Ben-Sasson en docto artículo sobre *The Generations of the Spanish Exiles on the Fate*[10] ha encarecido el gran valor social y nacional y la sagrada misión directiva que para sus correligionarios revistieron cerca de los soberanos cristianos personalidades como Don Isḥaq Abravanel. Este mismo nos relata al comienzo de su comentario al *Libro de los Reyes* sus denodados esfuerzos en Granada por conseguir de D. Fernando y Dª Isabel la abolición del decreto de 1492 que ponía a las comunidades hebreas ante el dilema de bautismo o salida de las tierras de España, Sicilia, Mallorca y Cerdaña. Es conmovedora su página: "Yo estaba a la sazón allí en la corte real y me afané en mi súplica hasta enronquecer mi garganta. Tres veces hablé al Monarca personalmente y le imploré diciendo: "¡Favor, oh rey! ¿por qué obras de este modo con tus súbditos? Imponnos fuertes gravámenes; regalos de oro y plata y cuanto posee un hombre de la casa de Israel lo dará por su tierra natal". Imploré a mis amigos que gozaban del favor regio para que intercediesen por mi pueblo, y los más destacados celebraron consulta para solicitar del Soberano con todas sus energías que retirara las órdenes de cólera y furor y abandonara su proyecto de perder a los judíos. Mas él como sorda víbora tapó sus oídos y en nada cejó. Además, la Reina, que estaba a su derecha como acusador fiscal,[11] le impelió con poderosa persuasión a ejecutar y rematar su obra iniciada. Nos esforzamos sin descanso; no tuve tranquilidad ni reposo, mas la desgracia llegó."

Creemos que ninguno de los anecdóticos y legendarios relatos sobre la dramática lucha de aquellos días entre los titánicos esfuerzos judíos y el tesón inconmovible de los Reyes, supera en emotiva grandeza la página de Don Isḥaq. Nada pudieron ni las

---

[10] En "Zion" XXV, 1961, 1, pp. 23 a 64.
[11] Nótese esta referencia tomada de Zacarías 3, 1.

riquezas ofrecidas ni la mediación de influencia de amigos como Boabdil, nobles tal vez como el del Infantado, o prelados como Pedro González de Mendoza, e incluso judíos prestigiosos como Abraham Seneor, a quienes Abravanel parece recurrió en un desesperado intento.

También los Monarcas debieron de intentar doblegar la tenacidad del arrendador portugués, inalterable en su lealtad al judaísmo. No por esto se le mostraron sañudos; antes al contrario, le hicieron objeto de un patente, excepcional patrocinio. Sin duda tenían aún presente la sustanciosa cooperación bancaria de Abravanel en la feliz empresa de Granada. Así lo prueba la serie de disposiciones con que, a lo largo del mes de mayo de 1492 y en los meses sucesivos Don Fernando y Doña Isabel trataron de dar justa solución a las reclamaciones de "Don Ysaque" sobre múltiples deudas que personas singulares y concejos tenían pendientes con el poderoso financiero. Los créditos de éste montaban, según uno de esos documentos, 1.021.956 mrs. y como los deudores mostrábanse remisos a pagar, con la intención que puede colegirse, Abravanel solicitó que "pues él se avya de yr de nuestros reynos, según que por nos está mandado", y él debía al Tesoro real sumas pendientes de liquidación como arrendador de rentas públicas, se aceptaran aquellos créditos a modo de compensación de las deudas que Don Ysaque tenía pendientes. Los Reyes acceden a la petición del judío "vista su nescesidad y la brevedad de su partida" y ordenan a Juan Ramírez de Tovar, juez ejecutor, la liquidación correspondiente.[12]

Más extraordinaria es la merced que le otorga el Rey desde Córdoba el 31 de mayo de 1492, por la cual ordena a los oficiales mayores y menores y los guardas de los pasos y puertos del reino de Valencia y el Principado de Cataluña, que, no obstante las disposiciones en contrario dadas, dejasen pasar libremente y sin impedimento alguno por aquellos pasos y puertos "al dicho Don

[12] La interesantísima carta real conservada en Simancas, R. G. S., 1492 — V, fol. 251, fue publicada por Baer, *ob. cit.*, pp. 409–410. (Han de corregirse algunos yerros leves de lectura: Covar por *Tovar*, Pedrazilla por *Pedrezuela*, Aires por *Arias*, etc.).

Ysaque e a su muger e fijos e casa" con mil ducados de oro e otras joyas de plata e oro que los valga e con las otras cosas que consigo levaren que no sean vedadas". Y un mandato similar se despachó a favor de Yuçe Abravanel, hijo político y sobrino de D. Isḥaq (cf. Baer, p. 411).

En relación con D. Isḥaq y el Cardenal de España dictaron los Reyes algunas disposiciones que merecen atención. Así el 20 de julio (junio dice el documento) de 1492, desde Valladolid expiden interesante iniciativa a las justicias a petición de Juda Abensimón, vecino de Sigüenza, sobre incumplimiento del contrato que a medias con D. Isaque Abravanel tenía, concerniente a la recaudación de rentas de los pontificados del arzobispado de Toledo y obispado de Sigüenza que pertenecían al Cardenal de España, antes de que los judíos abandonaran estos reinos.[13]

En 2 de octubre del mismo año D. Fernando y Doña Isabel, desde Zaragoza, noticiosos de que, a causa de cierto embargo que habían mandado poner en todas las deudas judías dejadas en estos reinos, su juez ejecutor Ramírez de Tovar tenía interrumpidas la comisión que los Reyes habíanle encomendado y el cobro de dichas deudas, remítenle nueva carta en que disponen que, pues es voluntad regia, que se cobren aquéllas, de ser líquidas y no intervenir en ellas logro ni fraude de usura, vea los aludidos contratos, obligaciones, etc. y si corresponden a deudas líquidas y sin logro ni fraude usurario, los lleven a pura y debida ejecución que a ello haya lugar. De esta suerte fueron exceptuadas de la suspensión general que afectaba al pago de las deudas de judíos (e. d. "a judíos") las que de Isaac Abravanel habían quedado — procedentes de rentas arrendadas — así como lo fueron las correspondientes al cardenal Mendoza y a la Iglesia de Toledo.[14]

Y en 8 de marzo de 1493 el real Consejo ordena desde Barcelona que se determine la demanda de Rodrigo de Haro, vecino de Caracuel, de la Orden de Calatrava, relativa a la fianza que había puesto por ciertos arrendadores del pan pontifical del Cardenal de

---

[13] Simancas, R. G. S., 1492 — VI (VII ?), fol. 146.

[14] Cf. Luis Suárez, *Documentos acerca de la expulsión de los judíos* (Valladolid, 1964), pp. 61 y 472-3 (R. G. S., 1496 — X, fol. 51).

España en 1483 (nótese la fecha); ausentados éstos, cítase a Don Isaque Abravanel, "a quien pertenecía la dicha deuda".[15]

Todavía en 23 de agosto de 1493 el Consejo desde la capital catalana disponía que el bachiller Alonso Pérez de Alcalá ejecutara el contrato que Fernando de Villarreal, vecino de Almagro, había de pagar a don Alvaro de Portugal, presidente del Consejo real, de ciertos maravedís que dicho vecino adeudaba al judío Isaque Abravanel, los cuales habían mandado entregar al citado D. Alvaro sus Altezas.[16]

Aún restarían por examinar otras disposiciones que no especifican claramente si se refieren a Isaac Abravanel o a su yerno Yuçef. Así, v. gr. las Instrucciones que con anterioridad a agosto de 1492 habianse dado a Luis de Sepúlveda, acerca de los múltiples fraudes cometidos por Gómez de Robles según denuncia formulada "por memorial que dio Abravanel" sin duda antes de partir de España.[17]

Aunque el índice del Archivo de Simancas, *Registro General del Sello*, vol. X (Valladolid, 1967) lo adscribe a Don Isaac, creemos que más bien ha de referirse a su sobrino y yerno Yuçef (bien conocido como vecino de Plasencia hasta su salida de España) la carta que desde Barcelona remitió el Consejo en 3 de junio de 1493 al corregidor de Plasencia para que determinase acerca de los maravedís que el judío Abravanel, recaudador que fue de dicha ciudad, cobró de las barcas de Albalá, las cuales habían sido restituidas a los propios de Plasencia cuando se redujo a la Corona, en cuya época teníalas ocupadas Fernando de Monroy.[18]

Otras veces el apellido Abravanel corresponde a Don Jaco, hermano de Don Yuçe, Yuça o Yuçef, no hermano de don Iṣḥaq, como afirma el Prof. L. Suárez.[19] A ambos hermanos, sobrinos

---

15 Simancas, R. G. S., Consejo, 1493 — III, fol. 205.

16 Simancas, R. G. S., Consejo, 1493 — VIII, fol. 117.

17 Cf. en L. Suárez, *ob. cit.* pp. 456-457, a base de doc. de Simancas, Diversos de Castilla.

18 Simancas, R. G. S., Consejo, 1493 — VII, fol. 218.

19 *Ob. cit.*, p. 50 (también habla de la mujer de Jacob cuando los docs. se refieren a la de Yuçe) y en el tomo XVII de la *Historia de España* de R.

de Don Isḥaq, defendieron en reiteradas cartas Don Fernando y Doña Isabel en junio de 1492 protegiendo su salida de España. Así el día 18 disponían[20] el desembargo de la "muger e fijos e bienes" del citado don Juça y de los bienes de don Jaco "e a todos sus factores, criados e fiadores" que por aquella causa se hallaban presos, embargados y detenidos; por cuanto habían respondido por ellos en fianzas bastantes sobre las rentas que recaudó en Plasencia, en 1487 y 1488, Luis de Alcalá y Fernand Nuñes Coronel, e. d. Rabi Mair Melamed, que tres días antes (el 15) había recibido el bautismo en Guadalupe con su suegro Abrahan Seneor, un hijo de éste y dos del propio R. Meir, todos ellos de manos del Cardenal Mendoza y el Nuncio pontificio.

El 20 del mismo junio los RR. CC. comisionaban al "contino" de su real casa Fernand Yañes de Alcover para que entendiera en las deudas que muchos vecinos de Plasencia y su comarca reclamaban a Yuçe Abravanel, a su mujer y a Jaco, hermano del mismo, llevados del "odio e henemistad que le tienen, non deviendoles cosa alguna".[21]

Quizá estos y otros actos menos públicos hicieran pervivir en los Abravanel la buena amistad de que dan muestra sus relaciones con españoles ilustres cuales el Gran Capitán Gonzalo de Córdoba y otros representantes de España en Italia.

Sirvan estas breves consideraciones también de grata conmemoración de la noble figura de Don "Ysaq Brauanel" uno de los valedores y sostenedores máximos de los judíos exiliados de la Diáspora hispana.

Menéndez Pidal (Madrid, 1969), p. 255. En el mismo error incurrieron Cassuto y Marx, como bien advirtió Netanyahu, *ob. cit.*, p. 287.

[20] R. G. S. 1492 — VI, fol. 96; publicado en Baer, *ob. cit.*, pp. 416–417, y Suárez, *Documentos...* pp. 435–436.

[21] R. G. S., 1942 — VII, fol. 95; publicado en Baer, *ibid*, pp. 417–418, y Suárez, *ibid,* pp. 437–438. Todavía otra carta real del 24 de junio protegía a don Jaco de otros desmanes: R. G. S. 1492 — VI, fol. 97; pub. en Baer, *ibid*, pp. 418–419 y Suárez, *ibid*, pp. 439–440.

JUIFS ET ARABES:
REFLEXIONS SUR LEUR RENAISSANCE
NATIONALE

ANDRÉ CHOURAQUI

LE CONFLIT JUDÉO-ARABE dure depuis plusieurs décennies. Il a commencé par opposer sournoisement aux Palestiniens les premiers pionniers juifs de retour en Palestine dans la deuxième moitié du 19e siècle. Il s'est aggravé au moment de l'établissement du Foyer national juif sur la Palestine. Il s'est institutionalisé et a pris les dimensions d'une guerre entre Etats au lendemain de la création de l'Etat d'Israel. Ces faits contemporains sont d'autant plus importants que le Proche-Orient constitue une région du monde sensible et importante, y compris au point de vue de la stratégie planétaire. Les événements qui s'y déroulent ont des conséquences mondiales. Cela tend à amplifier et à aggraver les échos de tout ce qui se passe dans cette partie du monde. Les relations judéo-arabes apparaissent ainsi, aux yeux de l'humanité, comme une longue série d'émeutes, d'assassinats et de guerres, le tout noyé sous le flot d'éloquence des propagandes. Compte-tenu des caractères psychologiques des antagonistes, il s'est déversé dans la région des centaines de milliards de mots qui, répercutés pendant près d'un demi siècle sur la planète tout entière, ont eu pour effet de fausser les perspectives réelles des problèmes historiques, sociaux et politiques, qui se posent réellement. C'est ainsi que le monde est persuadé que Juifs et Arabes sont des ennemis irréductibles, héréditairement opposés par des antagonismes sans issue. On est convaincu que Juifs et Arabes n'ont jamais eu et n'auront jamais rien d'autre en commun qu'une haine inexpiable. Des chercheurs, souvent très sérieux, comme par exemple le Colonel Harcavi, n'ont qu'à se plonger dans l'amoncellement des faits et des discours pour prouver au monde la haine irréductible que les Arabes vouent à Israel et aux Juifs. Les faits ne manquent pas: ce qui se passe depuis cinquante ans dans cette région du monde est connu de tous. Les émeutes, les guerres, les attentats perpétrés par les mouvements terroristes ont fait et continuent de faire des victimes trop nombreuses. Par surcroit, certains Etats arabes inspirent à l'égard des Juifs une politique aux résultats si néfastes que la conscience de l'humanité en est atterrée: les pendaisons de Damas et de Bagdad, les attentats contre les lignes civiles aériennes constituent des faits tragiques qui sont encore accusés par l'idéologie qui inspire certains des dictateurs arabes et des chefs de la Résistance palestinienne.

Le conflit judéo-arabe est bien réel, hélas, et ses racines sont profondes. Mais les faits, que nous venons brièvement de rappeler, aboutiraient par leur accumulation à une véritable et dangereuse mystification, s'ils nous faisaient oublier les véritables perspectives et les réalités profondes des relations réelles entre Juifs et Arabes.

Une première remarque que nous voudrions avancer ici a trait à la nature même des pouvoirs dictatoriaux. Lorsque l'on parle des "Arabes", on a tendance à confondre dans une même entité mythique des réalités bien différentes. La diversité est la loi fondamentale des différentes nations que le Panarabisme tente vainement de présenter sous un uniforme monolithique. Les conflits internes, propres à l'Egypte, à l'Iraq, à la Syrie, à la Jordanie, au Liban, sont bien connus. Ces contradictions internes sont encore aggravées par l'abime qui existe, dans tous les pays du monde et à toutes les époques, entre le pouvoir dictatorial et les masses qu'il entend diriger. Un quart de siècle de dictature mussolinienne n'a jamais changé les caractères profonds du peuple italien. Cette remarque est encore plus valable en ce qui concerne l'Egypte. Le théoricien francais de la Monarchie, Charles Maurras, faisait jadis la distinction entre le pays légal et le pays réel, pour souligner l'abime qui les séparait. Pour ce qui est des dictatures militaires qui règnent actuellement au Proche-Orient, la légalité du pouvoir se fonde sur la force des armées qui font et défont les régimes. Par nature, les dictatures sont fort éloignées des masses auxquelles elles entendent dicter une ligne de pensée et de conduite. Une police bien organisée et nombreuse, comme il en existe au sein de toute

dictature, peut organiser des manifestations impressionnantes. Il
ne leur est pas donné de changer la nature des choses ni les véritables perspectives de l'histoire et de la géopolitique. Toute propagande peut atteindre des sommets dans l'enseignement du mépris
et de la haine. Il n'est pas dit que ces proclamations soient auto-
matiquement adoptées par tous ceux auxquelles elles s'adressent
et qu'elles sont censées convaincre. Un passionnant sujet d'étude
serait d'examiner dans quelle mesure les slogans de la propagande
anti-sioniste et anti-juive des dictateurs arabes ont changé le comportement des masses. Cette étude reste à faire. Il est bien certain,
en tout cas, qu'il y a un vice de méthodes et de pensées dans le
fait de confondre la propagande d'un régime ou même les actes
d'un gouvernement avec la pensée et le comportement de dizaines
de millions d'hommes. La confusion est encore plus profonde quand
on projette, dans le passé et dans l'avenir, des généralisations hâti-
vement induites de faits isolés.

En second lieu, il conviendrait, avant de procéder à toute géné-
ralisation de quelque nature que ce soit, en ce qui concerne les
relations entre Juifs et Arabes, de les considérer dans l'ordre des
perspectives historiques réelles qui ont rapproché depuis tant de
siècles ces deux groupements humains que la renaissance de l'Etat
d'Israel a récemment mis face à face.

Les quelques réflexions suivantes ont pour but de rappeler quelques vérités essentielles que les analyses historiques du Professeur
Salo W. Baron ont mises en relief avec tant d'éclat et qui prennent
une importance nouvelle dans le conflit qui déchire actuellement
le Proche-Orient.

Pour l'historien, ce qui frappe davantage, ce n'est pas tant les
différences qui opposent Israel à Ismael, que le prodigieux parallélisme des vocations, des idées, des destins historiques et économiques de deux peuples, les Juifs et les Arabes, dont la longue
histoire serait entièrement à réécrire.

La première mention des Arabes dont nous ayions conservé la
trace apparait au IXe siècle avant Jésus-Christ, elle se trouve dans
une inscription de Shalmanasar III, en 853. Différents textes bib-
liques bien connus, font état des peuples de l'Arabie, et principale-

ment de ceux qui, au Nord de la Péninsule, étaient frontaliers d'Israel. Il est superflu ici de dire quels étaient à cette époque les liens qui unissaient les Juifs et les Arabes. La relation linguistique est bien connue. Les langues sont non seulement des soeurs, mais même des soeurs jumelles. Les cultures des Arabes du Nord, les Ismaélites, et des Arabes du Sud, les qahtanides, étaient en contact permanent avec la culture hébraique. Dès l'époque du roi Akab, les Sages d'Israel connaissaient, appréciaient, aimaient la sagesse arabe dont ils n'hésitèrent jamais à s'inspirer. Les ressemblances entre Hébreux et Arabes sont telles que des savants, dès 1781, n'ont pas hésité à lancer l'hypothèse discutable de l'existence d'une "race" sémitique dont Juifs et Arabes seraient les principaux représentants. James A. Montgomery et Duncan Black Macdonald ont récemment repris et se sont appropriés l'idée de Welhausen et de Robertson Smith, qui voyaient dans les tribus arabes actuelles le prototype le plus exact de ce que fut Israel à l'époque biblique. L'idée de l'origine arabe des tribus d'Israel est évidemment discutable et a été contestée par de nombreux savants, notamment par le Professeur Goitein dans le beau livre qu'il a consacré à "Jews and Arabs, their contacts through the ages". Ce qui est incontestable, c'est que le berceau d'Israel se situe avec Abraham dans la Péninsule arabique et, avec Moise, dans l'Egypte des Pharaons. Ce qui est encore plus incontestable et plus remarquable, peut-être, c'est que les Juifs et les Arabes ont vécu une aventure qui semble bien être unique dans l'histoire de l'humanité. Dans les deux cas, la religion nationale d'un peuple est devenue une religion d'essence universelle. Les Juifs ont commencé. Leur Dieu national, le Dieu d'Abraham, d'Isaac et de Jacob, par le canal et grâce à la prédication de l'Eglise chrétienne, est devenu le Dieu d'une religion qui inspire environ la moitié de l'humanité actuelle. La religion nationale des Arabes, grâce à la prédication de Mahomet, est devenue celle de centaines de millions de Musulmans, répartis dans le monde entier. Il n'existe pas, à ma connaissance, un troisième peuple qui ait partagé le destin des Juifs et des Arabes et qui soit devenu un peuple théophore, porteur et donneur de Dieu à l'humanité entière.

Les savants discutent pour savoir quel est le maillon qui raccorde

Mahomet à la chaine hébraïque. Qu'il ait été formé par des maitres juifs, des maitres chrétiens ou, comme le voudrait S.D. Goitein, par des rabbis qui auraient eu une connaissance profonde du Christianisme, il est certain que Mahomet plonge des racines très profondes dans l'héritage spirituel d'Israel. Dès lors, on comprend la profondeur du phénomène qui inspirera la symbiose religieuse et culturelle judéo-arabe. Un même Dieu, le Dieu d'Abraham, des traditions spirituelles parallèles, une morale qui s'inspire des mêmes impératifs spirituels, devaient conférer au Judaisme de l'exil et à l'Islam des caractères de grande ressemblance.

Les deux religions sont vouées au culte d'un Dieu transcendant: d'où la place faite, ici et là, à la loi, la *Halakha* juive et la *Shari'at* musulmane. Les recherches d'histoire religieuse ont mis en relief l'identité des structures internes du Judaisme et de l'Islam naissant. Les préoccupations des théologiens de ces deux religions se recoupent pendant tout le Moyen-âge. Les points communs deviennent d'autant plus frappants qu'à partir du 7e siècle, les Juifs abandonnèrent l'araméen, qui avait lui-même supplanté l'hébreu, pour parler l'arabe dans toute l'étendue de l'Empire musulman. On assiste alors à ce phénomène surprenant de théologiens juifs qui enseignent la religion de Moise dans la langue de Mahomet, du 8e au 16e siècle. Le Professeur Baron a analysé avec éclat les métamorphoses spirituelles, religieuses, intellectuelles et culturelles qui s'emparent du monde juifs après la constitution de l'Empire musulman. Les Arabes furent bien pour les Juifs le peuple de la médiation par excellence. Pendant toute la période d'ascension de l'Islam, les Juifs connaissent un épanouissement social et culturel qui favorise, sans aucun doute, leur survie au temps de l'exil. Et si, à certaines époques et en certaines régions, les Juifs eurent à subir un traitement rigoureux de la part de gouverneurs qui sévissaient également contre leurs propres coreligionnaires, il est bien certain que jamais les Arabes ni les Musulmans n'organisèrent contre les Juifs de persécutions systématiques semblables à celles de l'inquisition. Il n'a jamais existé, dans l'histoire arabe, rien qui rappelât, même de loin, les grandes persécutions qui ensanglantèrent à l'époque moderne les juiveries d'Europe orientale ou d'Allemagne. On peut dire, au contraire, qu'au sein de la Cité musulmane, les heurs et les malheurs étaient également partagés par les Juifs et par les Musulmans. Les inconvénients qui pesaient sur les Juifs du fait de la structure théocratique de l'Islam et du statut des *dhimmis* étaient compensés par d'autres avantages. Les Juifs, au sein des pays musulmans, constituaient des minorités très fortement organisées, jouissant d'une très large autonomie interne, ayant su organiser et répandre l'instruction à presque tous et jouissant de fortes relations extérieures et internationales qui leur assuraient un niveau de vie généralement supérieur au niveau de vie moyen des grandes masses musulmanes. Par surcroit, leur statut particulier mettait les Juifs en dehors des compétitions politiques qui ensanglantaient périodiquement l'histoire des pays où ils étaient établis. Les souverains arabes leur assuraient une protection systématique et généralement efficace. Pour aussi paradoxal que cela puisse apparaitre, depuis le 17e siècle surtout, les Juifs en terre d'Islam se connaissaient et étaient reconnus par leurs concitoyens musulmans comme une élite à certains égards priviligés. Et, si le mépris est une catégorie qu'il est difficile d'exclure des rapports humains, il est impossible de déceler la dimension de la haine dans le passé commun plusieurs fois millénaire des Juifs et des Arabes.

La règle générale de leurs relations semble être celle-ci: aux époques de prospérité, les Musulmans et les Juifs sont également prospères. Des épisodes tragiques, comme celui des persécutions sous la dynastie des Almohades, n'altèrent pas l'image d'expansion et de gloire fulgurante qui prévaut dans tous les domaines de la vie économique, de la culture et de la spiritualité durant quatre siècles, du 8e au 12e siècle. A partir du 17e siècle, le mouvement de décadence des pays musulmans va en s'aggravant, entrainant dans la chute les communautés juives qui, aux périodes de prospérité, avaient illustré d'une manière si brillante la pensée et l'histoire du Judaisme. L'histoire des Juifs et des Musulmans suit ainsi des courbes parallèles ascendantes ou descendantes selon les époques et les lieux.

Mais l'analyse la plus profonde nous révèle que la loi du parallélisme historique entre Juifs et Arabes n'a jamais été mieux illustrée

qu'à l'époque moderne à l'heure de la renaissance nationale des
nations qui font l'objet de notre présente analyse. La décadence
économique de l'Islam avait entrainé la perte de son autonomie
politique et l'instauration du régime colonial qui, sous une forme
ou une autre, régnait jusque dans la deuxième moitié du 20e siècle
dans la plupart des pays musulmans. L'on connait le rôle que la
révolution francaise et Napoléon jouèrent dans le mouvement de
résurrection nationale du monde arabe et du monde juif. L'expé-
dition de Napoléon en Egypte en 1789, comme le décret d'émancipation de 1791, marquent pour les Arabes et pour les Juifs le début
d'une ère nouvelle et d'un combat qui, pour les uns et les autres,
n'a pas encore pris fin: la lutte pour l'émancipation politique et
nationale. Pour les Juifs et les Arabes, pendant toute cette longue
période, l'ennemi, colonialisme d'une part, antisémitisme d'autre
part, portent un même nom: le racisme. La souffrance arabe et
la souffrance judaique, provoquées par des causes identiques, al-
laient donner naissance, pendant le 19e et le 20e siècle, à des mouvements intellectuels et politiques simultanés, parallèles et même
lorsqu'ils se dressaient l'un contre l'autre, de nature semblable. Car
tel est bien le paradoxe nouveau dans lequel l'histoire enferme les
Juifs et les Arabes: l'arabisme et le sionisme naissent de causes
historiques identiques qui agissent dans des contextes différents et
provoquent des effets dont les oppositions transitoires, n'empêchent
ni l'identité foncière, ni la très profonde complémentarité.

Prodigieux parallélisme: au contact de la civilisation occiden-
tale et du monde chrétien, Juifs et Arabes prennent simultanément
conscience de leur décadence et recherchent le salut d'abord dans
un retour aux sources de leur culture. L'hébreu était une langue
qui avait cessé d'être parlée depuis plus de deux millénaires. Dépuis
le 16e siècle, la décadence de l'arabe semblait irréversible. Du rang
de langue, elle était tombée dans toute l'étendue de l'empire musulman en poussière de jargons à peine articulés. De part et d'autre
les linguistes durent fournir le prodigieux effort qui a créé deux
langues modernes nouvelles, l'hébreu et l'arabe moderne, à partir
de deux langues sacrées traditionnelles qui avaient atteint leur splen-
deur en des époques dépassées. La renaissance linguistique s'ac-

compagne d'un effort de régénération intellectuelle, la *Nahda* arabe est contemporaine et à bien des égards identique à la *Haskala* des Juifs. Au Caire, à Beyrouth, à Damas, des penseurs, des traducteurs et des journalistes accomplissent le même effort que celui auquel Isaac Ber Levinsohn avait donné naissance en Europe orientale. Il faudrait faire une analyse comparée de la littérature arabe et hébraique à la fin du 19e siècle et au 20e siècle pour se rendre compte que dans des contextes différents, la problématique est la même et les solutions envisagées sont essentiellement de nature semblable. De part et d'autre, au contact de l'Occident chrétien, on aspire à métamorphoser deux mouvements religieux, ici le Judaisme et là l'Islam, en des mouvements socio-politiques, ici l'arabisme et là le sionisme, en vue d'aboutir à la libération des masses aliénées par les excès du colonialisme et du racisme et les rétablir dans la souveraineté des nations libres. La terminologie politique des leaders du sionisme et des théoriciens de l'arabisme est moins différente qu'on ne pourrait le supposer *a priori*. Les ressemblances essentielles se révèlent dès que l'on a dépassé les slogans des propagandes pour aboutir à l'analyse objective des vrais problèmes. Le conflit israélo-arabe, dans les vingt dernières années, a pu faire perdre de vue les vraies perspectives de l'histoire. Lui-aussi nait à partir d'une ressemblance essentielle: Juifs et Arabes aiment d'un égal amour le pays qu'ils se disputent.

L'analyse historique pourrait déjà souligner le rôle que ce conflit a joué: il n'est pas fait que d'ombres. On pourrait écrire l'histoire contemporaine du Proche-Orient par rapport aux péripéties de la guerre judéo-arabe. Le paradoxe est là: le mouvement sioniste progresse d'autant plus que le fouet de ses ennemis arabes le cingle mieux. Les assises politiques de l'Etat, ses fondements économiques et agricoles, sa puissance militaire et financière, auraient été tout à fait autres sans les coups d'éperons des Arabes. La résistance arabe a fait grandir le canton de 5.000 km^2 que les Juifs rêvaient d'avoir, conformément au plan de partage proposé par la Royal Commission en 1937: il est devenu un Etat de plus de 100.000 km^2, dont le monde entier connait désormais la puissance militaire et politique.

La réciproque est également vraie: le conflit palestinien confirme le rêve de l'unité arabe et aide à la constitution, en 1945, de la Ligue des Etats arabes. La défaite de 1947–48 réalise l'union du groupe d'officiers qui, autour de Neguib et Nasser, jurent d'abattre le régime corrompu de Farouk. Abdallah, roi de Jordanie, est assassiné à la suite de la victoire sioniste: sa mort tourne une page de l'histoire de son royaume. La haine d'Israel permet à l'Egypte de surmonter sa passivité, de se débarrasser de la monarchie et de proclamer la République en 1953, l'année-même où meurt Ibn Saoud. La campagne malheureuse de Suez, en 1956, aide Nasser à vaincre les résistances syriennes et à donner corps â son rêve éphémère, la République Arabe unie, qu'il fonde en 1958. Les Irakiens de leur côté, deux ans après Suez, parviennent à abattre la monarchie et à proclamer la République. La haine d'Israel inspire encore Nasser lorsqu'il adopte en 1961 ce qu'il définit comme le socialisme arabe qui inspire à l'extérieur les régimes de Ben Bella (1962–1965), de Boumédienne (depuis 1965), et favorisa les révolutions de 1963 en Syrie et en Iraq et de 1969 en Libie.

Depuis vingt ans, le sionisme et l'arabisme, en guerre l'un contre l'autre, interfèrent l'un sur l'autre d'une manière constante pour hâter les prises de conscience et pour accélérer le rythme des réalisations nécessaires.

Souligner les points communs entre l'arabisme et le sionisme, et parler de la complémentarité des intérêts entre Israéliens et Arabes, peut sembler un paradoxe à l'heure où chaque matin on déplore de part et d'autre des morts, des blessés, tout le long cortège de deuils que provoque toute guerre. Il en était de même en Europe en 1940, lorsque le Japon et l'Allemagne et l'Italie étaient en guerre contre le monde occidental tout entier. Parler à cette époque de la création d'une Europe unie aurait apparu non seulement comme une folie mais comme une trahison. Or, quelques années après la fin de la guerre, malgré des millions de morts et des haines qui apparaissent implacables, l'utopie a commencé à prendre corps: l'Europe est en train de se faire.

De 1940 à 1945, tout homme qui aurait parlé d'amitié entre l'Allemagne et le peuple juif, serait apparu comme un dément au comme un traitre. Les Allemands et les Juifs, qui n'ont pas la réputation d'être des peuples faciles, avaient vécu une tragédie qui n'a pas de précédent pour son horreur dans l'histoire universelle. Quelles années après, les liens étaient renoués, les hommes mêmes, qui avaient vécu ce drame épouvantable, devinrent les artisans de l'établissement de relations diplomatiques entre l'Allemagne et Israel et d'une amitié qui a donné ses preuves, notamment pendant la guerre des Six jours.

Les problèmes qui se posent aux Juifs et aux Arabes sont malgré tout beaucoup plus simples. Les rapports d'amitié et de coopération religieuse culturelle et économique ont chez eux une tradition plusieurs fois millénaire.

La région du monde qui sert de scène à leur renaissance nationale constitue une unité naturelle minuscule: la distance entre Amman et Jérusalem est comparable à celle qui sépare Jérusalem de Tel-Aviv. De Jérusalem au Caire, il y a quelques 460 kms, Damas et Beyrouth sont à quelques heures de la capitale d'Israel. Par surcroit, les torrents de paroles haineuses déversées par les dictateurs arabes n'ont jamais convaincu les grandes masses arabes. La cohabitation pacifique des Palestiniens et des Juifs, réunis depuis deux ans et demi dans une même entité étatique, donne la preuve que le désir de paix et la volonté de coopération sont les plus forts.

Plutôt que de rechercher une solution de partage statique qui perpétuerait en fait le conflit absurde et fratricide qui déchire le Moyen-Orient et constitue une menace pour le monde entier, les forces vitalement intéressées à l'établissement de la paix au Proche-Orient, devraient fonder leur politique sur un mouvement dynamique qui devrait commencer par établir un Etat de type fédératif entre Israéliens et Palestiniens. Ce noyau aurait pour vocation de réaliser une fédération des Etats du Proche-Orient. La fin du conflit actuel devrait aboutir non pas seulement à la stabilisation des frontières entre les nations actuellement en guerre, mais viser à la création des Etats unis du Proche-Orient. Lorsque Herzl parlait de la création de l'Etat Juif, le monde entier voyait en lui un utopiste ou un rêveur. Aujourd'hui, la vision des Etats unis du Proche-Orient peut encore apparaitre "chimérique". Mais nous sommes

au siècle où les utopies deviennent histoire. Nulle dictature n'a
jamais été éternelle. Les Etats unis du Proche-Orient constituent
une nécessité vitale pour les peuples qu'elle unirait: les Israéliens,
les Palestiniens, les Libanais, les Jordaniens, les Egyptiens et les
Syriens. Une telle fédération d'Etats pourrait changer l'équilibre
politique du monde en favorisant un regroupement général des
nations intéressées à une promotion et à une libération des pays
les plus pauvres de la planète. Toutes les données d'une telle révolution de l'histoire sont prêtes pour qu'elle soit mise en oeuvre et
réalisée en fait. Il n'y faudrait que beaucoup de volonté, du courage
et du travail. N'oublions pas le grand conseil de Herzl qui avait
prévu le regroupement auquel nous aspirons aujourd' hui: "Si
avous le voulez ce ne sera pas un rêve..."

THE HASMONEAN REVOLUTION POLITICALLY CONSIDERED
Outline of a New Interpretation

Martin A. Cohen

The Revolution associated with the Hasmoneans was in part a Jewish uprising against the Seleucids and partly an internecine struggle among the Jews themselves. From 168–165 B.C.E. the war against the outside foe overshadowed the internal strife, but the fratricidal antagonisms in Judea flared unobstructed before and after these critical years.[1]

A familiar line of explanations traces the roots of the struggles to the year 176, when Antiochus IV usurped the Seleucid throne. They depict the new monarch as a fanatical Hellenist, intent on imposing his customs and ideals upon the entire Seleucid realm. They say that his policies soon split Judea into Hellenist and anti-Hellenist camps. They depict Hellenists like Jason, Menelaus and their cohorts as arch assimilationists, contemptuous of their traditions and lusting to participate in Hellenistic customs. The anti-Hellenists, on the other hand, appear to them as glorious paladins of Judaism, fighting to preserve their inherited faith unchanged and unsullied by the ways of their foreign overlords.

Exigencies of space have necessitated the restriction of all notes to representative items. Fuller notes and bibliography will be found in a forthcoming work.

[1] See, for example, E. Bickerman, *Der Gott der Makkabäer* (Berlin, 1937), p. 8 and G. H. Box, *Judaism in the Greek Period* (Oxford, 1932), p. 39. Cf. also S. Zeitlin, Introduction to *The First Book of Maccabees*, ed. S. Tedesche and S. Zeitlin (New York, 1960), pp. 1, 36 and idem in *The Second Book of the Maccabees* (ed. S. Tedesche and S. Zeitlin), pp. 131 f., S. Zeitlin, *The Rise and Fall of the Judean State*, I (Philadelphia, 1962) (henceforth RFJS), 67 ff., and for a broad panorama of the problem in the context of its times, Salo W. Baron's *A Social and Religious History of the Jews*, I (New York, 1952), 212 ff., and II (New York, 1952), 3 ff.

Modern Jewish and Christian historians have rarely been impartial analysts of these events. In their parallel struggle against apathy and defection, they have invariably sided with the anti-Hellenists. In addition, they have often daubed their presentation with a Marxist coloration, blithely identifying the Hellenists as the Judean aristocracy and their opponents as the masses of the people. The Jewish struggle of the second century B.C.E. has thus been viewed simultaneously as a class conflict and a fight against assimilation. Some writers who have been particularly sensitive about the differences between Orthodox and Reform Judaism, have even gratuitously suggested that the Hellenists were the Reformers of their day and their adversaries the Orthodox Jews.[2]

Regrettably, our entire knowledge of the Hasmonean Revolution and the events immediately preceding (176–160 B.C.E.) derives from an extremely limited number of facts. Nearly all the primary information is to be found in I and II Maccabees and a few acceptable details in Josephus. These sources combined fall short of yielding a comprehensive picture of the events. They are woefully incomplete and frequently contradictory. At the same time the evidence they do contain exposes certain anomalies that challenge the traditional interpretations at critical points and suggest the need for a more coherent, if no less certain, reconstruction.[3]

The anomalies may be usefully grouped into six categories:

(1) The data in Josephus and I and II Macc. do not substantiate the claim that the struggle between the Hellenists and anti-Hellenists partook of the nature of a class war between the masses and aristocracy of Judea. They nowhere depict the Hellenist party and its supporters as coterminous with the aristocratic classes.

---

[2] Thus, for example, V. Tcherikover, *Hellenistic Civilization and the Jews* (Philadelphia, 1961), pp. 197, 234 and passim and E. Bickerman, *From Ezra to the Last of the Maccabees* (New York, 1962), pp. 107 ff., 126 f.

[3] The major differences in approach and details between I and II Macc. fall outside the purview of this study and will be treated more fully in the forthcoming work. There it will be argued, inter alia, that one cannot support the thesis of the historiographical superiority of either I or II Macc. The present study relies on data found in either I or II Macc. or without contradiction in both.

But they do point to popular support for the Hellenistic leaders and their aristocratic backers. II Macc. states that on assuming the pontificate, Jason immediately brought his countrymen (!) over to the Greek way of living (4:10), and this without apparent struggle or opposition. I Macc. corroborates this view, though it does not mention Jason by name. It speaks of the "lawless men" at this time who "persuaded many" to break the covenant and follow heathen practice (1:11). Later, at Antiochus' prodding, says I Macc., "many of Israel agreed to his kind of worship" (1:43). And when the king sent inspectors to enforce Hellenization, they were joined by "many of the people and everyone who was ready to forsake the Law" (1:52). Jason's magnificent welcome of Antiochus "with torches and acclamation" (II Macc. 4:22), further suggests popular support. Even after his deposition by Menelaus Jason was still strong enough to attack Jerusalem with the far from inconsiderable force of a thousand men (II Macc. 5:5). Josephus, who blames Menelaus for introducing "the Grecian way of living," has a majority of the people supporting Jason, and a substantial minority behind Menelaus (*Ant.* XII. 5).

II Macc. also implies substantial popular support for Menelaus. According to one of its statements (11:29), it was Menelaus and not Judah Maccabee or any other champion of Judaism who obtained the peace treaty from the Seleucids. Unless Menelaus commanded the allegiance of a large part of the Jewish populace, it would have been pointless for him to request the treaty or for the Seleucids to grant it.

Two additional considerations argue in favor of a trans-aristocratic constituency for the Hellenistic party.

One is the fact that, in deposing Onias, Antiochus preferred to retain the High Priesthood rather than institute martial law in Judea.

As they did with other subject peoples, the Seleucids permitted the Jews to maintain their traditions and self-rule and used these as mechanisms of control. The High Priest was the surrogate of the Seleucid rulers in Judea. He was responsible for the political stability of his country and the loyalty of his people to their overlords.[4] At least in this respect there was no essential difference in the Judean pontificate before and after 175 B.C.E. The maintenance and even lavish support of the theocracy[5] gave the Jews the illusion of self-determination. It also provided the Seleucids with control of a critical region at an expense far lower than would have been involved in a full-scale military occupation of the territory.

In this light, Antiochus' deposition of the High Priest Onias, attributed by II Macc. to Jason's bribe, is more readily explainable as the result of the failure by Onias and his party to provide the Seleucids with stability or loyalty or both. All that may be said for Jason's bribe, if given, is that it helped Antiochus choose between various possible replacements for Onias.

If we follow the traditional views that Judea's major problem was a struggle between the Hellenist-aristocrats and the anti-Hellenist masses, we would have to conclude that Onias' failure was a breach of loyalty to the Seleucids. Since he was on the side of the anti-Hellenists, he could not be charged with failure to maintain stability. On the contrary, he could be expected to control the masses much better than his replacement, the Hellenist Jason.

But if Judea were really torn by strife between a Hellenist aristocracy and anti-Hellenist masses, the theocracy would have offered little to the Seleucids. The Jewish aristocracy, though economically powerful, was numerically feeble and incapable of warding off a militant and united populace. If the masses as a group were constantly at odds with the ruling aristocracy and threatening the stability of the state, the Seleucids would have had to protect their position in Judea with a garrison approaching the size needed for full-scale military occupation. The fact that the Seleucids continued to support the theocracy under Jason and Menelaus suggests that the establishment classes attracted significant lower class support and thereby reduced the Seleucids' cost of control.

[4] E. Bickerman, "The Historical Foundations of Postbiblical Judaism," in L. Finkelstein, ed., *The Jews*, I (Philadelphia, 1960), 93. Cf. idem, *Institutions des Seleucides* (Paris, 1938), pp. 134 ff.

[5] Cf. II Macc. 3:2 f. and Josephus, *Antiquities* XII. 3.

The establishment classes would have included the so-called Hellenist groups. Obviously, in replacing Onias and later Jason, Antiochus sought to appoint men of the greatest possible loyalty to his regime. But this consideration would have meant nothing unless these men and their coteries of power could maintain internal stability in Judea.

This possibility, of course, cannot be conclusively established on the basis of current evidence, but it is far more reasonable than the oft-repeated and equally undemonstrable assertions about the class-structured battle lines in Judea.

The second consideration is the posture of the priesthood between 175–168 B.C.E. II Macc. speaks inclusively when it charges the priests with "thinking Greek standards the finest," "regarding as worthless the things their forefathers valued," "disdaining the sanctuary and neglecting the sacrifices," and "hurrying to take part in the unlawful exercises in the wrestling school after the summons of the discus throwing" (4:14). Since the priests neither abandoned their positions nor defected from Judaism, they would undoubtedly have rejected the charges of insufficient dedication and malfeasance in office. At the same time they could hardly have denied their public display of Hellenistic practice. Had the Jewish masses been granitically opposed to the priests' activities, the resultant restiveness would have rendered the priesthood useless to the Seleucids. Again, it would have been cheaper for Antiochus to remove the hierocracy and impose martial law. The fact that he did not do so suggests the possibility, if not the probability, that the priests' actions did not meet with general disapproval and that they too could still command considerable popular support. There was certainly no revolution against the priests between 175 and 168 B.C.E. In fact, the sources record no antihierocratic agitation in these years of turmoil and rebellion, though judging from their blanket condemnation of the priests, there is every reason to believe that neither I nor II Macc. would have failed to record such events had they occurred.

(2) Both the sources and the traditional explanations charge the Hellenists with defection from Judaism or compromising it with

"the Grecian way of living." The sources call the Hellenists "lawless" (I Macc. 1:11). They also refer to the High Priest Jason as "godless" and charge him with "abrogating the lawful ways of living" and "disowning the holy covenant" (II Macc. 4:11 ff.). We do not know how the Hellenists responded to these charges, but we can be certain that they did not accept them. Whatever their opponents said, the fact remains that Jason, Menelaus and their subalterns retained the Torah and continued to rule by the Torah. Nowhere does a leadership regard its rule as violating the constitution it supports.

Interestingly, for all their general condemnation, the sources do not cite a single instance in the years prior to 168/167 where the Hellenists advocated the abrogation of the Torah or flouted even one of its laws. They come close only when I Macc. 1:15 accuses the Hellenists of trying to hide their circumcision. Significantly it does not charge them with neglecting or discouraging the performance of the commandment upon the newly born. After the abolition of the Torah I Macc. claims that "many from Israel... offered sacrifice to idols and broke the Sabbath." From the statement that the group included "everyone who was ready to forsake the Law" (I Macc. 1:41 ff.), we may presume that it included former Hellenists, but we cannot be sure. In any case, these charges are not leveled for the period 175–168.

In addition, the Hellenists of 175–168 are charged with adding matters contrary to the letter and spirit of the Torah (II Macc. 4:11). The charge stems from the hankering of the Jewish aristocracy after privileges like the gymnasion and ephebeion, *polis* status for Jerusalem, and their enrollment "as citizens of Antioch" (II Macc. 4:9). It is understandable that the anti-Hellenists should have regarded these novelties as outrageous, but, as the Hellenists well knew, the letter of the Torah did not support their opponents' condemnation.[6]

(3) Furthermore, the evidence makes it impossible categorically

[6] See Lev. 18:3 and 20:3 (cf. Ezek. 5:7 and 11:12). The concept *ḥukkat ha-goy*, derived from these verses, could certainly have been reasonably defined in such a way as to exclude the practices of the Hellenists.

to ascribe to Antiochus the emergence of either Hellenistic proclivities or internal strife among the Jews.

The case for the existence of pre-Antiochian Hellenism is inferential but strong. It is based upon the realization that large numbers of men would not have accepted Hellenistic practice with alacrity unless they had long desired it. Nor would Antiochus, in his eagerness to cement greater unity in his regime, have offered what he regarded as the privileges of Hellenism to men unconditioned to his system of values.

The case for the internal strife in Judea prior to the advent of Antiochus derives from the account in II Macc. 3 of the quarrel between the High Priest Onias and his cousin, the Tobiad, Simon, the Temple governor, over the conduct of the Jerusalem market. II Macc. does not conceal the fact that the problem transcended the confines of a personal vendetta and pitted powerful groups against one another. The text reproves Simon for inviting Seleucus to confiscate the moneys in the Temple treasury and then charging Onias with conspiracy against the king. Nowhere is there a word about Simon's arrest or punishment, though, once again, II Macc. could be expected to have dilated on such events with relish, had they occurred. Judging from Simon's actions as well as his position and family strength, it appears that Onias faced strong and disruptive opposition. The internecine strife may well have pushed Judea to the brink of civil war.[7] II Macc. buttresses this inference with its statement that one of Simon's men committed murders, apparently with impunity, and that Simon was supported by no less a personage than Apollonius, son of Menestheus, the Seleucid *strategos* appointed over Coelesyria and therefore the king's representative in Judea. Appolonius did not require exceptional political acumen to recognize that his support would be unavailing unless Simon enjoyed substantial backing among his own people.

---

[7] See S. Zeitlin, RFJS, pp. 74 ff. and *The History of the Second Jewish Commonwealth*: *Prolegomena* (Philadelphia, 1933) (henceforth cited as P), pp. 19 ff., esp. p. 19 n. 6. I have not been able to find evidence for Zeitlin's assertion (P, p. 22) that "Simon and his brothers, the sons of Joseph, had lost their attachment of Judaism."

(4) In addition, the ascription of Antiochus' actions in Judea to his fanatical Hellenism is fraught with numerous problems. One wonders, for example, why Antiochus allowed some seven years to elapse from the time of his accession to the throne before he moved to interdict the Torah and practices related to it, the greatest obstacles to complete Hellenization in Judea. Besides, while the sources imply a relationship between Jason's appointment and Hellenization, they do not support the theory, occasionally advanced by scholars, that Jason's replacement by Menelaus meant increased Hellenization. From the perspective of elementary political procedure the story of Menelaus' bribe is insufficient to account for so momentous a political change.[8] We shall have occasion to reconsider these problems.

Besides, fanatical Hellenist though he may have been, Antiochus followed Seleucid custom in not eradicating the ancestral traditions of subjected groups. He apparently even permitted the Samaritans to retain the Torah after he had proscribed it for the Jews.[9] The question therefore arises whether explanations other than religious fanaticism are to be sought for Antiochus' actions.

(5) Similar anomalies are found for the period beginning with 165. Thus, after they had routed the Seleucid armies, regained and cleansed the Temple and then, in their hard-won freedom, presumably "restored the laws which were on the point of being destroyed" (II Macc. 2:22), the Jews, who had been "prepared to die rather than lose their liberty," (Ant. XII. 7) agreed to revert to the Seleucid yoke in return for the right to live "according to their ancestral customs."[10] These events, supported by I Macc. 6:55 ff., are documented by the letters in II Macc. 11. Further confusion results from the fact that the narrative introducing these letters has Judah Maccabee consenting to the Seleucids' peace proposals, while the letters themselves picture Menelaus and the Jewish people

8 II Macc. 4:23 ff. Cf. Zeitlin, P, pp. 23, 25.

9 Bickerman, *Der Gott der Makkabäer*, p. 24.

10 There is no basis for Tcherikover's claim, op. cit., p. 164, that Jason's reform involved "the complete abolition of the existing constitution and its replacement by a new one."

as the advocates of peace. In an attempt to resolve this anomaly, scholars have asserted that the peace arrangements were made with Judah Maccabee and preceded the purification of the Temple. This solution, however, not only fails to explain why Menelaus continued to rule; it violates the chronology and other details of both I and II Macc.[11]

(6) At least equivalent confusion results from the fact that after the peace agreement, Judah Maccabee, the "perfect champion of his fellow citizens," as he is called by II Macc. 15:30, continued to wage war until his death not only against the Seleucids but against many of his own people as well. Among his enemies there eventually appeared Alcimus, a legitimate Aaronide priest and Menelaus' successor in the pontificate. Because of his legitimacy, Alcimus was endorsed by none other than the Ḥasidim, the erstwhile allies of Judah and generally acknowledged as paragons of loyalty to the Jewish tradition. The Ḥasidim later broke with Alcimus, not on the question of the pontiff's legitimacy but because of his perfidy toward them.[12]

Furthermore, contrary to frequently appearing statements, Judah

---

[11] Some scholars, like Tcherikover (op. cit., p. 215) and Bickerman (*From Ezra to the Last of the Maccabees*, pp. 117 ff.) claim that the restoration of the Torah took place in the spring of 164 B.C.E. and that Judah's capture of Jerusalem and rededication of the Temple followed in December of 164. There is no reason or evidence to date Judah's capture of Jerusalem after the peace arrangements between Lysias and Menelaus' faction. II Macc. declares that Judah captured Jerusalem before and not after Lysias' offer (II Macc. 10:1 ff.) and that Lysias prepared to attack the Jews because Jerusalem had been captured (11:1 ff.). So too, I Macc. 4:41 ff. 6:63 ff. and Josephus. (S. Zeitlin, P, p. 35, RFJS, pp. 100 ff.).

[12] I Macc. 7:13 ff. Josephus (*Ant.* XII. 9) states without warrant that Alcimus was not of High Priestly stock. On the relationship of Menelaus (Onias-Menelaus) to Onias and Jason, see S. Zeitlin, ed., *The Second Book of Maccabees*, pp. 78 ff. What matters for this study is Zeitlin's conclusion that all these men came from legitimate Aaronide stock. We must defer to the forthcoming study the question of Menelaus' Benjamite origins raised by II Macc. Zeitlin's suggestion (P, p. 37) that Alcimus wooed the Hellenists because he knew the Ḥasidim would not support him against Judah Maccabee, is again based on the assumption that the Hasmonean Revolution was simply a struggle between loyal and renegade Jews.

was a fugitive in his continuing struggle. The troops under his command had been reduced and Jerusalem had become the stronghold of his enemies. II Macc., though pretending that Judah never lost a battle and never relinquished the leadership of the majority of his people, betrays the fact that in this stage of the war Jerusalem was beyond his sphere of control. After the agreement with Lysias, II Macc. mentions Judah in connection with Jerusalem only four times (12:31, 43; 14:23, 15:30). It places him in Jerusalem on only two of these occasions (12:31; 14:23) and in neither in a ruling capacity. The incidental character of these passages raises the suspicion that the connections are contrived. II Macc. discloses that Judah and his followers, including the Ḥasidim, were later accused of sedition by Alcimus, speaking on behalf of the Jews favorably inclined toward their government in Jerusalem. Alcimus even went so far as to declare that "as long as Judah lives, it is impossible for the government to find peace." (14:6 ff.).

Some claim that Judah Maccabee's continued fighting after the peace settlement was politically rather than religiously motivated.[13] This assertion not only lacks support from the evidence; it also runs counter to explicit statements, such as the one found in II Macc. 14:14. There Judah exhorts his men to fight nobly not

The Ḥasidim present a much greater problem than is generally recognized. Most scholars assume that this was a particularly pious group. No one has ever observed that far from being an objective description, the name Ḥasidim may have been self-adopted or bestowed by contemporary or subsequent admirers. In a context where the Torah was the constitution, the religious name Ḥasidim would be natural for a political party with a conservative bent, paralleling the name Loyalists in a modern secular polity. To the extent that conservatism is to be equated with piety, the Ḥasidim can be called particularly pious. The one item of evidence pointing in this direction is the Ḥasidim's insistence on living by the letter of the law and not fighting on the Sabbath. In this sense at least they sought to preserve the Pentateuch without innovation. By the same standard, the Hasmoneans, who advocated self-defense on the Sabbath, were not conservatives. Yet were they any less pious? An analysis of the identity and political position of the Ḥasidim must also be deferred to the forthcoming monograph.

[13] Thus, for example, J. Klausner, *Historiyah shel ha-Bayit ha-Sheni*, III (Jerusalem, 1963), 37 f.

only for "city, country and government," but also for "laws" and "Temple." In addition he chooses as his watchword the expression "God's victory."

There are additional anomalies here. Alcimus is called ungodly (I Macc. 7:8), as Jason had been, and his supporters, those favoring peace and living under the Torah are referred to as "those who harassed their people" (*ibid.* 7:22) and "those who had no regard for the Law" (!) (*ibid.* 9:23). Besides, with Alcimus, if not before, the old priesthood appears to have returned to its former positions and status. Since the priests are no longer explicitly faulted for their neglect of Judaism of defection to Hellenism, one wonders how to explain their apparent volte-face.

In addition, since the restoration of the Pentateuch, the goal of the revolution, had been accomplished, the question arises as to why men continued to fight on Judah's side. If the answer given is that they wanted the restoration of the Pentateuch only in an atmosphere of political independence, one may ask why so many other Jews, perhaps even a majority, were satisfied to return to the situation that existed before the war. Obviously, for large numbers of Jews fighting against the Seleucids independence did not mean as much as the Pentateuch, and many were content with the restoration of the Pentateuch under Hellenistic rule despite the continuing dangers of assimilation and the apparent return of the erstwhile Hellenists to positions of power.

The resolution of this panoply of anomalies and contradictions and the creation of a more comprehensive reconstruction is possible with the application of three often neglected but fundamental facts about the nature of the evidence and the context of the times it covers.

First, both I and II Macc. are passionately partisan texts. They stem from the closing years of the second century B.C.E., when the Hasmoneans, ensconced on both the pontifical and monarchical thrones, were in control of the Jewish establishment.[14] Each book

---

[14] On the two texts and the problem of the historicity of II Macc., see e.g., R. H. Pfeiffer, *History of New Testament Times* (New York, 1949), pp. 461 ff. and E. Bickerman, *Der Gott der Makkabäer*, pp. 29 ff. Zeitlin, in his introduc-

has a distinctive point of view: I Macc. appears to be an official apology of the Hasmonean dynasty, written from the perspective of the regnant John Hyrcanus (135–104), while II Macc. seems to have been composed as a defense of the Temple and its cognate institutions. Occasionally scholars cavil at these attributions, but few will deny that both books are the products of partisans of the Hasmonean house.[15] Josephus' treatment of the years 176–165 (*Ant.* XII. 5 ff), borrows heavily from I Macc., but even where it does not, as at the beginning of XII. 5, it reflects its partisan attitude.

The recognition of the bias in I and II Macc. impugns the credibility of their glorification of the Hasmoneans and the denigration of their opponents. To accept the characterizations of I and II Macc. uncritically would be tantamount to taking David ben Zakkai's excommunication of Saadia as the true picture of the Gaon, or Anan ben David's statements as the true picture of the Rabbanites, or the Inquisition's description of the New Christians as authentically reflective of their condition in Portugal or Spain. The indictments of the High Priests Jason and Menelaus as malfeasants and renegades appear to be pro-Hasmonean attempts to discredit their opponents by harping on the striking novelty of their Hellenistic activities and then implying a general acceptance of Hellenistic norms and values. The implication that the priests suddenly warmed to Hellenization and the explicit statement that with Jason's coming they abandoned the Torah testify to the development or extension of an antagonism to the point where anti-establishment classes could then or later make these charges. They also raise the question as to whether the Hasmoneans, themselves priests, were part of a group loyal to Onias after his ouster. II Macc. regards Onias as a model of righteousness.

Second, in the early second century the Pentateuch was not only

tion to II Macc. (p. 27) places the composition of that book during the reign of Agrippa (41–44 C.E.). Like others, C. C. Torrey speaks of "the strong Jewish bias" of I Macc. (*The Apocryphal Literature*, New Haven, 1945, p. 73), but fails to realize the fragmentation of the Jewish group.

15 See Zeitlin, P, p. 21.

a religious document for the Jews but the basis of their political life as well. The Pentateuch was the constitution of Judea. The Pentateuch and its derivative legislation were the "ancestral" laws referred to in the various Seleucid decrees.[16] The Sabbath, circumcision and other holy days and practices were not only religious institutions; they were as well societal miranda, to use the apt phrase of Charles E. Merriam. The modern distinction between politics and religion was unknown in Judea. Patriotism was expressed through loyalty to the Pentateuch; the man unfaithful to Torah, at least in its public aspects, was regarded as a traitor to the body politic. Since the days of Persian domination, Judea had been ruled by a hierocracy ideologically rooted in the Pentateuch, and the High Priest had served as the polity's chief executive.

Politically speaking, the controversy between the Hellenists and anti-Hellenists may be regarded as a struggle between establishment and anti-establishment factions for control of Judean society. Existentially, of course, the political side of a struggle cannot be separated from its social and ideological aspects. Yet, whatever the issues are in any struggle, its political manifestations reflect certain general patterns. For example, there is always a tension between the leadership in authority and opposition groups.

Viewed politically, the claim of the Hasmonean texts that their opponents were defecting from the Pentateuch and coddling the ways of the Hellenists completely parallel the charges of other political groups in history that their adversaries have assimilated to the ways and doctrines of the enemy.

It also becomes evident that Antiochus' actions against the Pentateuch can be understood politically, without recourse to explanations constructed on the monarch's real or alleged religious propensities. In proscribing the Pentateuch Antiochus was really suspending the constitution of Judea, and with it the Temple cult and the authority of the hierocracy. This meant the end of the façade of Jewish self-government and the necessity for imposing full military rule by the Seleucids. It was an expensive move for

16 Bickerman, *Der Gott der Makkabäer*, p. 53.

Antiochus. In addition to increasing restiveness among the Jews, it required an augmenting of the garrison in Judea.

Antiochus has been considered a madman at least since the punning Polybius called him Epimanes instead of Epiphanes.[17] But the fact is that in the political sphere he regularly displayed profound insight into his problems and sought pragmatic solutions. His failures in this area are attributable less to the vagaries of his thinking and emotions than to the insurmountable difficulties that affected the Seleucid regime even before his reign began. It may be satisfying to dismiss Antiochus' suspension of the Torah as an act of rank folly. But from Antiochus' perspective the decision, if hazardous, was nevertheless reasonable.

In the year 168/167 Antiochus' empire stood at a new nadir of debility. In the summer of 168, near Eleusis, across the Canobic branch of the Nile, the Roman legate, Gaius Popilius Laenas, forced the Seleucid monarch into an ignominious abandonment of his conquest of Egypt, which only a few years before lay almost fully within his grasp.

Antiochus' reign had been one of turmoil from the moment he seized the throne vacated by the assassination of his brother, Seleucus IV. His energies were constantly devoted to preventing insurrection within the motley states that comprised his empire and keeping foreign enemies like the Romans and Parthians at bay. Beginning with the year 173 Judea was increasingly drawn into the monarch's orbit of concern. In that year his sister Cleopatra, the regent of Egypt, died and an anti-Seleucid party came to the fore. Not content with the suppression of their domestic opponents, the anti-Seleucids threatened to annex Seleucid territories to Egypt. When they moved against Coele-Syria in 170/169, Antiochus made his first trip to Egypt. He overcame most of Lower Egypt, except for Alexandria, and set up a rival government at Memphis. Early in 168, Antiochus again marched into Egypt and was almost at

---

17 Polybius, *Histories* XXVI. 1 ff. (fragments), ed. W. R. Paton, Loeb Classical Library, V (Cambridge, Mass., 1926), 481.

the gates of Alexandria when his fateful meeting with the Romans took place.[18]

It is hardly coincidental that Antiochus' major actions in Judea, in 175/4, 172/1, 169/8 and 168/7, corresponded to the critical periods in his reign — the first to the time when he was beginning to consolidate his power after seizing the throne; the second to the threat posed by events following the death of Cleopatra; the third to his first trip to Egypt and the fourth to Eleusis and its aftermath.

Since Judea was a conquered state, the Seleucids and the changing Jewish establishment represented successively by the factors of Onias, Jason and Menelaus, always had to cope with desires for independence. As has always been the case with subjugated peoples vis-à-vis their masters, the opportunity for Jews to break away from Seleucid rule increased in direct proportion to the unrest in the Seleucid realm at large. Stated in other terms, the weaker the Seleucid government, the greater the chances for rebellion in the states under its domination.

Such a period of Seleucid weakness occurred during the interregnum between the assassination of Seleucus and Antiochus' effective attainment of the throne. At the time there were uprisings in various parts of the Seleucid realm,[19] and there is every reason to suppose that Judea was no exception. It is highly possible that an anti-Seleucid party arose seeking either independence or better conditions under the Ptolemies and willing for either purpose to enter into an alliance with Egypt. II Macc. hints at a dallying by Jewish leaders with the Ptolemies in the days of Seleucus IV when it says that Simon charged Onias with conspiracy against the king.[20] Though it favors Onias, the text chooses not to neglect

---

[18] On the chronology, see e.g., Tcherikover, op. cit., p. 186. Cf. M. Smith, "Palestinian Judaism from Alexander to Pompey," constituting chapter 4, section III of P. Grimal et al., *Hellenism and the Rise of Rome* (London, 1965), p. 253.

[19] E. R. Bevan, *The House of Seleucus*, II (London, 1902), 127 ff.

[20] II Macc. 4:1 ff.

this event, but rather to discredit the man responsible for it. This only serves to suggest the gravity and irrespressibility of the fact.

In any case, the opportunity for secession was present in Judea in 176. The appointment of Jason and the enticement of Hellenistic privileges can well be understood as measures intended to reduce subversion and retain Judea under the existing system of Seleucid control.

With Jason in charge of the government, the Onias faction became anti-establishment, that is, opponents of both the Jewish government and the Seleucids. It would be natural to suppose that this group kept pressure on Jason's regime and that it was ready, singly or in concert with other anti-establishment forces, to move to overthrow Jason at his first sign of weakness.

It is most likely that civil strife again erupted around 173/172, when Antiochus' attention was diverted to Egypt.[21] As a result of the unrest, Antiochus decided to replace Jason with Menelaus, who enjoyed the support of the Tobiads.[22] In this decision Jason's failure to maintain political stability was primarily at stake.

Jason's deposition threw him and his followers into the anti-establishment camp. Though compelled to take refuge in Ammon, the home territory of the Tobiads, Jason appears to have been actively preparing for a return. Nor did his departure stem the growing tide of rebellion in Judea, as is evidenced by the uprising against Lysimachus, the charges against Menelaus, and, possibly, Menelaus' execution of the former High Priest, Onias.[23] Antiochus' continued support of Menelaus can be attributed to the fact that unrest had reached the point where no other faction could be expected to insure a greater stability in Judea.

The volatility of Judean society led to fresh outbreaks when Antiochus first moved against Egypt in 169. II Macc. permits us

---

[21] Bevan, op. cit., pp. 134 ff.

[22] So says Josephus, *Antiquities* XII. 5, with justification.

[23] II Macc. 4:32 ff. The account of the murder of Onias by Andronicus is very likely fictional (see Zeitlin in *The Second Book of Maccabees*, p. 140), but the murder of Onias at Menelaus' command remains a possibility. Zeitlin believes that Onias was not murdered but took refuge in Egypt.

to discern two anti-establishment groups involved in the uprising. One of them, Jason's faction, forced Menelaus to retreat to the citadel only to be compelled to flee by a second, but unidentified group.[24] When Antiochus returned from Egypt, he crushed the rebellion and restored Menelaus to power. Responding to new troubles in 168, adumbrated though not clearly delineated in I or II Macc., Antiochus killed many Jews and put others to flight. He brought foreigners into Jerusalem and converted the city into a fortress. Since it had become apparent that no Jewish group could maintain stability and loyalty, the Seleucids had no alternative but to impose full military occupation on the land. Antiochus' actions in Jerusalem in 168 were followed within the year by his decree suspending the Jewish constitution. This hurled nearly all the Jews into the anti-establishment camp and precipitated their revolutionary union.[25]

Third, the Hasmonean Revolution and its precursory rebellions, though distinctive in their details, appear to follow the patterns of successful rebellions elsewhere in history, both in their gestation and post-natal development.[26] The sources of revolutions are manifold and complex, but the roots of all lie in men's grievances against

[24] II Macc. 5:5 ff. and Tcherikover, op. cit., pp. 186 ff. Tcherikover's belief that the unidentified group were members of a "people's revolt" is based on his conception of the fighting as a struggle between the Jewish masses and aristocracy and is hence unsupported by the evidence. Another possibility is that the mystery group was under the leadership of the Hasmoneans.

[25] II Macc. 5:11 ff. On the Akra, the headquarters for the Hellenizers in Jerusalem, see J. Simons, *Jerusalem in the Old Testament* (Leiden, 1952), p. 145. On the uprisings elsewhere in the Seleucid realm, see M. Rostovtzeff, *Social and Economic History of the Hellenistic World*, II (Oxford, 1941), 841.

[26] The modern sociological and political analysis of revolutions is a relatively new and still highly amorphous discipline. Most scholars focus to a greater extent on modern revolutions than on those of medieval or ancient times and seldom give sufficient attention to the psycho-sociological constants in revolutionary situations. See W. Laqueur, "Revolution," *International Encyclopedia of the Social Sciences*, XIII (New York, 1968), 501–507, especially the bibliography. Cf. also C. Brinton, *The Anatomy of Revolution*, revised ed. (New York, 1952), passim and bibliographical appendix (pp. 280 ff.) and N. Timasheff, *War and Revolution* (New York, 1965), passim.

their government. They generally begin when great social change affects large numbers of men adversely. As grievances spread, men gradually form themselves into anti-establishment groups ready to agitate for change. If conditions of life become desperate, these men may be willing to risk their lives and possessions for their redress. Some may wish to overthrow the constitution as well as the government. Others, frequently the majority, will wish to retain the constitution or constitutive principles of their society but at the same time give this constitution a new interpretation capable of satisfying their grievances and needs. Such groups will present a challenge and a threat to the establishment, with its entrenched, traditional interpretations of the constitution.

In time such anti-establishment groups grow, amalgamate or federate. Rebellious federations are often more united in their hostility to the regime than in the specifics of their grievances. Rebellions become revolutions when the dissidents have sufficient strength to overthrow the regime. But the struggle does not end with their victory. Once the common foe is removed, the various rebel factions are left free to fight among themselves for control of the society.

Neither I nor II Macc. is an analytical text. Neither is interested in a rounded sociological or political analysis of the Hasmonean Revolution or its antecedents. But the texts do identify at least six factions among the Jews in the year between 187 and 168, those of Onias, Simon, Jason, Menelaus, the Ḥasidim and the Hasmoneans. To these may be added the group that ousted Jason from Jerusalem in 169, if it is not to be identified with one of the others. The texts do not reveal whether any of the groups mentioned from 174 on were related to earlier factions, such as Jason's group to Simon's or the Ḥasidim to the followers of Onias.

But the texts make two facts clear. One is that all these groups were dedicated to the Pentateuch in the years 175 to 168. All of them sought to control Judea through the instrumentality of the Pentateuch. Like similar groups elsewhere in history, each of them can be expected to have championed a different approach to the Pentateuch constitution. The other is that at the height of the tevolt against Antiochus, in the years 168–165, all of them, with rhe exception of Menelaus' group, were, *regardless of their ideological inclinations*, politically anti-Seleucid. Before the revolution, at least three were at different times pro-Seleucid — the Onias group before the circumstances leading to the incident with Simon, the Jason forces before the deposition of their leader, and the Menelaus group. The Hasmoneans were always anti-Seleucid (In the uprisings of 169 Judah Maccabee was compelled to flee for his life from Jerusalem.) The Ḥasidim were anti-Seleucid before the revolution, unless they are to be identified with the Onias faction. The confirmed anti-Seleucid position of these groups made them the natural candidates for leadership in the swollen ranks of the anti-establishment and anti-Seleucid forces in the years 168–165. Under their leadership the diverse anti-establishment factions in Judean life formed a coalition against the common foe and for an identical goal, the restoration of the Pentateuch constitution (I Macc. 2:50). There is every reason to suppose that this coalition included aspirants to the pontificate, priests and lay aristocrats, both Hellenists and anti-Hellenists.[27]

Under Judah Maccabee, the united Jewish forces stunned Antiochus' troops with repeated defeats. They eventually captured Jerusalem, cleansed the Temple, appointed priests of Judah's choosing, restored the constitution and inaugurated a purge of their enemies. With Judah Maccabee still in command, the forces of the newly independent Judea proceeded to consolidate their gains and carry the war to Judea's hostile neighbors.[28]

At this juncture, an internecine struggle for control of Judean society broke out. Part of the coalition, eager to be restored to their old status and positions and understandably afraid that with

---

[27] A number of scholars have correctly recognized that the Hasmoneans and their followers were not untouched by Hellenism. Thus the name Maccabee, the name of Judah's friend, Eupolemus, and the world view of Judah Maccabee all show Hellenistic influence. See v.g., I Macc. 8:17, Zeitlin to I Macc., p. 38 and to II Macc., p. 25 and Bickerman, "The Historical Foundations of Postbiblical Judaism," pp. 108 ff.

[28] I Macc. 3:1 ff., especially 4:41 ff. and 5:1 ff. and II Macc. 10.

its increasing strength, Judah's faction might assume effective control of the state, hastened to make a league with Lysias. They promised to return Judea to Seleucid control in exchange for a restoration of their authority and the outlawing of Judah's faction.[29] Once again the Jews were split into substantial pro-Seleucid and anti-Seleucid factions. During the turmoil in the Seleucid realm in 163–162 Judah appears to have gotten the upper hand in Judea, but his opponents, "all the lawless and ungodly men of Israel" (I Macc. 7:5), led by Alcimus, informed the new king, Demetrius, of his threat, and, with the aid of a Seleucid army, put Judah to flight. Supported by the Seleucids, Alcimus and "all those who harassed their people...", took possession of the land of Judah" (ibid. 7:22) and ruled under the Pentateuch. To judge from II Macc. 14:3, which refers to Alcimus as having "formerly been High Priest," Alcimus may have been named High Priest a short time before these events, doubtless immediately after the death or deportation of Menelaus (II Macc. 13:4, *Ant.* XII. 9) and may have initially been prevented from ruling, or even deposed, by the forces of Judah Maccabee. In any event, Alcimus' effective rule did not begin until 162. In the year 160 Alcimus accompanied the army that defeated and killed Judah Maccabee (I Macc. 9:1 ff.).

For a while, until they were betrayed, the Ḥasidim, too, by their support of Alcimus, expressed their satisfaction with the Seleucid-Jewish entente. Of the various factions identifiable in 168, only the Hasmoneans remained undivertible in their opposition to the Seleucids after 165.

On the basis of available evidence there is no justification for the assumption that after 165 the Hasmonean faction's principal goal was the independence of Judea. For all we know the main thrust of their efforts was to gain control of Judean society, even if, like their enemies, they had to submit to Seleucid domination in exchange for this control. A mere dozen years after these events,

---

[29] For a discussion of the problem of the sequence and dates of the letters, see Tcherikover, op. cit., pp. 214 ff. My forthcoming study will deal with the texts and chronology in detail.

Judah's brother, Jonathan, did not scruple to subordinate Judea to the usurper of the Seleucid throne, Alexander Balas.[30] Jonathan had supported Alexander in his struggles against the Seleucid establishment. This establishment and the Hasmoneans had never been at peace. Other factions in Judea, like Jason's and Menelaus', had formerly been in league with these Seleucids. When, in 164, the Seleucids considered peace, it was therefore more natural for them to reembrace their old allies than to seek an accord with their perennial enemies. The Hasmoneans fought on against the coalition of Seleucids and Jews. If their immediate goal was independence, it was because they, rather than Judea, could not endure without it.

The fact that the Seleucids could succeed in their intent reveals the tenuousness of the Jewish confederation and the weakness of the position of the Hasmonean faction.

As for the rank and file of the Jewish armies, the explanation of their diverse reactions to the peace settlement is not to be sought in the artificial division between Pentateuch and politics, but in the different approaches to the Pentateuch constitution by the opposing factions in Judea. Since the government of Judea after 164 was essentially in the hands of the same groups that ruled prior to 168, it is natural to conclude that the men laying down their arms were content to return to the Pentateuch constitution as understood and applied before the revolution, while those continuing to fight under Judah felt that their grievances could be satisfied only by a radically different approach.[31]

On the determination of these grievances hinges not only a fuller understanding of the Hasmonean Revolution but of much of the subsequent history of the Jewish Second Commonwealth. The pertinent evidence here is so fragmentary and circumstantial that no reconstruction can be more than a study in conjecture. Yet reconstructions must be undertaken, for without some understanding of

---

[30] I Macc. 10:6 ff.

[31] Cf. E. Rivkin, *The Hidden Revolution: An Historical Reconstruction of the Pharisees*, to be published in the near future. Professor Rivkin has graciously permitted me to see and cite his manuscript.

this period, however hypothetical, it is impossible to elucidate many of the most critical aspects of the periods that follow.

In such a reconstruction two facts cannot be overlooked. First is the fact that the grievances producing the unrest in Judea in the 180s and 170s could have had nothing to do with the interdiction of the Pentateuch, which did not take place until 168/167. Nor did they in their entirety or perhaps even in the main have anything to do with Antiochus IV, for Antiochus did not ascend the Seleucid throne until 176. Furthermore, since the restiveness in the 180s was serious, it follows that the grievances in Judea were already of long standing.

Besides, whatever these grievances, it is clear that they were at no time shared by all the members of the lower classes. At all times, however, these grievances found supporters and spokesmen in members of the higher echelons of society who were seeking to oust the incumbent leadership. Such spokesmen included the Hasmoneans.

It has often been maintained that in the revolution of 168–165, the countryside supported the Hasmoneans while the townspeople, especially the Jerusalemites, backed their opponents. Yet II Macc. states that with the peace agreement and restoration of the Torah, "Lysias went back to the king and the Jews went about their farming" (12:1).

This item of evidence is insufficient to demonstrate anything: we do not know which Jews are meant and for how long they farmed. But it does suggest a question as yet not fully probed by scholars: could it be that the men satisfied with the peace arrangements belonged to the farming classes, while those supporting Judah came from the towns and especially from Jerusalem?[32]

The possibility that Judah Maccabee was a leader of urban

---

[32] Rivkin, op. cit., argues cogently for an identification of the Pharisees with the ideological leadership of the revolutionary factions in 168–165. See also his "The Pharisaic Revolution," in *Perspectives in Jewish Learning*, II (Chicago, 1966), 26–51; "The Internal City," *Journal for the Scientific Study of Religion* V (1966); and his Prologomenon in the reprint of Oesterley, Lowe and Rosenthal, eds., *Judaism and Christianity* (New York, 1969).

forces, or at least a town-oriented coalition, has appeal in the light of historical parallels. Regularly in history the movement of a region toward greater urbanization and the accompanying displacement of men from the farms to the cities has generated new needs in the growing urban classes which the constitution as previously understood could not satisfy and which the vested interests of intrenched power preferred to ignore. With the growth of these urban classes the resulting grievances flared into revolutionary outbursts.

The question also arises whether there is any relationship between the factions in Judea prior to 168 and at least the major factions in the post-165 period, the Hasmoneans and anti-Hasmoneans and the Pharisees, Sadducees and Essenes.

There is good reason to posit an intimate connection. An analysis of the political aspects of the Hasmonean Revolution lays the foundation for a new and clear understanding of the Pharisaic movement. It would be possible to demonstrate that Pharisaism represents the ideological aspect of the political struggle of the Hasmoneans. But this takes us far beyond the scope of this paper.

Difficult though the answers to such questions may be, they will be achieved with maximum possible objectivity if the historian is aware of the bias of the available sources, if during the course of his investigation he suspends his religious prejudgments about the personages involved, and if he treats his raw data with the same dispassion that he might employ when dealing with other aspects of history outside the focus of his ultimate concerns.

———

This article was completed in October 1969. For certain technical reasons connected with the printing, changes contemplated since that time could not be made. A revised version will be published in the near future. In the meantime attention should be called to the appearance of Morton Smith's *Palestinian Parties and Politics that Shaped the Old Testament* (New York, 1971), pp. 148 ff., with interesting attempts to identify party structure and activities at the time, and the more traditional approach of Menahem Stern, "The Hasmonean Revolt," in H. H. Ben-Sasson and S. Ettinger, eds., *Jewish Society Through the Ages*, pp. 92–106.

CHRISTIAN TRANSLATORS OF MAIMONIDES' *MISHNEH TORAH* INTO LATIN

A BIO-BIBLIOGRAPHICAL SURVEY

JACOB I. DIENSTAG

CHRISTIAN HEBRAISM has been a subject of study in modern Jewish scholarship for over a century. Beginning with F. L. Hoffmann's bibliography of Christian authors of Hebrew Grammars published in 1868,[1] followed shortly by Ludwig Geiger's work on the study of the Hebrew language in Germany,[2] this theme continues to be of profound interest to students of Jewish intellectual history. No less a historian than Professor Salo W. Baron, in whose honor we have the privilege to contribute this study, has enriched this subject with erudite excursuses in his monumental *Social and Religious History* beginning with volume six[3] and continuing in volume thirteen, which was recently published.[4]

This bio-bibliographical survey which is confined to Christian translators of Maimonides' *Mishneh Torah* — the only major work the Master wrote in Hebrew — reveals a curious paradox: whereas Christian interest in Maimonides' thought was focused on his philosophic work, *The Guide of the Perplexed*, during the Middle Ages — the so-called Age of Faith[5] — this interest shifted during

[1] F. L. Hoffmann, "Hebräische Grammatiken christlicher Autoren bis Ende des XVI. Jahrh. in der Hamburger Stadtbibliothek," *Jeschurun*, VI (1868), 33–48, 145–152.

[2] Ludwig Geiger, *Das Studium der hebräischen Sprache in Deutschland vom Ende des XV. bis zur Mitte des XVI. Jahrhunderts* (Breslau, 1870).

[3] Pp. 462 f., nn. 51–52; 466 f., n. 58.

[4] New York–Philadelphia, 1969, pp. 160–167; 390–397 (notes).

[5] Jacob Guttmann, "Der Einfluss der maimonidischen Philosophie auf das christliche Abendland," *Moses ben Maimon; sein Leben, seine Werke und sein Einfluss*, ed. W. Bacher, M. Brann, D. Simonsen & J. Guttmann (Leipzig, 1908), I, 135–230.

the Renaissance, the Reformation and the Enlightenment to his *Halakic* work, the *Mishneh Torah*. It was through the *Mishneh Torah* that Christian thinkers and theologians viewed normative Judaism. An interesting example of Christian acceptance of this code as an authentic document to be reckoned with, even in ecclesiastical matters, is provided by no lesser a personality than the poet John Milton. During a critical period of his life — when his wife Mary Powell left him the same year in which they were married (1643) — Milton, who was prevented by ecclesiastical law from divorcing her, did not hesitate to turn to Maimonides for legal support. It was through *Mishneh Torah, Hilkot Gerushin,* that Milton attempted to find a religious sanction for dissolving his marriage.[6] We do not attempt by this example to exaggerate the Judaizing tendencies or the purely intellectual aspects of Christian Hebraism. Undoubtedly, many Christian Hebraists were motivated by religious polemical considerations for they saw the main advantage of learning Hebrew as enabling them "to confound the Jews' perfidy, which, through false and frivolous arguments, they support with great audacity against ignorant Christians."[7] Whatever the reasons and motivations, the *Mishneh Torah* of Maimonides, as can be verified from the following survey, occupies a predominant role in Christian Hebraism.

In compiling this bibliography, we have examined the materials we describe. In a few cases only we relied upon the descriptions from reliable catalogues of existing libraries, pending receipt of microfilms or xerox copies. We were, therefore, compelled to omit a few Hebraists listed by Steinschneider[8] who relied in many

[6] "Hence it is that the Rabbis and Maimonides, famous among the rest, in a book of his... tells us that divorce was permitted to Moses to preserve peace and quiet in the family." In his "The Doctrine and Discipline of Divorce," chapter IV, *Works of John Milton*, vol. 3, part 2, ed. F. A. Patterson (New York, 1931), pp. 402–403.

[7] Heinrich von Langensein (Henricus de Hassia), *Opus de idiomate hebraico*, cited from an Erfurt MS by B. Walde in his "Christliche Hebraisten Deutschlands am Ausgang des Mittelalters," p. 10, quoted by S. Baron, op. cit., XIII, 163, 392, note 5.

[8] M. Steinschneider, "Christliche Hebraisten," *ZfHB*, I–V (1896–1901).

instances upon J. C. Wolf's *Bibliotheca Hebraea* and whose works we could not, reliably, verify either personally, or through existing printed catalogs of the British Museum, Oxford, and Bibliothèque Nationale. In the case of extremely rare books, we have designated their location.

It is my pleasure to express my profound appreciation to the libraries and their staffs who have made available their material to me. I am especially grateful to Hebrew Union College, Jewish Theological Seminary, Union Theological Seminary, General Theological Seminary, New York Public Library, Hebrew University, and Mosad Harav Kook in Jerusalem.

1

BASHUYSEN, HEINRICH JACOB (Hanau, Prussia, Oct. 26, 1679–c. 1750). Christian printer of Hebrew books and Orientalist.

In 1701 he was appointed ordinary professor of Oriental languages and ecclesiastical history at the Protestant gymnasium of Hanau, and in 1703 became professor of theology in that institution. In 1716 he accepted the position of rector and *professor primarius* at the gymnasium of Zerbst. Bashuysen was a member of the Academy of Berlin and of the London Society for the Propagation of the Gospel. He was a zealous promoter of Hebrew and rabbinical literature; and, among other works, he translated *Hilkot Sefer Torah*:

Heinrich Jacob van Bashuysen. Observationum sacrarum liber I. Agens de integritate Sacrae Scripturae imprimis Veteris Testamenti; quae occasione editionis, versionis et notarum R. Mosis Maimonidis tractatus ספר תורה seu de libro legis, (qui est II. Partis יד חזקה generalis Tituli, הלכות תפלין מזוזה וספר תורה, Cap. 7. 8. 9. 10.) nova methodo illustratur et defenditur, aspersis undique Antiquitatibus Judaicis, non ubique obviis, ita ut introductionis Biblicae vicem gerere possit. Francofurti a. M. 1708. [24], 152, [6] p.

BIBL. *Jewish Encyclopedia*, II (henceforth, *JE*), 574; Steinschneider, "Christliche Hebraisten," *ZfHB*, II (1897), 51.

2

BEKE, MATTHAEUS (Amsterdam, c. 1708). Biographical information unavailable.

Translated into Latin Maimonides' *Hilkot Yobel*:

הלכות יובל id est; Constitutiones de anno jubilaeo ex R. Mose

Maimonide. Hebraeo textui, versionem Latinam & notas addidit Matthaeus Beke... In quibus varia ex jure Hebraeorum, & quaedam theologico-philologica, nec non Quaedam V.T. loca & phrases N.T. illustrantur. Cum indice triplice. Lugduni Batavorum: H. Teering, 1708. [7] p. L., 143 p., [11] p. (Hebrew University).

3

BUXTORF, JOHANNES II (Basel, Aug. 13, 1599–Aug. 16, 1664).

Son of John Buxtorf, the elder (I). Before the age of thirteen he matriculated at the University of Basel, and in December of 1615 graduated as master of arts from that institution. He then went to Heidelberg, where he continued his studies. He succeeded his father, after the death of the latter, in the chair of Hebrew at the University of Basel. Like his father, Buxtorf II maintained relations with several learned Jews and corresponded with them. Among his correspondents was Manasseh B. Israel. He distinguished himself for his works on Hebrew grammar and translations of Hebrew works into Latin, among which are translations from the Letters and Responsa of Maimonides, documents related to the Maimonidean controversy, *The Guide of the Perplexed*, and *H. Ḥameẓ u-Maẓẓah*:

a) Appendix epistolarum aliquot insignium et eruditarum R. Mosis Majemonidis, R. Davidis Kimchii, R. Nachmanidis, R. Bechai, R. Samuelis Aben Tybbon... In Buxtorf Johann, "Institutio epistolaris Hebraica, sive de conscribendis epistolis Hebraicis liber...". Basileae: Sumptibus L. Regis, 1629, pp. 360–462.

b) Rabbi Mosis Majemonidis liber מורה נבוכים Doctor perplexorum; ad dubia & obscuriora Scripturae loca rectius intelligenda veluti clavem continens, prout in praefatione, in qua de authoris vita, & operis totius ratione agitur, pleniùs explicatur: primum ab authore in lingua Arabica..., in linguam Hebraeam... translatus: nunc vero nove... in linguam Latinam... fideliter conversus, a Johanne Buxtorfio, fil... Basileae, Sumptibus & impensis L. Konig, excudebat J. J. Genath, 1629. 20 p. 1., 532 p., [26] L. 4°.

c) הלכות חמץ ומצה R. Mosis Majemonidis.... In his "Dissertationes Philologico-Theologicae," Basilae: Joh. Jacobi Deckeri, 1662, p. 392–396. 4°.

BIBL. Steinschneider, *ZfHB*, II (1897), 94–95; *JE*, III, 446.

4

CARPZOV, J. BENEDICT (Leipzig, April 24, 1639–March 23, 1699). Protestant theologian.

He was a member of a family which, like the Buxtorfs, produced

a long line of distinguished scholars. He studied Hebrew under
Johannes Buxtorf II in Basel. In 1668 he was appointed professor
of Oriental languages at Leipzig and of theology (1684–99). He
edited and translated works on biblical exegesis and rabbinic
literature among which are:

a) הלכות תעניות Rabbi Mosis Ben Majemon Tractatus de Jejuniis
Hebraeorum cum interpretatione latina Jo. Benedicti Carpzovi.
Lipsiae, typ. J. E. Hahn, 1662. [3] p. L.; 41, [1] p.

b) Disputatio IV. ad R. Mosis Ben Majemon Cap. VII. Hilc. עכו״ם
Nun. XVI In his "Disputationes academicae..." Lipsiae, Impensis
haered. Friderici Lanckisii, 1699, pp. 133–150. An anti-Maimo-
nidean theological polemic.

BIBL. *JE*, III, 592; *Encyclopaedia Judaica*, V, col. 59 (henceforth *EJ*)
Steinschneider, *Cat. Bod.* p. 816.

5

CLAVERING, ROBERT (England, 1671–Oxford, July 21, 1747).

Was admitted to Lincoln College, Oxford, in 1693, after having
been at the University of Edinburgh. In 1715 he was elected Regius
Professor of Hebrew at Oxford and in 1729 he became Bishop of
Peterborough. He obtained permission to hold his professorship
and bishopric at the same time. In 1705, at Oxford, he published
a Latin translation of Maimonides' *Mishneh Torah, Hilkot Talmud
Torah* and *Teshubah*:

תורה ותשובה (!)הלכות תמלוד R. Mosis Maimonidis Tractatus duo:
1. De doctrina legis, sive educatione puerorum. 2. De natura &
ratione poenitentiae apud Hebraeos. Latinè reddidit, notisque
illustravit Robertus Clavering... Praemittitur dissertatio de
Maimonide ejusque operibus. Oxonii: E Theatro Sheldoniano,
impensis H. Mortlock, 1705. 12 p. L., 152, [1] p. 4°.

The Dissertatio de Maimonide was reprinted by Blasius Ugolino
in his *Thesaurus Antiquitatum Sacrarum*, vol. 8, Venetiis, Apud
J. G. Herthz, 1747, col. DCCIX–DCCXX.

BIBL. *JE*, IV, 110; *Dictionary of National Biography*, IV, 461;
S. Levy, "English Students of Maimonides," *The Jewish Annual*, 5701
(1940–1941), pp. 81–82 [= *Jewish Historical Society of England.
Miscellanies*, part IV: *Essays presented to E. N. Adler* — I, London,
1942, p. 74].

6

CRAMER, JOHANNES RUDOLPHUS (Elgg, Switzerland, Feb. 14, 1678–
Zurich, July 14, 1737).

Was first instructed in classical learning by his father, who was
a pastor of the Reformed Church. His father intended for him to

study medicine, but by the advice of his brother, professor of
Oriental languages at Zurich, he studied theology. He was admitted
into the ministry in 1699. The same year he accompanied his
brother to Herborn, where the latter had been appointed professor
of divinity. There he pursued his studies for two years. He then went
to study under Surenhusius in 1701 in Leyden where, as a result
of his great progress in Hebrew studies, he was unanimously chosen
to succeed his brother who died in 1702. In 1705 he was appointed
to teach sacred and profane history and in the following year
succeeded to the professorship of Hebrew in the Superior College.
In 1725 he became professor of theology in Zurich.

Among his numerous works is a translation of *Mishneh Torah,
Hilkot Bikkurim*:

הלכות בכורים, seu constitutiones de primitivis R. Mosis F. Mai-
monis... cum versione Latina et notis philologicis exhibitae à
J. R. Cramero. Lugduni Batavorum: H. Teering, 1702. 4°. 5 p. L.,
172 p.

BIBL. Jöcher, *Allgemeiner Gelehrten-Lexicon*, I, 2170–2171; *Chal-
mer's General Biographical Dictionary*, X, 460–461; Steinschneider,
Cat. Bodl., p. 849; idem, *ZfHB*, II (1897), 123; *Allgemeine Deutsche
Biographie*, IV, 148.

7

DITHMAR, JUSTUS CHRISTOPH (Rothenburg, Hessen–Darmstadt, March 13
1677–Frankfurt a/O, March 13, 1737).

Began his studies in his native town under his father's supervision till he was seventeen. He then proceeded to Marburg where
he studied Oriental languages and theology under Otto, the cel-
brated Orientalist, and Tileman, professor of divinity. Dithmar also
studied in Leyden and was afterwards appointed professor of law
of nature, and history.

A voluminous author in the field of his profession, Dithmar
translated Maimonides' *Hilkot Shebuʻot*:

הלכות שבועות id est, Constitutiones de jurejurando ex R. Mosis
Maimonidis opere היד החזקה dicto, latine redditae, variisque
notis illustratae a Justo Christophoro Dithmaro. Lugduni in
Batavis, Apud C. Boutesteyn, 1706. [8] p. L.; 226, [4] p. 4°.
Hebrew and Latin.

BIBL. *Chalmer's General Biographical Dict.*, XII, 135–137; *Nouvelle
Biographie Générale*, XIV, 326–327; J. C. Adelung, "Forsetzung
und Ergänzungen zu C. G. Jöchers allgemeinem Gelehrten-Lexicon", II, 710–712; Steinschneider, *ZfHB*, II (1897), 125.

8

ESGERS, JOHANNES (Amsterdam, Jan. 2, 1696–Leiden, May 28, 1755).
Studied in Leiden where he was appointed, in 1740, professor of
theology. In 1751 he became professor of Hebrew antiquities.
Besides his works on biblical exegesis and theology, Esgers translated *Mishneh Torah, Hilkot Sheḳalim*, his doctoral dissertation:
a) Dissertatio philologico-theologica, quae exhibet R. Mosis Maimonidis Constitutiones de siclis, Latinitate donatas, & notis
   illustratas; prima, secunda, et tertia. Quam... praeside... D.
   Francisco Fabricio... publico examini subjicit Joannes Esgers...
   Lugduni Batavorum: Apud P. Vander Aa, 1717. [1] p. L., 146,
   [10] p.
   Dissertation, Leiden, 1717.
   Contains Hebrew text and Latin translation of *H. Sheḳalim* with
   elaborate notes at end of each chapter.
b) רבי משה ב״ר מימון הלכות שקלים id est R. Mosis Maimonidis
   Constitutiones de siclis, quas Latinitate donavit & notis illustravit
   Joannes Esgers...
   Lugduni Batavorum: Apud Petrum Vander Aa, 1718.
   [4] p. L., 146 p., 3 L. 4°.
   Text in Hebrew and Latin.
*c) רבי משה ב״ר מימון הלכות שקלים id est... Constitutiones de siclis,
   quas Latinitate donavit & notis illustravit J. Esgers. Lugduni
   Batavorum: J. A. Langerak, 1727. 4 p. L., 146 p., 3 L.
   Hebrew and Latin.
   (*Hebrew Union College*, Cat., XVI, 654).
   BIBL. J. C. Adelung, "Fortsetzung und Ergänzungen zu C. G. Jöchers
   allgemeinem Gel.-Lex.," II, 935–936; *Nouvelle Biographie Générale*,
   XVI, 387. Steinschneider, *ZfHB*, II (1897), 149.

9

GEIER, MARTIN (Leipzig, April 24, 1614—Freiberg, Sept. 12, 1680).
Appointed as pastor of Thomas-Kirche in Leipzig. In 1661 he became professor and in 1665 was appointed to a high church position in Dresden. He was the author of works on biblical exegesis and
rabbinics and translated Maimonides' *Hilkot Abel*:
   De Ebraeorum luctu, lugentiumq. ritibus; e sacris praecipuè nec
   non R. Mosis B. Maimon tit. Efel, aliisq. Lipsiae: Haered H.
   Grossii, 1656. 12 p. L., 432 p. 17 L.
   — — [second revised edition]. Lipsiae: Haered, 1666. 12 p. L.,
   445, [1], p. 17 L. [third edition], Frankfurt, 1683.
   Reprinted in: *Thesaurus Antiquitatum Sacrarum*, ed. Blasio Ugolino, vol. 33, Venetiis, 1767, col. LXIII–CCLII.

294   JACOB I. DIENSTAG   [8]

Bibl. *Allgemeine Deutsche Biographie* (s.v.); Jöcher, *All. Gel.-Lex.* II, 903–904.

10

GENEBRARD, GILBERT (Paris, 1537–1597).

Catholic and translator of medieval Hebrew books into Latin. Among them are Maimonides' works:

a) שלש עשרה עיקרים שחבר הרמב״ם Symbolum fidei Judaeorum... Precationes... DCXIII legis praecepta. Paris, 1569.

b) Sexcenta Tredecim Praecepta Mosis... In: "Chronologia Hebrae-orum Maior, quae Seder Olam Rabba Inscribitur, et Minor, quae Seder Olam Zuata...," Paris: Apud M. Sonnium, 1584, p. 119–134.

Translation of the Six Hundred and Thirteen Commandments found in the beginning of the *Mishneh Torah.*

c) Hebraeorum breve chronicon sive compendium de mundi ordine et temporibus, ab orbe condito usque ad annum Christi, 1112. Capita R. Mose ben Maiemon de rebus Christi regis, Collectanea Eliae Levitis et R. Jacob Salomonis filii de eodem, quibus summatim explicatur, quicquid Judaei de Christo sapiunt. G[ilberto] Genebrardo... interprete. Parisiis 1572. This work also contains translation of *Mishneh Torah, Hilkot Melakim,* Chapters 11 and 12 referring to Jesus.

Bibl. M. Steinschneider, *Cat. Bodl.*, col. 1006–1008; A. E. Cowley, *Concise Cat...*, p. 209–210; Steinschneider, *ZfHB*, III (1898), 14–15, no. 195; Siegfried Stein, "Phillipus Ferdinandus Polonus," *Essays in Honour of J. H. Hertz*, (London, 1943), pp. 400, 403–405, 412.

11

GENTIUS, GEORGIUS (Dame, Querfurt, 1618–Freiberg, Sept., 1687).

Studied Oriental languages in Bremen and Arabic and Turkish in Leiden. As a result of his acquaintance with the Turkish ambassador in Holland, he obtained the opportunity to examine the literary treasures of Turkey. He also visited Greece and Persia. In 1648 he went to Venice and from there to Nürnberg, Hamburg, and Amsterdam. A renowned linguist, he served as an interpreter in the foreign ministry of his country and lived a very comfortable life from the lavish pension he received. The last years of his life, however, were spent in poverty and, upon his death, he was buried at the community's expense.

Besides translating Solomon Ibn Vergas' *Shevet Yehudah* (Amsterdam, 1651) into Latin, Gentius also rendered into Latin, *Mishneh Torah, Hilkot De'ot:*

הלכות דעות sive, Canones ethici R. Moseh Meimonidis, Hebraeorum sapientissimi, ex Hebraeo in Latinum versi, uberioribusque notis illustrati à Georgio Gentio... Amstelodami: Apud Ioh. & Cornelivum Blaev, 1640. 10 p. L., 160 p., 2 L.

Hebrew and Latin in parallel columns.

BIBL. Steinschneider, *ZfHB*, III (1899), 15. Jöcher, *All. Gel.-Lex.*, II, 925–926.

12

GIUSTINIANI, AGOSTINO (1470–1536). Corsican bishop, friend of Erasmus, Thomas More and Pico di Mirandola. Semitic Scholar who probably studied Hebrew under R. Elijah del Medigo.

Dedicated his life to publish the Bible with his translation, of which the Book of Psalms appeared in Hebrew, accompanied by the Greek, Aramaic, and Arabic; also the Book of Job with the Latin (Vulgate) translation and a new Latin version. In a note to Psalm 19:5 he mentions the voyage of Columbus and the discovery of America — the first time this fact was recorded in print. In 1520 he published the Latin translation of the *More Nebukim* based on the translation of Al-Ḥarizi, to which is added the oldest Latin translation of the "Six-Hundred Commandments" of Maimonides found in the beginning of the *Mishneh Torah*:

De CCXLVIII Preceptis...

In: Rabi Mossei Aegyptis Dux seu director dubitatium aut Perplexorum

Parisiis, 1520, leaves CXIIIa–CXVIIIb.

This translation was "amply used by Genebrardus (q.v.), though he altered his predecessor's Latin considerably and made additional explanations or corrections as e.g. on pos. 131, 174, 226; neg. 154, 183, 246..." (Stein, "Phillipus Ferdinandus Polonus...," p. 412).

BIBL. *Encyclopedia Hebraica*, X, 456–457; M. Steinschneider, *Cat. Bodl.*, col. 1564; Siegfried Stein, "Phillipus Ferdinandus Polonus..., p. 412.

13

HELENIUS, ENGELBERT (Helsingeland, Sweden, Oct. 8, 1700—Stara, Feb. 14, 1767).

Doctor of theology and bishop and son of a preacher. Studied in Uppsala where he specialized in Oriental languages. Served for some years as professor of philosophy and theology. In 1753 he was appointed Bishop of Stara in which office he remained till his death. His doctoral dissertation consisted of a Latin translation of Maimonides' *Mishneh Torah, Hilkot Kil'ayim*:

הלכות כלאים; seu, Mosis Maimonidae De miscellis caput sextum, ex ebraeo in latinum sermonem conversum, una cum brevi ex-

positione dicti Deut. XXII, 9. Praeside... Olavo Celsio publicae
bonorum censurae... sistit Engelbert. L. Halenius... ad d. 13.
Junii anni MDCCXXVII. Upsaliae, typ. Werner, [1727]. 2 p. 1.;
26 p.

Hebrew and Latin (Upsala. Universitet: Dissertationes, v. 1).

BIBL. J. C. Adelung, "Fortsetzung und Ergänzungen zu C. G. Jöchers
Allgemeinem Gelehrten-Lexicon," II, 1739; Steinschneider, *ZfHB*,
III (1899), 17.

14

HILPERT, JOHANN (Germany, c. 1627 — Helmstadt, May 10, 1680).

After serving as professor of Hebrew in Helmstadt, he was appointed as superintendent in Hildesheim. The author of various works on
theology and Jewish-Christian polemics, he translated Maimonides'
Hilkot Teshubah into Latin:

R. Mosis Maimonidae, Tractatus de Poenitentia, ex Ebraeo in
Latinum sermonem conversus à M. Iohanne Hilpert. Helmstadt,
typis Henningi Mvlleri [1651]. [18] leaves. Not paginated. 4°.

Latin only. (Hebrew University).

BIBL. Jöcher, *All. Gel.-Lex.*, II, 1609.

15

HIRT, JOHANN FRIEDRICH (Apolda, Sachsen-Weimar, Aug. 14, 1719–
Wittenberg, July 29, 1783).

Studied at Weimar and Jena theology, philosophy, and philology,
especially semitics. In 1758 he was appointed professor of philosophy
in Jena and in 1769 professor of theology. In 1755 he was called to
occupy the chair of professor of theology in Wittenberg where he
remained until his death. His voluminous writings consist of biblical
exegesis, Hebrew grammar, and antiquities. He also translated
Hebrew works among which is Maimonides' *Hilkot Ishut*:

הלכות אישות פרק עשירי sev Rabbi Mosis ben Maimon tractatus
de matrimonio Ebraeorum capvt decimvm. Adiecta svnt pvncta
vocalia et accentvs versio Latina nec non Annotationes mvltae,
ita vt instar commentationis de nvptiis Ebraeorvm et rebvs, qvae
cvm istis connexae svnt, qvibvsdam aliis, esse possit. Avctore
M. Ioan. Frider. Hirtio. Ienae: Apvd Io. Adam Melchier, 1746.
52, [4] p. 21 cm.

Hebrew and Latin in parallel columns.

(C.U.).

BIBL. *Allgemeine Deutsche Biographie*, XII, 481–482; *Nouvelle
Biographie Générale*, XXIV, 795–796; J. Adelung, "Forsetzung
und Ergänzungen zu Jöchers Gel.-Lex.," II, 2022–2025; Steinschneider, *ZfHB*, III (1899), 48.

16
HOUTING, HENRICUS (17th cent.)

Nothing is known of his life. He translated into Latin Mishnah, *Rosh ha-Shanah* to which he appended a translation of *Mishneh Torah, Hilkot Sanhedrin*:

Maimonides de synedriis & poenis. Accedunt variantes ad Maimonidem lectiones...

Appended to:

מסכת ראש השנה seu Tractatus talmudicus de festo novi anni ac calendarum consecratione itemque Maimonides De Synedriis & poenis. Accedunt variantes ad Maimonidem lectiones. Uterque ex hebraeo in latinum versus & prior notis illustratus ab Henrico Houting. Amstelodami, Apud Henricum & viduam Theodori Boom, 1695. 171, [3] p. (2nd pagination). Hebrew and Latin in parellel columns.

(Hebrew University).

17
LEUSDEN, JOHANNES (Utrecht, April 26, 1624–Utrecht, September 30, 1699). Dutch Biblical scholar.

He studied philosophy and theology, and especially Oriental languages at Utrecht, and then went to Amsterdam to perfect his knowledge of Judaism by intercourse with Jews. In 1650 he was appointed professor extraordinary of Oriental languages at Utrecht, and in 1653 ordinary professor. He collaborated with R. Joseph Athias in the publication of the Hebrew Bible (Amsterdam, 1660; 2nd ed., 1667), and translated Hebrew works into Latin, among them the "Six-Hundred and Thirteen Commandments" which are found in the beginning of the *Mishneh Torah*:

Johann Leusden: Catalogus Hebraicus et Latinus sexcentorum et tredecim praeceptorum, nempe 248 affirmativorum, et 365 negativorum, in quaetotus Pentateuchus ex sententia Judeorum divisus est [prout idem dispositus est à R. Mosche filio Majemonidis in praefatione Libri... Iad Chasaka.], translatus, & and in hunc ordinem dispositus a Johanne Leusden.

In his "Philologus Hebraeus...", Ultrajecti, 1657, pp. 357–447; Sexcenta et tredecim praecepta Mosaica, à Maimonide ex Pentateucho Hebraice olim excerpta, quae, additis locis Pentateuchi, Latine translata hic ordine exhibentur, auctore Johanne Leusden. Ultrajecti: F. Halma, 1686. 2 p. 1, 56 p. In his "Philologus Hebraeus", Ultrajecti, 1686.

BIBL. M. Steinschneider, *Catal. Bodl.*, col. 1605–1606; idem, *ZfHB*, III (1898), 113, no. 264; *New Schaff-Herzog Encyclopedia*, VI, 466; *EJ*, X, col. 829–830.

18

LEYDECKER, MELCHIOR (Middelburg, Zeeland, Holland, Jan. 25, 1642–
Jan. 6, 1721).

Studied in Middelburg, Utrecht and Leiden. In 1662 he was appointed preacher and in 1678 he became professor of theology in
Utrecht. Became deeply involved in the controversy of merging the
Dutch Reform church with the Lutherans. Among his many works
are his translations into Latin of Maimonides' *Hilkot Melakim*
and the "Six-Hundred and Thirteen Commandments" preceding
the *Mishneh Torah*:

a) R. Mosis Majemonidis Tractatus de Regibus hebraeorum eorum-
que bellis, praefertim de Rege Messia. Melchior Leydecker...
latine vertit & notis philologicis illustravit. Roterdami, apud
Petrum Vander Slaert, 1699. [4] p. L., 254, [2] p. 20 1/2 cm. 8°.
With polemical notes in reference to Maimonides' Messianic
theory and his opinion of Christianity and Jesus.

b) Reprinted in: Thomas Theodor Crenius [= Crusius'] Fasciculus...
Opusculorum quae ad historiam ac philologiam sacram spectant",
vol 9, Rotterodami, apud Petrum Vander Slaart, 1699, from beginning of vol to p [256].

c) De corpore juriis Mosaici secundum Judaeos. In his "De Re-
publica Hebraeorum", vol. I, Amstelaedami: Isaacum, Stockman,
1704, p. 295–307.
Six-Hundred Thirteen Commandments in Latin translation.

BIBL. Jöcher, *Allgem. Gel.-Lex.*, II, 2413–2415.

19

MAIUS, JOHANN HEINRICH (Durlach, March 11, 1688–Giessen, June 13,
1732).

Studied in Giessen, Altdorf and Jena. In 1709 he became professor
of Greek and Oriental literature in Giessen; in 1716 professor of
antiquities. Among the various Hebrew works which he translated
into Latin are parts of the *Mishneh Torah*:

a) הלכות שמיטה ויובל sive, R. Mosis filii Maimon Tractatvs de
ivribvs anni septimi et ivbilaei. Textum Hebraeum addidit, in
sermonem Latinum vertit, notisque illustrauit Io. Henricvs Maivs,
filivs, accessit, appendicis loco, Dissertatio de ivre anni septimi.
Francofurti ad Moenum: J. M. a Sande, 1708. [6] p. L., 20,
148 p. 4°.

b) הלכות ציצית sive, Ivra fimbriarvm, ex R. Mose ben Maimon
descripta, Latine reddita, atque notis illustrata, ab Ioanne
Henrico Maio, filio. Francofvrti ad Moenvm: I. M. a Sande,
1710. 36 p. 4°.

BIBL. Jöcher, *All. Gel.-Lex.*, III, 66–67; Steinschneider, *Cat. Bodl.*, no. 6201; idem, *ZfHB*, III (1898), 115.

20

MIEG, JOH. FRIDERICO (Germany, 1700–1788). Professor in Heidelberg. Was a student of biblical exegesis and rabbinics. He translated into Latin Maimonides' *Hilkot Shebu'ot*:

R. Mosis Maimonidis. Tractatus de Iuramentis, secundum leges Hebraeorum qui in Corpore Juris Maimoniano primus est partis sextae: latinè versus, à Joh. Friderico Mieg... Addita est praefatio, de juramentis Judaicis, quatenus ea admitti tuto in foris Christianorum possint. Heidelbergae, typis Joh. Christiani Walteri, Acad. Typogr. [1672]. [9] p. L., 146 p.; double leaf folded. 4°. (Hebrew University).

BIBL. M. Kayserling, "Les Hébraisants Chrétiens du xviie siècle," *REJ*, XX (1890), 266.

21

NORWICH, WILLIAM (England? — Leicestershire, 1675).

Graduated M.A. in 1629 and was a Fellow of Peterhouse, 1634–1641. He was Vicar of Cherry Hinton, Cambridgshire, from 1638 to 1641. In 1641 Norwich was appointed by Peterhouse as Rector of Stathern, Melton Mowbray, Leicestershire. When the struggle between King Charles I and the Parliament reached its height, Norwich unhesitatingly held to the King's cause. He was ejected in 1648, but after the accession of King Charles II was restored as Rector of Stathern.

A Latin translation of *Hilkot Teshubah* is attributed to him: הלכות תשובה Canones Poenitentiae Hebraicè à R. Mose Aegyptio descripti, Latinitate donati à G. N. Cantabriquiae, 1631. 3 p. L., 34 p. 12°.

A handwritten annotation in the British Museum General Catalogue of Printed Books, vol. 165, col. 375 gives Gulielmus [William] Norwich as the author of this Latin translation. (Cowley, p. 476)

BIBL. S. Levy, "English Students of Maimonides," *Jewish Historical Society of England. Miscellanies*, part IV: *Essays Presented to E. N. Adler* — I, London, 1942, pp. 66–67.

22

PRIDEAUX, HUMPHREY (Padstow, Cornwall, May 3, 1648–Norwich, Nov. 1, 1724). English Orientalist.

Was educated at Christ Church, Oxford (B.A. 1672; M.A. 1675; B.D. 1682), where he became lecturer in Hebrew in 1679. In 1683 he became rector of Bladon, Oxfordshire, in 1688 archdeacon of Suffolk, and in 1702 dean of Norwitch. Besides works on Mohammed and a history of the Jews, he translated into Latin, *Mishneh Torah, Mattenot An'iyyim* (to which is appended *Hilkot Issurei Bi'ah,* chapter XIII and XIV dealing with the laws of proselytizing and *Hilkot Melakim,* chapter VIII):

R. Moses Maimonides de jure pauperis et peregrini apud Judaeos. Latine vertit & notis illustravit Humphridus Prideaux... Oxonii, E. Theatro Sheldoniano, 1679. [16], p. L., 168 pp. 4°.

Bibl. S. Levy "English Students of Maimonides", *Jewish Annual,* 5701 (1940–1941), pp. 77–78 [= *Miscellanies of the Jewish Historical Society of England,* part IV: *Essays Presented to E. N. Adler,* London 1942, p. 68–69]; *Dictionary of National Biography,* XVI, 352–354; *New Schaff-Herzog,* IX, 246–247.

<h2 style="text-align:center">23</h2>

Ricius, Paulus (Germany, 16th century).

Convert to Christianity. After his conversion became professor of philosophy in the University of Pavia. Ricius was a prolific writer and translated various Hebrew works into Latin. Among them are the "Six-Hundred and Thirteen Commandments" which are found in the beginning of the *Mishneh Torah*:

a) Paulus Ricius... De sexcentum et tredecim Mosaice sanctionis edictis... Augustae Vindelicorum: Ionnes Miller, 1515. 4°. 42 leaves.

b) "In Tractatum de Sexcentis et Tredecim Mosaicae Legis Mandatis". In: Joh. Pistorius' "Artis Cabalisticae," vol. 1. Basilae: Per Sebastianun Henricept. [1587], pp. 221–257.

Like most converts from Judaism, Ricius attempted to convince the Jews of the truth of the Gospels, and in the above translation he altered and adapted the meaning so as to suit this purpose. (Cf. Positive Commandments 248; Negative Commendments 50, 117, 148, 177).

Bibl. M. Steinschneider, *Cat. Bodl.,* col. 2141–2143; Siegfried Stein, "Phillipus Ferdinandus Polonus," p. 440, 403, 404, 405, 412.

<h2 style="text-align:center">24</h2>

Scherzer, Johann Adam (Eger, Bohemia, Aug. 1, 1628–Leipzig, Dec. 23, 1683),

Studied theology in Altdorf, Jena and Leipzig. In 1667 he was appointed professor of theology. A prolific author on theology and biblical exegesis, he also reprinted Vorst's translation of chapters 1 and 2 of *Hilkot Yesodei ha-Torah,* including the anonymous commentary "Perush," attributed to R. Yom-Tob b. Abraham Ishbili: מעשה מרכבה Seu Opus Currus a R. Mose B. Majemonis, Prioribus duobus capitibus, de fundamentis legis traditum, & scholiastae notis illustratum.

In: a) Triforium Orientale... Leipzig, 1663. pp. [109]–154.

*b) Operae pretium Orientale... Leipzig, 1672.

c) Operae pretium orientale exhibens Commentariorum rabbinicorum, R. Isaaci Abarbenelis, & R. Salomonis Jarchii in Geneseos sectionem I. nec non R. Mosis Majemon. Theologiae, versionem cum notis, cui accessit Specimen Theologiae mythicae ebraeorum, cum indice loco s.s. Scrip. rerum ac verborum. Lipsiae, impensis Friderici Christiani Coelii, 1685, pp. [109]–154.

d) Selecta Rabbinica Philologica... cum versionibus & annotationibus... Jo. Adami Scherzeri,... sub nomine nec non indicibus... adjecta... a Jo. Georg. Abicht..., Lipsiae: Ap. Viduam J. Heinrichii, typ. J. H. Riehteri, 1705, pp. [105]–156.

Hebrew and Latin.

BIBL. Steinschneider, *ZfHB*, IV (1900), 151; Cowley, *Concise Catalogue*, p. 620; Jöcher, *All. Gel.-Lex.*, IV, 256–257.

25

SCHMID, SEBASTIAN (Lampertheim, Alsace, Jan. 6, 1617–1696)

Studied in Marburg, Wittenberg, Koenigsberg and Basel and specialized in Semitic languages and rabbinic literature. Served for some time as Lutheran preacher in Ensheim and was afterwards appointed as principal of the Gymnasium in Lindau, then attained the professorship in Strassburg. A prolific author of works in Biblical exegesis and Rabbinics, he translated into Latin *Mishnah*, *Sabbath* and *Erubin* with commentaries by Bertinoro and Maimonides:

a) משניות מסכת שבת cum commentariis... Mosis fil. Majemonis, et Obadjae de Bartenora, Latine versae a S. Schmidt, quibus textum Hebraeum addidit J. B. Carpzovius, Lipsiae: Expensis F. Lanckisch, excudebat J. E. Hahn, 1661. 8 p. L., 248 p.

b) משניות מסכת עירובין ... cum commentariis... Mosis fil. Majemonis, et Obadjae de Bartenora, Latine versae a S. Schmidt, quibus textum Hebraeum addidit J. B. Carpzov. Lipsiae: Expensis F. Lanckisch, excudebat J. E. Hahn, 1661, 6 p. L., 176 p.

and *Mishneh Torah*, *Hilkot Milah* and *Ḥameẓ u-Maẓẓah*, chapters 7–8:

c) *H. Milah*, In his "Tractatus de Circumcisione", Argent., 1661, pp. 230 ff. (Cowley, p. 622); "Tractatus de Circumcisione...", Editio secunda, Argentorati, Sumptibus Joh. Reinholdi Dulsseckeri, 1700, pp. 236–245.

d) Moses Majmonides Veteres Ritus, & quid hodie immutetur, tradit in Hilchoth Chamez umazzah cap. VII & IIX.
In his "Tractatus de Paschate," Frankfurt a.M., 1685, pp. 213–219.
Bibl. Jöcher, *All. Gel.-Lex.*, IV, 301–303.

26

Sonneschmid, Jo. Just. (fl. 1720–1770). Theologian of the Reform Church. Nothing is known of his life.

He translated Maimonides' *Hilkot Gerushin*:

הלכות גירושין seu Tractatus Maimonidis Ebraeorum jura divortii docentis versionem latinam locis parallelis Talmudicis illustratam... submittit M. Jo. Justus Sonneschmid... respondente Daniele Godofredo Wernero. Janae: Litteris Mullerianis, [1718]. 1 p. L., 46 p.

Bibl. J. Parkes, *Studies in Bibliography and Booklore*, VI (1962), 13, 24, note 226.

27

Ugolino, Blasuio (Venice, c. 1700– ?). Italian Roman Catholic Christian antiquarian. Of his life nothing is known, but there is little doubt that he was a Jew by birth.

His scholarly fame rests upon his *Thesaurus Antiquitatum Sacrarum* (34 volumes, Venice, 1744–1769). In this work he reprinted most of the seventeenth-century treatises on Jewish antiquities, besides obtaining fresh contributors, and translating much himself from Rabbinic literature, among which is Maimonides' *Hilkot Ebel, Kele ha-Miḳdash* and *Biat ha-Miḳdash*:

a) Mosis Maimonides Constitutiones de luctu... a B. Ugolino ex Hebraico Latine redditae.

In: Ugolino, Blasio. Thesaurus Antiquitatum sacrarum... vol. 33, Venetiis, 1767, col. I–LXII.

b) הלכות כלי המקדש והעובדים בו R. Mose ben Maimon Constitutiones de Vasis Sanctuarii et qui in eo ministrabant nunc primum cum Blasii Ugolino perpetuis notis philologicis.

In: Ibid., vo. 8, Venetiis, 1747, col. DCCCLXXXV–MXXXII.

c) הלכות ביאת המקדש, Ibid., p. MXXXIII–MCL.

Bibl. *JE*, XII, 338–339; *New Schaff-Herzog*, XII, 54.

28

Veil, Ludovicus de Compiègne de (2nd half of the 17th century).

Convert to Catholicism; afterwards to Protestantism. Lived at Paris, later at Metz. He was a descendant of the Rabbi Jacob Weil of Nürnberg. Having converted to Christianity while still a youth, he studied theology at the Sorbonne, and devoted himself to the interpretation of Maimonides' code *Mishneh Torah*, of which he translated into Latin:

1) Ex rabbi Mosis Maiemonidae opere quod Manus fortis inscribitur, tractatus tres. I. De Ieiunio. II. De solemnitate Expiationum. III. De solemnitate Paschatis. Ex hebraeo Latine conuersi à Ludovico de Compiègne. Parisiis: apud Petrvm Le Monnier, 1667. 5 parts in 1 volume.

2) Ex Rabbi Mosis Majemonidae opere, quod secvunda Lex, sive Manus Fortis inscribitur, Tractatus de Consecratione Calendarum, & de Ratione intercalandi. Ex Hebraeo Latine redditus à Lvdovico de Compiegne.
Parisiis, Apud Petrvm Promé, 1669. 16 p. L., 251, [1] p. 17 cm.
Hilkot Ḳiddush ha-Ḥodesh; in Latin only.
(Hebrew University).

3) Hebraeorum de connubiis jus civile et pontificium; seu, Ex R. Mosis Majemonidae Secundae legis, sive Manus fortis, eo libro, qui est de re uxoria, tractatus primus. Quem tractatus ex Hebraeo latinum fecit Ludovicus de Compiègne de Veille. Parisiis, Apud F. Muguet, 1673.
16 p. L., 206 p. 18 cm.
Book IV, 1: *H. Ishut*. Latin only.

4) De cultu divino, ex R. Mosis Majemonidae secunda lege, seu manu forti liber VIII. Dividitur in IX. tractatus... Accesserunt tabulae aere incisae in quibus exprimitur Hierosolymitani templi forma... descripta... ex hebraeo latinum fecit... Ludovicus de Compiegne de Veil. Parisiis: Apud G. Caillou, 1678. [8] p. L., 384 p. double plate, double plan. 23 cm. 4°. Latin only.

5) R. Mosis Majemonidae de Sacrificiis liber. Accesserunt Abarbanelis Exordium... in Leviticum: et Majemonidae tractatus de consecratione calendarum, et de ratione intercalandi. Quae ex Hebraeo convertit in sermonem Latinum, & notis illustravit Ludovicus de Compiegne de Veil. Londini: M. Flesher, 1683. 7 p. L., 450 p. small 4°. Book of Sacrifices, pp. 1–221; Book of Seasons, Treatise 8: Sanctification of the New Moon, pp. 339–424. Latin only.

6) De cultu divino liber, tractatus novem continens... ex Hebraeo Mosis Majemonidae Latinum fecit, & notis illustravit L. de C. de Veil. Parisiis, 1688.
(*HUC* cat. XXVI, 263).

7) De cultu divino. Ex R. Majemonidae Secundae legis... libro 8, In: Opuscula, quae ad historiam ac philologiam sacram spectant... fasc. 6–7 (ed. T. T. Crusius). Rotterodami: apud Petrum vander Slaart 1696. 1042 p.

Latin only.

(General Theological Seminary, N.Y.)

8) R. Mosis Majemonidae de sacrificiis liber. Accesserunt Abarbanelis Exordium... seu proemium commentariorum in Leviticum:
et Majemonidae tractatus de consecratione calendarum, et de
ratione intercalandi, quae ex Hebraeo convertit in sermonem
Latinum, & notis illustravit Ludovicus de Compiegne de Veil.
Amstelaedami: Petzold, 1701. [7] p. L., 450 p. 4°. Book of
Sacrifices, pp. 1–221; Book of Seasons, Treatise 8°. Sanctification
of the New Moon, pp. 339–424. Latin only.

9) R. Mose ben Maimon. Constitutiones de Domo Electa. In:
Thesaurus Antiquitatum Sacrarum, ed. Blasio Ugolino, vol. 8,
Venetiis: Apud Joannem Gabrielm Herthz, 1747, col. DCCXXVII–
DCCCLXXXIV; 2 leaves wood cut illustrations.

10) Maimonidis Constitutiones de Sanctificatione Novilunii cum
interpretatione Latina Ludovici Compiegne de Veil. In: *Thesaurus
Antiquitatum Sacrarum*, ed. Blasio Ugolino, vol. 17, Venetiis,
1755, col. CCXXXIII–CCCLXXII. *Hilkot Ḳiddush ha-Ḥodesh*.
Hebrew and Latin.

BIBL. *JE*, IV, 202–203; S. Levy, "English students of Maimonides",
Jewish Annual, 5701 (1940–1941), pp. 79–81 [= *Miscellanies of the
Jewish Historical Society of England*, part IV: *Essays presented* to
E. N. Adler — I, London, 1942, pp. 71–74]; Steinschneider, *ZfHB*,
III (1899), 114.

29

VOISIN, JOSEPH DE (France, 1610–1685).

Descendant of a distinguished family in Bordeaux. Attained the
degree Doctor of Theology and served as preacher. A distinguished
scholar in the classical languages, he immersed himself in rabbinical
studies and translated Maimonides' *Hilkot Shemiṭṭah we-Yobel*:

הלכות שמיטה ויובל De jubilaeo liber secundus... Tractatus de
quiete terrae anno septimo, & de jubilaeo R. Mosis Maiemonidis.
In: Voisin, Joseph de: Liber de Jubilaeo secundum Hebraeorum &
Christianorum doctrinam. Parisiis; apud Ludovicum Bollenger,
1665, pp. 293–445; reprinted, there, 1668, p. 293–445.
Hebrew and Latin in parallel columns.

BIBL. Jöcher, *All. Gel.-Lexicon*, IV, 1697–1698.

30

VORST, WILLIAM HENDRIJK (Holland, ?–Steinfurt, Oct. 1, 1652).

Son of the theologian Conrad Vorst (1569–1629). Served as preacher
in Leiden. Among his works is his Latin translation *Mishneh Torah,
Hilkot Yesodei ha-Torah*:

a) הלכות יסודי התורה רבי משה בן מיימוני Constitvtiones de Fvndamentis
Legis Rabbi Mosis F. Maiiemon. Latinè redditae per Guilielmum
Vorstium... Amstelodami: Apud Guiliel. & Iohannem Blaev,
1638. 4°. [4] p. L., 148 p.
Hebrew and Latin in parallel columns.

b) R. Mosis Maimonidis Theoremata de principiis juris divini...
Cum interpretatione Latina & notis. Guilielmi Vorstii... Amstelo-
dami, apud Janssonio-Waesbergios, 1680. [4] p. L., 148 p. 18½ cm.
small 4°.
Hebrew and Latin.
Spurious edition with preliminary leaves printed anew. (Hebrew
University & Union Theological Seminary). The first 2 chapters
were also reprinted by Johann Adam Scherzer (1628–1683), in-
cluding the anonymous commentary ("Perush" attributed to R.
Yom-Tob b. Ishbili):

c) מעשה מרכבה Seu Opus Currus à R. Mose B. Majemonis, Prioribus duobus capitibus, de fundementis legis traditum, & scholiastae
notis illustratum.

In: 1) Triforium Orientale... Leipzig, 1663. pp. [109]–154.
2) Operae pretium Orientale... Leipzig, 1672.
3) Operae pretium orientale exhibens Commentariorum rabbinicorum, R. Isaaci Abarbanelis, & R. Salomonis Jarchii in Geneseos
sectionem I. nec non R. Mosis Majemon. Theologiae, versionem
cum notis, cui accessit Specimen Theologiae, mythicae ebraeorum,
cum indice loco s.s. Scrip. rerum ac verborum. Lipsiae, impensis
Friderici Christiani Coelii, 1685, pp. [109]–154.
4) Selecta Rabbinico Philologica... cum versionibus & annotationibus... Jo. Adami Scherzeri,... sub nomine... nec non indicibus...
adjecta... à Jo. Georg. Abicht..., Lipsiae: Ap. Viduam J. Heinrichii, typ. J. H. Richteri, 1705, pp. [105]–156.

BIBL. Molhuysen, *Nieuw Nederlandisch-Biografisch Woordenboek*,
X, col. 1136; Jöcher, *All. Gel.-Lex.*, IV, 1712–1713.

31

VOSSIUS, DIONYSIUS (1612–1642).
    Son of the Dutch humanist and theologian, Gerardus Johannes
Vossius (1577–1649). Declined in 1632 a professorship of history
and rhetoric at Dorpat, and in the following year was appointed
historiographer to the king of Sweden.
    Vossius translated into Latin the *Laws of Idolatry* which is found
in Book I of Maimonides' *Mishneh Torah*:
a) R. M. Maimonidae: De idololatria liber, cum interpretatione

Latina & notis Dionysii Vossii. Amsterdami, J. &. C. Blaev, 1641. 6 p.l., 174 p., 1 l. 4°.

b) De idololatria liber, cum interpretatione Latina & notis, Dionysii Vossii. Amsterdami, apud. Ioh. & Cornelium Blaev, 1642. [6] p. 1., 174, [1] p. 20 cm. small 4°.

c) R. Mosis Maimonidae De idololatria liber, cum interpretatione Latina, & notis, Dionysii Vossii. Amsterdami, apud Ioannem Blaev, MDCLXVIII [1668]. 87 p. 40 cm. [With Vossius, Gerardus Joannes. De theologia gentili... Editio nova. Amsterdami, 1668].

d) R. Mosis Maimonidea De idololatria liber, cum interpretatione latina, & notis, Dionyssii Vossii [Amsterdam: Jaonnem Blaeu], 1668. 4 p. l., 174 p. 4°. [With Vossius, G. J. De physiologia Christiana... Amsterdam, 1669].

e) R. Mosis Maimonidae De idololatria liber, cum interpretatione latina, & notis, Dionysii Vossii. [Amsterdam], 1675. 4 p. l., 174 p. 4°. [With Vossius, G. J. De physiologia christiana... Amsterdam, 1669].

f) R. Mosis Maimonidae De idololatria liber cum interpretatione latina, & notis, Dionysii Vossii. Amstelodami: P. & J. Blaev, 1700. 68 p. 2°. [With Vossius, G. J. De Theologia Gentili et Physiologia Christiana, Amstelodami, 1700].

BIBL. *New Schaff-Herzog Encyclopedia*, XII, 228; Steinschneider, *Cat. Bodl.* 2710.

32

WITTER, HENNINGUS BERNHARDUS (Germany c. 1703).

His thesis in Jena consisted of a translation of *Mishneh Torah, H. Ḳiddush ha-Ḥodesh* with an introduction by the Christian Hebraist Johann Andreas Danz:

קידוש החודש sev, Novi lunii initiatio, qvam... ad mentem Talmudistarum, pro festis Judaeorum determinandis, parandoque ipsorum calendario e R. Mose Majmonide, speciminis loco transtulit, & praeside Iohanne Andrea Danzio... submittit avtor respondens Henningvs Bernhardvs VVitter... 21 Iulii, anni 1703... Ionae, Svmtibvs Bielckianis [1703]. [10] p.l., 96 p.

BIBL. Steinschneider, *ZfHB*, V (1901), 83; Zedner, p. 584; Cowley, p. 476; *JE*, VI, 304.

33

WOELDIKE, MARCUS (Schleswig, Nov. 25, 1699 — Copenhagen, Sept. 26, 1750).

Received his early training from his father, a Danish preacher, until 1716 when he continued his studies in the Academy of Copenhagen, Wittenberg (1717), Jena (1719), returning to Copenhagen in 1720. He was a preacher for several years and professor of theology.

Woeldike translated some rabbinical works into Latin among which is a part of Maimonides' *Mishneh Torah*:

R. Mosis Maimonidae tractatus מאכלות אסורות sive de cibis vetitis, in Latinam linguam versus notisque illustratus a Marco Wöldike. Hafniae & Lipsiae, Apud viduam B. H. C. Paulli, 1734. 12 p. L., 296 p.

Latin only.

BIBL. Steinschneider, *ZfHB*, V (1901), 83, no. 415; Jöcher, *All. Gel.-Lex.*, IV, 2037.

34

ZELLER, ANDREAS CHRISTOPH (Maulbron, Dec. 13, 1684–Dec. 14, 1743). Studied in Tübingen. After having traveled through Germany, Denmark, Holland, and England, he returned home in 1709. Has written various studies on Protestant and Catholic theology and translated into Latin the following work:

הלכות פרה אדומה R. Mosis Maimonidis Tractatus de Vacca Rufa Latinitate donatus & subjuncta ampliore hujus ritus explicatione quoad singulas circumstantias illustratus ab Andrea Christophoro Zellero... Amstelaedami: C. Petzold, 1711. 16 p. l., 544, [13] p. [Second edition]: Amstelaedami: P. Humbert & J. F. Bernard, 1713. [16] p. l., 544 p. 8°.

BIBL. Steinschneider, *ZfHB*, V (1901), 86; C. G. Jöcher, *All. Gel.-Lex.*, IV, 2174.

ADDENDUM

35

BENZELIUS, ERIK, the Younger (Uppsala, Sweden Jan. 27, 1675–1743). Historian-theologian and linguist; successively Bishop of Göteborg and of Linköping. After traveling in various countries, beginning in 1697, he returned to his native city in 1700, where he occupied the post of librarian (1702), successively Bishop of Göteborg and of Linköping, Professor of theology (1723), and Archbishop of Uppsala (1731). Benzelius, who was a member of the Academy of Sciences in Stockholm, was a prolific writer in various specialized fields, among which is his translation of Maimonides' H. Shekalim with elaborate notes:

Siclus Judaicus: id est Rabbi Mosis Majemonidis tractatus de siclis... capita duo; quae in idioma latinum transtulit et notulis

explicavit, jamque... Praes. Gustavo Peringer [afterwards Lilli-
blad]... disquisitione academica publicae censurae submittit Eri-
cus Benzelius Fil. Upsaliae: H. Keysers [1692]. [2] p. 1., 77,
[2] p. 8?.
Hebrew and Latin.

BIBL. British Museum Catalogue, vol. 15, p. 107; vol. 165, p. 375;
Jocher, *All. Gel. Lex.*, I, 977–978; Michaud, *Biographie Universelle*,
III, 679; Hans Joachim Schoeps, *Philosemitismus im Barock*, Tübin-
gen, J. C. B. Mohr, 1952, p. 150–151.

36

LANGENES, HENRICUS (Buiksloot, Holland, 1701–Benhuisen, Aug. 30,
1754).
Preacher of the Reform Church. He translated *Hilkot 'Arakin*:
Dissertatio Philologica exhibens R. M. Maimonidis Constitu-
tiones de Aestimationibus quam deo duce et a uspice, sub
Praesidio Davidis Millii... Publico examini subjicit Henricus
Langenes... 4 parts. Ultrecht: Apud Guilielmum vande Water,
1720–1723. [1] p. 1; 8, [4]; 9–16, [8], 17–28; [8]; 29–45, [5] p. 4°.
Hebrew and Latin.

BIBL. J. C. Adelung, Fortsetzung und Ergänzungen zu C. G. Jöcher's
Gelehrten-Lexikon, Band 3, col 1249–1250.

37

WALTHER, CHRISTIAN (Prussia, Germany, July 31, 1655– ?, Jan. 17,
1717).
Lutheran theologian. Studied in Königsberg and Jena (1673–77);
preacher at Königsberg (1681); member of the Academy of Sciences
in Berlin (1701) and in 1703 he was appointed professor of theology
at Königsberg. In 1704 we find him serving as inspector of the
Jewish synagogue. He published works in Biblical theology and
translated into Latin Maimonides' *Mishneh Torah, H. Milah, the
Laws of Circumcision*, accompanied by explanatory notes:
... R. Mosis Maimonidis; Tractatum de Circumcisione, cum
interpretatione Latina et annotationibus, exhibens, quam divina
favente gratia, rectore magnificentissimo... Domino Friderico
Wilhelmo... consensu superiorum, in illustri albertina, publicè
tuebitur, Christianus Walther... Respondente Christophoro
Rausch... Regiomonti, Typis Reusnerianis, 1705. [1] p. 1, 44 p.
London Library

BIBL. C. J. Jöcher, *Allgemeiner Gelehrten Lexicon*, IV, p. 1799;
M. Steinschneider, *ZfHB*, V, 53, no. 406.

INDEX

ADAM MICKIEWICZ'S
ANTI-JEWISH PERIOD

STUDIES IN "THE BOOKS OF THE POLISH NATION AND OF THE POLISH PILGRIMAGE"*

ABRAHAM G. DUKER

"The Pilgrims' Catechism"

"The Books of the Polish Nation and The Books of the Polish Pilgrimage" [= *KNP*],[1] Mickiewicz's propagandistic brochure, written from September to the middle of November 1832, appeared anonymously in December. Originally named "Catechism of the Polish Pilgrimage," it preached that Poland was the divine instrument for the realization of a new higher Christianity, and Poland-in-Exile — the émigré participants in the 1830–31 Insurrection ("The Great Emigration") — was the apostle and vanguard of the

* Thanks are due to the Lucius N. Littauer Fund, the American Council of Learned Societies, the American Philosophical Society (Penrose Fund), and the Wurzweiler Foundation for grants in support of my major study on the Polish Great Emigration and the Jewish Problem, of which this article is but a small part.

[1] In the original: *Księgi narodu polskiego i pielgrzymstwa polskiego*. Most references are to Zofja Stefanowska's edition, Wrocław-Kraków, 1956. Small roman numbers indicate chapters, and arabic ones lines. I also used Mickiewicz, *Dzieła* (Works), edited by Julian Krzyżanowski et al. (Warsaw, 1955) [= *D*] and the original incomplete draft, MS 19, in the Mickiewicz Museum in Paris. I wish to thank Dr. Jan Librach of the Polish Institute of Arts and Sciences in New York for obtaining the microfilm of MS 19; Miss Wanda Borkowska of the Polish Library in Paris for her generous help during my many visits to that hospitable institution; and the many nice people in libraries in Poland for their help in the summer of 1967.

Parts of MS 19 were published by Stanisław Pigoń, in Mickiewicz, *Dzieła wszystkie*, Sejm ed. [= *DW, S*] (Warsaw, 1933), VI, 535–50 [=Pigoń]. I regret that I have not been able to obtain Józef Kallenbach's edition of its original text, *Księgi narodu polskiego i pielgrzymstwa polskiego. Tekst pierwotny* (Paris [1905]).

people's political revolt which was to redeem mankind by introducing a new order built on Christian social reform rather than a
social revolution.

"The Books" is divided into two parts: (1) "The Books of the
Polish Nation from the Beginning of the World until the Martyrdom of the Polish Nation" [= *KN*], containing a Poland-centered
epitome of universal history and being the introduction to (2) "The
Books of the Polish Pilgrimage" [= *KP*], the guide book for the
exiles under arms. Written in biblical style[2] and published in the
form of a prayer book, *KNP* has had a profound influence on
Polish life. It was popular among the exiles and later among the
Polish military even in the Russo-Japanese and World Wars.[3] It
was translated into many languages.[4] Its revolutionary and anti-
Church tone led to its condemnation by the Pope and conservative
Catholics, while its anti-materialist and anti-rationalist positions
brought attacks from liberal and, later, Marxist quarters.[5]

[2] Zbigniew Jerzy Nowak's "Ze studiów nad księgami narodu i pielgrzymstwa
polskiego", *Roczniki humanistyczne, Prace z polonistyki*, no. 1, 1961, pp. 5–
124 [= "*ZS*"] is concerned with the biblical style and influence. Cf. also Wilhelm Fallek, "Szkice i studja o wpływie biblji na literaturę polską" in Pierwsze
gimnazjum męskie towarzystwa żydowskich szkół średnich w Łodzi, *Rocznik*,
1929–1930 (Łódź, 1930), pp. 194–205.

[3] On its popularity, cf. Juliusz Kleiner, *Mickiewicz*, II, part 2 (Lublin, 1948)
[= *M*, unless further identified], pp. 24, 87, 125 ff; Pigoń, loc. cit.; Stefanowska
as in note 5; Cf. also my *The Polish "Great Emigration" and the Jews. Studies
in Political and Intellectual History*" [=*PGE*], No. 1627, (Dissertation Series,
1956, University Microfilms, Ann Arbor, Mich.), p. 522, n. 16. The present
article is a far-reaching extension of a chapter in this doctoral dissertation
done under Professor Salo W. Baron.

[4] Pigoń, Introduction, *DW*, S, VI, 28–29; Stefanowska, Introduction, *KNP*,
Stefanowska ed., pp. LXI–LXX.

[5] Cf. Zofja Stefanowska, "Introduction", *Historia i profecja. Studium o
"księgach narodu i pielgrzymstwa polskiego" Adama Mickiewicza* [= *HIP*], (War-
saw, 1962), and her brief *Katechizm pielgrzymstwa polskiego* (Warsaw, 1955)
[=*KPP*]. Cf. also, Nowak, "ZS", pp. 5–17 for a review of evaluations, includ-
ing works by Kridl, Kubacki, Pigoń, Skwarczyńska, Tarnowski, Żółkiewski.
For a summary, cf. Wiktor Weintraub's *The Poetry of Adam Mickiewicz* (The
Hague, 1954), pp. 194–207, where Jewish implications are ignored. Pigoń's
O księgach narodu i pielgrzymstwa polskiego (1911) is still useful.

KNP carries a distinct anti-Jewish message, particularly noticeable when contrasted with *Pan Tadeusz* (1834), with its sympathetic
Jew Jankiel.[6] Significantly, *Dziady, Częśc III* (Forefathers' Eve,
Part III), Mickiewicz's preceding major work (March–April 1832),
contains only one direct allusion to Jews.[7] I will begin with the
covert anti-Jewish aspects of *KNP*.

History begins with a legendary pre-historic monotheism in a
primitive, free, ideal society. Paganization brought God's punishment of slavery and division, with Rome as the worst offender. Jesus
redeemed mankind and Christianity's victory initiated another ideal
period, the Middle Ages, when justice ruled again, Christians considered themselves one nation, with freedom expanding steadily, first
to the gentry, the cities, and eventually to all Christians. However,
the materialistic kings checked its expansion, abandoned Jesus and
engaged in war. Poland alone remained faithful, defended Christendom, and never fought for territory. Frightened by Poland's 1791
freedom Constitution, the "kings" martyred her. However, just as
Christ was resurrected after three days, Poland, the Lazarus among
the nations, was to arise soon for the third time since the partitions
and lead mankind to freedom.

The principles of the revolution and the behavior of the "pilgrim"
are outlined in the second part, *KP*. Its tone is set by the first
sentence, "the soul of the Polish Nation is the Polish pilgrimage."
A definition of the pilgrim follows.[8] As mankind's revolutionary

---

Space prevents the treatment or even the listing of the extensive literature
on influences of Mickiewicz's contemporaries as reflected in *KNP*. Very little
information on our problems can be gained from it.

[6] Cf. my "PGE", pp. 547–60.

[7] Cf. my "Some Cabbalistic and Frankist Elements in Adam Mickiewicz's
Dziady" [= "SCF"], *Studies in Polish Civilization. Selected Papers Delivered at
the First Congress of Scholars and Scientists Convened by the Polish Institute
of Arts and Sciences in America... 1966* (London, 1971), pp. 213–35.

My quotations are based on the translation by Dorthea Prall Radin in
Mickiewicz, *Poems*, ...edited by George Rapall Noyes (New York, Polish
Institute of Arts and Sciences in America, 1944), pp. 371–415.

[8] To cite: "But not every Pole in the pilgrimage is called a wanderer" or
"a man straying without a goal. Nor is he an exile... a man exiled by the

army, the pilgrims must maintain their soldierly virtues, remain united and ready to sacrifice their lives for Poland and humanity, avoid involvement in politics, social problems or discussions of the past, and protect themselves against demoralization from the West by retaining their national exclusiveness and even xenophobia.

The Two Histories

Mickiewicz's scheme of universal history, initiated in *KN*, is a radical "break from the religious tradition of the history of the world." Its purpose is to lead up to the election of Poland, partly by breaking "the then prevailing Judaeocentrism in the presentation of the first ages."[9] Mickiewicz ignores or reduces the chosenness of the Jews. Just as he leaves out the pagan beginnings of Polish history, so he omits the Jews' unique role in monotheism's history. Missing are the Covenant, the Patriarchs, Sinai, the Prophets, the destruction of the First Temple. Thus the history of Israel is eliminated not only from mankind's ideal period of prehistory. Jettisoned are not only the Jewish events and personalities that are part of Christian history, but also the strictly Christian views of the fall of man and the new revelation.

The Jews appear first in *KN* as the persecutors and tormentors of Jesus (61–62), when the new epoch that begins with his resurrection is introduced. They disappear again in the second ideal period, the Middle Ages, and reappear in connection with another crucifixion, that of Poland.[10]

The Jews are mentioned more frequently in *KP*. However, Second Commonwealth history is introduced with an emphasis on

decree of his own government... The Pole in the pilgrimage has not as yet a name of his own but it will be given to him later... Meanwhile the Pole is to be called a pilgrim, as he had made the vow of a journey to the holy land, his free Fatherland, he has sworn to wander until he will find her" (8–13).

[9] Stefanowska, *HIP*, pp. 75–76.

[10] Frederick II of Prussia is introduced as Judas (366–69). Casimir-Perrier, representing the principle of non-intervention, is identified as "that man who tore the friendship of the peoples like the Jewish priest (*kapłan żydowski*) who tore his cloak when he heard the voice of Christ" (395–96).

Judaism's formalism, the angry "Jewish" God and the customary derisive views on the Pharisees and Jewish scholars. Reflecting the émigré predicament is the obvious parallel drawn between the Israelite wanderings in the desert to the Holy Land and the Poles' European pilgrimage towards universal freedom. In contrast, another parallel of the two nations in exile, that of the Jews and the Poles, is rejected throughout the book, a rejection emphasized by contrasting the latter with the Jews and the Gypsies and by condemning Jewish selfishness and nasty cunningness in the tale of the forester. Furthermore, the European revolutionaries and liberals are identified as Jews or "persons of the Old Testament." There are also occasional comparisons of biblical and modern history, not complementary to Jews. In contrast, Polish history is highly idealized.[11]

The "Old Testament"

A key to Mickiewicz's treatment of the Jews in *KNP* is his usage of the term, *Stary Zakon* = "Old Testament", "Old Covenant" or "Old Laws" [= OT]. It is employed against Jews in several derogatory ways, as has been customary in Christendom. It is used to convey the classical Christian views of the contrast between Christianity, presented as the religion of love, and Judaism, as the faith of vindictiveness, materialism, and legalism. The alleged differences between the Jewish God of wrath and the Christian God of love are similarly emphasized through identification with the OT, as is Judaism's involvement with minutiae and formalism. The Pharisees, the doctors, and some Jewish customs are condemned as representative of the OT. Negative characteristics and persons are identified as associated with the OT or as influenced by it. Thus, per-

---

[11] As Stefanowska states: "The history of the Polish nation is the history of its mission conceived in the eschatological categories of the Fall, redemption and reintegration... The rhythm of Polish history dominates over the rhythm of the history of humanity... Poland's fall is even more important than the coming of Christ in the caesura in Poland's history" (*HIP*, pp. 76, 69, 73).

The Jewish people is not the only one to be demoted. Mickiewicz, the Napoleon worshipper, left out his hero in *KNP*. Stefanowska explains (*HIP*, p. 74) that his inclusion would have reduced Poland's position.

sons with OT attributes include non-Jews, followers of the French revolution, terrorists, as well as kings and tyrants and all those in the West who are opposed to the peoples' new religious revolution advocated by Mickiewicz.

The Jewish God and the Revolution

Chapter xviii in *KP* is most striking in this respect. It begins with the admonition to the Pilgrims: "You are among the foreigners, as the Apostles were among the idolaters." They are told to avoid both the politics of the "idolaters" (the governments in power) and the revolutions against them. The idolaters will be eliminated by the real revolutionaries, "Jews or persons of the Old Testament," who will be guided by the law of the angry Jewish Deity. To cite:

> Excite not yourselves so greatly against the idolaters, smite them with the word and others shall smite them with the sword; and those who shall smite them are the Jews (*żydzi*), or people (*ludzie*) of the old testament, who worship the Sovereignty of the people, and Equality and Freedom. They hate the idolaters, and have no love for their fellow men, and are sent to wipe out the idolatrous Canaanites. And they will crush their idols, and they will judge the idolaters by the law of Moses and Joshua, and Robespierre and Saint Just, exterminating them from old man to suckling child, from the ox to the whelp. For their God, who is called Omnipotence (*Wszechmożność*) of the people, is just, but angry and consuming like fire (*KP*, xviii, 1048–60).

In MS 19, Mickiewicz identified the idolaters as persons "who bow to power, offices, honors, and prosperity." He described the revolutionaries as Jews or at least as "Jews of the Old Testament."

> But God sent the Jews (*żydów*) to punish them [the idolaters who worship power, etc.]. And do you know who are the Jews? These are persons who worship the utmost lustre (*najaśniejszość*) of the common people, and equality, and liberty. They hate the idolaters, and as Jews of the old testament have no love for their neighbors, and are sent to exterminate the Canaanites.

And they will smash their idols and they will judge the idolaters by the law of Moses and Joshua, by the law of the old testament, exterminating them, from old man to suckling child, from the ox to the whelp. For their god who is called la souveraineté du peuple, that is the omnipotence of the people, is a god who is envious and consuming like fire (Pigoń, p. 545).

In editing, Mickiewicz softend somewhat the condemnation of the Jews by eliminating one reference to "the Jews of the Old Testament" and changed an attribute of the Jewish God from "envious" to "just." He identified more closely the French Revolution with the harsh OT and the Jews by adding Robespierre and Saint Just to Moses and Joshua.[12] Moses' humanitarian legislation

---

12 Stefanowska sees in this chapter "three moral-political positions represented by three groups: the idolaters, the Jews who are fighting them and the persons of the New Testament who are juxtopposed to the Jews" (*HIP*, p. 185). Mickiewicz, she holds, evaluates the historical role of the French revolution as positive, attributing to the 19th century's struggle for freedom the same significance that the OT had for Christianity, the continuity and completion of Judaism, and at the same time its negation and transvaluation" (pp. 186–87). She traces the idea of the two Gods, the angry and terrible God of the OT, the father, and the God of the Gospel, the Son, the God of love, light and goodness (pp. 87–89), to Boehme and Baader and mentions Marcion without any comments. The connection "of the Jacobin terror with the law of Moses serves to incorporate the French Revolution into the march of world history as a continuity of what had begun centuries before..." (p. 188). The analogy, she claims, is derived from St. Martin, who identified the French Revolution with the law of the OT. Mickiewicz, she claims, substitutes the fall of Poland for the fall of France (p. 192).

Missing in Stefanowska's classification are the radical and liberal opponents of the "idolaters" who too are Jews of the OT. Mickiewicz's view of the OT continuity leaves little room for ambivalence. Moreover, if the old regime and its adherents are the idolaters, "the Jews and Old Testament persons" who fight them are more than adherents of the French Revolution and not only symbolic "persons of the OT", but also Jews. Mickiewicz allows no shadings between the "Jews and OT persons" and draws no clear distinctions between radical revolutionaries and mild constitutionalists. England's freedom is also of OT kind. New Testament persons are opposed to pagans, Jews and OT people, but more so to the last two.

is not mentioned. The appearance of Jews, in the published version, as the cruel revolutionaries of Europe, true enough, together with non-Jewish "persons of the OT," preceded Zygmunt Krasiński's *Nieboska Komedja* (Undivine Comedy), published in 1835.[13]

This prophecy concerning the elimination of the idolaters by the modern inheritors of the French Revolution — Jews or persons of the OT — is followed by another parallel between the New Testament [= NT] and the New Law to be introduced by the pilgrims.[14] These are warned against the influence of the parliamentary democracies. England and France are presented as parallels to ancient Israel in following the petty ways of the OT, the Pharisees,

---

[13] An antecedent of the theme of the Protocols of the Elders of Zion, Krasiński's drama portrayed a successful proletarian revolution against Christendom and the social order by a secret cabal of Jewish converts to Christianity, aiming at world rule. Mickiewicz's criticism of Krasiński in his 1844 lectures at the College de France presents a vivid contrast from the poet's view in *KNP*. See my "The Mystery of the Jews in Mickiewicz's Towianist Lectures on Slav Literature" [= "MJ"], *The Polish Review*, VIII, 3 (1962), pp. 40–66.

Abbé Luigi Chiarini, an Italian educator and self-termed "expert" on the Talmud, exposed a Jewish world rule plot in a pamphlet (Anonymous, *O żydach czyli judaizmie...* Warsaw, 1819: 2nd edition: J., *O żydach i judaizmie*), where he also pointed to the Frankists as a second arm of imperialist Judaism. Cf. Raphael Mahler, *Divrei yemei israel. Dorot aharonim*, II, book 1 (Merhavya, 1970), 170, 222, 327. Chiarini was Krasiński's teacher. It is quite possible that Mickiewicz had read his works.

According to Norman Cohn, the Judeo-Masonic conspiracy myth raised by Abbé Baruel in consequence of the Simonini Letter of 1820 "passes into oblivion even among antisemites." The idea appeared again in Disraeli's *Connigsby* in 1844. Cf. Cohn's, *Warrant for Genocide. The Myth of the Jewish World-Conspiracy and the Protocols of the Elders of Zion* (New York, Torchbook ed., 1969), pp. 25–32. I have not come across any indication that the poet had been acquainted with Barruel.

[14] As "among the Jews in their capital, Christ and his law [-testament] arose, so in the capitals of the European liberals shall arise your law, your law of self-sacrifice and love" (*KP*, viii, 1061–64; Pigon, p. 545).

Kleiner points out the formula that foreigners are pagans in relation to the pilgrim apostles and that foreigners are OT Jews in relation to "the NT of freedom" (*M*, pp. 55–56).

and the Sadducees.[15] The parallels between Jesus and the messianic Polish bearers of a new message to humanity are introduced again.[16]

The term "Old Testament" is used in the comparison between the war-like policies of Europe and the biblical Jews.[17] However, the law of the Poles is different.

> For Ye say; All that is ours, is the Fatherland's; all that is our Fatherland's, belongth to the free Peoples" (1092–94).

In his criticism of the liberals for their inconsistency in approving the idea of the Insurrection while condemning its premature outbreak, Mickiewicz compares their arguments with those of the "doctors who reproached Christ and screamed: Is it right to cure on the Sabbath (*szabas*)? Is it right to fight Russia in the time of European peace?" (*KN*, 1083). The European parliamentary system is characterized as false and charity giving to "widows and orphans of Freedom" as loud and Pharisaic (*KP*, xviii, 1081–91). Parliamentary debate between Right and Left is an OT "thing," a mistake like the first Christians' expatiation "over circumcision

---

15 "For England and France are like Israel and Judah. For when you will hear the liberals quarrelling over the two Chambers, both about the hereditary Chamber and about the elective Chamber, and about the payment for the king, and about the freedom of the press, do not be amazed at their wisdom, it is the wisdom of the Old Testament. These are the Pharisees and the Sadducees who quarrel about trepha (*tref*) and about kosher, but do not understand what it is to love and to die for the truth" (1065–73).

16 "And when they hear You, the newcomers from the North, speaking of God and Liberty, then they become angry and shout, just as the doctors did at Christ, clamoring: Whence has come so much learning to that son of a carpenter and how could a prophet have been born in Nazareth? and how dare he teach us, the old doctors?" (1074–79).

17 "The English who love Freedom according to the Old Testament say: Let us take away the sea from the French, as Israel had taken away cities from Judah, and the French of the Old Testament [*starozakonni* — also used as a polite term for the Jews — A.G.D.] speak: Let us take away Rhenish lands from the Germans; and the Germans say: Let us take away Rhenish lands from the French; and similar things. Therefore, I say unto You, that they are infected with idolatry, the worship of Baal, and Moloch, and Balance of Power" (1095–1102).

and washing of hands" (*KP*, xix, 1125–28). He predicted a new baptism in the name of God and Freedom, which, unlike the other will save mankind (*KP*, xix, 1129–32).

Jews are consistently identified with the OT. The sectarian arguments of Pharisees and learned Jews about *trepha* and *kasher* are contrasted with their ignorance of "what is to love and to die for the truth" (*KP*, iv, 145–46), despite mass Jewish martyrdom under the Syrians and Romans, of which Mickiewicz knew. There are also references to the Pharisees' challenge of Jesus' right to be a learned man because of his father's occupation (*KP*, xviii, 1075–77) and to their shrewdness (*KP*, iv, 145–46). The early Christians' preoccupation with "circumcision and washing of hands" (*KP*, xix, 126–28) is in the same category. Thus to Stefanowska, the Pharisees represent in *KNP* "as they do in the evangelical polemics the old and merely formal rules and spiritless doctrinairism" (*HIP*, p. 185). Nowak calls attention to Mickiewicz's predilection for the use of "Pharisees, synagogues, crucifiers of Christ," as seen in his labeling of the Resurrectionist Fathers, an émigré monastic order, with whom he disagreed ("ZS", p. 118n.).

In contrast to the derogatory view of the OT, references to the Polish émigré and Israelite Exodus parallel emphasize the chosenness of the Jews. The Israelites are termed *lud Boży* — "God's people" (*KP*, xvii, 965, 969, 976). The Jews are called "a Nation chosen by God" in Mickiewicz's warning to the West, a parallel to Christ's threat of the replacement of the "Abrahamic Nation" by the Greeks and Romans following its rejection by God. (*KP*, xxi, 1246–50). The election of Israel was presented in order to emphasize his rejection.

Palestine is called the "Holy Land" in connection with the Crusades (*KN*, 91), Columbus' original ambition of regaining it for Christendom (*KN*, 190), and, of course, also with reference to the émigré-Israelite parallel (*KP*, xii, 968, 977). Joseph is identified as "the patriarch who liberated his brethren..." (*KN*, 271), in contrast to his namesake, the partitioning Austrian Emperor.

Contrast with Earlier Expressions

The anti-Jewish outbursts in *KNP* stand in drastic contrast to Mickiewicz's earlier expressions. In his anti-clerical 1819 poem, *Kartofla* (The Potato), the poet identified Jesus as "the Hebrew" (*hebrajczyk*) (*D*, VI, p. 41) and as "the Hebrew Man-God (*Mążobóg hebrejski*) who thundered out of Zion" (ibid., p. 45). But nowhere in *KNP* is he identified directly as a Hebrew or a Jew. In the poem, "To Joachim Lelewel" (1822), Mickiewicz mentioned the "spiritual Hebrews and sensuous Greeks..." (*D*, VI, p. 98), in connection with medieval chivalry and the crusaders. This spiritual characterization is replaced in *KNP* by accusations of materialism and formalism.

I will not enter into the problem of the use of biblical style.[18]

Chosen Nations

The treatment of nationalities in *KNP* is too vague to allow a consistent classification. The French, English, and Germans, the "older children" of the Christian Church, have sinned by greed and desire for world fame, in contrast to the good, freedom-fighting younger Catholic brothers, the Poles, Irish, Magyars, and "other believing nations." Evidently, the downtrodden non-Catholic Greeks and anti-Vatican Italians were not in that category.[19] Their treatment of Poland determined the standing of other nations. Many European states are mentioned in *KNP*: France, the main culprit, and England and the English—over twenty times. Slavophilism and anti-West sentiment evidently account for the few but

---

[18] Cf. Wacław Kubacki, "Styl biblijny ksiąg," *Żeglarz i pielgrzym* (Warsaw, ‹1954); Stefanowska, *HIP*; Nowak, "ZS". In his review of "ZS" (*Pamiętnik iteracki*, LVI, 4, 1965, 540–44), Stanisław Szczepański calls attention to Konrad Górski's complaints about "the lack of preparatory works that would show the influences of our Bible on the language and style of individual Polish writers and on our public's living speech." Cf. his *Z Historii i teorii literatury* (Wrocław, 1959), pp. 62–63. This may be due at least in part to the view that the Bible is a Jewish creation.

[19] In later editions the Belgians replaced the Hungarians, following Lammenais' *L'Avenir*. Cf. Kleiner, *M*, p. 57.

favorable mentions of Russia, Poland's chief partitioner.[20] She is to replace the West. Poland emerges as the Christ among the nations, the good Samaritan. Her resurrection will Christianize mankind.[21]

Two Nations in Exile

The parallel of the two nations in exile, the Jews and the Poles, had an ambivalent appeal. The precedents of Jewish survival and group solidarity gave the émigrés encouragement, but they resisted the analogy with a people doomed by Christian dogma to eternal perdition and low status. The Christian view that the Jews' long exile was the punishment for the rejection of Jesus clashed with Poles' hope for speedy redemption. Mickiewicz had been aware at that time of the parallel's encouraging aspect. In a lecture on the "National Spirit," read in November 1832, he pointed to the voluntary unity of the Jews as an example of "national feeling and thought that can unite people in every place and at all times."[22]

KNP reflects this ambivalence. Stefanowska argues that OT Israel "with its tendency to sin and idol worship that so often brings upon itself the wrath of the Lord" could not have served as "an image of the Polish nation, from the beginning to the end faithful to the God of its ancestors." She questions whether "that people, cruel and pervaded with the feeling of its own superiority" can present an analogy to the Poles' mission of liberation. The analogy with the Jews would have lowered the status of Jesus, chosen by Mickiewicz as the parallel to Poland (HIP, p. 78).

The answer is both more complicated and simpler. Mickiewicz's rejection of the Jewish parallel follows the Church's rejection of the chosenness of the Jews and her self-appointment as the New Israel. The idealization of the szlachta could not be maintained without the denigration of the Jews. Mickiewicz's anti-materialist

[20] Cf. Stefanowska, KPP, pp. 106–07; HIP, pp. 106, 117, 197.

[21] Cf., e.g., HIP, pp. 46–47, 51, 106.

[22] Cf. D, VI, 66. To cite: "We have the example of the Jews, who, nowhere utilizing political rights, are obedient to their rabbis and kahals [official communities], even in civil affairs, though they have every opportunity to break away from their rule."

stance could not but oppose the stereotyped materialistic Jews. If Poland was the Christ among the nations, Mickiewicz could not project the deicide Jews, so closely identified with anti-Christ, as her parallel. There may also have been an additional factor: dissociation from some radical Frankists, a subject that will be discussed below. To free himself from the embarassing dilemna, Mickiewicz rejected the parallel's contemporaneous validity. He used Christ as the parallel, thus eliminating the Polish-Jewish one. He also emphasized the Poles' superiority.

Mickiewicz reduced the span of Jewish history by eliminating its ancient period, except for the Exodus phase which he used for the enhancement of his own people's security and courage. He also denigrated the modern Jews, by stressing their cowardice and materialism and comparing them to the Gypsies.

The very title, "The Book of the Polish Pilgrimage," and the poet's view of the Polish uprootedness emphasizes "pilgrimage" rather than "exile." The history of biblical Israel in *KP* revolves around the Exodus. The parallel between desert Israel and the Emigration is thus accentuated. The "pilgrims" in Europe and the Israelites in the desert emphasize the hope for the Poles' parallel redemption. *KP* rests on this analogy, but its application is denied even to the post-Exodus Israelites. Omitted are not only the judges and prophets, but also the Cyrus restoration, that could have been presented as a precedent of hope for the Poles. The émigrés are portrayed as the pilgrims to the free world and not merely as selfish seekers of their own promised land or as returning sojourners like the Israelites.

The Polish pilgrimage is a repetition of the Exodus. First comes the setting of the parallel.[23] The comparison of both "pilgrimages"

---

[23] Chapter xvii of *KP* (964–76) begins: "You are on Your pilgrimage in a strange land, as was God's people (*Lud Boży*) in the wilderness... §Guard yourselves on the pilgrimage against complaining, grumbling, and doubting. These are sins. §You know, that when God's people was returning to the land of its ancestors, to the Holy Land, it was then on a pilgrimage (*pielgrzymował*) in the wilderness, and many of God's people were homesick and said: Let us return to Egypt; there we shall be in the land of bondage, but we will have

continues with the story of God's decision to punish, by death in the desert, "the people of God" who showed "no faith in their prophets" and "fear of mighty kings and men like men of giant races." (*KP*, xvii, 977–84). The pilgrims are warned against bickering and doubting, lest "they prolong the days of their pilgrimage" (989–91). They are also told to protect themselves against the frail and weak.

Following the biblical precedent of listing the recognition marks or symptoms of diseases, Mickiewicz presents the signs for recognizing the infectious pilgrims (922–95). He also urges at length that the pilgrims shun the "lepers" who should be separated from émigré offices for a certain period (1005–45). Their symptoms are disbelief in Poland's resurrection despite their participation in the Insurrection and Pilgrimage (*KP*, xvii, 998–1004). However, in MS 19, the poet stressed that the "sick" Poles are worse than pagans and Jews. The implication is that no one could be worse:

> There is among you a small number of persons worse than pagans and Jews (*żydzi*) and these people are the bad Poles, these are the infected, from whom you should flee....[24]

After the Exodus parallel, the analogy ends and the narrative resumes the excision of Jewish history until the appearance of Jesus. Nowak emphasizes ("ZS", pp. 65–66) the parallel between the émigrés and the Jews and Jewish Christians of the New Testament times. However, that between the émigrés and Exodus Israelites is brought out by far more strongly in the text.

Rejection of Jesus

The Jews' alleged treatment of Jesus is presented as a warning to the world and as an important aspect of the parallel between the Jews' rejection of Christ and the West's rejection of Poland.

---

abundance of meat and onions. §And the Holy Scripture tells that God, offended, prolonged the pilgrimage of the Nation, until all those who had longed [for Egypt] died in the wilderness; for none of them was to see the Holy Land."

[24] This passage is also omitted in Pigoń. Mickiewicz may have decided to replace it by the tale of the forester.

The nations of the West are warned that they would be replaced by Russians and Asians, should they not fight for freedom:

Said Jesus to the Nation chosen by GOD. Shouldst thou, Abraham's Nation, not follow me, then GOD will reject thy tribe and from stones he will raise sons unto Abraham; which signified that of Greeks and Romans he would make Christians.

And the Pole speaks to the French and the English: Should you, children of Freedom, not follow me, then GOD will reject your tribe and will raise up defenders of liberty from the stones, that is from the Muscovites and from the Asiatics.

For one who rejects the summons of Freedom, shall be cast forth from her countenance (*KP*, xxi, 1246–56).

The rejection of the Jews is thus clear and irrevocable.[25]

Blame for Crucifixion of Jesus

Some scholars hold that *KNP* blames the Romans for the crucifixion.[26] However, the evidence, even in *KN*, is against this asser-

---

[25] I shall not enter here into the problem of the figure of Christ — the social reformer — rather than God, supposedly introduced by the poet in order to fit "the inner logic of the composition" (Cf. Stefanowska, *HIP*, p. 75; Kleiner, *M*, p. 31). However, Microfilm 19 contains the words "being God" instead of "being the very best" that appear in the printed text. To cite: "But Christ, being God, had to sacrifice his blood through the most painful torture" (Cf. *KNP*, i, 45). The problem of Jesus's divinity in *KNP* awaits its solution.

[26] Pigoń claims that Mickiewicz "conceives" the crucifixion as exclusively the deed of the imperial system, remaining silent over the role of the Jews. (*Z epoki Mickiewicza, Studja i szkice*, Lwów, 1922, p. 115). Kleiner opines that "perhaps Mickiewicz had known the views of the defenders of the Jewish nation, that the Jews had not condemned the Savior, perhaps, the logic of the historiosophy of the 'Book' has led to that; in any case, the presentation of the judgement over Jesus deviates widely from the Gospel" (*M*, p. 31). He also calls attention (loc. cit., n. 2) to Elijah Hazan's emphasis in his preface to Moses Ascarelli's Hebrew translation of *KNP*, *Am Polones* (Paris, 1882) that "not the Jews but the Romans were the cause for Christ's death." Rabbi Hazan stated (p. xiv) that Mickiewicz "testified before his countrymen that it was the judges of Rome who judged in the name of Caesar of Rome

tion. Their main argument is that the judges are not directly identified as Jews. Thus:

> When CHRIST taught this his teaching of love, the judges
> who judged in the name of the Roman Emperor were terri-
> fied; and they said: We drove out justice from the earth and
> behold it returneth: let us slay it and bury it in the earth.

> Then they martyred the holiest and most innocent of men,
> and laid him in the tomb, and they cried out: Justice and truth
> are on earth no longer; who will now rise against the Roman
> Emperor? (*KN*, 39–68).

A prediction in *KP* that the Polish NT of "self-sacrifice and love"
will arise in the capitals of the liberals is based on the parallel,
"just as among the Jews (*żydami*) in their capital arose Christ and
his testament...."[27] Thus without directly stating that Jesus was a
Jew, Mickiewicz asserts that he flourished among the Jews. This
is followed by the criticism of the Pharisees and doctors. Nowhere
does the poet clearly declare the Romans responsible. The reader
raised in the crucifixion tradition will continue to identify the judges
as Jews. While Mickiewicz does not point here directly to the Jews
as the sentencers and crucifiers, he makes up for that omission in
another reference:

who passed the death sentence on their Christian legislator...." Hazan expressed his hope that Christian scholars would pay attention to Mickiewicz's
statement. Armand Levy initiated the translation (cf. Jerzy W. Borejsza,
Sekretarz Adama Mickiewicza — 1827–1891, Warsaw, 1969, p .160). Levy may
also have been responsible for the crucifixion guilt's denial in Hazan's introduction.

Similarly, Stefanowska traces Mickiewicz's alleged exoneration of the Jews
to his desire to "gain a new argument for the cause of the thesis on the connection of atheism with despotism and of religious faith with liberty" (*KNP*,
p. 7, note for lines 61–62).

I stated in *PGE* (p. 531) that "Mickiewicz abstained from holding them
[the Jews] responsible for the crucifixion...." I apologize for having deferred
to standard Mickiewicz studies.

[27] Stefanowska (*HIP*, p. 200) calls attention to the substitution in the text
of the word "murderer" (*zabójca*) for "suicide" (*samobójca*), originally in
MS 19.

Jerusalem, who murderest men who speak of Freedom, who murderest thy prophets; and the people, that murders its own prophets, smiteth itself in its own heart, like a mad suicide.

There shall come great oppression upon Judah and Israel (*KP*, xxii, 1328–31; Matthew 23:37).[28]

The parallel is obvious. Jerusalem of the New Testament days cannot be identified as any other but a Jewish city, and, understandingly, the people who allegedly had the habit of "murdering their own prophets" in that city can not be any other but the Jews. The punishment for the crucifixion is also indicated in the subsequent prophecy of the forthcoming "great oppression upon Judah and Israel." The responsible ones are identified. Frederick II is compared with Judas (*KN*, 366–369)[29] and Casimir-Perrier with "that Jewish priest" [Caiphas][30] (*KN*, 394–96).

Modern Jews

While in *KNP* the Jews of the Exodus were the nation chosen by God, modern Jews rank among the lowest on the scale of nationalities. The Jews are on the same level as the Gypsies. The

---

[28] MS 19 more specifically warns: "For the capital of freedom will be moved from the West to the North, should Jerusalem not mend her ways." The cited warning repeats for emphasis: "Jerusalem, Jerusalem...." The poet's hesitancy is revealed by the corrections in the next paragraph where some words and phrases, shown in brackets, are crossed out and changed:

Jerusalem [Judah and Israel] there will come great oppression upon Judah and Israel and [on your church] from your political structure one stone will not remain upon another (Pigoń, pp. 546–47).

The transfer of power and election from Jerusalem appears in the published text without the indication of the new locus, the North, presumably Russia, as in MS 19. Jerusalem is presumably the symbol for the West European capitals.

[29] Judas is also alluded to, but is not mentioned by name as the traitor among the apostles (*KP*, xiv, 780) and again by name as the treasurer of the Christians (ibid., 788).

[30] The phrase, "that Jewish priest", is absent in MS 19. Mickiewicz evidently decided to make Casimir-Perrier more despicable by the parallel with Caiphas.

most vivid illustration, this time pointing at the Polish Jews, is the tale of the forester.[31] Even the term, "Israelites," the polite identification during the emancipationist receptivity to Jews, is not employed in *KNP*.

In her discussion of names of nationalities in *KP*, Stefanowska remarks that the term *Żydzi* (Jews) refers to "those of the nineteenth century, all biblical names are omitted..." (*HIP*, p. 117). There are, however, several cases of identification of ancient Jews as Jewish (*żydowski*). The High Priest Caiphas is called *kapłan żydowski* — "Jewish Priest" (*KN*, 395). A Pharisee is identified as "a Jewish man versed in writing (*człowiek piśmienny żydowski*) which meant the same as crafty" (*KP*, iv, 145–46). Jesus arose among the Jews (*między żydami, KP*, xviii, 1061).

With reference to modern times, the category "Jews" (*żydzi, żydowie*) includes, as I have brought out, revolutionaries, non-Jews as well as "Jews, or people of the Old Testament," who are associated with the French Revolution or are its spiritual heirs. These are identified as Jews or "persons of the Old Testament." The emphasis on negative characteristics also occurs when using biblical parallels in modern situations. It pertains not only to revolutionaries. Mickiewicz tells that "the kings made an idol for the French and they called him Honor and that idol was the same one that was called in pagan times the golden calf" (*KN*, 133–36). In MS 19 the idol is associated directly with the modern Jews. There it is stated that the Kings made the idol Honor, that the "Jews cast it," and that "it was cast from pendants and women's bracelets."

This may be a hint concerning Jewish bankers or perhaps the Rothschilds. However, *KNP* disregards the growing influence of the Jews in western society, contrary to demands for involving Jews in Poland's liberation voiced in the early émigré stock-taking of the Insurrection's fiasco. These were pushed by Jan Czyński,[32]

---

[31] Cf. below, p. 330 [20].

[32] He was very active on behalf of Jewish emancipation and Polish-Jewish reconciliation. Cf. Marian Tyrowicz, *Towarzystwo demokratyczne polskie 1832–1863. Przywódcy i kadry członkowskie. Przewodnik biobibliograficzny* (Warsaw,

Bartłomiej Beniowski,[33] Maurycy Mochnacki[34] and others. At the time of the publication of the "Appeal to the Israelite People" of October 3, 1832 by the Lelewel-headed *Komitet Narodowy Polski* (Polish National Committee), Mickiewicz had been in close touch with Joachim Lelewel.[35]

The identification of the Western countries with the Jews of both the Old and New Testament is in line with Mickiewicz's general contempt for the West, also evinced during his Towianist period, as seen in his *Lectures on Slav Literature*.[36] However, it is much more severe in *KNP*.

Jews and Gypsies

The rejection of the Polish-Jewish exile parallel is also achieved in a more drastic way by contrasting the allegedly materialistic Jewish-Gypsy concepts of a homeland with the idealistic Polish ones:

> Ye hear that the Jews, and the Gypsies and people with a Jewish and Gypsy soul (*duszą żydowską i cygańską*) say: The Fatherland is where it is well. But the Pole saith to the Nations: "There the Fatherland is where it is ill"; for wherever there is

---

1964), pp. 113–15. On his Jewish interests see items listed in my "Polish Frankism's Duration: From Cabbalistic Judaism to Roman Catholicism and from Jewishness to Polishness" [="PFD"], *Jewish Social Studies*, XXV (1963), 298, 303, 304, 306, 315; my *PGE*, passim; and Mateusz Mieses, *Polacy chrześcijanie pochodzenia żydowskiego* (Lwów, 1939), I, 83–92.

[33] Cf. "Ha-kruz shel ha-emigratsia ha-gedola..." (The Polish Great Emigration's Appeal to the Jews, October 3, 1832), *Sepher yovel l' Yitzhak Baer—Yitzhak F. Baer Jubilee Volume on the Occasion of His Seventieth Birthday*, edited by S. W. Baron, et al. (Jerusalem, 1960), pp. 431–46; Mieses, op. cit., I, 18–25.

[34] Cf. my "The Polish Insurrection's Missed Opportunity: Mochnacki's Views on the Failure to Involve the Jews in the Uprising of 1830/31," *Jewish Social Studies*, XXVIII (1966), 212–32; and my *PGE*.

[35] On Lelewel and the Appeal, see note 33; On Lelewel and Mickiewicz, see Maria Dernałowicz, *Od Dziadów części trzeciej do pana Tadeusza. Marzec 1832-czerwiec 1832* in series, *Kronika życia i twórczości Mickiewicza*, ed. by S. Pigoń (Warsaw, 1966), p. 97.

[36] Cf. my article, as in n. 13.

in Europe oppression of freedom, and there is struggle over it, there is the struggle for the Fatherland and all should fight in that struggle (*KP*, xxi, 1222–27).

Zofja Skwarczyńska calls attention "parenthetically" to the "anti-Semitic accent" of this passage, "not the only one in the *Books*."[37] Kleiner sees in it "the rejection of the utilitarian, hedonistic patriotism, the transformation of the pain of the emigrant patriotism into a principle despite the judgement expressed by Jews and Gypsies..." (*M*, p. 59). In a posthumously published writing, Kleiner adds a German ingredient to this dictum on Jewish and Gypsy hedonism.[38]

The comparison between Jews and Gypsies furnished ammunition to anti-Semitic propagandists. Thus, Ignacy Chrzanowski wrote in 1929 that some persons utilize the love of the fatherland "like the Jews who exploit our goodness and naiveté for their national purposes...."[39]

Tale of the Forester

The denigration of the modern Jews is manifested most tellingly in the tale of the forester (*KP*, xv, 817–99), a parable on the West's betrayal of the November Insurrection, absent in MS 19. It portrays the Jews as cowards, liars, and materialists who cannot understand the meaning of altruism, of which only Christians are capable. In contrast, Poland is presented as the noble forester who protects the Jewish innkeeper and inn-residents (the European nations, particularly, France) against the highwayman (Russia). A brief summary of the tale is in order.[40]

---

[37] Cf. her *Mickiewiczowskie "powinnowactwa" z wyboru* (Warsaw, 1957) p. 538.

[38] Cf. his *Studia inedita*, ed. by Jerzy Starnawski (Lublin, 1964), p. 301.

[39] Cf. his "Trwałe wartości ksiąg pielgrzymstwa," reprinted in the émigré *Wiadomości polskie* (London), No. 1 (95), January 4, 1942, p. 6. The Nazis marked both the Jews and the Gypsies for genocide, but they did not have to borrow the pairing from Mickiewicz.

[40] The highwayman who was about to rob the Jewish inn was spotted by "a certain Christian", the alert forester, who fought, injured, and drove the robber away. Wounded, the forester crawled to the inn for aid, to warn the Jews of future attacks and to urge them to help him capture the robber,

It is safe to include the tale among Skwarczyńska's discoveries of "an anti-Semitic accent, not the only in the *Books*."[41] Other scholars have not been that frank and have avoided the investigation of Mickiewicz's anti-Semitism by tracing the work's anti-Jewish tone to his utilization of folk concepts and popular

should they fear to do it on their own. The innkeeper gave him bread and vodka and the Jewish youngsters (*bachury*) cried, ostensibly, moved by pity.

The Jews who had witnessed the struggle, unwilling to reward their rescuer, disbelieved the robber's murderous intentions; had he not paid a friendly visit to the inn? The forester explained that the robber is now aware that "in the house dwell Jews... a timorous and fainthearted nation." The resentful Jews answered that the brave David and Samson were Jews. The forester replied that these heroes were dead, but the living Jews were still in danger. The Jews then argued that the forester should have notified the authorities; it was their duty to protect the people and not his.

The Jews then contended that he had defended himself and not them. The forester replied that he had the choice of joining the robber, sharing the booty, keeping quiet, or staying home. The Jews then charged that he fought in expectation of reward. They promised to treat his wounds and to give him a silver thaler. The forester rejected their money and even offered to pay them for the bread and the vodka.

The Jews then accused him of pugnacity. He argued had he planned to fight he would have been better armed. The Jews then were astonished and said: "Say then and confess, why thou hast done this that thou hast done and what were thy thoughts for thou art a strange man." The forester answered: that they would not understand him,

this one thing I will not tell you, and even if I would tell you, you would not understand for of one sort is Jewish understanding and of another sort the Christian; but if you would be converted to Christianity, you would have understood my behavior by yourselves, without need to ask me. And so saying, he departed from them.

And as he walked, he groaned because of his wounds.

But the Jews said one to another: He boasteth that he is brave, but he groaneth; his wounds are not grievous and he groaneth only so that he might frighten our children.

The Jews (*żydowie*) knew that he was grievously wounded, but felt that they had done wrong, and they wanted to talk it into themselves — that they had done no evil. And they talked loudly, that they might deafen their conscience.

41 Cf. n. 37.

traditions. A few examples will help the understanding of Mickiewicz worship in Polish scholarship.

Kleiner, for instance, holds (*M*, p. 86) that the tale presents "a living characterization of both the forester and the Jews (whom the poet evaluates according to popular views, but whose characteristics he ascribes to precisely the non-Jewish societies the way later [Józef] Korzeniowski[42] will show Jews among the non-Jews in a negative meaning)...." Nowak notes that Mickiewicz adopted the style of the evangelical parables with stereotyped rather than individualized heroes. Examples are the designations "Pharisee" and "publican." "The Pharisees were known for hypocrisy and religious formalism, which replaced the essential religious-ethical culture" ("ZS", p. 87). He holds that in line with Mickiewicz's avoidance of individualization, "nationality has no significance here. Only the Jews [Chapter] (xv) act in accordance with their national mentality, formed according to the popular tradition" ("ZS", p. 88).

As for the tale, Nowak argues ("ZS", p. 100) that the Jews in it are greedy and that they mask this with hypocrisy. The most typical trait of Jewish character in this approach is contained in the view announced by the forester about the "timorous and faint-hearted nation. It would be difficult to establish the definite source of the characterization of the Jews in this fable... there is no doubt, however, that this time Mickiewicz... utilized an anti-Semitic folk tradition."[43] Nevertheless, Nowak insists that "it is impossible to

---

[42] In his play, *Żydzi* (The Jews, 1843), the honest Jewish banker confronts "an entire crowd of vulgar [Christian—A.G.D.] embezzlers, cheats, and usurers of aristocratic or gentry origin... They are the *real* Jews — that is, they possess those traits which tradition and immovable prejudice have attributed to the Jews, while Aron Leve is an honest man with deep feelings." Cited from Manfred Kridl, *A Survey of Polish Literature and Culture* (New York and The Hague, 1956), p. 339. Cf. also H. Wilczynski, *Idishe typn in der poilisher literatur* (Warsaw, 1928), pp. 41–44.

[43] Cf. "ZS", p. 100. The full text is as follows: "... there is no doubt, however, that the future creator of the sympathetic figure of Jankiel and the creator of the *Exposition of Principles* of 1848, with the known phrase about 'Israel, the elder brother,' appearing in the role of a moralizer, stigmatizing

speak here about the poet's anti-Semitism, the way, for instance, Czyński had proclaimed it in the Emigration" ("ZS", p. 100, n. 34).[44] Nowak also refers to a dialogue between "two types of mentality" in the tale ("ZS", p. 63).

Stefanowska does not comment on this aspect in her notes in *KP* (pp. 67–70). However, in the Introduction, she, too, traces the anti-Semitic accents to the utilization of folk notions, declaring that "the tale... that ascribes greed, cowardice and egotism to the Jews does not at all attest to the anti-Semitism of the poet (of which some accuse him). Mickiewicz had purposely taken over the widespread opinions about the Jewish national character, conforming the entire fable to a folk tale." She points to other examples of such adjustment, e.g. clothes and celebration of holidays (*KNP*, p. lvii). Later, she narrows the "national character" approach to a "definite" group: "The fabular description of the tale is taken from reality, it mirrors the social relations and patterns of a definite group of the Jewish population. However, does this mean that the tales are a true picture of life?" (*HIP*, p. 178). She sees common characteristics in the tales of the Good Samaritan and the forester (*HIP*, p. 185). She fails to consider the anti-Jewish intent of the tale.[45]

The folk characterization approach is not easily acceptable, though anti-Jewish stereotypes are common in Polish and Chris-

the behavior of the western powers in relation to the November insurrection and to the insurrectionists, utilized this time an anti-Semitic folk tradition."

On 1848, cf. my "The Polish Political Emigrés and the Jews in 1848," *Proceedings of the American Academy for Jewish Research*, XXIV (1955), 91–94.

[44] "ZS", p. 100, n. 34. Nowak cites here Kleiner's opinion (cf. p. 22) and even prints the ritual murder accusation lines from *Pan Tadeusz* (Book viii, lines 668–70) as another example of the "anti-Semitic folk tradition" (Cf. my *PGE*, pp. 551–52).

[45] She also sees the conflict in the tale as an illustration of the poet's view that a morality based on reason is subject to low materialistic motivations (*HIP*, p. 84). She also states that "if, for instance, the forester's deed is supposed to constitute an example of new political principles, of new relations between the nations, in the same fabular layer his motifs are sufficiently explained and the reader is not apt to share the amazement of the Jewish innkeeper" (*HIP*, p. 179).

tian folklore. Mickiewicz's portrayal of the Jews as ungrateful is unrealistic. Surely, the isolated, exposed, "timorous" rural Jews would have gladly rewarded their protector. Prudence alone should have induced them to do so. Mickiewicz ignores the specific Jewish locale and the milieu of the rural or small town Jew. There are very few Yiddishisms and references to Jewish customs in *KNP*.[46] Stefanowska's examples of clothes and holiday celebrations (Introduction to *KNP*, p. lvii) do not pertain to the Jews, ancient or contemporaneous. A comparison of the descriptions of the inns in *Pan Tadeusz* and in *KNP* may not be fair because of the differences in the poet's intentions in their presentation, but it is illuminating.[47] Mickiewicz was apt to make some mistakes, but he had a flair for the simple and primitive. The presentation of the Jews in the tale had little to do with folk tradition, except for the anti-Jewish ingredient. It is likely that Mickiewicz had wanted to accentuate it, for he added the tale when he edited *KNP* for the printer. It is not clear whom Mickiewicz intended to degrade more, the Jews or the West, Whatever the case, he was determined to denigrate the Jews.

No Equality for Jews

Mickiewicz's objection to Jewish equality in future free Poland should not come as a surprise. Thus the description of the progressive expansion of equality in *szlachta* Poland in the published text states that the intention of the makers of the Constitution of May 3, 1791, "the king and the knights, [was] to turn all *Poles* (my italics) into *szlachta* brethren, first, the burghers, and after-

---

[46] The Yiddishisms are: *szabas* (Sabbath); *koszer* (kasher, *KP*, 1071), *trepha* (ibid.); *bachury* (*bahurim*, lit. young men; meaning Jewish children), *KP*, xv, 841). Stefanowska (*HIP*, p. 120) writes about the Polish Lithuanian background of "the refuse-covered pavement of the small town, etc." This flavor is not so easily detectable. It is my opinion that she reads too much into the tale about the "forester together with the inn-keeper, the 'bachurim' and vodka... done deliberately in order to uncover what the patina of the messianic national tradition had hidden" (loc. cit.). The innkeeper's gift of bread and vodka to the forester is explalned by her as an illustration of a normal life situation (p. 177).

[47] *Pan Tadeusz*, Book IV, 172–209. Cf. my *PGE*, p. 551.

wards, the peasants" (*KN*, 342–45). The Constitution's authors "wanted to bring it to pass that every *Christian* (my italics) in Poland should become a noble and be called *szlachcic* (nobleman, gentryman), a sign that he is obligated to have a noble soul and always be ready to die for freedom" (*KN*, 347–450).

This denial of equality was not accidental. MS 19 reads: "And finally on the third of May, the king and the knights determined to make *all the people* (my italics) (*wszystkich ludzi*) brothers, first the burghers and the workers, the artisans, after that, the peasants." The word *Poles* (*Polaków*, my italics) was substituted in the published text for *people* (*ludzi*; my italics) and the words "workers" and "artisans" were left out. The word "workers" was crossed out in the original text.

Similarly, MS 19 states that the makers of the Constitution "wanted to bring about to pass that every *man* (my italics) in Poland should be called a Pole, that is a free man, and that he should be called a *szlachcic*." Mickiewicz crossed out the word, "man" (*człowiek*) and replaced it with "Christian" (*chrześcijanin*; *DW*, VI, p. 541). Thus non-Poles were excluded from the process of the ever-broadening equality. This may have been eliminated in deference to history. However, *KNP* is essentially non-historical. Furthermore, the poet could have indicated that inequality would no longer continue in Poland restored.

Elsewhere, Mickiewicz urged the pilgrims to remember that they were in exile in strange lands where they "were taken out of the protection of the law, that thou mayst know lawlessness; and when thou shall return to thy land, thou shallst say: Foreigners are joint lawgivers with me" (*KP*, iii, 94–98). No specific reference to Jews is included here.

Other Works of the Period

Mickiewicz's anti-Jewish stance in *KNP* is even more difficult to explain when we consider that it was written between *Dziady III* (Forefathers' Eve, Part III), which has practically no direct reference to Jews,[48] but contains Cabbalistic, if not Frankist, implications,

48 Cf. my article as in n. 7.

and *Pan Tadeusz*, with its patriotic Jankiel. An examination of Mickiewicz's minor works composed at about the same time is of help.

On March 23, 1832, about a half year before the commencement of *KNP* in September, he wrote the poem *Mędrcy* (The Wise Men), a sarcastic critique of the "proud" deicide Pharisees, without mentioning that term.[49]

More ominous is the poem *Nocleg* (Night's Bivouac), composed on March 29, 1832. Its theme is the capture by Polish insurrectionists of a French officer serving in the Russian army. In the background, there is a tree whose fruit "frightens the hungriest." From it "hang two Judas pears, one a Prussian, the other a Jew, who sweeps the ground with his earlocks."[50] The poem offers proof that the poet had not only accepted the émigré stereotype of the Jewish spy, but has also helped to disseminate it.

Between September and October 1832, Mickiewicz edited the Appeal of the Polish National Committee to the Russians of December 1832 (*D*, VI, p. 65–66), and possibly also the address to the Hungarian parliament (published on December 16), which he signed. It stands to reason that had he wished to do so, Mickiewicz could have also edited the "Appeal to the Israelite People" of October

---

[49] They did not only "want to capture God" at night in order to kill him, because the common people would have protected him in the daytime, but also sentenced the "son of Mary" to death. "They tore the mystical clothes off God, they chopped his body with mockery, and they punctured his heart with reasoning... After he was buried, he left their soul dark as a tomb... God lives, he died only in the spirit of wise men" (*D*, I, 349). This poem has usually been interpreted as evidence of the continuation of the poet's struggle against reason and atheism, but it is also open to other interpretations, as, for instance, of evidence of the poet's contempt for the formalistic learned Jews. In the same class is the poem *Rozum i Wiara* (Reason and Faith), written in 1832, a condemnation of the "proud researchers", again viewed as the triumph of faith over reason, but without references or hints to Jews (*D*, I, 351). I hope to discuss Frankist implications of the poet's defense of mysticism on another occasion.

[50] Cf. *D*, I, 354–56. There is the possibility of Mickiewicz's confusion of *pejsy* (*peot*—earlocks) with *cyces* (*tzitzit*-fringes on a "small *tallith*"), which were more likely to sweep the ground. Cf. my *PGE*, pp. 523–24, n. 18.

3, 1832[51] or at least he could have signed it. However, there is no record at all of his interest in that Appeal. In a Call to Compatriots, urging his fellow "Lithuanians" and "Ruthenians" to write memoirs, Mickiewicz emphasized the importance of gathering information on the attitudes to the past and future insurrections of the different elements in the population, "peasants, gentry, priests," youth, the provinces, but he did not mention the Jews.[52] At that time Mochnacki and others (possibly also Lelewel) had been very much concerned with the problem of involving the latter. In a poem to Francis Grzymała, Mickiewicz poked fun at those who would make "Polish peasants out of little counts, little Jews and little Orthodox priests" (*D*, I, p. 376), employing diminutives.

On the other hand, on November 10, 1832, Mickiewicz alluded in a positive way to the Polish-Jewish exile parallel in a speech on "The National Spirit" (*D*, VI, p. 68). He called attention to the voluntaristic unity and community of the Jews as an "example" of national unity.[53] This was stated in the midst of Mickiewicz's anti-Frankist attack.

Pielgrzym *Period*

This reference to Jews may perhaps be viewed as a prelude to the change in attitude during the brief "Pilgrim period," initiated when, in April 1833, Mickiewicz became editor of the *Pielgrzym Polski* (Polish Pilgrim), a spokesman for "Polish Christian Republicanism" and advocate of Polish self-reliance and preparation for a revolt which was sure to bring war and independence. Consideration must also be given to the attacks by the radicals and to the general turn to activist preparation in the homeland. A reliable indication of this change appears in the June 28, 1833 issue, where

---

[51] Cf. my article as in note 33. In fairness to Mickiewicz, it must be stated that it had taken much pressure by Czyński, Beniowski, and possibly also Ozjasz Ludwik Lubliner to force Lelewel to issue the Appeal. It is also possible that Lelewel's hostility to Jews at that time might have influenced Mickiewicz.

[52] *Pielgrzym polski*, Dec. 2, 7, 1832; reprinted in *D*, I, 84–87.

[53] Cf. n. 22.

equality of the Jews in free Poland was taken for granted by Mickiewicz.[54]

In his significant pragmatic article, "To the Galician Friends," written in November 1833, Mickiewicz includes the Jews among the classes of the population to whom the patriots ought to explain that "the cause of Poland is the cause of freedom and equality.... The prince, the count, the peasant, and the Jews, all are equally needed by us. Everyone of them is to be remade into a Pole" (*D*, VI, p. 184).[55] However, there is evidence in the article of hostility to converts,[56] written as it was during the battle against the radicals of Frankist descent. In an article on the "Constitution of May 3," published on May 8, 1833, the emphasis is on freedom for all.[57]

The Frankist Factor

Mickiewicz's passing anti-Jewish period included attacks on two radicals of Jewish descent, Jan Czyński and Tadeusz Krempowiecki.[58] There is little information available on his motivation for this attack. I have not come across any references in published

[54] In a humorous "reproduction" of the "Gazette of Szawle Voyevodaship" (Lithuania), a mock edition of an 1889 free Poland newspaper, the writer tells of his dismissal from his elective office of assistant judge in the small town of Traszkune because he did not know how to "decide a case about an ox between citizen Icek and citizen Jankiel" (*DW*, S, VI, 252–54). The citizenship of these Jews appears to be taken for granted, though still affording an occasion for humor.

[55] Kleiner (*M*, p. 279, n. 1) calls attention to the ideological closeness of this article to *Pan Tadeusz*.

[56] The printed version left out the passage in the draft urging the abandonment of "ancient prejudices against some religions, some classes of the inhabitants, for instance, a certain contempt for converts, for the children of the Greek clergy."

[57] Cf., *D*, I, 122–26. Mickiewicz describes one of the aims of the Poles at that time as "the extension of the rights of citizenship to all classes of the people" (p. 126).

[58] On Czyński, cf. above, n. 32. On Krempowiecki who had not been too friendly to Jews, cf., Mieses, op. cit., II, pp. 23–32; Tyrowicz, op. cit., pp. 336–37.

literature to Mickiewicz's own explanations of his attacks on the Frankists, except for a puzzling exception.[59]

Kleiner suggests (*M*, p. 132) that "perhaps Czyński's and Krempowiecki's Jewish origin influenced the accentuation of the negative Jewish characteristics in The Books." The two radicals criticized Mickiewicz's clerical and *szlachta* stand. Czyński also censured his anti-Jewish statements. Kleiner does not even hint at the reasons for Mickiewicz's need or decision to parry these attacks with anti-Semitic insults and to point his finger at the Jewish origin and alleged belongingness of his attackers. Nor does Kleiner reveal the sources of his statement or surmise. This is unfortunate because he could have based it on sources which may no longer be available or on oral tradition that Mickiewicz's worshippers have been seeking to destroy. His suggestion must nevertheless be pursued.

The Frankists' economic rise that commenced at the baptismal font and grew with their acculturation and assimilation led to increasing participation in Polish life and to status climbing. Economic and political success also brought with it hostility and suspicion, stimulated by their separatism. Czyński's and Krempowiecki's radical activities during the Insurrection and in the Emigration were intensely disliked by rightist and even moderate elements. The radicals' exposures in the French opposition press of Poland's gentry tradition and of the revolutionary leadership's neglect to involve the lower classes and the Jews in the Insurrection as causes for its defeat clashed with the conservatives' policy of restraint in criticizing the homeland and thereby revealing the shortcomings in its social order and risking the alienation of public opinion abroad.

It is generally assumed that the direct cause for Mickiewicz's

---

[59] Thus Mickiewicz gave punishment for the maltreatment of the peasants when reform was most needed as the reason. Punishment, he said, comes "from low, bad, spoiled" people, because "God sends the satans to punish and not the angels." At that time some Frankists had been landowners, but there is no knowledge that they had treated the peasants any worse than the genuine Christian owners. Could Mickiewicz have viewed the Frankist critics as the satanic instruments for exposing the evils of the landowners? If so, why should they have been punished for the maltreatment of the peasants?

chief outburst against the radicals[60] was their attack on *szlachta* Poland in speeches at the Paris commemoration of the Insurrection anniversary, November 29, 1832, in the presence of French dignitaries, including General Lafayette.[61] However, at that time *KNP* was still at the printer's. If Kleiner's conjecture is to be followed up, we must search for earlier incidents. The appearance of the two radicals at the Hambach Festival in May 1832, Czyński's publications, particularly his critical "The Night of August 15, 1831,"[62] have stimulated much talk in the Emigration and even caused the Literary Society to devote much of its meeting of November 15, 1832 to that brochure.[63] Czyński was also the author of several other publications.[64] An examination of *Le Populaire, La Tribune*

[60] Czyński was answered with the famous quatrain, *Wpół jest Żydem* (He Is a Half Jew), calling him "fully a scamp." Cf. *D*, I, 377; translation in my "PFD", p. 315.

Krempowiecki was treated worse. In the poem, *Do Franciszka Grzymały* (To Francis Grzymała), (*D*, I, 375–6). Mickiewicz refered to him by name and labeled his shortcomings as typically Jewish. The poet sought shelter from the attack of "the Jewish (*starozakonna*) war squadron." Krempowiecki's connection with the crucifixion was established by comparing him with a rabbi, "the greatest hero of the nation of the Hebrews who, when Christ, led by the Romans for contumely and scourging, dared in the synagogue to hit the unarmed savior in the face with his metal glove." Krempowiecki was also compared to another Jewish "hero" who in the poet's own times was admired by "the unbaptized," because he dared to show Prince Radziwiłł "a fig [with his hand] in his pocket." Krempowiecki, wrote Mickiewicz, stems from this Jew.

A third radical, Priest Kazimierz Aleksander Puławski (cf. Tyrowicz, op. cit., pp. 555–57) was also attacked in the poem.

[61] Krempowiecki's speech was published as *Discours prononcé à Paris le 29 Novembre 1832, anniversaire de la revolution polonaise* (Paris, 1833). Kleiner states that it appeared in *La Tribune*, without further details (*M*, p. 130, n. 11). Mieses gives some of its contents (op. cit., II, 30–31).

[62] *Noc 15 sierpnia*, Paris, 1832, was a report on the night of riots and terror in protest against the Insurrection's decline. It also appeared in French and German in 1832. Cf. Tyrowicz, op. cit., p. 114.

[63] Cf. Dernałowicz, op. cit., p. 121. Mickiewicz was present at the meeting.

[64] At least three brochures of his appeared in 1832 in German and French. Cf. Tyrowicz, loc. cit.

and other papers will reveal more about the radicals' activities. Understandingly, their Frankist descent presented a convenient target in the émigrés' acrimonious debate.

The dispute about Mickiewicz's alleged Jewish origin and contacts with Frankists in his childhood and youth may never be settled because of the destruction of sources and the reluctance on the part of his contemporaries and, later, of the Mickiewicz scholars to face these problems openly. However, indisputable are his intimate contacts with Maria Szymanowska, the pianist, in St. Petersburg.[65] Very little is known about the upheavals in the Polish Frankist sect after the death of Ewa, Frank's daughter, in 1816, and in consequence of the acculturation of the ostensible Catholics in Polish culture and of the ostensible Jews in the German and maskilic ones.[66] We can only surmise that the sect was split into a number of factions or groups, the "orthodox" cabbalistic believers in Frank, the "enlightened" outright sceptics who abandoned their belief in the false Messiah and in cabbalistic Judaism, but had not as yet accepted Christianity and would not return to Orthodox Judaism, and holders of various in-between opinions, including those who could no longer accept him as the messiah or God, but continued to respect him or even worship him because he was their emancipator. While the "enlightened" converts eventually came to desire total assimilation in the Catholic Polish community, even the more group- or tradition-centered "orthodox" Frankists avoided drawing attention to their background. They feared that the radicals' activities would interfere both with their continued separate existence or quiet absorption and we may assume that the majority, except for radical individuals, resented the actions of their leftist brethren. It may also be surmised that persons like Czyński and Krempowiecki had been more interested in absorption in the new democratic society of the future rather than in improving their standing among the aristocrats and gentry, an aim rather difficult of attainment, anyway.

65 Cf. my "PFD", pp. 305–06; my "SCF", (as in n. 7), n. 73.
66 Cf. my "PFD", pp. 306 ff., 317 ff., 320 ff., 323 ff.

Among Mickiewicz's Frankist friends and later relatives by marriage, Maria Szymanowska was very likely an "enlightened" Frankist, as she had few or no objections to exogamous marriage. Her cousin Franciszek Wołowski was a leading conservative and did not favor Jewish emancipation during the Insurrection, but his children married within the sect or converted Jews. Mickiewicz's wife Celina, Szymanowska's daughter, was more of a believing Frankist.[67]

We assume that Mickiewicz was of Jewish or, more specifically, Frankist origin. We know that he had been under the influence of Oleszkiewicz, a student of the Cabbala. There are also reports of other contacts with mystics, including Jews.[68] I have brought out that his *Dziady III*, written right before *KNP*, reveals cabbalistic and Frankist influences.[69] Why then the anti-Jewish and anti-convert tones in *KNP*? And why these intense reactions to the Jewishness of the two Frankist radicals, as Kleiner would have it?

Mickiewicz, we may assume, had not been immune from the effects of the propaganda of the radical Frankists. His true or alleged Jewish descent remained ostensibly hidden, yet had been whispered about among the initiates and the suspicious in the Emigration. Under normal conditions, having managed fairly successfully to hide his Jewish descent, Mickiewicz would have been expected to refrain from raising the convert issue. There must have been good reasons for his decision to join the anti-Jewish counterattack. I hope that I am not stretching my surmises too thinly by raising the possibility that he had feared the exposure of his origin. At that time non-participation in the Insurrection was viewed by the émigrés and their sympathizers as an act of betrayal and a cause

---

[67] Cf. my "PFD", pp. 325–27 and my "The Mystery of the Jews in Mickiewicz's Towianist Lectures on Slav Literature," *The Polish Review*, VII, (1962), 40–66.

[68] Cf. my "PFD".

[69] Cf. my "SCF". His contemporaries alluded to it, as, for example, the poet Zygmunt Krasiński in his letters to Cieszkowski, cf. *Listy... do Augusta Cieszkowskiego* (Kraków, 1912) I, 45; II, 35, 37. Cf. also Mieses, *PCPZ*, II, 119. I shall refrain from discussing Ksawery Branicki's claim.

for disqualification from émigré public life. Mickiewicz evidently feared that his enemies would expose his failure to fight for his country as well as his descent. As it had been impossible to silence the radicals, Mickiewicz tried the strategem of accentuating his contempt for Jews and, in particular, his hatred of the unpopular Frankists. In addition, he might have feared that his *Dziady III* could be interpreted by the Frankists as a signal that he was one of them or close to them. The initiates were capable of comprehending the cabbalistic and Frankist allusions in the work and a blunt dissociation through condemnation of the Jews, liberals and radicals could have served as a measure of self-protection. Perhaps Mickiewicz had also felt that he had gone too far in his mysticism in *Dziady III.* He was then entering a different stage, away from cabbalistic mysticism into one of direct patriotic Polish mystique. He was to return to his Jewish mysteries after his marriage. Meanwhile, with the increasing anti-convert tension in the Emigration, Mickiewicz felt the need of dissociating himself from the Frankists and Jews. His labelling of parliamentary democracy as Old Testament and of the revolutionaries in the West as Jews of the OT is not only proof of his own dissociation from the Jacobins and their contemporary successors, but can also be viewed as a move to lessen the impact of the radicals by implying that they were not true Poles and that, as converts, they were Jews of the OT and that all leftists and followers of the West should be suspect of following this doctrine. Could The Books have served the poet's emphatic assertion of his "true" Polishness and *szlachta* tradition as well as of his dissociation from both Jews and converts from Judaism?

H. M. BARATZ AND HIS VIEW OF KHAZAR INFLUENCE ON THE EARLIEST RUSSIAN LITERATURE, JURIDICAL AND HISTORICAL

D. M. DUNLOP

THE NAME OF H. M. BARATZ (German Markovich Barats, 1835–1922) has occasionally been mentioned in discussions of the Khazar problem,[1] but it is likely that the extent of his investigations in this difficult field has not as yet been realized, at all events in the West. The main reason no doubt is that his contributions before 1917 were printed in scattered Russian periodicals, and were never translated, and the three volumes of *Sobranie Trudov* (Collected Works) published by his son in Berlin and Paris between 1924 and 1927, also in Russian,[2] appeared at a time when the views of a pre-Revolution Russian scholar were not likely to attract a great deal of attention, either in his own or in a foreign country.[3] The notices about Baratz in such works of general reference as the *Jewish Encyclopedia* and *Encyclopaedia Judaica* are short and not particularly informative, except for his notable official career in Tsarist Russia, which concerns us here only in so far as we have to allow that what he wrote on early Russian legal history and his favorite subject, Jewish-Khazar influences on the development of law and literature in Russia, was almost exclusively the product of his leisure and retirement.

Baratz' early years were evidently those of a busy and successful practising lawyer. His first important published work was a long

---

[1] E.g. in *The World History of the Jewish People*, II Series, Vol. 2: *The Dark Ages* (Tel-Aviv, 1966), p. 351.

[2] Vol. II was the first published in Berlin, 1924; vols. I, i and I, ii only later (Paris, 1926 and 1927).

[3] Cf. Baratz' own remarks in the Author's Preface (dated July, 1921) to his Collected Works, I, i, V.

article or series of articles in the *Zhurnal Grazhdanskago i Ugolovnago Prava* (Journal of Civil and Criminal Law), St. Petersburg, 1884–85, on the foreign origin of the greater part of the Russian civil laws, at a time when, according to his son,[4] it was the almost unanimous opinion of Russian jurists that Russian legislation has developed independently of all foreign influences. The editor of the *Zhurnal*, Professor A. D. Gradovsky, qualified the contribution of Baratz as one of the "extremely interesting and bold conjectures with which science is forced to content itself, as long as the rich materials on the history of our codification still lie buried in the cellars of archives and heaped up among family papers."[5] The characterisation "interesting and bold conjectures" might well be applied to Baratz' later work. At the time of the articles in the *Zhurnal* he was concerned primarily with the great published codification of Russian law which had been completed earlier in the 19th century by Speransky, not directly with ancient documents, and it was doubtless to materials on Speransky's codification that the remark of Prof. Gradovsky referred. Yet it would seem that this investigation led Baratz to the subject which eventually became the dominant concern of his life. For not many years afterwards, in 1891, he published in the Proceedings of the Ecclesiastical Academy of Kiev a monograph on Hebrew elements in the works attributed to Constantine (Cyril), the Apostle of the Slavs (*Obraztsy evreiskago elementa v proizvedeniyakh pripisyvaemikh sv. Kirillu*; in the Collected Works, I, ii, 331–452). It was the first of numerous other works bearing on Russian Jewish history — with frequent glances at the Khazars — which now came from the pen of Baratz in close succession until his death at Kiev in 1922. More than a dozen were reprinted in the Collected Works. One or two other titles are mentioned in the obituary notice of Baratz in *La Tribune Juive* for April, 1922[6] by Maxim Vinaver, who had

---

[4] Leon Baratz, "Sur les origines étrangères de la plupart des lois civiles russes," *Publications de l'Institut de Droit Comparé de l'Université de Paris* (1re Série), (Paris, 1937), pp. 10–11.

[5] L. Baratz, op. cit., p. 40.

[6] Vol. II, no. 121, 1–2.

earlier been influenced by him.[7] This notice has the following not
unattractive description of Baratz towards the end of his life:

I had been keenly interested in the accounts of our common
friends, notably Koulicher, of this mysterious old man shut
up in his study and searching through ancient charters with
inextinguishable energy, commenting on texts so remote from
the terrible present.... I found him in a small apartment of
the place Sainte-Sophie (at Kiev), still young in appearance
(though he was already more than 75), very active, without a
single grey hair, showing great interest in all the news of the
learned world of the capital, entirely buried in his thoughts,
hastening to complete what he considered as important and re-
jecting everything which might distract him from this end.
He seemed like Archimedes studying his diagrams, and re-
pelling the importunate Roman soldier....

According to the testimony of his friends, Baratz was working
during these last years at a new book on the origins of the
Russian Chronicles.[8] In the summer of 1918 he read the first
chapters at a meeting of the Society of the Chronicle of Nestor.
When the Red armies bombarded the town of Kiev, Baratz,
shut up in a cellar, completed, by the light of a candle, his
researches on the origins of the Chronicles.[9]

The considerable body of work left by Baratz is mainly directed
to showing the influence of the Jews in ancient Russia, and is
particularly concerned with the attempt to trace this influence back,
if possible, to Khazaria. The idea of Khazar influence on Russian
culture was not absolutely original with Baratz, but he made the
most of it, developed it more fully than anyone else, and indeed,
as will be seen in the course of the present study, was inclined
to press it only too far.

---

[7] See L. Baratz, ibid., p. 16.

[8] Vol. II of the *Sobranie Trudov* contains the monograph of Baratz entitled
*O sostavitelyakh Povesty vremennykh let i eya istochnikakh, preimushchest-
venno evreiskikh* (On the writers of the *Russian Chronicle* and its sources,
predominantly Hebrew).

[9] Vinaver, op. cit., p. 2. Vinaver's tribute originally appeared in French.

Jewish-Khazar influence, like any other influence, had to be mediated. Baratz, recognizing this, cast around for probable or possible intermediaries and found three persons — mentioned by him in various works — of whom he thought it could be stated that through them Khazar, or at least Hebrew, elements (and behind what was Hebrew in the time and place, i.e. eastern Europe from the 9th century on, according to Baratz, one had to think of Khazaria) permeated the earliest Russian writing, juridical, i.e. the legal codes, and historical, i.e. the chronicles. We shall find it convenient to take each of these intermediaries in turn, and consider what is said of him by Baratz, for in this way we shall be able to cover many of his characteristic positions. But before doing so, two examples may be cited of alleged Hebrew influence on early Russian literary production. The first is from the well-known *History of Russia* of V. O. Kluchevsky,[10] who finds a connection between certain treatises of what he calls Byzantine-ecclesiastical origin which exist in Slavonic and the first Russian code of laws, the *Pravda Russkaya*.[11] For instance, he finds in an abstract of the Law of Moses, which is one of the treatises, "a clause relating to robbery by night which reads thus in the Book of Exodus: 'If a thief be found breaking up, and be smitten that he die, there shall no blood be shed for him. If the sun be risen upon him, there shall be blood shed for him.' "[12] Kluchevsky compares this with what we read in the *Pravda Russkaya* on the same subject (Article 40 of the so-called Expanded Version[13]): "If they kill any thief near the barn or in any other kind of thievery, they kill him like a dog; but if they hold him until dawn, they have to bring him to the prince's court. If they kill [the thief] and some people had seen him bound, they have to pay 12 *grivna* for the offense." In the original Short Version dating from the reign of

---

[10] English transl. of C. J. Hogarth, I, 131–32.

[11] Sometimes *Russkaya Pravda*, especially in the older writers. I am following Grekov and Vernadsky (see next note but one).

[12] Exodus, 22:2–3, Kluchevsky's translator has given the A.V.

[13] G. Vernadsky (transl.), *Medieval Russian Laws*, Records of Civilization, Columbia University, XLI (reprinted New York, 1965), p. 41.

Iaroslav (1015–54) this appears as (Article 38):[14] "And if they kill a thief in their own yard, or at the barn, or at the stable, he is [rightly] killed; but if they hold him until daylight, they have to bring him to the prince's court; and in case [they hold him till daylight and then] they kill him, and people have seen him bound [before he was killed], they have to pay for him." Kluchevsky says that the ordinance of Moses has become Russified in the *Pravda* to the extent of being adapted to local conditions and recast in native forms of expression,[15] and we can readily accept this. Certainly the enactment in the *Pravda* seems connected with the law of theft in Exodus 22:2–3, and we need only hesitate to follow Kluchevsky when he states that it follows the abstract of the Law of Moses, and not the Bible directly.

The second example of supposed Hebrew influence is given by Baratz, who discusses the story under 971 and 972 in the *Russian Chronicle*[16] of the forced wintering of Sviatoslav at the mouth of the Dnieper, the great famine which ensued there, and the death of Sviatoslav at the hands of the Pechenegs. It is somewhat surprising perhaps that mere oral tradition has preserved over two hundred years (i. e. till the compilation of the *Russian Chronicle*)[16a] such a detail as that during the famine the head of a horse should be sold at half a *grivna*. Baratz accounted for it[17] by comparing c. 25 of *Midrash Rabba*, according to which there were ten famines sent to the world, the tenth of which was in the time of the prophet Elisha and took place owing to an epidemic among the cattle. It caused an increase in the price of meat such that, agreeably with IV (II) Kings, 6:25, an ass's head

---

[14] Vernadsky, op. cit., p. 33. Kluchevsky apparently used a slightly different text of the Expanded Version.

[15] Op. cit., I, 132.

[16] *The Russian Primary Chronicle, Laurentian Text*, transl. and ed. Cross and Sherbowitz-Wetzor (The Mediaeval Academy of America, Publication No. 60, Cambridge, Mass., n.d. [preface dated 1953]), p. 90 = *Chronique dite de Nestor*, transl. Leger (Paris, 1884), p. 59 (c. XXXVI).

[16a] This places the compilation later than the date accepted below.

[17] *Sobranie Trudov*, II, 73–74.

was sold in Samaria for 80 pieces of silver. The author of the notice for the year 971 in the *Russian Chronicle*, says Baratz, substituted a horse's head for the ass's head just as, for example, in another code — that of King Casimir IV of Lithuania — it is said, instead of the precept of Deuteronomy, 22:1: "When you see a bullock or a sheep straying, return them to your brother," "Whoever sees a horse or a nag straying, etc.," while for simplicity's sake he has replaced the Biblical "80 pieces of silver" by "half a *grivna*" or, in one copy, "a *grivna*." The detail has been lifted from the Hebrew written source and put in the *Russian Chronicle*, and has therefore, for Baratz, no factual reference. It is a striking way simply of describing a famine. There is of course no means of knowing why the detail that the horse's head sold for half a *grivna* appears in the story in the *Russian Chronicle*, and there is no proof that it was inserted by someone who knew Hebrew. To say so is special pleading and will scarcely carry conviction. Yet this is cited by Baratz as a typical instance of borrowing.

We may now return to Baratz' three transmitters of Hebrew, eventually Khazar, elements into Russian literature. The first of these in point of time is the well-known 9th century figure, Constantine (Cyril), the Apostle of the Slavs, whose journey to Khazaria and subsequent missionary activities in Moravia, etc., are historical facts around which, as is natural, a great deal of legend has accumulated. Baratz seeks to connect him with the appearance of the ancient legal document called *Zakon Sudnyi Liudem*, "Law of Judging for the People," or to use Vernadsky's phrase "Court Law for the People," which "purports to have been drawn up for the use of the Bulgars shortly after their conversion to Christianity in the 9th century," and is regarded by Vernadsky as "a Bulgarian compilation of the Byzantine laws."[18] Kluchevsky, whose remark has just been quoted, gives the alternative title of the *Zakon Sudnyi Liudem*, viz. Constantine's *Sudebnik* or Code of law, and characterizes it as a Slavonic rendering of the penalties contained in the Ἐκλογὴ τῶν νόμων (Selection of Laws), which is a digest

---

[18] Op. cit., p. 5.

compiled in the early 8th century under the direction of the Icono-
clastic Emperors Leo the Isaurian and his son Constantine Copro-
nymus and which contains a number of ordinances relating to
family and civil law, as well as an addendum concerning penalties
for criminal offences.[19] Both the Eclogue and the *Zakon
Sudnyi Liudem* are among the treatises already mentioned, which
include the abstract of the Law of Moses, and whose Byzantine-
ecclesiastical origin is regarded by Kluchevsky as certain.

All this is different for Baratz. In the first place, the country
of origin of the *Zakon Sudnyi Liudem*, according to him, is in all
probability Khazaria. At the time of the life and activity of the
Apostles of the Slavs (Constantine and his brother Methodius),
as Baratz points out, the Khazar Khaqan and many of his people
had no doubt long professed Judaism, nominally at least;[20] and
he bases his surprising conclusion in regard to the place of origin
of the *Zakon Sudnyi Liudem* on a well-known passage of Mas'ūdī,
where the Arabic author has:

> The custom in the Khazar capital is to have seven judges.
> Of these two are for the Muslims, two for the Khazars judging
> according to the Torah, two for those in it who are Christians
> judging according to the Gospel, and one for the Ṣaqālibah
> (Slavs), Russians and other pagans judging according to pagan
> law, i.e. on theoretical principles.[21]

Baratz assumes that the passage refers to a single supreme court,
and goes on to argue that the different systems of law, being administered at the same time, could not but affect each other reci-
procally. Hence in Khazaria, he thinks, there must have appeared
a distinctive law at the base of which lay a mixture of heterogeneous
elements, and further that two of these elements — the Christian
and Hebrew laws — were bound to achieve predominance, the

---

[19] Kluchevsky, ibid., I, 131.

[20] See Dunlop, *History of the Jewish Khazars* (Princeton, 1954), (reprinted
New York, 1967), p. 115.

[21] *Murūj adh-Dhahab*, ed. Paris, II, 11 = ed. Cairo, 1384/1964, I, 179–80,
with variant *an-Naṣrāniyah* "Christianity" for *al-Injīl* "the Gospel"; transl.
C. Pellat, *Les Prairies d'or* (Paris, 1962), I, 162.

Christian[22] law thanks to its superiority over the legal concepts of Muslims and pagans — *imperio rationis* —, and the Hebrew law in some sense *ratione imperii*, owing to the fact that it was supported by the authority of the Khaqan and his magnates. Such, says Baratz, were the juridical norms functioning in Khazaria, which before the national acceptance of Christianity by the Russians and Bulgars were imbued in the field of secular legislation by the higher principles of Divine law, i.e. the Mosaic legislation and the New Testament, and were far from coinciding in this field either with the norms of Byzantine law, saturated as it was with the principles of barbarian (pagan) law, or with this same law, and served as the principal source of the *Zakon Sudnyi Liudem*.[23]

Secondly, Baratz calls attention to the fact that the *Zakon Sudnyi Liudem* has reached us in several recensions, and observes, what is no doubt true, that in its composition and extent it differs considerably from the original redaction. After examining this, he concludes that the *Zakon Sudnyi Liudem* in its original form presented, of itself, a complete code of the ecclesiastical and civil statutes functioning, according to his supposition, in Khazaria, compiled for simple people, whence also the actual name of the book, "Law of Judging for the People." He elsewhere endeavors, as he says, to confirm the influence of the Law of Moses and the *Zakon Sudnyi Liudem* on the juridical procedure of old Russia in general and, in particular, on the determination of the sphere of the department of the ecclesiastical court, indicating the fact that some terms and articles of the old Russian Ecclesiastical Statutes, which present real problems for investigators, may be understood only if one applies for help to the Hebrew language and the decisions of Mosaic-Talmudic law, and he instances as an example of such ideas and words, among others, the term *smilnoe* = *shiddukhin*, negotiations preliminary to betrothal.[24]

---

[22] Baratz does not stop to consider what Mas'ūdī may have meant by "Gospel law." Surely some ecclesiastical code must be intended, if Mas'ūdī's facts are right.

[23] *Sobranie Trudov*, I, i, 53 ff.

[24] Ibid., I, i, 56–62, 164.

Thirdly, Baratz turns to the question of the author or translator of the *Zakon Sudnyi Liudem*, and finds him to be none other than Constantine (Cyril), the Apostle of the Slavs. He argues that Constantine can be shown to have taken part in the completion of the translation of the collection of treatises which includes the *Zakon Sudnyi Liudem*, according to all probability the principal part, and must therefore be supposed to have had to do with this book.[25] It contains, he thinks, elements not only of Mosaic but also Mosaic-Talmudic law adapted to the religious-juridical consciousness of a nation just converted to Christianity, apparently accustomed to that and another law, and he makes much of the fact that Constantine was in a position to produce it, arguing at length that he possessed a knowledge of both Biblical and Talmudic Hebrew.[26] When the so-called Pannonian *Life* of Constantine speaks of him as as having used Aquila's (Greek) version of the Bible, what is really meant is the Targum of Onkelos.[27] Baratz also mentions that Photius, the teacher of Constantine, when young, studied with a Jew, according to Symeon Magister, and remarks that "nearer than all probability, this person belonged to people who came from places then subject to Khazar rule, the Crimean Peninsula or Taman (Tamatarkha]."[28] He has some remarks at this point about the epithet Χαζαροπρόσωπος applied to Photius by the Byzantine Emperor Michael III, also according to Symeon Magister,[29] suggesting that this means "Khazar person" or "Khazar chief," or again that what is intended may be "Khazarophil"(?).[30] Baratz adds that Michael goes on to call Photius μαρζούκα,[30a] "subtly hinting at the inclination of Photius to Jewish teaching," for this means "Rabbi Photius" in some Semitic dialect.[31] Baratz

---

[25] *Sobranie Trudov*, I, i, 3 ff., 6–7.

[26] Ibid., I, i, 62 ff.

[27] Ibid., I, ii, 445 ff.

[28] Ibid., I, ii, 431–32, 436–38.

[29] Ed. Bonn, p. 673.

[30] *Sob. Trud.*, I, ii, 440, 442.

[30a] So the Bonn text of Symeon Magister, pp. 673–4. Baratz writes Μαρσοῦχα.

[31] Ibid., 440.

returns to the term a page or two later, explaining it as two words: Mar + some equivalent of Photius = light-coloured, bright, perhaps Zakkai, in any case "Lord Photius."[32]

This is all quite interesting, and in part no doubt right. But it is in part also demonstrably incorrect. The long development on the origin of the *Zakon Sudnyi Liudem* is vitiated by the fact that Baratz apparently takes no account of the concluding words of Mas'ūdī, which are in contradiction of his idea that Christian and Jewish law came to predominate in Khazaria, for Mas'ūdī adds, after the words we have quoted above: "When a serious case is brought up, of which they have no knowledge, they come before the Muslim judges and plead there, obeying what the law of Islam lays down."[33] This cannot be set aside in favor of Baratz' imaginative construction, for which there is at most some general probability. To argue from the (quite possible) Hebrew knowledge of Constantine and his teacher seems irrelevant, when what is wanted for the argument is a demonstration that the former adapted the *Zakon Sudnyi Liudem* from a code of law which had course in Khazaria. This remains a speculation entirely without proof.

When Baratz comes to argue, from what is said in the Pannonian *Life* about Constantine having found Russian books at Kherson, that the ultimate aim of his mission was Russia and that he subsequently set out along the Dnieper to Kiev,[34] he is in the same predicament. He can advance no proof that Constantine did so, though this is perhaps formally possible, i.e. not in contradiction with known facts. But it seems a much more likely supposition that the Pannonian *Life* is mistaken about the discovery of Russian books at Kherson, or at most that this was unimportant. There is at all events no sufficient ground here for positing a mission of Constantine to Kievan Russia which is nowhere mentioned.

We now come to the second of Baratz' mediators of Jewish-Khazar influence in early Russian literature, the presbyter Gregory in the 10th century. Baratz points to elements in the first part of

32 Ibid., 443.
33 Mas'ūdī, loc. cit.
34 *Sob. Trud.*, I, ii, 483–84.

the *Russian Chronicle* extending to the death of Sviatoslav in 972, in particular notices of Byzantine and Bulgarian events and extracts from the *Chronicle* of George Hamartolus, the inclusion of which in the existing text is a problem. It used to be said that these were due to Nestor, a monk of the Pechersky monastery in Kiev at the end of the 11th and the beginning of the 12th century, who is stated in his *Life* to have known Greek. On the other hand, recently discovered authentic works of Nestor[35] bear no trace of familiarity with Byzantine chronicles. Further, Baratz finds it unnatural to think that treaties between Russia and Byzantium were first brought out and incorporated in the *Russian Chronicle* in the 11th or 12th century, at a time when interest in agreements concluded by heathen princes is likely to have been small in the ecclesiastical circles to which Nestor or his contemporary Sylvester belonged. (Sylvester has also been taken as the compiler of the *Russian Chronicle*.) Again, mingled with information about Byzantine and Bulgarian events given in the *Chronicle* only to 943 are extensive borrowings from Hebrew literature, regarded by Baratz as equally beyond the scope of Nestor and the other monks of the Pechersky monastery. Who then can be considered as responsible for the presence of these elements in the *Russian Chronicle*?

Baratz identifies this author as a certain presbyter Gregory, a Bulgarian, who appears to have been employed at first by the Bulgarian Tsar Simeon the Great and to have spent some time in Constantinople perhaps after the death of Simeon in 927. He became religious adviser to the Russian princess St. Olga, widow of Igor and mother of Sviatoslav, and accompanied her on her journey to Constantinople in 957, being received in her suite by the Emperor Constantine Porphyrogenitus. The literary work of Gregory included the translation into Slavonic of books of the Old Testament, the *Chronicle* of John Malalas and also, according to Baratz, the *Chronicle* of Hamartolus, which latter is followed, as admitted by

---

[35] A *Life* of Abbot Theodosius the Great of Pechersky and a narrative of the exploits of the princes Boris and Gleb.

other scholars, in the account given by the *Russian Chronicle* of the Russian expedition against Constantinople in 941.[36]

The narrative in the *Russian Chronicle* is said to draw also on the biography of Vasili Novy.[37] This Vasili was a saintly person who died in Constantinople in 944. Baratz is of the opinion that Gregory the presbyter, on his first visit to Constantinople, became his friend and later wrote his *Life*, attributed to a monk Gregory shortly after his death.[37a] His ground is as follows. In this *Life* the author narrates of himself that at one time there came over him doubt in regard to the truth of the Christian religion, for it seemed to him that the Hebrew faith, worshipping (one) God, is true and that he communicated his doubts to the blessed Vasili, who tried to dispel them, but that when they all still remained, he prayed that the Lord would reveal to him in a vision of sleep the state in the future life of the people of all faiths and creeds. From this story Baratz drew the conclusion that either Gregory was a Jew by birth who converted to Christianity, or, if he was born a Christian, a predilection in favor of Judaism appeared in him, as a consequence of the study of Hebrew religious books to which he had given himself up, at the suggestion perhaps of some Jewish teacher, as later happened to Nikita Zatvornik.[38] Thus we have reason to believe that the translator of Biblical books and the *Chronicles* of Malalas and Hamartolus, the author of the *Life of Vasili Novy* and the source of parts of the *Russian Chronicle* (derived, according to Baratz, from an earlier Chronicle of Kiev of which Gregory was editor, or a contributor) were one and the same person. Gregory the presbyter, remaining in Kiev, was associated with the church of St. Elias, the parishioners of which were his fellow countrymen, the Bulgars and Jewish Khazars converted

---

[36] *Sobranie Trudov*, II, 75 ff., 79. For the passage in the *Chronicle* see Cross, pp. 71–72, Leger, p. 35.

[37] Kluchevsky, I, 16.

[37a] Baratz quotes for this S. G. Bilinsky, *Life of Vasili Novy in Russian Literature* (in Russian) (Odessa, 1913), I, 69.

[38] For Nikita Zatvornik, Baratz' third mediator, see below, p. 362 [18].

to Christianity, and remained at his post also during the reign of Sviatoslav, outliving him even by one or two years.[39]

Turning now to the kind of information contributed by Gregory the presbyter to the *Russian Chronicle*, in the view of Baratz, we have already seen the baselessness of the attribution to a Hebrew-knowing author of the detail of a horse's head sold for half a *grivna* in the notice of the famine of 971–72. Baratz is hardly more happy in the sequel to the famine and the death of Sviatoslav, all of which is part of the same narrative. The Pecheneg prince Kurya and his men took the head of Sviatoslav, according to the *Chronicle*, and made a drinking-cup of his skull, overlaying it with gold. This, says Baratz, is merely an adaptation of some Bulgarian narrative of the battle of 811 in which the Bulgarians and their prince Krum defeated the Byzantine army and killed the Emperor Nicephorus I. The skull of Nicephorus was taken and mounted in silver for the Bulgar chiefs to use at their festivals instead of a cup.[40] Baratz suggests that Kurya, the name of the Pecheneg chief, may be a Bulgarian(?) version of Krum, and an inscription said to have been placed on the unfortunate man's skull, when it thus fell into the possession of his enemies: "Search for another's, destroy yourself," recalls to Baratz the Talmudic (Soṭa, 9a) "Whoever covets what is another's, to him they give not that which he desires, and that which he possesses they take away."[41]

If this means, as it appears to mean, that the reported outcome of the death of Sviatoslav, viz. that his skull was turned into a drinking-cup by his enemies, did not take place and is simply inserted into the narrative by a writer who knew of a similar incident in the past, i.e. Gregory the presbyter, surely Baratz violates the rule of all sound criticism that if what we find in a text is not impossible or self-contradictory and is not contradicted by other evidence, it has to be accepted. Evidently this was a practice of of the barbarians of the steppe and had been from time immemorial. Herodotus tells us that in his day (5th century B.C.) the same savage

[39] *Sob. Trud.*, II, 81.
[40] This is mentioned by Theophanes, ed. De Boor, p. 491 (A. M. 6303).
[41] *Sob. Trud.*, II, 73–75.

custom prevailed.[42] Baratz seems to have thought of the use made
of the skull of the Greek Nicephorus I after his death as unique.
But in this he was certainly in error. He shows himself here as not
only unduly sceptical of the reliability of the *Chronicle*, but far
too ready to seize upon what he thinks may be contributory to his
general contention, which defect, if once established, goes far to
detract from his credibility.

As is well known, the *Russian Chronicle* has a good deal to say
about the Slav tribes which at an early date occupied the territory
of what came to be Russia. These are mentioned by their names,
Polianians, Drevlians, Radimichians, Severians and others. They
are spoken of as existing chiefly in the 9th and 10th century, and
their circumstances can scarcely have been known except indirectly
when the *Chronicle* was compiled, as already mentioned, at the
end of the 11th or beginning of the 12th century. The notices of
these people are considered by Baratz to have been part of the
contribution to the *Chronicle* made by Gregory the presbyter.[43]

Speaking of the passage in the *Chronicle* where the laws and
customs of the Slav tribes are described, Baratz has the idea that
Hebrew sources can be detected. The Drevlians, Radimichians,
Vyatichians and Severians are, he says, represented in the *Chronicle*
with the same features as the people of Sodom and Gomorrah
in the *Book of Jashar*. As for the Polianians, their marriage customs
are represented as fully within the limits of the Mosaic-Talmudic
requirements, though they profess no revealed religion and retain
the customs of their fathers (מנהג אבותיהם). Baratz thinks that in
this description of the Polianians the writer has been influenced
by the Talmudic-Rabbinic idea that the other descendants of Noah
who observe the commandments of God given at Sinai are to be
recognised as "heterodox-devout", and as such, equally with the
Hebrews, have a portion in the bliss of the world to come. But this
is surely to read far too much into the simple descriptive passage.
In fact, the distinction between the Polianians, on one hand, and

---

[42] IV, 64.
[43] Indirectly, of course. See p. 356 [12].

the Drevlians, etc. on the other, is not made with absolute sharp-
ness.[44] The alleged Talmudic "custom of their fathers" or a similar
expression is said at the beginning of the section to be followed
by all these tribes alike. One may well doubt whether there is
clear Talmudic influence here.[45]

Again, the Polianians are stated a little later in the *Chronicle*
to have paid a tribute to the Khazars of one sword per hearth.
The Polianian swords were found to be double-edged, causing
alarm among the Khazar elders, since the Khazars themselves
possessed only single-edged swords, and they foresaw a time when
they would pay tribute to the Polianians. This has actually come to
pass, says the *Chronicle*, for they did not speak of themselves but
by a divine inspiration. In the time of Pharaoh, when Moses was
brought before him, the elders said to Pharaoh "This man will
subjugate Egypt," and it was so. Moses destroyed the Egyptians,
whose slaves the Israelites had formerly been. The Egyptians at
first ruled, but they were later ruled over by the Israelites. So the
Khazars to this day obey the Russian princes.[46]

All will admit that there is the clearest Biblical influence here,
but not everyone will be disposed to follow Baratz, who surprisingly
treats the story as an invention, on the ground, it might seem, that
it is in contradiction with positive reports of the *Chronicle* that
the Khazars took as tribute from the Polianians, Severians and
Vyatichians one ermine-skin[47] per hearth. The *Chronicle* of course
may very well mention the tribute of the Polianians as different
at different times. But this is not what he means, as is immediately
explained. The sword as the emblem or instrument of just punishment and vengeance is portrayed in the Bible as double-edged,
e.g. in Psalms 149:6–7: "And a two-edged sword in their hand,
to execute vengeance upon the heathen and punishments upon the

---

44 Cross has "The Drevlians, on the other hand..." (op. cit., p. 56), Leger
"Quant aux Drevlianes..." (op. cit., p. 10), which seems to be slightly different.
I have not seen the original Russian text.

45 *Sob. Trud.*, II, 96–97.

46 *Sob. Trud.*, I, ii, 503 ff., II, 98–99; Cross, p. 58; Leger, pp. 12–13.

47 Or squirrel- or beaver-skin (Cross, p. 59 = Leger, p. 14).

people" (A.V.). Again, Ehud in order to save the Israelites from the oppression of Eglon, king of Moab, made for himself a sword ("dagger," A.V.) which had two edges, with which he killed the king (Judges, 3:16). Further, in Haggadic works one comes upon sentences like the following: "With the sword with which the Egyptians smote the Israelites, they themselves were smitten,"[48] or "With the measure with which a man metes it is measured also to him. So Pharaoh commanded that every new-born infant among the Hebrews be thrown into the river; in return, the chariots of Pharaoh and his army were lost in the Red Sea."[49] It is with these and similar passages in mind that the writer (still Gregory the presbyter) has inserted this apocryphal story into the *Russian Chronicle*.[50]

So says Baratz. But who can doubt that, as an explanation of what we read in the *Russian Chronicle* concerning the tribute paid by the Polianians to the Khazars, this is merely misplaced ingenuity, determined by his over-riding idea of Jewish-Khazar influence in the *Chronicle*? Frequently the constructions of Baratz have at least an air of plausibility and, though not demonstrable, *may* represent the facts. In this case it will surely be allowed that in default of other evidence the story in the *Chronicle* must stand, as legendary perhaps — the opinion of at least one investigator[51] — but not to be explained away by any such cumbersome hypothesis as is offered by Baratz.

Again, Baratz examines the account which the *Russian Chronicle* gives concerning the funeral customs of the Radimichians, Vyatichians and Severians, appended to the account of their marriage customs which we have already noticed.[52] According to the *Chronicle*:

---

[48] Baratz quotes for this only the Latin equivalent from Buxtorf's *Lexicon Chald. Talm. et Rab.* (1639), p. 168.

[49] No reference is given in Baratz.

[50] *Sobranie Trudov*, I, ii, 503–05.

[51] A. A. Shakhmatov, in notes to his edition of the *Russian Chronicle*.

[52] The account of these funeral customs has been taken separately here because of the special character of the source alleged (Ibn Rustah).

Whenever a death occurred, a feast was held over the corpse, and then a great pyre was constructed, on which the deceased was laid and burned. After the bones were collected, they were placed in a small urn and set upon a post by the roadside, even as the Vyatichians do to this day.[53]

Baratz considers this as borrowed almost word for word from the Arabic geographer Ibn Rustah,[54] who has:

When one of (the Ṣaqālibah, Slavs) dies, they burn him in a fire. When there is a death, the women cut their hands and their faces with a knife. When the dead has been burned, they go to him next day and take the ashes from the place, putting them in a clay vessel (*barnīyah*) and setting them upon a mound. When a year has elapsed, they take about twenty jars of honey, more or less, and bring them to the mound. The people of the dead man assemble, and they eat and drink there. Then they depart.[54]

There is no reason to doubt that the same or similar customs are described. The Arabic is fuller and may be earlier. Ibn Rustah's date is given as A.D. 903, but he drew on some earlier account.[55] The Russian account forms part of the earlier undated part of the *Chronicle* (before 852). Even if we grant that the Arabic is earlier, which is by no means certain, it does not follow that the Russian account is borrowed from Ibn Rustah, as Baratz thought. Since for him Gregory the presbyter is the author of this account in the *Chronicle*, Gregory must also have known Arabic, a conclusion from which Baratz perhaps shrinks. At least he does not draw it. There is of course no evidence that Gregory knew Arabic, or that the information was taken from an Arabic source, e.g. Ibn Rustah or the original on which Ibn Rustah, a compiler, depended, and did not reach the author of the Russian account in some other way.[56]

---

[53] Cross, pp. 56–57 = Leger, p. 10.
[53a] Baratz uses the older, incorrect form of the Arabic name: Ibn Dastah.
[54] Ed. De Goeje, p. 143.
[55] Cf. *Hist of the Jewish Khazars*, p. 104 ff.
[56] *Sob. Trud.*, II, 97.

We shall be able to deal rather more briefly with Nikita Zatvornik, i.e. Nikita the ascetic, Baratz' third source of Hebrew influence in the early Russian books. For Baratz, it is this Nikita in the 11th century who above all introduced those reflections of Hebrew literature, post-Biblical as well as Biblical, with which the *Russian Chronicle* abounds, pointing therefore unmistakably to Jewish influence. The contributions of Nikita are never intermingled with accounts of early Russian history before the death of Sviatoslav or Byzantine-Bulgarian events, and can therefore, he thinks, readily be distinguished from elements due to Gregory the presbyter, already discussed. By the same token, Khazar influence here is at most indirect.

Assuming that the first, principal redaction of the *Russian Chronicle* was made at the Pechersky monastery in Kiev (using an earlier Kiev chronicle with which Gregory the presbyter was concerned), Baratz is unwilling to accept as its author either the monk Nestor or the Sylvester who, in a postscript added to the Laurentian manuscript of the *Chronicle*, stated that he wrote it in the year 1116.[57] According to Baratz, the author was Nikita Zatvornik, afterwards Bishop of Novgorod, though Nikita's name as a chronicler is nowhere found. For this paradox he is therefore confined to presumptive evidence. Nestor, whose authentic works, as already mentioned, are known, cannot be thought of as the author of a document in which the Old Testament is quoted extensively, any more than he can have been familiar with Byzantine chronicles,[58] and for the same reason apparently,[59] as well as his somewhat more tenuous claim, Sylvester is also excluded.

The Pechersky monk, Baratz goes on, who at the beginning of the 12th century redacted the *Chronicle*, introducing occasionally remarks in the first person, was Nikita, known from the Pechersky *Paterik* (Lives of the Saints) and from a letter sent by Polycarp,

---

[57] Cf. Cross, ibid., Introd. 4.

[58] Cf. above, p. 355 [11].

[59] See the remarks of Baratz, *Sob. Trud.*, II, 50 ff. for the studies of the Pechersky monastery at this time.

Abbot of the Pechersky monastery in the 13th century, to the archimandrite Akendin. According to the letter, Nikita applied for permission to withdraw into seclusion, and after some difficulty was granted his request, being consecrated in 1073.[60] (Baratz attempts to accomodate this with the notice in the *Chronicle* that the writer was accepted at the Pechersky monastery in 1051.[61]) While in seclusion he was tempted by a demon in the form of an angel, who at first, when he offered prayers, joined him, and afterwards began to try to persuade him not to pray at all, but to read books diligently and give useful instruction to the people, promising to pray to his Creator for his salvation. Nikita obeyed. Soon he felt the gift of enlightenment and instruction, and the word began to spread about him as a sage, whose prophecies came true. Princes and *boyars* began to come and listen to his admonitions. Afterwards it was discovered that in religious disputations none could compete with him. He knew by heart the books of the Old Testament and also knew well all Hebrew books, the books also of the New Testament he did not like either to read or to hear or talk about. The Pechersky fathers understood that he was deluded by devils and, gathering to the number of twelve most experienced brethren with the Abbot Nikon (1078–88) at their head, they prayed for the tempted one, held his demons back from him and brought him out from seclusion to a certain hostel, where he was cured. Having come to surpass all in virtue, he was finally consecrated Bishop of Novgorod. He became famous for the numerous miracles he performed, and now is revered as a saint.[62]

From this narrative Baratz derives certain conclusions. 1) Nikita not only displayed knowledge of all the books of the Old Testament (enumerated in Polycarp's letter), but was also fairly well acquainted with Hebrew in the proper, exclusive sense. 2) This suggests that he derived some of his knowledge from a Hebrew home, in other words that he was born a Jew. 3) The latter point is in some

---

[60] Date from Polycarp's letter quoted by Baratz.

[61] Cross, p. 142 = Leger, p. 136.

[62] *Sobranie Trudov*, II, 57 ff.

degree confirmed by the inability of later hagiographers, including the 16th century writer Marcellus, to discover anything about his birthplace and parents. 4) The demon who tempted Nikita was presumably a Judaizing Christian, more exactly a Hebrew Rabbinist converted to Christianity. The words directed to Nikita by the tempter nearly agree with the Talmudic sentence: "The study of the Law is equivalent to the fulfilment of all other religious duties taken together, including prayer."[63]

Thus, according to Baratz, Nikita was born in a Hebrew family, probably at Kiev or some locality near there, as a youth went through the Bible and some tractates of the Talmud, but displayed a special propensity for the study of the Kabbala — with reference to the miracles attributed to him. But not arriving at satisfaction and under the influence of a Christian missionary, he decided to become a convert to Christianity, and presented himself at the Pechersky cloister, where he was gladly received and christened by the Abbot Theodosius (i.e. in 1051), who occupied himself in catechising him, and by his gentle and indulgent demeanor bound the young novice to himself, so that he paid selfless devotion and deepest reverence to his father in God till his dying day — with reference to the panegyric of Theodosius in the *Chronicle*.[64] It is all ingenious and closely argued, and the original Judaism of Nikita may be taken as established. But from this to his editorship of the *Russian Chronicle* is a long way.[65]

Finally, we take Baratz' treatment of the account of the religious disputation held by Vladimir in Kiev in 986 according to the *Chronicle*, which issued in the conversion of the Russian ruler to the faith of the Greeks.[65a] This narrative was considered by Golubinsky, the historian of the Russian Church, and others to be an addition to the original form of the *Chronicle*, and Golubinsky actually noted that we may suppose "with some slight probability"

---

63 Baratz cites *Mishnah*, Tract. Pe'a, I, 1.
64 Cross, pp. 156 ff. = Leger, pp. 155 ff.
65 *Sobranie Trudov*, II, 58 ff.
65a Cross, 96 ff. = Leger, 69 ff.

that its author was motivated to compose it by the example of a similar narrative which he saw among the Jews of Kiev, namely an account of the Khazar conversion to Judaism about the middle of the 8th century.[66] Baratz adopts the suggestion of Golubinsky, and finds that it can be concluded not only "with great probability" (sic),[67] but, in his opinion, with complete confidence that the narrative in the *Chronicle* was influenced by the example of the story of the Khazar conversion to Judaism. He has in this case nothing specific to say about authorship, but since he finds traces in the narrative that use was made of the book *Cosri* (*Kuzari*) of R. Jehudah ha-Levi, written originally in Arabic in 1140 and only later[68] rendered into Hebrew by Ibn Tibbon (died after 1190), evidently Nikita Zatvornik is not to be thought of. Baratz points out "some turns of phrase and expressions" in the story in the *Chronicle* which he thinks are due to the influence of the book *Cosri*, or as he expresses it again, the narrative was composed by the author "in imitation of" the *Cosri*.[68a] The argument is too long to reproduce here, but may be regarded as special pleading. It would appear more natural to suppose that in similar circumstances (conversion to a monotheistic religion) among a people at much the same stage of development as the Khazars, at approximately the same time and in the same part of the world, the record would show some resemblances to accounts of the Khazar conversion, than that one of these was actually imitated.[69] There is at all events no evidence that the religious discussion before Vladimir did not take place.

This brings us to the end of the present examination of Baratz' views. The question which we have now to ask is, What light do his investigations throw on the Khazar problem? To this the reply must be, however reluctantly given: Very little. Here and there he

---

[66] Baratz (*Sob. Trud.* l, ii, 585) gives no clear reference.
[67] Apparently an oversight.
[68] Probably in 1167, cf. Steinschneider, *Die heb. Übersetzungen des Mittelalters*, p. 403 (§ 234).
[68a] *Sob. Trud.*, I, ii, 588.
[69] Cf. *Hist. of the Jewish Khazars*, pp. 250–51.

brings some light,[70] but as regards such central contentions as that the *Zakon Sudnyi Liudem* was originally in use in Khazaria and was translated by Constantine (Cyril), that important contributions to the first part of the *Russian Chronicle* were made by Gregory the presbyter, and that the redactor of the *Chronicle* at the end of the 11th century and the beginning of the 12th was neither Nestor nor Sylvester but Nikita Zatvornik, these remain interesting speculations which scarcely admit of proof or disproof with the information at our disposal. If Baratz' approach inspired entire confidence, his conclusions might be acceptable at least as hypotheses (he himself seldom or never presents them as other than established positions), but his method at all events for historical investigation is insecure, however suited it may be to forensic argument. Such and such was the case, e.g. in Khazaria a mixed code prevailed, or Gregory the presbyter was in touch with Bulgarian and Byzantine affairs, or Nikita Zatvornik was a Pechersky monk and was in a position to contribute Hebrew elements to the *Russian Chronicle* (proofs). What more natural than that such and such followed, i.e. Constantine (Cyril) took the code which he found in Khazaria and produced the *Zakon Sudnyi Liudem*, Gregory the presbyter contributed important items on Bulgarian and Byzantine affairs to the *Chronicle*, and Nikita was its principal redactor (no proofs cited, and none possible)? Such arguments have their uses, but do not yield anything like what we need for historical criticism. It would perhaps be enough for Jewish-Khazar influence on the *Russian Chronicle* as distinct from Christian ecclesiastical influence, if the *Chronicle* could be shown to contain Talmudic elements. So far as I have seen, Baratz has not been able to demonstrate a single instance. We are in fact, in spite of all that he adduces, left in uncertainty as to the identity of individual contributors of the undoubted Hebrew elements in very early Russian writings and as before have to suppose that these are due to the Biblical preoccupations of the ecclesiastics who composed the documents.

---

[70] On Μαρσοῦχα (μαρζούκα) and the parallel between the *Chronicle* and Ibn Rustah, though in both cases apparently the information is from others.

The position which Baratz takes up is certainly not unreasonable. He had made himself familiar with most of the sources and with the secondary material, chiefly Russian, which is calculated to throw light on the investigation, and therefore writes with wide knowledge of the facts. His style is for the most part simple and clear, his arrangement of the arguments well-ordered, his knowledge of the necessary languages at least adequate,[71] his industry unremitting. When he arrives at his conclusions, they are presented with clarity and force. Why then do they fail to carry conviction and sometimes appear fantastic? Why is it that after all he has very little to tell us which is reliable? The answer to these questions has already been indicated. It is not that Baratz lacked the ability to discover the truth (he obviously had great abilities), so much as that he was attempting to do something else. He is unwilling to content himself with examining the facts and after examination allowing them to speak for themselves, as the historian must, even when they tell him only a fraction of what he desires to know. Rather Baratz gives the impression of constantly trying to prove a case, using any argument which comes to his hand, without pausing to consider its validity at every stage, apart from its immediate utility. Having adopted the position, entirely unobjectionable as a hypothesis, that the Jews of Khazaria at some points and in some manner influenced the rising Russian literature, he has become an advocate rather than an analyst.

That Baratz had not more to show as a result of his labors is in part due also to the stage which the Khazar investigation had reached already in his time. It seems doubtful if the old, known documents have many more secrets to reveal. What is needed now is new material of the type of the Genizah document apparently bearing on the Khazars in Kiev, about which interesting lectures were given by Professors Golb and Pritsak at the spring meeting of the American Oriental Society at New Haven in 1967. It is to be hoped that this new Hebrew document will soon be made available to the public.

7   Latin, e.g., much better than his son's, who has (op. cit., p. 32) *mutatis mutandibus* and (ibid. p. 35) *de lege ferrenda*.

מסורת AND ITS HISTORICAL BACKGROUND

R. Edelmann

THERE ARE FEW FIELDS of biblical and Judaistic research where a clear definition of ideas and designations are so much needed as in the study of *Masorah*. The word *Masorah* itself has, as is well known, commonly been used to comprise so many different subjects of learning that it rightly could be described as covering the whole field of the "Philology of the Hebrew Bible" with its various aspects.[1]

When we, further, turn to the word *Masorah* in the sense of *Masorah marginalis* and *finalis*, it offers so many varieties, contradictions, inaccuracies — apparent as well as genuine — and all sorts of problems, both between the various statements themselves and in relation to the corresponding biblical text[2] that a very scrupulous and scrutinizing editorial work is necessary, even when one deals with the most authoritative masoretic manuscripts. The reason for these circumstances may be explained from the fact that, apart from the Bible texts from the Judean desert, no biblical manuscript known to us is older than the period which is considered as the heyday of the masoretic activities, i.e. when the *Masorah* had incorporated the ניקוד (punctuation) into its scope and become a matter of professional routine.[3]

If we go further back in order to try and find out the earlier stages of what is called *Masorah*, we shall find a number of statements scattered over the talmudic and midrashic literature, but

---

[1] Cf. R. Edelmann, "Soferim-Massorets, 'Massoretes'-Nakdanim," in *In Memoriam Paul Kahle* (Berlin, 1968), p. 116.

[2] Ibid. pp. 116 and 122.

[3] Ibid., p. 120.

also here it proves that it is necessary to begin with clearing up the ideas and to make out what it actually is all about as well as with sifting the literary sources in which these statements in relation to our question are found.

We can, for our purposes, leave out conditions in Babylonia and take under consideration only such statements found in the Babylonian Talmud and related literature which apply to the Palestinian tradition, because the subject had its origin in Hellenistic Palestine. The occupation with the consonantal text of the Bible was brought to Babylonia from Palestine only at a time when it already had gone through a considerable development in its homeland. We even know when it happened, viz. from the well-known note about the early Babylonian masoretes found in a number of masoretic texts.[4] Wilhelm Bacher,[5] who identified the name of the oldest of these masoretes as נקיי, Nakkai, made the authenticity of this list acceptable. According to it, the scribe Nakkai was exiled from Palestine during the Hadrianic persecutions and went to Babylonia, where he became the founder of the masoretic activities there.[6]

---

[4] Cf. G. E. Weil in *Textus*, II, 107–109. Weil does not mention the text in Cod. Hebr. XXXIV in the Royal Library of Copenhagen, fol. 1v: המסורת הזה (this text) שמסר דוסה בן אלעזר בנו של ר' אפסי שקבל מר' יהודה הבבלי שקבל משמעון אביו ושמעון מן המנונא שהוציאם בנהרדעא ורב המנונא ור' אדא קבלו שניהם מנַקְרֵי (misread by Baer and Strack in their edition of the "Dikduke Ha-Teamim", Lpz. 1879, §69, p. 56, as מנַקְדֵי) שהגלה מארץ ישראל לבבל שהגלהו רופס שלא תהא תורה בארץ ישראל ושכמו את התורה ואת הנביאים ואת הכתובים עשרים וארבע ספרים שלא טעו ושלא שנו בדקדוקיהם פסוקים שתי רבואות אלפים ושבע מאות וארבעים ושבעה לא פחות ולא יותר. (Rav) Hamnuna who is mentioned in this list as a pupil of Nakkai is not the Amora Rav Hamnuna who lived about 100 years later, cf. W. Bacher, in *Magazin für die Wissenschaft des Judentums*, 18. Jahrg. (1891), p. 58 seq., and *Die Agada der palästinensischen Amoräer*, 1. Bd. (1892), p. 2, note 1.

[5] In *Magazin f. d. Wissenschaft d. Judentums*, 17. Jahrg. (1890), pp. 169 seq.

[6] According to the list, Nakkai's pupil Hamnuna taught in Nehardea which seems to have been the oldest center in Babylonia for the cultivation of masoretic studies. It was the seat of Rav Nahman bar Jacob (d. 320) who was the son of a scribe in Samuel's law court (b. B.M. 16b) and himself a masorete. He kept up lively contact with Palestine, and his friend R. Yitzhak Nappaha from Tiberias and Caesarea, Palestinian centres of masoretic activities, used

Though the Babylonian *Masorah* later took a course of its own, different from that of Palestine, the Palestinian *Masorah* kept its superiority from the beginning. We can demonstrate this from the documents of Babylonian *Masorah* at our disposal,[7] as even from the Babylonian Talmud.[8] Thus in Kiddushin 30a we find a report of a discussion about a masoretic problem held at the beginning of the fourth century C.E. in Pumbedita. This discussion was held between Rav Joseph (d. 333) and other Amoraim, among them Abaye (d. 338). The question was whether the letter ו in גחון (Lev. 11:42), indicated by the סופרים to be the middle letter of the Pentateuch, belongs to the first half of the Torah or to the second half; and again, whether the verse beginning with והתגלח (Lev. 13:33) belongs to the first or to the second half of the number of verses in the Pentateuch.[9] In both cases the Amoraim reply that they were not experts, in distinction to the Palestinians who were experts. They said: בקיאי בחסירות ויתירות אנן לא (i.e. the Palestinians) אינהו בקיאי and they actually had a Torah scroll brought and had the letters counted in order to find out, thereby referring to Rabba bar bar Hanna (second half of the third century), who in the name

---

to stay with him during his visits to Babylonia. When the ישיבה of Nehardea was closed, it moved to Pumbedita, where another friend of Rav Nahman bar Jacob, R. Yehuda bar Yehezkel, who likewise was interested in masoretic matters, had founded a new ישיבה. There the Nehardeans were granted the privilege of occupying the first row (שורת נהרדעאי). J. Mann suggested in *JQR*, NS, VIII (1917–18), 352 seq. that this "row of the Nehardeans" was connected with the work of the "Eastern Massorah", which however seems to have been greatly influenced by Palestinian points of view.

Even a work like מסכת סופרים had its origin in Palestine, cf. M. Higger in his introduction to the edition of מ"ס (NewYork, 1937), p. 80. As for the *Ochla we-Ochla*, it is of a much later date than the period which is dealt with here.

[7] The relevant literature is listed in Weil, *Textus*, II, 103; see also *Textus*, III (1963), 74 seq. and VI (1968), 25 seq.

[8] On the differences between the biblical quotations in the Babyl. Talmud and the MT, cf. Isaiah Berlin, הפלאה שבערכין, II, edit. L. Rosenkranz, (Wien, 1859), s.v. מאה, and Akiva Eger's note on b. Shabbat 55b.

[9] About the meaning of this question see below, note 30.

of the Palestinian R. Yohannan (so in b. Shabbat 49b) had reported about a similar incident, obviously in Palestine.[10]

What we now have to deal with is the question: Who were these Masoretes? Or to say it more precisely: Who were those who first dealt with the biblical text in a similar way as the later Masoretes did?

The just mentioned discussion in b. Kiddushin 30a follows upon a Baraita which reads as follows: לפיכך נקראו ראשונים סופרים שהיו סופרים כל האותיות שבתורה. Here we do not have an attempt to explain the etymology of the designation of the early scholars, the סופרים; rather we have here a *characterization* of how they were working. The above report serves as an illustration to our Baraita. The סופרים counted the letters of the Torah, because they were responsible for the correctness of the biblical text. Thus R. Yismael once said to his pupil Meir (the later R. Meir) who was a לבלר by profession:[11] בני הוי זהיר במלאכתך שמלאכתך מלאכת שמים היא שמא אתה מחסר אות אחת או מייתר אות אחת נמצאת מחריב כל העולם כולו. To this Meir replied: בחסירות וביתירות בקי אנא. From Meir's reply it appears that he wanted to tell R. Yismael that he was not only aware of the importance of being careful as a לבלר, a scribe, in the writing of legal documents in order to avoid scribal errors by leaving out a letter or by writing a superfluous letter and thereby influence the legal case in question in a wrong way, but that he also knew the exact spelling of words in a Torah scroll, because the elaboration of certain Halakhot to a high degree was based on the spelling in the Torah text, especially on the *plene*, respectively defective writing.[12] By declaring himself a בקי בחסירות וביתירות Meir wanted to imply that he was not a mere לבלר, but that he even knew the halakhic implications of *plene* and defective writing

---

[10] Even in case the above-mentioned list of the earliest Babylonian masoretes should not be authentic, the very fact that it takes the history of the masoretic activities in Babylonia back to Palestine would prove that there was a necessity for producing a Palestinian origin thereof, in order to give it more authority.

[11] b. Sota 20a and b. Eruvin 13a.

[12] Cf. e.g. the discussions in b. Sanhedrin 4a–b.

of the words in the biblical text, i.e. that he was also capable as a סופר.

A close investigation of the usage of the words לבלר and סופר in the earlier sources, including the Targumim, proves that these expressions designated two different categories of scribes. The לבלר (*librarius*) was the ordinary scribe who wrote legal and other sorts of documents. This Latin designation, however, was not used after the tannaitic period.

As for the סופר, he seems to have been the successor of the member of the learned class of סופרים of the old society. But at the same time we can notice a change in his position in consequence of his more specialized activities during the tannaitic period, a process that was nearing its end during the second half of the third century C.E. During the tannaitic time the word סופר was used to designate both the scholar and the scribe, although we then can discern a tendency towards a differentiation in the usage of the word, insofar as in practically all cases the plural, סופרים, is used when the text speaks about scholars, whereas סופר, in singular, is used as a designation for a scribe.[13] We thus find in M. Yadayim III, 2 that the expression דברי סופרים includes a regulation made by the assembly in the attic of R. Hananya ben Hizkiya (בו ביום). In accordance with this we then are allowed to take Rabban Gamliel II's addressing his colleagues with the words הניחו לי סופרים ואדרשנה (b. Sota 15a) as an expression which must then still have been in use for scholars, although it perhaps in this case might have had an additional tinge of irony or solemnity. Also in the Baraita b. Berakhot 45b (b. Hullin 106a) תניא נמי הכי שנים שאכלו כאחת מצוה ליחלק. במה דברים אמורים כששניהם סופרים אבל א׳ סופר וא׳ בור סופר מברך ובור יוצא we have a rule from the tannaitic period which clearly uses the word סופר in the meaning of a man of knowledge. But at the same time, i.e. in the tannaitic period, and later, we find the word סופר in the sense of Scribe or Teacher of the Bible or both.[14]

---

13 Cf. the difference in the usage of *cleric* and *clerk* in English.

14 From various discussions in the Talmud, e.g. b. Menahot 29a seq., it appears that certain Amoraim, most, if not all of them from the period dealt

The Baraita in b. Kiddushin 30a quoted above, reads: לפיכך נקראו
ראשונים סופרים שהיו סופרים כל האותיות שבתורה. In b. Hagigah 15b
the Babylonian Amora R. Yehuda bar Yehezkel explains the verse
Isaiah 33:18: מאי דכתיב בהו ברבנן איה סופר איה שוקל איה סופר את
המגדלים: איה סופר [שסופר] כל האותיות שבתורה. איה שוקל ששוקל כל
קלים וחמורים שבתורה. איה סופר את המגדלים שהיו סופר שלש מאות הלכות
במגדל הפורח באויר. In b. Sanhedrin 106b it is R. Yehuda's Palestinian contemporary R. Yitzhak Nappaha who quotes the same
verse and gives the same explanation, only leaving out the introductory words מאי דכתיב בהו ברבנן. This expression adds considerably to the importance of the passage in connexion with our subject.

As for the first part of the explanation, viz. איה סופר [שסופר]
כל האותיות שבתורה, it is based on the just mentioned Baraita in
b. Kiddushin 30a. The second part of it: איה שוקל ששוקל כל קלים
וחמורים שבתורה makes us listen. This passage tells us that he שוקל
"counterbalanced" not only the קלים and the חמורים in the Torah,
but he did it with כל קלים וחמורים שבתורה, with all of them, just
as he counted the letters of the Torah and knew the number of
all of them (שסופר כל האותיות שבתורה). And in fact we find the
number of קלים וחמורים in the Bible indicated, viz. 10, both in
the tannaitic literature and in the masoretic lists[15] in the same way
as we have the number of the letters and the verses in the Bible
and in its parts given. That means that the סופר counted not only
the various components of the consonantal biblical text according
to formal, external aspects, but also the ideas and expressions in
it when they were of importance for halakhic and midrashic purposes. This is already said by the Palestinian R. Abbahu (second
half of the third century C.E.) in jer. Shekalim V, 2 (48c): אמר רבי
אבהו כתיב משפחת סופרים יושבי יעבץ (I Chr. 2:55) מה תלמוד לומר
סופרים אלא שעשו את התורה ספורות ספורות, and then he brings a
number of illustrations from various parts of the Mishnah:
חמשה לא יתרומו (תרומות) — חמשה דברים חייבין בחלה (חלה) — אבות

with here, were interested in orthographic and similar problems which were
of immediate importance for scribes at their work.

[15] Cf. *Das Buch Ochla W'ochla*, hrsg. von S. Frensdorff (Hannover, 1864),
nos. 182–183 and the notes p. 40 seq.

(שבת) מלאכות ארבעים חסר א׳, etc. This list could be made very long
if we include the whole Mishna and the tannaitic Midrashim, particularly the *Mekhilta*, in addition to the Agada by a number of
the Amoraim, first and foremost the Palestinian Amoraim of the
third and the beginning of the fourth century C.E. In this context
Ezra, naturally enough, appears as the סופר, the Counter, par excellence: אמר ר׳ אחא (בר חנינא?) כתיב: (Ezra 7:11) לעזרא הכהן הסופר.
מה תלמוד לומר סופר אלא כשם שהיה סופר בדברי תורה כך היה סופר
בדברי חכמים. This passage is to be found in direct continuation of
R. Abbahu's statement mentioned above. Accordingly, R. Aha
wanted to say that Ezra was an authority in everything in connection
with the Torah (דברי תורה) including the external text of it, as
well as in everything within the field of activities of the חכמים
(דברי חכמים). And he administered his learning by counting, grouping and classifying, just the way any other סופר did.

All the above quotations are dealing with what we are used to
call *Masorah*, but nevertheless we can make the striking observation
that the word מסורת is mentioned in none of them. (The word
מסורה is a post-Talmudic invention.) Let us therefore here take a
look at this word. It appears only a few times in the literature
dealt with here in another meaning than "Tradition," viz. (1) in
connection with the discussions in the Babylonian Talmud about
the exegetical principle of יש אם למסורת, i.e. about whether the
traditional writing of a word in the Torah, the composition of its
consonants is decisive as a base for the deduction of a Halakha,
as against the principle of יש אם למקרא, i.e. whether the way it
traditionally is pronounced should be essential;[16] (2) in R. Akiva's
statement, Avot III, 13: מסורת סייג לתורה, where מסורת, in accordance with his general position on the principle יש אם למסורת and
his interpretations of even the strokes on the letters (b. Menahot
29b), has the same meaning as above, viz. that the traditional
graphic representation of the consonantal biblical text in itself is

---

16 b. Pesahim 86b; b. Sukkah 6b; b. Kiddushin 18b; b. Sanhedrin 4a;
b. Makkot 7b; b. Zevahim 37b–38a; b. Keritot 17b. Some of these items are
only parallel quotations.

a warrant for the Torah;[17] (3) in a haggadic exegesis of Nehemia 8:8,[18] where the words ויבינו במקרא are explained as indicating the מסורת. Of special interest is a version of this interpretation given in *Gen. Rab.*, 36: רבנן דקסרין אמרי מיכן למסורת. The meaning of מסורת in this exegesis is not immediately clear, but from the context it seems to appear that מסורת also here means the same as in the aforementioned cases; finally, (4) מסורת is found in R. Samuel bar Rav Yitzhak's remark זו המסורת (מיד ה') on הכל בכתב I Chr. 28:19.[19] In the preceding verses, 11 till 18, the subject is a detailed "blueprint" of the Temple to be built by Solomon and its parts as well as a list of the quantities of gold and silver to be used for its equipment. Here at any rate the word מסורת cannot be understood as *Masorah*. More likely R. Samuel wanted to say that the drawings and the list, which David handed over to his son and designated successor, had the value of a document with a precisely worded text in an exact form. In the *Mekhilta* to Exod. 19:4 אתם ראיתם[20] the same meaning is expressed when the text says: ...לא במסורת אני אומר לכם לא כתובים הם לכם.

At any rate, in none of the cases where we might have expected to find a word used in the sense of *Masorah*, it is mentioned. It seems that what we call *Masorah*, at that time, still was called חסירות ויתירות, that this was then the *terminus technicus* for what later became the *Masorah marginalis* and *finalis*. חסירות ויתירות were used extensively both by scholars and by scribes, each from their point of view. The list brought by A. Marmorstein in the introduction to his edition of מדרש חסירות ויתירות, 1917, p. יא—י of those Tannaim and Amoraim who have used the defective and *plene* writing and other textual peculiarities of the biblical text in their exegesis gives us an idea of this. The scribes, on the other hand, were professionally interested in writing the exact number of letters in the Holy Text. The word מסורת seems to have meant:

[17] Cf. also W. Bacher, *Die älteste Terminologie* (1899), p. 108.
[18] Jer. Megillah IV, 1 (74d); b. Megillah 3a and b. Nedarim 37b; *Gen. Rab.* 36. The variants between these four versions do not matter in this context.
[19] Jer. Megillah I, 1 (70a).
[20] (מסכתא דבחדש, ב'), ed. Weiss, p. 71.

The consonantal text as it appeared in its graphic representation.[21]
This text was the concern of the סופר, the *scribe*, the copyist and
corrector of biblical manuscripts, the *counter*.

So far for the consonantal text. As for the oral representation
of the biblical text, the pronounciation of the words, the use of
the vowel-sounds, the cantillation and modulation of the text, it
seems to have been cultivated by other specialists, different from
the scribes, viz. by the קראים, singular: קרָא, reader. A definition
of a קרָא is given by R. Yehuda in b. Kiddushin 49a. According
to him the קרא is a man נביאי וכתובי בדיוקא דקרי אורייתא. A certain
ר׳ חנינה קרא appears several times in the Palestinian Talmud as
well as in the Bavli in passages of Palestinian origin.[22] Taking all
these facts into consideration it seems natural to assume that the
vowel-signs and the so-called accents in the biblical books were
introduced by these קרָאים who cultivated the pronunciation of
the consonantal text of the Bible and the modulation of the words
and the verses at the reading of the texts.

About the קראים we have further information. In the *Pesikta*,
(שובה קס״ה, ב׳) R. Nehemya interprets Hosea 14:3 קחו עמכם דְּבָרִים
by reading דַּבָרִים instead of דְּבָרִים. He says: קחו עמכם דַּבָרִים בעלי
דברים, קרָאים טובים דרשנים טובים. From here we can see that the
קרָאים, at any rate, belonged to the category of eloquent preachers
בעלי דברים, דרשנים טובים, i.e. because they mastered the possibilities of various ways of reading the words for homiletic purposes
(as e.g. דְּבָרִים and דַּבָרִים, to take one example among many others).
We can accordingly assume that the homiletic method of interpretation — אל תקרי — אלא, which is based upon the possibility of
reading a word in different ways, has had its origin with these
קרָאים. During the Middle Ages we find a number of people who
sometimes are called קרָא, sometimes דרשן and sometimes נקדן.
Their occupation is indicated by these designations and so they

21 About the etymology of מסורה ומסורת see Z. Ben-Haim, in *Leshonenu*,
XXI (1957), 283–292.

22 b. Berakhot 30b (b. Jevamot 40a; b. Ketuvot 56a); Jer. Kila'im IX, 7
(32d) (Jer. Shabbat X, 2 (10c)); b. Ta'anit 27b (b. Megillah 22a, here he is
called ר׳ חניא קרא).

seem to have been the successors of the קְרָאִים of the talmudic time. They were not סוֹפְרִים whether from a historic point of view nor by profession.

When we now take a look at those Amoraim who have made most of the aforementioned statements in connection with our subject we will find that they were living in Palestine or connected with it during the second half of the third and the beginning of the fourth century C.E. We will try and find the reason for this phenomenon.

In b. Avoda Zara 4a there is told a very informative story about the conditions in Palestine during the period in question, when the political and administrative power, including that of taxation, was in the hands of the Christians. R. Abbahu from Caesarea was in high esteem with the Christian authorities. They often challenged him with provocative questions about the interpretation of various passages in the Bible. He had recommended the Babylonian Rav Safra to them as a great scholar. When they, therefore, once met Rav Safra they also challenged him about the interpretation of Amos 3:2, but he could not answer, whereupon they started to maltreat him. R. Abbahu happened to arrive just then, and he saved R. Safra by explaining to the Christian officers that he was a great scholar in law matters (בתנאי, δευτέρωσις) but not in biblical passages. To their question why the Palestinians (אתון) then were so well versed in the Bible R. Abbahu answered: אנן דשכיחין גביכון רמינן אנפשין ומעיינין, אינהו לא מעייני i.e. we Palestinians live among you Christians, and because you make us discuss with you it is necessary for us to study thoroughly the Bible. The Babylonians, however, do not have this challenge and so they do not study the Bible so carefully.

We have here authentic evidence that because of a challenge from outside an intensification of the biblical studies, including — according to the other statements quoted before — the study of the outer text, took place in the period in question.[23] Besides, we

[23] There were other occasions during Jewish history when an intensification of the study of the Bible was due to a challenge from outside. This was the case during the later geonic period when the study of the Bible and of the

also have in R. Abbahu's statement a further confirmation of the fact that the study of the Bible in Palestine was superior to that in Babylonia.

Having now established where and when the occupation with the outer biblical text has reached its first culmination after having started during the early tannaitic period or even earlier, as well as having learned about the reason for this intensified occupation just there and then, we can proceed and ask: Why have these special Bible studies — and for that matter also other studies which were cultivated in the contemporaneous Jewish school — taken such forms and methods of counting and listing and grouping?

During the last decades much light has been shed by several scholars upon the relationship between various cultural manifestations of the Jews in Palestine and the cultural pattern of the contemporary non-Jewish world which was Hellenistic with a strong Greek population in Palestine itself and with a large Greek-assimilated Jewish diaspora. However much the rabbis endeavored to save the national Jewish religious and spiritual property from foreign impact, however much they fought Greek and Roman conceptions from penetrating into Jewish life and religion, they nevertheless used such external written forms and ways of expression, such methods of thinking and working which were common within the whole contemporary, Hellenistic, world of which Jewish Palestine appears to have formed a special part. We are therefore justified, if there methodically is not a necessity, to look to the Hellenistic surroundings in order to find the origin of some of the forms and methods applied to Jewish cultural

Hebrew language was stimulated by the polemics with the Karaites on the one hand and the rise of philological studies among the Arabs on the other hand. This occurred again in northern France during the 12th century when biblical studies, already renewed by Rashi and his family, received an additional stimulus from the interest shown by the christian scholars of St. Victor in Paris and others (cf. S. Smalley, *The Study of the Bible in the Middle Ages* (Oxford, 1952), pp. 78 seq. and passim, and H. Hailperin, *Rashi and the Christian Scholars* (Pittsburg, 1963), pp. 105 seq. See also R. Edelmann, "Das Buch der Frommen," in *Miscellanea Mediaevalia*, Bd. 4 (Berlin, 1966), p. 64.

property, *in casu* the statistical approach to the material of learning, including the outer text of the Bible.[24]

The term סופר leads us both into the sphere of the Jewish school and of the scribal profession, and when we turn to the Greek and Latin world in order to look for comparable phenomena, we will find similar conditions in abundance within the same fields of action. In Greek and Latin didactic literature the details of the treated material are grouped and classified and numbered to a degree which might not be understandable to us today,[25] if it could not be explained by the special method of learning by heart applied in the Antiquity.[26] And the same method of learning was used in the antique Jewish school.

The numbering and grouping of different categories of words, expressions and names according to certain points of view in the earlier talmudic and midrashic literature served pedagogical purposes; it was made in order to make the material easier to learn by heart, as we doubtless must consider all this literature as being closely connected with the contemporary Jewish school on its various levels and branches, respectively.

As for the scribal profession, the similarities in the methods of working within Jewish and non-Jewish book-making during the Hellenistic period were not less than within the methods of learning and teaching. About the Greek and Latin book we are rather well informed.[27]

At the end of the antique book there used to be a statement giving the number of the lines (στίχοι) in it. Thus Flavius Josephus,

[24] Cf. S. Lieberman, *Hellenism in Jewish Palestine* (New York, 1950), pp. 24 seq. See also: R. Edelmann, "Apophthegma and Chria in Talmud and Midrash," in the forthcoming Memorial Volume for Isidore Epstein.

[25] Cf. e.g. H.-J. Marrou, *Histoire de l'éducation dans l'antiquité* 2e édit. (Paris, 1950), p. 376 and H. Steinthal, *Geschichte der Sprachwissenschaft bei den Griechen und Römern mit besonderer Rücksicht auf die Logik.* 2. Aufl. 2. Teil (Berlin, 1891), pp. 205 seq. and 256 seq.

[26] Cf. Marrou, o.c., p. 231 and p. 366.

[27] Cf. e.g. Carl Wendel, *Die griechisch-römische Buchbeschreibung verglichen mit der des vorderen Orients* (Halle [Saale], 1949), (= Hallische Monographien. Nr. 3), with a bibliography on the subject p. (V).

at the end of his *Antiquities*, mentions that this work consists of 20 books (i.e. main parts) and 60,000 lines.[28] We can also find in antique books the counting of letters in a book and a statement about their number.[29] Even such a striking feature as the indication of the middle of the total number of lines in a book was known to the ancient world.[30]

These ways of describing a book emerged first in the Hellenistic world in the big library in Alexandria before they were taken over by the book trade for the fixation of the price of the books and by the professional scribes and their employers as a measure for the payment.[31] In the library the stichometry served biblio-graphical purposes. It was a means of describing a volume in order to indicate its size and to secure that the text thereof was complete.[31a] The number of the lines of each volume was carefully noted in the catalogue, alongside with the author's name, the title of the book and the number of volumes, in case the work in question consisted of more than one volume.[32]

It must have been a considerable task to accomplish all this counting which required a special routine. It must be assumed that a library of such proportions as that in Alexandria, and other big libraries as well, and, for that matter, also publishers who employed a number of copyists in their book workshops, employed specialists for doing all this counting — a counter, in Greek a Λογιστής, in Latin a *calculator*.

Apart from the fragments of Kallimachos' catalogue of the books

---

[28] It seems that both the פסוק and the στίχος originally designated the same part of the written page, viz. the line representing a poetic verse, cf. Wendel, op. cit., pp. 34 seq. and Th. Birt, *Das antike Buchwesen in seinem Verhältniss zur Litteratur* (Berlin, 1882), pp. 204 seq. For the Jewish book see: L. Blau, "Massoretic studies. III. The Division into verses," in *JQR* IX (1897), 122 seq.; see also, L. Blau, *Studien zum althebräischen Buchwesen* (1902), pp. 128 seq.

[29] Cf. Th. Birt, op. cit., pp. 160 seq.

[30] Cf. ibid., pp. 176 seq. As for the indication of the middle of the verses (letters) in the text of the Bible see above, p. 371 [3].

[31] Cf. Wendel, op. cit., pp. 41 seq.

[31a] Cp. above, note 4.

[32] Birt, op. cit., pp. 162 seq.

in the library of Alexandria, the Πίνακες, from where we know
the methods of cataloguing in this greatest of the libraries in
Antiquity, we unfortunately have little information about the
organization of the work in the Hellenistic libraries. When we
consult the Greek and Latin dictionaries[33] we learn that the
Λογιστής, and especially the *calculator* was connected both with
the school and with the book, and in both cases he in some way
or other occupied himself with numbers, with arithmetic, calculating
and accounting. But he was also a *librarius*, a scribe, and a *notarius*,
a shorthand writer. Accordingly, we doubtlessly do not go wrong
when we assume that a Λογιστής, respectively a *calculator*, also
was employed as a counter of lines and verses in libraries and in
publishers' workshops. In this respect, then, the Λογιστής and
the *calculator* would be like the סופר who, as we have seen before,
according to the view of the contemporary rabbis, was called so,
because he was a counter of verses and letters in the Torah. Counting was a professional technique connected with the making of
books and common to the whole ancient world.[34]

The subject of the סופר was the מסורת, the consonantal text of
the Bible as it appeared in its traditional graphic representation.

From the fourth century on conditions in Palestine deteriorated
and the interest in חסירות ויתירות became more and more a matter
of the professional סופר, the copyist and corrector of biblical books,
for professional purposes. During the geonic period the invention
of various systems of vowel-signs and "accents" gave the occupation with the outer biblical text a new direction, and a new subject
was created which was given the name of מסורה, indicating that
this subject was different from the מסורת, which was its object.[35]

---

[33] For Λογιστής see: H. Stephanus, *Thesaurus linguae graecae, nova editio*,
tom. V (Paris, 1843), s.v. and for *calculator* see, Forcellini, *Lexicon totius
latinitatis*, latest edition (Padua, 1940), s.v. and *Thesaurus linguae latinae*,
vol. III, s.v. Cf. also, Marrou, o.c., p. 550, note 13.

[34] Cf. Wendel, o.c., p. 149, s.v. *Zeilenzählung*.

[35] When in later texts the word מסורת sometimes appears instead of מסורה
it is due to a confusion of conceptions.

PLATONIC THEMES IN GERSONIDES' COSMOLOGY

SEYMOUR FELDMAN

IN HIS OPENING PRESENTATION of the controversy concerning creation Maimonides cites three distinct cosmological theories, the second
of which he attributes to Plato and some other Greek philosophers.[1]
The chief characteristic that differentiates this theory from the
Biblical and Aristotelian doctrines is that it asserts the creation of
the universe from some eternal matter.[2] Since the Platonic theory,
as understood by the medievals, asserted creation of some kind,
it was more acceptable to the medieval world than the eternity
hypothesis of Aristotle. But the Platonic notion of eternal matter
bothered them; for it was not clear whether this part of the Platonic
cosmology was compatible with the Bible.

Indeed, the dominant view in the three major philosophical-
religious traditions (Jewish, Christian and Muslim) was that God
created the universe *ex nihilo*. Quite early in the development of
Jewish theology the latter doctrine was advanced as the correct
interpretation of the first chapter of Genesis.[3] This view became the

---

[1] Moses Maimonides, *The Guide of the Perplexed*, trans. S. Pines (Chicago,
1963), II, 13.

[2] The interpretation of the *Timaeus* is notoriously difficult. But irrespective
of the correct interpretation of *Timaeus*, 48 e-53 c, the medievals interpreted
"the receptacle" to be some kind of eternal and formless matter out of and
within which the universe is alleged to have been created. Presumably this
interpretation was based upon Aristotle's identification of the receptacle with
matter (*Physics*, 209 b, 10). For a critical discussion of Aristotle's interpretation
see H. Cherniss, *Aristotle's Criticism of Plato and the Academy* (Baltimore, 1944),
chapter 2, especially pp. 112 ff.

[3] *Midrash Bereshit Rabbah*, I, 9; *Second Maccabees* 7:28; Philo Judaeus,
De Opificio mundi, VII; H. Wolfson, *Philo* (Cambridge, Mass., 1948), I, 300–310.

"official" view of the Church Fathers and the Muslim Mutakallimūn as well. Amongst the philosophers too this issue was of considerable interest. In the Jewish tradition, for example, Saadia Gaon attempted to defend creation *ex nihilo* by several philosophical arguments.[4] Judah Halevi and Maimonides, however, were not as certain with respect to both the incompatibility of the Platonic view with Scripture and the philosophical validity of the arguments in behalf of creation *ex nihilo*. To them what is essential is the belief in creation; the details are secondary.[5] There were, however, a few philosophers who adhered to the Platonic theory. Of this latter group Levi ben Gerson (Gersonides) was probably the most vigorous defender of the Platonic hypothesis.[6]

Another aspect of Plato's cosmology was also of considerable interest to the medieval philosopher. Plato held that although the universe had a temporal beginning it has no end: the world is everlasting.[7] Aristotle rejected this position and attempted to refute it, holding that anything generable must be destructible.[8] On this cosmological point Maimonides was again not sure, at least not as a philosopher. He *believed* that the universe is indestructible and that this view was the correct teaching of the Bible. But he recognized that many of his co-religionists held the contrary, and he refused to consider them as heretics. Accordingly, he was content to cite certain Biblical and Rabbinic passages that supported his view, without entering into a philosophical argument in behalf of

[4] Saadia Gaon, *The Book of Beliefs and Opinions*, trans. S. Rosenblatt (New Haven, 1948), pp. 46–70.

[5] Judah Halevi, *The Kuzari*, trans. H. Hirschfeld (New York, 1946), pp. 47–48; Maimonides, *Guide*, II, 25. Maimonides' attitude is particularly interesting. Although he opts for the *ex nihilo* view, he is prepared to accept the Platonic theory if the latter can be demonstratively proven. He suggests that the literal text of the Bible could be interpreted to fit the Platonic theory, if the latter were proven true.

[6] Abraham ibn Ezra suggests the Platonic theory in his commentary on *Genesis* 1:1. This interpretation of ibn Ezra (cf. Guttmann, *Philosophies of Judaism* [New York, 1969], p. 120) was rejected by Krochmal (cf. N. Krochmal, *Moreh Nebukei ha-Zeman*, ed. S. Rawidowicz [London 1961], pp. 306, 324).

[7] Plato, *Timaeus*, 31 b.

[8] Aristotle, *On the Heavens*, I, 9–12.

it.[9] This caution and tolerance, unusual for Maimonides in philosophical matters, are absent in Gersonides. For not only does
Gersonides side with Plato (as well as Maimonides), but he also
defends this claim with rigorous philosophical arguments. This
paper is devoted to a discussion of Gersonides' arguments in behalf
of these two Platonic theses: 1) the universe is created out of some
kind of eternal matter; and 2) the universe is indestructible.[10]

I

For the purposes of this essay creation *ex nihilo* shall be understood as asserting the non-existence of any "material cause" or
stuff, prior to creation from which God created the universe. Let
us construct the following "thought-experiment" to make this
notion clearer. Since *ex hypothesi* the universe had a temporal
beginning, let us imagine the very moment at which the universe
came into being. The doctrine of creation *ex nihilo* asserts that
"prior" to this moment there existed no corporeal substance which
acted as a partner in the creative act.[11]

Now there is at least one *prima facie* objection to such a theory,
an objection that was evident to the Greek philosophers who admitted the generation of the universe but postulated some kind
of corporeal substratum as the "stuff" out of which the universe
is generated. The ordinary cases of generation are all examples of
something coming from something else. This is evident both in
natural generation (e.g. flowers from seeds, earth and water) and
the crafts (e.g. statues from marble or bronze). To deny this
generalization is to run counter to our everyday experience. Gene-

---

[9] Maimonides, *Guide*, II, 27–30.

[10] Gersonides, *Milḥamot Hashem* (*The Wars of the Lord*), (Leipzig, 1866).
Hereafter abbreviated as *MH*.

[11] Naturally, since on this view time is created with the universe, terms like
"prior" or "before" are not really proper. But we may use these terms so long
as we take them figuratively. Cf. H. Wolfson, "The Kalam Problem of Non-
existence and Saadia's Second Theory of Creation," *JQR*, XXXVI (1945–46),
371–391; idem. "The Meaning of ex nihilo in the Church Fathers, Arabic and
Jewish Philosophy, and St. Thomas", *Medieval Studies in Honor of Jeremiah
Ford* (Cambridge, Mass., 1948), pp. 355–367.

ration consists in the emergence of a new form out of some pre-existent material or new individuals out of some pre-existent material and according to a definite structure or form. We don't observe the generation of a physical object from no previously existing matter. So it was quite natural for the ancient philosophers to formulate the law — *ex nihilo nihil fit*.[12]

Put in another way, it could be said that the doctrine of creation *ex nihilo* asserts a radical discontinuity in nature. For on this theory it is claimed that an incorporeal agent creates a corporeal substance without employing any material elements. Here too the Greeks seemed to have believed in a general principle according to which like produces like. For this reason Spinoza felt it necessary to ascribe to God the attribute of extension and to collapse the difference between God and the universe. But this route was not open to the medievals, for whom the incorporeality and trans-cendence of God were philosophical dogmas. Accordingly, Ger-sonides opted for a different way out — the notion of a primordial matter. In this way divine creation is brought in line with the notion of creation in the crafts and arts.[13] To Spinoza, however, this route led to a dead-end, and he ultimately rejected the entire doctrine of creation.[14]

The force of these *prima facie* objections, however, could be blunted if the defender of creation *ex nihilo* is prepared to accept certain discontinuities in and exceptions to the general course of nature. For example, it could be said that creation *ex nihilo* is simply a miracle, perhaps the greatest miracle of all. Or, put in a different, more philosophical way, if God is omnipotent he could create the world directly, i.e. without any secondary, or instrumental causes.[15] Indeed, creation *ex nihilo* is, on this view, the clearest

---

[12] Aristotle, *Metaphysics*, 1032 b, 30; Gersonides, *MH*, pp. 364–366.

[13] Gersonides, *MH*, p. 364.

[14] The problem that is fatal to any creation theory is how an *incorporeal* agent can act upon *corporeal* substance. For Spinoza there could be no such causal action; hence he rejected *any* kind of creation, voluntaristic or emana-tionist. Spinoza, *Ethics*, I, first six propositions. Cf. H. Wolfson, *The Philosophy of Spinoza* (New York, 1958), vol. I, chapter 4.

[15] This is an application of the Principle of Parsimony. Cf. Saadia Gaon,

example of divine omnipotence. An omnipotent God, it is believed, can bridge the gap between non-being and being; thus creation *ex nihilo* is a manifestation of the infinite power of God. This conception of nature and divine omnipotence was, however, not acceptable to Gersonides. In certain contexts he was prepared to introduce certain restrictions upon the scope of natural laws, as in his distinction between particular cases of generation, which are subject to the laws of Aristotle's physics, and the creation of the whole of nature, which is not subsumable *in toto* under Aristotle's theory of natural generation. But this kind of distinction he introduces quite sparingly. In general, nature is a rational system; indeed, even its creation is in some sense "rational," i.e. it does not violate good sense. This rationalism is so pervasive in Gersonides that it leads him to maintain that the doctrine of creation *ex nihilo* is not merely implausible, as the previous arguments contend, but actually absurd. It is not, therefore, a question of assessing the relative merits of alternative hypotheses, as it is for Maimonides; rather, one of these hypotheses is radically defective. This claim, therefore, entails that creation *ex nihilo* is not a genuine possibility; hence it does not fall within the scope of divine omnipotence. God can do only that which is logically possible.[16] To demonstrate the absurdity of the *ex nihilo* doctrine Gersonides marshalls several philosophical-scientific arguments.

The first set of arguments concerns the concept of a vacuum. Aristotle had pointed out that the belief in creation *ex nihilo* implies the prior existence of a vacuum. This can be shown as follows. This doctrine asserts that besides God there was nothing before creation; yet when the world is created it occupies a definite spatial region, since it is believed to be finite. Now, that which is empty

The Book of Beliefs and Opinions, p. 69. In his defense of the doctrine of creation *ex nihilo* Thomas Aquinas explicitly connects this thesis with the notion of divine omnipotence (Thomas Aquinas, *Summa Contra Gentiles*, II, c. 20–21).

[16] Gersonides implicitly accepts the definition of divine omnipotence explicitly stated by Maimonides: God can do whatever is logically possible. Cf. Maimonides, *Guide*, III, 15.

of any body but could be the place of a body is the void. Hence, the doctrine of creation *ex nihilo* implies the antemundane existence of the void. But, according to Aristotle and most of the medieval philosophers, the existence of a void is impossible.[17] And so creation *ex nihilo* is absurd.[18] The absurdity of this theory can be exhibited in a different way. Since all the parts of a vacuum are homogeneous, no particular part is more fitting to be the locus of the world than any other part. God's initial creative act, therefore, would spread throughout the *whole* infinitive void, resulting in an infinite universe. But for Aristotle and the Aristotelian medieval tradition the universe is finite.[19] Finally, even if it is granted that one particular region of the vacuum is occupied by the universe, there would still exist a void surrounding the universe. For, as before, no particular part of the remaining empty space is more fitting to be the locus for another body than any other part. Thus, either no other universe would be created, and a void would exist *extra mundum*, or *every* single point in this infinite space would be occupied, and the universe would be infinite. Since the latter consequence has already been excluded, the former consequence would ensue. Thus, the creation *ex nihilo* doctrine is committed not only to the existence of a void prior to creation but also to the existence of a vacuum *extra mundum*.[20]

The argument positing a vacuum *extra mundum* requires some comment. Although Aristotle believed in a finite but unbounded

---

[17] Aristotle, *Physics*, IV, 6–9; A. Koyré, "Le vide et l'espace infini au XIV siècle," *Archives d'Histoire Doctrinale et Littéraire du Moyen Âge*, XXIV (1949), 45–91.

[18] Aristotle, *On the Heavens*, 302 a, 1–9; Averroes, *Tahafut al-Tahafut*, trans. S. van der Bergh (London, 1954), vol. I, paragraph 89; Gersonides, *MH*, pp. 364–365.

[19] Gersonides, *MH*, pp. 364–365; Aristotle, *Physics*, 203 b, 27–29. These latter two arguments make use of a version of the Principle of Sufficient Reason: if there is a homogeneous vacuum there is no way to account for the creation of the universe. Cf. Leibniz, *Letters to Clarke*, III, paragraph 6, reprinted in *Leibniz Selections*, ed. P. Wiener (New York, 1951), p. 224.

[20] Gersonides, *MH*, *op. cit.* This was the view of the Stoics. Cf. Philo, *De aeternitate mundi*, 102.

universe, he denied the existence of a void beyond the universe. His main reason was that he wanted to preserve the uniqueness of this universe: if a vacuum did exist *extra mundum* then the existence of other worlds is more than just a possibility, since the vacuum is that which is empty of body but could be the place of a body. On independent grounds, however, Aristotle argues for the impossibility of a plurality of worlds, and then concludes that there is no vaccum beyond our universe.[21] Thus, for Aristotle, beyond the universe there is absolute, or sheer, nothingness. (Possibly the incorporeal gods reside there, but qua incorporeal they do not occupy space.)

This point was the occasion of some discussion even amongst Aristotle's ancient commentators. Amongst the medieval Aristotelians who accepted creation *ex nihilo* it was even more of a problem. Thomas Aquinas, for example, is quite alive to these arguments about the vacuum; but he rejects them. He maintains that creation *ex nihilo* does not commit one either to the existence of a vacuum *ante mundum* or *extra mundum*. Prior to creation there was no empty space, as there would be according to Aristotle (and Gersonides); and even after creation there is no empty space surrounding the universe.[22] The dimensions of the universe are created simultaneously with the universe, and there is no need to speak of them as potentially existing prior to creation.[23] This too was the answer of Gersonides' Jewish critics, Crescas and Abravanel.[24] On the other hand, Aristotle's definition of the void is so worded that a vacuum is implied if creation is admitted; for if the void is defined as that which is empty of body but could be the place of a body, then it is natural to conclude that if the world was created *ex nihilo* a void preceded creation. And since the universe is finite, a vacuum on this hypothesis would still exist *extra mundum*; for, as Aristotle

---

21 Aristotle, *On the Heavens*, I, 9, especially, 279 a, 12–20.

22 Thomas, *Summa Theologiae*, I, q. 46, a. 1, ad 4; idem, *In De Caelo et Mundo*, Liber I, Lectio XXI; Liber III, Lectio VIII.

23 Thomas Aquinas, II *Sententiarum*, d. 1, q. 1, a. 5, ad 4.

24 Ḥasdai Crescas, *Or Adonai* III, 1, 5; Isaac Abravanel, *Mif'alot Elohim* VI, 3. Cf. I. Efros, *The Problem of Space in Jewish Medieval Philosophy* (New York, 1917), pp. 85–86. (The latter has been translated into Hebrew [Tel Aviv, 1965]. In the Hebrew version the pages are 62–63.)

has shown, there cannot be any other worlds. Indeed, Crescas is prepared to admit, at least as philosophically unobjectionable, the existence of a vacuum *extra mundum*, which confirms Gersonides' contention that creation *ex nihilo* is committed to the existence of a vacuum at least *extra mundum*.[25] Gersonides, following Aristotle and Averroes, maintains that although the universe is finite it is not surrounded by a vacuum, even though this is a notion that is difficult to understand. "Beyond" the universe there is just nothing.[26]

The notion of a vacuum *extra mundum* is philosophically related to the first of many objections that Gersonides considers against his version of the Platonic theory. Let us assume that the universe has been created from some primordial matter. Has this matter been thoroughly exhausted or is there a surplus?[27] Already in Plato and Aristotle we find the view that there is no other matter besides our universe.[28] Origen, however, raises the following objection to this view: if all the primordial matter has been incorporated into the universe, isn't this just chance? Moreover, isn't it just chance

[25] Some of the Latin Scholastics appreciated the force of this objection. William of Burleigh, for example, realized that creation *ex nihilo* seems to imply the existence of a vacuum *extra mundum*. Cf. A. Koyré, "Le vide et l'espace infini au XIV siècle," pp. 75 ff.

[26] Gersonides, *MH*, p. 386; H. Wolfson, *Crescas' Critique of Aristotle* (Cambridge, Mass., 1929), pp. 421–422. In his supercommentary on *Averroes' Middle Commentary on Aristotle's On the Heavens* Gersonides points out that the hypothesis of a plurality of universes, which for Aristotle implied a vaccum *extra mundum* and is false, does not imply a vacuum. For between these universes there is absolute privation, or non-being (העדר פשוט), which excludes the possibility of any other bodies. Nevertheless, Gersonides rejects this hypothesis on different grounds. As we shall see, Gersonides believes that our universe does not exhaust all the available matter, even though this universe is unique. But, as his main argument suggests, he wants to deny also the existence of a vacuum *extra mundum* on *any* hypothesis concerning the number of universes. Cf. Gersonides, *Supercommentary on Averroes' Middle Commentary on Aristotle's On the Heavens* (Parma manuscript, 805), klal 8; *MH*, pp. 378–380.

[27] Gersonides, *MH*, p. 368.

[28] Plato, *Timaeus*, 32 c; Aristotle, *On the Heavens*, 278 b, 4–9, 23 ff; Philo Judaeus, *De aeternitate mundi*, 21.

that the primordial stuff was of the right amount so that enough matter was available for the creation of the universe? But to introduce chance into the creative act is to diminish God's omnipotence. Hence, creation must have been *ex nihilo*.[29]

These questions vex Gersonides, and he is not sure how to answer them. He agrees with the view of Origen. whom he does not mention, that it is not proper to subject God's creative act to chance: it cannot be mere accident that the primordial stuff was just the right amount as our present universe. But instead of concluding that the universe was created *ex nihilo*, as did Origen, he cautiously suggests that there is some surplus matter.[30] As we shall see, however, this surplus matter does not constitute another universe, or cosmos, as Aristotle feared it would; but it exists. Accordingly, in creation *some* of the primordial matter was fashioned into a cosmos, whereas the rest of it remains distributed throughout space.[31]

The second major philosophical argument levelled against the defender of creation *ex nihilo* is the argument from possibility. Briefly stated, the argument is as follows: prior to creation the world was possible, i.e. it could have been created. Now this possibility, or potentiality for creation, must inhere in some substratum; but matter is the bearer of all potentialities. Hence, prior to creation there must have existed something serving as the material matrix

[29] Origen, "Fragment on Genesis," preserved in Eusebius' *Praeparatio Evangelica* VII, 335 a–b; *On First Principles*, trans. G. W. Butterworth (New York, 1966), Book II, chap. 1, pp. 79–80. Cf. Wolfson, "Plato's Pre-existent Matter in Patristic Philosophy," *The Classical Tradition*, ed. L. Wallach (Ithaca, 1966), p. 419.

[30] Gersonides, *MH*, p. 372.

[31] Ibid., pp. 367–368. Gersonides' discussion of Origen's problems is puzzling. Neither Plato, Aristotle nor Philo are aware of Origen's problem. Of the Jewish philosophers writing in Arabic or Hebrew only Saadia, as far as I know, mentions the general question of the surplus matter; but he does not raise the issue of chance. (Cf. Saadia Gaon, *Commentaire sur Sefer Yesira*, trans. M. Lambert [Paris, 1891], pp. 18–19.) Nor does Averroes raise this problem in his commentary on that passage in *On the Heavens* where Aristotle claims that all the available matter is contained in the universe. Averroes, *Long Commentary on De Caelo* (Venice, 1562), ad locum.

from which the universe was created and as the recipient of God's creative act.[32]

The notion of a bearer of possibilities sounds strange to modern philosophical ears. But consider the following examples. We can say that a block of marble is potentially a statue of Hercules; analogously, we can say that an embryo is potentially a child. When the statue has been made and the child is born, each potentiality has been actualized. In both cases the potentiality, or possibility, is true of some material substrate, e.g. marble or a fertilized ovum. In this sense the medievals said that the possibility *inheres* in the material substratum. For Aristotle, matter is in general the bearer of potentialities, especially in the context of change and generation.[33]

Now there were two main ways whereby the defenders of creation *ex nihilo* attempted to meet this argument. One could simply reject the notion of possibility: either the concept of possibility is eliminated entirely or it is interpreted in a "subjective" manner. In either case, however, there are no potentialities for which a material substratum is necessary.[34] Or, one could interpret the possibility in question as simply the power of God to create the wolrd. As Thomas Aquinas puts it, it is not logically repugnant to ascribe this power to God. Thomas' interpretation rests upon a distinction between a passive potentiality for becoming a particular thing (e.g. the potentiality of a block of marble becoming a statue of Hercules) and the logical possibility that an agent can perform some act.[35] It is potency

---

[32] Gersonides, *MH*, p. 365; Averroes, *Tahafut al-Tahafut*, paragraph 100 ff.; cf. Maimonides, *Guide* II, 14, the "fourth method;" Thomas Aquinas, *De potentia*, q. 3. a. 1, 2nd objection. In Maimonides and Thomas this argument is cited as an argument in behalf of the eternity of the universe; Gersonides uses it to show the absurdity of *ex nihilo* creation.

[33] Aristotle, *On Generation and Corruption*, I, 3; *Metaphysics*, 1032 a, 20. Indeed, this is why for Aristotle matter cannot be created. Cf. Aristotle, *On the Heavens*, 302 a, 1 ff; Gersonides, *Supercommentary on Averroes' Epitome of Aristotle's Physics*, Book I.

[34] This was al-Ghazzali's objection to the philosophers. Cf. Averroes' *Tahafut al-Tahafut*, paragraphs 93 and 103.

[35] Thomas Aquinas, *Summa Contra Gentiles* II, 37, paragraph 5; *De potentia*, q. 3, a. 1 ad 2.

in the latter sense that is relevant in this context, and this kind of potency does not require a material substratum.

These various solutions are not acceptable to Maimonides, Averroes and Gersonides. They all believe in "objective possibilities," i.e. to say that x is possible is to say something true about the universe, even though x is as of yet an unrealized event.[36] Nor will it do to ascribe the possibility only to the agent: for there are here two distinct situations. It is one thing to say that a particular agent can do x; it is another thing to say that x can be produced.[37] Now, according to Averroes and Gersonides, the latter sense is primary: an agent can do something if that act is possible. Indeed, Thomas himself admits that omnipotence is defined as the ability to do whatever is possible. Hence, the ability of an agent to do some act implies that the act is a genuine possibility, and this has to be determined independently of the agent. This means that the possibility of creation is a feature that cannot be attributed to the agent alone, but must be attributed to some substratum in which it inheres, i.e. matter. (To say that this matter is itself created is to open the door to an infinite regress. Accordingly, let us keep the door closed *ab initio*.) Indeed, if God's creative act emanates from His overflowing goodness and grace, as all creationists believe, then, Gersonides contends, there must be something that is the recipient of this divine influx. In short, making something necessarily involves three components: an agent, or maker, some material that is the subject of the act of making, and finally the product. The advocate of creation *ex nihilo* dispenses with the second of these factors; the critic of this doctrine argues that this factor is a necessary element in any kind of productive activity, including the creation of the universe.[38]

---

[36] Averroes, *Tahafut al-Tahafut*, First Discussion, paragraphs 94–107.

[37] Maimonides, *Guide* II, 14; Gersonides, *MH*, p. 373. Maimonides maintains, however, that in the context of creation there is no need for a substratum for the second possibility; since what is true for natural generation need not be true for generation that is non-natural.

[38] Gersonides, *MH*, p. 373.

Nevertheless, Gersonides' doctrine is not free from difficulties. In accepting the Platonic notion of an eternal primordial matter Gersonides must come to grips with Aristotle's criticism of one aspect of this doctrine — the problem of the disorderly motion in the "receptacle", or primordial matter.[39] Whatever the correct interpretation of this notion, Aristotle construed it as implying that the primitive elements were in irregular motion. He claims this notion is absurd. For if these elements are in motion, this motion would have to satisfy *some* set of dynamical laws; but lawfulness implies order and form, and hence a cosmos would already be in existence.[40] Gersonides accepts this argument. But whereas Aristotle uses it against Plato's entire theory of creation, Gersonides restricts it to Plato's notion of disorderly motion. For Gersonides the primordial matter is neither in motion nor at rest, since neither state applies to it. The primordial matter is without form (the primeval chaos), and as such not capable of either motion or rest; for only a body with form is capable of these states.[41] Moreover, since this matter is formless, it does not constitute a cosmos, and so our universe is unique.

In evading Aristotle's criticism of Plato's notion of disorderly motion Gersonides seems to violate, however, one of Aristotle's fundamental principles — there is no matter without form.[42] Gersonides claims that this principle is not universally true. Firstly, as a matter of empirical fact there is even now a kind of matter that is formless: the matter between the celestial spheres, which has no form whatever and hence possesses no natural motion.[43] Indeed, this matter is the pristine remnant of the original primordial matter,

[39] Plato, *Timaeus*, 30 a.

[40] Aristotle, *On the Heavens*, 300 b, 17 ff; Gersonides, *MH*, pp. 362–63; cf. G. Vlastos, "Creation in the *Timaeus*: Is It a Fiction?", *Studies in Plato's Metaphysics*, ed. R. E. Allen (New York, 1965), pp. 401–419.

[41] Gersonides, *MH*, p. 374, reply to the 4th objection.

[42] Aristotle, *Physics* I, 6–9; idem, *On Generation and Corruption*, I, 3–5; Gersonides, *MH*, p. 370, fifth objection.

[43] In the astronomical portions of *MH* Gersonides introduces this matter to account for certain astronomical phenomena. Gersonides, *MH*, pp. 193–194.

whose other portions have been fashioned into the heavenly and earthly spheres.[44]

Secondly, it does no follow from Aristotle's own system that matter must always be "informed." To be sure this rule is true for sublunar matter, where earthly changes consist in transformations amongst contrary states or from the privation of a particular form to the possession of this form. But, as Aristotle insists, the heavenly bodies do not exhibit this kind of change, since they are not subject to privations or contrary states. Indeed, the heavenly bodies consist of a different element, the aether.[45] This difference suggested to some of the medievals that the general form-matter distinction is not applicable to the heavens, which can be considered to be *simple*.[46] This point is reinforced when we consider that for Aristotle forms can exist without matter, i.e. the unmoved movers, or in the medieval framework the Separate Intelligences. Now if forms can exist separate from matter, why not the converse?[47] Indeed, if it is appreciated that the heavenly bodies are simple it could be said that they are just matter.[48] Accordingly, even in Aristotle's own system the form-matter analysis is not universally applicable.

One standard objection to the primordial matter remains to be disposed of. If this matter is alleged to be eternal, then it would be equal in rank to God; indeed, it would be a god since it is eternal.

---

[44] Ibid., p. 367, p. 425. According to Gersonides this matter is formless not only in the topological sense but also in the deeper structural sense of Aristotle's notion of εἶδος. Since this matter has no natural motion, or intrinsic activities, it has no form, or essence; for according to Aristotle form is neither identified with or most clearly manifested in the recurrent activities of a substance. Hence, this matter has no form. (*MH*, p. 193, pp. 315–316. Cf. P. Duhem, *Le système du monde*, 2nd ed. [Paris, 1954], V, 221–222.)

[45] Aristotle, *On the Heavens*, I, 1–3; *Metaphysics*, 1069 b, 25–27.

[46] Averroes, *Tahafut al-Tahafut*, Fourth Discussion, paragraph 271. Wolfson, *Crescas' Critique of Aristotle*, pp. 594 ff. Gersonides, *MH*, p. 193.

[47] Gersonides, *MH*, p. 374, reply to fifth objection. This argument seems to be based upon Maimonides' second proof for the existence of a first unmoved mover. (*Guide* II, 1; cf. also the remarks of Efodi and Shem Tob *ad locum*.)

[48] Averroes, op. cit., quoted in Wolfson, *Crescas' Critique*, p. 595.

But this is polytheism.[49] This objection, Gersonides replies, can be easily dissipated. The term "eternity" does not mean or imply divinity. Even for Aristotle this is so, since the world may be eternal, but it is not considered divine or a god. God is divine not because He is eternal, but because He is capable of performing certain kinds of acts, and in fact does perform them. The primordial matter doesn't act at all (since it has no form), and consequently represents the lowest degree of reality, despite its eternity. Indeed, for Gersonides, matter is a source of evil.[50]

II

The second Platonic thesis that Gersonides defends is the incorruptibility of the universe. Here his task will be especially difficult, since he will have to counter the claims not only of the orthodox who maintain that this thesis puts restrictions upon God's infinite power, but also the arguments of Aristotle who attempts to prove the absurdity of the notion of a generated but incorruptible universe.

According to Aristotle and Gersonides natural destruction or corruption is the result of certain kinds of change: either the acquisition of a new form (substantial change) or the assumption of new qualities (alteration). In each case we have a passage from opposite states, either from the privation to the possession of a form or the passage from one contrary quality to another.[51] The heavens, however, do not possess contrary capacities such that they are subject to qualitative change. Nor do they ever assume a different form from the one they currently possess; that is, they do not suffer substantial change. Indeed, the only kind of change experienced by the heavenly bodies is locomotion; but this kind of change does not imply any novelty in the structure of these bodies.[52] Thus,

---

[49] Saadia Gaon, *Book of Beliefs and Opinions*, p. 48; Gersonides, *MH*, p. 370, third objection.

[50] Gersonides, *MH*, p. 373. This too is a Platonic motif, which in the hands of Aristotle became a strict equation. (Cf. Aristotle, *Metaphysics*, 988 a, 14–15. H. Cherniss, *Aristotle's Criticism of Plato and the Academy*, pp. 95 ff.)

[51] Aristotle, *On Generation and Corruption* I, 7; Gersonides, *MH*, p. 359.

[52] Aristotle, *Physics*, 261 a, 23–24.

for Aristotle, the heavens are eternal.[53] To Gersonides this argument establishes the thesis that the heavenly bodies are indestructible, which, as we shall see, is a weaker claim than the eternity of the heavens. If the heavenly bodies are not subject to change other than locomotion, then they are at least indestructible. Now if the heavens are indestructible, so must be the universe *in toto*; for if the earth could be destroyed while the heavens remain intact, the latter will have no object upon which to bestow its benefits, and hence would be gratuitous, which has been shown to be false.[54]

Now it might be objected that if the universe cannot be destroyed, God's power is thereby limited. Divine omnipotence is not only manifested, according to this view, in creation *ex nihilo* but also in God's capacity to destroy the universe if He wishes. Indeed, although Maimonides suggested that the universe is everlasting, he did say that God, if He wishes, could destroy it.[55] For him the indestructibility of the universe is a doctrine taught by Scripture, i.e. God has revealed to us that He does not wish to destroy the universe.[56] Gersonides' claim is stronger: it asserts the impossibility of destruction. This impossibility, however, does not diminish God's power. For what is impossible cannot be done, and the destruction of the universe, like creation *ex nihilo*, is an impossibility.

Let us suppose that God could destroy the universe. The question can be raised, what *motive* could He have for doing so? If someone

[53] Aristotle, *On the Heavens*, 270 a, 13–35.

[54] In his proofs for creation Gersonides argues that the heavenly bodies have positive influences upon the earth. (Cf. Gersonides, *MH*, pp. 359, 310–316).

[55] Maimonides, *Guide* II, 27. Maimonides defends the possibility of its everlastingness by restricting Aristotle's theorem that whatever is generated is corruptible to natural phenomena and generation. The creation of the universe, however, is not a natural occurrence, or generation. Gersonides provides a different kind of argument, as we shall see.

[56] This is similar to Thomas' view, according to which the world is not subject to natural corruption but only to supernatural annihilation if God so wills. Annihilation, for Thomas, is the contrary of creation: both are supernatural events. (Cf. *Summa Theologiae*, I, q. 104, a. 3–4; idem, *Commentary on Aristotle's Physics*, trans. R. Blackwell, R. Spath and W. Thirkel [London, 1963], paragraphs 986, 1147.)

makes something he destroys it either because the product is un-satisfactory in some respect, or out of a fit of anger, or from vengeance. Neither of these possibilities can be attributed to God. Firstly, God created a world that is as perfect as it can be. Indeed, to say that he could destroy the world and make a better one is to diminish God's power. For why didn't He make the better one in the first place, especially since God is good?[57] In the second place, God is not subject to anger or revenge; hence He could not destroy the universe as the result of these passions. Thus, there is no reason that God *could* have for annihilating the universe. The impossibility of this event resides in its incompatibility with the notion of a perfect and good God.[58] In this respect, it sould be emphasized, Gersonides' claim is even stronger than that made by Plato, who makes the everlastingness of the universe dependent upon divine will.[59]

The second stage of Gersonides' argument, however, is more difficult. He must now show that Aristotle's cosmological theorem — whatever is generated is destructible, and conversely — is false.[60]

[57] Although Maimonides allows for the possibility of the destruction of the world, he expresses revulsion for the view that God created a succession of worlds, presumably because this doctrine opens the door for doubt upon God's perfection and wisdom. (Maimonides, *Guide* II, 30; Wolfson, "The Platonic, Aristotelian and Stoic Theories of Creation in Halevi and Maimonides," *Essays in Honor of the Very Rev. Dr. J. H. Hertz* [London, 1943], p. 436.) This suggests that Maimonides was moving towards Gersonides' position, according to which the destruction of the universe is inconsistent with God's nature. (Cf. Philo, *De aeternitate mundi*, 39–44.)

[58] Gersonides, *MH*, pp. 359–361. Gersonides' arguments anticipate Leibniz' principles of sufficient reason and perfection, although Leibniz himself did not consistently develop their implications; for Leibniz accepted Thomas' notion of the supernatural power of annihilation. Gersonides, however, correctly saw that if God acts for a reason and if He chooses to create our universe because it is the best possible world, then it would be inconsistent with the nature of God to ascribe to Him the power to destroy this universe. There is no restraint on God's power here; just the realization that God cannot do what is impossible. (Cf. Leibniz, *Monadology*, paragraphs 4–6; *Letters to Clarke*, V, paragraphs 73–76.)

[59] Plato, *Timaeus*, 41 a-b.

[60] Aristotle, *On the Heavens* I, 9–12; Gersonides, *MH*, pp. 403–415.

In the defense of this theorem Aristotle marshalls several arguments, of which two are especially crucial: 1) a metaphysical analysis showing that the concept of a generated but indestructible world is absurd; 2) a logical analysis of the terms "generated" and "destructible" showing that they are "coincident," or coextensive.

The first argument is presented in several different versions, all claiming to show the absurdity inherent in the Platonic conception of the universe. Now *ex hypothesi* such a universe exhibits two contrary capacities in so far as it is a created universe: the capacity for existence and the capacity for non-existence. Now, when a substance can sustain, or have, contrary properties, these capacities must be finite, or limited, in duration; otherwise these capacities would be simultaneously realized. Let us consider first the case when the universe *ex hypothesi* has not yet been created. Now in this situation we have the two contrary possibilities of existence and non-existence obtaining throughout all of infinite time prior to creation. But since in infinite time all possibilities are realized, the capacity for existence would be realized prior to creation, which is absurd.[61] Suppose further that the universe has been created. As a created substance it is obviously something that could have not existed, i.e. it has the capacity for non-existence. Now if it is alleged that the universe endures *ad infinitum*, this capacity for non-existence *will* be realized sooner or later, for capacities are future-directed. But this is absurd, since *ex hypothesi* the universe is indestructible.[62] Put differently, contingency is an *inherited* property: if the universe is created, i.e. contingent, there is always the possibility of its destruction.

In rebuttal Gersonides replies to the first case by pointing out that Aristotle's argument is an *ignoratio elenchi*. The theory of creation does not assert that creation takes place *in* time; rather, it asserts that time was created together with the universe. Thus, Aristotle's first objection is irrelevant. Indeed, all the stock arguments of this type are equally beside the point, e.g. why did God

---

61 Aristotle, *On the Heavens*, 283 a, 20–24.
62 Ibid., 283 a, 11–19; 283, b 13–14.

create the universe at this moment and not at another? Or, since no moment is more propitious than another, the universe has not been created at all but is eternal.[63] All these arguments assume what the theory of creation definitely denies: the ante-mundane existence of time.[64]

The second case, however, is more difficult to dispose of. It would seem that Aristotle is right in saying that contingency is an inherited property, that a substance which was once non-existent should be so again in the future. Nevertheless, Gersonides contends that this argument rests upon a confusion between the concepts of contingency and of corruption. A substance that can and cannot exist is, to be sure, a contingent substance. It would be obviously absurd to say that a substance of this sort is eternal, for, as Aristotle says, an eternal substance is a necessary existent, and conversely.[65] But an incorruptible substance is not necessarily an eternal substance; analogously, a contingent substance is not necessarily a corruptible substance. For Gersonides, then, these concepts are not identical, as they are for Aristotle. Indeed, Aristotle often uses these concepts interchangeably throughout his criticism of Plato, without realizing that these equations have to be defended.[66] Gersonides agrees that on the hypothesis of creation, the universe is contingent; but this means merely that it has been generated, that it was once non-existent. The "capacity for non-existence" has been realized, so to speak, in the non-eternity of the universe. The world's contingency is then expressed simply in the fact of its creation. But to admit this is not to imply, at least without further argument, that the world cannot endure infinitely *a parte post*. Indeed, this is the crucial

[63] Aristotle, *On the Heavens*, 283, a 11–14; Averroes, *Tahafut al-Tahafut*, First Discussion, passim; Leibniz, *Letters to S. Clarke*, III, paragraph 6, in *Selections*, ed. P. Wiener, p. 224.

[64] Gersonides, *MH*, p. 406 bottom. Cf. Thomas Aquinas, *Summa Contra Gentiles*, II, c. 35.

[65] Aristotle, *On Generation and Corruption*, 337 b, 35–338; a 4.

[66] Aristotle, *On the Heavens*, 279 b, 18 ff.; 282 a, 23 ff. It is only from 282 b, 10 ff. that Aristotle attempts to prove these equations. But, as we shall see, these proofs are guilty of a *petitio principii*.

point: whereas for Aristotle eternity and infinite duration are identical notions, for Gersonides they are different. The former is equivalent to infinite duration *a parte ante* and *a parte post*. To Gersonides, however, infinite duration is also a feature of a substance that is incorruptible, i.e. a substance that exists infinitely only *a parte post*. The contingency of the universe (i.e. the possibility of its non-existence) derives from the divine act of creation which, Gersonides stresses, is free. That is, to say that the world is contingent is to say that God was free in producing it. The universe is contingent not in the sense of being capable of destruction, as Aristotle maintains, but simply because it is not eternal. Eternity and contingency, then, are incompatible features of a substance, and Aristotle is right in saying that it is impossible for a contingent substance to be eternal; but this is not the issue. What is in question is the possibility of a generated and *incorruptible* substance, which is, to be sure, contingent. Aristotle's arguments, however, have so far not established its impossibility.[67]

Aristotle's second major argument against the possibility of a generated but incorruptible world consists in a linguistic analysis of the relevant concepts.[68] Let us consider the terms "always existing" (i.e. eternal) and "never existing" to be ontological extremes, or contraries. The contradictory of the former is "that which is capable of not existing at some time," whereas the contradictory of the latter is "that which can exist at some time." Now if the latter two predicates are (non-simultaneously) applicable to something, then that thing will have the capacities of existence and non-existence, i.e. contingency, and hence will be the intermediate entity

[67] Gersonides, *MH*, pp. 405–408. The notion of a generated but incorruptible universe differs, then, from the notion of an eternal but contingent universe that Thomas alleges to be a possible, i.e. non-self-contradictory, concept. (Thomas Aquinas, *Summa Theologia*, I, q. 46, a. 2, ad 1, where Augustine is quoted as reporting this view.) This was the view of Avicenna who maintained that the universe is contingent *per se* but eternal *ab alio*, i.e. through its eternal cause, God. (Wolfson, *Crescas' Critique*, pp. 680–684.) Averroes rejected this notion of Avicenna, and as far as I can tell, so did Gersonides. (*MH*, pp. 312–313.)

[68] Aristotle, *On the Heavens*, 281 b, 33–282 a, 13; 282 b, 13–283, a 3.

between that which always exists and that which never exists.[69] Aristotle then identifies this intermediate entity, or term, as the generable *and* the destructible.[70] From this identification he then concludes that "generable" and "corruptible" are convertible predicates.[71]

Gersonides maintains that this argument is not valid. Aristotle is wrong in identifying the intermediate term with the generable and the destructible. For *any* generated substance is something that can and cannot exist (non-simultaneously), and, therefore is, contingent. Whether this substance is destructible or indestructible is irrelevant. And to assume that every contingent is corruptible is to beg the question, as we have already seen. Consequently, Gersonides' hypothesis of a generated but indestructible universe describes a world that is also intermediate between a world that is eternal and a world that cannot exist, just as much as the notion of a generated and destructible universe. Gersonides suggests that Aristotle should have begun his analysis with the terms "existence" and "non-existence", which are the most general and basic ontological categories. Then he would have seen that under the former notion we have the sub-classes of eternal and of contingent beings; and of the latter category the generated and incorruptible is an instance, just as much as the generated and corruptible.[72]

---

[69] Ibid., 281 b, 32–282 a, 13.   [70] Ibid., 282 b, 10–12.

[71] Ibid., 282 b, 9–10.

[72] Gersonides, *MH*, pp. 410–411. Aristotle's other proofs for the convertibility of "generable" and "corruptible" are also invalid. Either they presuppose the previous argument, which has been shown to be invalid, or are invalid on other grounds. Consider, for example, this indirect proof: if it is premised that anything generable or destructible is contingent, Aristotle concludes that whatever is ungenerated or indestructible is eternal, from which it could be inferred that "generable" and "destructible" are convertible. (*On the Heavens*, 282 a, 23–38.) This argument, however, is invalid, since it presupposes that the *only* intermediate term between "eternally existing" and "never existing" is "generated and destructible." (*MH*, p. 410.) Nor is Aristotle's direct proof (*On the Heavens*, 282 b, 9–24) any more successful, since in addition to the premise that "the generable and the destructible" is *the* intermediate ontological predicate, it introduces the additional premise that the contingent, e.g. the generated, must be finite in duration, which is an obvious *petitio principii*.

If we now try to form a general picture of Gersonides' cosmology we see that it asserts the existence of a universe that endures infinitely in one direction only, i.e. *a parte post*. But for Aristotle the notion of a "one-sided" infinite is absurd, and at this point in this dialectic an argument crops up that gives Gersonides considerable difficulty. It would seem that a magnitude, e.g. a length, that is infinite in one direction, i.e. at one of its termini, is "smaller" than, or a part of, a magnitude that is infinite in both directions. But for most medievals, and most likely for Aristotle too, infinite magnitudes are all equal. Hence, an infinite part of an infinite whole would qua infinite be equal to the whole; however, this is absurd, since according to common sense the whole is greater than any of its parts. Consequently, the notion of a universe that endures infinitely *a parte post* only is absurd.[73]

This argument can be spatially represented as follows: Let line A represent the duration of a universe that is temporally infinite in both directions, i.e. Aristotle's conception of an eternally existing universe; let line X represent the duration of a universe that is temporally infinite in one direction only, *a parte post*.

A

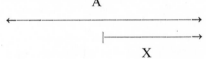

X

The argument contends that since X is shorter than A it is a part of A. But *ex hypothesi* X is infinite and qua infinite it is equal to A. Thus, the part is equal to the whole, which is absurd.

To dissipate the force of this objection Gersonides levels three arguments against it. Firstly, the objection is equally valid against the eternity hypothesis. Consider any instant on A; it demarcates

---

[73] Gersonides, *MH*, pp. 405–407. This argument does not appear explicitly in Aristotle, although the denial of a one-sided infinite is stated in *On the Heavens* 283 a, 10–11. For a discussion of the principle that infinites must be equal see H. Wolfson, *The Philosophy of Spinoza* (New York, 1958), I, 286–291; S. Feldman, "Gersonides' Proofs for Creation of the Universe," *PAAJR*, XXXV (1967), 131–132; N. Rescher and H. Khatchadourian, "Al Kindi's Epistle on the Finitude of the Universe," *Isis*, 1965, pp. 426–433.

two segments each infinite but "smaller" than the whole. That is, the present delineates two parts of time, each infinite, yet as parts presumably smaller than the whole of time. Accordingly, whatever conviction the argument carries is equally pertinent to Aristotle's own theory. Secondly, although from a strict numerical, or quantitative, point of view X is no greater than A, it is possible to consider X "smaller" in so far as it is terminated at one side. In so far as X has a terminus it is a "part" of A, although the term "part" has to be construed in a loose sense.[74]

Finally, Aristotle's argument is again an example of an *ignoratio elenchi*: it assumes that time is infinite *a parte ante* as well as *a parte post*, and that, for the Platonist, the universe exists in only one part of this infinite dimension. But this is not the case. It is not alleged that the universe was created in time, which is infinite in the past and then continues *ad infinitum*. Rather, it is claimed that time had a beginning: there is no infinite time *a parte ante*. Aristotle's argument is, therefore, irrelevant.[75]

[74] Gersonides, *MH*, p. 406; Wolfson, *Crescas' Critique*, pp. 423–424. Although Cantor's theory of transfinite numbers has opened up to us diverse realms of infinite numbers, it is possible to employ the modern theory as a means to elucidate Gersonides' point. The fundamental notion here is that of an infinite set A set K is infinite if all the members of a proper sub-set of K can be matched one-to-one with all the members of K. Accordingly, the set of integers N is infinite since a proper sub-set of N, the series of positive integers, can be matched one-to-one with all the members of N. In this sense, the set of positive integers is as large as the set of integers, although the latter contains the former. But in another sense N is "larger," since it also contains the set of negative integers, which is also infinite; hence N encompasses two sub-sets that are each infinite. Although the terms "larger" and "smaller" are mathematically inappropriate here, one might say that N is "richer", or more inclusive, than any of its sub-sets. To the degree that one of the sub-sets is impoverished it is thereby a "part" of the whole. In our particular case this would mean that just as the set of positive integers does not exhaust all of the set of integers, so too X, infinite time *a parte post*, doesn't exhaust all of A, and thus can be considered as a "part" of A.

[75] Gersonides, *MH*, p. 406, bottom. Gersonides refutes the thesis of infinite past time in an earlier stage of his argument against Aristotle's theory. Cf. chapter 11 of *MH*, Book VI, part 1. (Cf. Feldman, "Gersonides' Proofs for Creation of the Universe," pp. 125–137.)

CONCLUSION

Gersonides' cosmogony turns out to be one of the more unique and and bold theories of creation in the Middle Ages. He defends the doctrine of the primordial matter vigorously, which brings him into conflict not only with his more traditional co-religionists for whom creation *ex nihilo* had become a dogma, but also with Aristotle for whom Plato's cosmology was utterly defective. In his criticism of the traditional dogma of creation *ex nihilo* Gersonides forges out a path that Spinoza was to pursue even farther. For both thinkers the notion of creation *ex nihilo* is too radical a break in nature. Similarly, in advocating the Platonic thesis of the indestructibility of the universe Gersonides defends it in a strong form going far beyond the more modest statements of Maimonides or even Plato. Again, Gersonides points in the direction of Spinoza, for whom also the destructibility of the universe is utterly impossible. Spinoza took the steps that Gersonides was unwilling to take — the complete denial of creation and the elimination of genuine contingency in nature. But in his version of Plato's cosmology Gersonides approaches and prepares the way for Spinoza's radical break with the medieval world.

GARCIA DE ORTA — A MILITANT MARRANO IN PORTUGUESE-INDIA IN THE 16TH CENTURY

WALTER J. FISCHEL

A. *The Exodus of Portuguese and Spanish Jews to India*

THE HISTORY OF THE JEWS IN INDIA, at least from the 16th century on, can be properly appraised only if it is recognized that their fate and destiny, their rise, growth and decline, were conditioned by the steady flow towards India of waves of immigrants from the European and Asiatic diaspora at various periods in history.

This correlation and interdependence of the Jewish scene in India with events within the Jewish diaspora are most glaringly illustrated in the following study which aims at investigating the exodus of Jews from Portugal and Spain to India in its relevance to the rise of Jewish settlements in territories under Portuguese rule in India and adjacent territories in Asia from the early 16th century on.

It is an established fact that some of these refugees from Spain and Portugal, New-Christians, Marranos, Judaisers or Jews, who had reached, towards the end of the 15th and the early part of the 16th century, the region of the Eastern Mediterranean and the European and Asiatic provinces of the Ottoman Empire, moved even further East and South, into the area between the Persian Gulf and the Arabian Sea and between the Indian Ocean and the Archipelago and the Straits of Malacca.

The trend of this migratory movement of Spanish and Portuguese refugees to India and beyond at the beginning of the 16th century is well attested in Portuguese sources. When the Portuguese captain Pedro Alvares Cabral captured a ship near Calicut in 1501, he found among her passengers "a Jewess of Seville who told him that she had fled from Spain, by reason of the Inquisition, into

Barbary and Alexandria of Egypt; and then to Cairo and in(to) India...." Since the Captain refused to put this Jewess ashore after a few days she cast herself into the sea and was drowned.[1]

There were captured near Mount d'Ely on a ship bound for Calicut in 1510, two Castilian Jews who had left Spain in order to settle in India. They were interviewed by Affonso d'Albuquerque who, having been impressed by their linguistic abilities and their knowledge of political and economic aspects of India and Asia, took them into his service and employed them as interpreters, agents, and confidential advisors, compelling them, of course, to become Christians. They became known as Alexander d'Atayde and Francis d'Albuquerque and played a prominent part in the exploration and expansion of the Portuguese power in Asia.[2]

The Portuguese historian, G. Correa,[3] observed in 1510 that "there are many Spanish Jews along the Indian Ocean" (Judeu hispani in mari indica iam); and beyond the Indian Ocean, in the major strategic and commercial key positions in Portuguese-Asia, especially in Malacca and Ormuz an ever-increasing number of Portuguese and Spanish refugees seem to have been absorbed.

Ormuz, that island situated at the entry and exit of the trade route through the Persian Gulf, conquered by the Portuguese in 1514, attracted a considerable number of Spanish and Portuguese Jews. Gaspar Barzaeus, who came as a Jesuit missionary to Ormuz in 1549, encountered there a large Jewish settlement and noticed "many Jews from Castille"[4] who had arrived from Venice, Constantinople, Alexandria or Jerusalem. It is significant that he deliver-

---

[1] See "Carta de El Rei D. Manuel," in *Documentos sobre os Portugueses em Mocambique e na Africa Central* (1497–1840) (Lisbon, 1962), I, 58–59; also reported in other sources.

[2] Gaspar Correa, *Lendas da India*, ed. L. Felner (Lisbon, 1860–1922), III, 252; IV, 139ff.; about their activities in the service of the Portuguese cause, see also *The Commentaries of Affonso d'Albuquerque*, trans. and ed. W. Birch (London, 1877), II, 228–230.

[3] Correa, *Lendas*, II, 134.

[4] For further details and bibliography see the present writer's study in *JQR*, n.s., XL (1950), 379–394.

ed his famous "Trinity Sermon" in the Ormuz synagogue in the Portuguese language.[5]

Malacca, conquered by the Portuguese in 1511, commanding the narrow straits between the Malayan Peninsula and Sumatra, a central port on the trade routes to South Asia, also emerged at this juncture as the seat of a Jewish settlement. Francisco Xavier, the Jesuit missionary who visited Malacca at various times between 1544 and 1548, met there a well-established Jewish community with a synagogue and rabbis of Spanish and Portuguese origin.[6]

Many of the Jewish immigrants in Ormuz or Malacca used their new haven, however, only as a temporary station, as a stepping-stone for their ultimate goal, namely the mainland of India.

The presence of Portuguese Jews on the mainland of India is attested by the fact that the early Portuguese Governors and Vice-roys of India had no difficulties in finding on Indian soil suitable and qualified Jews of Portuguese and Spanish origin whom they could employ as agents, informers, guides, interpreters and letter carriers and whom they did entrust with delicate diplomatic assignments to the King of Portugal.[7]

The case of the Portuguese Marrano merchant and diplomat, Alvaro Mendes, later known as Don Solomon b. Yaish, who entered the service of the Hindu ruler of Golconda (between 1530–1555) and amassed a great fortune by farming the diamond mines in this territory, can serve as a further illustration of the dispersion of Portuguese Jews in India.[8]

[5] For the Portuguese text of this "Trinity Sermon" see G. Schurhammer, in *Archivum Historicum Societatis Iesu* (Rome, 1933), pp. 291–309, and again in his *Orientalia* (Rome, 1963), pp. 413–435.

[6] About Xavier's repeated visits to Malacca see G. Schurhammer, *Franz Xavier, Sein Leben und Seine Zeit* (Freiburg, 1955), II, 599–647; especially pp. 618 ff. (Subsequently quoted as *F.X.*)

[7] The Portuguese and Jesuit sources refer to many Jewish agents in India in the service of the Governors of Goa, Nuno da Cunha (1529–38) and Martim Affonso de Sousa (1542–45). Frequently mentioned is "the Jew Manasse;" see G. Correa, *Lendas*, IV, 212–214; 404–407; Schurhammer, *F.X.*, I, 671–675; II, 491.

[8] On this merchant-adventurer, see L. Wolf, "Jews in Elizabethan England," *Transaction of the Jewish Historical Society of England*, XI (1927), 1–91; also

Some of the Portuguese and Spanish refugees settled even in the cities of Northern India, which at this juncture prospered and flourished under the enlightened and tolerant rule of the Moghul Emperor Akbar the Great (1542–1605).[9] The bulk of the Portuguese and Spanish refugees, however, seem to have moved to the West Coast of India, to Diu,[10] Chaul,[11] Ahmadnagar,[12] Cochin,[13] and, above all, to Goa[14], situated, about 250 miles South of Bombay.

B. *The Move towards Goa*

The earliest recorded Jewish connection with Goa was established, however, before the coming of the Portuguese through that Jewish agent of Polish parentage, known in history as Gaspar da Gama, or Gaspar of the Indies, who, in the service of the Muslim ruler of Goa, Yusuf Adil Shah of the Bijapur dynasty, was commissioned by his master, in his capacity as a Shahbandar, to spy on the fleet of Vasco da Gama when it was laying at anchor in September 1498 at the Anjediva Island, opposite Goa. When Gaspar da Gama's intentions became known, as a result of his confession obtained under torture by Vasco da Gama and his brother Paul, he was for-

---

F. Heymann, *Der Chevalier von Geldern* (Amsterdam, 1937), pp. 58 ff., 85 ff.; *Encyclopedia Judaica*, I, 226 ff.

[9] About Jews and Judaism at the court of the Moghul Emperors, see W. J. Fischel, in *PAAJR*, XVIII, (1949), 137–177.

[10] About Isaac of Cairo, alias Jorge Pinto, one of the most prominent Jewish agents of Portuguese origin, whose activities are connected with Diu, see below, p. 431 [25].

[11] See G. M. Moraes, *A History of Christianity in India* (Bombay, 1964), pp. 162–165; Gerson da Cunha, *Notes on the History and Antiquities of Chaul and Bassein* (Bombay, 1876), pp. 8–9.

[12] Ahmadnagar, see below, p. 429 [23].

[13] According to the *Notisias dos Judeos de Cochim* by Mosseh Pereyra de Paiva (Amsterdam, 1687), there arrived in Cochin already at the beginning of the 16th century (1512), the first members of the Castiel family from Spain, who played later a leading role as Mudaliars in the Cochin community.

[14] For the general background, see J. N. de Fonseca, *An Historical and Archaeological Sketch of the City of Goa* (Bombay, 1878); D. L. Cottineau de Kloguen, *An Historical Sketch of Goa* (Madras, 1831; republ. Bombay, 1922); B. Penrose, *Goa — Queen of the East* (in Portuguese and English) (Lisbon, 1960).

cibly taken to Portugal, converted to Christianity and then served the Portuguese Crown in a variety of functions until about 1510.[15]

However, after the conquest by the Portuguese in 1510, Goa became the capital of Portuguese Asia and the residence of the Portuguese Viceroys, and attracted many Portuguese and Spanish Jews, New-Christians or Marranos, who hoped to find there a life of security and tranquillity.[16]

The size of the Jewish exodus from Portugal and Spain to Goa in the early decades of the 16th century must have assumed considerable proportions, as can be gauged by the reaction which their presence evoked in Portuguese secular and ecclesiastical circles. In the missionary literature of that time, in the correspondence of the Provincial and Municipal Councils of Goa with the Portuguese authorities in Lisbon, and in other sources, the numerical strength of the New-Christians in Goa has become a major issue. Bitter complaints were sent to the Portuguese authorities about those "homens de Nação" or "gente da Nação" or "gente da Nação hebréa" — by which "Christãos Novos", New-Christians of Jewish descent are meant — and severe restrictions against them were requested.[17] Already in 1519 a decree by the Goanese authorities was issued barring New Christians from holding any municipal office in Goa or any other official appointment in the various Portuguese-

[15] For details see F. Huemmerich, *Diario da Viagem da Vasco da Gama* (Porto, 1945), II, 242–306; and W. J. Fischel, *The Jews in India, Their Contributions to the Economic and Political Life* (Jerusalem, 1960), pp. 15–30.

[16] About the presence of Portuguese and Spanish Jews in Goa and other parts of Portuguese-Asia see the extremely important collection of documents in G. Schurhammer, *Die Zeitgenoessischen Quellen zur Geschichte Portugiesisch-Asiens und seiner Nachbarlaender zur Zeit des HL Franz Xavier* (1538–1552) (Leipzig, 1932; Rome, 1962); *Documenta Indica*, ed. J. Wicki, Vols. I–XI (1540–1580) (Rome, 1948–1970); *Documentação para a História das Missões do Padroado Portugues do Oriente*, ed. A. da Silva Rego, 12 vols. (Lisbon, 1947–1958).

[17] See *Archivo Portugez-Oriental* (1595–1609), ed. J. H. de Cunha Rivara (New Goa, 1876); *Documentos Remettidos da India*, vol. I (Lisboa, 1880); vol. II (Lisboa, 1884), with many references to these terms; and C. R. Boxer, *Portuguese Society in the Tropics* (Madison and Milwaukee, 1965), with an important chapter on the municipal council of Goa (camera de Goa), pp. 12–41.

controlled fortresses in Asia, except with the authorization of the King.

In 1527, in a letter from Goa to the King of Portugal, strong opposition was voiced to the concentration of the local trade and commerce in the hands of New-Christians, to their big stores in the "Rua Directa"[18] in Goa, and their detestable practices in buying up the salary claims of the poor soldiers for exhorbitant prices, as well as to their dealings with Turks and Arabs, all to the disadvantage of the Christian-Portuguese population.[19]

Similar complaints against the New-Christians and their practices continued to be heard all through the early decades of the 16th century. In a report to the Portuguese King in 1540, a leading clergyman listed as the three factors which were apt to bring ruin to the Portuguese rule in India: the delay in payment to the soldiers, the low moral practices of the Portuguese who marry Indian women though they have wives at home, and the presence of so many New-Christians in Goa. He informed the King about the deplorable situation, that India was full of New-Christians who stuck together very closely and that the influx of White Jews (judeu albi) from Turkey and Persia to Cochin and other places was detrimental to the interests of the Crown.

While the opposition against New-Christians and Judaisers within the Portuguese possessions was based at the beginning mainly on economic grounds, their numerical strength, their unfair competition, their monopolistic practices, and their solidarity amongst themselves, there soon entered a new element into this discussion, namely the religious aspect.

Mention should be made that the Portuguese came to India not only as conquerors and merchants in search of spices but also as "bearers of the Cross" in search of Christians. No sooner was the civil authority of the Portuguese firmly established when the ecclesiastical authorities tried to assert their influence in India. Francis-

---

[18] About this major street, see the map and illustration in Penrose, *Goa*, pp. 67–75; and Schurhammer, *F.X.*, II, 190–191.

[19] For these and the following references, see the material in G. Schurhammer, *F.X.*, II, 157, 190–91 ff.

cans, Augustines, Dominicans and later Jesuits began to propagate the "True Faith" among the multitudes of Heathens and Moors. Among the objects of this missionary zeal were not only the native Hindu population, but also the relatively small and scattered settlements of Jews in the Portuguese possessions of Ormuz, Malacca, Goa, Cochin and elsewhere.

It was observed that "certain rich New-Christians who lived in Goa were carrying on the Judaic ceremonies scandalously and with the likes of whom India was becoming contaminated" and that many of them adhered secretly to the "ley de Moise" and were thus "prejudicial to our faith".

Alarmed by this state of affairs, the ecclesiastical authorities in Goa advocated the transfer of the Inquisition, which had been established in Lisbon in 1536,[20] to the transoceanic Portuguese possessions in India. Francisco Xavier, the foremost apostle and organizer of the Jesuit activities in Asia, was one of the earliest who, confronted with the heresy and impiety of these New-Christians whom he had met in Malacca, Goa, and elsewhere, had advocated the establishment of the Indian Inquisition. In various letters from Malacca from 1545 on to King João III he stated that "in order that those who live in Goa may be good Christians it is necessary that your Majesty send the Holy Inquisition thither [to India] because there are many who live according to the Mosaic Law... without any fear of God or shame before the world."[21]

The Vicar-General in Goa, Miguel Vaz Coutinho, a fanatical enemy of the New-Christians, wrote in 1549 that "there are so many New-Christians here who live according to the Mosaic reli-

---

[20] The religious situation in Portugal at the end of the 15th and beginning of the 16th centuries is portrayed in all its details by Schurhammer, *F.X.*, I, 597–627; on the Portuguese Inquisition in Lisboa, see also A. Herculano, *Historia da Origem, Establecimento da Inquisição em Portugal*, ed. David Lopez, 3 vols. (Lisbon, 1896–97), and Cecil Roth, *History of the Marranos* (New York, 1960).

[21] For the text of Xavier's letter from Malacca to João II, King of Portugal, of May 16, 1545, see Silva da Rego, *Documentação*, III, 351; G. Schurhammer, *F.X.*, II, 734; also Sebastiam Gonçalves, *Primeira Parte da Historia dos Religiosos da Companhia de Jesus*, ed. J. Wicki (Coimbra, 1962), III, 154–155.

gion without fear of God or shame before the world... and there are so many of them scattered all over our fortresses that we need the Holy Inquisition."

While these calls for the Inquisition remained unheeded by the Pope for the time being, the first auto da fé in Goa had already taken place even before the formal establishment of the Inquisition. Its first victim was a baccalaureus of medicine by the name of Jeronimo Diaz who, accused by the Bishop D. João Affonso de Albuquerque in 1543, of secret adherence to the Jewish religion, was found guilty by an Ecclesiastical Court and sentenced to be burned at the stake. Having confessed his guilt, the sentence of Jeronimo Diaz was, however, mitigated by his first being strangled.[22]

The intensity of the religious fanaticism and the persistent demand of the Goanese ecclesiastical authorities[23] over a period of almost two decades led finally, in 1560, to the establishment of the Inquisition in Goa,[24] which lasted, except for a provisional suspension from 1774–1778, for almost 250 years until its final liquidation in 1812.

C. *Garcia de Orta in Goa and His Work*

The Acts of the Inquisition of Goa, as far as they have been preserved, have not yet been systematically subjected to a thorough

---

[22] See Correa, *Lendas*, IV, 292–294; Lucio d'Azavedo, *Historia dos Christãos-Novos Portugueses* (Lisbon, 1921), pp. 98–99; and the sources mentioned in note 16.

[23] Goa became a Metropolitan See in 1557 and in 1559 Goa was constituted a bishopry; in 1560 D. João de Albuquerque was made Primate of all the Indies and the first Inquisitor arrived in Goa.

[24] About the establishment of the Goanese Inquisition in 1560 and its activities, see Alessandro Valignano, *Historia del Principio y Progresso de la Compañia de Jesus en las Indias Orientales* (1542–1564), ed. J. Wicki (Roma, 1944); A. Baião, *A Inquisiçao de Goa* (1569–1630), vol. I (Lisboa, 1949), vol. II (Coimbra, 1930); for the latest survey of the Goa Inquisition, see A. K. Priolkar, *The Goa Inquisition, Being a Quartercentenary Commemoration Study of the Inquisition in India* (Bombay, 1961) which contains, in part 2, Claude Dellon's account of the Inquisition in Goa.

investigation in their relevance to the Marrano colony in Portuguese India.[25] Yet what has become accessible has revealed the presence of a large number of New-Christians, Marranos, or Judaisers who had moved from Portugal and Spain to India in the early part of the 16th century.

Among the many prominent individuals who lived in Goa under the shadow of the Inquisition, none arrests our attention more than Garcia de Orta,[26] that Portuguese physician and scientist of Marrano parentage who was destined to make an indelible impression on the world of scholarship during his 34 years of residence in Portuguese India (1534–1568).

The parents of Garcia de Orta, Fernão (Isaac) de Orta and Leonor Gomez, were Spanish Jews who had fled Spain in the wake of the expulsion of the Jews in 1492 and had taken refuge in Castelo de Vide in Portugal, a frontier town. When King Manuel I, in 1497, had ordered the mass conversion of all his Jewish subjects, they too became New-Christians. They had four children: three daughters — Violante, Catarina (b. 1513) and Isabel — and one son, Garcia de Orta, born around 1500 in Castelo de Vida. He studied medicine at the Universities of Salamanca and Alcala and, after having practiced medicine in his home town for some time, went to Lisbon where he occupied a University position teaching Logic and Natural Philosophy for about eight years.[27]

When Garcia de Orta was invited, in 1534, by his illustrious friend

---

[25] For a rather fragmentary listing of the auto da fé's in Lisbon and in Goa in which Jews were involved see E. N. Adler, "Auto da Fe and Jew," *JQR*, XV (1908), 413–439; also F. D. Mocatta, *The Jews of Spain and Portugal and the Inquisition* (London, 1877).

[26] The documents as well as the literature spell his name in various forms, sometimes Garcia da Orta, Garcia de Orta, Garcia Dorta, or even Garcia Horta.

[27] The condensed biographical sketch is based on: Conde de Ficalho, *Garcia da Orta e O Seu Tempo* (Lisboa, 1886); Augusta da Silva Carvalho, "Garcia d'Orta," *Revista de Universidade de Coimbra*, XII (1934), 61–246; Harry Friedenwald, "The Medical Pioneers in the East Indies", in *The Jews and Medicine*, Essays, (Baltimore, 1944), vol. II, pp. 430–447; C. R. Boxer, *Two Pioneers of Tropical Medicine: Garcia d'Orta and Nicolas Monardes* (London, 1963).

Martim Affonso de Sousa, the newly-appointed Captain-Major of the Indian Ocean, to accompany him as his personal physician, he accepted this offer and left for India on March 12, 1534, never to return to Europe again.

Martim Affonso de Sousa, together with Garcia de Orta, arrived in Goa in September, 1534, at the time of the Governorship of Nuno da Cunha, and for the next four years Garcia traveled with his "amigo constande" to Cambay, Bassaim, Chaul, Salsette, Diu, Cochin, Ceylon and participated in all the various expeditions and campaigns to which de Sousa had been assigned at this juncture.

The "Wander Years" of Garcia de Orta came to an end when his friend de Sousa was called back to Lisbon in 1538. Garcia de Orta decided, however, to stay in India and he made Goa his new residence, spending almost thirty years of his life there until his death in 1568, interrupted only by frequent visits to Bombay and Ahmadnagar.[28]

In 1542 he married his cousin Brianda de Solis, the daughter of Henriques de Solis,[29] a Jew by birth, a wealthy and influential Portuguese merchant who came to India in his capacity as "ship writer" appointed by the Portuguese King, together with his daughter Brianda. Garcia de Orta had two daughters by this marriage. A few years later, in 1548, Garcia de Orta brought his mother, Leonor Gomez, and two of his sisters, Isabel and Catarina, and their respective husbands, from Lisbon, where they had experienced great hardship and, having been exposed to denunciations, were temporarily imprisoned by the Lisbon Inquisition. They established

---

[28] It should be mentioned that prior to Garcia de Orta's settling in Goa, other members of his wider family had already moved to India or to Portuguese-controlled territories and achieved distinction and standing in Socotora, Ormuz, Dabul etc.; see Carvalho, "Garcia d'Orta," pp. 80–81.

[29] The families of the de Solis and Fernandez Lopez de Orta, relatives of Garcia de Orta, played in subsequent decades a leading role in the affairs of India; see P. S. S. Pissurlencar, *Assentos do Conselho do Estado da India*, 1618–1750, 5 vols. (Bastora-Goa, 1953–57); and *O Chronista de Tissuary*, ed. J. H. da Cunha Rivara (1866), I, 92 ff.; Carvalho, "Garcia d'Orta," pp. 134–139; 220–223.

residence in Goa, in the vicinity of Garcia de Orta's home in Rua dos Namorados.[30]

During his long sojourn in Goa, Garcia de Orta practiced medicine, working in the Royal Hospital of Goa, but devoting his free time to research and scholarship. He did not occupy an official position in the city, though he was called at various occasions to serve as physician to the Viceroys.[31] His professional help was also sought by many of the leading Christian dignitaries and notables in Goa and he had free entry to the highest circles of the ecclesiastical and secular society with many of whom he became friendly.

His fame as a physician spread soon beyond the borders of Portuguese Goa, and it was in particular the Muslim ruler Burhan ad-Din Nizam al-Mulk (1508–1553), of Ahmadnagar who invited Garcia de Orta at various occasions to his court.[32]

In recognition of his services as a physician to the Portuguese Viceroys and Christian dignitaries, the Portuguese Viceroy João de Castro (1545–48) bestowed upon him, probably in 1548, the island of Bombay, then a small, insignificant, fishing village, and made him Lord of the Manor of Bombay, probably for the years 1548 to 1554. As the new Lord of the Manor of the island, it was incumbent upon Garcia de Orta to pay a certain quit rent to the government during the period of his ownership, in order to improve the land.[33]

Garcia de Orta must have been very proud of this property in Bombay, explicitly referring to Bombay (then known as Bombaim

---

30 This street was not far from what became later known as Casa da Inquisicão; G. Schurhammer, *F.X.*, II, 157; Carvalho, "Garcia d'Orta," p. 89.

31 Though he was never the official court physician of the Viceroy, the sources sometimes refer to him as "medico do rei or vicerei da India"; see F. Schurhammer, *F.X.*, II, 197.

32 About Ahmadnagar see below, p. 429 [23].

33 On Bombay under Portuguese rule see J. Gerson da Cunha, "The Origin of Bombay," *Journal of the Royal Asiatic Society, Bombay Branch.* Extra number, XX (1902), 368; A. X. Soares, "Garcia d'Orta, a Little Known Owner of Bombay", *Journal of the Royal Asiatic Society, Bombay Branch,*" XXVI (1921–22), 195–229; and Julio Gonçalves, "Garcia de Orta e a Sua Illa de Bombaim," *Boletim de Geografia de Lisboa,* ser. 81, nos. 7–12 (1963), 203–212.

or Mombaym) as "the land and island which the King our Lord made me a grant of, paying a quit rent." He let the tenant of his possession in Bombay, Sinão Toscana, appear in Goa with a basketful of mangoes, "from a mango tree in that my island which gives two crops, one at this time and one at the end of May." He mentions Bombay again as "This, my island."[34]

Garcia de Orta visited this island frequently whenever his duties in Goa allowed him to travel and built on his leased property in Bombay a splendid house near the spot where to-day the garden of the Town Hall of Bombay Castle stands, with a museum of art objects, a garden with a botanical collection, and a large library.[35]

It was there as well as in his house and garden with many medicinal herbs in Goa that the foundation was laid for that great work of his *Coloquios dos simples e drogas he cousas mediçinais da India*, which established his fame and made him "the first European writer on tropical medicine and a pioneer in pharmacology."

In the form of a dialogue between himself and a certain fictitious Dr. Ruano, the author gave a careful description, in 57 "Coloquios," or chapters, of the medicinal plants and drugs in India and of tropical diseases and other matters of botanical, pharmaceutical, and medicinal relevance, the like of which had never been written before.[36]

[34] The references to Bombay in his *Coloquios* are in Nos. 22, 28 and 34.

[35] During my stay in Bombay in 1963–64 and again in 1971, I crossed at various occasions that site which, over four centuries ago, was Garcia de Orta's possession. At a meeting under the auspices of the Bombay University History Professor's Association on August 27, 1963, the distinguished educator and scholar, G. M. Moraes, lectured on Garcia de Orta and proposed to urge the Municipal Corporation of Bombay to honor the memory of Garcia de Orta by endowing a chair of medicine in his name at the University of Bombay. To the best of my knowledge, no action has yet been taken on this suggestion.

[36] See Louis H. Roddis, "Garcia da Orta — The First European Writer on Tropical Medicine and a Pioneer in Pharmacognosy", *Annals of Medical History, New York*, N. S. I (1929), 198–207; and F. A. Fluckiger and D. Hanbury, *Pharmacographia — a History of the Principal Drugs of Vegetable Origin met with in Great Britain and the British Isles* (London, 1879), who evaluate the work as follows: "The 'Colloquies' are above all notable by reason of the richness of information and the exactitude of the descriptions. No one

His work, published in April 1563 in Goa,[37] dedicated to the then Portuguese Viceroy, D. Fr. Coutinho (1561–67), approved by Aleixo Dias Falcão, the great Inquisitor of Goa, prefaced by the court physician of the Portuguese Viceroy, Dimão Bosque, and enhanced by an ode in honor of the author, composed by no less a person than the famous Luis de Camões, the author of the "*Lusiades*", who stayed in Goa from 1561 to 1607, was hailed as one of the greatest cultural achievements of the 16th century, as a work which brought the greatest honor to the author's country, Portugal, as "uma das grandes glorias da sciencia portugueza."[38]

In appreciating Garcia de Orta's work, Sir Clements Markham remarked: "Among the Portuguese worthies who have established for their country a claim to permanent remembrance in connection with the history of India and the Further East, the name of Garcia da Orta stands in the first rank. While da Gama and Albuquerque have won imperishable renown for Portuguese valour and statemanship, and Camões has raised an immortal literary monument in connection with Portuguese Indian achievements, Garcia da Orta and Pedro Nunes have done equal service to their country in the departments of scientific research."[39]

has as yet described the drugs of India with greater care, nor collected with regard to them information of greater value than Garcia. Always when we treat of Indian drugs it will be necessary to turn to Garcia; in spite of its defects which for the greater part must be attributed to the time in which he wrote, the 'Colloquies' will always occupy a place of honour in the history of Pharmacopoeia."

[37] A scholarly edition of the *Coloquios* was issued by Conde de Ficalho, *Coloquios dos Simples e Drogas por Garcia da Orta*, 2 vols. (Lisbon, 1891 and 1895); an English translation of the *Coloquios* based on this edition with introduction and index was published by Sir Clements R. Markham (London, 1913).

[38] See R. Da Rocha E Sa, "Garcia Da Orta Em Diu", *O Oriente Portuguez*, IX (1912), 276; also D. F. Lach, *Asia in the Making of Europe* (Chicago, 1965), I, 193, who mentions Garcia de Orta as "possibly the most learned Portuguese to reside in India permanently in the 16th century;" Cecil Roth, *The Jews in the Renaissance* (Philadelphia, 1964), p. 226, regards his work as "probably the greatest scientific monument of the Portuguese Renaissance."

[39] See Markham in *Revista de Historia*, Lisbon, Vol. II, No. 5 (1922), p. 5.

D. *Garcia de Orta and his Secret Adherence to Judaism*

While Garcia de Orta's reputation has been firmly established in the annals of scholarship,[40] a whole web of problems connected with his personal life and with his religious attitude and his position within the colony of Marrano-Jews in Goa, has remained obscure and controversial.

His early biographers portrayed him as a happy man, as a devout Catholic who attended mass regularly, and as a man unaffected by and disinterested in the external, political or ecclesiastical events surrounding him, pursuing his scholarly activities in splendid isolation, unmarried and wedded only to his research.

Gerson da Cunha, one of his earliest biographers, summed up Garcia de Orta's life story in the following words: "Garcia de Orta died a bachelor in Goa, about 1570, aged eighty. The Lord of the Manor of Bombay lived thus to a ripe old age, receiving love and regard of all in the splendid dignity of his venerable age.... Besides writing his immortal "Coloquios" and possessing the beautiful island of Bombay he had the privilege to live long. To become an octogenarian is a supreme achievement everywhere, especially for a European in India. Garcia de Orta lived long and died happy. That is his short but true epitaph."[41]

A. X. Soarez stated: "Surrounded by distinguished friends, enjoying the respect of the highest in the land, cared for by numerous servants and attendants, affluent in circumstances, keen on the study of the East, its habits of life, its varied customs, its flora and its fauna, and writing down his researches and his observations in his "Coloquios," d'Orta lived a quiet and, to all appearance, an

---

[40] All the various aspects connected with the *Coloquios* and its author, its relationship to the work by Cristobal d'Acosta, the various editions and translations, with a selected bibliography, have been investigated again by prominent experts on Garcia de Orta in "Número Especial Comemorativo do Quarto Centenário da Publicação dos Coloquios dos Simples," *Revista da Junta de Investigações do Ultramar*, Lisbon, XI, No. 4 (1963); and in *Boletim da Sociedade de Geografia de Lisboa* (1963), issued at the occasion of the 400th anniversary of the appearance of Garcia de Orta's *Coloquios*.

[41] See Gerson da Cunha, "The Origin of Bombay," p. 112.

uneventful life."[42] Conde de Ficalho, the meritorious editor of Garcia de Orta's *Coloquios* and the author of a comprehensive biography of him, followed closely this line of portrayal.

These appraisals and evaluations of Garcia de Orta's personal life have proven, however, to be in almost every detail erroneous and untenable in the light of newly discovered documents. Far from leading a life of happiness, Garcia de Orta's life was one of great affliction and tribulation and he spent his stay in India, especially in its later stage, in steady terror and fear for his own safety and that of his family, for the simple reason that he adhered secretly to Judaism and lived the life of a militant Marrano.

This was brought out by the monumental biography, written in 1934, by the Portuguese scholar Augusta da Silva Carvalho, on the occasion of the 400th anniversary of Garcia de Orta's arrival in India, based on unpublished and hitherto inaccessible Acts of the Inquisition of Goa, and in particular on the dramatic confessions of Garcia de Orta's own sister Catarina and her husband Lionel Perez before the Inquisition, immediately following the death of Garcia de Orta in 1568.[43]

The testimonies before the Inquisition made it convincingly clear that Garcia de Orta had often expressed the view that the Law of Moses was the true law, that one should live therein and keep the Sabbath and the festivals on the appointed days and, above all, Yom Kippur, that one should put on clean clothing and shirts on the Sabbath and add more oil to the lamps than usual. Lionel Perez conveyed in his testimony Garcia de Orta's convictions that he had heard from him repeatedly that "the Old Testament prophecies were not yet fulfilled, that Christ was not the son of God, that the

---

[42] A. X. Soares, "Garcia d'Orta," pp. 225 ff.

[43] Carvalho, "Garcia d'Orta" (see note 27); for the complete text of the "Processo da Inquisicão de Catarina d'Orta em Goa, No. 1283 dos processos de Lisboa," see Carvalho, pp. 202–215; also pp. 159 ff. Other important documents pertaining to Garcia de Orta's family in Portugal, New-Christians, and secret Judaisers, which were used by Carvalho, include: No. 5217, Evora, of the year 1563; No. 3326, Evora, of the year 1566; No. 10312, Lisboa, of the year 1587; No. 12081, Lisboa, of the year 1571; No. 229, Lisboa, of the year 1594; No. 7411, Lisboa, of the 1600; and No. 648, Lisboa.

Jews had not killed him but that he had died of old age and that he was the son of Miriam and Joseph." It was also revealed that Garcia de Orta's mother, Leonor Gomez, secretly practiced Judaism, that she used to prepare the meat in a special fashion, that unleavened bread was used at the proper occasion and that she had trained her children in the Mosaic law. Catarina also gave a full account of the circumstances of her brother's funeral service in 1569, and described how, according to Jewish tradition, he was shrouded in a special garment and sheet and shirt prior to the funeral services.[44]

Catarina incriminated not only herself, her late brother, and other members of her family, but mentioned also many other relations, who as New-Christians living in Goa continued secretly to practice the Jewish law.[45] She was sentenced to be burned at the stake on October 25, 1569 and thus had to pay the penalty for her dual life. It is stated "Catarina d'Orta, a Portuguese woman, a New Christian of Castelo de Vide, daughter of Fernão d'Orta and Leonor Gomez, married to Lionel Gomez, and dwelling in Goa, because she is an impenitent Jewess is given over to secular justice. Inquisitor Alx. Dias Falcão."[46]

Thus Carvalho could show convincingly in the light of documents from the Inquisition that Garcia de Orta, the son of New-Christian parents, continued in Goa to live a dual religious life and, while pretending to be outwardly a devoted and pious Catholic, was in his heart and in his secret practices a militant Marrano Jew with a deep emotional attachment to his Jewish heritage.

With this discovery, Carvalho has completely revolutionized the

---

[44] This is a résumé based on the Inquisition Acts No. 1283.

[45] Apart from the immediate family of Garcia de Orta, reference is made to other New-Christians living in Goa such as Jorge Pinto, Duarte Peres, Beatriz de Solis, Garcia Roiz, Simão Roiz, Filipa Gomez, Bastião Mendes, Violante Pimentel, Francisco Pimentel, Diogo Soares, Lope Soares, Francisco Vaz, Affonso Pinto, Francisco Roiz, Manuel Lopez, Leonel Gonzales, Alvara de Castro, Damian de Solis and others.

[46] It is significant that the Inquisitor who presided over the trial was none other than the very Aleixo Dias Falcão, who, in 1563, approved the publication of Garcia de Orta's *Coloquios*.

hitherto held image of Garcia de Orta. It was regarded as "verdadeirmenta sensacional."[47] Friedenwald, refering to Carvalho's work, stated "The Jewish origin of Garcia de Orta had never previously been known or even suggested in any of the publications during more than three centuries."[48] I. S. Révah exclaimed "who would have thought to include the great physician and botanist, Garcia de Orta, into the ranks of Marranos"[49] and credited Carvalho by his utilization of the data supplied by the Inquisition Acts to have integrated definitely Garcia de Orta "dans l'histoire du crypto-judaisme péninsulaire."[50] C. R. Boxer[51] hailed the discovery, as a portrayal of Garcia de Orta "as he really was and not as he is commonly represented as having been."[52]

The confession and testimony of Catarina de Orta before the Inquisition have revealed not only the secret Marrano life of her brother and her family, but have established also definitely the hitherto uncertain date of Garcia de Orta's death. Prior to Carvalho's discovery, the biographers were almost unanimous that "no records have been kept of the time and place of his death" and the lack of such records was even interpreted "as it were to give him

---

[47] See A. Iria, "Dos biógrafos portugueses de Garcia de Orta", *Comemorative Volume* (Lisbon, 1963), pp. 849 ff.

[48] Friedenwald, in *The Jews and Medicine*, p. 441.

[49] See I. S. Révah, "Les Marranes," *REJ*, CXVIII (1959–60), 72.

[50] See also the same author's study, "La famille de Garcia de Orta," *Revista da Universidade de Coimbra*, XIX (1960), 407–420, in which Carvalho's genealogical data are supplemented and corrected.

[51] C. R. Boxer, *Two Pioneers*, p. 6.

[52] While G. Schurhammer, the foremost authority on Portuguese-India (*F.X.*, II, 199, note 21 and 157, note 62), subscribes completely to Carvalho's findings, some eminent Portuguese scholars continue to adhere to the views held prior to the discovery of Carvalho's Inquisition documents; thus A. da Silva Rego in his "Garcia da Orta e a ideia de toleráncia religiósa", (*Numéro Especial Comemorativo*, XI [1963], 663–676) maintained "Garcia da Orta era Catôlico e era portugues," and regarded him as "verdadeiro e sincero Católico" (p. 674). He attributes the treatment meted out to Garcia de Orta by the Inquisition to "indevidas acusaçoes;" see also A. Martins, "O Catolicismo de Garcia de Orta", *Brotéria, Revista contemporánea de Cultura*, Lisboa, LXXVII, No. 1 (July 1963), 35–46.

additional claim to greatness — the date of his death, like that of his birth and likewise the place of his burial are to us unknown and this oblivion he shares with many great names in history."[53] Now, however, it has been definitely established that he had died in the first half of 1568 at the age of about 69 years, and was buried in Goa near or in the famous "Catédral da Sé." Thus the damaging evidence against Garcia de Orta could not have had any effect on him anymore, and it was rightly said that his natural death saved himself from arrest and trial.[54]

It can well be assumed that the Goanese authorities were fully aware of Garcia de Orta's Marrano life and had collected ample evidence about this aspect, but were reluctant to make a case against him, probably out of consideration for the prestige, standing and reputation he enjoyed in all Portuguese circles.

Garcia de Orta himself once, in 1558, had a highly unpleasant and explosive encounter directly with the ecclesiastical authorities, when a rich merchant in Goa, Diogo Soares, one of the earliest Portuguese New-Christians and a friend of Garcia de Orta, was summoned before the tribunal, under suspicion of being a secret Jew and observing Jewish laws. The Inquisition had ascertained that he was eating meat on forbidden days, refused to eat fish on Fridays, and when requested by the Inquisition to explain his attitude, he told that he was advised by Garcia de Orta, his physician, not to observe the various dietary practices of the Church. Garcia de Orta was questioned about this case and had to admit that for health reasons he suggested this cure. Nevertheless, Diogo Soares was accused of being an apostate and was imprisoned, together with his son Lopo (born in Goa in 1534), for four years.[55]

Yet, twelve years after Garcia de Orta's death, the Inquisition[56] decided to act, and ordered his mortal remains to be exhumed and

---

[53] See Gerson da Cunha, "The Origin of Bombay," p. 112; Soares, "Garcia d'Orta," pp. 226–27.

[54] Cecil Roth, *The Jews in the Renaissance*, p. 226 and p. 356.

[55] See Carvalho, "Garcia d'Orta," pp. 105–106.

[56] The Inquisitor at this juncture was not anymore Aleixo Dias Falcão, but Bartolomeu da Fonseca.

burned in an auto da fé at Goa. His ashes were carried to Mandobi, where they were cast into the sea as posthumous punishment for a militant Marrano who had escaped his fate during his lifetime. The verdict proclaimed on December 4, 1580 reads: "Garcia d'Orta, doutor, cristão novo portugues, por judeu entregue seus ossos a justica secular. Relaxado" (to be surrendered to secular justice to be burned).[57]

Thus, the shadow of the Inquisition which had motivated Garcia de Orta to leave Lisbon[58] and which had accompanied him all through his stay in India did not even spare him after his death.[59]

E. *The Re-examination of his* Coloquios

In the light of the firmly established fact of Garcia de Orta's secret Marrano life, it has to be asked, how did Garcia de Orta, the son of Marrano parents who had fled Spain and Portugal because of the Inquisition, react to the religious policy of the Portuguese authorities, the intolerance, tension and persecution which prevailed throughout the years of his stay in Goa? Is his experience or state of mind mirrored and reflected in his *Coloquios*, and to what degree, if at all, could any data be extracted from it which might have any bearing on his religious convictions?

The new perspective on his life, as supplied by the documentary evidence, allows us, first of all, to assume that Garcia de Orta's original departure from Portugal in 1534 was not solely motivated by the feverish yearning that many Portuguese had at this juncture to go to the mysterious East to look for fortune and new opportun-

[57] Carvalho, "Garcia d'Orta," pp. 132–34, describes dramatically how the ashes of Garcia de Orta were carried through the very street where his funeral had passed with great pomp just twelve years earlier.

[58] See Augusta d'Esagny, in *Bulletin, Institute of the History of Medicine, Johns Hopkins University*, Baltimore, V (1937), 483–487.

[59] During my visit to Goa in the fall of 1963, shortly after Goa had ceased to be a Portuguese territory, I was guided by my distinguished friend, Dr. P. S. S. Pissurlencar, the former Director of the Portuguese Archives in Goa, through all the sites in Old Goa which were connected with Garcia de Orta's life and death, such as Rua dos Judeus, Casa da Inquisição, Casa de Garcia de Orta, Rua Directa, Catédral da Sé, etc.

ities, to see new people and countries, or by his intellectual curiosity to study the physical world of medicinal plants and drugs, diseases and their cures. It seems rather that Garcia de Orta, in addition to all this, felt the precarious and insecure situation of the New-Christians within the Portuguese society, which indeed reached its climax in the establishment of the Portuguese Inquisition in 1538, and, following the trend set by many other New-Christians or Marranos, he migrated from Portugal to seek a new haven of refuge in India.

It is obvious that Garcia de Orta, residing in Goa from 1538 until his death in 1568, far from being merely "a disinterested spectator," was an eye-witness of all the manifold manifestations of the intolerant attitude of the Portuguese authorities, of the persecution and hunt for apostates, heretics, Judaisers, and New-Christians, the destruction of Hindu temples and burning of their books. Garcia de Orta must have been well acquainted with the contemporary scene in all its grim and tragic aspects, and deeply perturbed and shocked, in particular when the Inquisition was finally established in 1560. He could not have failed to learn of the tragic fate which had been meted out to a fellow physician in Goa, the New-Christian Jeronimo Diaz, at the public auto da fé in 1543, nor could it have remained a secret to him that a relative of his, Francisco de Orta,[60] accused of heresy and practicing Judaism, was burned at the stake in Lisbon in 1563.

It is clear that his *Coloquios* would never have received the imprimatur and approval of the ecclesiastical authorities in Goa had it contained even the slightest derogatory remarks about the religious attitude of the Portuguese of his time.

Yet equipped with the knowledge of the author's secret militant Marrano life, his *Coloquios* should be re-examined and be subjected to a new critical approach, in order to ascertain whether they could yield and reveal any facts relevant to his innermost religious feelings.

In approaching his *Coloquios* from this angle, it is to be noticed, first of all, the conspicuous absence of any Christological elements

[60] Processo da Inquisição de Evora, No. 5217, published by Carvalho, "Garcia d'Orta," pp. 201–2.

and of any reference to the Trinity. When the author refers to God he uses such simple phrases as "God willing," "if God should spare me," or "in the name of God." On the other hand, he emphasizes, almost ostentaciously, his own close contacts with Christian leaders in Goa, with Dimão Bosque, the official physician of the Viceroy,[61] with the Vicar-General of India, Miguel Vaz, whom he called "no less virtuous than learned," though he was notoriously the most fanatical enemy of the New Christians.[62] He stressed his relationship with Father Ambrozio of the order of the preaching friars,[63] and above all, with Francisco Xavier, whom he called "Maestro Francisquo," stating that "conversion to Christianity was increased by Master Francisco, theologist, who was a principal of this holy company jointly with Father Ignacio, whose virtues and sanctities, if they were written down, would make a large book. This Christianity is now fostered and encouraged by fathers and brothers of the company of Jesus and is honored by the martyrdom of some of the religious of this company."[64]

Such flattery of religious leaders in a treatise on drugs and medical plants seems rather strange and unwarranted, but was probably motivated by reasons of expediency, to ascertain the approval of the ecclesiastical authorities for the publication of his work.

His *Coloquios* contain frequent references to the Bible, to Palestine, to Judea, and some Jewish aspects.[65] He showed a sound knowledge of Jewish law when, in speaking of the Parsees in Bassain, he stated that since "they (the Parsees) do not circumcise

---

[61] Col. 42 and 58; about him see Jaime Walter, "Dimão Bosque, Fisico-mor da India e as Sereias", *Studia Revista Semestral*, Lisboa, No. 12, (1963), 261–271.

[62] Col. 35; for further details about him see Schurhammer, *F.X.*, II, 154 ff. and 380 ff.

[63] Col. 50.

[64] Col. 35; these and the following quotations are based on the English translation of the *Coloquios* by Sir Clements Markham (London, 1913).

[65] Col. 7, 9, 22; in some passages (see Col. 9) he indicates also a certain knowledge of Hebrew. His Hebrew name is said to have been Abraham, derived from a careful examination of his various signatures; see Carvalho, "Garcia d'Orta," p. 126.

nor are they forbidden pork... they are not Jews."[66] He made also a daring statement when, in comparing the Greek and Hebrew civilizations, he pronounced: "The Greeks were the first writers on human things, though the first who wrote on divine things were the Hebrews."[67]

Garcia de Orta mentions in his *Coloquios* some of his Jewish informants whom he interrogated in regards to medical plants and drugs in this part of the world without giving, however, their names. He repeatedly made statements such as "I asked an apothecary who was Spanish in language but Jewish by his false religion who said he was from Jerusalem...."[68] In another context he refers to "some Jews who came here (Goa) and said they were inhabitants of Jerusalem; some of them were sons of physicians, others of apothecaries." In another passage he stated "When I came from Portugal I asked a Christian who had been a Jew, being a Spaniard and a resident in Cairo, how many Christians and how many Jews there were in Cairo...;" in reporting about his visit to "the cities on the coast" (Cochin on the Malabar Coast) he stated: "while walking in these cities on the coast, I saw a Jew-merchant from Turkey who told me...."[69]

These Jews to whom Garcia de Orta referred were undoubtedly refugees from Spain and Portugal, who may have come to Goa via Jerusalem but who were, as their language indicates, of Portuguese or Spanish origin and who lived as secret Jews in Goa, a fact which

---

[66] Col. 54.

[67] Col. 54.

[68] For these and the following references to his Jewish informants see Col. 2, 4, 9.

[69] See Col. 13; "These cities of the coast" refer to Garcia de Orta's visit to Cochin together with his friend, Martim Affonso de Sousa in the early years of his stay in India. It is disappointing that this is the only reference to a Jewish merchant in Cochin since Garcia de Orta could hardly have missed a meeting with the members of the ancient Jewish community in Cochin. The presence of Jews in Cochin was noticed by numerous Portuguese and Western travellers, but, trying to avoid publicly and in his writings any identification with the Jews, his silence, though suspicious, is understandable.

Garcia de Orta would not have revealed in order not to arouse any suspicions as to his own association with them.

F. *His Visits to Ahmadnagar*

In the light of his well-documented Marrano life, Garcia de Orta's frequent visits to Ahmadnagar, to his friend and patron, the Shi'a Muslim Sultan Burhan ad Din Nizam al-Mulk(d. 1553), called by him and the Portuguese sources Nizamoxa or Nizamaluco, also assume new meaning.

This ruler, a patron of learning and scholarship, made his Court a centre of Indo-Muslim culture, a meeting place of scholars, scientists, physicians and philosophers where, in an atmosphere of complete religious tolerance, scholars of all denominations could meet and discuss their problems.[70] To this meeting-place of East and West many a Marrano Jew from Spain and Portugal seems to have flocked.

Garcia de Orta was invited at frequent intervals to the Court and served as physician to the Sultan and his son, whom he taught the Portuguese language. He must have enjoyed the exchange of views with the Sultan and the many Muslim, Indian, and European physicians and philosophers as well as the accessibility of ancient manuscripts for his specific research, housed in the Sultan's huge library.

His frequent visits to Ahmadnagar,[71] to which he travelled by way of Chaul, the only port of the kingdom, 30 miles south of

---

[70] For the historical background see T. W. Haig, "The History of the Nizami Shahi-Kings of Ahmadnagar", *Indian Antiquary*, Bombay, XLIX–L (1920–21); R. Sewell, *A Forgotten Empire* (London, 1900; Bombay, 1962); see also Aziz Ahmad, "The Muslim Kingdoms of Deccan and Gujarat," *Journal of World History*, VII (1963), 787–793. Very informative are the chapters on Ahmadnagar in Ficalho, *Garcia da Orta*, pp. 221–247; in Soarez, "Garcia d'Orta," p. 221; and in Carvalho, "Garcia d'Orta," pp. 99 ff.; 147. For the latest work on this dynasty see Radhey Shyam, *The Kingdom of Ahmadnagar* (Bombay, 1966), especially pp. 57–103, devoted to the rule of Burhan Nizam Shah. The author, strangely enough, did not mention Garcia de Orta's close friendship with the ruler and his frequent visits to his court.

[71] All through his *Coloquios* repeated mention is made of his visits to Ahmadnagar and its ruler; see Col. 2, 3, 10, 24, 36, 49, 50, 59.

Bombay, were motivated apparently not only by his friendship with the Sultan or the high rewards in terms of remuneration for his professional help as a physician to the Sultan or the scholarly benefits, but by another consideration of utmost personal relevance. It seems that Garcia de Orta was induced to spend as much time as possible at the Court of the Sultan in Ahmadnagar because it gave him the opportunity to breathe the air of religious freedom and tolerance and to escape the bigotry, fear, tension, and suspicion to which he and his family were subjected in Goa. Being beyond the reach of the Portuguese ecclesiastical authorities, he could throw off the mask of his dual religious life at the Court of the Shi'a Muslim ruler and could openly practice the Jewish religion and its ritual (if he so wanted) which he could observe in Goa only secretly and at great risk to his life. There he could associate, free from the Goanese inquisitorial surveillance, with numerous Jews or former Jews among the assembly of scientists, physicians, and merchants who either lived in, or passed through, this cultural center.[72] He could even dare to state unhesitatingly that "there are Jews in the territory of Nizamaluco."[73]

During his stay in Ahmadnagar, Garcia de Orta became the friend of a very colorful personality who had come from Portugal to India and was also a Jew by origin, namely Sancho Pires. This Sancho Pires,[74] after his arrival in Goa, served the Portuguese under Nunha da Cunha as an artillery man but deserted the Portuguese and entered the service of the Muslim ruler Nizam al-Mulk in Ahmadnagar, who promoted him to the position of a general in the Cavalry, and who made him his confidant and favorite. When Sancho Pires fell sick and needed medical care and treatment, the Sultan assigned Garcia de Orta to this task, excluding his own physicians out of fear that they might kill Sancho Pires. It was

---

[72] See J. B. Amáncio Gracias, "Médicos europeus em Goa e nas córtes indiánas nos séculos XVI a XVIII," *O Oriente Portuguez* (Bastora, 1939), pp. 1–57.

[73] Col. 54; since it was beyond the reach of the Portuguese Inquisition, Garcia de Orta could mention their presence without hesitation.

[74] See Col. 51, 54 and Carvalho, "Garcia d'Orta," pp. 95, 100.

through this professional care that Garcia de Orta became well acquainted with Sancho Pires and reported in his *Coloquios* a conversation which he had with him. Garcia de Orta let Ruano ask about him, whether he was a Muslim or a Christian. Garcia de Orta answered "In secret he told me he was a Christian, and he ate with me things forbidden to Moors, and spoke ill of them. He was not circumcised, though all supposed that he was, but I have seen, and he was not."

Actually, Sancho Pires was neither a Muslim nor a Christian but originally a Jew and a New-Christian. The fact that Sancho Pires was uncircumcised would not contradict his Jewish origin, since many New-Christians avoided the circumcision of their children. Though there was no need to hide the facts, Garcia de Orta wanted to make him appear a good Christian, stressing that he bequeathed many gifts to Portuguese churches and charities.

Of all the references to Jews found in Garcia de Orta's *Coloquios*, none supplies a more striking and glaring illustration of the way in which Garcia de Orta tried to camouflage, hide, and protect his Jewish friends than the case of a Jew by the name of Isaac of Cairo. In several places in his *Coloquios*[75] he mentions that this "Isaac a Jew born in Cairo," was sent by the Portuguese Viceroy on a special mission to Portugal to bring the news of the death of the Sultan Bahadur in 1537 to the King's notice and that he was "a discreet man and learned in many languages."

The mission of Isaac of Cairo (overland by way of Suez) to the King of Portugal is well attested by the Portuguese historian Gaspar Correa, who calls him "Isaquito of Cairo, a Jew, a prudent man."[76]

The Acts of the Inquisition have established the identity of this Isaac of Cairo beyond any doubt and proven that behind this name was actually hidden Jorge Pinto, a Portuguese Jew, a Marrano, born in Castelo de Vida, the very home town of Garcia de Orta, who had escaped to Flanders in Belgium in company with Clara Dias, a sister of Lionel Peres, the husband of Garcia de Orta's

[75] See Col. 32; 43.
[76] G. Correa, *Lendas*, III, 792, 848.

sister. It was in Flanders that Jorge Pinto returned openly to Judaism before he moved on to Goa, where he arrived, probably in 1538, as a young man, said to have been dressed as a Muslim and assuming the name of Isaac of Cairo, though secretly adhering to Judaism.

Garcia de Orta was, of course, well acquainted with the real identity of Jorge Pinto, alias Isaac of Cairo, the more so since they were first cousins. For his and Isaac's protection, for reasons of precaution and prudence, Garcia de Orta thought it safer, however, to make Jorge Pinto a native of Cairo and thus to eliminate any suspicion on part of the ecclesiastical authorities in Goa.[77]

These are but a few illustrations derived from his *Coloquios* which can serve as additional evidence of his Marrano mentality, and which supplement and confirm the confession made by his sister.

The death of Garcia de Orta and his exhumation in 1580 did not terminate the association of Goa with Jews and Jewish history. Despite the continued fanaticism and persecution and the steady, threat of the Inquisition throughout the 17th and 18th centuries, the colony of Jews and Marranos in Goa increased considerably, as attested by the accounts of missionary sources and European travellers to India covering this period.[78]

---

[77] Processo da Inquisição de Catarina d'Orta em Goa, No. 1283, published by Carvalho, "Garcia d'Orta," pp. 92–94; pp. 202–215.

[78] For further details see my forthcoming comprehensive work on *The Jews of India.*

JEWISH HISTORIOGRAPHY IN THE NETHERLANDS IN THE 17TH AND 18TH CENTURIES

LEO AND RENA FUKS

JEWISH HISTORIOGRAPHY in the Netherlands in 17th and 18th centuries is closely linked with its environment. The young Republic of the Seven United Provinces, hardly free from Spanish domination, soon became the center of world trade in the first half of the 17th century. The port of Amsterdam was always full with ships from all parts of the world and its inhabitants were used to see foreigners of all colors and statures walk along its canals. Dutch trade and prosperity reposed on the sound principles of free trade and tolerance. Even while the Dutch Reformed Church was the official church in the Republic, there remained freedom for all creeds, from Catholicism to Judaism.

From the 15th century onward the inhabitants of the Low Countries (the Dutch speaking part of Belgium included) were the most literate of Western Europe thanks to the activities of the Brethren of the Common Life.[1] In the 17th century a fully developed system of communal primary schools procured the knowledge of reading, writing and arithmetic to the greater part of the Dutch children, boys and girls alike. It is because of the literacy of the common people and its interest in religion, politics and seafaring that Amsterdam became the center of European book-printing and the daily press. So much news came in with the ships from abroad, so many people were interested in this news and were able to read it, that from 1618 onward several papers were published regularly, much earlier than in other European cities.[2] The same applies to

[1] A. Hyma, *The Brethren of the Common Life* (Grand Rapids, Mich., 1950).
[2] M. Schneider, *De Nederlandse krant van "Nieuwstijdinghe" tot dagblad-concentratie* (Amsterdam, 1968).

the Jewish press: The *Gazeta de Amsterdam* and the *Dinstagishe und Freytagishe Kuranten* were the first Jewish papers ever published.[3]

The great interest the Dutch took in the life of their country can also be seen in the large number of tracts and pamphlets they wrote on all kinds of subjects. Not only learned people took to their pens whenever they thought it necessary to illuminate their co-citizens; practically everybody who could write also disposed of his right. The absence of censureship (only a mild form of repressive censure was executed) and the cheapness of printing made it possible that the common Dutchman could express his views on whatever he thought right or wrong.

The fact that the country had only recently achieved its national unity and independence during the war with Spain 1568–1648, and the vastness of its overseas empire, made Dutch historiography less theoretical than in other countries. At the universities, of course, the renaissance art of historical writing in Latin was continued without much originality; but outside the learned world several well-educated men wrote histories of the Dutch people, especially of the heroical struggle for freedom from Spanish domination. These histories, written in Dutch, are noteworthy for the use of original sources, sometimes inserted in the text or given as appendices.[4] Accounts of travels to Asia and America were also very popular. In Dutch historical and semi-historical literature of the period we see a great predilection for facts and reliable information, characteristics which are also to be found in Dutch Jewish historiography. The fact that no historical work is written in Hebrew in our period also points to the influence of Dutch popular historiography. The Sephardim who settled in Amsterdam from 1593 on-

---

[3] L. Fuks, *De Joodse Pers in de Nederlanden, 1674–1940*. Introduction to the catalogue of the exhibition "Joodse Pers in de Nederlanden en in Duitsland". (Amsterdam, 1969), pp. 7 sqq.

[4] A handbook on Dutch historiography is unfortunately not yet written, though several monographs on historians exist. The only short survey on the subject we can recommend here is by Ph. de Vries in *Historische Winkler Prins Encyclopedie* (Amsterdam, 1957), pp. 74–89.

ward always remained a relatively small group. They were soon outnumbered by the Ashkenazim after 1632.

When surveying Jewish historiography in our period, the differences between the two Jewish groups in the Netherlands become clearly evident. The Sephardim are by far the more cultured group and they produce three historians in the period: the Spanish poet Daniel Levi de Barrios (nr. III), David de Fonseca (nr. VII) and the Hebrew poet David Franco Mendes (nr. X). The latter wrote his historical works in Portuguese. De Fonseca and Franco Mendes are typical representatives of well-to-do Sephardim of the 18th century. They described the life of their community, their learned rabbis, their rich and generous merchants and they recorded how the regulations of the congregations were composed and altered. Neither political events nor social circumstances are mentioned and the existence of the Ashkenazic community is overlooked.

Ashkenazic historiography, written in Yiddish for the common people, is more informative. Much interest is shown for political events and their importance for the position of the Jews. Poverty, the greatest problem of Dutch Jewry in the 18th and 19th centuries, is extensively mentioned and the Sephardic community and its rich representatives are treated with great respect. Of the authors of Yiddish histories only Menaḥem Man Amelander (nr. IX) was a learned man. Braatbard (nr. VIII) was a small broker and Zalman Prinz (nr. XII) a cooper.

Only a man who was born and bred far from the Amsterdam scene could reconcile the differences. This man was David Nassy (nr. XIII) who lived in the Dutch colony Surinam. He wrote an excellent history of the Jews in Surinam, of Sephardim and Ashkenazim together, uniting the cultural level of the Sephardim with the social consciousness of the Ashkenazim.

One must be aware of the fact that probably many popular historical works have disappeared in the course of time. We have proof of two lost manuscripts of Zalman ben Moses Prinz (nr. XII), of a Hebrew translation of a Portuguese chronicle by David Franco Mendes (nr. XI) and of two lost printed works in Yiddish. The one is a description of the privileges of the Jews in Naples and

Sicily, printed by the sons of Solomon Proops in Amsterdam, 1740, the second a Yiddish translation of a history of the first settlement of the Sephardim in Amsterdam, originally written in Portuguese (nr. VI), piinted by G. J. Janson and I. Mondovy in Amsterdam, 1768. Of both editions only the title-pages have survived.[5]

Our period ends with the year 1795 when the French revolutionary army swept away the Republic of the Seven United Provinces. The National Assembly of the new Batavian Republic granted equal civil rights to the Dutch Jews in September 1796. A new era in the history of Dutch Jewry had begun.

*   *   *

The Jewish historiographical works which originated in the Netherlands in the 17th and 18th centuries which we were able to find, are listed here chronologically. We know, of course, that our list is not complete and do hope that it may soon be supplemented.

I. *Narrative of the rescue of David Curiel from the hands of a murderer. Amsterdam, 20 Adar I 5388 (March 15th, 1628).*

The chronicle was written immediately after the event, in Portuguese, by David Curiel himself, Not much later Moses Guideon Abudiente of Hamburg translated it into Hebrew and added a Hebrew poem *Mizmôr ledawid* of six stanzas of four lines each.

In the library Ets Haim / Livraria Montezinos of the Sephardic community in Amsterdam three copies of the Portuguese and two of the Hebrew text repose: a) Hs. 47 B 11[16]: 16,1 × 9,2 cm.; 4 ff.; neat small 17th century hand; no title. At the end of f. 4v signed: "David Curiel".

b) Hs. 49 B 9: Cazo de David Curiel/ com o alemão em 20/ Adar risson anno 5388 em/ Amsterdam.

---

[5] The first reposes in the Bibliotheca Rosenthaliana, University Library of Amsterdam, in the collection of broadsides (Ros. Ebl.–C–10), the latter is in the possession of Mr. J. H. Coppenhagen in Jerusalem, but a photocopy is also in the Bibliotheca Rosenthaliana.

16,6 × 25,9 cm. (obl.); 11 ff.; 17th century hand. At the end of the text on f. 11r,v the Hebrew poem *Mizmôr ledawid*.

c) Hs. 49 B 10: Copia/ da milagroza historia/ aconteçeu a o muy inclito e nobre/ senhor David Curiel cuya prodigioza vida escapou/ a providencia devina e força/ des pessimas garras de hum/ fasinerozo enemigo/ em 21 adar risson/ do anno 5388/ corresponde a 1628.

   23,1 × 18,5 cm.; 7 ff.; 18th century hand. The copyist calls himself in the colophon on f. 7v: Abraham de Moseh Curiel.

d) Hs. 47 B 11[15]: 16,1 × 9,2 cm.; 13 ff.; neat small 17th century Sephardic cursive hand; no title.

   Hebrew translation of the Portuguese text with the Hebrew poem by M.G. Abudiente.

e) Hs. 47 E 51: The same text written in the form of a megillah by a professional scribe on vellum. 164,5 × 14,7 cm; text written in 11 columns of 22 lines each.

The Portuguese text has been published by L. C. Fabião[6] in 1965, the Hebrew text by Gabriel Polak[7] in 1857.

Fabião holds that b) is the oldest version and possibly the original autograph of David Curiel. We are more inclined to consider a) as the original because of the signature of David Curiel at the end of the text. The 18th century copy by a greatgrandchild of the author has been made to perpetuate the memory of the miraculous event.

David Franco Mendes (cf. nr. X) mentions the described events extensively in his history of the Sephardim in Amsterdam[8] and relates that the Curiel family used to remember the event — which took place on the day of Purim — each year during the Purim feast by reading the "Curiel-megillah" after the Esther-Megillah.

---

[6] Luis Crespo Fabiao, *O caso de David Curiel com o alemão. Curioso manuscrito inédito seiscentista, da autoria dum Judeu portugués de Amsterdao* (Coimbra, 1965).

[7] *'Ezba' 'elôhîm* (Königsberg, 1857). M. Steinschneider, *Die Geschichtsliteratur der Juden in Druckwerken und Handschriften* (Frankfurt/M., 1905), par. 152, p. 116. (Further quoted as *StGL*.)

[8] *Memorias da Estabelicimento...* cf. nr. X.

In another manuscript of the Ets Haim Library (Hs. 48 E 27) *Libro de Nota de Ydades* by Ishack de Matatiah Aboab which contains a detailed genealogy of the Aboab family, we find on f. 9v that David Curiel, alias Lopo Ramirez, was born in Lisbon on May 11th, 1594. He arrived in Amsterdam in 1614. In 1617 he married Rahel Naar and after her death in 1651, Rahel Aboab. His first marriage was childless, from his second marriage eight children were born.

Curiel was an important merchant of jewels in Amsterdam. One day a German introduced himself as a prospective buyer of diamonds and, while in Curiel's office, tried to stab him to death and make away with several stones. Curiel, though severely wounded, ran after him in the streets and with the help of gentile neighbors the villain was caught and handed over to the Amsterdam court. The favorable attitude towards the Jews in Holland is clearly illustrated by the end of the chronicle. After the execution of the German who was duly sentenced to death, the corpse was handed over to the medical faculty of the University of Leyden. David Curiel was officially invited by the faculty to be present at the "anatomical lesson" performed on the corpse of the German. The chronicle, though limited in scope, has a distinct flavor of authenticity and gives a lively description of Jewish life in Amsterdam in the early 1620's.

II. *Hebrew poem describing the hardship of the Jews in Brazil during the siege of Recife by the Portuguese in 1646 by Haham Isaac Aboab da Fonseca.*

ב״ה / זכר עשיתי לנפלאות אל ורב טוב / לבית ישראל אשר גמלו ברחמיו
וברוב / חסדיו במדינת ברזיל בבא עליהם גדודי / פורטוגאל עם נבל נאצו
שמו להשמיד / להרוג ולאבד את כל אשר בשם ישראל / יכנה טף נשים ביום
אחד בשנת ועל / כל איש אשר עליו הַתָו / אל תגשו: / אני הצעיר וקטן /
יצחק אבואב. / נעתק בשנת התפ״א.

19,5 × 14,8 cm.; 26 ff.; neat 18th century Sephardic cursive hand (most probably copied by David Franco Mendes). The historical poem on the first 8 ff., followed by some prayers and a thanksgiving poem by the same author. Reposes in the Ets Haim library

Hs. 47 C 12[1]. Published by M. Kayserling from this manuscript in 1902.[9]

Isaac Aboab da Fonseca was born in Castro d'Ayre (Portugal) in 1605. In 1612 he came to Amsterdam and became a pupil of Rabbi Uziel. The Sephardic congregation Beth Israel appointed him as their rabbi in 1626 and he remained in office when the three Sephardic congregations in Amsterdam were united in 1639. He served the new community Talmud Torah until his death in 1693, with an interruption of twelve years from 1642–1654.

When the Dutch conquests in Northern Brazil became united and established, many Sephardim of Amsterdam decided to emigrate to the new colony. Isaac Aboab and Moseh Raphael d'Aguilar went with them as rabbis in 1642. Until 1654 when Recife was conquered by the Portuguese, Aboab remained head of the Sephardic congregation *Ẕûr yisrael* in Recife. In 1646 he lived through the siege of Recife by rebellious Portuguese and in the poem he describes the hardships, battles and deprivations the inhabitants of the city had to suffer until two Dutch men-of-war came to their rescue. Aboab also mentions some of these events in his introduction to the Hebrew translation of Abraham Cohen Herrera's *Puerto del cielo* which appeared in Amsterdam in 1655, shortly after his return from Brazil.[10]

III.   *Daniel Levi (Miguel) de Barrios, Opuscula. Amsterdam,* 1683–84.

In the two copies A and B which slightly differ in contents, many poems and some prose pieces on the history of the Sephardim and their institutions can be found. The differences and bibliographical peculiarities of the few copies which are still extant[11]

---

[9] *Hagôren* III (Berditshev, 1904), 158–174; *StGL*, par. 165, p. 119.

[10] *Sefer ša'ar hašamayim...* printed by Emanuel Benveniste (Amsterdam, 1655), introd. f. 2r; cf. also C. R. Boxer, *The Dutch in Brazil* (Oxford, 1957), pp. 181, 274; A. Wiznitzer, *The Jews in Colonial Brazil* (New York, 1960), p. 142.

[11] The Ets Haim Library also possesses the volumes A and B. One copy reposes in the British Museum, London, and two copies in the Bodleian Library, Oxford.

are recently summed up by Miss Dr. W. C. Pieterse in her thesis on de Barrios.[12] We follow here the copies A and B of the Bibliotheca Rosenthaliana, Ros. 19 G 11 and 12.

In copy A:

1. Triumpho del Govierno Popular,/ y de la Antiguedad Holandesa./ Dedicalo en el Año de 5443 [1683]./ Daniel Levi de Barrios./ A los muy ilustres Señores Parnasim, y Gabay/ del Kahal Kados Amstelodamo,/ Ishac Belmonte. Iacob Abendana de Brito/ Iacob de Pinto./ Ishac Levi Ximenes./ Abraham Gutierres. Mordechay Franco./ Iosseph Mocata./ [ornament]/ De La Ley los Hebreos son las Flores,/ abejas los Maestros, que en las Hojas/ se sustentan por sus Mantenedores.

8°: 68 pp.

A short history of the Jewish people until the expulsion of the Jews from Spain in prose.

2. Several pieces describing the 'hermandades' learned and charitable societies with the Sephardic communities of Amsterdam and Rotterdam [13]. Preliminary: Tabla de las sacras Hermandades del Kahal Kados Amstelodamo, 2 pp.

a) Corona de la Ley (Keter tôrah). 16 pp. Prose.
   Learned society founded by Rabbi Saul Levi Mortera in 1643.

b) Tora Hor. Pp. 17–52. Prose and poetry.
   Learned society founded by Dr. Ephraim Bueno and Abraham Pereira in 1656.

c) Yesiba de los Pintos. 4 unpaginated pp. Prose.
   Seminary founded by Abraham and Emanuel de Pinto in Rotterdam in 1647.

d) Meirat Henaim. Pp. 57–96. Prose and poetry. (Hebr. text by Ishac Saruco on pp. 63, 64.)

---

12 W. C. Pieterse, *Daniel Levi de Barrios als geschiedschrijver van de Portugees–Israelietische Gemeente te Amsterdam in zijn 'Triumpho del Govierno popular'* (Thesis, Amsterdam University, 1968).

13 On the societies of the Sephardim in Amsterdam, cf. J. M. Hillesum, "Vereenigingen bij de Portugeesche en Spaansche Joden te Amsterdam in de 17e en 18e eeuw," *Jaarboek Amstelodamum*, I (1901), 169–18 3.

Learned and charitable society.

e) Hermandad de huerfanas. 4 unpaginated pp. Poetry.
Charitable society for the care of orphans (girls only).

f) Abi Yetomim. Pp. 17–45 [should be 47]. Prose and poetry.
Hebrew text on pp. 24 and 42.
Charitable society for the care of orphans, founded in 1648.

g) Gemilut jassadim. Pp. 49–71. Prose and poetry. Hebrew text
on p. 56. Charitable society founded by Moses Belmonte in
1639.

h) Temime darex. 16 unpaginated pp. Hebrew poem on p. 4
and list of members on pp. 9, 10.
Charitable society founded in 1665.

i) Jonen Dalim. Pp. 65–94. Prose and poetry.
Charitable society.

j) Maskil el Dal. Pp. 92–146. Prose and poetry.
Charitable society founded in 1676.

k) Sahare Sedek. Pp. 145–148, 6 unpaginated pp. Poetry. Hebrew
poem on p. [5]. Learned society.

l) Keter Sem Tob. 8 unpaginate pp., pp. 151–158. Prose and
poetry. Learned society founded in 1679.

m) Resit Jokma. Pp. 159, 160. Prose and poetry.
Learned society also called Baale Tesuba, founded in 1682.

3. Govierno poli-/tico/ judayco./ En Amsterdam año de 5444./
Descrivelo Daniel Levi de Barrios,/ a los muy Ilustres Señores
Parnasim y Gabay/ del Kahal Kados de Talmud Tora.
4 unpaginated pp.
Short description of the situation of the Sephardic community in
Amsterdam in 1684.

4. Triumpho del Govierno popular/ en la Casa de Jacob./
Descrivelo Daniel Levi de Barrios./
Pp. 1–26. Prose and some poetry.
Short history of the first settlement of the Sephardim in Amsterdam.

5. Xebra de Bikur Jolim. Pp. 27–34. Prose and poetry.
Short history of one of the oldest societies of the Sephardic community in Amsterdam.

6. Vida de Ishac Huziel,/ Jaxam del Kahal Kados Amstelodamo/

en la Sinagoga de Bet Jahacob./ descrivela/ Daniel Levi de Barrios.
Pp. 33–52. Prose and poetry. Hebrew poems on pp. 39 and 51.
Biography of Isaac Uziel (d. 1622) rabbi of Beth Jacob, the oldest
Sephardic congregation in Amsterdam.

7.   Historia Universal Judayca.
Pp. 1–22. Prose.
Short history of the Jews in several countries after the expulsion
of the Jews from Spain in 1492.

8.   Govierno popular judayco 5444 [1684].
Pp. 23–48, 8 unpaginated pp. Prose and poetry.
Description of the history of the Sephardim in Amsterdam, of the
new synagogue (inaugurated in 1675) and list of martyrs which
were executed by the Inquisition in Spain.

9.   Hes Jaim/ Arbol de Vidas/ Del Kahal Kados Amstelodamo.
Pp. 61–102. The five first pages prose, rest poetry.
Description and history of the school and seminary of the Sephardic
community in Amsterdam.

In Copy B:
10.   Hermosura de Moços (tiferet baḥûrîm),
Pp. 15, 16. Poetry.
Description of the learned society, which was founded in 1684.

Daniel Levi (Miguel) de Barrios was born in Montilla (near
Cordova) in 1635 and baptised there. He died as a Jew in Amsterdam
in 1701. His tragic life, not unlike that of so many Marranos of
his time, but intensified by his artistic endowments, has recently
been the subject of two studies by K. R. Scholberg.[14] He draws a
moving picture of the unfortunate poet who gave up a satisfactory
career as captain in the Spanish army in Brussels to be able to
live freely as a Jew in Amsterdam. The proud captain and successful
poet had to pay for this step with everlasting poverty and endless
troubles with the parnassim (governors) of the Sephardic community

---

[14] Kenneth R. Scholberg, "Miguel de Barrios and the Amsterdam Sephardic
Community," *Jewish Quarterly Review*, LIII (1962); Id., *La poesia religiosa
de Miguel de Barrios* (Ohio State University Press s.a. [about 1963]).

who censured his books. He had to eke out a living by writing laudatory poems for rich Sephardim.

De Barrios always had a predilection for history. This appears
not only in his works on non-Jewish themes like *Flor de Apollo*,
Brussels, 1663 and *Coro de las Musas*, 1672, but also in a history of
England which he published in Amsterdam: *Historia real de la
Gran Bretaña*, Amsterdam, 1688. In the Bibliotheca Rosenthaliana
reposes a probably unpublished historical work of de Barrios, a
short history of Spain in verse.[15]

Opinions varied on the reliability of de Barrios as an historian
in the course of time. Until the end of the 19th century his works
on the history of the Sephardim in Amsterdam were generally
considered as important sources and were frequently quoted in
historical works.[16] But with the advance of study in the field in
the 20th century, when the records in the archives of the Sephardic
community and in the notarial archives of Amsterdam began to
be used, many facts came to light which did not seem in accordance
with de Barrios' tales. Most historians of Dutch Jewry before the
second world war, therefore, held him in low esteem.[17]

From the work of Miss Pieterse who for the first time systematically compared de Barrios' historical work with controlable facts

---

[15] Hs. Ros. 115: 20,5 × 16 cm.; 39 ff.; Spanish text; 17th century hand.
Metros/ cronologicos, genealogicos, y geo/graficos, del Imperio español/ desde
su principio, hasta el año de/ 1672./ Y compendio/ de las cosas mas notables
que suce/dieron en tiempo de sus Reyes, y/ dominadores./ Descrivese/ desde/
Adam hasta Don Carlos segun/do, que al presente reyna en España./ El
capitan Don Miguel de Barrios.

[16] David Franco Mendes in his *Memorias* (nr. X) quotes him frequently
and so does H. J. Koenen in his *Geschiedenis der Joden in Nederland* (Utrecht,
1843).

[17] We can only quote here some of the most important authors: J. S. da
Silva Rosa, *Geschiedenis der Portugeesche Joden te Amsterdam, 1593–1925*
(Amsterdam, 1925); I. Prins, *De vestiging der Marranen in Noord-Nederland
in de 16e eeuw* (Amsterdam, 1927); many articles by A. M. Vaz Dias and J.
Zwarts; the chapters on the history of the Sephardim by J. d'Ancona in
Geschiedenis der Joden in Nederland, I, ed. by H. Brugmans en A. Frank
(Amsterdam, 1940).

of the records, a more favorable view in de Barrios' historical reliability emerges. Miss Pieterse[18] proves that de Barrios was mostly correct in the rendering of his facts and dates, especially when he wrote about his contemporaries. His data on several learned and charitable societies are the only evidence of their existence. Sometimes, of course, de Barrios' poetical drive carries him away in his descriptions, mostly in his biographies which are written in a strong laudatory vein and in his work on the synagogue. But on the whole de Barrios must be considered the most important historian of the Dutch Sephardim in the 17th century.

IV. *Description of the Jews of Cochin on the Malabar Coast by Mosseh Pereyra de Paiva, Amsterdam* 1687.

Notisias/ dos/ Judeos de Cochim,/ mandadas/ por/ Mosseh Pereyra/ de Paiva,/ Acuya Custa se imprimerão./ [ornament]/ Em Amsterdam,/ estampado em casa de Ury Levy em 9 de Ilul 5447.

4°; 16 pp.; at the beginning approbation of Rabbi Isaac Aboab, also dated 9 Elul 5447 (August 18th, 1687).

An early 18th century copy in manuscript with the same text and title, but without the approbation, reposes in the Ets Haim Library (Hs. 48 E 13). A Yiddish translation of the text appeared 10 days after the original one, also published by Uri Phoebus Halevi. No copy of this edition has been preserved, as far as we could ascertain, but a second Yiddish edition, Prague 1688 [19] and a third one, Amsterdam 1713, bear witness of its existence. Of the third Yiddish edition a unique copy reposes in the Bodleian Library in Oxford (Opp. 8°. 1131) which bears the following title:

קעניס / דער יהודים פון קושין / גישיקט דוריך משה פרערא דפייבא / נדפס / בבית ע″י המחוקק הגביר החב″ר אורי פייבש / בלא″א החב″ר אהרן הלוי זצל הח / ביום יט אלול *תמז* לפ″ק / אונ׳ איז ווידר העז דרוקט ע″י שמואל בן יודא / שמש ע″ה / ביום א ג סיון *תע″ג* לפ″ק / בק″ק / אמשטילרדם.

8°; 16 unfoliated leaves.

---

[18] W. C. Pieterse, op. cit., pp. 133 sqq.

[19] M. Steinschneider, *Catalogus librorum Hebraeorum in Bibliotheca Bodleiana* (Berlin, 1852–1860), nr. 6540[2], p. 1981; *StGL*, par. 198, p. 132.

This second Yiddish Amsterdam edition, printed by Samuel ben Juda Shamash apparently is identical with the original Yiddish one. It has been translated literally from the Portuguese text, with the approbation of Isaac Aboab. Two facsimiles of the Portuguese text have been published, resp. in 1923 and 1924.[20]

About the author Mosseh Pereyra de Paiva no data are known, except that he was a member of a commission of three which was sent to Cochin by the Sephardic community of Amsterdam to make inquiries on the spot. Since 1663, when Cochin had been conquered by the Dutch, many rumors about the existence of a Jewish community had circulated. It is amazing that the Sephardim had no information on the Cochin Jews before 1687, because the Dutch traveller Jan Huygens van Linschoten had already mentioned the Jewish communities in India in his itinerary of his journey to East India 1579–1592 which appeared in 1596.[21]

The narrative of Pereyra de Paiva is soberly written. It contains a lot of information on this forgotten remnant of Judaism. The questions which were put to the Cochin Jews, as they are to be found on pp. 13–15, have undoubtedly been compiled beforehand in Amsterdam. The answers are very instructive on the history and customs of the Cochin Jews who were known to be descendants of Jews of Majorca, expelled in 1370.

The "Notisias" caused a sensation among Amsterdam Jewry. This can be judged by the eagerness with which they bought the booklet. The contacts between the Sephardic community of Amsterdam and the Cochin community remained very close throughout the 18th century.

[20] One with introduction by Moses Bensabat Amzalak (Lisbon, 1923) and the second by Louis Lamm (Berlin, 1924).

[21] *Itinerario voyage ofte Schipvaert van Jan Huygens van Linschoten naer Oost ofte Portugaels Indien 1579–1592*, ed. by H. Kern (The Hague, 1910). *Werken uitgegeven door de Linschoten-Vereeniging*, II, 186 sqq. For other 17th and 18th century literature cf. "Geschiedkundige narichten betreffende de blanke en zwarte Jooden te Cochin, op de kust van Malabar... door Adrianus's Gravezande," *Verhandelingen uitgegeven door het Zeeuwsche Genootschap der Wetenschappen te Vlissingen*, VI (1778), 517–586; Introduction of Amzalak's facsimile-edition.

V. *Description of the "Undertakers Rebellion" in Amsterdam in 1696. Probably translated from the Dutch by Joseph ben Jacob Maarsen and published in 1707 by the compositor Jacob, son-in-law to Jacob Maarsen.*

אײן בשרייבונג / פון דיא רעבלײרייא צו אמשטרדם / איר / ליבה לײט זעלט
וואש איך אייך דא אם טאג טוא ברעגנגין: / אײן גישיכֿטניש וואו מעניך אײנר
האט מוזן דרום העננגין: / איבר אײן אויך רור אודר רעבלרייא צו
אמשטרדם: / דיא גיוועזן איז (בשנת֗ תנ״ו) עש איז נאך ניט זער לאנג / לאנג
גיליטן. עש ווייש נאך דר מעניך אײנר דר פֿון צו זאגין: / יונג אונ׳ אלט. וויא
עש זיך דער מיט האט צו גיטראגין: / איך זעלבשט האב עש מיט אייגן אויגן
גיזעהן: / וויא עש איז צו גיגאנגין. אונ׳ וואש אליש איז גישעהן: / זוא דאש
איר קײן וואנרט שקר וערט דרײן גיפֿינדן: / זעלכֿש וויל איך מיר וואול בײא
לײב שטראף פֿאר בינדן: / אונ׳ אויך האב איך עש ניט אויש מײן קאפף
גישריבן אליין: / זונדרן וויא איך עש האב גיפֿונדן אין אײן גלחת֗ ביכֿליין: /
אלזו האב איך עש מעתיק גיוועזן ממש אות֗ באאות֗: / כדי מן ניט זאגן זאל היר
אודר דאר זײנן גרוישי שטות֗: / איך ווייש גיוויש אונ׳ צווייפֿל אויך גאנץ ניט
דראן: / וואש מן דר פֿאר גיבט. קיינם וערט גירייאן טאן: / דארום לאזט
אייך אייער געלט ניט פֿרדרישן: / פֿילײיכֿט וער איך זעלבר מוזן געלט דר
בייא אײן שיסן: / האב עס ניט גטאן אום רווחים נייארט אויש ליב
האברייא: / וואו מיט איך גיהורזאמר דינר בלײבי איטליכֿם גיטרייא: /
ובמצות / הפועל הזעציר יאקב חתן יאקב מארשן ע״ה: / נדפס באמשטרדם /
בשנת תס״ז לפ״ק:

8°; 16 pp.

The only known copy reposes in the Bodleian Library Oxford Opp. 8°. 1062. The translator is most probably Joseph ben Jacob Maarsen, who adapted and translated many popular Dutch works into Yiddish in the first half of the 18th century.[22] The source he used for this work is the anonymous: Historie/ van den/ Oproer/ te Amsterdam/ voorgevallen,/ door den Stads Gr. Achtb. Overheid en trouwe/ Borgers loffelijke wijze/ gestild, zedert den 31sten/ January 1696. The booklet appeared in Amsterdam and Rotterdam

---

[22] *StGL*, par. 204, p. 134; J. Shatzky, "The Prefaces to Joseph Maarsen's writings," *YIVO Bleter*, XIII (Sept./Oct. 1938), nr. 5–6, 379 sqq.

in 1696.[23] The translation into Yiddish is indeed almost literally as Maarsen stated in his rhymed title-page.

The booklet contains a description of the rebellion of the Amsterdam proletariat against new regulations from the magistrate concerning funerals which were considered to be discriminatory against the poor. The number of undertakers was to be drastically reduced and they and their helpers were to be officially appointed by the magistrate. The poor inhabitants of Amsterdam, always restive and somewhat unruly, first did protest before the magistrates. Some of their claims were granted, but the duped undertakers incited the masses and they attacked the town hall. This was the beginning of three days of rioting, looting and burning of houses in Amsterdam. It ended with the invasion of the house of the rich Sephardi de Pinto, where the plunderers were caught by Jewish and non-Jewish defenders. The leaders of the rebellion were hanged and soon order was restored in the city of Amsterdam.

The work is a typical example of a mixture between a pamphlet and a history. It has the flavor of the eye-witness, of having been written on the spot, yet it gives several sources, among others the complete text of the regulations concerning funerals and it adds reflections on the causes of rebellions in general. That this kind of semi-historical literature was as popular with the Dutch Jews as with the gentiles appears clearly from the fact that even ten years after the event Maarsen's booklet was sold out and survived only thanks to the collector's zeal of Rabbi David Oppenheim of Prague.

VI.   *History of the first settlement of the Sephardic Jews in Amsterdam; first Portuguese edition, Amsterdam 1710–1711.*

The original edition, written by Uri de Aron Halevi the well-known Hebrew printer Uri Phoebus Halevi, and probably printed

---

[23] The events are also mentioned in David Franco Mendes, *Memorias*, p. 118 and in Menaḥem Man Amelander's *Še'erit yisra'el*, 2nd ed. (Amsterdam, 1771), chapter 34, f. 93. A detailed article on the rebellion was written by J. F. Gebhardt jr., "Het 'Aansprekers-oproer' van 1696", *Amsterdamsch Jaarboekje voor 1899*, pp. 100–157.

by Moses Dias,[24] reposed as an unique copy in the archives of the Sephardic community in Amsterdam before the second world war. It has not been found since. Sigmund Seeligmann and J. S. da Silva Rosa, the former librarian of the Ets Haim library, bear witness to its existence and so does a copy in manuscript of the first edition in the Bibliotheca Rosenthaliana: Hs. Ros. 277; 20,6 × 16,2 cm.; 3 ff; 18th century writing; no title. The first page bears the inscription "Memoria para os siglos futuros". At the end of the text on f. 3v is written:

"Amsterdam em 10 de Kisleff 5471 [December 2nd, 1710] Uri de Aron Alevi filho do HH asalem R. Mosseh Uri Levi fundadores deste santo K.K. que el Dio aumente por muitos annos. Amen." Then follow two declarations in Portuguese on the trustworthiness of the text and the merits of Uri and Aharon Halevi, the first signed by David de Ishac Cohen de Lara, Amsterdam "a 32 de Homer A° 5433" (May 4th, 1673) and the second by Ishac Aboab "os 20 de Homer de 5434" (May 19th, 1674).

A second edition of the Portuguese text appeared in 1768:

Narração,/ da vinda dos/ Judeos Espanhoes/ a Amsterdam,/ conforme a tradição verdadeira,/ que re-/cebeo de seus genitores, o Senhor/ Ury de Aharon A Levy,/ E o publicou a o Munodo [sic!] no A° 5471./ E agora traduzido no nosso sacro idioma por/ & impresso por ordem, & despeza de/ Mosseh Levy Maduro./ [ornament]/ Em Amsterdam/ Na Officina Typographica de G. J. Janson,/ Em Caza de I. Mondovy, A° 5528.

This unique copy reposes in the Ets Haim Library, EH 20 E 46.[24]

The booklet consists of 4 pp., at the end of which the above-mentioned approbations appear. Its counterpart, the Hebrew translation of Isaac Cohen Belinfante, which appeared in 1773, has disappeared and we only know it from a facsimile-edition of 1933.[25] The same printers, G. J. Janson and I. Mondovy, paid by

---

[24] For a detailed description of the editions and translations cf. S. Seeligmann, "Über die erste jüdische Ansiedlung in Amsterdam," *Mitteilungen zur jüdischen Volkskunde*, hrsg. von M. Grünwald, XVII (N.F. II, 1) (Berlin, 1906), 1–13.

[25] *Narracão da Vinda dos Judeos Espanhoes a Amsterdam*, with introd. by J. S. da Silva Rosa (Amsterdam, 1933). Reprinted text from the Library of

the bookseller Mosseh Levi Maduro, also printed a Yiddish translation, probably at the same time as the Hebrew one. Of this
Yiddish edition only the title-page has been preserved.[26]

Title of the Hebrew edition:

זכרון / מעשה רב / מן ביאת היהודים הספרדים / לאמשטרדם ואיך נשתלשל /
ישובם פה עד היום / אשר קבל מפי אבותיו הקדושים זי״ע הגביר / אורי
בכ״ר אהרן הלוי והדפיס טופס / המעשה בלשון לעז בשנת התע״א / כאשר
העידו עליו חכמי / הדור זצו״קל : / וילך איש מבית לוי הוא הגביר משה לוי
מאדורו / ה״י מוכר ספרים ויקח רשות משבעה טובי העיר / ה״ה פרנסי
ומנהיגי קהלתנו יע״א ובהסכמת מ״ו אב״ד נר״ו / להדפיסו עוד בלשון לעז
כראשונים. ולהוסיף בזאת ההדפסה / העתקתו בלשון הקדש. לשון הזהב
והאדרת. גברת כל / הלשונות. לבי היא לכל הארצות: / בשנת התק״כח
ליצירה / באמשטרדם / נדפס ע״י גיררארד יוהאן יאנסון / ובבית הבחור
ישראל מונדווי:

Title of the Yiddish edition:

מעשה / וועלכש איזט דיא וואהרי ערצילונג וויא / אונד אויף וועלכה ווייזה
דיא / (יהודים) ספרדים / זיינן קומן זיך צו ביזעצן בק״ק אמשטרדם / וועלכש
טרייאליך טראנצליטהרט אויש דען / שפאגישע אין יודיש טייטש זעהר אן /
גנאהם צו לערנן אונ׳ צוערקענן דיא גנאדע גאטש איבר / זיין פֿאליק
(ישראל). גלייך אין אונזר הייליגה (תורה) / שטיהט (ואף גם זאת בהיותם
בארץ אויביהם לא מעסתים [Sic!] / ולא געלתים לכֿלותם). דז איז צו זאגן
וועז איר ווערט זיין / אין לאנד אייארה פֿיינד. ווערט דער ליבה גאט דאך
ניט / אן אייך פֿראומוווערדגן אונד ווערט אונש טוהן איבר / בלייבן ביז זיין
הייליגה ווילן ווערט זיין אונש צו שיקן / דען (גואל צדק במהרה בימינו)
אמן: / נדפס ברשיון אלופי׳ פרנסים ומנהיגים / דק״ק ת״ת ספרדים יע״א: /
ע״י הגביר משה לוי מאדורו ובניו / מוכרי ספרים בק״ק אמשטרדם: / נדפס
ע״י גיררארד יוהאן יאנסון / ובבית הבחור ישראל מונדווי:

On the reliability of the text of the "Memoria" a controversy
arose between J. M. Hillesum, librarian of the Bibliotheca Rosenthaliana and the Portuguese scholar Cardozo de Bethancourt.[27]
Hillesum contested the reliability of the text and Cardozo de

the Portuguese Jewish Seminary Ets Haim, Amsterdam, Vol. I. The edition
was limited to 100 copies which also have become very rare.

[26] Photocopy in the Bibliotheca Rosenthaliana.

[27] J. M. Hillesum, *Uri Ha-Levi. De eerste Mohel, chazzan en predikant der
Portugeesche Joden te Amsterdam in het jaar 1593* (Amsterdam, 1904).

Bethancourt defended it. Later, when other facts had come to light, Cardozo de Bethancourt and the "Memoria" proved to be right.[28]

Da Silva Rosa[29] holds that the "Memoria" had existed as a family-chronicle in the Halevi family. As all direct descendants of Uri Halevi had the right to be members of the Sephardic congregation in Amsterdam, it may have been important for members of the family to stress this point and draw again attention to the great merits of Uri Halevi for the first Sephardim in Amsterdam. The tale is well written and tells the story of the Marranos who found Uri Halevi in Embden. He went with them to Amsterdam and guided their return to Judaism.

The story is used by de Barrios in his Triumpho del Govierno popular en la Caza de Jacob, p. 8 and by David Franco Mendes in his Memorias da Estabelicimento, p. 1 and onward.

VII.   *History of the Sephardic Jews in The Hague, 1698–1726.*

Manuscript reposing in the Bibliotheca Rosenthaliana Hs. Ros. 80 25 × 19 cm.; 64 pp. written in Spanish; no title; 18th century hand.

The manuscript most probably was written by David de Fonseca, son of Abraham Hisquiau de Fonseca, one of the first members of the Sephardic congregation in The Hague. J. H. Buzaglo,[30] who used this manuscript, states that there existed a second part of the manuscript with a continuation of the history, but this was already lost before the Second World War. Of the author no data are known. He wrote his history soberly and in the form of a chronicle. He keeps strictly within the bound of his subject and does hardly refer to Dutch history. At the end he gives the complete text, in Portuguese, of the first regulations of the Hague congregation of 1726 and also a list of its members. He also adds a minute description of the inauguration of the new Sephardic synagogue at the Princessegracht which took place the 9th of August, 1726.

---

[28] J. S. da Silva Rosa, Introduction facsimilie edition.   [29] Ibid.

[30] J. H. Buzaglo, "Bijdragen tot de geschiedenis der Portugeesche Israelieten en hunner gemeenten te 's Gravenhage van ± 1690 tot ± 1730," *Die Haghe* (1939), p. 29.

VIII. *Chronicle for the years 1740–1752 by Abraham Chaim ben Zvi Hirsh Braatbard,* Amsterdam, 1753.

.1740—1752 / פון / אײן נייאי קורניק

Colophon: "אני הקטון אברהם חיים בר צבי הירש יצ״ו ז״ל בראטבאַרד
ממשפחת קוברין, שנת תקי״ג לפ״ק, אמשטרדם."

Manuscript in Yiddish reposing in the Bibliotheca Rosenthaliana, Hs. Ros. 486.

22,5 × 16,5 cm.; 164+2+24 ff.; Ashkenazic cursive writing.

The manuscript was found by L. Fuks shortly after the Second World War. It probably had belonged to a Dutch Jewish family who could not read it. That could be the reason why this important sample of Jewish historiography in the Netherlands remained unknown before the Second World War.[31] Some data on the author also were found by chance. On the fly-leaf of a Yiddish translation of a Pentateuch, printed in Amsterdam in 1749, which is in the Bibliotheca Rosenthaliana, a genealogical list of the Braatbard family, begun by our author and continued by his sons, is written. From this list we know that the author's father Zvi Hirsh Braatbard died in 1751. Abraham Chaim, the author, was born in May 1699, he married Sipra Hymans in 1729 and they had nine children, six daughters and three sons. Abraham Chaim died in 1786. The records of a special tax which was levied in Amsterdam in 1746, which are in the municipal archives of Amsterdam, tell us that Zvi Hirsh or in Dutch Hartog Samuel was a moderately well-to-do broker and money changer. He lived in Uilenburg, the Jewish quarter of the city.

The author was probably born and surely reared in Amsterdam. The language of his chronicle is real Dutch-Yiddish, full of ex-

[31] L. Fuks first mentioned it in "Ajn naje kronajk foen 1740–1752. Uit de kroniek van Abraham Chajim, zoon van Tsewi Hirsch Braatbard van den huize Couweren," *Maandblad voor de geschiedenis der Joden in Nederland*, I, 2 (1947), 45–49. Parts of the chronicle in Dutch translation and with introd. by the same: "De Jiddische kroniek van Abraham Chaim Braatbard (1740–1752)," *Jaarboek Amstelodamum*, XLVIII (1959), 113–171. And: *De Zeven Provincien in beroering. Hoofdstukken uit een Jiddische kroniek over de jaren 1740–1752 van Abraham Chaim Braatbard* (Amsterdam, 1960), Meulenhoff Minerva Pockets, 3.

pressions which only a Dutch Ashkenazic Jew could use. From
the orthographical faults in Hebrew words we must infer, that his
Jewish learning was not extensive. But in his chronicle he reveals
himself as a very intelligent man, a keen observer of the events of
which he was a witness. He was most interested in the politics of
the Dutch Republic which he considered as his fatherland.

His chronicle is divided into 295 short chapters and is for the
greatest part devoted to the description of political events in
Holland: a) The war with France which ended in 1747; b) the
subsequent Restoration of William IV of Orange as Stadhouder
of the whole country; c) the struggle for democratization of local
and general government which failed in 1748; d) the new taxation
and the revolt against it in the same year. As practically all Dutch
Jews, Braatbard is a fervent adherent of the House of Orange and
he defends and reveres the Prince with all his heart. As the movement for democratization was closely connected with a movement
for restoration of the power of the crafts-guilds, the membership
of which was usually denied to the Jews, Braatbard is very much
opposed to the movement and its leaders. One of these, a certain
Daniel Raap, he always describes as Haman de Raap. But even
if he is a partisan in the struggle, Braatbard is not blind for the
faults in the existing system.

The rest of the chronicle is filled with local events: the conflict
between members of the Jewish fishvendors' guild "Mazal dagim"
and the gentile vendors; conflicts in the Sephardic community over
the appointment of a new cantor; murder and crime in Amsterdam;
epidemics, cold winters, expensiveness of victuals and other recurring events in the daily life of common people. The expulsion
of the Jews from Prague in 1744 is extensively mentioned and so
are the measures the Dutch Jews took to help their brethren. At
the end a description of the inauguration of the new Ashkenazic
synagogue in 1752 with all prayers and poems which were recited at
the occasion, is added. This chronicle gives a true picture of Ashkenazic life in Amsterdam in the middle of the 18th century. The
author has a keen political interest, is well informed about the
causes of events, and takes his political opponents seriously.

IX. *History of the Jewish people in Yiddish from the destruction of the second Temple until 1740 by Menahem Man Amelander b. Solomon Halevi, Amsterdam, 1743.*

כתר מלכות / והוא חלק שני / מספר יוסיפון / בלשון אשכנז / חברו ויסדו
האלוף התורני והמדקדק. איש חי רב פעלים. ה״ח כ״ש כהר״ר מנחם מן בן
שלמה הלוי / נר״ו. ונקרא שמו בישראל. / ספר שארית ישראל / איר ליבה
לייט טוט גשווינד לויפֿן. אונ׳ טוט אייך באלד / אזו אייך מעבֿטיג (סבֿר)
קויפֿין. דען דא אין / ווערט דר צילט אלי דיא דיא וואונדר גשיכטן. דיא גאט
האט / אן אונש יהודים טאן ריבֿטן. פֿון דיא צייט דש יוסיפֿון / האט אויף
גהערט צו שרייבן. אונ׳ וואו מיר יהודים אין / גלות האבן טון בלייבן. דען
מיר יהודים זיין פֿר שפרייט / גווארן. אין אלי עקין פֿון דר וועלט (מזרח
מערבֿ צפֿון / דרום). וויא זיא ווערן גמעלט. (הש״י) זאל ווייטר היטן / דיא
איבר בלייבונג פֿון ישראל. אונ׳ זאל אונז שיקן / אונזר רעבֿטר (גואל). דז
זאל גשעהן אין קארצי / טאגין. דרויף וועלן מיר אמן זאגין: / נדפס
באמשטרדם / במצות ובהוצאות הני שלשה אחים. ה״ה הנעלה כ״ש / כמר
יוחנן סופר סת״ם. והב״ח כמר מרדכי גומפיל / והב״ח כמר שלמה זלמן. בנים
של הנעלה כ״ש כמר גבריאל בן המנוח כהר״ר לנג דוד זלה״ה: / בבית ובדפוס
המשותפים האלופים הקצינים ה״ה הנעלה כהר״ר נפתלי והירץ לוי
רופא עם חתנו / התורני היקר והנעלה כהר״ר קאשמן יצ״ו: / בשנת בבית
אלהים נדלך ברגש לפ״ק:

8°; IV+ 148 ff.; (f. 146v–148r index of chapters).

The work is preceded by a Hebrew approbation of Rabbi Aryeh Leib, rabbi of the Ashkenazic community in Amsterdam, in which he gives consent to the three brothers Yoḥanan the scribe, Mordekay Gimpel and Solomon Zalman to publish the work of the learned grammarian Menaḥem Man ben Solomon Halevi. It is dated Wednesday 13 Elul 502 (September 12th, 1742). Then follows on f. 1v a Hebrew preface of the printers and an acrostichon, giving their names Herz Levi Rofe and his son-in-law Kosman. On f. 1v, 2r a Hebrew preface of the author, also with acrostichon, followed by a Yiddish introduction with a Yiddish acrostichon at the end on f. 4v.

The author Menaḥem Man Amelander ben Solomon Halevi was a learned man, a disciple of Rabbi Moses Frankfurt, the well-known Amsterdam rabbi and printer who also had a great predilection for writing Yiddish. Of Amelander's life few data are known.

He compiled a Yiddish commentary on the Old Testament which
appeared in the Bible-edition *Magišê minḥah* in Amsterdam, 1725–
1727. He also wrote some other commentaries.[32] In 1776 his commentary *Ladaʿat ḥokmah* on *Rešît ḥokmah* by 'Eliah de Vidas
appeared in Amsterdam. The title-page bears his name without the
addition ז״ל so we may infer that Amelander was still alive in 1776.
This fact complicates matters concerning the second enlarged
Amsterdam edition which appeared in 1771. The printer Kosman
ben Joseph Baruch states in his introduction (verso-side of the
title-page) that he wrote the additions himself until 1770:

"עש איז נון לערך דרייסיג יאר גליטן דש דיזוש ספר שארית
ישראל ע״י האחים כהר״ר יוחנן וכ׳ זלמן וכ׳ גומפל בני המנוח
גבריאל ז״ל בייא מיר גדרוקט איז. אונ׳ דורך דעם דש זער אנגענעם בייא
דען עולם וואר. איז עש שוין פֿר לעגנשט אויש פֿר קויפֿט אונ׳ קיינש מער
בנמצא. ע״כ האב אויף פֿר זוך פֿון גאר פֿיל ליב האברש רעזוולפֿיהרט אום עש
זעלבה ווידר אויף בייאש צו דרוקן. אונ׳ אום עש נאך אן גענמר אן דען עולם
צו מאכֿן. זוא האב אלי דיא לשון הקודש ווערטר באותיות מרובעות גדרוקט
וויא אויך אלי דיא שמות פֿון דיא אומות אונ׳ לענדר:
גם האב דא בייא אין אין בזונדרר פרק גדרוקט אלש וואש אחינו בני ישראל
אין עולם ווידר פֿארן איז נאך עש דרוקן פֿון עש ערשטי שארית ישראל פֿאר
זוא ווייט מיר בוואושט איז. ובפרט בקהלתינו ק״ק אמשטרדם יע״א. צוויפֿל
ניט אודר ווערט אן דען עולם זער וואול גפֿאלן. אונ׳ האפֿה דאש הש״י מיר
וויטר זאל מזכה זיין נאך מער ספרים צו דרוקן לזכות את הרבים אחינו בני
ישראל. עד ביאת הגואל. במהרה בימינו אמן וכן יהי רצון:"

"It has now been about thirty years ago that this book *Šeʾerît*
yisraʾel has been printed by me ordered by the brothers Johanan,
Zalman and Gimpel, sons of Gabriel. Because this has been well
received by the public, it has been sold out long ago and is not to
be found anymore. Having been asked for it by many lovers [of
history] I decided to reprint it. And to make it even more attractive
to the public I have printed all Hebrew words and names of persons

---

32 Cf. *Seërith Jisrael of Lotgevallen der Joden in alle werelddelen, vanaf de*
verwoesting des tweeden tempels tot het jaer 1770 door Menachem Man ben
Salomo Halevi. Naar de tweede, vermeerderde uitgave uit het Joodsch-Duitsch
vertaald door L. Goudsmit Azn, met talrijke aanteekeningen door G. I. Polak
(Amsterdam, 1855) (this is a Dutch translation of the 2nd ed.), p. 5.

and countries with square characters. I have also added everything which happened to our Jewish brethren in the whole world since the first edition of *Še'erît yisra'el* in a new chapter, as far as it was known to me. And particularly what happened in our community in Amsterdam. I do not doubt that the readers will like it and I hope that the Lord will give me strength to print more books for the weal of our Jewish brethren until the Redeemer will come, may it be soon in our days, amen, and may this be His will."

As we have no exact data on Menaḥem Man's life, it is difficult to understand why he did not write the additions to his chronicle. He must have been pleased that his *magnum opus* was reprinted during his life-time. We also do not know whether he knew of the second unrevised edition of his whole work in Fürth, 1767, printed by Ḥayim ben Zvi Hirsh. Kosman ben Joseph Baruch does not mention this edition at all, but that may be for business' sake. Perhaps Menaḥem Man who in 1771 must have been about seventy years old — his first literary activities being in the twenties of the 18th century — felt not well enough to undertake the writing of the new chapter? Or had he lost interest in historiography?

In a copy of the first edition of the work which is in our private collection, additions in manuscript are added at the end in a very neat small Ashkenazic hand and beautiful square characters. Part of these additions have actually been printed in the 36th chapter by Kosman in the 2nd edition, the last two leaves have not been published. Perhaps this is Kosman ben Baruch's copy, or otherwise it is the work of one of the numerous "lovers of history" in Jewish Amsterdam, who recorded the important events of their times. We shall see later (cf. nr. XII) that one continuation of *Še'erit yisra'el* had been made by Zalman ben Moses Prinz the cooper.

Še'erit Yisra'el is generally considered to be the most important sample of Jewish historiography in the 18th century.[33] Though

33 M. Grünbaum, *Jüdischdeutsche Chrestomathie* (Leipzig, 1882), pp. 361–379; M. Erik, *The history of the Yiddish Literature, 14th–18th century* (Warsaw, 1929), p. 377 (Yidd. text); I. Zinberg, *The History of Jewish Literature* (Wilna, 1935), VI, pp. 63–65 (Yidd. text).

Menahem Man was no *maskil avant la lettre*, he made the utmost of his possibilities within the limits of his time and environment. In his introduction he describes the reasons which induced him to translate the *Sefer Yosipon* and to write his continuation. He reveals himself as a real historian. The knowledge of history makes people wiser and serves as an example for the generations to come. He also states that he had used only reliable sources, Jewish as well as non-Jewish.

A separate study would be required to go into the sources Menahem Man used and to analyse his historical method. We can only state shortly that he compiled Jewish history in a readable and understandable way for the general public. His last chapters on the history of the Jews in Germany and Holland in his own time are still of value for the students of Jewish history. The great popularity of Menahem Man's work is amply proved by the numerous editions in Yiddish and Hebrew.[34]

X. *History of the Sephardic Jews in Amsterdam from their first settlement (c. 1593) until 1769 by David Franco Mendes.*

Memorias/ do estabelecimento e progresso/ dos Judeos/ Portuguezes e Espanhoes/ nesta famosa cidade de/ Amsterdam./ Nellas se narrão as fundaçoens das suas esnogas,/ as instituiçoens das suas academias e escollas/ para instrucção da mocidade; os seus illustres/ professores na theologia etc. as suas varias cazas/ de piedade; a nobreza de alguns particulares/ e varios successos memoraveis; recupilados de/ papeis antigos impressos e escritos./ No anno 5529 por David Franco Mendes.

The unpublished manuscript reposes in the Ets Haim library Hs. 49 A 8. 27,5 × 21 cm.; I + 111 ff., Portuguese text.

The author was born in 1713 [35] and married his cousin Rachel

---

[34] *StGL*, par, 242, p. 147; also *Sheairith Yisrael* complete ... Hebrew translation with notes and preface by Hayim Hominer (Jerusalem, 1964), where 7 Yiddish and 9 Hebrew editions are listed, except the above mentioned Dutch translation of 1855.

[35] Cf. D. R. Montezinos, "De werken van David Franco Mendes," *Joodsch-Letterkundige Bijdragen*, i, nrs. 3,4,6,7,8, 1867; J. Melkman, *David Franco Mendes, a Hebrew poet* (Thesis, Amsterdam University, 1951).

Dias de Fonseca in 1750. He died in Amsterdam in 1792. Franco Mendes was a merchant and sworn translator for Portuguese and Dutch at the court of Amsterdam, as appears from two nautical dictionaries in French, Portuguese and Dutch which repose in manuscript in the Ets Haim library. He devoted his spare time to the cultivation of the Hebrew language in prose and poetry, especially the latter. He was a member of a Hebrew literary society in which Hebrew poetry of quality was produced, had great knowledge of Jewish law and was a collector of pieces concerning the history of the Sephardim in Holland. Besides, he was a talented calligrapher and copied skilfully several works. At the end of his life he worked on a Hebrew encyclopaedia *Ahavat David* of which no traces have been found besides a mention in the Hebrew journal *Hameasef*, for which he wrote several articles. In 1769 he probably was secretary of the Sephardic community in Amsterdam for a short time and had then access to the secret archive of the community. As Franco Mendes' endeavors in Hebrew poetry culminated in his tragedy *Gemûl 'ataliah* (Amsterdam, 1760), so his historical work is best represented by his *Memorias*.

His chronicle reveals the outlook of a well-to-do Amsterdam Sephardi of the second half of the 18th century. He is a *laudator tempori acti* knowing that the old splendor of his community was waning. His political views are very conservative and as practically all Dutch Jews he is an adherent of the House of Orange. When one reads his history it might seem that all Amsterdam Sephardim were rich, learned, noble and charitable and that life in the Dutch Republic was ever nice and prosperous. Of the increasing poverty of the Amsterdam Sephardim, one of the greatest problems of the community in the 18th century,[36] no mention is made. Some events of Dutch history are mentioned, mostly in connection with the princes of Orange, but the political developments in the Dutch

---

[36] The poverty was so great that the Sephardic economist Isaac de Pinto developed a plan to ship the poor Sephardim to the Dutch colonies in West-India to relieve the burden of the Sephardic community in Amsterdam. He published this plan in a pamphlet: *Reflexoens politicas tocante a constituição da nação judaica....* (Amsterdam, 5508 [1748]).

Republic are completely neglected. Franco Mendes used several
Dutch sources, mostly histories of Amsterdam, Pierre Bayle's
Dictionnaire Historique and several pieces from his own collection
which he calls "Collecção de Antiguidades." After 1750 the work
consists only of annotations which he probably planned to work
out later.

In one sense Franco Mendes differs favorably from his fellow
Sephardim: He has a rational attitude towards his Ashkenazic
brethern and considers contacts with them necessary. Hence his
friendship with Wessely and his cooperation with the *Hameasef*.
Though burdened by the past and the prejudices of his environment, Franco Mendes is one of the Amsterdam Sephardim who
saw a glimpse of the time to come. Politically unable to cope with
the new ideas which blew over from France to Holland which
affected also many cultured Jews, he sensed the coming renewal of
Hebrew language and letters by a new generation of Ashkenazim
and sponsored it with all his might.

From his *Memorias* Franco Mendes culled several biographies
of rabbis of the Sephardic community and translated them into
Hebrew. In the *Hameasef* are published:

a) Rabbi Mosseh Rephael d'Aguilar   תולדות החכם מהורר משה
Hameasef, 1785, pp. 15, 16, 26, 28   רפאל די אגילאר זצל.
b) Balthasar Orobio de Castro   תולדות החכם המפואר אראביא ז"ל
Hameasef, 1788, pp. 219–223
c) Jacob Judah Leon (Templo),   תולדות החכם מהו׳ יעקב יהודה
ibid. pp. 296–301   ליאון זצ"ל
d) Menasseh Ben Israel,   תולדות הרב מנשה בן ישראל
ibid., pp. 167–172

XI. *Chronicle of the rebellion in Amsterdam against William V
of Orange and his restoration by the Prussian army in 1787 by
David Franco Mendes.*

Memorias/ succinctas/ da consternação de/ nosso KK de Amster-
dam/ nas tribulaçoens desta cidade a provin/cias unidas no anno/
prodigiozo de 1787./ Impeçada a felice/ tranquilidade/ que a divina

magestade/ fez succeder a ellas./ no fim do mesmo anno.
Manuscript reposing in the Ets Haim library. Hs. 49 B 19.
18,9 × 13,2 cm.; 17 ff.; Portuguese text.

Though no mention of the author is made, it must have been written by David Franco Mendes. The handwriting is the same as in the *Memorias* and also the style conforms. Moreover, D. Montezinos[37] mentions a Hebrew translation of the work with a statement by the author, which reposed in the library of the literary society To'elet in Amsterdam but which has been lost during the Second World War.

In the chronicle the events in Holland and particularly in Amsterdam in 1787 are described. Because he was an eye-witness, the author's personality emerges more clearly than from his previous work. He describes the causes of the rebellion, mainly the lost war with England, 1780–1784, which fed the already pending crisis. What Franco Mendes fails to see is that the completely corrupt government with an incapable and idle Prince of Orange at the top was not able to cope with the emergencies. The feelings of the Patriots which wanted more democracy became ever more embittered, the influence of the new French political ideas became stronger, and 1787 the clash came. Most cities in the province of Holland rebelled against the Prince of Orange who fled to one of his castles in Gelderland. This rebellion was accompanied by riots in the cities with the customary looting and burning, until Frederick, king of Prussia came to the rescue of his brother-in-law and restored the old order in Holland with his army.

The author, naturally, gives much vent to his indignation against the rebels and rejoices with the restoration of the Oranges. He concludes his chronicle with the wish that the Amsterdam Jews may live long in prosperity under the House of Orange. But fate did grant neither longevity nor prosperity to the Orange old regime. In the winter of 1794–1795 the French revolutionary armies crossed the frozen rivers and made an end to the Dutch Republic. The

---

[37] Montezinos, op. cit., p. 45. Neither the Portuguese nor the Hebrew manuscripts are listed by Melkman, op. cit., in his enumeration of Franco Mendes' works, pp. 157–160.

chronicle has some points of local interest in the description of
the defence of the Sephardic and Ashkenazic synagogues in Amsterdam.

XII.　　*Yiddish chronicle for the years 1784–1788 by Zalman ben
Moses Prinz, Amsterdam 1788.*

קראניק / מן שנת תקמ״ד עד שנת תקמ״ח לפ״ק / דש וואונדרליך קראניק איז
זיין לעבן אין דיא וועלט ניט / גיוועזן / וויא איהר עז אויך ווערט אונטיר
פֿינדן מיט לעזין. / אונ׳ דז קראניק פֿון דש איינן יאהר. / איז מער פֿאר
גיפֿאלן אלז אין זיבציג יאר איז גיקומן צו פֿאר. / אונ׳ דער ווייל דש נס וואר
אזוי גרויש אלז וויא אין מצרים / בייא פרעה. / דארום אויך האב איך דש
וואונדרליך קראניק אויף גשריבן / אלז עז זאל זיין לא תשכח מפי זרעו. /
אונ׳ אלז איר לייט דא אין בישטעדין אייר געלט. / דער קעגין ווערט איר
אויך דריין פֿינדן וואונדר זאכֿן דש / זיין לעבן איז ניט גיוועזין אין דיא
וועלט. / אונ׳ וואז איר לייט דא פֿר אויז גיבט אזו ווערט איר לייט / האבין
קיין חרטה. / דער קעגין ווערט איר אויך וואונדר זאכֿן דריין פֿינדן דש / איז
ניט גשעהן למן היום הוסדה ועד עתה. / אונ׳ דר ווייל מיר אין דז זעלבגה
יאהר תקמ״ז וגם תקמ״ח / וואָרן אין אלן שראאמה. / מיר האבן דיא זעלבגין
צייט ניקש אנדרשט פֿר אונש גזעהן / כלם אחוזי חרב מלמדי מלחמה. / אונ׳
מיר וואָרן פֿון וועגין פֿאָרבֿט שכרת ולא מיין. / נור דער נאך האבן מיר
גיזעהן תשועת ה׳ בהרף עיין. / אונ׳ מיר וועָרן האפֿין עז זאל ניט ווידר אזו
איין שרעקניש / קומן אין אונרין מדינה. / שנת / ימ̇לא ̇שחוק פינו ו̇ל̇שוננו
ר̇נה / נעשה על ידי זלמן בן משה פרינץ.

Unique copy reposing in the Bibliotheca Rosenthaliana, Ros.
1895 J 28. 8°; I + 8 ff.

Published with abridged Dutch translation by M. Roest Mzn in
1875.[38]

The title informs us that the author was so impressed by the
events of 1787 (the restoration of William V of Orange by the
Prussian army) that he compares it with the crossing of the Red
Sea by the Children of Israel. In his introduction on the verso-side
of the title, he repeats his awe for the miracles the Lord has wrought.

---

[38] M. Roest Mzn, "Losse bijdragen tot de geschiedenis der Joden in Nederland, I. Een kroniekje van de jaren 1787–'88," *Israelietische Letterbode*, I,
nsr. 2,3,4,5,6 (August–December 1885); J. Shatzky, *The decline of the Yiddish
language and literature in Holland* (Wilna, 1938), pp. 256 sqq. (Yidd. text).

He presents himself here as living in Uilenburg next to Jetje the midwife. Like Franco Mendes he also wishes that the House of Orange may reign long and happily.

The epilogue on f. 8v is most revealing for the motivation of historiography as it was felt by ordinary Ashkenazic Jews in Holland in the 18th century:

דער ווייל מיר השם ב״ה אין מיין גדאנקין האט גיגעבן אום צו שרייבן דש נס
חדש. זייט ווישן רבותי דש האב איך ארויש גינומן אויז מיין בוך וואש איך
איין נאמן האב גיגעבן שארית עם קדוש. דארום אויך איר ליבן קינדר. דש
גימיינן קאנטעפט פון דש קראניק דש איך האב ביטראכט זייט ווישן רבותי
איך בין נאר איין אום גלערנטיר מענש איין פעסיר בינדר. אונ' וואש איין
מענש אלש איך איך בין דז טוא איך אייך זאגן. איך טוא אלן טאג פר דיא פרנסה
דעם רייף שלאגן. דארום אויך אלז איר לייט אין טעות מעכט פינדן אזוי
זעלט איהר לייט אן מיר עקסקוזירירין. אונ' איך פר זוך איר ווערט מיר
רעקומאנדירן. דש זייט איר לייט אויך פון זינב. דער ווייל מיין נאמן איז זלמן
בן משה פרינץ. אונ' דש זאג איך דער בייא. מיין גרויש בוך צו צו הערן איז
איין גרויש ליפהאברייא. אונ' דא שטינן וואונדר זאכן אין בימעלט. דש בוך
קען יעדר איינר הערן פר וויניג געלט. אונ' איך האב נאך איין אנדרן קראניק
דש נאהך עז שארית ישראל בימעלט. אונ' איז אויך אזוי גרויש. דש שרייבט
ביז ר' משה חזן אויז. אונ' מיט דער צייט. אלש איהר לייט אין עש אנדרן
קראניק אויך ליפהאברייא אין העט אזו בין איך אם ירצה השם ברייט. אונ'
דער ווייל מיר דא האבן בייא גיוואונט זעלכן ניסים כנגד יציאת מצרים. אזוי
האפ̇ין מיר אויך אום צו בילעבן בנחמות ציון ובנה ירושלים. ועם כל ישראל
אחינו במהרה בימינו אמן.

"Because the Lord, praised be He, induced me to describe the new miracle, you must know, gentlemen, that I took this from my book Šeʾerît ʿam qadôš. When you see the simple form of the chronicle you must know, gentlemen, that I am but an illiterate man, a cooper and all day long I have to earn my living by fastening staves. Therefore, if you might find a fault, you will pardon me. I pray you to recommend me, if you will, my name is Zalman ben Moses Prinz. And I tell you, I have written a big book for my own pleasure, wherein miraculous stories can be found. Everybody can hear [tales] from this book for little money. I have also written another chronicle as a continuation of Šeʾerit Yisraʾel which is kept until the appointment of Rabbi Moses the Cantor [Moses ben Phoebus Glogau, 1786]. And if you have liked the other chronicle, I am willing with God's help [to print it] when the time comes. And while you have witnessed miracles like the exodus from Egypt, we do hope also to witness the consolation of Zion and the rebuilding of Jerusalem, with all our brethren of Israel, soon in our days, amen."

We see that our author Zalman the cooper had great literary and historical ambitions and we are certain that he was not the only one among his kinsmen. We also see that *Še'erit yisra'el* was indeed a very popular book and that it inspired many people to continue it.

The chronicle of Prinz is written in a very popular vein. He even inserts typical Jewish jokes which were told in the streets. His facts are the same as those David Franco Mendes tells in his chronicle, but the outlook of the author is somewhat different. Franco Mendes and Prinz do agree in their hatred for the Patriots and rebels and their love for William V and the old order. But Prinz records many facts which Franco Mendes probably had not seen at all: dearness of victuals and water and all other evils which always accompany troublesome times and which are felt most bitterly by the common people. Prinz adds at the end of his chronicle a detailed description of the festivities in Amsterdam after the victory of William V of Orange.

XII. *History of the Jews in Surinam by David de Isaac Cohen Nassy, Para-Maribo 1788.*

Essai historique/ sur la/ Colonie/ de/ Surinam,/ Sa fondation, ses révolutions, ses progrès, depuis/ son origine jusqu'à nos jours, ainsi que les causes/ qui depuis quelques années ont arreté le cours/ de sa prospérité; avec la description & l'état ac-/tuel de la Colonie, de même que ses ré-/venus annuels, les charges & impots qu'on y/ paye, comme aussi plusieurs autres objets/ civils & politiques; ainsi qu'un tableau/ des moeurs de ses habitants en général./ Avec/ l'Histoire de la Nation Juive Portugaise & Al-lemande y Etablie, leurs Privilèges immuni-/tés & franchises: leur Etat politique &/ moral, tant ancien que moderne: La/ part qu'ils ont eu dans la défense &/ dans les progrès de la Colonie./ Le tout redigé sur des pieces authentiques/ y jointes, & mis en ordre par les Régens/ & Réprésentants de ladite Nation Juive/ Portugaise./ Première partie./ A Paramaribo/ 1788.

Reposes in the Bibliotheca Rosenthaliana Ros. 19 G 38.

8°; 2 vols; I: XXXVIII+192 pp.; II: 197 pp.

Soon after the original edition two Dutch translations appeared, resp. in 1791 and in 1802.[39] A facsimile edition appeared in Amsterdam, 1968.[40] The authorship of David de Isaac Cohen Nassy stands above doubt, although his name is not stated in the title. Nassy himself described it as "my unfortunate booklet" in a memorandum to Governor Wichers of Surinam in June 1790.[41]

David de Isaac Cohen Nassy is a direct descendant of the first Jewish colonist in Surinam, David Nassy, who had left Amsterdam in 1642 for Brazil and had settled in Surinam after the Portuguese conquest of Recife in 1654.[42] The first David Nassy received a charter from the Directors of the Dutch West-India Company to found a colony "on the island Cayana or other places on the Wild Coast of West-India" in 1660.[43] The Nassy family has remained in Surinam ever since and played an important role in the life of the Jewish community.

Our historian was born in February, 1747 in the "Jooden-Savanne" (a region with many Jewish plantations along the Surinam river) and died in Paramaribo in March 1806.[44] His father Isaac Cohen Nassy was official notary (jurator) of the Portuguese Jewish Nation in Surinam and he taught his son himself, as he was to

[39] S. Seeligmann, "David Nassy of Surinam and his 'Lettre politico-theologico-morale sur les Juifs'," *Publications of the American Jewish Historical Society*, XXII (1914), 27–29.

[40] Published by S. Emmering.

[41] R. Bijlsma, "David de Is. C. Nassy, schrijver van de 'Essai historique sur Surinam'," *Bijdragen voor Vaderlandsche geschiedenis en Oudheidkunde*, V, 6 (1919), 219 sqq.

[42] *Essai*, II, Pieces justificatives, pp. 111–122.

[43] Ibid.

[44] Bijlsma, op. cit.

succeed him in the office. But David Nassy, after marrying a relation, Esther Abigail Cahanat Nassy, bought a plantation "Tulpenburg" for which he had to borrow a great sum in Holland. The enterprise did not prove to be successful and, after an epidemic among his negro slaves, he had to sell the plantation very cheaply in 1773.

Nassy went to Paramaribo and became sworn translator for Spanish and Portuguese at the Court of Justice in Paramaribo, but he had to flee soon, as he was pursued by his creditors. He settled again in the Savanne, where his creditors could not reach him, studied medicine from books in his private library and associated with the local Jewish physician who already practiced there. In 1778 he became secretary of the Sephardi community, but had still to stay in the Savanne. Only in 1784 when his debts were superannuated, Nassy could return to Paramaribo. He began a pharmacy, founded a literary society "Docendo Docemur" under the special protection of governor Wichers[45] and was very active in the Sephardic community. In this period he wrote the *Essai historique*. After the death of his wife in 1789 the pharmacy did not flourish any more, and in 1792 Nassy departed with his daughter Sara to the United States, much regretted by his friends in Paramaribo. He settled in Philadelphia as a physician and became a correspondent of the American Academy of Medicine. Later he went to St. Thomas, then a Danish colony, and received his medical license from the official royal physician there. Finally back in Paramaribo in 1796, the governors of the Sephardic community granted him the title of doctor medicinae. During his stay in Philadelphia Nassy had heard of the revolution in the Netherlands in 1795. He immediately wrote a memorandum on improvements for the colony of Surinam and sent it to the government of the new Batavian Republic.

In Paramaribo Nassy returned to his old office as secretary of the Sephardic congregation and remained alert in the cause of Jewish emancipation. When a pamphlet against civil rights for the

[45] The text of the prospectus issued by the new society is published in the *Essai*, II, 176–183.

Jews reached him, which was written by a member of a patriotic club in Dordrecht, he immediately reacted with an apologetic "Lettre-Politico-Morale sur les Juifs"... Paramaribo, 1798.[46] In 1799 Nassy married Ribca de David de la Parra, a young girl of 24. A most interesting fact about this marriage: the ketubah (marriage-contract) was written in Dutch, the first of its kind. Few months after his marriage he retired from his office, but remained a member of the governing board of the congregation. After retirement from all offices, he died in March 1806 and was buried in the cemetery of the Jooden-Savanne.

Nassy was an extraordinarily gifted man. Born and educated in Surinam, far from the centers of European civilization, he did not only acquire great mastery in many languages, but became a physician as well. His extensive library which was sold in 1782 and of which the catalogue reposes in the notarial archives of Surinam,[47] consists of all the great works on philosophy and history from Bayle to Voltaire. Classical literature, French, Portuguese and Spanish *belles lettres* are also well represented, as well as medicine and physics. The catalogue ends with some Hebrew prayer books. This was the intellectual world of an enlightened Sephardi, a champion of political and social emancipation of the Jews. When challenged, he set it as his tasks to describe his country Surinam and the history of its Jewish inhabitants. The result of his endeavors was the best historical work ever written on the subject until our days.

The challenge for the writing of the book came from Europe: In May 1784 the French *Gazette Littéraire* which was read avidly by the cultured Jews of Surinam, published a review of M. J. Bernouilli's French translation of the work of C. G. Dohm, *Über die bürgerliche Verbesserung der Juden*. It was ordered in Holland and finally, in February 1786, some copies of the much desired work arrived in Surinam. It was read and studied in the literary society "Docendo Docemur" and the members were so enthusiastic, that they wrote Dohm a congratulatory letter. This letter reached Dohm

46 Seeligmann, op. cit., pp. 25 sqq.
47 Bijlsma, op. cit., pp. 224 sqq.

via Holland and he answered it. Both letters are published in the preface of the *Essai*, pp. XIX–XXIV. In his letter Dohm asked for information on the Jews of Surinam, and wanted to be informed on their rights and economic situation. This incited the learned society, *in casu* David Nassy, to compile his work which became the apogee of Jewish historiography in the 18th century.

Nassy divided his work in two parts, preceded by a preface and introduction. The first volume is devoted to the history of the Jews in Surinam, the second volume to the geography, economic development and social and cultural situation of the colony. At the end of Volume II (pp. 88–96) a list of exported goods from Surinam from 1700–1788 is added, complete with the ships which departed from the colony for Holland. The list is followed by an enumeration of all governors and high officials which ruled the colony from 1665 until 1788. The rest of the work is filled with "Pièces justificatives," important documents on the history of the Jews in Surinam.

Though the work had been conceived as an Apology for the Jews and a plea for political emancipation, the *Essai* itself is a most useful history, dealing critically with a wealth of material, both from the archives of the Sephardic community and from the official government archives of Surinam. For the description of the island no better man than Nassy could have been found, with his profound knowledge of the interior of the country and its inhabitants.

Nassy's *Essai* also represents the end of an era in Dutch Jewish history. His plea for emancipation of 1788 was fulfilled in 1796 when the Dutch Jews — inclusive all Jews dwelling in the Dutch colonies — were granted equal civil rights with the rest of the Dutch population.

DOCUMENTS ON ROUMANIAN JEWRY, CONSUL PEIXOTTO, AND JEWISH DIPLOMACY, 1870–1875

LLOYD P. GARTNER

ONE OF PROFESSOR SALO WITTMAYER BARON'S most enduring interests as an historian has been modern diplomacy and the Jewish question. Since his *Die Judenfrage auf dem Wiener Kongress* fifty years ago, numerous studies from his pen have illuminated the place of Jewish questions in 19th century international affairs, and have shown how emancipated Jewry worked within the concert of nations to relieve and liberate their people. This small contribution in that field is a tribute of esteem and affection to a great teacher and scholar.

The plight of Roumanian Jewry prompted emancipated Western Jewry to extensive diplomatic effort in the period between the Treaty of Paris of 1856 and the Treaty of Berlin of 1878. The first treaty, which concluded the Crimean War, gave broad autonomy to Moldavia and Wallachia, known as the Danubian Principalities, under the supervision of the consuls of the signatory powers. Article 46 of the Treaty of Paris proclaimed Jewish emancipation in those lands. This provision did the Jews little good, however, for the regime of the Principalities vigorously opposed it and by chicanery and deception circumvented and outwitted the ineffective consuls. The Treaty of Berlin twenty-two years after the pact at Paris settled the Balkan crisis and the Russo-Turkish War, and recognized the accomplished facts of Roumanian unity (since 1866) and independence. In the most specific terms, the emancipation and equality of the Roumanian Jews was a set condition for the full international recognition of the new Balkan state.[1]

[1] Standard accounts of the founding of the Roumanian state and related diplomatic history are T. W. Riker, *The Making of Roumania: A Study of an International Problem 1856–1866* (London, 1931); William L. Langer, *European*

This seemingly triumphant achievement resulted from the diplomatic activities of French, English, German, and American Jews far more than from Roumanian Jewish efforts. The Jewish community in that country had grown greatly during the 19th century, mainly by virtue of immigration from Russia and Galicia. Except for a thin upper stratum of priviliged bankers and merchants in Bucharest, the "emancipated" Jews, who numbered about 200,000 in 1870, were actually treated as rightless aliens. Even if they possessed homes and businesses and had dwelled in Roumania for years, they and their Roumanian-born children ranked no higher than squatters liable to summary expulsion and the pillaging of their belongings. Not only did the Roumanian government treat tolerantly occasional outbreaks of violence against Jews, but it also skillfully employed the threat of anti-Jewish legislation to repress any inclination Roumanian Jews might manifest to protest their ignominious status.

Efforts to aid Roumanian Jewry reached their fullest stage with the appointment of an American Sefardi, Benjamin Franklin Peixotto (1834–1890), as the first United States Consul posted to Bucharest. Serving without official salary, Peixotto and his educational and philanthropic projects were privately supported. Funds came from B'nai B'rith of which he had been president (Grand Sar) in 1863–1864, from the banking brothers Joseph, Jesse, Abraham, and Isaac Seligman and other American Jews, and from some Jewish sources in England and Germany. Peixotto's American Jewish base was the quasi-representative Board of Delegates of American Israelites. To its secretary, his friend Myer S. Isaacs (1841–1905), he

Alliances and Alignments 1871–1890, 2nd ed. (New York, 1950); B. H. Summer, *Russia and the Balkans 1870–1880* (New York, 1937); Richard V. Burks, "Romania and the Balkan Crisis of 1875–1878," *Journal of Central European Affairs*, II, 2 and 3 (July and October, 1942), 119–134, 310–320; W. N. Medlicott, "The Recognition of Roumanian Independence, 1878–1880," *Slavonic and East European Review*, XI (1932–1933), 354–372, 572–589. The best account of the Jewish position is Isidore Loeb, *La situation des Israélites en Serbie et en Roumanie* (Paris, 1876), usefully supplemented by Joshua Starr, "Jewish Citizenship in Roumania (1878–1940)," *Jewish Social Studies*, III, 1 (January, 1941), 57–79.

poured out his heart in correspondence (some of it printed below), as he also did to Adolphus S. Solomons (1826–1908) and Simon Wolf (1837–1922) in Washington. Peixotto's principal European connection was Sir Francis Goldsmid, M.P. (1808–1879).[2]

The following documents concern Peixotto's and other diplomatic activities, as well as the condition of Roumanian Jewry. All except Document V come from the papers of the Board of Delegates of American Israelites and the Sang Collection, both at the American Jewish Historical Society, Waltham, Massachusetts. Grateful acknowledgement is herewith given to the Society and to Mr. Sang for generously making these materials available. They are printed verbatim, without grammatical or other corrections.

I

Shortly before leaving San Francisco to take up his mission in Roumania, Peixotto expressed to Isaacs his conception of the work he was to undertake, and the goals he proposed.

San Francisco June 28, 1870

My Dear Friend

Your brief letter of the 17th is read. I have to thank you and dear Adolph [Solomons] for the interest you take in the sufferings of our brethren of Roumania, it is *them* not *me* you serve by any and all you do to promote the success of the appointment made by the President. No "empty sceptre" would do those wretchedly persecuted people any good. Authority in name and not in fact would be a gross outrage, a mockery. Not only would the fair fame of our country be tarnished but that which is still dearer, *Israel's* would be blurred and disgraced. The Consul to Roumania to do good must have the means with the official Varnish. He must be American Consul for outward form and what prestige such position may possibly confer — but *American Israelite* and Jew to the core to do practical good. His work lies in winning the love of those poor people of his of whom there are countless hundreds, of doing them charity in many ways, by money, by words of counsel, by going down to them not being above their reach. His main instru-

<hr/>

[2] A detailed account of the Peixotto mission, with extensive bibliography, may be found in my "Roumania, America, and World Jewry: Consul Peixotto in Bucharest, 1870–1876," *American Jewish Historical Quarterly*, LVIII, 1 (September, 1968), 25–117 (abbrev. Gartner, "Peixotto").

mentality for good would be in his successful inauguration of schools among them *a la Alliance Israelite*. Disseminating modern thought, liberalizing the mind, reaching into their hearts by showing them how they may still be Jews without the frightful social *costumes* and customs which they persist in retaining. I believe when my thoughts for these people are placed before the *Alliance* Cohn and Cremieux will warmly sustain me. But is it not possible for the B[oard] of D[elegates] of Am[erican] Israelites to inaugurate something for them. Cannot a Roumanian School Fund be established? Must we go abroad to the B[oard] of Deputies of London or the Alliance of Paris? Or cannot all three of these be united in the work — contributing thereto? Will not the Board of Delegates of American Israelites second the Government of the United States. The Govt. gives the shadow — the official trappings — will not the Board make that shadow substance — afford the means to make effectual the good the office may be made to do?

A meeting of some 12 or 15 of the prominent Israelites of this city has been called for tomorrow evening at the instance of Rev Dr Elkan Cohn, Abraham Seligman, Alexander Weill and A. Hollub[3] who have issued a private note which reads as follows: "The present unfortunate condition of our brethren in Roumania exciting deep sympathy, and the President of the United States, having exhibited commendable interest in their behalf, we have thought it our duty to call together a few prominent co-religionists with a view of sustaining the Government. To this end you are invited to attend a meeting Wednesday evening 8 P.M." This is signed by the gentlemen I have before named. You will please make no use of this communication other than to a similar private end. The object of the meeting is to determine if concert of action cannot be had through which the leading public spirited Israelites of the principal cities can be united in the object of sustaining the mission to Roumania. Of course my relation to the mission will preclude my presence but I will let you know the result as soon as I hear it. If New York Phila Cincinnati Chicago St. Louis & perhaps one or two other cities can be reached through enough of their public-spirited men who are possessed of ample fortune — it is not designed to approach any others — then this mission may prove a success. — provided, the Nomination is confirmed. Did I not believe it possible that some practical good — decided and positive — could be accomplished — I would not urge this undertaking. Nor would I urge it did I in this view stand *alone*. But when practical men like Abraham Seligman and Alexander Weill believe

---

[3] Elkan Cohn (1820–1889) was Reform rabbi in San Francisco; Abraham Seligman was one of the banking brothers; Weill and Hollub could not be identified.

in it and urge it with all their hearts — I am confirmed in my belief. At the same time I am anxious to know how you view the matter and how it is viewed by others. In this you must separate the *personal man* from the man whom the mission calls, if there be a better man than the one whose name is now before the Senate let him stand forth or be brought forward, and gladly willingly will I withdraw. I am not afraid of the consequences of this mission upon myself. When it shall please Heaven that I return from it, if I go — my power for good will be so greatly and potently advanced that I shall be richly repaid for the sacrifice. Nor will those whom I love best on earth my wife and children suffer from it — a few years in Europe — the benefit of a European education for my darlings will be an *advantage* not a disadvantage.

I have tried to look at this question in all its aspects and the result is — my determination to go if it be possible & can have the mission so placed as to make it potent for good. I have grave doubts however of there being sufficient disinterestedness and unselfishness existing to secure the end desired and while I shall lament for the unhappy ones of Roumania that they could not have secured *a friend*, I shall probably rejoice in the sacrifice *saved me*.

One word more. I am told by an enlightened Hungarian who lived six years in Bucharest that Adolph Buchner is the son of an unprincipled man, that he himself was a dissipated young man educated & having the entrée to many Boyar families — a Sec'y to Mr Czapkay formerly our Consul there who came also from this city — who lives now in Europe. I cannot believe it would be well in any event to have such a person represent this country or Am Israelites. One who has never trod our soil or nothing of our institutions.[4] My dear Wife thanks you for your ever kind remembrances. So do I. To yours remember *us*. And to Adolph [Solomons] — kind friend — good heart. And to your brother Isaac — and to your venerable Father.[5]

Ever most faithfully your friend
B. F. Peixotto

II

The privileged stratum of Roumanian Jewry possessed the veneer of French culture prized by the Roumanian upper class. They were

---

[4] Concerning Czapkay, and Buchner's attempt to secure the consulship before Peixotto volunteered, see Gartner, "Peixotto," 39–45.

[5] "Isaac" is Myer S. Isaacs' younger brother and later law partner. Their father was the Rev. Samuel M. Isaacs (1804–1879); see Moshe Davis, *The Emergence of Conservative Judaism* (Philadelphia, 1963), 340–342.

also organized into a Bucharest branch of the Alliance Israelite Universelle. The letter sent by this group to the venerated head of the Alliance, Isaac-Adolphe Crémieux (1796–1880), describes eloquently and quite accurately the devious oppressiveness of the Roumanian government. The man of Bucharest proposed petitioning the European powers to intervene and reaffirm Jewish rights under the Treaty of Paris, and to prevent local outbreaks they urged passage of a law imposing responsibility upon villages and towns as a whole for such occurrences.

Consul Peixotto and the Alliance did not get on well, as their disparaging remarks about his "energies" evidence.[6]

ALLIANCE ISRAÉLITE UNIVERSELLE

Comité Central   Bucarest, le 11 Mars 1872
Bureaux   *M. Peixotto, dont il est souvent question*
Rue de Trevise, 37   *dans cette lettre, est le consul des Etats-*
                          Unis à Bucharest. Il est israélite

Monsieur le Président,

Après avoir reçu les tristes nouvelles des émeutes dont nous avons été encore des victimes à Ismail, à Cahoul et à Vilcow en Bessarabie, le comité de l'Alliance a résolu de secour nos malheureux confrères avec tous les moyens dont nous disposons et à demander comme mesure de protection générale une loi qui rendrait dans l'avenir les communes seules responsables des émeutes dirigés contre nous. Nous sommes allés chez M. Peixotto pour le prier de soutenir notre demande auprès du prince et d'agir chez les consuls dans le même sens.

On nous a dit que tout le monde et prêt à agir pour nous et que le Ministère actuel qui se compose des meilleurs éléments d'ordre qui se trouvent dans le pays et qui offrent les plus sûrs garanties pour nous rendre justice a déjà agi, que de troupes et un procureur général ont été déjà envoyés sur les lieux de désordre.[7]

Nous avons répondu que les troupes arriveront comme toujours trop tard et que le procureur trouvera difficilement des coupables, mais s'il en trouve que ce seront des juifs mêmes par la simple raison que sans israélites une émeute contre eux n'est pas possible. Et supposons qu'il

---

[6] Tension between Peixotto and the privileged Roumanian Jews was constant. His circle was composed of middle class *maskilim*, generally of Germanic culture. Gartner, "Peixotto," pp. 27, 61–66, 82, 88–91, 102.

[7] The Ministry was installed in 1871 and was of the conservative, i.e. landed proprietary, party. Gartner, "Peixotto," p. 60.

trouve des chrétiens coupables, on peut être sûr que plus ils seront condamnables plutôt ils seront délivrés. Le jury devant lequel ils seront appelés fait perdre aux Juifs tous les procès qu'ils ont contre les chrétiens, et dans le cas présent, il regardera comme un devoir patriotique et glorieux d'acquitter les pillards avec leurs instigations.

Les troupes, nous dit on, empêcheront au moins la propagation des émeutes. Les émeutes se sont arrêtées d'elles-mêmes. Il faut savoir qu'on nous consomme comme un artichaut, une feuille après l'autre. Les meneurs qui ont provoqué ces pillages ne veulent pas que leur oeuvre destructive embrasse beaucoup de villes en même temps. Ils craignent que l'étendu du mal ne fasse sortir l'Europe de sa torpeur et secouer enfin sa grande longanimité. En intervenant pour nous, elle éteindra le feu par lequel ils troublent le pays à leur profit.

Les Ministres assurent que dans l'interêt de l'ordre, qui est une condition vitale de leur propre existence, ils rendront justice aux Israélites. Vous savez, Messieurs, que depuis 6 ans de nombreuses émeutes ont été excités contre nous, presque chaque ville en Roumanie en compte une ou deux. Tous les ministres, près dans tous les partis politiques du pays, ont dit dans les mêmes phrases et de plus forts encore, sans les tenir jamais. Par une triste expérience qui s'est répétée au moins 12 fois, nous sommes forcés d'avoir la conviction que toutes les promesses étaient fausses. Elles n'avaient qu'un but: fidèle à la politique orientale on cherche à trainer en longueur une affaire qu'on ne veut jamais résoudre. On laisse agir le temps qui émousse l'interêt et amortit et enterre l'objet. En attendant on paie largement en promesses, et si on va loin, on commence à faire un peu de justice pour s'arrêter et finir immédiatement. Soyez sûrs que cette fois-ci, comme tous les cas précédents, nous n'obtiendrons pas la satisfaction désirée.

On a promis de nous soutenir auprès du gouvernement, de demander la déliverance du rabbin d'Ismaïl et la condamnation des coupables. Nous avons dit que nous n'espérons rien de la libre volonté du gouvernement, mais que les consuls doivent le forcer a rendre justice. Preuve éclatante que sa mauvaise volonté persiste, qu'il reste attaché à la même tactique que tous les ministres ont suivi jusqu'à présent et qui consiste a nier même que les Roumains persécutent les Israélites. M. Catargiu ministre président, a dit dans la Chambre qu'il a passé une nuit blanche à cause de la terrible insurrection des Grecs d'Ismaïl et de Galatz contre nous. Ce sont donc, selon lui, les Grecs qui nous persécutent et non les Roumains. Or les Grecs sont nos amis, nous sommes émancipés dans leur pays. Les Grecs de Galatz n'étaient pas mêmes pas présents pendant les émeutes à Ismaïl. Ceux de cette ville ont donné asile aux Israélites, et à Cahul et à Vilcov il n'y a pas d'habitants grecs. Donc ce sont des accusations fausses faites pour excuser les vrais coupables.

L'insomie de M. Catargiu ne venait pas de ce que le sang impur des juifs a été versé a Cahul, mais bien de ce que le sang pur des chrétiens a coulé, vu que les Orthodoxes du pays s'appellent des chrétiens pur sang.[8]

Nous avons décrit notre position. Nous sommes ici hors de la loi, et notre sort dépend de la fidélité et de l'énergie de la police, institution la plus corrompue. Le gouvernement même avec la meilleure volonté, ne peut à présent nous protéger partout. Il n'a que 20000 soldats à sa disposition, dont un tiers est engarnison à Bucarest et à Jassy, le reste ne suffit pas pour nous protéger dans le pays entier, qui à une etendue de 2300 lièves. Nous avons deux catégories d'ennemis. Les ennemis du pays qui veulent démontrer que la Roumanie ne peut exister comme un état indépendant, et les ennemis du Prince et du Ministère. Les uns et les autres veulent arriver à leur but par le même moyens, en troublant l'ordre par les émeutes, qui si elles sont dirigées contre nous, réussissent le plus facilement. Avec une somme minime, on achète un meneur qui se compose une petite bande de malfaiteurs dont le nombre s'augmentera par la canaille, les fanatiques religieux et une partie de nos concurrents de chaque commune qu'il veut attaquer. L'entreprise est facile, l'impunité et le gain assurés. Telle est notre position déplorable dans le présent encore plus menaçant dans l'avenir. Pour remedier à cette intolérable situation il nous faut une loi qui nous regardons comme l'unique moyen pour nous sauver dans le moment actuel. Il faut rendre chaque commune responsable pour les émeutes qui y ont lieu contre nous. C'est aussi elle qui doit payer immédiatement notre indemnité.

Cette loi nous rendra partout la sureté, parceque l'immense majorité des habitants qui a laisse agir jusqu'à présent les petites bandes qui nous ont pillés, croyant que ces choses ne la regardent pas, vu qu'elle n'était pas menacée, se dira pour nous et nous protègera — sachant bien au fond que c'est elle qu'on pille et qu'elle sera condamnée par la nouvelle loi. Seulement par la responsabilité impose aux communes, l'Italie a pu se sauver du brigandage dans les Calabres contre lequel elle avait envoyé en vaine une nombreuse armée. En Valachie même sous le gouvernement du prince Stirbey quand les impôts étaient minimes et l'armée en proportion, la même loi a délivré le pays des brigands et des voleurs dont il était rempli.

On nous dit que cette mesure pouvait s'employer facilement alors mais qu'à présent la constitution offre de très graves obstacles. Par une autonomie excessive dont [...] a doté les communes, mais que les Ministres

---

[8] The Ismail and Cahul riots of January, 1872, originated in an accusation by an apostate that Ismail Jews had stolen and desecrated a chalice. Large-scale plundering and physical attacks ensued, and the episode became an international incident. Gartner, "Peixotto," pp. 68–74.

prendront peut être d'une main plus ferme les rènes du gouvernement.

Notre situation a l'intérieur est notablement empirée. Nous ne sommes pas sûrs du jour en lendemain contre une nouvelle émeute. Il est vrai que le parti rouge d'ici après la chûte de la commune de Paris, a perdu une partie de son influence, mais le vent déchaîné par lui est devenu orage. Du reste à qui demander ici une amélioration de notre sort!

Le Prince n'est pas contraire à notre émancipation, mais dans un état constitutionel il ne peut rien faire sans le Ministère.

Le Ministère dit qu'il voudrait faire quelque chose pour nous mais qu'il depend de la Chambre. Nous connaissons les sentiments de la Chambre contre nous, elles les a manifestés dans la loi sur le monopole du tabac, permettant qu'un Juif puisse devenir fermier général, mais défendant qu'il emploie un seul coreligionnaire dans cette entreprise. Elle a décidé aussi que dans la nouvelle ville "Corabia" qu'elle veut fonder sur le Danube, les Israélites ne pourront acheter aucun terrain. Parmi les Députés et Sénateurs il y a certainement des hommes justes. Comment se fait-il que pas un ne parle franchement pour nous? Laissons la justice et l'humanité de coté, parlons d'un sentiment qui se trouve même chez quelques animaux, la Pitié. Admettons tous les mensonges proférés pendant les derniers évènements contre nous! C'étaient les Grecs, non les Roumains, qui[...]contre nous etc. Messieurs les Députés savent que 200 familles ont été rendus misérables si malheureuses qu'elles souffrent de la faim et du froid. Comment se fait-il que pas un d'entre eux n'ait eu assez du pitié pour ces malheureux pour proposer à la Chambre de voter une somme quelconque pour les soutenir dans leur misères. Jugez vous mêmes ce que nous avons à attendre.

La France occupée de ses propres malheurs ne peut pas s'occuper beaucoup de nous.

La Prusse favorise beaucoup le Ministère actuel qui lui a rendu un service très important en arrangeant l'affaire Strousberg dans laquelle 200 millions de francs sont engagés qui appartiennent à ses sujets. Une pression de sa part sera difficile à obtenir. L'Autriche est en train de conclure avec la Roumanie des traités d'un grande portû. C'est le traité postal et télégraphique qui a été signé avant hier. Le Ministère actuel est d'accord avec les planes de l'Autriche. Jugez si le moment est bien choisi pour le consul autrichien d'agir contre le Ministère qui disposə dans ces questions de la majorité de la Chambre de manière que sa volonté fait loi.

En Angleterre nous avons un très noble défenseur qui nous fait beaucoup de bien. Nous voulons parler de Sir Francis Goldsmid. Mais le Consul anglais ne suit que pour la forme les instructions qu'il reçoit de son gouvernement. Ses sentiments envers nous sont plutôt ceux d'un oriental que d'un anglais.

La sympathie de l'Europe se refroidit, malgré qu'il n'y ait jamais eu un moment ou nous avions plus besoin d'elle qu'à présent.

Malgré ces circonstances défavorables, nous nous sommes dit qu'il est impossible que l'opinion européenne ne vienne pas à notre secours si on trouve le moyen juste de la décider. Tout est là.

Sachant que le monde ne connaît pas et ne croit pas assez a nos intolérables souffrances, nous pensions avoir trouvé ce moyen dans une exposition vraie et complète de notre déplorable position adressée d'une manière officielle au monde. Nous nous sommes imaginés que nous parviendrons à notre but par des petitions.

Nous sommes allés chez M. Peixotto et ne trouvant pas là l'énergie nécessaire pour l'execution de notre projet, nous nous sommes adressés à d'autres consuls. Nous leur avons dit que les Israélites sont decidés à rédiger des pétitions, les indigènes au Prince, au Ministère et au Corps législatif, que les Israélites étrangers feront la même chose auprès de leurs Consuls et auprès des puissances garantes.

Dans ces pétitions nous exposerons succinctement les cruelles persé-cutions que nous avons endurés jusqu'à présent. Nous dirons qu'on ne nous a pas rendu justice, et que nous n'en demandons plus pour le passé. Mais nous prions qu'on nous accorde au moins une garantie pour l'avenir, qui mette notre vie et nos biens toujours menacés, à l'abri. Que la responsabilité communale serait ce moyen.

Ils nous ont demandé si nous sommes pénétrés de la gravité de cette démarche? Oui, c'est un appel à l'intervention étrangère, un attentat à l'autonomie du pays, il en résultera probablement une émeute contre nous; elle sera la dernière, et il en vaut mieux une pour finir, que 14 comme nous les avons eues. Nous sommes poussés par le sentiment de notre conservation. Personne ne pourra nous reprocher une défense si légitime. Depuis 6 ans on nous a mis le couteau à la gorge, nous avons crié et à present le couteau coupe déjà profondément. Les prochains Pacques sont pleins de dangers pour nous. S'il faut succomber, il vaut mieux pour nous succomber en nous défendant. Que nous n'en pouvons plus et que nous sommes décidés. (Notre plan était que les Israélites indigènes fassent d'abord leur petition — elle aurait été sans résultat. En attendant nous aurions été informes par vous, si les Israélites étrangers doivent la même démarche, et quand, bientôt, on après la prochaine émeute qui n'aurait pas tardé a se présenter.)

Notre démarche eut un résultat inattendu. Le lendemain nous apprîmes d'un source certaine que M. Catargiu, à qui notre résolution inébranlable fut communiqué, en avait été extrêmement agité, sachant parfaitement à quels dangers notre pression exposerait le pays, et il a promis que le ministère même prendra l'initiative et proposera la responsabilité communale à la Chambre.

Figurez-vous notre joie!

Cette joie a été diminué notablement les jours suivants parce que nous avons appris que la loi demandée sera singulièrement modifiée, qu'elle figurera dans la loi communale qui doit être soumise ces jours-ci à la Chambre que le Ministère propose: "Que la commune est responsable pour chaque acte de violence qui aura lieu chez elle."

Nous nous sommes plaint de cette modification qui ne mentionne pas même les Israélites. On nous a dit que malheureusement on ne peut pas faire mieux si on voulait proposer une loi plus favorable aux Israélites et on n'obtiendra rien. Nous disions que des mesures énergiques souvent (?) peuvent nous sauver. L'intervention serait l'unique mesure tout à fait sûre, mais... "nous parlâmes d'une note collective vous pourrez l'obtenir — nous dit-on — mais probablement signée seulement de trois puissances garantes." Or si la Russie manque, notre position serait emp[...]

Les choses sont là. En attendant notre commune enverra une deput[...] au Prince parce que M. Peixotto nous a dit qu'il veut nous parler.

Les promesses en Roumanie ne valent rien. Ce sont seulement les faits positifs qui comptent. Nous attendons de très petits résultats, en nous reservant l'action future.

Recevez etc.

III

In July, 1872 the Roumanian Committee of Berlin proposed a Jewish international conference to consider the Roumanian Jewish question. The possibility of mass emigration from Roumania to America was added to the conference's agenda after Peixotto raised the subject unofficially with the Roumanian government. The latter's loud-spoken agreement and its mocking offer of free passports seriously impaired Peixotto's standing in Western Jewry. However, he continued to advocate large-scale emigration publicly and privately, as in the following letter to Myer S. Isaacs:[9]

Private
Bucharest 19th Sept 1872
My dear friend
    Your warm advocacy evinced many times to promote the welfare of

[9] Gartner, "Peixotto," pp. 79–86, 90–94, 98–101, 105; idem, "Roumania and America, 1873: Leon Horowitz' Roumanian Tour and Its Background," *Publications of the American Jewish Historical Society*, XLV, 2 (December, 1955), 57–89.

our unfortunate brethren of Eastern Europe and especially of Roumania is likely to result in something definite through one of the means of relief you have with others suggested and which you repeat in the *Messenger* of Aug 23 in your article entitled the "Emigration scheme."

For some years before leaving America I had been deeply impressed (witness my answer to M Cremieux Spring of 1870)[10] with the expedieney and practicability of emigration as a means of relief to the suffering people of our faith crowded in Eastern Europe. Since coming to this country I have been strengthened and confirmed in these views and it has rejoiced my heart exceedingly to see many noble men in our country both Christian and Israelite, embrace and endorse the project.

The recent painful events in Roumania and the great difficulty of obtaining *direct armed intervention* with the continued miseries of our people and the prospect of radical relief being delayed unless the friends of Israel and humanity *unite* and *combine* and apply more than *one* remedy, has finally determined me to advocate with all the force I am capable of partial emigration as an additional and very powerful means of amelioration and *of more speedily acquiring the rights of those remaining.*

Inquiring of the Roum Govt at the instance of several letters recd from our brethren in America and in Europe on the subject I have found that they are not averse to promoting the object while the Roumanians affect to receive with delight but their joy is not so real or in no sense to be compared with the delight and enthusiasm of our brethren at this prospect of final relief and already 404 families have registered their names for emigration nearly all of them are engaged in industrial pursuits embracing *glaziers, painters, tin-smiths, joiners, carpenters, tailors, shoemakers, hat-makers, stone-cutters, farmers* etc. etc. All that is now needed is the means and as to these I think it not impossible to secure such by a grand combination of all the Hebrew Societies of Europe co-operated with by America. Ere this is recd you will no doubt have recd from the Berlin Roumanian Com an invitation to attend a General Conference to be held in Brussels on the 28th–29th proximo. Such a letter addressed to the Bd of Delegates & particularly our dear friend Mr Hart and yourself I know has been sent as well as invitations to other American representative Israelites. I do hope & pray God that you will send a delegate and that it will be yourself or one whose heart is as thoroughly kindled to the cause of Israel as yours. I shall make every effort to be present myself though my leaving here is attended with difficulty. Empowered by the Bd of Delegates or other American

[10] This letter, in the Board of Delegates of American Israelites collection, had been written before Peixotto presented himself for the consulship.

societies I would try to represent you if instructions were sent me but only in the event of your own inability to send a representative. I enclose a copy (translated) of the Berlin Committee letter to me. In complying with the request of the Com in so far as America is concerned I have given the following names: Benj. I. Hart Myer S. Isaacs Joseph Seligman Philip Heidelbach A. S. Solomons Rev Dr M. Jastrow Simon Wolf, Abraham Seligman, Henry Greenebaum.[11] The last two names I gave because I thought perhaps Mr A. Seligman might now be in Berlin & if requested would attend the Conference & Mr Greenebaum's name as he is known in Berlin. In my letter I said that in the event of none of these gentlemen who were representative American Israelites, not being able to attend they would probably decide to send some other who would fully enter into their views and who would be familiar with the ideas and wishes at present prevailing in the U. States among our brethren. You will see that I am anxious that an American representative coming fresh from the heart of the people should be present. It is important such should be for he will go back and report the spirit and doings, the heart & soul of the Conference. I beg you dear Myer therefore immediately on receipt of the Berlin Committee's letter to convene a meeting of the Ex Com of the Bd of Delegates take this subject into consideration and resolve to find & send a delegate. The expense could well be made — the time required would not be long and the object *great*.

You will receive this letter on the 8th leaving but little time to decide, but if the delegate or delegates will leave N.Y. on the 16th Oct they will (*sic*) be ample time to reach Brussels.

I have at length induced the Prince to pardon the three remaining Ismail Israelite prisoners Haim David, Abraham Preismann & Israel Weisman. They were liberated Tuesday evening. My remarks on this subject (in to-morrow's Roumanische Post) I beg to recommend for reproduction in the *Messenger*.[12] From the first moment after their condemnation the Prince promised to pardon these poor men. You know he did carry this out in so far as the Rabbin & Mr Goldschlager was concerned but *really was afraid* to exercise his authority toward the others. I have never ceased to plead for them both with him the Princess

11 In addition to the familiar names, Benjamin I. Hart was President of the Board of Delegates; Philip Heidelbach was a Cincinnati banker and merchant; Henry Greenebaum (1833–1914) was a Chicago banker and merchant; Marcus Jastrow (1829–1903) was the rabbi and Talmudist in Philadelphia.

12 Isaacs edited the weekly *Jewish Messenger*, established by his father in 1859. The sentences of the prisoners convicted of the alleged desecration had previously been reduced by Prince Charles. Gartner, "Peixotto," pp. 72–74.

and the Minister of Justice. It required great delicacy and I fear I was sometimes too zealous for one holding an official position but you see I have triumphed — as perseverance and an unconquerable purpose must triumph in the end.

Love to all & in trust believe me dear Myer
Ever your faithful friend

Benj. F. Peixotto

M. S. Isaacs Esq,
N.Y.
[Added in margin]
The Roumanian Hebrew haters stop at nothing they have now hired one of our own people to write against me. He has succeeded to have his letter published in the first instance in the Archives Israelite (*sic*) (of course by imposition) only to give it *more force* now that it is reproduced in all the Roumanian journals.[13]

IV

The Board of Delegates formulated its policy towards immigration when it was invited to the Brussels conference. It endorsed the organized movement of employable men and their families on a comparatively large scale. However, the conference sharply rejected emigration as a solution of the Roumanian Jewish problem, adhering to the policy of demanding emancipation and promoting internal Jewish reform. Isaacs' comment on the reception of Jewish immigrants in the United States during the 1830's and 1840's — which, being born in 1841, he must have heard rather than experienced — is quite interesting, although it finds little support in early sources.

BOARD OF DELEGATES OF AMERICAN ISRAELITES
Office of the Executive Committee
243 Broadway
New York, Oct. 9, 5633, 1872

My dear Friend,

Your letter reached me yesterday and simultaneously I had a note from Berlin upon the same subject. Mr. Hart & I called on Mr. [Joseph] Seligman to see what the Roumania Committee would do. We have determined to be represented at Brussels, although it is too late for any

[13] Gartner, "Peixotto," p. 78, note 13.

of our New Yorkers to cross the sea. Mr. Isaac Seligman of London[14] will be with you at Brussels and some other gentlemen representing the Roumania Committee.

As for instructions, I scarcely know what to say. The call is so general and the subject so comprehensive, that every thing is to be left to the discretion of the Conference. Our representatives will not be authorized to distinctly pledged us to any definite action — save to express what we all believe most earnestly, the conviction that American Israelites will be prompt, cordial & liberal in extending a substantial welcome to the emigrants. And there is a condition which underlines our action — that the emigrants be families or individuals having an occupation or a trade — the class you indicate among the 400 families now registered. If such came hither they will get what the Germans & Poles of thirty or forty years ago did not enjoy — a warm, kind reception and a helping hand.

I have written to Mr. [Isaac] Seligman (in addition to the formal letter of which a copy is sent to you) the suggestions which occur to us respecting emigration. If that is considered (as I imagine it will be) a prominent and indispensable means of relief, it is understood that you & Mr. Seligman will insist that it be not exclusively to America, and that emigrants be selected from the industrial classes. Only those having a trade or occupation will be welcome to America. The Russian emigrants who to the number of 500, have arrived here in detachments have shown themselves capable of becoming useful citizens and an assistance has given them a start.[15] It will be precisely thus with the Roumanians. Let a Committee be formed in Hamburg or some other German port, whence they may be transported to U.S. Then let this Committee register the emigrants — ages, names, occupations, no. in family, whether they are willing to settle in agricultural districts. Let no emigration commence until April, which will give us time to organize & find at least some homes.

I would suggest a conference at Vienna next July — giving ample means to the Israelites everywhere to be represented. By that time, something may have been accomplished in the way of emigration & addresses to the Powers of Europe.

Please write to Mr. Seligman if you are unable to attend at Brussels. I would intimate to you that this Committee will refund your travelling

---

[14] Isaac Seligman (1834–1927) lived in London where he represented the brothers' banking interests.

[15] On this early Russian Jewish migration, see J. Lipschitz (E. Lifschutz), "An Unsuccessful Attempt of a Mass Immigration to the United States," (Yiddish) *Yorbukh fun Amoptayl* (New York, 1938), pp. 38–59.

expenses to & from Brussels if you are there as its representative — of course, you would bear in mind that our funds are not extensive. —

I am delighted to learn of your success in liberating the three remaining Ismail prisoners.

In behalf of my dear wife, I wish you & yours a Happy New Year and hope & pray that you may be able to render yet further services to humanity and receive the approval of God and man.

Faithfully Yours,
Myer.

V

One of the approximately thirty-five delegates to the Brussels conference was M. Krasnopolski, an otherwise unknown businessman of Galatz.[16] The Jewish community of that city furnished him with a letter of accreditation and introduction, together with a most interesting memorandum for the conference which presents three main subjects:

1. A classification of Roumanian society into four strata: landowners, petty officials, small merchants, and the peasantry. The composition and outlook of each class and its attitude to the Jews are discussed incisively and with wit. Governmental policy is also frankly discussed.

2. Galatz Jewry, which the memorandum estimates at 8,000 in a population of 100,000 (more likely, 70,000). The struggles between the Jewish community's "party of progress" and the "lower class of people" are treated from the standpoint of the former. Jewish livelihoods are also touched upon.

3. In its final paragraph the memorandum enthusiastically endorses Peixotto's emigration proposals. No less than 2,216 persons registered to go to America, provided their fares were paid.

[16] The virtually unknown history of this (and other) Roumanian Jewish communities has been considerably advanced by the publication of *Pinkas Hakehillot. Encyclopedia of Jewish Communities. Rumania. Volume I.* (Jerusalem: Yad Vashem, 1969), pp. 90–99. See also E. Feldman, "Jewish Guilds in Moldavia in the 19th Century" (Hebrew with English abstract), *Fourth World Congress of Jewish Studies, Papers,* II (Jerusalem, 1968), pp. 219–222 (Hebrew), English section pp. 197–198 (English). An early source is *Narrative of a Mission of Inquiry to the Jews from the Church of Scotland in 1839* (Edinburgh, 1843), pp. 343–375.

The city of Galatz was a free port near the mouth of the Danube which grew considerably during the 19th century. It was the home of a variegated population from Russia and the Balkans. While the history of Galatz Jewry has barely been explored, it is known to include many anti-Jewish disturbances. The Jews had undergone a full-blown blood libel in 1859 with three days of rioting and pillaging, in which several were murdered. Some Jews were forcibly drowned in 1867, and in 1868 yet another pogrom shook the city's Jewish community. These events called forth international protests.

Jewish communal life was unsteady and plagued by disputes throughout this period. Governmental authorization to the community was repeatedly granted and withdrawn. Inter-synagogal rivalry, quarrels over the kosher meat tax, and religious differences were constant, while the Talmud Torah and the hospital established by the "progressive" group had very checkered careers until the close of the century. One interesting feature of Jewish life was the large and active craft guilds. A measure of stability was attained by Galatz Jewry from 1873, when Peixotto organized an active local B'nai B'rith lodge and a communal council was also formed.

This six-page document is located in the Jewish Historical General Archives, Jerusalem, class mark Rm 63, and I am indebted to that institution for permission to publish it. The generous help of Dr. Rudolf Glanz in deciphering Krasnopolski's memorandum from its very blurred and faded letter press copy is gratefully remembered.

Galatz, 21 Oct: 1872

Euer Wohlgeboren,

Wir vernehem mit besonderem Vergnügen dass das "Berliner Comite" eine Einladung zu der am 29 u. 30 d.M. in Brüssel stattfinden den Conferenz — die Interessen der Israeliten Rumäniens betreffend — ergehen liess.

Es freut uns (...) dass Sie dieser Einladung folge werden leisten und wünschen wir Ihnen von ganzen Herzen dass der Allmächtiger Ihre Hin- und Herreise segnen möge!

Zugleich wollen wir uns erlauben, Sie zu ersuchen, (der) Dolmetsch unserer innigsten Gefühle bei sämtlichen Herren Abgeordneten der Conferenz sein zu wollen und ihnen Allen den wärmsten Dank auszudrücken für das rege Interesse das sie für unsere rumänischen Glaubensgenossen hegen; auch sind wir von den besten Hoffnungen beseelt dass die Bemühungen diesmal gewiss Früchte tragen und der gordische Knoten endlich zu unserer Zufriedenheit gelöst werden wird!

Wir ertheilen Ihnen hiemit auch Vollmacht alles in unserem Namen thun zu wollen was Sie zweckentsprechend finden und erlauben uns noch ausserdem schliesslich einige Notizen zu gefl. Kenntnisnahme beizulegen.

Sie ersuchen bei dieser Gelegenheit den Ausdruck unserer hochachtung annehmen zu wollen, zeichnen ergebenst

Die Mitglieder des Israel.
Gemeinde-Vorstandes in Galatz

Sr. Wohlgeboren
Herrn M. Krasnopolski
Galatz

MEMORANDUM

Obwohl allen Herren Abgeordneten der Conferenz in Brüssel die Lage und Leidensgeschichte der rumänischen Israeliten bekannt ist, möchten wir wünschen beifolgenden Notizen, wenn thunlichst, zur Sprache bringen zu wollen. Damit die Herrn auf manches, davon [besinnen] welches vielleicht im Laufe der Zeit vergessen [wurde], und was unseren Erachtens zur Erläuterung der Situation von Nutzen sein dürfte.

Die Einwohner Rumäniens zerfallen in vier Klassen, folgender (sic): 1. Der führende, "Boyaren Stande", [dessen Mitglieder] sich als Gutsbesitzer bewährt, entweder hohe Staatsämte bekleidet oder in dolce far niente seine Zeit hier und im Auslande zubringt. 2. Dem [Beamten?]-stand", von denen es eine enorme Zahl gibt welche (sic) die Regierung zu reduziren nicht im Stande ist. Hier aber heisst Jemand ein Amt verleihen soviel [...] 3. Den "Klein-Kaufmann-stande", der den Detailhandel betreibt. 4. Den "Bauernstand", oder den Landmann.

Alle vier Klassen lebten stets in Eintracht und Harmonie mit der jüdischen Bevölkerung [...], den hiesigen Verhältnissen angemessen, bis Bratianu ans Ruder kam. Dieser, in der Folge zusehend dass seine Stellung bei Hofe erschüttert wurde, suchte ein Mittel sich eindeseits bei den Grossen in Gunst [zu stellen], anderseits [sich] bei den andern Volksklassen populär zu erhalten, und brachte die [...] Judenfrage aufs Tapet. [Er tat das] indem er die [sich] im Lande (zu bilden erfolgenden?) Comites zur Verfolgung der Juden unterstützte. Er reüssirte auch vollständig damit [;] nur seit damals gelang es den unausgesetzten Hetzereien Bresche auf Bresche in unsere Rechte zu schlagen trotz den grossherzigen Bemühungen der Alliance Isr: Univ. und insbesondere der hochverehrten Herrn Crémieux, Montefiore &c. &c.

Es folgte die entsetzenerregende *Noyade* in Galatz, die *Vertreibung* der Juden aus den Dörfern und vom flachem Lande, die *Zerstörungen* und *Plünderungen* der Synagogen und jüdischen Wohnstätten in Galatz-Bucharest-Berlad-Tekutsch-Bacau-Bottaschan &c., und erreichten ihren Kulminations-punkt in Ismaïl-Cahul-Wilcow.

Alle Interventionen der Consuln fremder Regierungen, alle Proteste derselben, führten zu nichts. Die Regierung in Bucharest wusste stets auf eine oder die andere Weise die Sache zu verdrehen und todt zu schweigen. Das höchste was man ihr an Konzessionen abzwingen konnte, waren bisher-Versprechungen, die aber nie in Erfüllung gingen. Die Rumänen wissen: promettre c'est novel [?] mais tenir c'est bourgeoise! *Schuld an allem Übel trägt die Regierung!* Es wird dem jeweiligen Ministerium und den Kammern nie conveniren, gutwillig auch nur die kleinsten Rechte, die wir bessassen und man uns nach und nach raubte, zurückzustatten. Ein Teil der *Boyaren* ist uns zwar gut gesinnt, aber ein anderer der an die Juden verschuldet ist, glaubt auf diese Weise, durch Verfolgung, u.s.w., den Aufenthalt derselben zu verleiden, und dadurch, wenn [sich] auch nicht seiner Schulden zu entäussern, doch wenigstens sich zu rächen. Aus anderen Bewegsgründen werden wir von der *Beamten* gehasst und verfolgt. Diese fürchten nämlich bei Gewährung von Rechten an die Israeliten, [sie] grossenteils ihre Posten verlieren [würden], welche von den bei weitem fähigeren und intelligenteren Juden eingenommen werden würden. Zweiten ist es ihnen schon deshalb daran gelegen die Juden in ihrer misslichen, deprimierenden Lage zu erhalten, weil sie dadurch Geld bei unsern Glaubensbrüdern bei jeder Gelegenheit und unter jedem Vorwande erpressen [können] summen die beiweitem ihren Gehalt übersteigen unter ihnen die Mittel verschaff auf grossem Fusse leben zu können. Solche Tatsachen können nur diejenigen begreifen, welche hier zu Lande leben und mit dem Verhältnissen betraut sind. Dagegen höhern Orts appelliren fruchtet nichts, allen solchen Petitionen werden von vornherein kein Gehöre geschenkt und der Jude ist und bleibt der Willkur der Beamten preisgegeben.

Der Kaufmannsstand ist uns aus blossem Brotneide gehässig. Da er ungebildet und des Lesens und Schreibens unkundig [sind] muss seine (*sic*) Tätigkeit bloss auf Localkäufe und Verkäufe en detail beschränkt bleiben, weil er mit dem Auslande nicht in Relation treten könne. Er ist daher in dieser Beziehung von dem Juden, Griechen, Deutschen etc. die den ganzen Ex- und Import in Händen haben, abhängig. Da aber gegen die anderen Nationen nichts ausrichten kann, hatte er all seinen Hass auf Andere gerichtet und sucht auf diese Art sich Mästrodomo zu [...] typ.

Was den Bauerstand anbelangt, so mischt er sich in keine Politik, und will wie der rumänische Landmann den Juden in seinen Rechten kränken und drücken, trotzdem ihm dieser manchmal Veranlassung dazu gibt. Aber weil der Grieche, Bulgare und Armenier den Bauern malträtiert und erbarmungslos schindet, so zieht er den bei weiten menschlich fühlenden Juden vor, der sich mit ihm gutwillig [?] [...] auch müssen wir die Dorfgeistlichkeit lobend erwähnen, die ein durch Aufreizungen predigten &c. das Volk zu Verfolgungen anfechten.

Deshalb ist & bleibt alle Schuld wie oben angedeutet, nur der Regierung zuzuschreiben, und auch sie allein ist im Stande von oben herab auf ihre Beamten hinzuwirken, dass "gleiches Recht für Alle" geübt werde, wenn wir auch "gleichen Pflichten" wie Alle unterworfen sind und [wir] erwarten auch mehr im Verhältnis zu den christlichen Mitbürgen besteuert werden.

Dass die Presidenten der Tribunale keine Haüser und Grundstücke auf Juden übertragen wollen, hängt von deren blossen Willkür ab, da darüber kein Gesetz existiert, und die Meinung ein und desselben Gerichthofes divergiren, ist auch der metallene Unter [...] zins der an die Herren verabfolgt wird. Geld ist der goldene Schlüssel der hier überall Tür und Tor offnet.

Zu Licitationen bei Munizipalitäten wegen verschiedene Octrois [...] zu Stadtverschönerung u. dgl. werden keine Israeliten zugelassen. Bei einigen Kreisen können sie ja mitlizitieren, müssen aber *christliche* Agenten in dem Bureaus [...] anstellen.

Tausenden und Aber-Tausenden von Israeliten wurde durch das jüngst eingeführte *Tabaksmonopol* jeder Nahrungszweig abgeschnitten, weil diese weder in der Verwaltung, noch bein Verschleiss engagiert würden dürfen.

Es heisst nun die Kammern werden ein *Spiritus-Fleischmonopol* votieren in welchem Falle [wird] wiederum zehntausenden Israeliten ihr Erwerbszweig entzogen, und wegen der Fleischfrage in die grösse Verlegenheit kommen.[17]

Da vereinigen sich unsere Feinde einen grossen Theil der Israeliten ohne Lebensunterhalt zu lassen; und beschweren wir uns bei den Lokalämtern erhält man keine Antwort; wenden wir uns Ausland, so heisst es: wir wollen fremde Intervention ins Land bringen.

Was unsere Lage in Galatz speziell anbelangt, so ist bei einer Bevölkerung von circa 8,000 Seelen (unter circa 100,000) unser Gemeindewesen hier wie in den meisten Städten des Landes in zerüttersten Verhältnissen, und nur aus dem einfachen Grunde, weil die Munizipalität keinen gehörigen Schutz verleiht und wir müssen es leider zur Steuer der Wahrheit sagen, einige Intriganten der niederen Volksklasse zerstören allemal, was

---

[17] The Roumanian regime enacted legislation in 1873 denying tobacco and liquor licenses to aliens, i.e. Jews, and enforced this policy spasmodically. The principal use of the law was as political blackmail. Gartner, "Peixotto," p. 95.

die Fortschrittspartei nach schweren Kämpfen errungen und geschaffen hat. Schon mehrmals hatten wir Schule, Spital-angelegenheiten in Ordnung, aber ebensooft wurden sie jedesmal aufgelassen weil die Unterhaltungskosten bloss von der *Koscherfleischsteuer* bestritten werden und diese nur *solange* eingehoben werden kann solange keine Zerwürfnis in der Gemeinde vorkommen. Wir waren bis jetzt beispielweise auch nicht im Stande unsere seit 13 Jahren zerstörte *Synagoge* aufzubauen, desgleichen konnten wir bei allen Bemühungen bei der Munizipalität, der Kammer und dem Ministerium nicht reussieren einen *Tempel* zu errichten, wozu wir bereits seit Jahren ein Grundstück, Baumaterialen und Geld haben, bloss weil nach dem altem verrosteten Gesetze ein jüdisches Bethaus so und soviel Meter von der nächsten Kirche entfernt sein muss und dies hier nur knapp der Fall ist. Was würde der Fall sein, wenn bei einer Entfernung von einigen Metern jetzt eine Kirche errichtet würde. Würden da nicht in einigen Jahren die Niederreisung der älteren Synagoge von den Christen verlangt werden?, und bis wir prozessieren ist die Niederreisung ein fait accompli — und die Rumänen werden Recht behalten! — Ist schon Alles dagewesen!

Seit [ein] paar Monaten ist unser Gemeindewesen wieder Complett und haben wir unser Spital restauriert, desgleichen wieder am fünften November a:c: unsere *Schule* eröffnet, wo wir in vier Classen ausser hebräisch noch rumänisch und deutsch unterrichten lassen. Die Kinder der hies. Israeliten sind beiweitem talentvoller und aufgeweckter als vielleicht anderswo und [sie] würden bei den Wohltaten des Unterrichts allen Anforderungen Ehre machen. Die rumänischen Schulen besuchen nur eine kleine Zahl, weil sie von den christlichen Schülern beschimpft werden. Manche Kinder besuchen Pensionate, die meisten geniesen Privatunterricht zu Hause und viele studieren in Ausland.

Unsere Rabbinen huldigen noch lange nicht den Fortschritt und sind deshalb meist die Veranlassung zu Streit und Zwistigkeiten in der Gemeinde. —

Den *Erwerbszweig* der hiesigen Israeliten betreffend, gibt es bloss Banquiers, dann einige Geldverleiher, hierauf folgt eine ziemliche Zahl Kaufleute in Manufactur — Colonial kleiderwaren, Spirituosen, Holz [und] andere Landesprodukte, desgleichen zwei Getreide Exporteurs und mehrere Sensale. — Die meisten aber sind Handwerker jedweden Gewerbes als: Schneider, Schuster, Tischler, Schmiede, Kempscher, Glaser, Uhrmacher, Maurer etc. etc. Dann folgen Fiakerkutscher, Wasserführer, Arbeiter, Dienstboten, und Proletariat wie es nun einmal in einer Hafenstadt üblich ist.

Manches Handwerk wird von Juden speziell betrieben, sodass wenn wir, z.b. Donnerstag u. Freitag Feiertage haben und darauf Samstag, so ist faktisch Niemand im Stande die Lücke auszufüllen.

Seitdem nun die *Auswanderungsfrage nach America* aufs Tapet geb-
racht wurder, haben sich einstweilen 623 Familien mit zusammen 2,216
Personen angemeldet, *freie Überfahrt conditionierend* können wir diesfalls
vielleicht bis 1,000 Familien rechnen. ALLE SIND FEST ENTSCHLOS-
SEN JENSEITS DES OCEANS SICH EINEN HERD ZU GRÜN-
DEN! Wir wollen nun den Beschlüssen der hohen Versammlung nicht
vorgreifen und erwarten mit Ungeduld die Resultate sowohl die Aus-
wanderer als die Zurückbleibenden!!!

VI

Consul Peixotto spent freely both on communal and charitable activities and on an elaborate scale of living which he believed necessary to establish political ties and exert influence. Often in financial
straits, he was forced to plead with English, American, and German
backers for additional funds. Despite their dissatisfaction with his
extravagance and their disapproval of his enthusiasm for emigration, it is clear from the letter sent by Isaac Seligman to Myer S.
Isaacs that European Jewish leaders thought it essential to maintain
the American Consul at his post.[18]

                              Lincoln House
                              Clarence Road
                              Clapham Park, S.W.
                              April 13 [18]73
My dear Sir!
    I have been requested by several gentlemen who take a warm interest
in the welfare of the Roumanian Jews to enter into strictly confidential
communication with you, and to ascertain through you, the views of
our American Coreligionists.
    Mr Peixotto has written several very pressing letters to some leading
Jews here, concerning his financial status, and it is with a view of sustaining him in his present position that the united action of the Jews
of America and of Europe is sought to be enlisted. —
    I am desired to communicate to you the following points:
    1 How much does Mr Peixotto receive per annum from the american
jews?
    2 Mr P's resignation would place the Roumanian Jews in a position
of danger as the numerous and influential enemies of the Jews would
believe that the interest in the Roumanian Jews is withdrawn from them

---

[18] Gartner, "Peixotto," pp. 66–67, 77–78, 102 n. 25, 105.

by the earliest and most active friends of the unemancipated Roumanian Jews. —

3 European Jewish associations being, with the exception of the Alliance Israelite, in a state of infancy, it would require years before the good initiated by the American philanthropists could be effectually, and on an independent footing, accomplished by those associations. —

4 It is therefore of vital importance to sustain Mr Peixotto in his honorable post and it is equally important that the American and the European men of heart and mind should join hands in keeping Mr Peixotto in his mission and in enabling him to subsidize the "Roumanian Post" which has done *much* good. —

You will greatly oblige me by communicating the above to the leading members of the Roumanian Committee and the Board of Delegates, and informing me as soon as possible of their views. —

I remain, my dear Sir,
Yours very sincerely
Isaac Seligman[19]

M. S. Isaacs Esqre.

VII

Early in 1875, Peixotto, discouraged by slow progress towards Roumanian Jewish emancipation and harassed by financial problems, sought to return home. Myer S. Isaacs' letter of encouragement, printed below, reflects the Consul's depressed state. Peixotto actually remained in Bucharest until June, 1876.

Law Offices
ISAACS & SANGER
243 Broadway

Myer S. Isaacs   Rooms 9 and 10
Adolph L. Sanger
Isaac S. Isaacs

New York, March 11th, 1875

My dear friend,

I am awaiting a letter from you in response to mine advising you of the action proposed to be taken by the N.Y. Committee. My letter conveyed to you a reply in *anticipation.*

I do not in any wise share in your despondent view respecting your position on returning to America. I believe that you have had (irrespective of the service to our people & humanity) an admirable oppor-

---

[19] No reply has been located.

tunity of preparing yourself to fill a high position, diplomatically. And if your political affiliations are as decided as they used to be, there is abundant scope for an honorable ambition.

Again — in journalism, as well as in the law, there is a fine field. Your residence and experience abroad are invaluable in directing your usefulness at home.

I need not say that you have still some firm friends here. I am unaware of a single element of antagonism. Lukewarmness as to Roumania there undoubtedly is. That does not in any respect imply dissatisfaction with you.

[Julius] Bien promised to address the D.G.L.'s,[20] so as to secure a reasonable contribution to the Roumania Fund. [Simon] Wolf has had no end of personal trouble — his wife's melancholy illness being of itself sufficient to concentrate his thoughts on home.

Thank God, our little circle in New York progresses and thrives. We have excellent letters from my brother Abm. who appears to be enthusiastic as well and industrious in his studies, and patiently preparing himself to carry on his father's work.[21]

Adolph's[22] wife has been suffering from asthma and nervous prostration since their second daughter was born, some two months ago. She is, however, recovering.

Merry Purim to you all and may the next bring with it the joy of an American home coupled with the delights of news from the Danube that Haman is forever doomed.

Yours faithfully,
Myer

---

20 Bien, a B'nai B'rith leader, was to speak before the order's District Grand Lodges, or regional divisions.

21 Abram S. Isaacs (1851–1920) became Professor of Semitics at New York University.

22 Apparently Adolph L. Sanger, the writer's law partner.

JEW AND NEGRO:
NOTES ON THE MOBILITY
OF TWO MINORITY GROUPS
IN THE UNITED STATES

ELI GINZBERG

WHEN PROFESSOR BARON was appointed Miller Professor of Jewish History at Columbia University in 1930, the University did not have among its tenured faculty more than a handful of Jews. In the large department which he joined Professor Baron was the only one. On the entire Faculty of Political Science one could not count five Jews and similar small numbers were characteristic of the Faculties of Philosophy and Pure Science and the professional schools.

Lionel Trilling recently told me that it took the personal intervention of President Butler to make a place for him in the English Department. In the School of Business, Dean McCrea worked for several years to prepare the ground to appoint Nathan Isaacs but at the end of that time, Harvard had beat him to the punch. I became the first tenured Jewish member of the faculty of the School of Business and that was at the end of World War II!

One of the recent radical transformations in the American occupational structure has been the increasing appointment, absolutely and relatively, of Jews to university positions during the last quarter century. When the son of one of my close friends, a distinguished academician on the West Coast, wanted to come East to college in the late 1960's his father wrote to a friend on the Yale faculty to inquire whether his boy would feel at home in such a Wasp environment. The reply pointed out that five of the key eleven deans were Jewish! With Levi's appointment at Chicago and Brown's at the California Institute of Technology even the barrier to university presidencies at elite institutions had been broken.

There is no mystery about the forces responsible for this revolution: a vast expansion in the post-war period in the demand for academic manpower; a relatively smaller number of young people coming through graduate schools in the 1950's as a result of the lower birth rates of the depressed 1930's; a relative overrepresentation of Jews among college and university students which reflects their urban location, family income, and cultural tradition; the recent use of objective criteria to assess performance particularly in mathematics and the natural sciences which helped moderate the subjective factors in appointments; the reduction in religious prejudice as a concomitant of the changes wrought by World War II; and the substantial lag in academic salary levels which made a college or university appointment less attractive to members of the in-group who faced attractive alternative opportunities.

Within the context of our larger concern it might be useful to follow up the tack of delineating the forces that contributed to the penetration of Jews into academic work in the recent past with a brief consideration of the contemporary scene with regards to the Negro penetration of the academic establishment. We know that a large number of distinguished and an even larger number of not so distinguished colleges and universities are now seriously attempting to add Negro members to their staffs. The problem that they face is the very small number and still smaller percentage of Negro students enrolled in the major universities which train tomorrow's academicians. Columbia's distinguished physics department has yet to produce one Negro Ph.D!

There are other parallels and differences from the earlier Jewish breakthrough. Many white institutions seeking Negro staff are located in small towns. Many able Negroes are disinclined to live in a small town particularly because of its probable impact on their children. Surely similar considerations played a part earlier in the occupational decision-making of Jewish intellectuals.

The same forces that have propelled colleges and universities to seek able Negroes have led other major employers of trained manpower — government, corporations, nonprofit institutions such as foundations, hospitals, and welfare organizations — to compete for the same limited supply of well trained persons. And in an inflationary market, the academic world frequently loses out. One important university recently sought to attract a Negro graduate in his early thirties who had just completed his studies at a prestigious law school. The candidate told an intermediary that there was no point to his entering into discussion with the University unless it was able to pay at least $24,000 as an opening salary!

There appear to be more differences than parallels between the penetration of Jews and Negroes into academic life. The parallels relate to the reduction in prejudice and the increase in demand; the differences are a function of the unique role of the racial revolution in creating opportunities for Negroes and the relatively thin supply of trained persons able to take advantage of them.

Since Professor Baron joined the Columbia faculty we have seen a marked increase in the number of young Jewish scholars — and some not so young or so scholarly — appointed to academic posts in Hebraica, Semitics, Jewish Religion. Many Negroes are now being appointed to teach "Afro-American Studies." We do not yet know whether these two developments have much or little in common with respect to either initiation or objective.

This essay aims to look at not one phase of the occupational structure but at the whole of it and to see what lessons, if any, can be extracted about the ways in which two distinctive minority groups, Jews and Negroes, have succeeded over time in improving their position. Since much of what follows is more conceptual than empirical, we shall make explicit at least two dimensions and the matrix that underlies this analysis. As to time, the relevant period for the Jews is the three score years from 1890 to 1950. The Negro story began in 1940 when, for the first time, industrial America was willing, if only under governmental prodding, to make room for Negro industrial labor. A time span similar to that required by the Jews to penetrate broadly the upper levels of the occupational hierarchy would bring us to the year 2,000, the year selected by the late Martin Luther King as the one which might mark the end of gross discrimination in American life. The whole of the relevant Jewish experience is back of us, but with regard to the Negro we must extrapolate from the happenings of the last thirty years to the probable and possible happenings of the next thirty. This is not a preferred approach; speculations about the future interest all men although they are not part of the daily regimen of historians.

The analytical model which we will employ is a deliberately simple one consisting of four categories: the geographical distribution of the group; its characteristics; the nature of the economy; and special factors. Again, our primary interest is to explore the parallels and differences in occupational and income mobility of Jew and Negro.

With respect to geographical considerations, the mass of Jewish immigrants located in the major urban centers along the Eastern seaboard and in the large cities of the Midwest and Far West. As such they were well positioned to grow with the large city which has been among the fastest growing sectors of the American economy. Hard as it is to believe today, critical services, especially educational services, were better in the crowded city than in the sparse country-side. The Jewish immigrants thus had access to schools that could help them on their way. In New York City they had the special advantage of a tuiton-free college with a high academic standing.

As late as 1940, about 8 out of 10 Negroes were still living in the South, primarily in the rural areas. In the past three decades about 3 out of these 8 have relocated to the large cities in the North and West and of the 5 who remained in the South the majority have moved off the farm and out of rural areas into the cities.

The difficulties of the Negroes have been compounded by the fact that ever since Emancipation, they have been heavily concentrated in the South, a region which President Franklin Roosevelt defined as late as the 1930's as the nation's Number One Economic Problem! The South has been traditionally a manpower surplus, tax poor area; matters of race aside, the Negro thus was in a poor position to achieve access to expanding jobs or even to acquire the basic education and technical skills which determine a man's occupational options. My friend, the late Dr. Charles Johnson who was President of Fisk University, used to say that the distribution of the limited number of tax dollars available was so uneven that the whites in Mississippi and elsewhere in the deep South were educated off the backs of the blacks.

We might sensibly raise the question why, if conditions were so bad in the South, Negroes stayed there rather than relocated. After all, the Jews had a much longer trek when they left Vilna or Kiev to come to New York or Chicago. However, in response to our question we must remember that the Civil War was fought and won by the North among other reasons to keep the Negro out of the West. As hostilities grew to a close, President Lincoln strongly appealed to Negroes to remain in the South. After the end of hostilities, when some Negroes moved into Kansas, their reception from the settled population was so hostile and their inability to cope with the climate so abysmal that most of those who did not succumb to these forces had to beat a retreat. Over the following decades a slowly increasing number of Negroes did relocate out of the South; nevertheless when Northern recruiters sought to increase the emigration to help meet manpower stringencies in the North during World War I, they were run out of town at the muzzle of a gun. The South still wanted cheap Negro labor. It took the combined efforts of the decline of cotton culture in the Old South, the introduction of the automobile, the cessation of uncontrolled immigration from Europe and the boom of World War II to bring about a redistribution of Negro population.

It was the good fortune of the Jews — and of all the other immigrants from Europe — that the American people opted in their favor against the Negro. They were given preference when the country needed massive increments to the domestic labor force. The Negro was deliberately excluded and confined to Southern farms.

On the question of group characteristics, the idealized picture of the Jewish minority is that of a tight family structure, a love for learning, highly developed mutual aid, cleanliness, and low incidence of criminality and other counter-productive behavior such as addiction to alcohol, sexual promiscuity, drugs.

We will leave it to the young Jewish members of SDS from affluent homes to enter a denial of this description of Jewish virtues and strengths. But for the sake of illuminating our subject we must explore some of these presumed characteristics.

The Jewish immigrants who came to the United States had learned how to live and survive, economically and physically, under adverse circumstances and they had been able to keep a strong intellectual tradition alive and flourishing. Moreover, it is true that there are close bonds within and among Jewish families and that for the most part Jews tended to be law-abiding and not dissolute. However, the critical elements are not the quality of family life or the relatively low criminality and social pathology index; they do not include even the self-help organizations characteristic of the enlarged family and the community. Other immigrant groups shared most of these virtues. The two critical points were the ability of many Jewish youngsters to do well in school and the ability of many others to demonstrate a penchant for business. We have called attention to the availability of reasonably good schools in the places where Jews settled. We now mention the opportunity that Jews found to exploit the interstices in the industrial and commercial economy from peddling to moviemaking.

In contradistinction the Negro has been forced to build everything from the ground up within the last hundred years — his family, community, literacy, ambition, self-respect and the other sine qua non of personal and group survival and prosperity. There is no parallel in human society to the magnitude of this challenge. It is true, as many observers have been quick to point out, that family disorganization, sexual promiscuity, criminality, the substantial absence of self-help organizations, are widespread among the Negro minority. While these characteristics might explain why many Negroes remain at the bottom of the socio-economic ladder, they tell us little about many others who are free of such pathology. But two points of difference now become clear: coming out of a background of farm tenancy, Negroes have had little or no op-portunity to develop business acumen; and forced to attend grossly inferior schools they have been handicapped in using the educa-tional route to mobility. Once these two factors are in place, little remains to be explained except the horrendous costs of several hundred years of slavery, segregation, and discrimination that have taken their toll in human life, ambition, energy.

What happens to a minority depends in considerable measure on the rate at which opportunities are opened up for the majority. We have noted the advantages that accrued to the Jews and the disadvantages confronting Negroes because of their respective lo-cations. Now we must look more closely at the changing structure of the economy when Jews and Negroes were beating on the door for admission.

Most of the Jews who arrived in the New World around the turn of this century had little education and less skill. But at that time the American economy was much more responsive to a man's ability and willingness to work than to his credentials. There were conspicuously few college men among the great captains of indus-try, commerce, and finance.

In addition, the first and second generation of American Jews had a head start in getting an education. Many overinvested in education. They had more to offer than the economy of the twen-ties and the thirties required. But when the explosion came in 1940 — and the demand for professionals expanded rapidly — a large number of Jews were in an excellent position to take advan-tage of the burgeoning occupational opportunities. Moreover, many others came from families which had been able to put aside some savings so that they were able to take advantage of the booms in real estate, the stock market, and in business activity generally.

By the time Negroes came North in large numbers in the 1940's, the demand for unskilled labor had leveled off with the end of the war and actually declined thereafter. The former Negro farm worker did not find a blue-collar job waiting for him in the in-creasingly sophisticated economy of the North. Besides, only a small number of Negroes, natives and in-migrants, had the breadth and depth of education and skill training that made them even weak competitors for the rapidly expanding white collar positions. History had been an ally of the Jews; it was an enemy of the Negro.

But one must avoid oversimplifications. In some respects recent trends have favored the Negro. For instance the entire period from 1940 to date has been one of substantially uninterrupted expansion in employment and income. Secondly, with immigration tightly controlled, Negroes turned out to be the key residual labor force (white women excepted) to fill many of the new openings. Thirdly, since the presidential election of 1948 political leaders in the Democratic Party have been sensitive to the growing importance of the Negro minority and the passage of the 1957 Civil Rights Act proved that the same lesson had finally been learned by Republican Senators and Representatives from Northern states. More recently there have been unmistakable signs of the growing political strength of Negroes in the South. Despite Moynihan's insightful observation that firmly entrenched civil service systems make it more difficult for Negroes to "cash in" on their new political power in the form of more and better government jobs, the simple fact is that they have made striking gains in the governmental sector.

I cannot prove it, but I believe that since 1940 the Negro has made more absolute and relative progress, measured in terms of occupational achievement and family income, than any minority within a thirty-year time span. And I do not exclude Jews from this generalization. A few pieces of evidence: writing in 1940, Myrdal pointed out that the best hope for a Negro was to get on a federal relief project! In 1970 about 1 out of 4 Negroes is a white collar worker compared to 1 out of every 2 whites. The Negro is still underrepresented, but the gap is being steadily reduced. With respect to income, the impact since 1939 has been even more striking. In that year the earnings of a median Negro family totaled $489 or 44 percent of the white average; the data for 1967 show $5100 and 62 percent. In 1940 almost all Negroes were poor; by 1970 about 2 out of 5 outside of the South will have joined middle-income families and even in the South this will be true of about 1 out of 5.

On the education front the average years of schooling completed at the end of the 1960's among the younger age group of whites was 12.5 and for non-whites 12.1 — hardly a significant difference. About 3 out of 4 whites and 3 out of 5 Negroes are currently graduating from high school. The figures for college graduation is about 1:7 for whites, 1:12 for Negroes. These figures do not disclose however the differences in the quality of education received (amounting to two to three years) or the very small numbers of Negroes who have gone on to complete their work for a doctorate.

There are a great many poor Negroes and many of them are likely to remain in or close to poverty for a long time to come. But the more relevant finding is that a great many other Negroes have made substantial progress and more are likely to do so in the next 30 years. This assumption is predicated on the maintenance of a high level of economic growth.

Before drawing a few conclusions from this exercise about the comparative mobility of Jews and Negroes it is essential that we make explicit a few of the unique dimensions of the Negro experience in the United States.

Many Jews who change their name can no longer be identified as members of a minority group. It must be exasperating even to sophisticated Negroes to hear Jewish commentators equate American prejudice based on religion to that based on race. Until recently there has been a difference of several orders of magnitude between the two. In the middle of 1950's the dean of one of the Negro colleges in the Atlanta complex told me that he was never confident that he would return alive from his frequent trips into the countryside which he took to study voter behavior. It was an act of bravado for him to enter the lobby of my hotel and we both were probably injudicious when we sat together in the front of his car and drove through the white sections of the city. This was only fifteen years ago in the most progressive city in the South! Translated this means that segregation made it very difficult for

Negroes to feel secure, to develop self-esteem, to protect their sanity.

Drawing on my personal experiences with racial prejudice, I recall the uncertainty with which a friend and I drove up to the Grove Park Inn in Asheville, North Carolina in the middle 1930's and inquired if Jews were welcome; we were told that they had been accepted for the last few years as a result of the depression! It was not until after World War II that the Columbia University Club removed the special hurdles that had previously kept the Jewish membership to a very small number. And I remember General N——— in World War II screaming over the phone that he didn't like "New York shyster tricks" because of a decision that had gone against him. An unpleasant episode, but hardly a threat to my security, self-esteem, or sanity.

Jews, who have suffered so much over so many centuries should be more sensitive about conditions in the United States and should be able to distinguish between religious prejudice that leads to exclusion from clubs and racial prejudice that has often spilled over into murder. Some years ago when the American Jewish Committee looked for a project which would justify its sizable budget and staff, I suggested that since discrimination against Jewish students applying to medical schools had largely vanished, they look into anti-Semitism in the Executive Suite and this subsequently became a major project of the Committee for a period of years. But the Negro community must still fight for elementary rights on every front — political, legal, housing, economic, social. It has made substantial gains and it will doubtless make more in the years ahead. But the Negro still faces discrimination, segregation, deep-seated hostility.

Despite the differences in the basic position of Jew and Negro in American society, the conclusion to which this analysis points is that if the nation does not lose its way, the conspicuous mobility of Negroes in the last thirty years will continue in the next thirty years. By the year 2,000, not all Negroes will be professionals or even white collar workers. And they may be able to boast of only relatively small numbers who have achieved outstanding recognition in academic, scientific, and business life. But even while forced to live on the periphery of American life they have shown marked strength in the artistic, literary, athletic, religious and political realms and there is every likelihood that their talents here as elsewhere will blossom as the obstacles they confront are lessened and removed.

We do not here calibrate how well Negroes will do over three score years of expanding freedom relative to the success of the Jewish minority. But if history is an even imperfect guide to the future, the outlook for the United States and for its Negro minority is much more auspicious than the recent conflagrations in our cities suggest. This optimistic conclusion is strengthened by the analysis which we have undertaken that has revealed many similarities in occupational mobility between these two quite different minorities.

The critical issue that remains open is whether America, which has always been able to make room for and accept successive minorities, will continue true to its tradition and finally accept the Negro or whether it will choke on the irrationalism of race. We hope that the nation which welcomed Dr. Baron and millions of other immigrant Jews and non-Jews and provided them with opportunities to develop their full potential, thereby strengthening itself, will do the same for that largest of all minorities — the Negro — who has been waiting in the anteroom since 1619.

BIBLIOGRAPHIC NOTE

The data and analysis underlying this interpretation have been dealt with in extenso in the following of my publications:

Agenda for American Jews, Columbia University Press, 1950.

The Negro Potential, Columbia University Press, 1956.

The American Worker in the 20th Century: A History Through Autobiographies, Free Press, 1963.

The Negro Challenge to the Business Community, McGraw-Hill, 1964.

The Troublesome Presence: American Democracy and the Negro, Free Press,1964.

The Middle Class Negro in the White Man's World, Columbia University Press, 1967.

Mobility in the Negro Community, U.S. Civil Rights Commission, 1968.

Business Leadership and the Negro Crisis, McGraw-Hill, 1969.

"The Black Revolution and the Jew," *Conservative Judaism*, XXIV, 1 (Fall 1969).

NEW SOURCES ON THE PALESTINIAN
GAONATE

SHELOMO DOV GOITEIN

"You wrote history with such zeal that
You have become history yourself."

THIS VERSE, addressed to the famous Muslim historian Tabari (d.
923), appropriately describes the master to whom this volume is
dedicated. His performance cannot be duplicated. Standing on the
crossways of continents, cultures, and eras of history, and equipped
with the intellectual and moral powers to master these contrasts,
Salo W. Baron has created a lifework that is unique. His jubilee is
a festive occasion for Jewish scholarship, and I regard it as a pleasure
and privilege to participate in this homage.

*   *   *

It is no exaggeration to say that the most revolutionizing addition
to our knowledge of Jewish history brought about by the findings
of the Cairo Geniza was the new information provided by it on
the yeshivas in general, and that of Jerusalem in particular. The
yeshiva of the tenth and eleventh centuries designated itself rightly
as *sanhedrin*. The two terms are identical not only in literal meaning,
but also according to their historical semantics. The yeshiva of
those days was not a school for students, but was the highest
council of the Jewish people, a body uniting the role of high court,
parliament, and academy — a combination not without certain
parallels in other medieval societies. The head of the yeshiva, the
Gaon, was the leader of the Jewish community, not only spiritually,
but administratively as well, inasmuch as the appointment of the
communal officials and the confirmation in office of the local

leaders were in his hand, namely in countries and districts that were under his *reshūth*, or authority.

The Muslim government had nothing to do with these developments. The Gaon, and the local spiritual and communal heads (mostly a *hāvēr* or *dayyān*) also, needed confirmation by the government — any government — because the judges of a minority group were part and parcel of the public juridical system and as such had official status. But how the minority groups wished to organize their communal life was left to their own devices, not because the Muslim government was liberal, but because in general it did not concern itself with the inner affairs of its subjects — Muslim and non-Muslim alike — except as far as matters of revenue and security were concerned.[1]

When we learn so much about the Palestinian gaonate during the Fatimid period we should by no means assume that this was due to the fact that Egypt and Palestine had become independent of Baghdad. They had enjoyed a high degree of independence from Baghdad long before under the Tulunid and Ikhshid viceroys and under a number of strong provincial governors. As the Ben Meir controversy proves, the Palestinian yeshiva was very much alive long before the advent of the Fatimids, and in all the larger cities of the countries that once had been Byzantine, such as Alexandria, (Babylon-) Fustat, Damascus, (Lod-) Ramle, the "large" or main synagogue, namely the one in which the local chief judge had his seat, invariably was the Palestinian, that is, the one that recognized the authority of the yeshiva of the Holy Land. The Babylonian,

---

[1] Information on the Palestinian gaonate culled from the Cairo Geniza documents is presented in detail in my book *A Mediterranean Society: The Jewish Communities of the Arab World, as Portrayed in the Documents of the Cairo Geniza*, vol. II, *The Community*, published by the University of California Press in fall, 1971. Specifically, chapter v, section A, 1 (the yeshiva and the gaonate as administrative and spiritual center of the Jewish people); ch. vi, secs. 7–8 (organization, syllabus, and teaching methods in Jewish higher learning); and ch. vii, secs. B and D (functioning of Jewish judiciary and communal organization within the framework of the Muslim state).

or Iraqian synagogue everywhere was the secondary, "small" synagogue and was originally not permitted to have an independent *dayyān* of its own.[2]

The rich information about the Palestinian gaonate during the eleventh century is only due to the fact that the Geniza documents for that period are profuse, while we have very few documents preceding the advent of the Fatimids. The situation is exactly the same with regard to trade. Historical considerations induce us to assume that Jewish trade in the Mediterranean during the tenth century was at least as important as that of the eleventh century; yet we have many hundreds of Jewish business letters concerned with international commerce from the eleventh century, but practically none from the tenth. Anyone studying intimately the documents related to the Palestinian gaonate will recognize that they reflect the waning and end of a long tradition and not the beginning of a new development.

As soon as the "Egyptian fragments" (as the Geniza papers were first called) made their appearance in the early 1890's, Jewish scholarship became aware of the significance of the new material on the yeshivas and the gaonate. The most prominent Jewish historians, such as Solomon Schechter, David Kaufmann, and Samuel Poznanski, dedicated studies to the subject, and Jacob Mann devoted to it the major part of his book *The Jews in Egypt and in Palestine under the Fatimids* and returned to it again in his *Texts and Studies*. Simha Assaf, although concentrating mainly on the responsa of the Babylonian Gaons, did not neglect the history of the Palestinian yeshiva. S. Abramson's recent *Bamerkazim*, 1965, and other publications by contemporaries prove that the subject is by no means exhausted. Salo W. Baron's monumental *History of the Jews* surveys and sifts the whole material, as far as it had been known until 1958.

It is natural that during my long preoccupation with the Geniza documents, mostly those written in the Arabic language, I had

---

[2] Documents illustrating this situation are found in my article "The Struggle between Congregation and Local Community," *J. Schirmann Jubilee Volume* (Jerusalem, 1970), pp. 69–77.

opportunity to collect much additional source material on the
Palestinian gaonate and its role within the Jewish community of
the Fatimid empire. There is also no doubt that a comprehensive
and systematic history of this venerable institution is a desideratum
of Jewish and general historiography. Still, I believe, the time has
not yet come for this undertaking. In addition to documents that
are mainly and directly concerned with the subject there are references to it in private and business letters. Such references are sometimes of significance for the chronology of the events or shed
significant sidelights on their course or character. Moreover, I
doubt whether the literary Geniza treasures have already been
searched sufficiently in that direction. But work on the documentary
Geniza material is now well under way and it stands to reason
that in not too distant a future the more significant part of the
eleventh century correspondence will have been brought under
control. And constant research is going on with regard to the literary Geniza.

Things being so, I prefer now to make available to interested
scholars the material on the Palestinian gaonate collected by me
without waiting for the opportunity of a comprehensive presentation. In what follows a group of documents is discussed that originated between approximately 1020 and 1036. It vividly illustrates
the communal role of the yeshiva and the relationship of the Gaons
with the local communities and of both with the government.

1. A REPORT ON AN EVENTFUL MONTH
OF HOLIDAYS IN JERUSALEM

written by the later Gaon Solomon b. Judah
at a time of tension and when he himself still was "Third".
TS NS (= Taylor–Schechter Collection, New Series) Box 320, f. 16
The report is written in the unmistakable hand of Solomon b.
Judah (Gaon ca. 1026–1051) in Arabic characters with a few inserted
Hebrew words. But several Hebrew words are written in Arabic
script. Next to no diacritical points are provided and the task of
deciphering is rendered even more difficult by the writing having

been effaced or covered with stains in many places. Beginning and end are lost. Still, all the main points of the report can be established with certainty.

As the content reveals, at the time of the writing Solomon b. Judah still was "Third". According to Mann, *Jews*, I, 71, there was only one Gaon between Joshiah b. Aaron, who signed a document in Ramle in 1015 and was still in office around 1018, when the rebuilding of the churches and synagogues was permitted by al-Ḥākim, the mad Fatimid caliph, and our Solomon b. Judah, namely Solomon ha-Kohen.[3] But from a still unpublished, very important document from 1028, it appears that a Gaon, named Ṣādōq, ruled, albeit for a short time, between the two Solomons. Thus, the Gaon referred to in our report must have been Solomon ha-Kohen, and the president of the court most probably Ṣādōq.[4]

The letter translated here is of interest insofar as it presents a detailed picture of occurrences in Jerusalem during Tishri, the month of pilgrimage. We learn about prominent pilgrims and visitors from the Maghreb, Damascus, and Rūm (Europe or Byzantium); about the official conveyance of titles by the yeshiva, first at its meeting in the house of the Āv, or president of the court, and then, publicly, on the solemn convention on the Mount of Olives on the seventh day of Sukkoth; about the expulsion and final readmittance of the Egyptian spiritual leader Elhanan b. Shemarya; and, above all, about the exact order in which the three highest dignitaries of the yeshiva and one layman conducted the various sections of the services and delivered a derāsh, that is, a combination of sermon, lecture, and disputation.

The purpose of this letter, which no doubt was addressed to a

---

[3] TS (Taylor-Schechter Collection) 13 J 1, f. 2, see Jacob Mann, *The Jews in Egypt and Palestine etc.* (cited hereafter as Mann, *Jews*), II, (Oxford, 1922), 49. For a complete edition and further discussion of this document see S. Shaked, *A Tentative Bibliography of Geniza Documents* (Paris–The Hague, 1964), p. 114.

[4] TS 13 J 7, f. 25, l. 18. I intend to publish this document presently together with another batch of new sources on the Palestinian gaonate. Permission to build the destroyed synagogues in the time of Joshiah: see Mann, *Jews*, II, 72.

notable in Egypt, obviously was twofold. It tried to explain to him how the yeshiva handled the affairs of Elhanan. It had long been known that these relations were not the best, and that Elhanan, who headed a midrash (but not a "yeshiva"!) in Fustat, had assumed prerogatives reserved to a Gaon, such as lecturing with the aid of a broadcaster, or *meturgeman*. Our letter describes how matters came to a head and how finally a reconciliation was achieved.[5]

Secondly, it seems to me that by detailing all the honors given to him during the holidays and the pilgrimage to Jerusalem, Solomon b. Judah wanted to emphasize his candidacy for the gaonate. We should not forget that Solomon did not belong to one of the three gaonic families of Palestine, but was a foreigner from Fez, Morocco, and therefore always encountered strong opposition — as did Saadya, the Egyptian, in Baghdad. At the seat of the government he was indeed known as Solomon al-Fāsī.[6]

Translation

TS NS Box 320, f. 16

(The numbers refer to the lines of the original. The margin is not a direct continuation of the text.)

(1).... This letter of mine comprises an account of all that happened. (2) The president of the court and the Maghrebis arrived two days before the New Year. On the New Year my lord, (3) the head of the yeshiva was not permitted (by his physician) to go down to the synagogue. I did not wish that the 'Ibbūr should be made in my house, since we had assembled in the house of the president of the court, (4) and his brother al-Sahl did not like me because he was a partisan of the Shuway' family. Abu 'l-Khayr, the son of the Tāhertī, was present with us and we prayed for him as

---

[5] See S. Abramson, *Bamerkazim u-va-Tfutsot* (Jerusalem, 1965), pp. 105–155, 175–179. A series of new Geniza documents emanating from Elhanan b. Shemarya or related to him is contained in my article "Elhanan b. Shemarya as Communal Leader," *Joshua Finkel Jubilee Volume* (New York, 1973).

[6] TS NS Box 320, f. 45, l. 5; see below, p. 526 [24].

(5) "member (of the yeshiva)." On Saʿīd b. Isrāʾīl al-Ḥarrāz (probably to be read as Kharrāz) we conferred the title... and on... Yaḥyā of Damascus the title "Seventh."

(6) On Rosh ha-shanah, I and the president of the court went down to the synagogue, and at the time of the reading of the Torah we repeated publicly that Elhanan would be expelled because of judgments (illegally given by him?). (7) I presided over the ceremony of the blowing of the shofar. The president of the court delivered the sermon on Sabbath *Shūvā* (the Sabbath between New Year and the day of Atonement), and during the ten days of atonement I was constantly in charge of...

(8) On the Day of Atonement did my lord, the head of the yeshiva, go down to the synagogue. The president of the court conducted the reading of the Torah, I the Musaf service, al-Kharrāz — Minhah, (9) and our lord, the Gaon — Neʿilah. The president preached on the first(?) day of Sukkah (= Sukkoth) and I on Sabbath ʿAssēr (the Sabbath during the half-holidays).

(10) My lord, the head of the yeshiva, delivered the sermon on the Mount of Olives on the day of ʿArāvā (= Hoshana Rabba, the seventh day of Sukkoth). Only few pilgrims were present. Meanwhile, Elhanan had arrived, but we chased him away so that he found himself (11) in an indescribably humiliating position.... Finally, he testified before the assembly that he... (12) to this yeshiva. And when.... Afterwards, we were friendly with him and called him up (13) to the reading of the Torah. On the 8th of Marheshvan did the president of the court conduct the *geshem* (prayer for rain during the winter season).

On the day after the holidays I was called (14) in great haste to Salmān, the Son of the Scholar, may God have mercy upon him, for he was in a grave state of illness. He testified before us (15) that he possessed nothing and that he was a poor man and that his brother and sister were his heirs. He died on Friday night.

On Sabbath... (16) I delivered the sermon and on the Hoshana day we confirmed the son of Elhanan as Fourth. (17) The son of the Rūmī Rav and... And we confirmed Abu 'l-Khayr...

(Margin) (And please excuse me for...) and being late in writing, but these were the holidays, and God knows that I did not cease to mention you in (my prayers).

(On a separate piece of paper the left lower corner of a letter is found which is also in the Arabic and Hebrew hand of Solomon b. Judah and bears even his usual motto *Yeshaʿ rāv*, "Complete salvation." But the pen is thinner, the writing less careful, and the letters are slightly smaller than in the text translated above. I doubt that the two fragments belong together, although they are listed under the same shelf mark in the Library. As far as the fragmentary state of the piece permits, I provide a translation at the end of the Commentary. The first three lines are in Arabic letters; in line 4, the writer changes to Hebrew in the middle of a word. The fragment contains a request to help a man).

COMMENTARY

(The numbers refer to the lines of the original)

(1)   The end of the sentence visible says that the letters from Fustat have been delivered and read, but not yet answered because of the holidays, as stated at the end.

(2)   The president of the court of the yeshiva sat most of the time in Ramle, the administrative and economic capital of the country. The Maghrebis, that is, pilgrims from Qayrawān and other places in North Africa, also sojourned most of the time in Ramle, since the pilgrimage normally was combined with business.

(3)   The recipient of the letter certainly knew about the state of health of the Gaon of Jerusalem.

The details about the ʿIbbūr (declaration that the coming year would be a leap year) are of interest in view of the discussion of the matter in a gaonic commentary saying that the decision whether there should be an ʿIbbūr year used to be made in Av, a month before the Jewish New Year, see Mann, *Texts and Studies* (Cincinnati, 1931), I, 316, n. 11. From a Geniza fragment, TS Loan 11, l. 17, edited by Mann, *ibid.*, it appears that the public announcement was made on the Mount of Olives on the Hoshana Rabba day. The fragment of the gaonic commentary, referred to above, was edited in full by S. Assaf in his *Responsa Geonica*, (Jerusalem, 1952), p. 154, to which Professor S. Lieberman kindly drew my attention. The procedure reported here, where the formal decision was made in the house of the president of the court a day before Rosh Hashana, and not in Av, simply had its reason in the fact that only during the month of pilgrimage did all the members of the yeshiva, or most of them, assemble in Jerusalem. The formal decision in the house of the president of the court no doubt was followed by the solemn public announcement on the Mount of Olives three weeks later, see Bavli, Sanhedrin 12a and b.

(4) Sahl and Abū Sahl were common Jewish names. But al-Sahl (with the article) is absolutely exceptional.[7] Therefore, we are permitted to identify this al-Sahl with the father of Isḥāq b. al-Sahl, a prominent notable in Jerusalem, who was in close correspondence with Abraham b. ʿAṭāʾ (or Nathan), the Nagid of Qayrawān,[8] and with the famous Berachia family of the same city.[9]

The Shuwayʿ family is known from several Geniza documents as inimical to the Gaon Solomon b. Judah. It was indeed in their mansion where the pilgrims, dissatisfied with Solomon's handling of public affairs at the assembly on the Mount of Olives, convened and paid homage to his rival Nathan b. Abraham.[10] For this reason Solomon excommunicated them together with other dissenters.[11] This enmity was transmitted even to Solomon's grandchildren.[12] On the other hand, the Gaon protected a member of

---

[7] See *Tarbiz*, XXXIV (1965), 168, n. 17.

[8] TS 10 J 9, f. 26, ll. 16 and 32, ed. S. D. Goitein, *Tarbiz*, ibid. pp. 168–169.

[9] Bodleian manuscript Heb. d 65 (Cat. 2877), f. 9, l. 4, ed. S. Assaf, *Jacob N. Epstein Jubilee Volume* (Jerusalem, 1950), p. 179.

[10] University Library Cambridge, Or 1080 J 45, l. 21 (to be published together with other new documents on Nathan b. Abraham).

[11] TS 16.261, l. 27, ed. J. Mann, *Texts and Studies*, I, 339. Mann, ibid., p. 325, read the name Shaviʿah; but Shuwayʿ is an Arabic diminutive of Shūʿa, which is an abbreviation of the Hebrew name Yeshūʿā. In the letter cited in the next note the Gaon uses the names Shuwayʿ and Shūʿa interchangeably.

[12] Bodl. MS Heb. c 28 (Cat. 2876), f. 67 (ready for publication).

this family in Jerusalem against the high-handed actions of an over-reaching Muslim, as was indeed Solomon's duty as highest representative of the Jewish community.[13] From another letter of his it appears that he had special regard for this man and because of him treated the Shuway'–Shū'ā family less harshly than it deserved.[14]

Our letter shows that this enmity existed already at a time when Solomon was still "Third," and that the family of the president of the court also was involved. We can well imagine how the newcomer from Morocco made a great impression in Jerusalem because of his learnedness and his exceptionally beautiful Hebrew (he was also a *payṭān*); the old families first received him with open arms, but were dismayed when they discovered that he pushed their own members aside in his aspiration for the highest office, which he indeed finally obtained.

Abu 'l-Khayr was the kunya, or by-name of Moses, one of the four sons of Barhūn (the North-African form of the name Abraham) Tāherti, one of the most prominent families of Qayrawān. He constantly commuted between Qayrawān and Fustat and was a staunch supporter of the yeshiva of Jerusalem, to which he once transmitted a sum of 58 dinars (worth about 6,000 dollars in purchasing power today).[15] Moreover, as the son of the city of Jewish scholarship, Qayrawān, and scion of a noble family he certainly also possessed a certain degree of Jewish learning. No wonder, then, that the yeshiva makes him here one of its members, or, as the technical procedure was, accompanied his name, while praying for him (or, as we would say, making him a *mi she-berakh*) with the word *ḥāvēr*.[16]

(5) Two prominent persons by the name Sa'īd b. Isrā'īl (also in Hebrew, Saadya b. Israel) were active at that time: one, an

---

[13] TS 13 J 19, f. 3 (edition prepared).

[14] Bodl. MS Heb. b 11 (Cat. 2874), f. 1. The name of the elder concerned was Mevōrākh.

[15] ULC Or 1081 J 24, verso, l. 21: *mathībat al-Shām*.

[16] Spelled here *ḥ'wyr*, which is exceptional and linguistically significant. The usual Arabic rendering is *ḥ'byr*.

uncle of the famous "vizier" of the Fatimids, Abū Sa'd, the youngest of the three senior Tustari brothers. He cannot be meant here. For the Tustaris were Karaites. This has been assumed long ago by Samuel Poznanski, was corroborated repeatedly by Alexander Scheiber of Budapest and myself, and is now established beyond any doubt by a Geniza document prepared for publication by the late S. M. Stern, in which the Rabbanite writers say about Abū Sa'd's brother "he is not of our religion."[17]

The man referred to here is no doubt identical with Saadya b. Israel who is praised in a letter of Solomon b. Judah Gaon, TS 13 J 17, f. 17, ll. 5–8, as "a great benefactor, who pleases God, whose house in Jerusalem is open to everyone calling on him." *Ḥarrāz*, found only here, means, according to an Arabic dictionary written in Spain during the 13th century, "writer of amulets" (see Dozy, *Supplément aux dictionnaires arabes*, s.v.). Since, however, the corresponding word for amulet, *ḥirz*, has not yet been found by me in the Geniza, I prefer to read *Kharrāz*, shoemaker, cobbler, a family name as common among the well-to-do Jewish merchants of the Geniza period as Shoemaker and Shuster are frequent family names here today.

The title conferred on Saadya probably meant something like "benefactor." It must be Greek, since it ends in *ṭs* and is too long for a Semitic word. The possibilities of reading are *b/t/th/n/y-'/gh/g-k/d-'-ṭ/z-s/sh*. Perhaps the author of *Greek in Jewish Palestine* might find the solution. (Alif ' may render *a* or *e*, so-called Imāla.)

(6) "I and the president" — in Arabic invariably "I" is said first, even in "I and my father," despite the profound reverence of the Muslims for their parents.

(7) Constantly — reading and translation doubtful.[18] The illegible expression probably designated Ashmurot (or Selihot, as the Ashkenazim say).

(9) '*Assēr* — so called, of course, after the beginning of the Scripture lection of that Sabbath (Deut. 14: 22).

---

[17] TS Arabic Box 30, f. 278, ed. S. M. Stern, *Revue des Études Juives*, CXXVIII (1969), 215, l. 24 and the lamented author's note, ibid., p. 211.

[18] I read *wdmnt*, taking it as *wa-admant*, with elision of Alif.

ʿArāvā — named also Hōshaʿnā (without Rabbā), see below,
l. 16. ʿArāvā was perhaps the Babylonian name, see *Siddur Rav
Saadya Gaon* (Jerusalem, 1941), p. 239, l. 1. It is still used so by
the Yemenites.

(10) Elhanan, namely b. Shemarya, see above, and below,
ll. 11–13.

Judgments — *aḥkām*. One would prefer *aḥrām*, "bans", meaning
that several scholars had pronounced a *herem* on Elhanan. But
the third letter clearly is a *k*, not a *r*.

(13) According to Bavli, Taʿanith 4b the prayer for rain (*ṭal
u-maṭar*) starts in Palestine on 7 Marheshvan, and this is the usage
to the present day. I hesitantly suggest that in that particular year,
as often, the 7th fell on Friday; the *ṭal u-maṭar* was indeed inserted
in the prayer, but the solemn *geshem* prayer was reserved for the
Sabbath when the service was fully attended. (After typing this
I received Professor Lieberman's kind letter of January 11, 1970,
with this explanation: the 7th fell on a Sunday, the subsequent
Monday was observed as a fast, as usual in the weeks after the
holidays, therefore the solemn prayer was postponed to that day,
and on it the president of the court, the scholar highest in rank
(the Gaon being ill) officiated. I prefer Dr. Lieberman's explanation;
for if the service had been held on a Saturday, it would have been
referred to by the name of the weekly Scripture lection, and not
as 8th Marheshvan. Dr. Lieberman's explanation stands even if
there was no fast on Monday. Abundant Geniza sources prove that
everything of importance was done in the synagogue on Monday
or Thursday when attendance was general because of the reading
of the Torah).

(14) Salmān — probably a pilgrim from Egypt, or an old man
from there who passed the end of his days in the Holy City.

Son of the Scholar — a family name (Ibn al-Talmīd) borne also
by other persons living in the eleventh century.

(15) The deathbed declaration was directed on the one hand
to the government to show that the dying man possessed nothing
in Jerusalem, on the other hand to the Jewish authorities in Fustat,
where he probably was the proprietor of a house, from which he

derived his maintenance in old age and which he now left to his brother *and sister* (not exclusively to his brother who would be the heir according to Jewish law).

On Sabbath... — no doubt, the writer repeats here that he preached on the Sabbath of Sukkoth. It was their habit to repeat things important to them even more than once in a letter, and in a way, as if they had not been mentioned before.

Fourth — reading doubtful, might be "Sixth." Elhanan had indeed the title "Sixth"; see Mann, *Texts and Studies*, I, 200; then, "son of" would be redundant. But since most persons are referred to in Arabic as "Ibn," such a slip is not difficult to explain. On the other hand, we never hear of a son of Elhanan. Abu 'l-Kayr — Tāhertī, see l. 4, above.

(On a separate piece of paper, see above, p. 510 [8]).

Translation

TS NS Box 320, f. 16, fragment, left lower corner of a sheet.

(1) ... (forgive) whatever wrong he might have done.

(2) ... He is grateful for your benefactions and expresses his gratitude everywhere.

(3) ... Make an effort to help him — God will reward you — and do not forsake him

(4) ... translated into (continued in Hebrew script) the Holy tongue: *kol ha-mithaddēsh* (may mean many things)

(5) ... (East) and West, may have mercy and compassion. Best greetings to you and ...

(6) ... My (son; or: my lord, the Gaon) greets you and your beloved[19]

(7) ... (do not put him off) from month to month, but let him take every month.

Complete Salvation![20]

---

[19] Hebrew *metāv*, for the more commonly used *metē sōdō*, Job 19: 19, "his intimate friends".

[20] Solomon b. Judah's regular motto, see Mann, *Jews*, I, 179.

FRAGMENT OF A LETTER BY SOLOMON B. JUDAH

TS NS Box 320, f. 16. See p. 515 [13]

2. REQUEST BY A GAON OF JERUSALEM FOR CONFIRMATION IN OFFICE

by the New Caliph (Aẓ-Ẓāhir, 1021–1036)

TS 24.43.

This is the second, lower leaf of a long letter. It was pasted on on an upper leaf that is lost. The fifty lines preserved are at most one half of the original length, but they contain all the essentials; the proems of the letters of the Gaons addressed to communities often were longer than the proper text. As its contents proves, our letter emanated from a Gaon writing under the fourth Fatimid caliph of Egypt, aẓ-Ẓāhir, for the writer asks for a rescript of installation, the likes of which were given by the caliph's three ancestors and predecessors and were still preserved in the yeshiva. The section containing this request is translated in full below. The preceding parts, which are anyhow largely effaced, are given in summary.

A. *End of the Proem*

Lines 1–10. Greetings to the notables of Fustat and to "both communities," obviously meaning Rabbinites and Karaites (*shetey ha-kittōt*), for the last and most extended greetings are addressed to David b. Isaac, known from other documents as *pe'ēr shetey ha-pē'ōt*, "Pride of the two denominations," a Karaite and prominent figure in the Fustat Jewish community for at least twenty years.[21] At the time of the writing of this letter he must have been still at his beginnings, for the Gaon mentions that he has written a letter to him and to his father.

The names of three other notables greeted are legible, albeit with great difficulty: Japheth (ha-Levi) b. Toviah (l. 1) al-Nīlī (the

---

[21] At a "United Karaite-Rabbanite Appeal" for the Jews of Jerusalem, arranged in the capital of Egypt, he donated 20 dinars, more than anyone else, see *A Mediterranean Society*, II, Appendix C, sec. 4, where further details about him are found.

[22] Mann, *Jews*, II, 98 and 103.

indigo merchant); he signed documents in Fustat in 1028 and 1037.[22]

David (ha-Levi) b. Aaron (l. 2); he and Solomon b. Ḥakīm, as well as Muḥsin, both mentioned below, were members of a committee of seven parnasim, headed by the two leaders of the Fustat Rabbanite community, Ephraim (b. Shemarya) and Samuel (b. Avtalion), at the time of Joshiah Gaon.[23]

Solomon b. Ḥakīm al-Fāsī (of Fez, Morocco). Hay Gaon inquired about him in a letter dated Adar, 1007, and he signed documents in Fustat in 1022 and 1029.[24]

Ll. 10–13. After mentioning that, besides the letter, addressed, in the Hebrew language, to the Karaite notable David b. Isaac, he had written another one during the mōʿēd, the intermediate days of the holiday week,[25] the Gaon continues that he had written a third letter, and when the member of the yeshiva, Toviah, would arrive from Jerusalem, he would write again, doing everything his correspondent in Fustat had asked from him. Clearly an affair involving both Rabbanites and Karaites is referred to, and the secession of the representative of the merchants Muḥsin, which forms the main topic of our letter, had something to do with that affair. The letter was dispatched from Ramle, where the Gaons often presided over the court in person, and it is interesting to note that the writer did not want to act before he was informed about the opinions of the Jerusalem members of the yeshiva.

B.   *The Secession of the Representative of the Merchants*
     from the Palestinian Synagogue of Fustat

Ll. 13–34. The main part of the letter deals with one issue: the vow of the representative of the merchants Muḥsin b. Ḥusayn,

---

[23] TS 20.104, l. 5. Ready for publication.

[24] Hay Gaon, see Mann, *Texts and Studies*, I, 126. The signatures of Solomon b. Ḥakīm in Mann, *Jews*, II, 97 and 99.

[25] The question of abstaining from work on the half-holidays is much discussed in the Geniza papers, and actual testimonies pro and con are to

"known as the son of the sister of Sham'ān,"[26] not to participate in the public service of the Palestinian synagogue of Fustat. One of the most extensive, most carefully styled and beautifully written Hebrew documents in the Geniza is a bill of release given to him in 1025–26 by Turayk, daughter of Abraham.[27] She declares to have lived in his house for ten years entirely at his cost and that neither he, nor his three sons, nor his three daughters, called Sarwa ("Cypress"), Fā'iza ("Favorite"), and Nabīla ("The noble one"), nor his wife Fahda ("Female Cheetah"), daughter of Judah ha-Kohen, known as al-Athāribī,[28] the clothier, owed her anything.[29] This Muḥsin still was a very influential man at the time of

be found. The material is presented in *A Mediterranean Society*, III, chap. viii (in preparation).

[26] Muḥsin's full name is established beyond doubt by multiple occurrence in the calligraphic document described in the next note and in several other Geniza papers. Here a part of it is effaced or its reading doubtful. Thus it seems to me that his father is called here Ḥasan, and not Ḥusayn, as usual. Such deviations occur sometimes. He is always referred to as "Sham'ān's sister's son," presumably because he took over his uncle's business and possibly also office of representative of the merchants. I have never seen the name Sham'ān elsewhere (which is, of course, not the Arabic equivalent of Heb. Simon; that is Sim'ān). I assume both Sham'ān and his nephew have come from the north of Syria (Aleppo etc.), where, at that time, Jews had often strange Arabic names and where they were engaged in big business. Muḥsin's father-in-law came from a town half-way between Aleppo and Antioch, see n. 28, below.

[27] I pieced this precious document together from three different fragments, two in the Taylor-Schechter Collection: Glasses, TS 20.169, and Volumes, 10 J 8, f. 9, and one in the British Museum, BM Or 5542, f. 6, see Mann, *Jews*, II, 78, n. 7.

[28] Al-Athārib was a town between Aleppo and Antioch, see Yāqūt, *Geographical Dictionary*, I, 114.

[29] Turayk had legal heirs who might claim that she could not have lived for such a long time in Muḥsin's house without having deposited with him or his female relatives a large sum in advance, and that, after her death, that money belonged to them. Similar declarations, in which aged persons who had been mercifully harbored by other people, free them of all claims, are found elsewhere in the Geniza. The strange name, which means "little Turk" (in the masculine!) describes its bearer as being of fair complexion, that is, beautiful.

the Gaon Solomon b. Judah. The absence from the synagogue of the representative of the merchants meant a great financial loss for the community, since the pledges for contributions usually were made during the service; in addition, it augured ill of communal strife. Therefore the Gaon assembles a formidable array of quotations from Talmud and Midrash to the effect that private prayer could never replace the regular attendance at the public service. This shows, by the way, that Muḥsin did not intend to defect to the Iraqi synagogue or to the Karaites. We find him indeed later a staunch supporter of the Palestinian Gaon, although strongly opposing the Rabbanite fanatics of Ramle who incited to anti-Karaite demonstrations by divulging false accusations.[30]

C. First Postscript

Ll. 34–38. The addressee had sent a gift to one of the members of the yeshiva. The Gaon discreetly remarks that there are four to five others worthy of such a consideration.

D. Second Postscript: Request for Confirmation in Office

Translation

May our lord, the king, son of kings,[31] be exalted forever; may his days be prolonged and his years multiplied and his reign endure longer than that of other kings of the nations; may his enemies be subdued and his fame increase. May he find healing and be restored to good health, gain strength and his mind be set to peace so that he may enjoy his reign and find pleasure in his

---

[30] TS 13 J 19, f. 16, l. 33. This is one of the most important still unpublished letters of Solomon b. Judah Gaon. Professor D. H. Baneth has prepared a complete edition of this difficult document, but with his usual thoroughness wishes to clarify certain points. He has kindly presented me with his transscript, translation, and commentary.

[31] Imitation of an Arabic phrase, referring to the Fatimids' claim to be descendants of the seven Imāms, the heavenly inspired rulers of Islam according to the Shiʿite theory.

office.[32] For he pays attention to his subjects and in particular to the servants of the crown who have been known to him and also to his fathers, may they rest in glory. Three of his ancestors have been beneficient to us, and their rescripts are with us, the rescript of his great-grandfather, that of his grandfather and that of his father.[33] Let him complement those by his own rescript. May his Creator help him and make all his crowds submissive to him; may his prayers be accepted, and his favor be spread over us, over you and over all the people of our God.

Your welfare and that of your son[34] may wax forever, and also the welfare of all your friends and beloved; the leaders of the people, the heads of the community, and the elders of the congregation — all are greeted by their name and rank[35] and the rest of the congregation, young and old.

May Salvation come quickly!

Commentary

The letter must have been written some time after aẓ-Ẓāhir ascended the throne. It cannot have emanated from Joshiah Gaon,

[32] Aẓ-Ẓāhir, like his father al-Ḥākim, was a psychopath and committed crimes which, before 1933, were believed to be possible only in a complete madman. Once he invited all the palace girls, 2,660 in number, to a party, then ordered the doors to be locked and bricked up, so that all the girls died of suffocation and starvation, Stanley Lane-Poole, *History of Egypt in the Middle Ages*, (London, 1914), p. 136. This happened near the end of his short life. Our letter proves that the subjects of that monster had been aware of his malady already at the beginning of his reign.

[33] The first Fatimid ruler over Egypt and the adjacent countries was al-Muʿizz (d. 975), succeeded by his son al-ʿAzīz (d. 996), and grandson al-Ḥākim (d. February 13, 1021). "Rescript" translates the biblical *nishtewān* (Ezra 4: 7; 7: 11), an originally Persian word, properly used here as an equivalent of Arabic *tawqīʿ*.

[34] The word *ḥmwdk* (ḥamūdekhā), "your son", was erroneously corrected into *hmlk*, "the king," who was the topic of the previous lines. But a caliph cannot be referred to with the phrase used in the letter which corresponds to our "kind regards to."

[35] That is, give them my greetings in a way, as if I had mentioned everyone by his name and honorific title (given to him by the yeshiva or by a state authority).

for the letters coming from his chancery were written in an entirely different style and the one that is preserved to its end does not contain the motto used here.[36]

Since Joshiah must have been still alive around 1018 (see above), it stands to reason that the Gaon writing here was his immediate successor, Solomon ha-Kohen b. Joseph Āv bēth dīn. According to Mann, *Jews*, I, 70, his family had come from Iraq, which would explain the astonishing fact that our letter is written in a pure Babylonian style of handwriting. The motto *yesha' yūḥash* has been found by me thus far (in this period) only in two letters of Abraham, son and representative of the later Gaon Solomon b. Judah. He might have married a daughter of the Gaon Solomon ha-Kohen and, having done so, adopted his motto, thus manifesting a double claim to office in the yeshiva, being son of the "Third" and son-in-law of the incumbent Gaon.[37]

When the writer of our letter remarks that he was known to the caliph's fathers we should take this with a grain of salt. He possibly had appeared in an audience of the caliph al-Ḥākim shortly after he had acceded to the gaonate, but he might have happened to be in the Egyptian capital at the time of a public audience of al-Ḥākim's predecessor(s), while he was still president of the court, and as such would have led the Jewish delegation.

---

[36] See Mann, *Jews*, II, 66–72, also TS NS J 92. Mann, ibid., p. 66, says that the verso of the interesting document TS 13 J 14, f. 10 is blank and that it was "probably" sent to Egypt. But verso is not blank, but contains the address in Arabic characters, written, I admit, in an extremely involved and fleeting script: "To my lords and elders, the elders of the Synagogues, may God prolong their lives etc., from Joshiah b. Hārūn (Aaron), the head of the yeshiva. To al-Fustat." While preparing the new edition of Mann, *Jews*, for re-impression by Ktav Publishing House, New York, I was not yet aware of this omission.

[37] Letters with this motto of Abraham b. Solomon: ULC Or 1080 J 265 (written by him in Egypt), TS 10 J 11, f. 28v (a fragment). He seems not to have survived his father very long and not to have attained a rank higher than Fourth. Such mottoes, which served as 'alāma, or indication who the issuer of the letter was, were normally found only in letters of caliphs, Gaons, or Nagids, see S. M. Stern, *Fatimid Decrees* (London, 1964), Index, s.v. 'alāma.

The late S. M. Stern makes mention of TS 24.43 in the article referred to in n. 17, above. He had partly copied it, but did not contemplate its publication.

The yeshiva often sent representatives to the adjacent countries for settling important lawsuits, for instance, Hananya Āv in 1007.[38]

The modern reader of the letter might ask, why was it necessary to enlist the help of a notable in order to obtain the caliph's rescript, why was it not given at the government's own initiative after the caliph's ascension to the throne, and why was it necessary at all, seeing that the incumbent already had been confirmed in his office by a former ruler. The answer to all this is that everything (except the collecting of revenue, of course) was done in this way in the Muslim state. Every interested party had to ask for its rights, and every right was granted as a favor of the ruler. The Gaon himself could not apply. This would have been bad form; the old principle "do not seek honor (i.e., office)" was as valid in Islam as in Judaism. Finally, the confirmation of all incumbents in office by a new ruler (or their replacement by others) was as common a practice in the Muslim state as the well known occurrences in the United States when a president from another party takes office.

An exact parallel to our document, which must be dated around 1022–24, is a decree of the same caliph aẓ-Ẓāhir from 1024 in which he granted to Coptic monks the same privileges that they had enjoyed under his three ancestors and predecessors (see S. M. Stern, *Fatimid Decrees*, London, 1964, pp. 15–22).

3. THE OFFICE OF THE HEAD OF THE JERUSALEM YESHIVA

As Defined in a Testimony to be submitted to the Government

Dropsie University, Geniza Collection, 354.

A fragment in Arabic characters, beginning, end, and right side torn away.

The Arabic text of this important document has been restored by conjecture (the complemented parts appear here in parentheses),

---

[38] MS Mosseri L 134, see Mann, *HUCA*, III (1926), 266. Now included in vol. II of the new edition of Mann, *Jews*, see n. 36, above.

translated into Hebrew and its content been discussed in *Eretz-Israel*, 10, Jerusalem 1971. We provide here an English translation, for its script and style are identical with TS NS Box 320, f. 45, presented below, and both documents, no doubt, emanated from the same source and were written approximately at the same time. Moreover, Dropsie 354 is the most important Geniza document found thus far illustrating the official position of the Jerusalem Gaonate within the Muslim state.

Translation

1 (Having been requested,) we, all together and each separately,
2 (to deliver this testimony,) namely all those writing their witness and signing
3 (at the end of this document, say) that what they know and understand and are able to testify
4 (with regard of the leadership of) the community known as the Rabbanite Jews,
5 (and which they testify herewith) is that all the judgments in their lawsuits in the course
6 (of the years and all matters of marr)iage and divorce, and the curbing of anyone remiss in the keeping
7 (of their religion and "the encouragement to act properly) and the prohibition of acting improperly,"[39] the removal of the evildoer by ban and the lifting of the ban,
8 (the issuing of reponsa and the public ex)pounding of the Scriptures, the appointment of cantors for the synagogues to lead
9 (their congregations in prayer, and of shohets) in charge of the ritual killing, and the dismissal of anyone deserving it,

[39] A phrase found originally in the Koran and later developed in Islamic law as conferring authority to interfere wherever the obedience to the injunctions of religion seems to be slack.

10   (the appointment of "members" of the yesh)iva, of judges,[40] and of dayyānīm and the defining of their competence according to[41]

11   (..., and the supervision of the acts of the parna)sim[42] and the conduct of the "trustees"[43] — all this is within the competence of the head of all

12   (the Rabbanite Jews in every) period and time, on whose leadership the entire community is agreed, namely

13   (the dignitary whose) office is called "Head of the Yeshiva" and whose son is his....[44] And the undersigned also know

14   (that the Rabbanite) Jews are not permitted to disapprove of, or to object to his decisions or actions

15   (or any order [?] emanating) from him. He also has the right to delegate his authority in any town or country to any one reliable

16   (who will provide) him with any help he might request from him. [The rest is torn off, but not much can have been lost.]

4. THE OFFICE OF THE JEWISH CHIEF JUDGE OF ALEXANDRIA

As Described in a Testimony to be Submitted to the Government
TS NS Box 320, f. 45.

[40] This word (*ḥukkām*), which designates both judges and governors, is crossed out. In Jewish usage it comprised the notions both of dayyān and lay judge.

[41] "According to" is crossed out; therefore it is impossible to know what was written at the beginning of the next line.

[42] The parnasim of those days were the social service officers in charge of communal property (such as houses donated to a synagogue) and administering the funds for the needy.

[43] The *ne'emānīm* were entrusted with the money and the goods deposited with the courts.

[44] There is a remote possibility to read *mustawfī*, "administrator." Abraham acted indeed in this capacity for his father, the Gaon Solomon b. Judah. But since I have not yet read this word in a Geniza document in this sense, I cannot acquiesce in that reading.

The fragment is in Arabic characters and a draft, as is evident from the fact that it is not completed and written on a page showing remainders of writings in Hebrew characters. The reverse side contains the fragment of a legal deed in Hebrew characters, in which two partners, one of whom is called Maḥfūẓ (corresponding to Heb. Shemarya), l. 4, release Yeshū'ā, son of Sa'dēl, Head of the Congregations, ll. 6 and 14, from all claims. This Yeshū'ā signed TS 16.191, a document issued around 1,000. This means that our draft in support of the Alexandrian judge was written in Fustat on the mostly blank verso of a legal document no longer needed. As said before, this and the preceding document discussed here are identical in style and script. They were made out, no doubt, in the capital of Egypt on the same occasion and for the same purpose.

Translation
TS NS Box 320, f. 45

1   ... for Joseph the Aaronite[45]...)
2   may God have mercy upon him.[46] And Joseph did not cease to administer the affa(irs of the Alexandrian community until the times of)
3   Joshia, the head of the yeshiva, may God be pleased with him[47] and after the latter's (death in the times of Solomon, the Aaronite).
4   And when Solomon, the Aaronite, the head of the yeshiva, died and the office passed (to Solomon b. Judah)
5   of Fez,[48] the present incumbent — may God increase his

---

[45] Arabic *Hārūnī* ("from the tribe of Aaron") corresponds to Heb. Kohen.

[46] Blessing for a dead person. The predecessor of Joshiah, who had first appointed Joseph ha-Kohen as dayyān of Alexandria, is referred to. The words are deleted in the manuscript, no doubt because the formula had already been written at the end of the preceding line.

[47] Another blessing for a dead person.

[48] Solomon b. Judah Gaon was called al-Fāsī by his Babylonian colleague Hay Gaon and in other Geniza letters, e.g. ULC Or 1080 J 45.

splendor —, he appointed Joseph, the Aaronite, (to be chief of the Rabbanite Jews)

6 in the port-city of Alexandria, namely as judge[49] in all matters that he had administered up till then,[50] (to wit,) decisions on

7 their civil cases, the conclusion of marriages and the enactment of divorces in accordance with the rites of their denomination, the appointment of cantors (and officiating in)

8 their synagogues, and of persons administering[51] their emoluments, and the dismissal of anyone deserving it in his opinion. And when anyone opposes him,

9 (no action can be taken against Joseph) except by the head of the yeshiva, who has appointed him and invested him with his authority.

10 And when we were asked to testify by one who has authority to do so, we wrote this our testimony (...)

11 (...) and we signed for him[52] and signed ourselves on the day...

Commentary

At the end of the testimony on the privileges of the head of the yeshiva (above, no. 3, Dropsie 354, l. 15) it was stated that he had the right to delegate his authority over a city or country to anyone

---

[49] The words for judge and decision used here, *nāẓir* and *naẓar*, lit. "seeing into a case," cf. Heb. *le-ʿayyēn be-dīn*, may refer in Islamic law both to a qadi and to an administrative judge.

[50] The text has *mʾ ḥwh ʾlyh*, but one expects mā huwa ʿalayh (with ʿayn, not *alif*).

[51] Eight partly effaced letters. For *budhil lahum*, the clerk wrote originally *bdhlhm lhm*, a dittograph which he corrected by deleting the first *hm*. The parnasim responsible for the payment of the community officials are referred to.

[52] The concluding phrase is a standing formula in such testimonies of a general character. The words "and we signed for him" refer to a person that had been mentioned at the beginning of the document as one of the participants in the testimony, but was not able to sign, for instance, because he had meanwhile left the capital for travel abroad. The man concerned certainly was a V.I.P. known to the government, wherefore one was eager to have him included.

he regarded as reliable. In our document we clearly see that the local dayyān acted as the deputy of the Gaon. In fact, the dayyān's privileges are very similar to those of the Gaon. They are only more limited in scope and entirely subject to the overriding authority of the head of the yeshiva of Jerusalem.

Joseph ha-Kohen of Alexandria, whose time is indicated by the reference to three Gaons who re-appointed him in his office, is well known. Several letters, written by the beautiful hand of his son and successor Yeshū'ā, but issued by Joseph in the name of the Palestinian and Babylonian congregations of Alexandria to the two corresponding congregations in Fustat, have been preserved.[53] Also the fragment of another such letter, sent to another country, of which only the exordium is extant.[54] A considerable number of letters emanating from, or referring to his son and successor have also been preserved (mostly still unpublished), and repeatedly mention is being made in them of his father Joseph both during his lifetime and after his death. We learn from them the interesting fact that Joseph, unlike his son, never received the title ḥāvēr, or member of the yeshiva, and also that Yeshū'ā repeatedly incurred much opposition in the Alexandrian community; but his authority was staunchely upheld both by the Gaon Solomon b. Judah and his rival and later successor Daniel b. Azarya (1051–1063).

Only one change of government occurred during the incumbency of Solomon b. Judah, namely the accession to the throne of the caliph al-Mustanṣir in 1036. Consequently, our document, as well as no. 3, translated above, must have been written in that year or sometime afterwards.[55]

---

[53] See the references in Mann, *Texts and Studies*, I, 366 ff.

[54] TS 10 J 15, f. 16, with greetings from his son Yeshū'ā.

[55] Between Solomon ha-Kohen and Solomon b. Judah there was another Gaon, named Ṣādōq, see n. 1, above. But he can have been in office only for a very short time, not long enough for being officially installed by the government. Therefore, no reference is made to him here.

המקורות

1. דו״ח על אירועים בחודש תשרי בירושלים
כתבו שלמה בן יהודה גאון בהיותו עדיין "שלישי"
TS NS Box 320, f. 16 ט״ש (אוסף טיילור־שכטר), סידרה חדשה
(בחלק האנגלי, עמ׳ 508—510 [6—8])

1 عليها وقوف الأجوبة عنها وكتابي هذا يقتضي شرح جميع ما [جر]ى [وهوان]

2 قبل راس السنة بيومين وصل ا ب بيت دين والمغاربة ولما كان فى راس السنة لم يكن به مولاي اذن

3 الريس نزول الكنيسة ولم اوثر انا كون العبور فى داري باجتماعنا فى دار اب بيت دين ولم يرض

4 اخوه السهل منى لانه غضبان لبنى شويع وحضر معنا الشيخ ابو الخير بن التاهرتى وصلينا عليه

5 حـاوير ولصينـا على سعيد بن اسرائيل الحراز لعكاطس صلينـاو . . . يحيى الدمشقى **שביעי** .

6 ونزلت انا واب بيت دين الكنيسة ووقت السفر اكرزنا جاهر طرد الحانان بسبب احكام .

7 وتقدمت انا **תקיעות** وسبت **שובה** درس **אב** ودمنت السوا . . . ي ** י ימי תשובה.**

8 ويوم كفور نزل مولاي الريس الى الكنيسة وتقدم **אב אחרי מות** وانا **מוסף** والحراز **מנחה**

9 **ואדוננו גאון נעילה** واول يوم **הסוכה** درس **אב** وسبت **עשר דרשת** انا ويوم **ערבה**

10 درس مولاي الريس فى الجبل وكان الحجاج قليل وكان الحانان قد وصل وانتهرناه وهو عليه حال لا

11 يوصف الى مـا . . . . قد تكررا واشهد الجمع على نفسه ان . . .

12 بهذه المثيبة ولما . . . . وبعد ذلك بسطنا له وجه واطلعناه [الى

13 **ספר תורה** ويوم **ח מרחשון** صلى **אב** بيت دين **גשם** وغـد العيد احضرت س[ريعا

14 عاجلة (!) الى عند سلمان بن التلميذ رحمه الله لانه كـان مثقل فى الوجـع واش]مهدنا

15 ان ليس له شيء وانه فقير وان وراثه اخوه واخته وتوفي ليلة السبت وس[بت . . .

16 درست انا . . . . ويوم **הושענא** اكرزنا بن الحانان **רביעי**(؟) . . .

17 بن ا **אלרב אלרומי** . . . . . . واك[رنا] ابو الخير . . . . تأخرى فى ايام العيد وقد علم الله انى ما ودعت ذكره فى وسط . . . .

LETTER BY SOLOMON B. JUDAH
TS NS Box 320, f. 16. See p. 529 [27]

2. בקשת גאון ירושלמי מיהודי בעל השפעה במצרים
להשיג אישור ממשלתי למשרתו
ט״ש, סידרת הזגוגיות TS 24.43
(בחלק האנגלי עמ׳ 517—521 [15—19])

שלום אל רבנא יפת בן רבנא טוביה הידוע אלנילי	1
ובכתבו ובאהבה ואל דויד בן אהרן	2
שלמה בן חכים אלפאסי ולכל	3
תפילותי ימים ולילות	4
הקהילות הם	5
שתי הכיתות המושלמים לשרייהם זקניהם	6
...הם ושאר הקהילות גדולם וקטנם ברכות ותפילות נשמעות	7
בעדך ובעד כל אוהביך ואהוביך ובעדם ובעד כל ישראל וגם	8
(רמ?) המעלה שרינו רבנא דויד בן יצחק אשר	9
...בלשון קודש על שמו ועל שם אביו אותיותיו. וזה בתוך המועד	10
כתבנו... שלישי ובבוא החבר האדיר ר׳ טוביה מירושלים אנו ניכתוב	11
כל הראוי לכתבו וכל הראוי לחפצך כמ...ך ייעשה. ובעד רבנא	12
מוחסן בן חסן (אבן אכת ? ש)מעאן פקיד הסוחרים אשר אמרת כי	13
נישבע	
שלא שאין נשבעין לבטל את (המצוה)x	14
(א)בל (נשבעין) לק(יימה כב ב)שבע(תי) ואקיימה וגו.x ואמרו חכמ(ינ)	15
זלב	
כל מי שהוא מתפלל (אחורי ? בית) כנסת ניקרא שכן רעx דכתיב	16
על כל ש(כני הרעים) הנוגעים בנחלה ועוד אמ חכמ (בת)למוד	17
הירושלמיx כל המתפלל בביתו ולא בבית הכנסת כאילו מקיף עליו	18
חומה שלברזלx	19
בבתי (כניסיות ובתי) מדרשות ואמרו חכמ זל בפירוש זה הפסוק	20
כל (מי) שהוא נהו(ג?) להתפלל בבית הכנסת וניתעכב יו(ם) אחד הקבה	21
מש... מדוע ב)אתי ואין איש קראתי ואין עונה	22
ומא... ופודיהו ממגורו. ומצילו מזעמי עם	23
גם משטינו... ככת הקצור קצרה ידי מפדות וכו׳.x א	24
דומה דודי לצבי ואומ קול דודי הנה זה בא מדלג על ההרים פ (=פירוש)	25
שקב	
מזכיר למתפללים בבית הכניסת זכות אבות וזכות אמהות.x ובכל	26

27 יום ויום שלוחיו שליוצרינו משקיפין על בתי כניסיות מן החלונות

28 ומן החרכים. (ככֹת מ)שגיח מן החלונות מצֹיץ מֹן הֹחרֹכים. וכֹת

29 ואתֹה קדֹוֹש יושב תהילוֹת ישראל. וכיון שאדם מתאחר מבית הכנסת

30 הקדֹוש (ברוך הוא כו׳)עֹס עליו דכֹת נֹידרשתי (ללֹא) שאלו נֹמצ(אתֹי)

31 ל(לֹא ב)קֹש(וֹני...   בתי כניסיות

32 ובתי מדרשות דכֹת (וֹא)הֹי להֹם מקדֹש מעֹ(ט   עוֹנֹש כל

33 המתאחרים מן הכניסת   ואתה שלום וביתֹך שלום

34 וכל אשר לך שלום   והזריזים מקדימים למיצוות. דכֹת ועֹץ

35 חיֹיֹם תֹאוֹוֹה בֹאֹה. ואודיעֹך יקירנו שארבעה וחמֹשה חבירים

36 שלנו כולם יריאי שמים וחכמי תורה ראויים לכל מעֹלה נאה

37 ואיך נפריד מהם אחד ונטיל ביניהם מריבה ומחלוקות. ומחלוקֹת

38 בית דינֹא חרבן עולם. והישועה קרובה. והמשתלֹמֹא קרוב. ואדונינו

39 המלך בן המלכים. ישֹוגֹב לֹנצח. ויוֹארכו ימיו. ותרבינה שנוֹתֹיו.

40 ותֹימֹשֹך מֹלֹכוֹתֹו עֹל כל מלֹכי הגֹוים ויפֹלו אויבֹיו ויֹכֹנעֹו קמֹיו. ויֹאבדו

41 משֹנֹאיֹו ותֹרֹום ידו. ו(יֹג)דֹל כבֹודו וימֹצֹא רֹפֹואֹות. ותֹעֹלֹות בֹאות.

42 ויֹתֹאזֹר כֹוֹחֹו. ותֹיֹשֹקֹוֹט רוֹחֹו ויֹיֹנֹעֹם בֹמֹלֹכֹוֹתֹו. ויֹתֹעֹנֹג בֹמֹמֹשֹלֹתֹו.

43 כֹי שֹם בֹלֹא עֹל צֹאן מֹרֹעֹיֹתֹו ו((.))עֹל עֹבֹדֹי מֹלֹכֹוֹתֹו הֹיֹדֹועֹים לֹו גֹם

44 לֹאֹבֹותֹיֹו הֹיֹקֹרֹים בֹמֹנֹוֹחֹתֹם. כֹי שֹלֹוֹשֹת אֹבֹותֹיו גֹמֹלֹוֹנֹו טֹוֹבֹה.

45 אֹשֹר נֹיֹשֹתֹוֹוֹנֹם עֹיֹמֹנֹו. נֹיֹשֹתֹוֹרֹוֹן זֹקֹן אֹבֹיֹהֹו. וֹזֹקֹיֹנֹהֹו. ונֹיֹשֹתֹוֹרֹוֹן אֹבֹיֹהֹו.

46 יוֹשֹלֹם בֹנֹיֹשֹתֹוֹוֹנֹיֹהֹו. יֹעֹזֹרֹהֹו קֹוֹנֹיֹהֹו. ויֹכֹרֹע לֹפֹנֹיֹהֹו כֹל הֹמֹוֹנֹיֹהֹו.

47 ויֹקֹוֹבֹל רֹבֹנֹיֹהֹו ויֹוֹפֹרֹש עֹלֹיֹנֹו ועֹלֹיֹך ועֹל כֹל עֹם אֹלֹינֹו חֹיֹנֹיֹהֹו.

48 ושֹלֹוֹמֹך ושֹלֹום חֹמֹוֹדֹך (תֹוֹקֹן בֹטֹעֹוֹת: הֹמֹלֹך) יֹגֹדֹל לֹעֹדֹי עֹד. ושֹלֹום כֹל   אֹוֹהֹבֹיך ואֹהֹוֹבֹיך

49 ושֹלֹום שֹרֹי עֹם וֹרֹבֹי עֹדֹה וֹשֹבֹי קֹהֹל כֹל אֹחֹד מֹהֹם בֹשֹמֹו גֹם

50 בֹמֹעֹלֹתֹו ושֹאֹר הֹקֹהֹילֹות קֹטֹון וֹגֹדֹוֹל.   יֹשֹע יוֹחֹש

בירור מובאות אחדות
(המספרים מתיחסים לשורות כתב היד)

14 צירוף לשון המשנה: "אין נשבעין לעבור על המצוות", נדרים ט״ז, ע״א, ולשון הברייתא "יכול נשבע לבטל את המצוה", שם, ע״ב.

15 נשבעין לקיימה: נדרים ח׳, ע״א. נשבעתי: תהלים קט״ו, קד.

16 הפסוק בירמיה יב, יד, מובא בברכות ח׳, ע״א כסמך לדרש "כל מי שיש לו בית כנסת בעירו ואינו נכנס שם להתפלל נקרא שכן רע." במקום שלא נשמרו האותיות יש רווח יותר מכדי המלים (אחורי בית), על כן שמתי סימן שאלה.

18 בירושלמי ברכות פ״ה, ה״א, לפנינו (מהד׳ קרוטושין): ״אמר רבי יוחנן
המתפלל בתוך ביתו כאילו מקיפו חומה של ברזל״, עיין לוי גינצבורג,
״פירושים וחידושים בירושלמי״, כרך ד, עמ׳ 144: ״חומה של ברזל:
המפסקת בינו להקב״ה ומגנה תפלה ביחיד״. כך פשוט מהמשך הדברים,
וכך הבין כותב מכתבנו. אך מלכתחילה, כוונת ר׳ יוחנן היתה אולי הפוכה,
כלומר לשון שמירה, עי׳ ירוש׳ ב״ק, סוף פרק ד, ד, ע״ג: ״כל שמירה
שאמרה תורה, אפילו הקיפו חומת ברזל וכו׳״, ודרשו דברי ר׳ יוחנן אחר
כך לעניינו. ועיין ליברמן, הלכות הירושלמי להר״מ, עמ׳ ל״ה, אות ב׳.
ועיין מ״ש גינצבורג לפני כן בח״ג, עמ׳ 361.

19 אפשר אולי לשחזר יתר השורה.

22 מדוע באתי ואין איש (ישעיה נ, ב) נדרש בברכות ו׳, ע״ב: ״בשעה
שהקב״ה בא בבית הכנסת ולא מצא בה עשרה מיד הוא כועס.״ כנראה יש
כאן רמז למקום דומה, אך לא מזדהה.

24 הקצור קצרה: ישעיה, שם, ובוודאי המשך הדרש.

25—26 שיר השירים ב, ח, נדרש בראש השנה י״א, ע״א: ״הרים — אבות.
גבעות — אמהות״. שאר המובאות פשוטות.

38 בית דין: לפנינו (דרך ארץ זוטא סוף פרק ט׳): אבא שאול אומר, מחלוקת
בתי דינין חורבן העולם. ומלת ״בתי דינים״ ביארו דיינים מומחים, כפי
שיוצא מן המאמר הקודם: ״תלמידי חכמים הדרים בעיר אחת, והם בתי
דינים״. לא דקדקו בהבאות.

38 והמשתלם — כלומר, הנותן לבני הישיבה יקבל שכרו בקרוב.

43 כי שם בל — דניאל ו׳, ט״ו.

3. משרת ראש הישיבה הירושלמית
כפי שהוגדרה בטיוטה של בקשה אל הממשלה הפאטימית

דרופסי אוניברסיטי, כ״י גניזה, מס׳ 354

(בנוגע למקור עיין בחלק האנגלי, עמ׳ 523—524 [21—22])

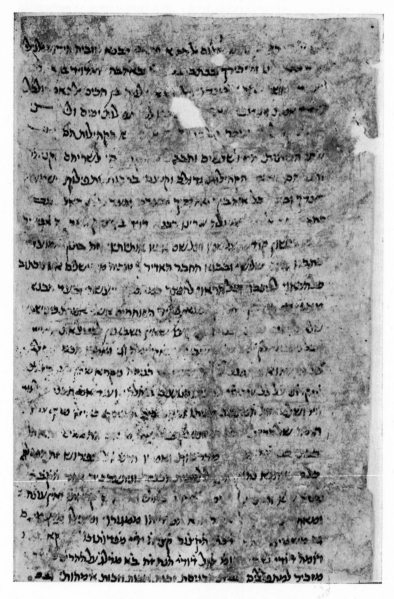

LETTER OF A GAON OF JERUSALEM
TS 24.43. See pp. 531–532 [29–30]

LETTER OF A GAON OF JERUSALEM (CONTINUATION)
TS 24.43. See pp. 531–532 [29–30]

4. משרתו של דיין אלכסנדריה
כפי שהוגדרה בטיוטה של בקשה אל הממשלה הפאטימית

ט״ש, סידרה חדשה   TS NS Box 320, f. 45

(בחלק האנגלי, עמ׳ 526—527 [24—25])

وفاته و ب[عده ن]صب ليوسف الهاروني [1

[[رحمه الله]] ولم يزل يوسف الهاروني القيم با[مورهم . . . الى ايام   2

يوشيا راس المثيبة رضى الله عنه و بعد [وفاته فى ايام سليمان الهارونى] .   3

ولما توفى سليمان الهاروني راس المثيبة وكان التصرف [لسليمان بن يهودا]   4

الفاسى الباق الى اليوم ادام الله عزه قلد ليوسف الهارونى [مقـــدم على اليهود   5
الربانيين]

فى ثغر الاسكندرية ناضر (= ناظر) فى جميع ما هوه اليه من [التصرف . . .   6
والنظر]

فى احكامهم وعقد نكاحاتهم وطلاقاتهم على سنن مذهبهم ونصب حزانين [و . . .   7
فى]

كنائسهم ومن يتولا ما بذل لهم وعزل من يرا عزله وعند مخالفة احدهم له .   8

] الا راس المثيبة الذى نصبه وقلده و . . .   9

] ولما سالنا سائل جاز سؤاله كتبنا شها[دت]نا بما   10

] علمنا]به وكتبنا خطه وخطنا فى يوم [11

שולים   اذ لا يجوز]

اعتزل]

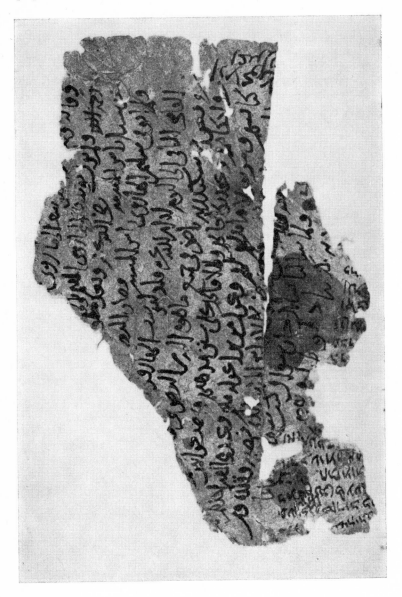

TESTIMONY ON THE OFFICE OF THE JEWISH JUDGE
OF ALEXANDRIA
TS NS Box 320, f. 45. See p. 536 [34]

"THIS SONG"

JUDAH GOLDIN

ON THE PHRASE את השירה הזאת of Exodus 15:1, the Mekilta[1]
comment as it has been preserved is almost frustratingly difficult,
and, what is more, it has been so for a long, long time. Has
Mekilta de-Rabbi Simeon (henceforth, MRS) been of some help
perhaps? Not a bit. With a few virtually trivial variants, it reads
like the Mekilta (of R. Ishmael), and thus naturally compounds
bewilderment: how come that what makes no sense is simply
repeated?

What is the Mekilta comment? It begins seemingly as follows:
"THIS SONG. Now then, is there only one Song? Are there not
indeed ten Songs?" את השירה הזאת, וכי שירה אחת היא, והלא עשר
שירות הן. Even before proceeding with the remainder of the passage,
one is certainly entitled to ask in turn: What can the Mekilta
possibly mean? Supposing there are a number of other songs, so
what? After all, the biblical verse is reporting that at the miracle
at the Reed Sea Moses and the children of Israel sang this particular
song of Exodus 15. That on other occasions other worthies in
Israel sang other songs is perfectly natural. What therefore is both-
ering the Tannaim when they come upon "This Song" as they
read Exodus 15:1? That this puzzled at least the author of Midrash
ha-Gadol is clear from the way he remarks, "THIS SONG: evidently
there are also others," מיכלל דאיכא אחריתי.[2] The late Mordecai

---

1 The text I use is the Lauterbach edition, though I keep consulting the
Horovitz-Rabin edition as well; and the edition of *Mekilta de-Rabbi Simeon*
is that by Epstein-Melamed.

2 *MhG*, Exod., ed. Margulies, p. 285. And note that in *'Efat Ṣedeq* also
there is no question, "Now then, is there only one song"; however, cf. the

Margulies was quite right in his comment ad loc., that this sentence is wanting in the sources and is very likely the emphasis of the author of the Midrash ha-Gadol. But that author too is of no help, for he continues at once, with ‏והלא עשר שירה היא, אחת שירה וכי תניא‎ ‏שירות הן‎. Our difficulty therefore remains. Perhaps, however, as the Mekilta text proceeds immediately after its initial question, some clarity emerges. Let us see.

Are there not in fact ten Songs, the Mekilta had asked presumably: whereupon to leave nothing hazy, it undertakes to tell us what the ten songs are. The first is that referred to in Isaiah 30:29; the second is the one in our verse, Exodus 15:1; third is the one referred to in Numbers 21:17; for the fourth, see Deuteronomy 31:24 f.; the fifth, Joshua 10:12 f., where, although the word "song" does not appear, a poetic quotation is transmitted;[3] the sixth is found in Judges 5; the seventh is spoken of in II Samuel 22:1 ff.; the eighth in Psalm 30:1;[4] the ninth in II Chronicles 20:21;[5] as for the tenth, which is the song for the Age to Come,[6] we are referred to Isaiah 42:10 as well as Psalms 149:1.[7]

Very well, we now know what the ten songs are. Observe, however, that our primary difficulty has not disappeared: so what?[8] What's wrong with "This Song" in Exodus 15:1, even though for other occasions there were and are other songs?

commentary in Horovitz-Rabin ad loc. According to Kasher, *Torah Shelemah,* XIV, 289, this "evidently there are also others" occurs also in the Ms. of ‏מדרש הביאור‎.

[3] And there may even be a play on the word (*Sefer*) *ha-Yashar* (*hyšr*). Cf. Peshitta. By the way, note how the verse is quoted in *Midrash ha-Gadol.*

[4] For the long digression at this point, see further below.

[5] Cf. preceding note.

[6] In other words, presumably it has not yet been sung! Note indeed that the author of *We-Hizhir* (20a–b) therefore introduces his quotation of the "ten songs" passage as follows: "Our sages said, *Nine* songs were recited." Thus when he cites the tenth song, it is unambiguously "for the Age to Come."

[7] Note, however, that *Yalquṭ ha-Makiri* on Ps. 18:1 (52a) quotes Isa. 48:20 instead of this Psalm verse.

[8] That I am not alone in asking this, is evident from the comment by Rabbi Abraham, the author of *Be'er Abraham,* ad loc. See further below.

Bewilderment only increases when we reach the concluding remarks of the Mekilta comment. For immediately after quoting Psalm 149:1, the Mekilta says: "For all the songs[9] referring to past events the noun used is in the feminine, [because] even as a female brings to birth, so the triumphs in the past were succeeded by subjugation; but the triumph which is yet to be will not be succeeded by subjugation. That is why the noun used for it is in the masculine, as it is said (Jer. 30:6), 'Ask ye now, and see whether a man doth travail with child': [for] just as no male gives birth, so the triumph which is yet to come will not be succeeded by subjugation, as it is said (Isa. 45:17), 'O Israel, that art saved by the Lord with an everlasting salvation.'"[10]

That there should be reflection on the gender of the noun for song-in-the-future, coming right after the statement on the Tenth Song, that it will be the Song for the Age to Come, is not out of the ordinary, certainly as midrashic texts are generally organized. Mention a theme, and by association a related thought will be introduced. And if the verses "speaking of" the Song for the Age to Come used for the word "song" not *shirah*, in the feminine (as Exodus 15:1, for example, reads), but *shir*, in the masculine, then the concluding remarks are midrashically apt. The trouble is that among the ten songs listed by the Mekilta, there are a couple which their prooftexts call quite explicitly *shir*, in the masculine, not *shirah*. Note carefully the biblical text for the first song, Isaiah 30:29 (for the sixth song, Judges 5:1 is noncommittal and it would be pressing a little desperately to enlist the support of *'ashirah* of 5:3; if anything 5:12 embarrassingly speaks of *shir*); Psalm 30:1, the prooftext for the eighth song, reads plainly *shir*.[11] What sense therefore does the Mekilta's conclusion make?

One thing is fairly certain: the author or compiler of the Tanḥuma was already a victim of the confused and confusing text and

---

9 *MRS*, "triumphs," *teshuʿot*, may reflect some unease with the reading *shirot*.

10 Note that this whole conclusion is not supplied by *Yalquṭ Makiri*, loc. cit.

11 Nor does the alternative (ר״א) referred to by *MhG* get us out of the difficulty: *shir* ha-shirim.

he is of no help to us. In pericope Be-Shallaḥ, although he has helped himself liberally[12] to Mekilta material, he omits the section quoted above on the masculine and feminine forms of the word for "song." My guess is, because he's utterly bewildered by it. The way he presents the ten songs (in Be-Shallaḥ 10) is interesting[13] but no remedy at all. He reports in commentary on Exodus 14:15, that at the Sea ten miracles were performed for the benefit of the Israelites; correspondingly [!], he tells us, the Israelites recited ten songs. Thereupon he quotes the first eight songs of the list familiar to us, and then goes off on a tangent. When shortly thereafter he begins to comment on 15:1, he follows the Mekilta order once again, and thus arrives at *'et ha-shirah ha-zot*, where we read: "THIS SONG. Now then, is there only one Song? Are there not indeed ten Songs, as specified above," כדמפרש לעיל. He repeats song number eight, and goes on as the Mekilta does;[14] finally he specifies songs nine and ten. Date the final compilation of the Taḥḥuma as you please;[15] the trouble is already there, and our initial problems are still with us.

That the author of the Leqaḥ Ṭob was ill at ease with the midrash is evident at a glance. "'*Et ha-shirah ha-zot.* There are ten songs," he informs us, and lists the ten we are familiar with. No question like "Now then, is there only one Song," and so on; plain statement of fact, "There are ten songs." Despite this, however, he is still at the mercy of his source, as his very attempt to make sense of it reveals. For after he has quoted Isaiah 42:10[16] for his tenth

---

12 See the reference in the following note.

13 See Zunz-Albeck, *Ha-Derashot be-Yisrael*, pp. 366 f., and 110 et seq.

14 Note, by the way, that apparently the Jehoshaphat song of II Chron. 20 he does not count as one of the ten songs, though he does refer to it. For him, the ninth song is Solomon's "Song of Songs;" and his tenth song, which is also of the Future, is Ps. 98:1. The author of *We-Hizhir* does not refer at all to Jehoshaphat, and his ninth song is also Solomon's Song of Songs. As for the eighth, he too cites Ps. 30:1, but attributes it to no one!

15 See note 39 in Zunz-Albeck, p. 368. Cf. also *Deut. R.*, ed. S. Lieberman, Introduction, p. xxii f.

16 He does not quote Ps. 149:1 after it.

song (which is for the Age to Come), he continues: "This song is
different (משונה שיר זה), for the noun used for it is in the masculine,
while for all the (other) songs (וכן השירות כולן) the noun used is
in the feminine — for it is like a female who brings to birth (כשם
שהנקבה יולדת) — because all the (past) triumphs were succeeded
by subjugation. But in the Age to Come there will be a triumph
which will not be succeeded by subjugation, as it is said (Isa.
45:17), 'O Israel, that art saved by the Lord with an everlasting
salvation.' That is why [in Isaiah 42:10] it is written *shir ḥadash*
[in the masculine], for it is like a male who does not give birth."
He even quotes Jeremiah 30:6 at this point. Clearly therefore, he
attaches this male-female remark to the verse of the tenth song.
But surely, the list he quoted explicitly had verses with *shir* in the
masculine, as we observed; the problem he himself must have
noted, as his very משונה שיר זה so lamely and hopelessly seeks to
solve. *Hadara qushya le-dukta*, we are back where we started!

The author of Sekel Ṭob tries even harder, and from the way
he presents his comments I fear I have to accuse him of double-
talk. First (ed. Buber, p. 191) he says: "'*et ha-shirah ha-zot*. Why
is this said? For nine other songs are spoken of לפי שנאמר
תשע שירות אחרות; but this one they recited at the Sea. And why
is the word for song (*shirah*) in the feminine form? To tell thee,
that even as a female gives birth, so the triumphs in the past were
succeeded by subjugation; but as for the triumphs [sic] in the future,
the word used for their songs (שיריהן) is in the masculine, because
they are not succeeded by subjugation, as it is said (Isa. 30:29),
'Ye shall have a song (*shir*) as in the night when a feast is [the
feast was? will be?] hallowed'; and it says (Ps. 98:1), 'A Psalm.
O sing unto the Lord a new song'; and it says (Isa. 45:17), 'O Israel,
that art saved by the Lord with an everlasting salvation.'" This is
not cricket, as one might say — hiding behind the unspelled-out
"nine other songs" and relocating the Isaiah 30:29 verse without
so much as an if-you-please. And what *does* he mean by triumphs,
in the plural, in the future? Then, second (pp. 200 f.), he quotes
the commentary of the Sages (ורבותינו דרשו), as we are already
familiar with it, and here is how he concludes: "The tenth [n.b.

העשירי! and not העשירית] in the Age to Come. And once it [the song? the triumph?] begins it will never again be interrupted (וכיון שמתחלת אין לה הפסק), as it is said" — and he quotes first Psalm 149:1, then [I guess] Isaiah 42:10, and finally Isaiah 26:1, "In that day shall this song (*shir*) be sung." No help from this quarter.

Nor is there any from Yalquṭ Shimeoni (242); it reads almost word for word like the Mekilta. There are some differences, it is true. For example, after song number three and its prooftext, no more numbers, ordinals, are supplied. Instead we read, "And [the one] that Moses recited" (Deut. 31:24 f.), "and [the one] that Joshua recited" (Josh. 10:12), "and [the one] that Deborah and Barak recited" (Judg. 5), and so on until we get to the tenth song where once again we read, "the tenth" etc. Further, for the songs of David and Solomon the reading is as follows: "And [the one] that David recited, 'And David spoke unto the Lord' (II Sam. 22:1), 'A Psalm, a Song at the dedication of the House' (Ps. 30:1).[17] And [the one] that Solomon recited, as it is said (I Kings 8:12 ff.), 'Then spoke Solomon.' " But the Yalquṭ concludes no differently from the Mekilta.[18]

That neither first aid nor any other kind is forthcoming from the Midrash ha-Gadol we have already seen. And that we are dealing with a long-established and accepted text is evident not only from these sources which we have reviewed but from the fact that MRS, as we said right at the outset, reads as does our Mekilta.

Let us consult the commentators. R. Moses of Frankfort[19] explains why among the ten songs Miriam's song is not listed; as for the question, what sense does the Mekilta conclusion make,

---

[17] In this fashion the *Yalquṭ* apparently avoids the necessity to digress briefly as the *Mekilta* does, and in turn can comfortably ignore the long digression (cf. above, n. 4) present in the *Mekilta* as it continues.

[18] The variants are trivial.

[19] In his commentary זה ינחמנו. I am using the recent (date?) reprint of the Warsaw edition, 5687. And cf. the commentary עץ יוסף in the *Tanḥuma*, s.v., עשר שירות.

he says:[20] "This is the answer to the question raised above, 'Now then, is there only one Song?' And the answer is, the reason it says *'et ha-shirah ha-zot* is not to imply that there aren't others. On the contrary, there are many [others]. But it is written (in Exod. 15:1) *ha-zot* [this, fem.] to indicate feminine gender, for it [the song, or, the triumph] was succeeded by subjugation; hence *ha-shirah ha-zot*. But for the Age to Come [the word for song] is in the masculine, as it is written, 'Sing unto the Lord a new song (*shir ḥadash*),' for it will be in a new idiom (בלשון חדש, or, it will be in the masculine gender, *ḥadash*), in the masculine, hence, Sing unto the Lord *shir ḥadash* and it is not written *shirah ḥadashah* [in the feminine]." But how does this answer *our* question? What about those songs among the ten that are called *shir*? And where does R. Moses get the idea that the Midrash in commenting on *'et ha-shirah ha-zot* of Exodus 15:1 principally intends to explain the reading *shir ḥadash* [and not *shirah ḥadashah*] of some other verse!

Like R. Moses of Frankfort, R. Judah Najar[21] also recognizes that the concluding reflection of the Mekilta on the masculine and feminine forms of the word for "song" is meant to serve as a reply to the initial question, But is there only one *Shirah*, are there not indeed ten? He too, however, acknowledges that among the ten Songs cited by the Mekilta, some are called *shir*. He admits he has his problems and therefore is grateful (והנאני) to the author of the Yefeh To'ar (R. Samuel Yafeh Ashkenazi) for *his* explanation ad Exodus R. 23:11, that the midrashic exegesis is occasioned by the words *zot* and *ḥadash*. To put it mildly, the Yefeh To'ar (which is as a rule a splendid commentary on the Midrash) leaves us still almost where R. Moses left us, in the dark.

R. Isaac Elijah Landau[22] apparently recommends eliminating

---

[20] S.v., כל השירות כולן.

[21] In his commentary שבות יהודה.

[22] In his edition (Wilna, 1844) and commentary בירורי המדות. On this edition, cf. J. N. Epstein's introduction to *MRS*, pp. 14 f.

the question "Now then, is there only one song",[23] and, under catchword *'et ha-shirah ha-zot* remarks, "The word *ha-zot* excludes others, for there are ten songs (*shirot*)." This is surely as flat a comment as can be made, and leaves our question unanswered. Later, under catchword "the tenth etc." (*ha-ʿaśirit we-ku'*) he says, "And possibly this too qualifies (excludes, ממעט) the word *zot*, for in the Age to Come the Song will not be in the feminine, for no subjugation will follow; there will be only a *shir ḥadash* (a new song, in the masculine)."[24]

R. David Moses Abraham[25] is no more enlightening. "In many places" [in Scripture], he says, "*zot* occurs for purposes of exclusion" (דזאת בכ״מ מיעוטא). As regards the theme of masculine and feminine forms for the word "song," he has some mystical thoughts, but he does not solve our problem.[26] As far as I can make out, the Malbim seems to have no comment to offer. R. Abraham of Slonim[27] also senses the real difficulties and is manifestly unable to resolve them.[28]

Is the matter hopeless? I do not think so. Is the Mekilta text corrupt? I do not think so, although I believe that it has been clumsily preserved, and I think this can be proved, by the Mekilta text itself.

From the way the Mekilta commentary on *'et ha-shirah ha-zot* concludes, it is evident that some reflection on the masculine and feminine forms of the word for "song", *shir* and *shirah*, is in the Tanna's mind. And, truth to say, it is worth asking oneself — particularly if one approaches a biblical text midrashically — why

---

[23] See also above, n. 2. And so too, apparently, R. David Moses Abraham; see below.

[24] On his comment in מיצוי המדות, see below (last note).

[25] In his מרכבת המשנה (Jerusalem, 5725).

[26] Note, however, that in his commentary on the Isa. 30:29 proof-text, he is fully aware of our problem.

[27] In his באר אברהם (Warsaw, 5687).

[28] I. H. Weiss in his edition of the *Mekilta* says almost nothing. Friedmann's faute de mieux explanation gets us nowhere: מוכרחין אנו לפרש דלאו קושיא היא, כיון דלא תירץ מידי, אלא סגנון לשון הוא דנקט בלשון תמיה, לחזק העניין.

does the verse say *'et ha-shirah hazot* in Exodus 15:1 and not *'et ha-shir ha-zeh*? To be sure, *shirah* is not an uncommon word; on the other hand, *shir* is certainly the more frequent term. I regret that even with the help of the lexica I am unable to perceive any significant distinction in semantic range between *shir* and *shirah*.[28a] Whether or not there is one, the midrash, however, would not let pass a phrase like *'et ha-shirah ha-zot* if one could just as easily have said *'et ha-shir ha-zeh*, particularly if the more common word for "song" is *shir*. So the Mekilta (or the source the compiler of this particular treatise drew on)[29] must have asked, "Why *'et ha-shirah hazot*?"[30] And to this question came the retort: "But does *ha-shirah ha-zot* occur once only," is it a hapax, does it occur only here? Why, it occurs ten times in Scripture! — And the fact is, this observation is correct! The feminine absolute form *ha-shirah*, specifically *ha-shirah ha-zot*, occurs ten times in Scripture, as even a glance at Mandelkern's Concordance will reveal.[31] The words והלא עשר שירות הן do not mean "Are there not indeed ten Songs," but "Does not indeed the expression *ha-shirah ha-zot* occur ten times?"[32] In other words, if you ask why *'et ha-shirah ha-zot* and not *'et ha-shir ha-zeh*, best recall that *'et ha-shirah ha-zot* occurs not only here, it's not a freakish use; it occurs ten times!

Nevertheless, the midrashic question is still a question: whether *ha-shirah ha-zot* occurs once or ten times, one has a right to ask, why was not *ha-shir ha-zeh* adopted by the verse? And the Mekilta answered: On all occasions when *ha-shirah ha-zot* was used, the triumph, the joyful occasion, was followed by a reversal of fortune,

---

28a However, cf. A. Ehrlich, *Miqra' ki-Pheshuṭo* on the Pentateuch, p. 4, top.

29 My reason for this parenthetical remark is that both the *Mekilta* and *MRS* read "alike;" hence one source underlies both.

30 Perhaps thus: את השירה הזאת, למה נאמר.

31 Cf. also *BDB*, p. 1010 b. As for Ps. 42:9, it is not *hšyrh hz't*, and above all, note the *qeri*!

32 With this idiom of עשר שירות הן cf. *ARNB*: א', מ"ט; עשרה נקודות בתורה (מ"ט, א'), וראה נוסחא א', נ', ב'), עשר תולדות בתורה (מ"ט, ב'), י"א יודות שבתורה (נ"א, א). Cf. also such constructions as M. *Nega'im* 13:1, which does not mean that here are ten houses, but there are ten different conditions regarding a בית המנוגע.

by subjugation. But the song which will be sung in the Age to
Come will celebrate a triumph that will not be succeeded by subjugation. For the song then, in that Age, the word will be *shir*,
in the masculine, for it will be as with a male, he does not give
birth. In that day Israel will be "saved by the Lord with an everlasting salvation," as Isaiah said.

This was the original and complete Mekilta commentary on
'et ha-shirah ha-zot, and read this way the beginning and end fit
perfectly, like a lid on a kettle (if I may appropriate a midrashic
expression). The midrashic question was a natural one, and its
answer furnished a midrashically reasonable explanation for the
particular biblical idiom. And, by the way, in that state of the
text, no more than the other nine songs, the tenth too was thought
of as a song *not* of the Age to Come. For the *additional* song for
the Age to Come there was a verse or there were verses using
the word *shir*, and those verses may very well have been Isaiah
42:10 and Psalm 149:1, exactly as the Mekilta reads to this very
day.

But if this seemingly radical amputation of a whole in-between
section is correct, how in the world did our preserved Mekilta
get to read as it does? Only on the surface is this a hard question.

Already, at a very early stage — who can say how early; maybe
already in later tannaite times, possibly by amoraic times, and
absolutely certainly not too long after the time of Saadia Gaon,[33]
perhaps even while he was yet alive[34] — the correct meaning of

---

[33] Cf. *Teshubot ha-Geonim*, ed. Harkavy,⧧ 66, pp. 30 f. Saadia is dead by
the time this responsum is written: note ‏ג״ע‏. As to the problem of the Song
of Abraham, cf. *Agadat Shir Ha-Shirim*, ed. Schechter, p. 10, and especially p. 29.

[34] Note in Kasher, XIV, 289: ‏וכן פי׳ להדיא רס״ג מובא בפי׳ לאחד מהקדמונים:‏
‏והגאון רצה לדרוש עשר שירות מטעם השירה הזאת, כי אמר נראה מזה שיש שירות‏
‏אחרות וכו׳‏. And I would say that it is likely that Simon ben Isaac of Mainz
(10th and 11th centuries) also got his idea of the ten songs (familiar to us)
from exegesis of the Shirah. See his poem (*Zulat*) ‏אי פתרוס בעברך‏ (*Maḥzor
for the Seventh and Eighth Days of Passover* [Roedelheim, 1827] pp. 87b-
90b). Note ibid. the slightly variant list (absence of our fourth song, and for
the eighth I Kings 8:12).

והלא עשר שירות הן was forgotten, and woodenly, mechanically the clause was interpreted as, "Are there not indeed ten songs?" And once that misunderstanding occurred, what happened was inevitable.

"Ten songs."[35] What *are* the ten songs, a student of the Mekilta wondered. This question indeed is not easy to answer. Take a look not only at the Mekilta and the sources dependent on it, but also at the beginning of the Targum to the Song of Songs,[36] at the geonic responsum referred to in a preceding note,[37] at Kasher's *Torah Shelemah*, XIV, 289–290, at Louis Ginzberg's *Legends of the Jews*, VI, 11, note 59. In other words, while there was a general tradition to the effect that there were "ten songs," there were, it seems, variant "lists" in circulation; and as a result, it is no wonder that "helpful readers" would undertake *on the margins* of their copies to spell out what the ten songs were. That such puzzlement is not necessarily post-talmudic can be seen, for example, by variant explanations of the Ten Utterances Abot 5:1 tells us the world was created with.[38]

But would correct meanings be so "quickly" forgotten and misunderstanding of והלא עשר שירות הן happen "early"? Yes, indeed. There are not a few traces of forgetting and misunderstanding and guessing in our classical sources (and it would be foolish to dismiss this as a possibility). "There are seven types of Pharisee," a baraita (תנו רבנן) reports,[39] and it is anybody's guess, in the Talmud too, not only what the terms mean but even how to pronounce (or even transcribe!) the names. Such being the dilemma, it is not surprising that a modern scholar can even come up with

---

35 Needless to say, we are dealing with a typical round number.
36 Cf. *Midrash Zutta* on Canticles (Wilna, 1925), p. 6 f., and Buber's n. 32 ad loc.; *Agadat Shir Hashirim*, p. 10.
37 ויש שקיבצו שירות הרבה.
38 Cf. C. Taylor, *Sayings of the Jewish Fathers*, I, 78. See also *ARNB*, p. 90, and Schechter's note ad loc.; Ginzberg, *Legends*, V, 63, n. 1.
39 B. *Soṭah* 22b, and for parallels cf. *ARNA*, 109, and Schechter's note ad loc., and *Fathers According to Rabbi Nathan*, pp. 153 and 213.

sexy conjectures.[40] Once upon a time Antigonus of Soko admonish-
ed his contemporaries, "...and let the fear of Heaven be upon
you."[41] If he could see how he is quoted by Abot de-Rabbi Natan,
in both versions, he might shudder. "Three days before the festivals
of the heathen," the Mishnah[42] lays down, "it is forbidden to
transact business with them." But what *is* the word for heathen
festivals, and what exactly does it mean?[43] Already Rab and Samuel
can't agree in their explanations. There is no lack of other instances.[44] There is nothing reckless, then, in assuming (naturally only
if the state of the sources gives reason for such assumption) that
even by the third century misunderstanding could occur.

Let us return to the ten songs. Having misunderstood the statement והלא עשר שירות הן, a "learned" reader decided to spell out
on *the margin* of his copy of the Mekilta text what the ten songs
were (and he assumed that the tenth referred to by the Mekilta
was the Song for the Age to Come). And to begin with, that is
all that list was, a marginal explanation of "ten songs." But
before the Mekilta of R. Ishmael and the Mekilta of R. Simeon
were drawn up in the form more or less as we have inherited
them — for the texts of both Mekiltas on *'et ha-shirah ha-zot*
incorporate that list — some copyist who failed to recognize that
the list *was* only marginal, and *not* original to the Mekilta (at least
here), embodied it in the Mekilta text itself. He thus sundered
the beginning from its end and created our problem for us, and
for our predecessors no less — as the Tanḥuma and Leqaḥ Ṭob
and Sekel Ṭob and Yalquṭ Shimeoni and Midrash ha-Gadol
demonstrate.

There is no need for me to argue at length that into our classical

---

[40] Cf. N. Tur-Sinai in *Mordecai M. Kaplan Jubilee Volume* (Hebrew part),
p. 86 et seq.

[41] *P.A.* 1:3, and cf. E. J. Bickerman in *Harvard Theological Review*, XLIV
(1951), 153 ff. *ARN*, pp. 25 f.

[42] *'Abodah Zarah* 1:1.

[43] Cf. W. A. L. Elmslie, *The Mishnah on Idolatry* (Cambridge, 1911), pp.
2 f., 18 f.

[44] Cf. briefly *History of Religions* (Chicago, 1965), IV, 281–287.

texts have been interpolated passages which did not belong there originally, for since the early thirties of this century this has been convincingly demonstrated by Ch. Albeck, J. N. Epstein, S. Lieberman,[45] and especially L. Finkelstein in his fundamental studies of the texts of tannaite midrashim.[46] Our texts suffer often from lacunae; they suffer from improper additions as well: the itemizing of the ten songs in connection with 'et ha-shirah ha-zot is merely a particularly vivid instance of such addition.

And concerning this addition of ours we may say one thing more: it was infectious. For within the framework of the ten songs that found their way into the Mekilta text, still another addition was made. It is easily recognizable; what is significant, however, is that it too cannot have been terribly late, for it too appears both in the Mekilta and MRS.

The eighth song, we are informed, "was the one Solomon recited." A song that Solomon sang, one would think, should not be hard to find.[47] But our marginal annotator did not choose the easy way out. He had a tradition that Solomon's song was Psalm 30, and he refused to suppress it. But does not Psalm 30:1 belong to David? Only if we punctuate it, let us say, as do the Septuagint, the Vulgate,[48] the Jewish Publication Society Version (I would too, I suppose). The translators of the King James Version, on the other hand, rendered the sentence, "A Psalm and Song at the dedication of the house of David." They may have gotten the idea from the view favored by Ibn Ezra above others reported by him:

---

[45] Who incidentally calls attention to the fact that על עצם הדבר של תוספות תוספת במדרשי הלכה כבר העיר הרש״ש בהערותיו לבבלי ע״ז ל״ח, א׳ לתוספ׳ ד״ה לעולם Cf. the reference in the following note.

[46] See, for example, his study in *JQR*, XXXI (1940–41), particularly pp. 231 ff., and the references he supplies to the works of the other scholars, as well as his own earlier researches. See also his *Sifra According to Codex Assemani* (1956), Introduction, p. 9 et seq. I have read carefully the study by B. Z. Wacholder, "The Date of the Mekilta de-Rabbi Ishmael," *HUCA*, XXXIX, 117 et seq., and remain unconvinced.

[47] Cf. the ninth song in Tg to Cant. 1:1, and see also *Agadat Shir Ha-shirim*, 10. And note too the "alternative" suggestion in *MhG*. Cf. also *We-Hizhir*, 20b.

[48] Cf. Sabatier's note on the Versio Antiqua.

ultimately however, the *hint* [49] for that syntactical understanding derives from the Mekilta:

"'A Psalm; a song at the dedication of *ha-bayit le-Dawid.*' Was it then David who built it? On the contrary, was it not Solomon who built it...? Why, then, does Scripture say, 'A Psalm; a song at the dedication of the House of David?' Only because David gave over his life to it, to have it built; that is why it goes by his name." For this fact, that David had the building of the Temple on his mind and in his plans, there are prooftexts; hence it is in a profound sense fitting that the House should be named after him even though in the strict and literal sense it was built by Solomon.[50] For, now the Mekilta *and* MRS[51] declare, "You will find the same true of every man, that whatever he gives over his life to, goes by his name." And the Mekilta (so too MRS) does not merely declare this but goes on to demonstrate the truth of it by the case of Moses; and it's quite a while before we return to the subject at hand, namely, the listing of songs. Even an amateur can recognize that we are once again on a detour from the main course, despite the fact that the Tanḥuma too contains the "Moses passage."[52]

Who is responsible for *this* interpolation? Who indeed? Perhaps this too was a marginal annotation incorporated by that first copyist who could not resist leaving things where they were and

---

[49] "Hint," for of course Ibn Ezra refers to David's house, and not to the Temple (as the *Mekilta* takes it). Rashi says, שיאמרוהו הלויים בחנוכת הבית בימי שלמה; Radaq: חברו דוד שיאמרוהו בחנכת בית המקדש.

[50] Note the "clever" adaptation by *Tanḥuma* (followed in this respect by *We-Hizhir*): "Did then David *dedicate* it? Was it not Solomon who *dedicated* it?" But, of course, that avoids the whole issue and renders the question and answer almost otiose.

[51] The *MRS* variants ad loc. are slight. *We-Hizhir* too has a brief digression at this point, but quoting only the passage about Miriam, "Aaron's sister," from the *Mekilta* on Exod. 15:20.

[52] But not *Leqaḥ Ṭob*, not *Sekel Ṭob*, not *Yalquṭ Shimeoni*, not *Yalquṭ ha-Makiri* (on Ps. 18, 52a; not even on Ps. 30:1, 96b, does he exploit the opportunity to enlarge on Moses). On the "Moses passage" see *Midrash Tannaim*, p. 96 (and p. 212 briefly), and cf. Hoffmann's לקוטי בתר לקוטי, p. 13.

dragged in what was better left out. Perhaps it was another copyist. The notion is after all not alien to Mekilta thinking, as is evident from the Mekilta (and MRS!) comment on Exodus 15:20, "Aaron's sister."[53] However, congenial as this notion may be to Mekilta thinking and teaching, in explanation of *'et ha-shirah ha-zot* and in the list of ten songs it is marginal, and by having been brought *into* the text, it interrupts the principal discussion. And that interruption too is not modern: as we have said, it is already to be found in MRS as well, and, as we saw, in the Tanḥuma too.[54]

Let us therefore return to what first occasioned our present study. As the Mekilta text on *'et ha-shirah ha-zot* has been preserved, it is in a sorry state. Beginning and end of the original comment were separated from each other because of a misunderstanding and the consequent insertion of what did not belong. It all began with a misunderstanding. The misunderstanding was clearly early. Later (but not too much later) came interpolation, and this deepened misunderstanding. Remove *that*, and the original Mekilta shines with clarity.

'Et ha-shirah ha-zot: [Why is it said (*'et ha-shirah ha-zot*, rather than *'et ha-shir ha-zeh*)?]

But does (this term) *shirah* occur only once, [here, in Exodus 15:1]? Does not indeed the word *shirah* occur ten times [in Scripture]! [Why then should its occurrence here call for comment?]

For all the songs referring to past events the noun used is in the feminine, [because] even as a female brings to birth, so the triumphs in the past were succeeded by subjugation; but the triumph which is yet to be will not be succeeded by subjugation. That is

---

[53] Note however that in *MRS* the example of Simeon and Levi, Dinah's brothers, does not occur. As for the Cambridge ms. reading, it does not get that far; cf. *MRS*, ed. Epstein-Melamed, p. 238. On the idea of giving over one's life to Israel, see also Pisḥa, I (I, 10 f.) and *Sifre Deut.* 344, ed. Finkelstein, p. 400.

[54] As for the brief enlargement on the ninth song, it is hard for me to decide (although my instinct tells me that here too we have something that was originally marginal) — because it occurs in *MRS*, *Tanḥuma*, *Sekel Ṭob* 201, *Yalquṭ Shimeoni*.

why the noun used for it [for example, in Isaiah 42:10 and Ps. 149:1] is in the masculine, as it is said (Jer. 30:6), "Ask ye now, and see whether a man doth travail with child": [for] just as no man gives birth, so the triumph which is yet to come will not be succeeded by subjugation, as it is said (Isa. 45:17), "O Israel, that art saved by the Lord with an everlasting salvation."[55]

[55] And by way of postscript (cf. above, note 24) perhaps this may be added: *maybe* the clause (שבחו גאולים) שירה חדשה of the Prayer-Book does not mean "The redeemed (from Egyptian bondage) sang a new song" (see both עץ יוסף and עיון תפלה in סדור אוצר התפלות who recognize that the expression *shirah ḥadashah* calls for comment, but their explanation seems to me forced: why *new* only if the real emphasis is on *first*; cf. also the comment in *Abudraham*, Jerusalem, 5719, pp. 89 f.; Baer, ad loc., senses that some thought expressed in the *Mekilta* is relevant here, but he is of no help in making it clear), but something akin to, "The redeemed (from Egyptian bondage) sang a Song of the New Age," to wit, ה' ימלוך לעולם ועד. In other words, this would be an interpretation of *shirah not* like that of the *Mekilta*, that only *shir* in the masculine is to be associated with the song for a Future Age. Per contra, note that Yannai does not hesitate to use *shir* for the song of the redemption from Egypt: כאשר שוררנו שיר, עוד כן נשיר וכו' (*Piyyute Yannai*, ed. Zulay, p. 263).

I can't tell whether שירה חדשה does or does not occur in *Seder R. Amram Gaon* (cf. ed. Hedegård, Lund, 1951, p. 29, of the Hebrew text, trans., p. 68). Possibly it does. It does occur in *Maḥzor Vitry*, p. 66. It is not in Saadia's *Siddur* (ed. Davidson, Assaf, Joel, Jerusalem, 1941, p. 16); it is not in Maimonides' Order of Service (cf. D. Goldschmidt in *Studies... Schocken*, VII [Jerusalem, 1958], 193).

Judah ha-Levi was certainly familiar with the expression; see the second line (and refrain) of his שירה חדשה גאולה לפסח (*Selected Poems*, ed. Brody [Phila., 1928], p. 139).

As for the so-called reading שירה חדשה in the Passover Haggadah, cf. D. Goldschmidt in his edition ad loc., p. 54, n. 17, and the critical apparatus in Kasher's *Haggadah Shelemah*, pp. 66 f.

ERRATA

ENGLISH SECTION: VOLS. I and II

		Instead of	*Should be*
Title Page		Jerusalem 1974	Jerusalem 1975
		New York and London 1974	New York and London 1975
Reverse of Title Page		Copyright 1974	Copyright 1975
Foreword			
line 26		te	the
29		Russel	Russell
Table of Contents			
page 1	line 11	of *Qol Sakhal*	of the *Qol Sakhal*
	13	Dropsie College	Dropsie University
	20	CANTERA, FRANCISCO BURGOS	CANTERA BURGOS, FRANCISCO
	20	Ishaq	Isḥaq
	22	CHAOURAQUI, ANDRE	CHOURAQUI, ANDRÉ
		(Alliance Israelite of Jerusalem)	(Alliance Israélite of Jerusalem)
page 2	line 8	FUKS, LEO and RENA, FUKS	FUKS, LEO and RENA FUKS
	15	GOITEN	GOITEIN
	20	GRUENWALD	GRUENEWALD
	26	Emanuel's	Emmanuel's

TABLE OF CONTENTS OF THE HEBREW SECTION

page 4	line 20–21	On Persecution of the Jewish Religion	On Persecutions of the Jewish Religion
	23	"Ha-kane"	"Ha-Kane"
	37	Vespesian	Vespasian

קלי שכל

Reverse of Title Page   Copyright 1974

Copyright 1975

הקדמה		אהרה הנכון	אהרן הנכון
page 1	line 10	of *Qol Sakhal*	of the *Qol Sakhal*
	12	Dropsie College	Dropsie University
	19	CANTERA, FRANCISCO BURGOS	CANTERA BURGOS, FRANCISCO
	19	Ishaq	Ishaq
	22	:eur	leur
	29	FUKS, LEO and RENA, FUKS	FUKS, LEO and RENA FUKS
page 2	line 1	*Un versity*	*University*
	4	GRUENWALD	GRUENEWALD
	10	Emanuel's	Emmanuel's